W9-CND-321

WADE HAMPTON

CONFEDERATE WARRIOR,
CONSERVATIVE STATESMAN

Walter Brian Cisco

Brassey's, Inc.
Washington, D.C.

Library of Congress Cataloging-in-Publication Data

Cisco, Walter Brian, 1947–
    Wade Hampton : Confederate warrior, conservative statesman / Walter Brian Cisco.— 1st ed.
        p.   cm.
    Includes bibliographical references and index.
    ISBN 1-57488-626-6 (alk. paper)
    1. Hampton, Wade, 1818–1902.   2. Generals—Confederate States of America—Biography.   3. Confederate States of America. Army—Biography.
4. Governors—South Carolina—Biography.   5. Legislators—United States—Biography.   6. United States. Congress. Senate—Biography.   7. South Carolina—Politics and government—1865–1950.   I. Title.

E467.1.H19C57 2004
975.7′041′092—dc22
[B]   2004051839

ISBN 1-57488-626-6

(alk. paper)

Printed in the United States of America on acid-free paper that meets the American National Standards Institute Z39-48 Standard.

Brassey's, Inc.
22841 Quicksilver Drive
Dulles, Virginia 20166

First Edition

10 9 8 7 6 5 4 3 2 1

In memory of my grandparents:
Lillie M. and John S. Love
and
Lillie S. and Henry Cisco

Contents

Illustrations

List of Maps

The Wade Hampton statue located on the grounds of the South Carolina State House. Sculptor Frederick Wellington Ruckstahl completed the work in Paris, France. It was dedicated November 20, 1906. *David Cisco*.

Acknowledgments

I APPRECIATE all those willing to assist a writer in his quest. Particularly deserving of thanks are the staffs of the South Caroliniana Library Book Division, the Thomas Cooper Library Government Documents Department, the South Carolina Department of Archives and History, the Southern Historical Collection, and the Library of Congress Manuscript Division. David Cisco's photographic expertise has again been invaluable.

I acknowledge, too, the truth of I Chronicles 29:11–12.

"CONSIDER EVERYTHING CERTAIN WHICH IS POSSIBLE"

The Hampton Heritage

On Friday, April 11, 1902, the people of Columbia, South Carolina, awakened to the prospect of another glorious spring day. Blessed by a brisk breeze, sunshine, and a profusion of flowers, spirits could only be bright. Over breakfast they read a newspaper account of the previous day's local excitement. A huge crowd had gathered at the railroad station to cheer Theodore Roosevelt on his way home from Charleston's Interstate and West Indian Exposition. All eyes had been on South Carolina during the presidential visit. North-South divisions seemed finally forgotten. The twentieth century was full of promise.

But as Columbians prepared for another day, their morning routine was interrupted. The news was sad, although not unexpected. Many were first alerted by a sorrowful tolling of bells. Others saw flags falling to half-staff. Quickly word spread. Workers began draping in black the portico and columns of the State House. Mourning streamers drooped from the Confederate soldier monument. By telephone and telegraph the tidings traveled across the state, the South, the nation.

"I have learned with profound regret," said President Roosevelt, "of the death of Gen. Wade Hampton."

Soon condolences were pouring in. "I grieve with you for the revered and beloved dead," telegraphed former-Confederate first lady Varina Davis. "Accept my profound sympathy," said Gen. James Longstreet, adding that

Hampton was "the greatest natural cavalry leader of our or any other country." Surviving Confederate generals Stephen D. Lee, Thomas L. Rosser, Joseph Wheeler, Bradley Johnson, and Fitzhugh Lee also wired expressions of sympathy.

The next day newspapers all across the state bordered their columns in black as South Carolinians went into mourning. Hampton was eulogized by numberless friends. In death he had no enemies. With trembling voice U.S. Senator George Vest of Missouri announced Hampton's passing to fellow senators, declaring that his "memory will live for centuries to come." Sen. John L. McLaurin pronounced Hampton "the best loved man in the history of South Carolina." The state's senior senator, Benjamin R. Tillman, would travel by rail to the funeral. "It is the one way I can show regard and respect for the memory of Gen. Hampton."

Services were scheduled for four o'clock on Sunday afternoon in Trinity Episcopal Church. Hampton's home on the corner of Barnwell and Senate streets would be opened for a few hours before the funeral so that friends might view the body and pay their respects. Troops of the state militia were detailed to control the crowd as a line of 6,000 filed through the parlor. A contingent from Camp Hampton, United Confederate Veterans (UCV), served as honor guard. On the casket were arranged three calla lilies and a sprig of laurel taken from a tree near the ruins of Hampton's boyhood home, Millwood. In the center of the casket was a wreath of roses and carnations sent by the Paul McMichael Chapter of the United Daughters of the Confederacy. On Hampton's breast lay flowers picked from the long-abandoned garden at Millwood. Decorating the mantle were sprays of lilacs from Hampton's old home, Diamond Hill. These blossoms had been lovingly gathered by family servants. A newsman wrote that "faithful negroes were in tears when they saw their old master lying dead." The reporter told how "men, women and children, white and black, came to join in the review and to leave their floral offerings."

In mid-afternoon the funeral procession formed on Senate Street in front of Hampton's home. A single band led the way, followed by Confederate veterans, some wearing their old uniforms. Immediately behind the hearse were twenty survivors of the Hampton Legion, then family members in carriages. One hundred women carried floral tributes, two wagons transporting the larger arrangements. Marching behind were men of the Sons of Confederate Veterans, Citadel cadets, students from South Carolina College, politicians, and militiamen. Governor and staff trooped in full uniform. The six city blocks to Trinity Church were lined with a mass of mourners. Conservative estimates numbered the crowd at 20,000.

Bishop Ellison Capers, Hampton friend and former Southern brigadier, conducted the service. Fewer than 1,500 were able to find a place inside the church, leaving countless thousands standing in the street. A choir sang

"Rock of Ages" as the casket was carried down the aisle, the words taken up by all. In a voice "choking with emotion" Bishop Capers read familiar words from scripture, "I am the resurrection and the life, saith the Lord: he that believeth in me, though he were dead, yet shall he live: and whosoever liveth and believeth in me, shall never die."

On his deathbed Hampton had requested his favorite hymn be sung at this service. It was penned by John Henry Newman. Its message had struck a cord in Hampton's heart. The words seemed to mirror his own mourning over loss, his struggle with pride, his hope, and the triumph of his faith. The strains of "Lead, Kindly Light" now filled the church.

> Lead, kindly Light, amid the encircling gloom,
>   Lead thou me on;
> The night is dark, and I am far from home,
>   Lead thou me on.
> Keep thou my feet; I do not ask to see
> The distant scene; one step enough for me.
>
> I was not ever thus, nor prayed that thou
>   Shouldst lead me on;
> I loved to choose and see my path; but now
>   Lead thou me on.
> I loved the garish day, and, spite of fears,
> Pride ruled my will: remember not past years.
>
> So long thy power hath blest me, sure it still
>   Will lead me on
> O'er moor and fen, o'er crag and torrent, till
>   The night is gone.
> And with the morn those angel faces smile
> Which I have loved long since, and lost awhile.

The casket was carried outside to the Hampton cemetery plot. Here rested the remains of parents and grandfather. Under an ancient oak were buried Margaret and Mary, Hampton's wives. Brother Frank, cut down at Brandy Station, lay beside his Sally. Here too lay Preston, whose death in battle at Burgess's Mill broke his father's heart.

Surrounding Wade Hampton's open grave were his surviving family and fourteen UCV flag bearers. Mourners completely filled the cemetery as well as Gervais and Sumter streets, all trying to view the final act. The choir sang as his casket was lowered into the ground and as gray-headed veterans shoveled earth into the grave. One lady fainted, overcome with emotion. Flowers were placed over the mound. There was a six-foot-tall floral cross. Another display took in the shape of a cavalry sabre. There was such an abundance that flowers covered nearby graves; wreathes even hung on trees. Then, just as the sun began to set, two soldiers played "Taps." A prayer by Bishop Capers ended the service, and the crowd began to drift away. For two days and two nights, city police remained on duty in the church yard as visitors continued to come.

One editorial writer tried to understand the old man's hold on these people. Wade Hampton, he concluded,

> lived a life his fellow countrymen knew to be good and great. The things they aspired to do he had done. They borrowed glory of his achievements, and they were grateful. . . . The people loved him because he represented them as they knew they should have been, rather than as they knew they were.[1]

IT WAS DURING the High Middle Ages, when Englishmen first felt a need for surnames, that members of the Hampton family chose to be known by the place where they lived. During the reign of Æthelred the Unready, the little Staffordshire village of Hampton became the site of a monastery paid for by one Lady Wulfruna. The town thereafter became known as Wulfruns-hampton and, eventually, Wolverhampton. It is today an industrial center of some quarter million people.[2]

Over the years Hamptons would leave Wolverhampton to settle in other corners of the realm. Near London in Twickenham Parish, County Middlesex, in the time of Elizabeth I, William Hampton was born. He made a good living as a wool merchant, but by age twenty-nine determined to seek a greater fortune in the New World. The Virginia Company of London encouraged immigration to the colony by promising fifty acres for every person whose way was paid. William secured for himself a substantial homestead by investing in passage for eight other men. They set sail in the fall of 1620 aboard the *Bona Nova*. William's wife, Joane, and their children joined him early the next year at the tiny settlement of Kecoughton.[3]

It was no place for the fainthearted. Just as the colony was recovering from a typhus epidemic, an Indian attack wiped out one-third of the white population. Fortunately for the Hamptons, the raiders were stopped before reaching their village on the James River. In the spring of 1623, Joane gave birth to a son they called Thomas, their last child and the first Hampton to be born in America. The family went on to prosper, accumulating land, planting tobacco, and probably purchasing a few slaves.

When Thomas was sixteen he sailed to England to study for the Anglican ministry. He returned to become a prominent clergyman, serving Wilmington Parish for nearly a half century. Reverend Hampton accumulated— through inheritance and his own diligence—plantations that afforded a comfortable income. His firstborn son, John, was commissioned a captain of the militia in Gloucester County, helped put down Bacon's Rebellion, and continued the Hampton tradition of growing tobacco.[4]

The name Wade entered the family lexicon when John Hampton Jr.—the captain's son—married Margaret Wade of New Kent County. The first of their twelve children was christened John Wade Hampton. When he was just thirteen years old, "died our beloved oldest son Wade Hampton of a Lingering Fever," wrote the grieving father in the family Bible. "God's will be done."[5]

Second-born son, Anthony, demonstrated ambition and an ability to lead. He farmed, learned surveying, and drilled the local militia. In 1741 the twenty-six-year-old married Elizabeth Preston on her twenty-first birthday. Restless, searching for new land and fresh opportunities, Anthony moved his growing family from Tidewater Virginia north to Loudon and then south to what is now Halifax County. Later he built a home on the Dan River in Rowan County, North Carolina, where his neighbors chose him to command their frontier militia company. In 1755, at the height of the French and Indian War, Captain Hampton and his men spent the summer campaigning against Indians in the foothills of the Blue Ridge Mountains. Respected in his community, he became known as one who stood up for colonial rights. Elected to the North Carolina general assembly, Hampton served only six weeks; the governor dissolved the body in March 1773. Many Americans were demanding liberty, if not yet independence. Hampton was probably one of those who still pledged allegiance to an empire he found increasingly difficult to obey.

Anthony Hampton and his extended family made a good living trading the accoutrements of European civilization for Indian deerskins and furs. To be nearer their source of trade, he decided in 1773 to make one more move, this time to the sparsely populated frontier of South Carolina. Traveling with Hampton and wife, Elizabeth, were their little grandson John Bynum, son Preston and his wife, Betty, and fifteen-year-old daughter Elizabeth and her new husband, James Harrison. Hampton's younger sons Henry, Wade, and Richard probably joined their older brother Edward on the trek south about this time. They cleared land and began building new homes near the Tyger River in Ninety-six District, less than a mile from the Cherokee Nation.

These gentle hills and dark forests were only beginning to echo with the rhythm of the steel ax, music of the fiddle, and the laughter of children. Down rutted roads from Virginia, Maryland, and Pennsylvania traveled other families lured by the promise of one more fresh start. This Carolina upcountry was a land of which coastal dwellers had only heard tales. Here the night was ruled by screaming "tygers," fearsome beasts as big as a man. Monumental boulders protruded from verdant hillsides, where erosion exposed burnt-red earth. Hazy on the horizon hung jagged blue peaks—proud, ancient, and somehow foreboding. On sultry summer nights lightning bugs, darting and dancing, worked their magic until a crash of thunder broke the spell, heralding an onslaught of rushing wind and blinding rain charging down from those mountains in the distance.

As self-sufficient upcountrymen grew in numbers, nervous British authorities began bolstering old ties with the Cherokees. Traders Edward and Preston Hampton routinely journeyed to the Cherokee towns and made no secret of their Whig sympathies. There, on a spring day in 1775, they were surprised by a force of white Tories and Indian warriors. The young men were robbed, made sport of, and then taken to an Indian village deep in the mountains. Just as these "enemies of the Crown" were about to be transported to confinement in Pensacola, West Florida, they managed to escape. When once again among friends, they warned of Indian trouble, but as the months passed and nothing happened, settlers began to let down their guard.[6]

In Charles Town the independence movement was rapidly gaining strength. In November 1775 royal governor Lord William Campbell fled his Meeting Street home and sailed away, the great seal of the province tucked under his arm. By year's end patriot militia had taken possession of forts guarding the city. But the empire would not let go without a fight. On June 28, 1776, a powerful fleet of British warships opened fire at the hastily constructed battery on Sullivan's Island protecting Charles Town Harbor. Built of palmetto logs and manned by Col. William Moultrie's Second Regiment, gunners in the little bastion somehow managed to repulse the king's armada. Six days later the Continental Congress signed Jefferson's Declaration of Independence.

Defeated on the coast, loyalists used their Indian allies to strike in the South Carolina upcountry. On the morning of July 1, 1776, Anthony and Elizabeth Hampton were caring for their infant grandson. The baby's mother, Elizabeth Hampton Harrison, lived with her parents while husband James recruited men for the militia. At the moment she was visiting the nearby Sadler family cabin. Preston had stopped by the Hampton place, leaving his wife and children at home. His younger brothers were away. Nine-year-old John Bynum was there with his grandparents. Anthony Hampton was probably surprised, but not alarmed, when the party of Indians rode up. He scarcely had time to be afraid. Without warning, tomakawk blows split the skulls of the old man and his wife. Son Preston was shot to death. The celebrating savages began ransacking the house, trying on clothes, drinking stolen brandy, and scalping and multilating the corpses of their victims.

Elizabeth Harrison and Mrs. Sadler heard the commotion. Cautiously, they approached through a canebrake in time to witness the final scene of horror. The young mother saw a brave grasp her infant by the feet and swing him through the air to smash his brains out against a tree. Mrs. Sadler's firm hand kept Elizabeth's scream from escaping her mouth as the two backed away and rode for help.

An armed party returned to find charred ruins and four bodies strewn across the yard. Young John had been kidnapped. Other families nearby suffered similar fates as the rampaging Indians crippled the British cause by killing settlers indiscriminately. Capt. Aaron Smith, his wife, and their five children were slaughtered along with five slaves. Jacob Hite was cut down, his family and slaves were kidnapped, and his wife's naked body was found later. It was said that Preston Hampton's widow, Betty, was discovered wandering and out of her mind, the Indians having butchered her two children.[7]

At the time of the massacre, according to a family tradition, Wade and the other brothers were serving with the patriot army near Charles Town. When news came of the carnage, they rushed home with vengeance in their hearts. From across the Carolinas rose a cry to punish the savages and stamp out the Indian threat once and for all. Eleven hundred South Carolina militiamen shouldered flintlock rifles and muskets. Citizen-soldiers from North Carolina dropped their plows and joined the expedition. The hard-eyed frontiersmen fell upon Cherokees whenever they found them—killing, burning villages, destroying crops. It was a brief, one-sided campaign. Indian survivors signed treaties in the late summer and fall of 1777 that brought an end to the bloodletting and a return of hostages.[8] Wade Hampton already had the look of a hardened veteran, and the Revolutionary War had only just begun.

ON THE DAY of the horse race, young frontiersmen gathered from miles around, bragging, betting, and showing off their riding skills. Wade and Richard longed to join the fun, but their father had given the boys a job they must do first. There was a field to prepare for planting, and he told his two youngest sons to hoe the ground up to a certain distant stump. Their hearts sank. It would be impossible to accomplish the task and still make it to the race. Then one of them had an idea. It is easy to imagine Wade selling the scheme to his brother. Quickly they ran to the stump, dug it up, and dragged it back to the already-hoed portion of the field. They were off to the races, having obeyed their father's instructions to the letter.[9]

Wade—"the first Wade Hampton"—was probably born on May 3, 1754. It is less certain whether he was a native of Virginia or North Carolina, his family being on the move around the time of his birth. One tradition assumed that he received "a thorough education," but more likely he was exposed only to the rudimentary schooling common on the frontier. Hampton was unusually intelligent, shrewd, and would become widely read. "He seems to have availed himself of every opportunity to acquire knowledge," wrote one who knew him later, "and is able to converse with ease and spirit, on most subjects. . . . His acquaintance with good authors is very considerable. . . . His language is more than ordinarily pure, forcible, clear and concise."[10]

Wade Hampton was an extraordinarily ambitious young man. In 1777, after the Indian campaign, he and brother Richard operated a small business trading with the South Carolina backcountry. Based first in Charles Town, after a few years the young merchants moved to Granby, near the center of the state, in an area called the Congarees, in Saxe Gotha Township. They must have been well thought of by their neighbors for both brothers were elected to South Carolina's Third General Assembly in 1779. Wade Hampton would serve in the state House of Representatives for much of the next decade. Businessman and lawmaker, he also found time for the patriot cause, serving from 1777 as paymaster in Brig. Gen. Thomas Sumter's Sixth Regiment.[11]

The British capture of Charles Town on May 12, 1780, was a severe setback for those supporting American independence. And it was a threat to the livelihood of merchants like Wade Hampton. Apparently to avoid confiscation of his property within British lines, he put his signature on a declaration of loyalty to King George III, proclaiming himself "a true and faithful Subject of His Majesty." Many other rebels also signed. In Hampton's case it was almost certainly understood by friends as a temporary expedient, and soon he had repudiated the oath and stood again openly on the patriot side. Not long afterwards he was apprehended by Redcoats. As the king's men escorted him to Charles Town—where he faced certain hanging as a traitor— the desperate prisoner grabbed a musket, overpowered his six guards, and dashed to freedom.[12]

In the spring of 1781 Hampton set to work raising a regiment of South Carolina state troops, traveling even to Rowan County, North Carolina, to sign up volunteers. Slaves confiscated from Tories were offered as an enlistment bonus, with rewards ranging from three and one-half slaves per year for a colonel to one for a private's ten-month enlistment. General Sumter, writing about this time from his camp in Waxhaw, South Carolina, entrusted Hampton with a letter to Maj. Gen. Nathanael Greene. In it Sumter described Hampton as "a Valuable and Intelligent officer . . . on whose information you may Rely—and to whom you may communicate with Safety." Hampton returned to Sumter with Greene's confidential reply.[13] His previous "defection to the king" was obviously not taken seriously by those who knew him.

In April of that year Hampton, now a colonel commanding a force of dragoons, surprised the enemy at Friday's Ferry on the Congaree River, winning a small victory. In July General Sumter ordered American cavalry to probe to the very outskirts of Charles Town, hoping to pressure the British to pull troops out of the upcountry. Hampton and his men rode to St.

Hampton's grandfather, the first Wade Hampton. *Edward L. Wells, Hampton and His Cavalry in '64 (Richmond, Va.: B. F. Johnson Pub. Co., 1899).*

James's Church, Goose Creek, on Sunday morning, July 15, surprising and capturing British soldiers and local Tories in the congregation. From there Hampton's horsemen galloped down the peninsula as far as the Quarter House. The raid may have had little strategic value, but it did encourage patriots and create alarm within Charles Town's garrison.[14]

On September 8 British and Americans faced each other at what would be the decisive battle of Eutaw Springs. At one point in the action, South Carolina state troops became demoralized when their commander, Col. William Henderson, was severely wounded. Hampton took over, rallied the men, and led a gallant charge that netted nearly one hundred prisoners. His men were badly mauled but hailed as heroes. Although Redcoats held the field as the sun set, Eutaw proved a strategic victory for the patriot cause in the South, for afterwards the British never ventured from their Charles Town base. General Greene praised Hampton in his report, and the Continental Congress voted its thanks "to the officers and men of the state corps of South-Carolina . . . for the zeal, activity and firmness by them exhibited throughout the engagement."[15] "Wade Hampton," writes one historian two centuries later, "was unquestionably the outstanding American officer on that bloody and crucial occasion." With the enemy now on the defensive, Hampton's military duties became routine in the months following the fight at Eutaw. Elected again to the South Carolina House of Representatives, Hampton regularly attended sessions held in the village of Jacksonborough.[16] By the end of 1782, the British abandoned Charles Town. The war was over.

Sometime shortly before the end of hostilities, Hampton married the widow Martha Eppes Howell; she was about thirty years old and the mother of a young son. She lived in Richland District, not far from Granby, and had inherited from her parents some 2,500 acres and two homes called Mill Place and Greenfield. Just after their first wedding anniversary, Martha died. No children had been born to them.[17]

In 1786 the widower married eighteen-year-old Harriet Flud, daughter of a wealthy planter from Santee. Hampton built for his young bride a fine and well-furnished home on property he had inherited from Martha and called it Woodlands. Off Bluff Road, east of the Congaree River, they lived in near isolation. Wade Hampton relished this kind of independence and self-sufficiency. "Four miles," according to Hampton, "is close enough for a neighbor."[18]

Hampton was accumulating wealth in the form of land and slaves at a rate that probably amazed even him. He retained a variety of business interests, but after he married Martha, agriculture became his primary pursuit. Eventually, he would possess over 12,000 acres in Richland—pine and hardwood forests, useless swamp, and fertile farmland. He grew corn, indigo, hemp, barley, peas, and cotton. Eli Whitney's invention of an engine to separate seed from lint soon made cotton Hampton's most profitable crop. A visitor to Woodlands described a plantation village and church for the slaves, and a multitude of barns and storage sheds. Water powered a saw mill, grain mill, cotton gin, and presses. With his profits Hampton bred race horses and speculated in land. His entries did well at the Charleston track. More importantly, his gambling in the real estate market also paid off. He seemed to have a knack for buying huge tracts of land and selling it at just the right moment. He went on to invest in the stock of the Yazoo Company. The state of Georgia was disposing of vast stretches of wilderness for pennies an acre, and the Yazoo Company became the principal purchaser. State legislators were charged with profiting from the deals, either as stockholders themselves or simply as the recipients of bribes. Reformers would later attempt to rescind the sales, and Congress tried to get involved, but the U.S. Supreme Court ultimately ruled that the transactions had indeed been legal. Hampton once again made money, although association with the Yazoo venture badly tarnished his reputation.[19]

In middle age, after four years of marriage to Harriet, Hampton finally became a father. Wade Junior was born on April 21, 1791. A little more than two years later a second son, Francis (called Frank), was born. But on October 31, 1794, Harriet died, the victim of what the Charleston *City Gazette* called "a short but painful illness." She was only twenty-six.[20] Six years later Hampton began a courtship that may have raised a few eyebrows. The object of his affections was Harriet's step-sister Mary Cantey. Longtime Hampton friend Aaron Burr informed daughter Theodosia that from what he had heard Mary was "a charming young girl." Fifty-year-old Hampton married his twenty-two-year-old former sister-in-law on Independence Day, 1801. Mary became mother to her two young nephews, Wade and Frank. Over the next fifteen years she would bear six children of her own. The first, a daughter, the couple named Harriet.[21]

Never satisfied with what he had, Hampton went on to purchase and develop sugar plantations in Louisiana and Mississippi. Houmas in Ascension Parish, Louisiana—with 148,000 acres and nearly twelve miles of frontage on the Mississippi River—became the greatest of all the Hampton holdings. In an era when possession of perhaps fifty slaves would qualify a Southerner for admission to the planter elite, the first Wade Hampton came to own upwards of 1,000. His Louisiana plantations alone were said to provide a return of $100,000 in a single year—at a time when an annual salary of $2,000 might be considered a comfortable middle-class income. It is difficult to disagree with contemporary characterizations of Hampton as "the richest planter in the South."

Justly or not, Hampton was criticized by some for mistreating his work force. A traveler named James Stuart claimed to have talked to former Hampton overseers who quit rather than "assist in the cruel punishment inflicted upon his slaves." According to Stuart, Hampton "stints them in food, overworks them, and keeps them almost naked." Virginia's Edmund Ruffin, himself no foe of slavery, expressed satisfaction that Hampton's "cruelty" had been "exposed."[22]

Despite talk of abusing slaves and cheating the public in the Yazoo affair, Hampton still enjoyed a long career in politics. Voters perhaps remembered the colonel's heroic role in the Revolutionary War as they reelected him year after year to the South Carolina House of Representatives. Never a legislative leader, he attended sessions only when they did not interfere with his other interests. Wade, Richard, and John Hampton were all delegates to the state convention that convened in 1788 to consider the proposed Constitution of the United States. The brothers heeded the arguments and warnings of anti-Federalists and voted against ratification. Charleston and the low country, through a long-standing system of rotten boroughs, effectively controlled South Carolina politics. Conservatives in this region favored the new Constitution and had the delegate votes to put the state in the new union. Nearly everywhere else in South Carolina, the underrepresented majority opposed ratification.

Wade Hampton won a seat in the U.S. House of Representatives in a February 1795 special election. The new congressman was as anonymous in that body as he had been in South Carolina's general assembly, although he did serve on committees involved with defense issues. Defeated for reelection in 1796, Hampton was elected to the Eighth Congress in 1802, only to lose again two years later. In 1800 he was a presidential elector for the successful Republican ticket of Jefferson and Burr.[23]

Although a Republican, Hampton's public policy decisions usually turned on pragmatism rather than ideology. As a trustee of the newly chartered South Carolina College, he was once asked to support a man for the presidency of that institution because the aspirant was "a staunch Jeffersonian Republican." Hampton was irritated. "I want none of your staunch republicans at the head of our college; nor your staunch Federalists neither," he declared. "I know of no necessary connection between party politics and literature; and till a candidate presents some better recommendation for the office than staunch republicanism, I shall employ my influence to keep him out of it."

Hampton described himself as "a loose Christian." He made occasional contributions to local congregations and eventually joined Trinity Episcopal Church. Although his pronouncements were often at variance with scripture and historical Christianity, he was never hesitant to express himself. His was the cocksure philosophy of the self-made man. "One of the principal maxims of Col. Hampton's life," wrote one familiar with his views, "and which he strongly recommended to me has been to *consider everything certain which is possible*."[24]

It must have come as a surprise to most when Hampton in 1808 chose to reenter active military service. At fifty-four he was long exempt from even militia drill, but growing British belligerency probably stirred his anger, patriotism, and pride. Writing to Thomas Sumter, then South Carolina's senior U.S. senator, he asked his old friend "barely to mention my wish, to the proper department." The wish resulted in a colonel's commission. After some hand-wringing over who might outrank him, the new colonel accepted responsibility for overseeing recruiting in his home state and superintending the defenses of Charleston. Storm-battered Fort Moultrie, the city's premier fortification, was described at the time by one engineer as "a heap of rubbish of no other value than the bricks that might come in use again." Hampton began to make improvements and ordered the erection of new batteries, all the while remaining involved in the day-to-day management of his own business affairs. In May 1809 he was promoted to brigadier general and a few months later ordered to New Orleans.[25] "War hawks" continued to agitate for war with Great Britain, and Congress finally passed a declaration in June 1812. President James Madison recommended Hampton and three others for promotion to the rank of major general, and the Senate quickly confirmed the nominations. Still, Hampton was disappointed to receive orders giving him responsibility for defending Norfolk, Virginia. He coveted nothing less than command of an army on the Canadian front.[26]

U.S. strategy called for the liberation of British North America. In 1812 Canada was invaded at three points, but the attacks were not coordinated, and all failed. The offensive would be renewed the next year. In June 1813 Hampton was summoned to Washington where Secretary of War John Armstrong offered him Military District Nine near Lake Champlain. Hampton's army consisted of 4,000 regulars and some 1,500 militiamen. One problem surfaced immediately. Hampton was frankly contemptuous of overall commander James Wilkinson and insisted on reporting directly to the War Department. Secretary Armstrong chose to keep peace among his subordinates by leaving the question unsettled. Generals Wilkinson and Hampton were set to launch their invasions from upper New York and converge on Montreal. Headquartered at Chateaugay—less than ten miles from the Canadian border—Hampton marshaled his forces.[27]

That they might first "spy out the land," Hampton's men collared two brothers, Jacob and David Manning, and brought them before the general. Hampton proposed that David ride as far as Montreal and bring back a report on British strength. Manning refused.

"Are you not an American?" asked Hampton. A Tory, Manning had fled to Canada after the Revolutionary War in order to avoid persecution.

"Yes, I was born on the American side," answered Manning, "and I have many relations, but I am true to the British flag."

An exasperated Hampton pointed to his legions camped outside the window, determined to have the last word. How far, he demanded to know, could an army of that size go?

"If it has good luck," replied Jacob Manning, "it might get to Halifax."

Everyone in the room knew the British kept prisoners of war in that Nova Scotia town. A furious Hampton ordered the brothers locked up for three days. It happened that their guard was a local militiaman and friend of the Mannings and, without hesitation, let them go. They promptly rode to British headquarters to tell all they knew of American strength and strategy.[28]

Hampton divided his command into two brigades—one under Brig. Gen. George Izard of South Carolina, the other led by Col. Robert Purdy— and on October 21 ordered them across the Canadian border. Each column moved down the Chateaugay River—Purdy on the east bank, Izard on the west. Apparently the Manning brothers' intelligence report had little impact on British preparedness. Opposing Hampton was a force of only 1,600 French Canadians under the command of Lt. Col. Charles de Salaberry. The colonel had but 460 of his men deployed. Hampton ordered Purdy to hit the enemy from the right. When he heard the rattle of musketry, Hampton would order Izard into action with the rest of the men. Frustrated by dense woods and incompetent scouts, Purdy was late, and his troops were repulsed by the few enemy soldiers they encountered. Izard's men then traded volleys with a concealed foe, but casualties were few on either side. Greatly overestimating the number he faced, a fearful Hampton called off the attack. De Salaberry was amazed and relieved to see the invaders retreating to their own country after but five days on Canadian soil.[29]

A few weeks later Wilkinson was defeated at the battle of Chrysler's Farm, extinguishing American hopes of conquering Canada. Poor intelligence, an uncooperative attitude, and indecision all contributed to Hampton's debacle on the Chateaugay. "The reckless daring that had characterized him as a twenty-seven-year-old colonel in the heat of battle at Eutaw simply deserted him as a fifty-nine-year-old general in the cold woodlands of Canada," concludes one historian. Not that Hampton was without strengths as a commander. Strict in discipline, he insisted that his men display a soldierly appearance and pay attention to duty. "The outlines of his character were sharp and well defined," remembered Col. Winfield Scott. "In mind vigorous, prompt, intrepid, sagacious, but of irritable nerves." Just after the defeat Hampton resigned his commission and returned home.[30] What if he had not been so cautious, if his troops had swept aside the little band of French Canadians, if Montreal had fallen to the invading Americans—the lost opportunities must have haunted Hampton for the remainder of his life. Victorious, the general would have been an instant hero, the kind of man American voters traditionally promote to the White House. And if Montreal had fallen, the borders of the United States might have advanced to encompass Hudson Bay.

General Hampton's sons Wade Jr. and Frank had buckled on swords and followed their father into service once war was declared. Frank would rise to the rank of captain before leaving the army in 1815. A drinker, dueler, and spendthrift, a year later he was dead. Young Wade served as a second lieuten-

Hampton's father, Col. Wade Hampton Jr., circa 1835. From a portrait attributed to William Scarborough. *Historic Columbia Foundation Collection.*

ant in the First Regiment of Light Dragoons, but doffed his uniform when the general resigned. Looking after his father's Louisiana plantations, Wade found himself in New Orleans in December 1814. With the British landing troops and threatening the city, he threw in with a militia company. On January 7, Maj. Gen. Andrew Jackson invited Hampton to join his staff. The next day the ragtag American force—outnumbered 2 to 1—routed the attacking Redcoats, neither side aware that a peace treaty had been signed in Ghent, Belgium, two weeks before. In his report Jackson thanked the twenty-three-year-old Hampton. In one story often told by the family, Hampton galloped to Washington in ten and a half days with news of the victory.[31]

Learning of his son's participation in the battle of New Orleans must have been a proud moment for the old general. Wade Jr. had too often disappointed his father. He was educated first by tutors, then at Moses Waddel's illustrious academy at Willington, in preparation for study at South Carolina College. Wade was a sophomore there in 1807 when he returned one night to the campus "intoxicated to delirium, raving and storming like a Bedlamite," according to a witness. His father's position as trustee may have saved him on that occasion. Two years later he was denied promotion to the senior class for having skipped examinations. This time his college career was over.[32]

Before and after service in the War of 1812, young Wade traveled extensively, helping to manage his father's far-flung empire. All was not business, however. It may have been at Charleston's Washington Race Course that this most eligible of bachelors first met Ann Fitzsimons. Three years younger than Wade, Ann was one of ten children born to Christopher Fitzsimons and Catharine Pritchard. The Irish-born Fitzsimons parlayed an inheritance and earnings as a Charleston cotton factor into a fortune in land and slaves. In 1807 he purchased a large house in the city that had been built a century earlier by William Rhett, the swashbuckler who cleared the coast of pirates.

Young Wade managed to make a good impression when he had to. "I am very much pleased with him," wrote Fitzsimons to Wade's father. "He appears as steady as a man of forty years of age and I think very free from the vices that our young men of his age are generally addicted to." He reported that others in Charleston "speak highly of his manners and good conduct."

Wade Hampton Jr. and Ann Fitzsimons were married at the bride's home on March 6, 1817. As a wedding present Ann's father gave them a 730-acre plantation near Augusta, Georgia, with seventy-five slaves. Not to be outdone, General Hampton presented the couple with 3,000 acres in Richland District, South Carolina. There, not far from the road that led from Columbia to Pressly Garner's ferry over the Wateree River, he built for them a two-story home they called Millwood. Nestled among the pine trees, some four miles from the village of Columbia, Millwood was perhaps as yet incomplete, unfurnished, or too isolated for Ann. Whatever the reason, as the time approached for the birth of her first child, she chose to return to the security of her parent's home in Charleston.[33]

In the spring of 1818, handsome homes and soaring steeples, pastel and white, rose proudly behind the great city's protective sea wall. As Charleston merchants prospered they had moved their families from living quarters above waterfront offices to fashionable new homes on streets like Ashley, Meeting, and Montagu. There, salty ocean breezes gave way to the spring-time fragrance of Carolina jessamine and the heavy scent of gardenia. Visiting planters docked their boats in the pond that connected Queen Street to the Ashley River. East Bay Street, on the Cooper River side of the Charleston peninsula, was crowded with craftsmen, vendors, sailors, and stevedores. The harbor bristled with masts. Ships departed Charleston's wharves loaded with cotton, rice, and tobacco. Southern consumers bought English wool, Jamaican rum, linen from Ireland and Germany, Scottish plaids, and Barcelonan silk. Along with books, bonnets, and barrels of wheat, ships brought news from around the globe. The editor of the *Times* of Charleston opined that erelong "Europe will again become the theatre of war and bloodshed—when Russia, marching her millions to the field, will strike for univeral empire." Napoleon's empire of the French was but a memory, Bonaparte himself imprisoned on the island of Saint Helena. Yet, most of the world knew nothing of republican liberty. King George III still sat on the British throne. With Napoleon out of the way, the dynastic order in Europe had been resurrected by the Congress of Vienna. A traveler quoted in the Charleston *City Gazette* complained of an anti-American dictatorship in "Buenos Ayres." The newly independent United Provinces of Rio de la Plata is a country "as far removed from liberty as before the Revolution."

As the year 1818 began, Spain seemed everywhere in retreat. General Jackson's punitive expedition against the Seminole Indians was fast becoming an outright invasion of Spanish Florida. The Stars and Stripes commanded new respect. There were twenty united states now, with a total population approaching nine million. Possibilities appeared endless. Philip Freneau, poet of the American Revolution, gazed westward and exclaimed,

> What wonders there shall freedom show,
> What mighty States successive grow!

The Hampton family's expectations were, for now, more immediate. On Saturday, March 28, 1818, at the Fitzsimons' home on Hasell Street in the Charleston neighborhood known as Rhettsbury, Ann Hampton gave birth to a son. Like his father and grandfather, he was christened Wade Hampton.[34]

The birthplace of Wade Hampton III, Hasell Street, Charleston, South Carolina.
*Edward L. Wells, Hampton and His Cavalry in '64 (Richmond, Va.: B. F. Johnson Pub.
Co., 1899).*

2

"DEEP IN UNFATHOMABLE MINES"

Learning to Be a Gentleman

I t is easy to picture the boy at his grandfather's knee, listening wide-eyed to tales of Indians and Redcoats, frontier dangers, heroic deeds, and courage in battle. American history became as real to little Wade as the old general's sword. Yet, there was one corner of Wade's world he feared to tread. Little more than a toddler, he had become the victim of a Muscovy duck—the undisputed dictator of the Millwood pond. The old drake bullied the child—running, hissing, and snapping. That some thought the scene amusing only deepened his resolve. One day at a Columbia store, Wade spied a toy sabre. It was but a replica of the real article, but had an unsharpened iron blade, a scabbard, and a belt. He convinced his parents to buy it for him. Returning home, Wade buckled on his new weapon and sallied forth to meet the enemy, determined never again to flee. He unsheathed the blade. The drake charged as usual, but was surprised by his blows. Repulsed, the huge bird turned to attack again. More hits were scored. Soon the boy was the pursuer, circling to cut off retreat, continually slashing away until at last the old tyrant lay dead. Wade's parents could only smile and shake their heads; he was, after all, a Hampton—a warrior.[1]

As a small child, Wade was in the care of Mauma Nelly, a faithful and beloved servant who would later nurse all the Hampton children. It would be a large family. Christopher (Kit) was three years younger than Wade. Harriet Flud was born in 1823, Catharine (Kate) Pritchard in 1824, Ann M. in 1826, Caroline Louisa in 1828, Frank in 1829, and Mary Fisher in 1833.[2]

Wade would be the big brother they all looked up to. He was on the back of a horse almost as soon as he learned to walk. By age four he had his own mount, a pony named Button, and rapidly developed extraordinary riding skills. A story tells of Wade as a young man attempting to mount his horse as it plunged and reared on a Charleston street. He "vaulted into the saddle without touching the stirrup, and before the excited creature knew it, was firmly seated, cantering up the street a hundred yards or so, the horse and he had come to a perfect understanding."[3] Wade loved the outdoors. He would come to relish fishing and hunting, especially the pursuit of big game.

Wade and the other children may have received their primary education from tutors at Millwood. Learning was prized in the Hampton family, and there was certainly ample opportunity for reading in a home that boasted a large library. In 1828 Dartmouth graduate Rev. Rufus W. Brailey and associate H. L. Dana opened Richland School at Rice Creek Springs, fifteen miles northeast of Columbia. It was determined that Wade and Kit should attend, although that would require their living away from home for the first time. The village of Rice Creek Springs boasted a public house, a cluster of summer cottages, postal service, and biweekly stage connections to Columbia. The 1830 school catalog listed eighty young scholars. Most were from South Carolina, but others came from Georgia, Louisiana, and Pennsylvania, as well as Greece and Spain. Future South Carolina governor James Hopkins Adams attended, as did James Chesnut Jr. of Kershaw District, who was destined to be a U.S. senator and Confederate brigadier. Richland School's students were divided into groups of twelve, each supervised by one teacher. Styled after a European gymnasium, the school had departments of elementary, classical, belles lettres, scientific, commercial, agricultural, military, and physical education. The young men wore handsome uniforms. Each had a brass-buttoned blue coat with a standing collar; white pantaloons in summer, blue in winter. Richland School would enjoy a brief career,[4] but Wade profited from his time there, preparing for admission to South Carolina College.

The college had opened its doors in Columbia three decades earlier, over the years increasing in size and reputation. The town was growing too. South Carolina's capital had been moved from Charleston soon after the Revolutionary War to be nearer the center of the state. There a new community was fashioned from farmland and forest. Charlestonians might look down on what they saw as a country village—a place where pine trees and wood facades fronted muddy streets. Still, Columbians had vision and their own civic pride. "Columbia is a very flourishing town," wrote a Northern visitor in 1831, "and one of the handsomest in the United States, and the citizens are industrious, polite and hospitable." There were bakers and blacksmiths, apothecaries, grocers, lawyers, tailors, and doctors. The United States Hotel stood at the corner of Richardson and Lady streets. Boarding houses provided more modest lodgings. In the early 1830s Columbians read about tariffs and debated nullification in the *Southern Times and State Gazette, Columbia Telescope,* and the *South Carolinian.* On Washington Street the Methodists had raised a fine brick sanctuary and a two-story Sunday school building. The Baptist church stood at the southeastern corner of Plain and Sumter streets. Presbyterians, long active in the capital, had opened a seminary. The Columbia Female Academy offered higher education to young women.[5] Just a few blocks southeast of the capitol stood the tree-shaded brick buildings of the South Carolina College.

Chartered in 1801, the first classes were held four years later. The state-supported school had succeeded in bringing together young men from all sections of South Carolina, as its founders intended, serving to unify the state. Wade would begin his studies as the college entered the severest trial in its history.

In November 1833 college president Thomas Cooper resigned. Advocating free trade and championing state sovereignty—even to the point of disunionism—his views were gradually gaining ground. Yet, many were alienated by his irreligion. It was not in his nature to be conciliatory. "His life had been spent amid storms and tempests," wrote one who knew him, "and the howling of the wind and muttering sound of the thunder were music to his ears." Directed by the legislature, college trustees conducted an investigation and public hearing on Cooper's conduct as president. Although acquitted of any wrongdoing, the strife and negative publicity embarrassed the school. Of 114 students in 1832, ninety reported to class in February 1833. Only three sophomores returned that fall. No longer president, Cooper remained on campus as lecturer of chemistry, his mere presence keeping controversy alive. Total enrollment declined to fifty-two in the spring of 1834 and to a pathetic twenty that fall. "[T]he close of the year 1834 found the College in a deplorable condition," said one observer. "It was almost deserted."[6] Only drastic measures could save the school. Trustees asked for the resignation of the entire faculty. From the ruins there would come a complete reorganization and new beginning.

Legislators did their part by providing funds to renovate buildings, enclose the campus with a brick wall, and increase salaries. Robert Woodward Barnwell, a Harvard-educated lawyer and former congressman, was chosen as president. "The students . . . extended to him a regard and esteem which have never been surpassed," said one contemporary. "So universally popular was he in the State," wrote a later historian, "that under his administration public confidence in the institution was restored and criticism almost extinguished."[7]

A competent faculty began to be assembled. Henry Junius Nott, a genial professor of belles lettres and logic, was rehired. New Yorker Thomas S. Twiss would teach mathematics and natural philosophy.[8] Isaac W. Stuart, a Yale graduate, was named professor of Greek and Roman literature. Educated at

Columbia College and Rutgers Medical School, William H. Ellet replaced Cooper as professor of chemistry. Described by a fellow faculty member as "a man of genius and learning," he led his students in experiments with telegraphy, explosives, and photography.[9] A critical part of the reorganization was that "Christian influences . . . pervade the Campus," that the specter of Cooper be forever exorcised. To accomplish this task, young Episcopal minister Stephen Elliott was hired to teach evidences of Christianity and sacred literature. Educated at Harvard and South Carolina College, Reverend Elliott, observed a friend, "could indulge the feeling of brotherhood towards all who loved the Lord Jesus Christ in sincerity."[10]

Most distinguished of the new professors was Francis Lieber. Born in Brandenburg, a graduate of Berlin University, young Lieber had served in the Prussian Army, fighting at Ligney, Namur, and Waterloo. He immigrated to America in 1827, living in Boston, New York, and Philadelphia. He made his intellectual reputation editing the thirteen-volume *Encyclopedia Americana*. Although reluctant to teach in little Columbia, he frankly needed the job. The South Carolina professorship of history and political economy he thought of as a temporary expedient. Yet, he would stay for two decades, years spent doing his most important writing.[11]

When he first arrived on campus, Lieber found that his furniture had not been delivered to his four-room faculty residence. The Hampton family came to his rescue, lending beds. Soon he was invited to go on a long deer-hunting expedition with the Hamptons. A later professor, Maximilian LaBorde, described Lieber as "kindly-natured, free to forgive, and incapable of malice." The Prussian disliked slavery, although he was discreet enough to keep such feelings to himself. Free trade he advocated in class and out, to the applause of all South Carolinians. Lieber attended the Hampton family's Episcopal church. Evangelical Christianity—Calvinism in particular—he privately despised.[12]

Author of *Manual of Political Ethics* and *On Civil Liberty and Self-Government,* Lieber came to be known throughout America as an advocate of a strong national government. Ironically, it was a reputation he made while teaching in a state where secessionism was gaining ground. In class Lieber was respectful of his students' predisposition towards limited government and the rights of the states. His lecture room was filled with maps and globes, decorated with busts of luminaries such as Homer, Socrates, Shakespeare, Milton, Luther, and Washington.[13] If the professor won no converts to his vision of nationalism, students were challenged in their long-held assumptions and forced to defend their particularism, some perhaps emerging with a new confidence in their convictions.

It is not certain when Wade began his college studies. Most applicants were sufficiently prepared to be admitted to the sophomore class. Yet the school was in disarray during what would have been his sophomore (or even freshman) year, and existing records for that period make no mention of his name. It was possible for well-prepared students to be admitted as juniors. We know that on January 4, 1835, Wade wrote to a friend, Peter Della Torre, encouraging him to enter college now that the faculty reorganization was complete, adding "I commence my studies tomorrow." Two months later Wade joined one of the debating societies, under normal circumstances the act of a new student. Less than two years later he graduated.[14]

The junior class studied, among other things, Cicero, Juvenal, Homer, Demosthenes, descriptive geometry and conic sections, chemistry, criticism and rhetoric, moral philosophy and logic, and sacred literature. Seniors went on to geology and minerology, astronomy, history, political economy, and metaphysics. Compositions in both English and Latin would be required "at such times as the faculty may appoint."[15] It was the kind of broad, classical education designed to produce cultured gentlemen, leaders in all walks of life.

Wade joined the Clariosophic Society, one of the college's two literary and debating clubs. They met weekly in a large room over the chapel. Maxcy Gregg was another older member described by Wade as "an intimate friend of mine & who is one of the smartest young men in the state." Clariosophics raised money for expenses and philanthropy through dues and a system of fines imposed on members. Punishable infractions ranged from such things as sitting with feet in the aisle (a 12.5¢ fine), all the way up to failure to perform as an orator (a $1.00 penalty). Some members managed to compile a long record of offenses. A few had none. Wade was about average, running up a tab for such things as "reading a book in the Hall" and, on his seventeenth birthday, "talking aloud." There are no existing records of the topics of specific debates in which Wade may have participated. According to a former student and teacher, the debating societies "have stimulated the mental energies . . . far more than is done in the collegiate course of instruction." The societies, he would conclude, "are the nursery of eloquence," giving "the first impulse to many of the distinguished men of Carolina."[16]

There were only eleven in Wade's 1836 graduating class, but by then total enrollment had rebounded to 142. South Carolina College had not only survived, but was prospering as never before. "The state of the college discipline is now excellent," boasted Governor George McDuffie in 1836, "and the conduct of the students for the present year has, with few exceptions, been highly exemplary." Wade stood in the middle of his class academically. Each graduate was required to display learning and polish by making a formal speech. Wade's was titled "Oration on the Character of Tasso." Poet of the Italian High Renaissance, Torquato Tasso is best known for *Jerusalem Delivered,* an epic poem that extolled the ideals of Christian chivalry. The hero is Godfrey, a warrior anointed by the archangel Gabriel to lead a host of divided crusaders to ultimate victory. It is a story meant to inspire. Three months short of his nineteenth birthday, in chapel ceremonies, Wade Hampton was presented the A.B. degree, *artium baccalaureus,* or bachelor of arts, of South Carolina College.[17]

Wade Hampton's career in public service began just a month after graduation. Although it involved few real responsibilities, there was now a title to precede his name. On January 7, 1837, incoming governor Pierce Mason Butler made staff military appointments, positions more honorary than active, but certainly bringing welcome recognition. The adjutant and inspector general's order appeared in newspapers across the state. Wade Hampton was among those appointed "Aids de Camp to the Commander in Chief, with the rank of Lieutenant Colonel. They will equip themselves within thirty days from the reception of this order, and report to Head Quarters, for duty, after which they will be commissioned and obeyed and respected accordingly."[18] He must have cut quite a figure in the smart blue uniform of the South Carolina militia, set off with epaulets, sword, and gleaming brass buttons that bore the palmetto emblem.

Wade's diploma from South Carolina College carried the signature of his father. The second Wade Hampton, like his own father before him, served as trustee. There is a story told of one college student who made regular rides out to Millwood after classes each Friday, perhaps to visit with young Wade. Although a policy seldom enforced, owning a horse was a violation of school rules. Trustee Hampton welcomed his guest, but could not simply wink at so flagrant an infraction.

"I think you had better sell that horse," the elder Hampton advised the student. Of course, he did. On the following Friday the young man went again to the stable in Columbia, this time to *hire* a horse. To the boy's surprise, a fine thoroughbred was led out and he was handed the reins.

"Colonel Hampton sent this horse here," explained the liveryman, "and said he was to be kept for your use as long as you are at college."

James De Veaux, a promising but struggling artist and friend of young Wade, once toured the galleries of England and France at Colonel Hampton's expense. Arriving in Liverpool, he presented a letter of credit to a shopkeeper named Forde. "But," said the astonished Mr. Forde, "Col. Hampton does not limit your credit in this letter."

De Veaux coolly replied, "I did not expect he would, sir."[19]

The second Wade Hampton "was a complete model and specimen of the old time, outspoken, open-handed gentleman," remembered an acquaintance. South Carolina politician Benjamin F. Perry recalled that "his home was full of company, and he delighted in the companionship of his friends." Although not a public speaker, Wade Hampton Jr. "was pleasant and agreeable in conversation." An unsigned tribute, probably written by one of his daughters, describes him as having "that peculiar trait (inherited by his son Wade III) of drawing and influencing all with whom he was thrown." A peacemaker, he intervened to stop many duels, "all feeling that their honor was safe."[20] His liberality and benevolence contrasted with his father's reputation for sharp business dealings.

The second Wade Hampton had served his father long and well, sharing in the management of the Hampton empire, spending much time at Houmas. From the Louisiana plantation he mailed regular reports to the old general, detailing the progress of the sugar crop, the digging of drainage ditches, the weather. Only rarely did he comment on family matters. The first Wade Hampton had withdrawn from public life, and as he entered his eighties, he was perceived as being "quite childish" and "rather churlish." Still, to one observer, he "seemed to be a thin, wiry, fiery horseman, who sat as easy and erect as any youth of one-fourth his age."

On one of his last trips to Virginia, the general stopped at a friend's house for the night. Early the next morning Hampton was found sitting under a tree, one of his host's turkeys hanging from a branch. "I had to kill him," he explained. "He was strutting about and beating all the smaller fowls, and I could not endure it. It was not fair play."[21]

There were those who might recognize in the offending bird the old general himself.

Hampton saw a doctor nearly every week during the last year of his life, finally dying on February 4, 1835. His estate, valued at a then-astronomical $1,641,065, was divided equally among wife, Mary, and children Caroline, Susan, and Wade Jr.[22]

The second Wade Hampton held the rank of colonel in the state's militia, the kind of duty expected of a man of his station. And although he continued to manage his plantations and even invest in mines and railroads, he seemed better suited to spending money than accumulating it. Breeding and racing horses became his passion. Active in the South Carolina Jockey Club, "no one can be fonder of fine horses than Col. Hampton," said a fellow aficionado. "He is not only a gentleman of high character, but of great liberality on the Turf." Hampton on one occasion donated a magnificent silver cup for use as a prize. Another time he gave the club the $1,200 that his entry had just won that they might make improvements to Charleston's Washington Race Course.[23]

To escape the oppressive Carolina summer the family took extended trips to the mountains of Virginia. At fashionable White Sulphur Springs, they built a cottage and enjoyed hunting, fishing, and mingling with socially elite vacationers.[24] But it was back home at Millwood that the Hamptons redefined hospitality.

The original structure was renovated in 1838 and expanded with the addition of wings. Six massive columns gave Millwood the Greek Revival appearance then in vogue. Benjamin F. Perry described his arrival at a Hampton party. "The company was invited at eight o'clock in the evening. When we

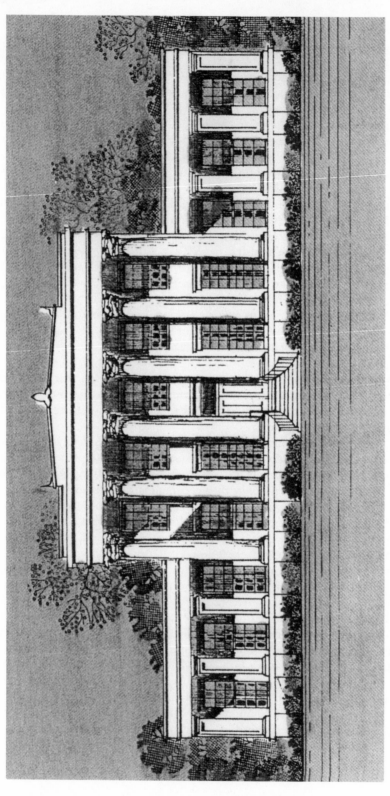

A conjectural rendition of Millwood after the 1838 renovations. *Virginia G. Meynard, The Venturers (Greenville, S.C.: Southern Historical Press, 1981).*

reached the avenue leading from the public road to his [Wade Hampton Jr.'s] house, we saw on both sides of it, huge lighted torches of pine, making the road as bright as if it were mid-day. The supper was most luxurious and very handsomely decorated."

Just four miles from the capital, Millwood was a favorite meeting place for politicians. Antebellum South Carolina had no organized political parties. Personalities were as important as issues in deciding the outcome of elections. In the absence of party loyalty, shifting coalitions and alliances determined votes in the all-powerful general assembly. Made up of a Senate and House of Representatives, South Carolina's general assembly chose the governor, lieutenant governor, state officers, U.S. senators, and even presidential electors. The second Wade Hampton, master of Millwood, could have had nearly any office he desired, but chose to exercise his influence behind the scenes. "For more than twenty years he was the great Warwick of South Carolina," remembered Perry. "He preferred making governors to being one himself."[25] The colonel had been elected to the state Senate in 1826, but served only a single term of four years. There he was a member of committees on agriculture, banks, grievances, accounts, and the military.[26] But Senator Hampton would face one question during his time in office that eclipsed all others.

That issue was protective tariffs. High federal tariffs on imported goods forced Southerners to buy from Northern manufacturers. Consumers in South Carolina were paying inflated prices so that Northern manufacturers might grow and prosper. To be sure, duties were the government's primary source of income, and Congress had the constitutional authority to regulate commerce. But Southerners argued that a permanent, high tariff was patently unfair and even destroyed commerce. In the summer of 1827 protest meetings were held across the state. The South Carolina general assembly in December drafted a mildly worded resolution opposing the tariff, urging that "the State Legislatures be watchful, and to remonstrate with Congress when necessary." Complaints went unheeded. The following May Congress passed the infamous "Tariff of Abominations," raising import duties to 50 percent. South Carolinians were indignant. In the state House of Representatives, a young firebrand from Colleton District, Robert Barnwell Rhett, demanded action—even secession if need be.[27]

South Carolina's John C. Calhoun was serving as U.S. vice president. He had been formulating a reasoned case against the tariff. Protectionism he branded "a breach of a well-defined trust," a system "grossly unequal." It was up to the sovereign states "to determine, authoritatively, whether the acts of which we complain be unconstitutional; and, if so, whether they constitute a violation so deliberate, palpable and dangerous, as to justify the interposition of the State to protect its rights." South Carolinians, although "anxiously desiring to live in peace" and "to preserve and perpetuate the union of the states," must protest the present tariff "as unconstitutional, oppressive, and unjust."[28]

Calhoun carried his sixty-page report to the leaders of South Carolina's general assembly. On December 17, 1828, the South Carolina Senate, meeting as a committee of the whole, took up the issue. "After considerable time spent in discussion," recorded the clerk, a resolution was agreed upon declaring that "the tariff acts of congress, for the protection of domestic manufactures, are unconstitutional and should be resisted." The method of resistance? That "other states be invited to cooperate with this state" in making that determination. A special Senate committee was then appointed, with one member from each of the state's nine congressional districts. Members of the committee were charged with drafting a declaration that "will clearly elucidate the principles of South Carolina." The vote on the resolution was thirty-four in favor, six opposed. Wade Hampton Jr. voted aye. He was also chosen to serve on the special committee. That committee studied Calhoun's document, making only minor changes. Two days later, on December 19, 1828, the state Senate and House of Representatives voted to adopt *The South Carolina Exposition*.[29]

After Senator Hampton left office, the tariff issue continued to fester. South Carolina unionists were opposed to protectionism, but seemed unwilling to do more than complain. Growing numbers of others entertained thoughts of leaving a union they felt had become a burden. Calhoun understood what was at stake. He conceded that a state might secede from a compact it had voluntarily joined, but he was intent on saving both the Union and constitutional government. Perhaps if South Carolina were to nullify an unconstitutional law—to suspend its enforcement within the borders of the state—that very act might force change. Problematic—even desperate—nullification was the prescription of a man who loved and wanted to preserve unchanged the Republic of the Founding Fathers.[30]

The second Wade Hampton supported Calhoun's leadership, although his aged father was pessimistic that "clamours against the Tariff" would ever succeed. On November 24, 1832, a convention of the people of South Carolina nullified the new tariff, but delayed the effective date of their action two months, allowing time for negotiations. President Andrew Jackson threatened force, Calhoun resigned the vice presidency (quickly returning to Washington as a senator), and both sides prepared for war. An eleventh-hour compromise tariff bill, put together by Henry Clay, was accepted by South Carolina in early 1833. The crisis had passed, ended by an accommodation that settled nothing permanently.[31] The constitution itself had been the product of compromise rather than consensus. Did sovereignty—ultimate political power—reside with the people of the United States or the people of the individual states? The issue remained unresolved. The first Wade Hampton had voted against ratification of the constitution. His son now had to wrestle with problems made unavoidable by that document's inability to deal with sectionalism. The next generation, that of Wade Hampton III, would pay the ultimate price.

As the crisis over nullification neared an end, Ann Fitzsimons Hampton delivered her eighth child, Mary Fisher. There were complications. The thirty-nine-year-old mother never recovered, dying a few weeks later. Wade was almost fifteen, preparing for South Carolina College. He would, of course, feel the loss. But it would affect the younger children most. The second Wade Hampton never remarried. The little girls, none older than ten when she died, would grow up without a mother's care and guidance.[32]

Soon after his college graduation, it is said, Wade Hampton III read law, although he never attempted to pass the bar exam and practice. He may have studied in the office and under the guidance of his uncle John Smith Preston, Columbia attorney and Harvard Law graduate. Even an elemental knowledge of the law would serve Hampton well.

The young Wade was described as tall and handsome, with light brown hair. "His eyes were large, and gray in color, but having a 'suspicion' of blue, when in repose, and could be on occasion steel-gray," remembered a friend.

> His voice in conversation . . . had that smooth, flowing-water sound. . . . Standing just six feet in height, broad-shouldered, deep-chested, well proportioned in waist, and narrow hipped, with legs which, if he chose to close them in a grip, could make a horse groan with pain, he possessed an iron constitution, and great muscular strength, gifts of nature and inheritance, never marred by any excess, and kept in vigor by habits of out-of-door exercise. Tobacco he used in no form, and wine or liquor very sparingly.[33]

The third Wade Hampton traveled extensively, on business for his father and on vacations with the family. It was at White Sulphur Springs that he met Margaret, the youngest daughter of Sarah Preston and her late husband, former congressman Francis Preston. Wade and Margaret had probably known each other since childhood. The Prestons were a family long prominent in southwestern Virginia, and it was Margaret's brother John, the attorney, who had married Wade's aunt Caroline in 1830. Wade and Margaret courted at the Virginia resort. They were married in a ceremony at the bride's home in Abington, Virginia, on October 10, 1838. Both were twenty years old. Tradition called for an extended wedding trip, after which they settled back in South Carolina.

Wade confided to James De Veaux that he was "married and happy." "God bless you, and *keep* you so," replied his friend, "you deserve to be *doubly blessed*—first for your kindness toward others, and secondly for the *peculiar care* you have taken of *yourself*, as your act of 10th October most fully proves." James recalled "glorious times together, in our bachelor state," riding, hunting, eating, and drinking.

Wade Hampton III's first wife, Margaret Preston. *Virginia G. Meynard, The Venturers (Greenville, S.C.: Southern Historical Press, 1981).*

[M]y dear Wade, if you are not always happy 'twill be your own fault—with means sufficient for all rational uses—friends (poor and rich) ready to advance you in any route, that *taste, pleasure,* or *ambition* may suggest, and with all this, and more, the lady of your love, your *first* matchless choice.[34]

The newlyweds called their home Sand Hills. It was just outside Columbia on that stretch of land thought once to be a prehistoric coastline, but no description of the house remains. Colonel Hampton and his children stayed a few miles away at Millwood. U.S. Senator William Campbell Preston, eldest of the Preston brothers, regularly returned to Columbia when the Senate was not in session. Susan Hampton, youngest of General Hampton's daughters, had just married John Lawrence Manning. They were regular visitors at the Columbia town house John and Caroline Preston shared with Caroline's widowed mother. Later additions to that structure would make it nearly as impressive a venue for entertaining as the legendary Millwood. Over the years, what became known as the Hampton-Preston house saw countless family births, weddings, deaths, and funerals.[35]

Wade Hampton III kept busy with the management and expansion of his cotton plantations in Mississippi. Bayou Place, Wild Woods, Otterbourne, and Richland totaled some 8,168 acres. He owned Bear Garden, a 2,000-acre hunting preserve in the Magnolia State, as well. But Mississippi summers were as sweltering and malarial as those in his own state. In 1845 Wade Hampton, brother Kit, and their father purchased 2,300 acres in North Carolina and there built a hunting and fishing lodge. At an elevation of 3,200 feet, it provided them a relief from the lowland heat. A former slave and companion of the third Wade Hampton remembered how "the master was a pow'ful man for hunting bear and deer." It was said he could sling a dead bear over a horse's back single-handedly. The Hamptons called their retreat the Valley. On summer Sabbaths there were no neighborhood churches to attend, but the third Wade Hampton habitually refrained from fishing or hunting on that day, playing with children instead. The Hamptons kept livestock on the property, including two bulls named Brutus and Cassius. Once Cassius got caught in a thicket and broke his neck struggling to escape. The area came to be known by the name of the unlucky beast. In mountain parlance, "Cassius" soon became (with the accent on the first syllable) "Cashiers," and the name stuck.[36]

Bear hunts in the swamps of Mississippi might last a month or more. They were held annually, when the crops were in and after frosts had eliminated mosquitoes. "Wade Hampton [III] also brought a good many negroes with him," remembered a participant, "and at night there was music and dancing and all kinds of plantation songs from the fiddlers, and banjo players around campfires." In his lifetime Hampton is said to have been present at the death of 500 bears. Most he killed himself. He dispatched thirty or forty with his knife, and during one of these encounters, he was injured in the forearm.

> 'Now if you are not familiar with the bear, be careful. Don't take him into close quarters. Put a ball through his heart before he can reach you with his paws; but if you fail to do this, stand not on the order of your going—leave! And, by the way, whatever you do, save the dogs.'[37]

Wade and Margaret Hampton had their first child in 1840, a son, and carried on tradition by naming him Wade. Margaret seemed contented in her role of wife and mother. A second son, Thomas Preston, was born two years later. The family would call him simply Preston.[38]

Their father was involved in an 1841 incident that earned applause from his neighbors. The third Wade Hampton was in Columbia when a fire broke out in a blacksmith's shop and quickly spread, consuming buildings from Plain to Taylor streets. Hampton climbed to the roof of a threatened structure and began fighting the flames. He was aided by a sailor named Neville who happened to be in town visiting relatives. The two of them were able to save the building, but "presented a sad appearance when they came down from the roof," remembered a bystander, "hair and whiskers singed, clothing soaked with water, blackened and burned. The crowd cheered them heartily."[39]

The conflagration had spared the wooden sanctuary of Trinity Episcopal Church, where the Hamptons and Prestons worshipped. The families were generous in their support of Trinity and would later contribute to the building of the larger Gothic edifice that replaced the first structure. The Hamptons offered to pay for the new church themselves, but Rector Peter Shand naturally wanted the whole congregation to participate. Dr. Shand spoke at the laying of the cornerstone, in which was placed a Bible and Book of Common Prayer. "Here may worldly anxieties and worldly strifes find no entrance—the passions of our corrupt nature be hushed into silence." The Hamptons and Prestons maintained family plots in the church cemetery. The second Wade Hampton would later back a nondenominational plan to support a missionary to blacks in the district, build a church, and provide religious instruction for his own slaves.[40]

Hampton's public piety contrasted with brother-in-law James Henry Hammond's lack of faith. "I have not a Christian's hopes or feelings," confessed Hammond, "the comforts of Religion are wholly wanting to me." Son of a transplanted New Englander, Hammond graduated from South Carolina College in just two years. In a college debate he once argued against the question, Should seduction be punished by death? In 1830 he set out to marry Catherine Elizabeth Fitzsimons, Ann Hampton's young sister, described as "a homely sixteen year old Charleston heiress." It took many tears for Cath-

A youthful Wade Hampton III. Miniature by an unknown artist, circa 1840. *Manly Wade Wellman, Giant in Gray (New York: Charles Scribner's Sons, 1949)*.

erine to overcome her family's opposition. The marriage made Hammond the master of Silver Bluff plantation in Barnwell District. Political ambition soon led him to a seat in the U.S. Congress.[41] He was a man on the way up.

Hammond kept a private journal, virtually unknown until its 1988 publication and appalling in its revelation of his long liaison with one of his slaves, Sally, beginning when she was eighteen. When Sally's daughter Louisa reached the age of twelve, Hammond took her for a mistress as well, fathering children by them both. His sordid affairs remained well-kept secrets.[42]

The Hamptons were close to Catherine and James Hammond, often visiting them at Silver Bluff and in the home Hammond maintained in Columbia. Elected to the two-year term of South Carolina governor in 1842, Hammond began to spend more time in the capital. For the most part the second Wade Hampton was open and cordial. Yet caution appears in his letters, hinting that perhaps he felt something was not quite right in Hammond's solicitous attitude towards his daughters.[43]

It may have been at the races in Nashville in October 1843 that Catharine Hampton went to her father and told him what she had been keeping a secret for months. On April 13, her uncle James, the nineteen-year-old charged, had attempted to seduce her.[44]

According to one account Catharine's father threatened Hammond with death. Son Wade and brothers-in-law John Manning and John Preston each wanted to kill Hammond themselves. William Campbell Preston is said to have intervened, calming, reasoning with the outraged father. Hammond reported receiving on November 1 a letter from the second Wade Hampton "denouncing me in the coursest terms" and severing all relations. Hammond tried to patch things up with a message sent by way of John Preston, but was immediately rebuffed. In that letter Hammond made references to "dalliances with his Daughters, using the plural."[45]

Hammond did not know what to expect next. The girls' father, a churchgoer, was supposed to be against dueling and private justice. The murder of a governor, and the reason for it, would be the talk of the nation. Still, Hammond nervously pocketed pistols. At the conclusion of the legislative session, he raced to the safety of his Barnwell District home.[46]

Soon the governor learned that the father's vengeance would be more subtle than the violence he had feared. The Hamptons, Mannings, and Prestons are "pursuing me with the bitterest persecution," he complained in his journal. Catharine's father was orchestrating the destruction of Hammond's political career. John Manning and John Preston "have gone all over the state," Hammond wrote that summer, "and are generally believed." Sometimes he felt like "coming out with the *whole truth* and fighting my way through." Back in Columbia for the next legislative session, in November 1844, Hammond thought others cool towards him. He kept looking over his shoulder. At his successor's inauguration he stayed close to the militia escort, keeping a sharp eye on his enemies, for "from their movements I rather apprehended an attack after the ceremony." The former governor once again beat a hasty retreat out of town.[47]

In later journal entries Hammond revealed his version of "the whole truth." He claimed that for two years he had engaged in sexual intimacy with four of his Hampton nieces. Initiated by Harriet when she was about eighteen, the games included sixteen-year-old Catharine, fourteen-year-old Ann, and even thirteen-year-old Caroline. The girls strove to outdo each other in sexual teasing and intimacy that "extended to everything short of direct sexual intercourse." Finally, in April 1843, Catharine "took offense at a familiarity." Surprised, Hammond said that he immediately recognized "the full extent of my past indiscretions" and stopped.[48]

Without revealing details, Hammond defended himself in correspondence with loyal friends. William Gilmore Simms rallied blindly to his side. A few months earlier Simms had advised Edgar Allen Poe to beware of bad associations, "subdue [his] impulses," and cherish his wife—excellent advice to a man he hardly knew. As time passed Hammond's conscience stopped bothering him, giving way to bitterness and frustration. John Preston and "young Wade" were, according to Hammond, "two fools universally acknowledged as such." "Both their wives hate me," he whined, "because I have always held them in contempt, and they have perhaps been the instigators." Hammond speculated that the second Wade Hampton knew only of the April 1843 incident. "I question whether he has even said one word to the girls on the subject. . . . A man of any sense would have been led by this [Hammond's letter] to probe the whole matter to the bottom. But Hampton is not such." Hammond complained of his own wife's unwillingness to mend the breach with the Hamptons. She feared that her husband might continue to pursue the girls. The long-suffering Mrs. Hammond finally left her husband over his refusal to give up the slave girl Louisa.[49]

Hammond spent the next fourteen years in political exile. "He seemed to be disgusted with the State and everything in it," wrote Benjamin F. Perry. In 1857 Hammond narrowly out-polled Francis Pickens for a seat in the U.S. Senate, finally overcoming what the defeated candidate called "that private feud" everyone knew at least something about.[50]

Hammond's journal is the only major source of information we have on the scandal. Of Catharine's side of the story, the true extent of the girls' involvement, the family's ordeal—we can only speculate. The Hampton children grew up privileged, cherished by an overly indulgent father. The girls had entered adolescence motherless, probably bored and unsupervised, artless if not innocent. They would emerge from the trial seemingly chastened and subdued, even depressed. Harriet died in 1848, only twenty-five years old. Catharine, Ann, and Caroline each lived into the twentieth century. None of the four ever married.[51]

The third Wade Hampton rallied to the defense of his sister, reacting in loyalty and love as expected of an older brother. He and his extended family drew even closer in the aftermath. But he must have asked that most human of questions, Why? Why had this calamity come upon his family? Why must such unhappiness afflict those he loved? As he grappled for answers, perhaps he turned to the faith that sustained his own father. The words of an old Episcopal hymn promised comfort to those who would but trust in God.

> Deep in unfathomable mines,
>   With never-failing skill,
> He treasures up his bright designs,
>   And works his gracious will.[52]

"FLAGS WERE WAVING IN EVERY DIRECTION"

Hampton Chooses Secession

Margaret Hampton chose to return to the home of her mother in Abingdon, Virginia, during the summer of 1845 for the delivery of her third child. On September 7, Sarah Buchanan Hampton, called Sally, was born. One month later, down in Columbia, Susan Hampton Manning died soon after giving birth to a son. Grieving over the loss of his sister and ill himself, the second Wade Hampton was also concerned about his brother-in-law John Smith Preston. John and Caroline Preston had moved to Louisiana in 1840. Responsibility for managing the vast Houmas plantation left Preston physically exhausted and emotionally drained. Legal challenges to his ownership of the land, cases that would drag through the courts for years, added to his burdens. The elder Hampton thought that a change of scene might help. He suggested that the Prestons, accompanied by Wade and Margaret Hampton, vacation abroad. They took him up on the idea. But by the late spring of 1846 Margaret was expecting another child, making a sea voyage and extensive travel impossible. It was agreed that Wade alone should accompany the Prestons across the Atlantic.[1]

They departed in midsummer, armed with letters of introduction. Hampton kept his wife and sisters apprised of their travels. From London in late July, the twenty-eight-year-old told his wife that he had received an invitation to meet the Duke of Wellington at a large, formal reception. Hampton thought Wellington, then seventy-two, a "kind looking old man." "How I

did wish that your magnificent beauty could have shone in that great hall,"
he wrote to Margaret, "to shame the diamond covered brows of the haughty
princesses." At Madame Tussaud's museum Hampton inspected Napoleon's
watch, his toothbrush, and the sword Bonaparte carried during the French
invasion of Egypt. "In another room we saw his military carriage in which he
made the campaign of Russia—I sat in it." Hampton heard a speech by
Henry Peter Broughm, Edinburgh-born reformer and foe of slavery. He had
breakfast with poet and raconteur Samuel Rogers, then eighty-three. Hampton wrote, "Rogers is one of the most delightful charming old men I ever
saw, . . . [He] talks beautifully and is very fond of America. He seems to be a
link between the present and the past."[2]

The party lingered for two weeks in London, but still Hampton was
unable to see all that he wished. He was particularly impressed with the
Tower of London, Westminister Abbey, Saint Paul's Cathedral, Apsley
House, and the park at Hampton Court. He confided to sister Harriet that
"men all over England are not one bit better looking than our country men.
Indeed I have found out that the English are as great boasters as the Yankees
whom they laugh at so much." He was unable to remember the titles of
all the noble ladies he met, "and called them 'madam,' in my republican
simplicity."

At Oxford University Hampton was overwhelmed by the half million
volumes of the Bodleian Library. He visited Stratford-on-Avon, paid his
respects at Shakespeare's grave, and took a rose leaf as a keepsake for Margaret's mother. He missed his family. "I must try to bring you over," he wrote
to Margaret. "I know you would enjoy everything so much. What will we do
with those three or four little rascals, bring them too? We ought to have come
when we first proposed to do so. You stopped me twice," he teased, "so it is
but fair that you should send me over." He bought presents for family members. Little Wade he admonished to be "a good boy and take care of Preston & Sally. How I do miss them, especially my little Sally, my dear
playfellow. I fear she will forget me. By this time she is walking alone I
hope; & talking too. Make her learn to talk of me." He was glad to report
that John Smith Preston "is quite well and in good spirits, much better than
I have seen him for a long time. He has lost that morbid feeling that gave
him so much trouble and his family such uneasiness."[3]

One family story has it that while in England Hampton "visited a
museum where the curator showed him a long bow which he said had not
been strung since the days of the yeoman." The American tourist promptly
proceeded to string the bow and "passed the arrow through it, destroying
the old curator's story."[4]

Soon after his return to South Carolina, a son was born to Wade and
Margaret Hampton. Named John Preston, within a year the child was dead.
Tragedy struck again on June 2, 1848, when Wade's sister Harriet died at

Millwood. When a daughter was born to the Hamptons eleven days later, the grieving brother named the child after his deceased sister. Life was, as the Bible said, "a vapour, that appeareth for a little time, and then vanisheth away."[5] Yet in all of his afflictions, the third Wade Hampton managed to endure with faith unshaken. He was becoming the one that family members turned to for leadership and strength. Little did he know that his own trials were only beginning.

Four years later on June 27, 1852, Margaret Hampton died. The cause is not known. At age thirty-four Wade Hampton III was a widower. His four unmarried sisters would care for the surviving children. Son Wade IV was eleven, Preston nine, Sally almost seven, and Harriet four. The next year little Harriet died. She had been the special favorite of her aunt Mary Fisher Hampton, who took her loss particularly hard. "Your love of, and devotion to her, exceeded a mother's," wrote Mary's father.

> But my dear child you should remember that to grieve for this child, so dear to us all, is selfish. Who can doubt that our loss is her gain. Removed from a world, which to her had been little more than a scene of suffering & of pain, her spirit is now at rest, on the bosom of her mother & in the company of her god.[6]

As the Hamptons comforted one another in their losses, America at mid-century was growing ever more divided. Few could have foreseen the problems that would accompany victory in the war with Mexico. On August 8, 1846, Pennsylvania congressman David Wilmot proposed that slavery be prohibited in territory acquired from Mexico. Passed by the House, defeated in the Senate, the Wilmot Proviso created a furor in the South. Calhoun demanded that the territories, the common property of all the states, be administered without discriminating between the sections. He warned that if "the alternative is forced upon us of resistance or submission, who can doubt the result. Though the Union is dear to us, our honor and our liberty are dearer." Southerners, said Greenville unionist Benjamin F. Perry, must "declare that any interference on the part of the Federal Government with slave property will be the cause of an immediate dissolution of this great and hitherto glorious Union." The dispute over slavery in the territories was seen by Southerners as but part of a larger campaign being waged against them. At Calhoun's suggestion a statewide meeting would be held in Columbia on May 14 and 15, 1849. Delegates resolved to be on their guard since "a vast power, sleepless in activity and remourseless in purpose, is organized and moving against them." The second Wade Hampton and four other prominent citizens were elected at this gathering to the Central Committee of Vigilance and Safety.[7]

The Compromise of 1850 proved to be a disappointment to Southerners.

California was admitted as a nonslaveholding state, and other concessions were made in exchange for the Fugitive Slave Act—a law that Northern states routinely chose to ignore. Secessionists demanded that South Carolina act. A group of moderates met in Columbia in the fall of 1850 to urge caution, recommending that Gov. Whitemarsh B. Seabrook not take precipitate action. The third Wade Hampton was host to James Chesnut Jr. and his delegation from Camden, and he probably attended this meeting himself. Debate raged on. The Southern Rights Association declared in 1851 that "South Carolina entered this Confederacy as a sovereign and independent State, and that, having been wronged, she has the perfect right to withdraw from it." The following year, for the first time since the nullification crisis, a convention of the people convened in South Carolina. Although delegates drew back from immediate secession, they voted overwhelmingly for an ordinance that affirmed state sovereignty. South Carolina, they proclaimed, had become a part of the Union "in exercise of her sovereign will," could depart the same way, and was answerable only "to the tribunal of public opinion among the nations of the earth."[8]

Although the third Wade Hampton was not prominent in these deliberations, he was at this point opposed to South Carolina's leaving the Union. His caution was shared by a majority in the state. "I took a very active part against the secession movement," he stated almost two decades later, "and used all the influence I had against it." His greatest responsibility remained the management of four plantations in Mississippi, where he often spent the spring and summer months. Scores of surviving letters to his favorite sister, Mary Fisher Hampton, reveal much about the man. He relied on Mary Fisher for news of the family, and he expressed his love and concern for them in every letter. "We must all now strive to be as much together *here* as possible & to prepare to spend a blessed eternity as one united family." He could tease too. "You must not think I write to you because you asked me to do so or because I care for you, or for any such foolish reason." He shared his feelings about the losses he had suffered, particularly the death of wife Margaret. "Memory, when I shut out external things, in an instant brings up the happy past. . . . Again I hear the voice and see the smile that once was dearer to me than all else on earth." But he would not dwell on his grief or be consumed by it. "All must be for the best. I hope at some future time to see this clearly. Now I must strive to bear as all have to do."[9]

Sarah Strong Baxter, twenty-one-year-old daughter of a prominent New York City family, visited Columbia in 1854. Sally, as she was called, attracted the attention of twenty-five-year-old Frank Hampton. By the time she returned a year later, she and Frank had announced their engagement. They were married in New York City in December, returning to live first at Millwood, then Woodlands. Sally was beautiful and well educated. As a teenager she had counted among her admirers English novelist William Makepeace

Thackery, becoming his inspiration for the heroine in *The Newcomes*. Twice her age, Thackery was initially upset over Sally's engagement, but upon meeting Frank he relented and even bought them a wedding gift. "Hampton is a fine young fellow," wrote Thackery, "good looking burly honest not a literairy cove—Last year when the cholera was on his plantation he would not leave it but staid and nursed his poor black people by whom he is adored."[10]

Sally Baxter Hampton described her new life in letters to her family.

> The ease and liberality with which everything is conducted makes it seem so natural that one forgets what is in reality great magnificence. . . . We sit down every day fourteen to twenty at dinner—people come and go, stay or not as they please and it all passes off as a matter of course.

The Hampton family, she wrote,

> seems to me the most remarkable of any I ever saw—four unmarried sisters—each utterly different from the other and yet it is impossible to say which is the most attractive. Such highbred elegance and with sufficient more than ordinary cleverness, such perfect femininity and womanliness.

Sally was suffering from tuberculosis, but the disease would not be diagnosed for several years. She related to her father "how tender and gentle" her husband and her brother-in-law were to her during a recent illness.

> Half a dozen times in a day brother Wade will come to my room to inquire about me and always with some suggestion for my comfort that shows he really thinks about it. Now that I am out and about, tho' still suffering from the pain, he watches me, sees when I am tired and notices the least indication of pain.[11]

Sally—New Yorker turned South Carolinian—recognized an irrepressible conflict between the sections over slavery. "Anybody who stops to investigate can't but see how utterly impracticable to the southern mind is any idea of compromise, and how northern fanaticism on this subject is ever to be moderated Heaven above knows."[12] Both Wade and Frank had reputations for being paternalistic masters who treated slaves as individuals and as fellow human beings. Bondsman Jonas Weeks remembered Wade Hampton as a "good man" who dealt "kindly" with his slaves and fed them well, and they "loved him" in return. Abolitionists preferred to dwell on slavery's abuses, even as they ignored its long history. Southerners knew the institution had existed since the dawn of time, that "the glory that was Greece and the grandeur that was Rome" had been built by slave labor. Slavery was regulated in Old Testament days, tolerated by the New Testament church, defended by philosophers, and practiced by America's Founding Fathers. Both North and

South had been slave-owning during the colonial period. Slaves, purchased in Africa from their African owners, were transported to the New World by New England slave traders. Slavery was gradually ended in the North only when it became unimportant economically. South of the Mason-Dixon Line, it was a very different matter. One historian writes,

> Whether or not slavery was essential to the South, it was essential to the South to have the power to maintain slavery. If the North could control the one, she could control all. This was the issue, the tragedy, that slavery had become the proving ground of the South's fight to maintain her rights as a minority within the Union.[13]

In the spring of 1859, Frank and Sally Hampton, searching for a healthful climate, vacationed in Cuba. At their Havana hotel Sally met antislavery activist Julia Ward Howe, who was traveling with her husband. Mrs. Howe remembered hearing of Sally Baxter Hampton, "a great belle in her time, and much admired by Mr. Thackery." She described Sally now as "a lovely lady, with pathetic dark eyes and a look of ill health."

"Are you *the* Mrs. Hampton?" asked Howe.

"Are you *the* Mrs. Howe?" Sally replied.

"We became friends at once," wrote Howe. "The Hamptons went with us to Matanzas, where we passed a few pleasant days." The two couples later journeyed together to Charleston and from there to the Hampton's Columbia home. "Wade Hampton called upon Dr. Howe," remembered Mrs. Howe, "and soon introduced a topic which we would gladly have avoided, namely the strained relations between the North and the South."

"We mean to fight for it," she quoted Wade Hampton as saying, without telling what was said to provoke his response.[14] In two years Julia Ward Howe would pen "The Battle Hymn of the Republic." By then what had once been "strained relations" had become an apocalyptic mission of divine judgment meted out by the righteous North upon a wicked South.

The third Wade Hampton remained interested in South Carolina College. In 1853 he wrote to college president James Henley Thornwell. "I desire to manifest my gratitude to my Alma Mater by placing under its protection, some at least, who tho worthy of an education, are unable to procure one." It was a sentiment Thornwell could appreciate. As a youth he had himself been the recipient of such help. Later college catalogs list the availability of five scholarships, two funded by Hampton. "These are awarded by the Faculty to young men of more than ordinary merit and attainments. . . . They are not designed to be simply aids to indigence, but compliments to excellence."[15]

One winter morning in 1858 the second Wade Hampton, now almost sixty-seven years old, entered the Millwood library and spoke to his daughters.

"Father is very unhappy," he said, "I dreamed last night I had done a mean thing & God knows, I did not think, that even in a dream, I would do a mean thing."

On the afternoon of February 9, while reading his Bible, he died.[16] Wade had to console his sisters as he himself grieved over the loss of his father. "You may be assured that I shall do all in my power to comfort our dear Sisters," he wrote to Mary Fisher Hampton. "Their wishes shall be my law, and my time shall be at their disposal. I feel that I can not better prove my love for him we have lost, than by caring for those beloved daughters who were so dear to him." He was sure that his father had

> become a *christian,* for he did believe in the savior and was only withheld from an open profession of his faith by his conscientious fear that he was not *good* enough to become a member of the church. But his heart was changed, & I hope & think God knew that he was fit to be a member of *his* church in Heaven, & took him to himself. We have always been a most united family & I feel that this will but draw closer the bonds that have bound us together.

It was Wade's prayer that his sisters were "*looking forward with hope.* It would be wrong for you, young as you are, to despond, for there may be much happiness in store for you." On Good Friday he wrote to Mary Fisher, regretting that he could not be in Columbia to join them "in the beautiful and impressive services of our church." He assured his sisters of his prayers.

> I hope God will bless you all and reward you for your devotion to the father who loved you so much. I believe that *he* is happy. I *know* he was spared much trouble, and I feel that our Father in Heaven *must* have acted wisely. All that seems dark to us now, will at some future time, be clear.[17]

Unlike his father, the third Wade Hampton would not remain a widower. Mary Singleton McDuffie had been twenty-one when her father died in March 1851. Congressman, governor, senator, and oratorical genius, George McDuffie became a political legend in South Carolina. He spent a lifetime battling protective tariffs, the growing dominance of the industrial Northeast, and the power of the federal government. Wade Hampton, twelve years older than Mary, became interested in her when he was asked to help in managing her father's estate. "You need have no fear of giving me trouble," Wade assured Mary in March 1856. It would be a protracted and stormy courtship. For a time he had competition from young Charleston lawyer James Johnston Pettigrew. Near the end of the year Sally Baxter Hampton wrote that Wade "is supposed to be on the verge of espousals with the witty demoiselle."[18] Something went awry, for on Saint Valentine's Day, 1857, Wade wrote Mary a melancholy poem.

Mary Singleton McDuffie, Hampton's second wife, from an 1846 portrait attributed to John Wesley Jarvis. *Historic Columbia Foundation Collection.*

To Miss Mary McDuffie

When the birds to their southern homes so bright,
Were planning their flight last November,
They promised me, a fair lady to see,
And tell me if she could *remember*.

They said they would warble their lovliest tone,
When such beauty and grace they discover,
And the sweetest song, that their notes could prolong,
They would sing, when around her they hover.

Each morn should their melody open her eyes
Like a welcome of sunshine and gladness
And at eve she should hear, tones most plaintive and clear,
While they whisper to her of *my* sadness.

Ah me! Will she listen *to day,* and believe
In the notes of their musical letters?
Will her smile come to bless? or must I confess
To the wish—that I *never had met her.*[19]

In a letter that fall Wade encouraged his sister to visit Mary and put in a good word for him. By the end of the year, all was well, and the two were married on January 27, 1858. They planned an extended wedding trip to Europe that summer, but probably changed their plans when Mary was found to be pregnant. They vacationed instead in Virginia. A son, George McDuffie Hampton, was born January 16, 1859, at Millwood. Wade soon began construction of a home for Mary on one hundred acres near Columbia, probably on the old Sand Hills property. "Go up to my house and hurry on the workmen," he admonished sister Mary Fisher Hampton. "See too what furniture is needed." It would be a Greek Revival structure, with a large two-room library. Among his growing collection of books were volumes that had been in the library of King George III, some bearing the monarch's signature. The Hamptons called their home Diamond Hill.[20]

Wade Hampton, wife Mary, and their infant son were involved in a serious accident in September 1859. Apparently returning from a mountain vacation, they were sixteen miles from Pickensville, South Carolina, when their buggy overturned. The baby was unhurt, and Mary was only bruised, but Hampton suffered a dislocated shoulder. It was dark, and "I had to lie where I fell for 12 hours, not being able to move at all." A doctor finally came to his aid, "but my arm & shoulder were in a terrible condition." Boarding a train on the Greenville & Columbia Railroad, they were forced to delay the journey an additional day because "the jolting of the train pains me greatly."[21]

Hampton seemed always in a hurry, rushing from one responsibility to another. He was a member of a militia company called the Richland Light Dragoons. Such units typically were composed of the local elite and usually best described as uniformed social clubs. It was, nevertheless, the kind of service expected of a man like Hampton. He had been elected to the South Carolina House of Representatives in 1852. Perhaps a family member had suggested that political activity might take his mind off the recent loss of wife Margaret. Again, for a man of his position legislative service was also expected. He would take the oath alongside such men as Benjamin F. Perry, a respected Greenville unionist, and states' rights stalwart Olin M. Dantzler of St. Matthews. In the Charleston delegation was old friend, Peter Della Torre.[22]

Members of the general assembly were chosen in a two-day election held the second Monday and Tuesday in October every two years. Representatives served for two years, senators four. The general assembly convened annually on the fourth Monday in November, completing its business before Christmas. The first act of the Fortieth General Assembly, meeting in a brief extra session, was to choose presidential electors pledged to New Hampshire Democrat Franklin Pierce. Three years later the House, by a one-vote margin, approved a bill that would have permitted South Carolina's voters to choose among presidential candidates. Hampton sided with the majority, but the Senate failed to go along.[23] South Carolina would remain the only state where the general assembly cast the vote for president and vice president.

As a legislator Wade Hampton was more active and outspoken than his father had been. He served on the House committees on federal relations, agriculture, redistricting, and the Senate-House Conference Committee. Although often on the losing side when the votes were taken, Hampton consistently supported such things as improvements to the state's modest system of free schools, establishment of a penitentiary, and construction of a new capitol.[24] One of his favorite causes was care for the mentally ill.

Chartered in 1821, the South Carolina Lunatic Asylum was only the second such institution in America. Located in Columbia near the edge of town, its main building had been designed by noted Charleston architect Robert Mills. Francis Lieber served as chairman of the board of regents, and the asylum enjoyed a reputation for humane and enlightened treatment. When overcrowding became a problem in the 1840s some began to talk of relocating. Hampton would have none of that, urging expansion of the existing facility. It was an uphill battle, but the 1850s did see new construction. Hampton's support of the asylum went beyond the issue of state spending in his own district. He took a genuine interest in the welfare of patients. In 1856 Hampton insisted that a physician's report be completely reprinted, *omitting* the names of patients. The House agreed. In December 1859 Dorothea Dix, author and crusader for better treatment of the insane, visited Columbia.

"This General Assembly have heard of the arrival in Columbia of Miss Dix," read a Hampton-sponsored resolution, "whose philanthropy and charities have earned for her a world-wide reputation." At Hampton's suggestion the legislative library would be put at her disposal during her stay.[25]

In his November 24, 1856, message to the general assembly, Gov. James Hopkins Adams urged a reopening of the foreign slave trade. His words were controversial from the moment he uttered them. Many of slavery's staunchest defenders thought his proposal ill-advised. The importation of slaves into the United States had been banned since 1808. Adams claimed that an increasing worldwide need for cotton made it impossible for the South to meet the demand with existing manpower. With supply lagging, prices would be driven up. This might seem like good news for Southern planters, he said, but in the long run higher prices would encourage cotton production in the East Indies, Egypt, Brazil, and Algeria. The South needed more laborers, ran his argument, to maintain "the monopoly which we have so long enjoyed."[26]

House reaction was cool. For the time being a special committee would study the matter. Hampton was profoundly disturbed by Adams' proposal and wanted to bury it in committee. Later he tried to postpone it indefinitely.[27] South Carolinians were deeply divided on an issue that served only to inflame the North. James Henley Thornwell, now professor at Columbia Theological Seminary and copastor of the Presbyterian church, regretted that the question "has been agitated at all." Renewed importation would bring in "lawless savages" to demoralize American blacks. "Capital and labour with us are not distinct. The slave is as really capital, as he is labourer. To reduce his value, therefore, is not simply to cheapen labour, it is to reduce the amount of capital. The country will be no richer by the foreign importation." Nor could Thornwell countenance involving Africa in inevitable bloodshed "and the additional crime of man-stealing."[28]

The issue continued to simmer. Hampton considered leaving the general assembly, but was encouraged by friends to run for a seat in the state Senate in 1858, and he won. He shared with James Johnston Pettigrew his concern that "the *agitators* will urge the Slave Trade foolery" in the legislature and promote Adams to the U.S. Senate. Hampton felt no personal hostility towards Adams, but believed "his principles are mischievous" and out of the mainstream. "I think that those of us who are not of the *Ultra* party, *can* & *should* take control of the state." That summer he wrote to old friend professor Francis Lieber, asking for books that might help him prepare a case against reopening the slave trade. Lieber considered the trade a "crime and infamy" and took aim at the underlying assumption that importation of slaves would strengthen the South's political position in the struggle with the North.

> We are told, and profess to believe, that boastfulness, pride, cruelty, truthfulness, simplicity of heart, love, charity, are vices or virtues, but only privately

so; for boastfulness becomes a public virtue, and the moment we pretend to profess a thing for our country, we pretend to think of it as patriotism.

The professor concluded with an admonition to his former student. "Do what you can in your sphere and your line to avert this slur on humanity."[29]

Hampton did just that in a long and impassioned speech in the Senate chamber on December 10, 1859. "I confess to a strong desire to place upon record my unalterable and uncompromising opposition to a measure that is, I honestly believe, fraught with a greater danger to the South than any other that has ever been proposed." His arguments echoed Thornwell's. The trade would "involve cruel and inhuman practices . . . and demoralize the slaves now owned in the United States." Unity was needed in the face of Northern threats, not a divisive proposal such as this.

> The South has pressing need for all of her sons. Cannot some platform be found broad enough and strong enough to sustain us all? Show me such a one, and I will sacrifice everything but principle and honor to place myself upon it by the side of the true patriots of the South.

Reopening the foreign slave trade must not become *the* issue simply because "it lacks . . . that most essential element of success, *truth*." In opposing foreign slave trade, Hampton did not question the morality of slavery itself or express doubts about the institution's future.[30]

Later Thornwell would attempt to put the controversy in perspective. "The agitation on this subject at the South has been grievously misunderstood. One extreme generates another. The violence of Northern abolitionists gave rise to a small party among ourselves, who were determined not to be outdone in extravagance." Most Southerners remained against renewal of the foreign trade—not because buying and selling slaves was itself immoral, but because it would involve "a system of kidnaping and man-stealing, which is as abhorrent to the South as it is to the North."[31]

Hampton's most significant words were spoken near the conclusion of his Senate address. He was speaking in the aftermath of John Brown's raid on the federal arsenal at Harpers Ferry, Virginia, and that abolitionist's abortive call for a slave uprising. Brown relished the role of martyr. His trial and conviction for murder and treason brought to light widespread Northern sympathy. On the day of the terrorist's hanging, church bells tolled in the North while antislavery zealots sang his praises and compared him to Christ. Conservatives were stunned. These abolitionists were "trampling the Constitution and the Bible alike under their feet," continued Hampton, even as they "impiously appeal to a *higher law* than is found in either, to sanction their enormities."

I have not, sir, heretofore apprehended a dissolution of the Union—I have always desired its preservation. . . . But—I say this with deep conviction of its truth, though with profound regret—unless an entire revolution of public sentiment takes place at the North—unless that spirit of hostility towards us, that seems to have spread like some dread pestilence through-out their land, is rebuked, speedily and effectually by the good and true men of the North . . . unless that religion which preaches rapine and murder is superseded . . . I do not see how the Union *can be* or *should be* preserved.[32]

Five days later the South Carolina Senate resolved,

That, in view of recent events, and the present state of things in this Union, growing out of the agitation of the question of African slavery, the General Assembly deem it a fit occasion for declaring that the interests and safety of the Southern States imperatatively demand that they should unite for the common defence.

The vote was unanimous. Senators also reasserted the state's right of secession.[33]

In the election year of 1860, South Carolinians began to view with alarm the growing strength of the Republican Party. Nearly everyone in the state agreed that secession was a constitutional right. Now they began to consider the possibility of exercising that right in response to a victory by Abraham Lincoln in the presidential contest. These were opinions fully shared by Wade Hampton.[34]

Candidate Lincoln faced a fractured opposition. In April the Democratic national convention met in Charleston, but soon broke up over the issue of congressional protection of slavery in the territories. The Northern faction would reconvene to nominate Illinois senator Stephen Douglas. Southern Democrats backed their own candidate, vice president of the United States John C. Breckinridge. A fourth party, calling themselves Constitutional Unionists, nominated Tennessean John Bell. Despite their differences, the specter of a Republican presidency horrified Southerners. Lincoln rejected compromise or accommodation, and his view of America as a "house divided" repudiated the Founding Father's acceptance of diversity within the Union. With Lincoln in power the federal government would drop any pretense of sectional neutrality. His party had become abolitionism's political vehicle, backed by a disparate coalition that included antislavery zealots, anti-black racialists, and Northeastern protectionists. South Carolinians came to believe that the White House in Republican hands portended a very different America. A Lincoln triumph promised nothing less than revolution. As election day neared and Republican success appeared likely, opinion in South Carolina quickly began to coalesce. Most regretted that it had come to this, but the overwhelming majority concluded that South Carolina could not remain part of a union dominated by "Black Republicans." Either in concert with other states—or unilaterally—South Carolina must secede in response to a Lincoln victory.[35]

South Carolinians were nearly unanimous in support of Breckinridge. On October 12, 1860, Gov. William Henry Gist had issued a routine call for the legislature to meet on November 5 to choose presidential electors. On the appointed day, after making their choice, he asked them to remain in session that they might learn the outcome of the election and call a secession convention if Lincoln won.[36] The telegraph soon flashed the news. The Republican candidate swept the Northern states, winning by an electoral landslide, although his popular vote total nationally barely surpassed 39 percent.

On the assumption that the extra session would concern itself solely with choosing Breckinridge electors, Hampton departed in October for his Wild Woods, Mississippi, plantation. He planned to return for the regularly scheduled session he knew would begin, as always, on the fourth Monday in November. There had been some talk of lawmakers remaining in session. "Try to find out about the Legislature & let me know what it is thought will be done," Hampton wrote to Mary Fisher Hampton as he traveled west by steamboat. After arriving in Mississippi he wrote to his sister, on November 4, reporting on crops and talking about family. He added,

> I am in expectation of hearing very soon what the Legislature will do and if the Session is continued until the fourth Monday in November. I must go on though I shall dislike to do so. If they only remain in Session, for a few days, then there will be no necessity for me to be there.

A week later he received news that the general assembly had indeed remained in session.[37] They were deliberating how to proceed with perhaps the most momentous decision in American history—the dissolution of the Union.

Candidates chosen in South Carolina's legislative election, held October 8 and 9, had been committed to calling a secession convention in the event of a Lincoln victory. But should South Carolina secede immediately and alone, or should secession be accomplished in cooperation with other states? Cooperationists, wanting more time for concerted action, argued for assembling a convention in mid-January. Immediate-state-actionists preferred a December convention, but were willing to go along with the later date if needed to maintain unity. On November 9 the Senate gave second-reading approval, by a 44–1 vote, to a January convention bill.[38] But even now the mood was changing. South Carolina was about to reassert her leadership of the secession movement.

On November 7 federal judge Andrew G. Magrath and District Attorney

James Conner resigned. Their refusal to serve under a "Lincoln tyranny" created much excitement. Governor Gist's cousin, States Rights Gist, had just returned from an interstate diplomatic mission to other Southern governors. Assurances by many of these leaders that secession in South Carolina would be followed by secession elsewhere seemed to make cooperation a moot point. A huge prosecession rally on the evening of November 9 at Charleston's Institute Hall, an event attended by many Georgians, demonstrated Southerners' uniting for secession.[39] Perhaps as important as any factor in South Carolina's final dash to independence was the work of the Minute Men.

The Minute Men were one of two groups particularly influential in the months leading to South Carolina's declaration of independence. Pamphleteering was done by the 1860 Association. Demonstrating for secession was the primary mission of the Minute Men. During the fall Minute Men organizations sprang up in Columbia, Greenville, Charleston, Laurens, Newberry, Camden, Graniteville, Limestone, and other towns. Prospective members were required to sign the Minute Men constitution, to "solemnly pledge, 'our LIVES, our FORTUNES, and our sacred HONOR,' to sustain Southern Constitutional equality in the Union, or, failing that, to establish our independence out of it." Organized statewide on October 3, this semisecret, paramilitary body engaged in some drilling. Members were "to procure a Colt's Revolver, a Rifle, or some other approved fire-arm." But the Minute Men were most effective in agitation for secession. A prescribed regalia was worn during street demonstrations. Torchlight parades were a favorite activity. Minute Men carried signs in a Newberry procession proclaiming "Prepare for the Issue" and "South Carolina Is Expected to Lead." Parades and demonstrations were held nightly in Columbia during the legislature's deliberations over the convention bill.[40]

Public demand and rapidly unfolding events were even having an effect on cautious legislators. Opinion in the capitol began to shift in favor of a plan to hold an election for delegates on December 6, with the secession convention itself to meet on December 17. The South Carolina House of Representatives met as a committee of the whole on Saturday, November 10, and voted 91–14 in favor of this early-convention plan. Approval by the full House was then unanimous. That evening every senator voted for the early-convention bill. Formal ratification in joint session would come three days later, but with the legislature's vote on November 10, South Carolina had decided to lead the secession parade.[41]

The special legislative session adjourned on November 13. Wade Hampton was back in Columbia by Saturday, November 24. On that day the Richland Light Dragoons met and voted unanimously to offer their services to Governor Gist. Despite the impending crisis there is no record that their offer was immediately accepted or that the company participated as a unit in coming hostilities. The November 24 resolution was signed by Capt. Wade Hampton, commanding officer of the Dragoons. At seven o'clock in the evening on the following Monday, November 26, Hampton was on hand to answer the Senate roll call as the regular legislative session began.[42]

That same evening Wade Hampton and John S. Preston attended the meeting of the Columbia Minute Men, signed the constitution, and became members. Although he never questioned South Carolina's right to secede, Hampton had been criticized by some for a reluctance to embrace independence. Now he would make it clear that his conservatism should not be misconstrued. He agreed that Lincoln's election made secession necessary. A reporter from the *Daily Southern Guardian* covered the event.

> Col. Hampton thanked them for the kind and warm reception he received from a constituency who had ever honored and confided in him. He stated that when he left here he expected nothing more would be done at the extra session than the formal record of the State, giving her vote for Mr. Breckinridge. Just as he was leaving he heard it intimated that probably the extra session would be prolonged and that some action would be necessary. He made every arrangement to receive telegraphic dispatches from home. A message was sent to him on the 5th, which did not reach him until the 11th, when he immediately hastened home. If, however, he had lost the honor of assisting in the counsels of the State, he was determined to be here in time to share in any danger that might threaten her. The business was urgent that called him away, and he felt it was due to his constituency and to himself to make this explanation truly and honestly.
>
> Then he turned from personal considerations to the important and grave issues before the country. When he passed along the Southern States on his way out West, he found in those States party divisions as to the candidates for the Presidency. Here there existed no such divisions. The State was about to vote for Breckinridge, not because he was the nominee of a party, but because he represented a principle—a principle that was stronger than the Union. South Carolina had uttered no threat—had made no aggressive war. She goes forth with equality in the Union or independence out of it, inscribed upon her banners; her armor, Truth and Justice; and her shield, The Constitution, putting her trust in the God of Nations.
>
> He said that he fully concurred in the action that the State had taken. On his way out he had met with a State Senator, and stated to him that if Lincoln was elected President, he should unhesitatingly vote for a State Convention. When asked in Mississippi what South Carolina would do, he had always replied that a State Convention would be held, and that South Carolina would secede. He made but one exception to this programme— that if Mississippi or Alabama desired to lead, South Carolina would give them the privilege.
>
> On his way home the scene was different. Flags were waving in every direction, indicative of resistance. He met the blue cockade everywhere from

Memphis to Columbia. In Memphis he met a young citizen from this city, who told him there were a hundred men ready to march to the aid of South Carolina if necessary. The last man he met was a Kentuckian who was about to return home, and who told him that if Kentucky did not come up to the aid of this State, he would come and fight for her, and, if his life was spared, would remain with her.

He concluded by saying that it was time for the State to move—for us to go out of the Union; and pledged his life, his fortune, and his honor, to stand by her and maintain her rights.[43]

Preston then delivered a fiery speech to the Minute Men. He had declined to run in the election for convention delegates, although he favored immediate secession. He even dismissed the constitutional need for convening a convention, insisting that the legislature could act alone. John Lawrence Manning, husband of the late Susan Hampton Manning, was elected to the convention from Clarendon District.[44]

On December 11 Hampton reported to his Senate colleagues that the Richland District House and Senate delegation, as host to the upcoming convention, had arranged a meeting place in Columbia. Charlestonians had already begun to lobby for holding the gathering in their city. Columbians were quick to respond. "Some people have a very contracted idea of the capacity of Columbia," complained the editor of the *Southern Guardian*. "During fair week we accommodated some two or three thousand visitors. We certainly can afford lodgings for the members of a State Convention." Ominously, the same issue of the newspaper mentioned that the Board of Health was keeping track of "the disease alluded to yesterday." Several cases of smallpox had been reported.[45] The convention would hold only its first session in Columbia. Because of the danger posed by smallpox, it adjourned to reconvene in Charleston. Over the bitter protests of Hampton and others, the general assembly followed its example.[46]

Sally Baxter Hampton witnessed the march towards secession with a breaking heart. "I am no Southerner heaven knows," she wrote to her New York family on the eve of secession, "& at heart if not abolition at least anti slavery but I must concede that the tone of the South has been most firm—calm—manly & decided." To prominent New Yorker Samuel Ruggles, she expressed her despair. "I see daily Carolinians of all ages & parties—The members of both House & Senate—(the Legislature of So Ca being you know now in session) come out to our House for a few quiet hours & are glad perhaps of a chance to open their hearts." Although they expressed to her their sadness that in days "this great nation will cease to have existence—Yet with all this, is mingled, a calm self-determination & heroic bravery one cannot but admire."[47]

That word—"calm"—kept appearing. Sally Hampton noted, "Men are too calm, too quiet, too grave to be undertaking anything but a move for life or death."[48] Professor Thornwell spoke of a "calm serenity" exhibited by convention delegates. "In the midst of intense agitation and excitement, they were calm, cool, collected, and self-possessed. They deliberated without passion, and concluded without rashness. They sat with closed doors, that the tumult of the populace might not invade the sobriety of their minds." Those "stirring scenes with which the streets of Charleston were alive," contrasted sharply with "the calm and quiet sanctuary of this council."[49]

At one-fifteen on the afternoon of December 20, 1860, in the hall of the Saint Andrew's Society on Broad Street, the convention of the people of South Carolina voted unanimously for independence.

James Buchanan, president of the United States, was attending a gala wedding reception at a Washington residence on the afternoon of December 20. The social elite of the nation's capital had been invited. Suddenly, there was a commotion in the entrance hall. Someone was shouting, leaping up and down, waving a telegram over his head. Buchanan asked another guest to find out what had happened.

"It appears, Mr. President, that South Carolina has seceded."

The president fell back into his chair, gripping the arms, his face pale, his voice low and hoarse. "Might I beg you to have my carriage called?"[50]

4

"STAND UP FOR SOUTH CAROLINA"

The Legion Goes to War

With the signing of the Ordinance of Secession, South Carolina became, in the words of convention president David F. Jamison, "an Independent Commonwealth." Yet the new republic's integrity would be compromised so long as four military installations remained under foreign—United States—control. Maj. Robert Anderson commanded eighty-four soldiers of the U.S. Army at Fort Moultrie, overlooking the entrance to Charleston Harbor. Anderson was also responsible for an obsolete fortification called Castle Pinckney, the city arsenal, and the impressive but incomplete Fort Sumter. President Buchanan, unwilling to recognize secession's legality, but fearful that he might begin a war over it, strove to maintain the status quo until his successor took the oath of office. But six days after South Carolina's secession, Anderson abandoned Moultrie by night and retreated to the more defensible Fort Sumter. Gov. Francis Pickens responded to his "treachery" by ordering the militia to seize Moultrie, Castle Pinckey, and the arsenal. State forces then began to erect batteries that would surround Anderson and command approaches to the harbor. Buchanan made one attempt to supply the beleaguered outpost, but the ship chartered for that purpose—the *Star of the West*—was driven off by South Carolina artillery fire on the morning of January 9, 1861.[1]

During these weeks of postsecession euphoria, Wade Hampton seemed unsettled and unsure of what role he should play. He continued to serve in

55

the Senate as the extraordinary session of 1860 stretched into the new year. According to Sally Baxter Hampton, writing on January 11, her brother-in-law "reprobates most strongly the firing on the 'Star of the West' & is entirely disgusted with the manner in which matters are conducted down there." Yet, five days later Hampton reported for the Senate Committee on Foreign Affairs (formerly the Federal Relations Committee) approval of a resolution supporting Pickens. Lawmakers "fully endorse the action and course of his Excellency, the Governor of the State, in regard to the occupation of the forts and arsenal lately in possession of the United States, and tender to him our hearty support in the present crisis."[2] But passing resolutions would not secure South Carolina's liberty. Hampton wanted to take a more active part. The forty-two-year-old and his two sons volunteered as privates in a company that was forming, called the Congaree Mounted Riflemen, but "hundreds" begged Hampton to raise a command of his own. A brief item appeared in the December 29, 1860, *Daily Courier*. "Among the earliest dispatches tendering services and volunteers for the defence of Charleston, on Thursday [December 27], under the indignant excitement caused by the dereliction of Major Anderson, was one from Col. Wade Hampton, of Columbia." The honorary title of colonel had been bestowed decades earlier. Hampton may have still been connected with the Richland Light Dragoons, but just what "services and volunteers" he was then prepared to offer is unknown.[3]

On the eve of war, few in South Carolina had any real military training, and the state was woefully unprepared to defend her new independence. The governor might, of course, call forth the militia to repel invasion. Made up of ten infantry divisions, supported by artillery and cavalry, the South Carolina Militia seemed formidable on paper. There were a few commanders who did a creditable job, and some companies were well drilled and smartly uniformed. But too often, especially in rural areas, arms and uniforms were lacking altogether, and training was ignored. Four Saturday mornings of drill and one review was the most training a typical militiaman could expect in a year—certainly inadequate preparation for the task South Carolinians faced in the winter of 1860–1861. During the crisis over Anderson's redeployment, the governor kept Charleston's Fourth Militia Brigade under arms, causing many complaints among its citizen-soldiers. In mid-December the general assembly began raising the Volunteer Forces of South Carolina. An infantry regiment was being enlisted by authority of the secession convention. And in late January legislators voted into existence the Regular Army of South Carolina.[4] Mobilization was proceeding by fits and starts with little overall planning or leadership.

The Palmetto State would soon have help. During January Mississippi, Florida, Alabama, Georgia, Louisiana, and Texas followed South Carolina's lead by seceding. On February 4, delegates met in Montgomery, Alabama, to form the Confederate States of America. A provisional constitution was adopted, Jefferson Davis of Mississippi was inaugurated as president, and an officer was dispatched to Charleston. Brig. Gen. Pierre Gustave Toutant Beauregard arrived on March 1 to take command of the South Carolinians surrounding Fort Sumter.

In early April Abraham Lincoln ordered a fleet of ships loaded with troops, guns, and supplies to sail for Sumter. He knew well that the move would force Confederates to take action. Before the fleet arrived—and after Anderson refused to surrender—Davis ordered General Beauregard to reduce the fort. The Confederate president had little choice. Lincoln's successful reinforcement of Sumter would have made a mockery of Southern independence. Batteries surrounding Anderson's garrison opened fire on the morning of April 12, and the next day it was over. Having maneuvered the South into firing the "first shot," Lincoln called for troops to march against the seceded states. Northerners rushed to arms, Confederates vowed to defend their country from invasion, and the Upper South rallied to the Confederate cause.[5]

During the Sumter bombardment Lt. William Campbell Preston aimed the Fort Moultrie gun that brought down Anderson's flagstaff. Preston's grandmother Mary Cantey Hampton, eighty-one-year-old widow of the first Wade Hampton, was delighted when she heard the news. Described as "the mildest, sweetest, gentlest of old ladies," she fired off a telegram from Columbia that read simply, "Well done, Willie!"[6]

Wade Hampton did not witness his young cousin's feat. He departed in March for Mississippi, seeing to his business interests. He wrote to Mary Fisher Hampton from Mobile, Alabama, on March 27. "Tomorrow is my birthday," he noted, "and I am getting old and no better fast." He wrote again from his Wild Woods, Mississippi, plantation on April 9. He gave her few hints, but he was formulating a plan.[7] Returning to Charleston about the third week in April, Hampton conferred with General Beauregard and Governor Pickens. He secured letters of introduction from them addressed to the Confederate president.[8] Armed with these missives "of a most complimentary character," he raced to the Southern capital at Montgomery, Alabama. He would lay before the president a plan to raise his own command for military service.

What Hampton proposed was the organization of a "legion"—over 1,000 strong—composed of infantry, cavalry, and light artillery. In the military parlance of the day, a legion would most often be made up of infantry and cavalry, deployed as an independent command. Hampton wrote to his sister on April 24, saying that he had been "very well received" in Montgomery. The day before, he had been "called out twice along the road & made to speak." More importantly,

> My plan has been laid before the Presdt & the Sec. of War [Leroy Pope Walker] & I think they are both inclined to aid in carrying out my views.

The Adjutant General [Samuel Cooper] speaks highly of it & has promised to give me a full plan for organization. Col. [George Allen] Deas, who is drawing up the paper calls the Regiment "Hampton's Legion" & I hope soon to see it in the field. The Sec. of War says he will do all in his power to assist me & the Presdt. is very friendly. I trust that I may yet have the opportunity of proving that I can do the State some service. I want a place where I can do real hard work; not one where the only duty is to wear a uniform.

On April 27, Hampton, accompanied by James Chesnut Jr., had a final meeting with Davis.[9]

Just three days later Hampton was back in Charleston. His family was filled with pride and excitement. Mary Fisher told sister-in-law Mary McDuffie Hampton, "I know the Hamptons Legion will do great things." Hampton promised his sister that he would be home in Columbia by week's end, but "I want to put the Legion on foot before I leave."[10]

On May 3, a notice, submitted by Hampton, appeared in the *Daily Courier:*

As various inquiries have been made in reference to the Legion which the President has honored me with a commission to raise, I beg you to allow me to give through your paper such information as may be necessary to those who wish to enlist in this corps.

The object of those who are engaged in this matter is to raise an independent legion, to consist of six companies of infantry or voltigeurs, four of cavalry, and one of flying artillery, the field officers to be appointed by the President and each company to elect its own officers, who will then receive commissions from the President.

As soon as the organization of this corps is complete it will be received into the Provisional Army of the Confederate States for one year, unless its services should not be required for so long a time, in which case the President can disband it. The Legion is to serve wherever it may be ordered by the President, and is to be on precisely the same footing, except as to its peculiar organization, as the rest of the Provisional Army. The cavalry will furnish their own horses and, as far as possible, their own arms and equipments. Each man must have a saber and two Colt pistols. Should any horses be lost in the service they will be paid for.

The infantry I wish armed with Enfield rifles, and the Governor has kindly promised to furnish them as far as he is able to do so, and he will also provide the battery. As soon as the companies report themselves ready for duty they will be ordered into camp for the purpose of drilling together. It is very desirable to have this corps ready at an early day, as I have every reason to hope that it will at once be ordered into active service.

A table of organization followed. There would be 120 men in the artillery, 340 in the cavalry, and 600 infantry "voltigeurs" (styled after the elite foot soldiers of the French Army). Aggregate strength, including field officers and staff, would be 1,095. Pay ranged from $195 per month for the colonel commanding, to $11 for artillery and infantry privates. Cavalrymen made an additional dollar per month. A letter from the Confederate war secretary was published, along with the governor's response. "I have said to Col. Wade Hampton that I would accept the regiment with legionary formation which he proposes," wrote Walker, "if it would be acceptable to Your Excellency." Pickens answered handsomely.

> I hereby state that it will not only be agreeable to me but I will take great pride in it, as no one could with more propriety be selected as commander of such a force than Colonel Hampton. I will contribute everything in my power to aid in its formation. . . . It is intended to be an independent corps, ready for service anywhere.[11]

Still, Hampton fretted. "So many troops have already been taken," he said on April 30, "that I fear I shall have difficulty in getting as many as I need." The editor of the *Courier* was more optimistic. "The 'Hampton Legion' is progressing favorably," he reported, "and, in some arms of the service, the only difficulty will be in selecting the complement from the number of applications." Hampton and his second-in-command, Benjamin J. Johnson, "are so well known that all our young men who seek honorable service are eager to be enrolled under their command."[12] Only four days later Hampton told Secretary Walker that "there have been already tenders of very many more troops than I am authorized to accept." At the end of the month the *Courier* reported that "over thirty companies of seventy-five men each have offered themselves for enrollment in this Legion." Hampton inspected militia units that asked to join, selecting those "best prepared for immediate service." Vacancies in understrength companies filled up quickly when it became known those units were going into the Legion. They would report to Columbia for drill, that they might be ready "at a very early day to respond to any call."[13]

So many companies volunteered that Hampton was able to insure that most regions of the state were represented. Charleston's elite and well-drilled Washington Light Infantry became Company A of the Legion's infantry battalion. Thirty-one-year-old James Conner, former U.S. district attorney, was captain. Oscar Lieber, son of Professor Francis Lieber, broke his unionist father's heart by joining.[14] From Edgefield came the Watson Guards, now Company B, under the command of Harvard Law graduate Martin Witherspoon Gary.[15] Capt. Brown Manning, younger brother of John Laurence Manning, led Clarendon District's Company C.[16] The Gist Riflemen of Union, under twenty-eight-year-old Capt. Henry J. Smith, became Company D.[17] Hampton visited Greenville in late April, staying several days with

Col. Wade Hampton, commander of the Legion. His collar insignia appears to be that of a Confederate colonel. Shoulder straps showing a palmetto signified a colonel in South Carolina state service. *Manly Wade Wellman, Giant in Gray (New York: Charles Scribner's Sons, 1949)*.

Benjamin F. Perry. Toliver L. Bozeman had just been elected colonel of the militia's Third Regiment. Bozeman gave that up to lead Company E of the Legion.[18] Also from Greenville came the Davis Guards under Capt. William L. M. Austin. At fifty-seven, Austin was perhaps the Legion's oldest company commander. The Guards became Company F.[19]

A large crowd gathered on the public square in front of the Planter's Hotel on June 6 to see about fifty of the Edgefield Hussars depart. Twenty-five or thirty more would join them en route to Columbia where they would become Company A of the Legion cavalry. Twenty-five-year-old lawyer Matthew Calbraith Butler, son-in-law of Governor Pickens, was in command. Serving, too, was John R. Niernsee, Austrian-born architect of the new South Carolina State House. Brothers Wade Hampton IV and Thomas Preston Hampton found a place with the Hussars. "It is ours to act, and not to speak," young Captain Butler told the appreciative Edgefield crowd. "You will hear from us. Farewell!"[20] Cavalry Company B, under Capt. John F. Lanneau, was recruited in Greenville. "I am glad to hear such good accounts of the troop," Hampton wrote to Perry, "& shall be very much pleased to be able to accept them."[21] From the coastal village of Beaufort came Capt. Thomas E. Screven's Company C. Thirty-one years old, Screven had graduated with honors from South Carolina College, where he had roomed with States Rights Gist, now the state's uniquely named adjutant general.[22] Completing the cavalry battalion was Company D from Richland District, Capt. Thomas Taylor commanding. Rev. James Henley Thornwell's sixteen-year-old-son, Gillespie, rode with them.[23]

The Washington Artillery of Charleston was one of South Carolina's elite and venerable units. After Fort Sumter some of its members were so anxious to see further action that they began organizing a battery of light artillery for service out of state. By mid-May about fifty had joined this spin-off company, and as soon as word spread that it was to serve in the Hampton Legion, vacant positions quickly filled up. The Washington Light Artillery was first commanded by twenty-four-year-old Citadel graduate James Franklin Hart. West Point–educated Stephen Dill Lee responded to Hampton's newspaper notice. He was elected to lead, but would be detained with other duties, leaving Hart in command for now.[24] The Washington Light Artillery paraded through the streets of Charleston, escorted by the Washington Artillery and the German Artillery, on its way to board the Columbia train. "The Palmetto Brass Band was in attendance," reported the *Courier,* "and played some of their liveliest tunes." A red-and-white silk guidon was presented to them, patriotic speeches were made, and "the cars moved off amid the loud and prolonged cheers of the spectators."[25] Despite the governor's promise to provide the guns, Colonel Hampton was reported to have purchased two rifled cannon for his artillery company—"the best products of the Tredegar Works," said the *Courier.* Tredegar was also to provide four howitzers. Four

British-made Blakely rifles were on order, paid for by Hampton. Hampton had also ordered, at his own expense, 200 Enfield rifles with bayonets and 20,000 cartridges. The admiring newspaper editor could only conclude, "With such a force there can be no such word as fail."[26]

The second-in-command of the Legion was Lt. Col. Benjamin Jenkins Johnson. A year older than Hampton, Johnson was a low-country planter, lawyer, and legislator. Like Hampton, he was without military training, but possessed an ability to lead. Lt. Theodore Gailliard Barker was named adjutant and in June was sent on ahead to Richmond, Virginia, the new Confederate capital and the Legion's expected destination. Capt. Claudius L. Goodwin was quartermaster. Capt. Thomas C. Beggs served as commissary. John T. Darby was surgeon, assisted by Henry W. Moore and Benjamin W. Taylor.[27]

All of the companies of the Legion rendezvoused at "Camp Hampton," on the old race course at the Woodlands property. When the first Wade Hampton built Woodlands for his young bride back in 1786, he had chosen the isolated location with the comment, "Four miles is close enough for any neighbor." Now the old place hosted over 1,000 guests. Legion commander Hampton was ill in early June and, in the absence of Lieutenant Colonel Johnson, Captain Conner of the Washington Light Infantry took over briefly.

"We are the pets of the ladies here," boasted Conner, "and are the crack corps of the Legion." He informed his mother on June 13, "I have drilled the boys pretty hard, and you would scarcely know them, they have improved so much. We can out drill anything in Charleston, except the [Citadel] cadets." The entire Hampton family adopted the Legion as their own.

> They send us baskets of vegetables and bottles of milk, and homemade biscuits, and preserves, and all sorts of good things. . . . Miss Hampton sent out to say that all the washing for our company should be done at Millwood. Another day she sends out a champagne basket full of books, novels, etc.

One sultry June day many of the boys did not feel like drilling in the summer sun, reported Conner. His orderly sergeant

> assembled the sick and those who pretended to be, and asked them how they were. All quite sick—feeling very bad. Any appetite? No appetite—all gone—can't eat anything. "Well," says he, "Very sorry; Miss Hampton has just sent a basket of nice things for the sick. The things won't keep, and as you are too sick to eat, I will distribute them among the well as a lunch."

Connor could not praise the Hampton sisters enough.

> If we were only to say the word, those Miss Hamptons would give up their house and grounds [nearby Millwood] and servants and anything we

wanted. Their whole heart is in the Legion, and if anything was to happen to the Legion it would break their hearts. Our boys just believe in them. The whole company is devoted to them.

Connor wrote of attending a party and a "glorious supper" hosted by Frank and Sally Baxter Hampton at Woodlands. He spent another evening at the Hampton-Preston town house in Columbia. "The Misses Preston exerted themselves to make everybody feel at home. The walks in the garden were beautiful with the soft moonlight on them, and the fountains all playing."[28]

To sixteen-year-old Pvt. John Coxe of Company F, Wade Hampton seemed

> a young man—fully grown up, to be sure, but still without pompousness or egotism. His hair and beard were dark, and so were his eyes, which had a peculiar natural snappy motion that attracted attention. He wore mustaches and side, or "mutton chop," whiskers. . . . He was rather tall and otherwise well proportioned. His voice was tenor and ringing.

The young private remembered too how "it was said that he paid from his private purse the entire expenses of this our first camp."

The officers and enlisted men ate together. "The bread was supplied by a bakery in Columbia, and negro cooks stewed fresh beef in huge camp kettles." Lieutenant Colonel Johnson led them in "severe company drills." A recovering Hampton "usually took command at dress parades, and every evening fine ladies and gentlemen from the city came out to see us on parade." The militia traditionally dressed in dark blue, and each company of the Legion for now retained its own similar, yet distinct, uniform. The Washington Light Infantry wore gray. Havelocks were issued to all of the men while they were at Camp Hampton, contributing a degree of uniformity.[29]

Captain Conner was anxious to be off to Virginia, "for it is going to be a short war, and we may just as well see a little bit of it before the curtain drops on the performance." His Charleston pride was irrepressible. "If those confounded country fellows were better drilled, they would move us on at once I expect, but they are all horribly green.[30]

On June 10 Hampton wrote to General Beauregard asking that Capt. Stephen D. Lee be relieved of his duties and allowed to assume command of the Legion artillery. Hampton also resigned as Beauregard's aide—an honor the general had bestowed on a number of prominent men upon arriving in South Carolina. Colonel Hampton reported that "the Legion in which you so kindly interested yourself, is now organized." He begged that it be attached to Beauregard's command. "And I hope, Sir, that you will find my men, though inexperienced, not unworthy of this place."

Finally, word was received that the Legion would depart on Wednesday, June 26. That day the men were up at dawn and marched out of Camp Hampton in the midmorning heat. Burdened with their arms and knapsacks, they trudged down sandy roads to the Columbia terminus of the Charlotte and South Carolina Railroad. Some straggled on the way. By noon a crowd had gathered at the depot to see them off. Connor said,

> I was moving about looking after things, and I heard someone say, "There he is, there he is!" and about eight ladies bore down upon me, shook hands, and introduced themselves and each other. They were the mother, sister, aunts, cousins, etc., of a young fellow that was going with me. And the cautions I got about taking care of him, and what a good boy he was, and what a pet he had been, and would I look after him, and a whole lot of such directions. I thought they would all kiss me before they got through.[31]

Departing this day along with the Washington Light Infantry were the Davis Guards and the Gist Riflemen. The contingent was under the command of Lieutenant Colonel Johnson. Hampton and the remainder of the Legion would follow the next week. On this day Hampton, still recuperating from his illness, made a short speech. South Carolina College chaplain Robert W. Barnwell Jr. offered prayer. "I was delighted when the cars left," confessed Conner, "and took me from an admiring circle of weeping women."[32]

Stops were made in Charlotte and Raleigh, where ladies brought food and drink to the sweltering troops. "You have no idea how good a thing water is," wrote Conner. "I never before appreciated the blessings of good water and plenty of it." They reached Petersburg, Virginia, on Friday morning and were treated to a picnic.

> Notwithstanding the number of troops that have passed through, we created a sensation. They had a palmetto flag hung across the street, and as we went under it, we gave three cheers that astonished them. They took us to a beautiful hill, with a spring of water as cool as ice, and a shady grove, and gave such a dinner. . . . Lord how we ate!

The troops finally reached Richmond in a midnight downpour and soon were asleep on the floor of a tobacco warehouse. They were learning how to be soldiers. "A certain amount of grumbling is absolutely necessary," concluded Conner. "I don't care what you do, or how well you have arranged for the comfort of the men, there are always some men who will grumble." The remainder of the Legion, under Hampton, departed Columbia on July 2 and detrained in Richmond on July 4.[33]

The Legion camped about two miles southeast of the center of Richmond in an area called Rocketts, not far from the terminus of the York River

Railroad. Soon they were receiving visitors. Mary Chesnut, wife of South Carolina politician James Chesnut Jr., came on Independence Day. "How very nice our Carolina gentry are. Today I found them charming—indeed, I felt so proud of them." Colonel Hampton kept busy procuring equipment and supplies and selecting horses. He assured his sister Mary Fisher on July 13 that "I have been improving and now am quite well." He lived in camp with his men, although often was found in town. "We are getting on quite well, and our men are contented and in good spirits," he assured her.[34] Yet one noncommissioned officer complained publicly "of cold, of hunger, of partiality and of restrictions on the freedom of speech." Some had yet to realize that they were off to a real war, not a summertime militia review. Young Private Coxe of Company F remembered Hampton as "conspicuous for his diligence and care for the comfort of his men, as well as [for] quelling an incipient mutiny in the artillery company." "The Hampton Legion all in a snarl," wrote Mary Chesnut, "about, I forget what—standing on their dignity, I suppose. I have come to detest a man who says, 'My own personal dignity—self respect requires—' I long to cry, 'No need to respect yourself until you can make other people do it.'"[35]

On July 16 President Jefferson Davis visited the Legion to present their flag formally. The banner was said to have been made from silk dressses belonging to Surgeon John T. Darby's wife. "Our flag is a magnificent one," wrote Pvt. Richard Habersham of Company C. "It is on a blood red field, the Palmetto and Crescent being worked with silver cord." The Legion infantry formed three sides of a square with the cavalry off to one side and the artillery on the other. Davis, according to Conner, "presented the colors in a capital speech—a real fighting speech. . . . We then formed in column and passed the President, and he expressed himself highly pleased with the drill and material of the Legion."[36]

It had been bold—some might say foolhardy—for Confederates to establish their capital in Richmond, less than one hundred miles from Lincoln's White House. By late May federal forces had occupied Arlington and Alexandria and were building fortifications to protect Washington. Brig. Gen. Irvin McDowell took command of U.S. troops gathering there. A Union force under Brig. Gen. Robert Patterson threatened Harpers Ferry. Confederate troops were concentrating near the northern Virginia railroad junction of Manassas behind a stream called Bull Run.

General Beauregard, "Hero of Sumter," arrived at Manassas in June. He deployed his 15,000 men on a six-mile front behind the Run. Patterson found that Brig. Gen. Joseph E. Johnston's 10,000 Southerners had withdrawn from Harpers Ferry. Beauregard expected to be attacked and needed Johnston to join him. McDowell—prodded by impatient press, public, and politicians—marched south with 37,000 troops. He counted on Patterson's army to prevent Johnston from linking up with Beauregard. McDowell made his

The flag of the Hampton Legion. The side with the palmetto and crescent was red, the reverse blue. *Glenn Dedmondt, The Flags of Civil War South Carolina (Gretna, La.: Pelican Pub., 2000).*

headquarters at Centreville, just north of Bull Run. He ordered a feint toward the stone bridge that crossed the Run; then with two divisions, he planned to fall on Beauregard's left over the ford at Sudley Springs. Johnston had eluded Patterson and come to the aid of the main Confederate army. Now reinforced, Beauregard planned an attack of his own on the right. Both commanders gave orders for the action to begin on the morning of July 21.[37]

Early on July 19, men of the Hampton Legion were awakened by newspaper boys shouting the news of impending battle. Quickly they broke camp. "You'll hear from me again after we've finished the affair at Mannassas, or never see me again," Private Habersham wrote hastily to his parents. "I have a position just under the flag, and woe be to the Yankee who tries to take it."[38] The Legion men hurried to the downtown Richmond depot of the Central Railroad, but were made to wait far into the night. There would be no room for the men's baggage, or even their rations. Only the infantry companies would go by rail. The cavalry was at a training camp near Ashland, twenty miles from Richmond. The artillery had to take the road, ensuring its late arrival. And orders were received that all those company flags must be left in Richmond. "This goes hard with our boys," wrote Conner, "as they had set their hearts on carrying their flag into the fight."[39] The Legion would be identified on the battlefield by their single shining crimson banner, emblazoned with palmetto and crescent.

The train bumped along slowly, making frequent stops, the men packed into boxcars. People along the way came out to greet the troops, and a quartet from the Davis Guards sang patriotic songs. Among the newest in their repertoire was "Dixie." Sleep was difficult. There was little food, although water was plentiful. At about eleven o'clock on Saturday morning, the train reached Trevilian Station and was delayed there until late afternoon. Hampton telegraphed ahead to Gordonsville, telling the tavern keeper to have 600 meals waiting for his men when they got there. It was too much to ask. When the hungry troops jumped from the cars, said Private Coxe, "instead of a sumptuous supper awaiting us there we found only a few negro women standing about with pies, cakes, and sandwiches for sale. . . . I saw Colonel Hampton come out of the little tavern with a very wry face." Around daybreak they reached Manassas. A few were able to find something for breakfast. Ammunition, brought all the way from Columbia, was issued. Distant cannon fire could be heard. One soldier remembered that it was Sunday morning, back home people were preparing for church, and "prayers were ascending in our behalf."

"We were then addressed by our Colonel as follows: 'Men of the Legion; I am happy to inform you that the enemy are in sight.' He then exhorted us to strike boldly, to remember the cause in which we were fighting, to stand up for South Carolina."[40]

McDowell's flanking of the Confederate left proceeded clumsily, but had at least got underway. Beauregard's advance on the right started late and soon dissolved in confusion. The Union feint on the stone bridge did not fool Confederate brigadier general Nathan G. Evans. "Shanks," as he was called, left a small force at the bridge and, without orders, hurried to Sudley Springs just in time to stall the Yankee attack. Evans held 13,000 at bay with his 1,000 men, but was soon reinforced by the brigades of Brig. Gen. Barnard E. Bee and Col. Francis S. Bartow, both of Johnston's command.

Hampton was ordered to march his 600 men in the direction of the stone bridge, but even before he reached Portici—the Lewis house—a scout told him that the enemy was turning the Confederate left. He shifted towards that threatened flank and came to the support of a two-gun Confederate battery. His men were under fire for the first time. One private said that enemy artillery shells "were hissing like serpents." When Hampton became fearful for his right, he ordered the Legion to the Robinson house on the Warrenton Turnpike and positioned his men along the road. Shells and bullets continued to fill the air. Sergeant Cleveland of Company F was hit in the stomach. "The ball struck the big brass buckle of his belt and made a great noise," remembered a comrade. Lieutenant Colonel Johnson was placing

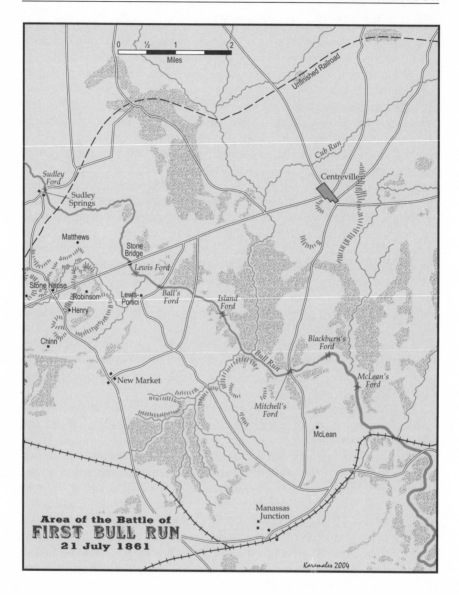

men in position when a bullet smashed into his temple. Now that they were close enough to return fire, "we opened on them—each man firing and loading as fast as he could," wrote one soldier of the Legion.[41] The enemy was driven back to the cover of some trees. Another exchange of fire followed on the left. A strong force of Federals formed up to attack, "but a single volley dispersed them in great confusion," reported Hampton. An enemy battery

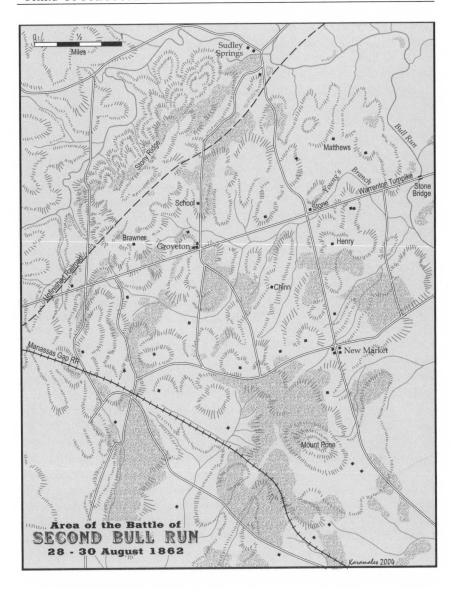

Area of the Battle of
SECOND BULL RUN
28 - 30 August 1862

Karamales 2004

unlimbered down the turnpike to the left, but out of range of the Legion's muskets. Seeing this, Hampton ordered his men back to the hill at their rear. There they were attacked from the right and narrowly avoided being surrounded. "The commands of General Bee and myself," reported Evans, "were now completely scattered, when we were timely covered by Hampton's Legion and other re-enforcements." The Legion's stand drew attention. The colonel of a Georgia regiment made a deal with his hard-pressed men to hold their ground as long as "the S. C. battalion" would.[42]

Both Bee and Evans advised Hampton to fall back from his exposed position. He did so, forming a defensive line with the remnants of their own and Bartow's brigades. The Hampton Legion had endured for two hours the fire of an enemy far superior in numbers. "Never," wrote a survivor from Company A, "have I conceived of such a continuous, rushing hailstorm of shot, shell, and musketry as fell around and among us for hours together."[43] The Legion had also inflicted a punishing fire on the enemy. At one point Hampton's horse was shot and killed. "I cannot understand how in such a fire anyone escaped," wrote 1st Lt. James Lowndes of Company A. "The bullets rattled around like hail." After losing his mount Hampton grabbed a rifle and shouted, "Watch me, boys; do as I do." He took careful aim and began bringing down enemy officers."[44]

Beauregard and Johnston had ridden to the roar of battle, arriving in time to help rally the confused and demoralized. By late afternoon sufficient reinforcements had arrived for Beauregard to order a charge. Although their ranks were thin and all were exhausted, the men of the Legion formed up one more time. Under intense fire they reached the Henry house. From there they poured repeated volleys into the enemy. Hampton then ordered his men to charge the battery that had been plaguing them for so long. Just as the assault began, Hampton was struck in the temple over his left eye by a shell fragment or buckshot. A soldier standing six feet away thought him "badly wounded." Hampton himself would later downplay the injury as "slight," but he was forced to relinquish command to the senior officer present, Captain Conner of Company A. Advancing with the Eighteenth Virginia Infantry on their left, the battery was taken.[45]

The Union reverse quickly turned to defeat, then to panic and total collapse. "Such a rout I never witnessed before," reported Union brigade commander Col. Samuel P. Heintzelman. "No efforts could induce a single regiment to form after the retreat was commenced." Confederates were exhilarated, but too exhausted to mount an effective pursuit. Elements of the Legion advanced two miles beyond the stone bridge before the day ended. Private Coxe, the teenager from Greenville, joined "the remnant of Hampton's Legion" as it returned to Manassas Junction, "where it found something to eat and, better, rest." One soldier who met Hampton just after the battle found the colonel "sitting his horse well, his clothes were bloody and his head bandaged, but his voice was strong, and he expected to take the field again in a short time." The doctors feared to attempt removing the metal fragment from Hampton's head. They dressed the wound and ordered him to rest.[46]

President Davis could not bear the suspense of waiting in Richmond for the battle's outcome. He and a single aide boarded a train and headed for

Manassas. "Sunday night," wrote Conner, "Davis and Beauregard came to Hampton's tent and thanked him for the handsome manner in which the Legion had behaved. Hampton told me that they were so complimentary that he had not ventured to write their remarks to his wife lest he should appear vain." In his official report Beauregard noted that the line had been "stoutly held" by the Legion, even "after having previously been as far forward as the turnpike." Hampton demonstrated "soldierly ability," continued Beauregard, the Legion being among the commands he compared to veterans. Johnston too lauded Hampton for "efficient service in maintaining the orderly character of the retreat" after holding the turnpike.[47]

Hampton himself praised the "unflinching courage" of his men, "only equaled by the gallantry of the officers whom they so trustingly obeyed."[48]

Wild stories made the rounds in Richmond in the aftermath of Manassas. There was talk of cowardice and incredible bravery, of carnage and lost opportunities. The facts were that McDowell suffered around 3,000 killed, wounded, captured, and missing out of 37,000 engaged. He also lost 28 artillery pieces, 500 muskets, half a million rounds of ammunition, tons of supplies, and 9 flags. Confederates numbered about 35,000, and their total casualties were perhaps 1,000 fewer than the enemy's. The Hampton Legion lost 123 men, including 19 dead. That casualty rate exceeded 20 percent—one of the highest suffered in the Southern army that day.[49]

After the battle diarist Mary Chesnut recorded the comments of Caroline Preston's "furiously patriotic" maid, Maria. The black Carolinian complained,

> These colored people say it is printed in the papers here that the Virginia people done it all. Now Mars Wade has had so many of his men killed—and he wounded—it stands to reason that South Carolina was no ways backward. If there was ever anything plain, that's plain.[50]

It was plain too, that the war would not be over as quickly as so many on both sides had assumed. The defeat only steeled the resolve of millions in the North. Southerners became too confident.

The Legion went into bivouac, its white tents covering the green fields. Colonel Hampton was soon back to work. The Legion was finally joined by the Washington Light Artillery, which Stephen Lee quickly put into rigorous training. Recruits arrived. The colonel had received word a few weeks earlier that the Legion would be granted two additional infantry companies.

Just after the battle Hampton telegraphed his family, minimizing the seriousness of his wound. "It is very hard to think of you so far from us and suffering alone," replied sister Caroline. "Take care of yourself dearest Brother, remember how very valuable your life is." Wife Mary and sister Mary Fisher visited in early August. "He met us in Richmond," reported Mary, "and I went with him to his camp, situated within a few miles of Manassas. Mary [Fisher] went on with us. We staid in a farm house, and were quite comfortable." Mary Fisher wrote that she

> found him well except [for] a very red eye. The doctors tell us it will be some time before it is quite well. . . . The ball is still *under* the eye, and I do not think it will be well until it is taken out. But the doctors say it must be let alone, and of course they know best.

She resolved to show her gratitude to God for sparing her brother's life "by a closer walk with Him."[51]

Hampton described his injury in a letter to a family friend, Mrs. Mary Singleton. "I escaped by almost a miracle. Had this shot struck one ½ inch higher up it would have gone through my head. . . . I fear I shall always suffer from it—as I have had fearful neuralgic headaches of late, all the pain coming from this wound." He also had something to say about leadership.

> You must not believe a word about my being "reckless." I am the personification of discretion. But to make men fight well the officers must *lead*. I am very glad to feel that I now have the confidence of my men & I know that they will follow me anywhere.

He had contempt for the misinformation that circulated after the battle. "Nobody saved us & for hours we were fighting the main columns of the enemy. We held them in check for two hours & thus gained this most precious time."

In this first engagement Hampton had shown himself a natural leader, a fearless fighter, and a tactician quick to respond to changing battlefield conditions. His military career seemed to hold promise. Still, for Hampton army service was only a duty—a job that had to be done. He expected recognition, but insisted that glory was not worth the pursuit.

> This is the most atrocious & unnatural war ever waged, & if it does not soon cease its horrors will exceed those of any previous war recorded in history. It is fearful. And the sights after a battle are too horrible to think of. I want to see no more of them.[52]

5

"A MAN FOR HARD WORK"

Infantry Commander

S oon after the triumph at Manassas, it became known that Hampton
would add two companies of infantry to the Legion. "We learn that
quite a large number of young men have already formed an association for the purpose of raising at least one, if not both, of these companies in
Charleston," reported the *Courier*. From that city's German-American community volunteers stepped forward under the command of Capt. William K.
Bachman. "There was not a man in the company," remembered Bachman,
"who owed allegiance to the Confederate States, every man being a foreigner
and unnaturalized." Still, they "volunteered unconditionally" to serve for
the duration of the war. On September 10, the unit was solemnly presented
with a flag, speeches were made in English and German, and the men were
given a patriotic send-off at the Northeastern Railroad Station.[1] But they
would not remain foot soldiers. In October Hampton took delivery of two
of those rifled field guns, with a large supply of ammunition, that he had
ordered from London. Determined to expand the Legion's artillery contingent by the creation of an additional battery, the newly arrived Germans
became Company B. The Legion infantry would be reinforced later by the
Claremont Rifles from Stateburg, Capt. James G. Spann commanding, and
by the Zouave Volunteers from Richland under Capt. L. Cheves McCord.
These units became infantry companies G and H, respectively.[2]

"We had our new uniforms and new sabers and rifles," remembered a
Legion cavalryman. Yet the horsemen remained at Ashland during the July
21 battle. In the aftermath of Manassas, they scouted as far as Vienna, but

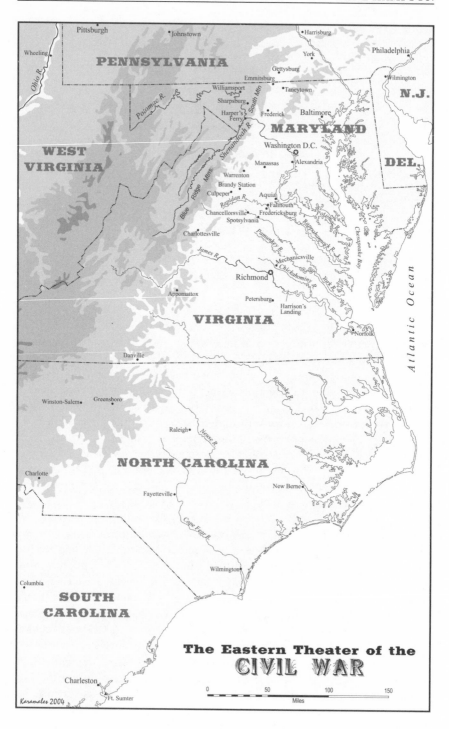

The Eastern Theater of the CIVIL WAR

found few Yankee stragglers or plunder and in a few weeks rejoined Hampton. In August Chaplain A. Toomer Porter was sent on a mission to procure uniforms for all. He succeeded in having them made at the Industrial School for Girls in Charleston. Coats and trousers were of a gray cotton and wool material. Trimmed in yellow—traditional for voltigeurs—some coats had buttons emblazoned with an eagle and a "V." Other uniform buttons were of the traditional palmetto design. Issued in October, the uniforms would be supplemented as time went on from a variety of sources as they wore out.[3]

Recovering from his head wound, Hampton remained with his men at their camp east of Manassas Junction. They were well supplied with army rations, although "some mouths watered for more tasty things," confessed Pvt. John Coxe. Farmers in the neighborhood noticed that poultry was disappearing, and feathers were accumulating around the tents of those South Carolinians. One afternoon in early August, before dismissing the men from drill, Hampton called the Legion to attention. Sadly, their colonel presented the evidence of pilferage.

> You must know that such misconduct on your part grieves my heart beyond measure. And I do hope that I have heard my last complaint on such an unsavory subject. If any of you men are so delicate as to be unable to eat the camp fare, come to me and I will, if necessary, divide the last dollar I have with you to enable you to purchase finer food."

Thoroughly ashamed of themselves, there was no further thievery.[4]

In the late summer heat, many, including Hampton, were stricken with what was described as "bowel trouble" and others with typhoid fever. For two weeks the colonel rested at a nearby farm house, although almost every day he rode to camp. "I am improving quite fast now," he wrote to Mary Fisher on September 4.

> I only want my strength back again to be quite well. I do not know what there was in the attack to pull me down so suddenly and completely. But I was entirely prostrated and for some days suffered very much. . . . The sick men are getting better, though there have been several deaths.

Even with so many on sick call, Hampton refused to reduce the guard. Requiring healthy soldiers to perform the extra duty made the colonel for a time most unpopular.[5]

Hampton was soon back to active leadership. During a reconnaissance in early September he led a mounted scouting party down a road only to find that it terminated abruptly in a farm yard. "Four females rushed out and attempted to explain the course we should have taken," recounted Lt. James Lowndes. The twenty-six-year-old lieutenant was delighted when the "youngest and prettiest" of the girls volunteered to personally show them the way back. Hampton "accepted so fair a guide with great readiness," but not without casting a wary eye on his infatuated lieutenant. "[T]he column countermarched leaving the Colonel, myself & the guide in the rear," continued Lowndes, "but he soon got rid of me by sending me to the front with a very unnecessary message. As we started she asked him very innocently, 'Sir, do you belong to the Hampton Legion[?]' " The frustrated young man could not resist answering for his commander.

"[N]o—the Hampton Legion belongs to him."[6]

The Legion would be ordered to the army's right flank, south of the Occoquan River and overlooking the Potomac. At Freestone Point on the Potomac, Hampton erected a battery of three guns, having the work done at night. Hidden by trees were two field guns and a 32-pounder captured at Manassas and dubbed "Long Tom." Only when the work was complete were the trees felled, unmasking the position. Early on the morning of September 25, the battery was discovered. A Union gunboat quickly steamed upriver, returning with six other vessels. They opened fire at ten o'clock. For the first time—and outgunned—the Legion artillery went into action. As Hampton was tying up his horse, a Yankee shell exploded but ten feet away, showering him and the animal with dirt. His artillerymen returned a well-aimed fire. The uneven duel went on until one o'clock in the afternoon when the Union flotilla withdrew. One gunboat was beached, another disabled and towed to safety. "Long Tom's" range astounded the enemy, some shots nearly reaching the Maryland shore. Based on the little battery's rate of fire, one Union commander thought he had faced four guns. Hampton reported to his sister,

> We had a warm little brush and drove the whole concern off, luckily without any damage to us, though one big shell *scared* me very much. The generals all seem pleased with the manner in which the affair was managed and I am entirely satisfied with the conduct of my men.[7]

The companies of the Legion pitched their tents in the vicinity of Bacon Race Church and a tiny community called Maple Valley. There they would remain through the winter. First assigned to Earl Van Dorn's division, later to that of James Longstreet, Hampton's command was in each case brigaded alone—in recognition of the Legion's "independent" status. His men continued to construct fortifications on the Occoquan. "But we had a good time," remembered one private, "Captain Beggs, our commissary, kept us plentifully supplied with rations." Hampton was given responsibility for a long stretch of the river, and he remained vigilant, reconnoitering on horseback and even by rowboat when necessary. He discovered a new ford on the Occoquan and made recommendations for improved defenses. Where the two rivers come together, the water is more than a mile wide. "Across the Potomac opposite our camp in Maryland was a Federal camp," remembered one of Hampton's men, "and when weather conditions were favorable we could hear their drums, bugles, and brass band."[8]

There was a sharp skirmish with patrolling Union cavalry on December 18, and again on New Year's Day, 1862. On the latter occasion about one hundred blue-clad horsemen were ambushed by twenty of the Legion's cavalry. Hampton recounted that, while leading reinforcements into the fray,

> I rode on a bunch of Yanks, who fired on me when I charged. . . . We broke their squadron and emptied several saddles and if I had only taken more of my men with me, I would have cut the party to pieces. . . . Unless we look them up, they don't seem disposed to fight.

He thought that snow would probably preclude further enemy advances and predicted foreign recognition of Southern independence by spring. "I look for the breaking up of the Yankee Government," wrote Hampton, "& it will be a blessing to mankind when this occurs."[9]

Hampton had been distressed to learn of the Union capture of Port Royal, South Carolina, in November. He tried in vain to have the Legion transferred there. He expressed to Mary Fisher his longing to return and fight on the soil of the Palmetto State. "I have looked for nothing but disaster since that fool Pickens was elected Gov. It will be only through the mercy of God that we get over our troubles safely, if we do get over them." The Legion, he was sure, could do good work back home in South Carolina. "My men are crazy to go and if they could meet the Yankees *there*, not many would be spared. One of the companies has run up a *black flag*, indicating that no quarter is to be asked or given."[10]

A different flag arrived in camp in late November. Ladies in Matanzas, Cuba—Confederate sympathizers with some acquaintance with the Legion—sent the banner through the blockade. A soldier of the Legion reported,

> It is a beautiful Confederate flag—the "stars and bars"—made of elegant silk, and exhibits exquisite workmanship. Its appearance was hailed with genuine enthusiasm by those who were present, and the compliments bestowed upon it and the lovely dark-eyed Senoritas whose fair hands wrought its silken folds would have been gratifying to their patriotic hearts.

Colonel Hampton graciously thanked the donors in a public letter, assuring them that "we shall cherish it for their sakes, and, if need be, defend it with our lives."[11]

Hampton was handed another gift in early December. Joseph E. Johnston, commanding general of the Department of Northern Virginia, sent Hampton a sword. "It is a beautiful one," responded the colonel, "and I trust it may do good service whilst in my hands." Hampton considered the weapon a loan, "and I shall try to return it untarnished."[12]

The Confederate flag presented by the ladies of Matanzas, Cuba, to the Hampton Legion. *Glenn Dedmondt, The Flags of Civil War South Carolina (Gretna, La.: Pelican Pub., 2000).*

On Christmas Day, 1861, Hampton reminded Mary Fisher,

> Since I left home, six months ago, the hand of our Father in Heaven has protected me from many and great dangers. He has kept me from falling, in battle when so many fell, and in the midst of great sickness, He has granted to me strength and health. I strive to be thankful for these unmerited mercies and I pray to be made worthy of them.

His family was constantly on his mind. At year's end he urged wife Mary and his sister to come to Virginia. "I must have McDuffie too." In a letter to Mary Fisher on January 3, he included lifelike sketches of a little dog—the camp mascot—for his four-year-old son's amusement. Although McDuffie would remain in Columbia, near mid-January Hampton met his wife in Richmond for a brief reunion.[13]

In January Johnston reorganized the Potomac District. On January 14 Colonel Hampton was given command of a full brigade. His command would be composed of the Legion and three infantry regiments: the Fourteenth Georgia, Nineteenth Georgia, and Sixteenth North Carolina. For the first time the Legion was brigaded with infantry regiments—a more practical arrangement certainly, but one that eroded its status as an independent, mixed command. Hampton was now exercising the responsibilities of a brigadier general, and his brigade would soon become part of a division commanded by Brig. Gen. William Henry Chase Whiting. Assignment of another artillery battery would increase the strength of Hampton's command to some 2,600 men.[14]

But Hampton had no intention of abandoning his Legion. On February 1 he wrote to Secretary of War Judah P. Benjamin requesting help in bringing the Legion itself up to brigade strength. A reorganized Legion would "consist of from two to four regiments of infantry, each regiment to have a company of artillery and one or two of cavalry. This would give force enough to constitute a very strong brigade, and yet the formation of it would not preclude its being thrown with other troops." In January Hampton had met with Davis in Richmond and received the president's blessing for his plan. The problem was the availability of troops. Secretary Benjamin informed Hampton that he had no "unattached regiments" to offer him.[15] The colonel initially hoped to recruit additional men in South Carolina, but manpower reserves were growing thin.[16] Hampton's plan languished. The great wave of patriotic enthusiasm during the Confederacy's first spring had swept tens of thousands into the field. Now state authorities were having difficulty meeting quotas. In April 1862 Congress passed the first Confederate conscription act, requiring able-bodied white males from eighteen to thirty-five to serve for three years or the duration of the war. Those already in the army who failed to reenlist would be mustered out and immediately drafted.[17]

One portion of that act—in the time-honored tradition of the prewar militia—permitted companies and regiments to choose their own officers. Throughout the army elections wrought chaos. Hampton feared that Lt. Col. James B. Griffin, acting commander of the Legion, would be one of those voted out. "I am very sorry for this as he is a good officer & I like him very much. But, by some means, he has not become popular with the men."[18]

In the midst of the disorder caused by elections, reenlistments, and reorganization, the army was ordered to retreat. On February 19 Johnston met with Davis and the Confederate Cabinet. Johnston insisted that the Manassas–Bull Run–Occoquan line could not be held much longer. He left the meeting understanding "that the army was to fall back as soon as practicable," although the general was cautioned to save his cannon and supplies. It was unclear what new defensive line he might establish.[19] Without communicating further with the commander in chief, Johnston decided to begin his withdrawal on Saturday morning, March 8.

Whiting gave Hampton his orders, urging him to get the wagons rolling Friday night. The colonel was recovering from another bout of illness. His brigade was posted along a twelve-mile front, supplies piled up at Bacon Race Church, 130 sick had to be evacuated, and he was short of transportation. As they got under way, Hampton was forced to destroy—lest it fall into enemy hands—fifty-nine army tents, other property belonging to his men, and some ammunition. He reported,

> With the means at my disposal, I moved, literally in the face of the enemy, four regiments of infantry, three batteries, containing 31 guns and gun-carriages, and 120 cavalry . . . over roads that were scarcely passable, a distance of 50 miles. There was no straggling, no confusion, and after the first day's march no loss of any property. . . . My greatest regret is that I cannot say the same as to private property, for it seems to be a hard case to make the soldier bear a loss which was caused by no fault of his own.

Maj. Stephen D. Lee, acting as brigade chief of staff, insisted that most of the army property lost was of little value.[20]

"The difficulties surrounding Colonel Hampton were indeed great," Whiting told his superiors. "An extended line, insufficient transportation, an active and superior enemy in his front, incessant skirmishing all along his outposts; his army was watched and shelled from the enemy's fleet." Hampton's performance met with the West Pointer's unqualified approval. "It is due to that distinguished, active, and vigilant officer to say that here, as everywhere, he conducted his brigade with consummate judgment, precision, and skill."[21]

Elsewhere in Johnston's army tons of supplies were lost, and many heavy guns were simply abandoned, infuriating the president and his War Department. New positions were taken along the Rapidan and Rappahannock rivers. Hampton could only agree with his superiors that Fredericksburg could not be held, except "by winning a battle before the enemy arrive, the town being perfectly commanded by the heights on the opposite bank of the river." But there was a new and imminent threat. Union major general George B. McClellan, McDowell's replacement, had begun landing troops at the tip of the peninsula—that large neck of land southwest of Richmond between the York and James rivers. There, a 105,000-man army was under the protection of the federal navy's heavy guns. As rapidly as he could, Johnston dispatched his outnumbered army to the peninsula to block McClellan.

During April, Confederate major general John Bankhead Magruder's stubborn resistance had taught McClellan to be cautious. McClellan would lay siege to the Southern lines around Williamsburg. But Johnston came to believe that his own position on the lower peninsula was vulnerable. He ordered a retreat to begin on the night of May 3. Delayed by mud, Confederates would abandon fifty-six more heavy guns. The battle of Williamsburg became a series of rearguard actions resulting in 2,239 Union, 1,560 Confederate casualties.[22] "The Yankee cavalry made its appearance [on May 4]," recounted Maj. Gen. Daniel Harvey Hill, "but after being charged by Hampton remained quiet and civil the balance of the day." In the melee Gillespie Thornwell of Company D of the Legion cavalry "was wounded four times by

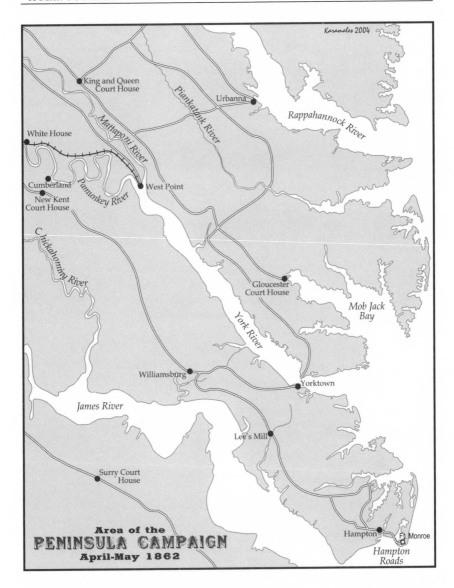

Karamales 2004

King and Queen Court House

Urbanna

Piankatank River

Rappahannock River

Mattaponi River

White House

Cumberland

New Kent Court House

Pamunkey River

West Point

Chickahominy River

Gloucester Court House

Mob Jack Bay

York River

Williamsburg

Yorktown

James River

Lee's Mill

Surry Court House

Hampton

Ft. Monroe

Hampton Roads

Area of the
PENINSULA CAMPAIGN
April-May 1862

their sabres, and, when surrounded, declared he would die before he would surrender."[23]

Early on May 7 Federals began disembarking large numbers of troops—protected by the firepower of their York River gunboats—near West Point, below the landing that served Eltham plantation. If the maneuver succeded they might be able to flank the main column of Johnston's retreating army.

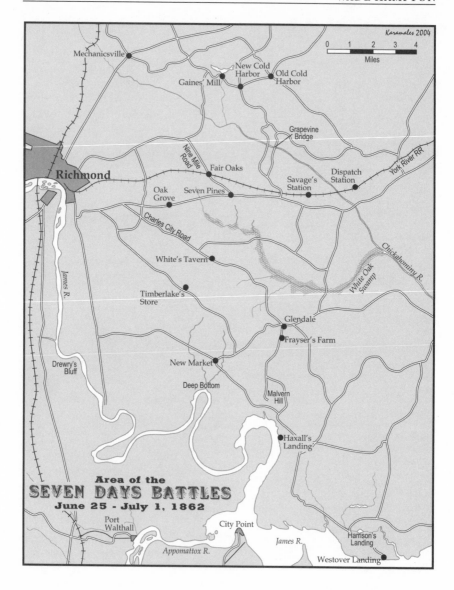

Whiting was ordered to throw them back, and he called upon the brigades of Hampton and Brig. Gen. John Bell Hood. The enemy was in dense woods and too far inland to be supported effectively by naval guns. Hood attacked on the left, down the Brick House and Barhamsville roads. Hampton advanced on the right with the Legion infantry and the Nineteenth Georgia. Lt. Col. Griffin commanded the Legion, and Lt. Col. Thomas C. Johnson commanded the Georgia infantry—both under the direction of Hampton. Steadily the Yankees were driven back. Hood repulsed a counterattack on his left. Hampton's force beat back a threat to their right. Having driven the enemy one and a half miles, inflicting many casualties and taking forty prisoners, Hood withdrew as ordered. Hampton was also preparing to retire when the Federals made one more thrust. "My men returned this fire, and, responding to my order to charge with a cheer, drove the enemy back." It was handsomely done, with only four Confederates wounded and none killed. "I would respectfully state that Colonel Hampton," wrote Hood, "with about 400 of his Legion, forced the enemy on the right to return to the protection of their gunboats." Whiting referred to the "conspicuous gallantry" of Hampton and his "small number of brave troops." The next day Johnston reported to Gen. Robert E. Lee, the president's military adviser, recommending Hampton for promotion to brigadier general.[24]

Back on February 2 Johnston had complained to Adj. Gen. Samuel Cooper that one of his divisions and five of his brigades were "without their proper generals." Hampton, he said, was one of several colonels "fully competent to command brigades." Hampton had been in charge of a brigade, performing a brigadier general's job, since January. Yet, to him advancement was problematic. "If the Presdt. now offers me promotion," he told his sister on March 25, "I shall refuse it, unless he makes my commission date back to the time at which I took command of this Brigade." Was he petulant that his plans for augmenting the Legion had been stalled? In the same letter he expressed a willingness to return to his Legion and reorganize it himself, still confident that with it "good service can be done."[25]

He may have yet hoped for favorable news from Davis on expanding the Legion. "Nothing has been said to me by the Presdt.," he wrote to Mary Fisher on May 21, "& I begin to think he means to back out. I wish he would come to some determination, as my position is not a pleasant one." He expressed fear that Griffin and Conner would "both be thrown out" as a result of elections. "If so, I should prefer to give up the command *even if they elect me*. Suppose they throw me out too: how would you like that? I could then go home & attend to my business."[26]

On May 23 the president appointed Wade Hampton a brigadier general in the Provisional Army of the Confederate States, to rank from that date. Hampton declined the promotion.[27]

The next day Hampton issued a general order from "Headquarters, Hampton Legion." It had been one year since these South Carolinians first answered his call. Perhaps he finally understood that the Legion would not become a brigade, but must be broken up. "Whatever may be the future of the several arms, the Commanding Officer feels sure that the members of the Legion will not forget the family tie, which as an independent and isolated Command, has so long and so happily bound them together in the war."[28]

Still in charge of his brigade, Colonel Hampton had work to do. Johnston had fallen back to lines that were, in some places, little more than three
miles from Richmond. Yankee soldiers could see the capital's church spires.
McClellan had to be stopped. "If we whip him here—& I have no doubt but
that we shall—we will have every prospect for peace," Hampton confided to
his sister.

> But I do not like to think of peace until we have carried the war into Yankee-
> dom. *They* should be made to feel the horrors of the war & then perhaps
> peace would be lasting. When I think how much our people are suffering
> my heart burns with indignation & I have the most vindictive feelings
> towards the whole Yankee race.[29]

On the eve of battle Hampton penned a note to Mary Fisher. "I have
but a moment in which to write to you before going out to attack the enemy.
My Brigade is ordered to lead & I hope it will prove itself worthy of the
position." He seemed to be saying good-bye for the last time.

> Whatever the result to our army may be, it may please God to take me. Rest
> assured then should this be the case, that I have always loved you very
> much & thanked you for the devotion to me & mine. Keep up your care to
> all the dear ones I leave. Tell the girls & Sally that I send my love & blessing
> to them. I have done my duty as a soldier & none of my name need be
> ashamed of me. God bless & keep you all.[30]

The Chickahominy River, east of Richmond, flows generally southeast-
ward. McClellan had positioned three corps north of the river, two to the
south. Since heavy rain on May 30 made the river difficult to cross, Johnston
determined to attack those Union forces to the south. His plan was complicated. Maj. Gen. Benjamin Huger's division would march down the Charles
City Road, protecting the Confederate right. Maj. Gen. Daniel Harvey Hill's
division, in the Confederate center, would advance on the Williamsburg
Road in the direction of a tiny settlement called Seven Pines. On the left two
divisions of Longstreet's corps, reinforced by Whiting's division, would press
down Nine Mile Road, pass Fair Oaks Station on the York River Railroad,
and then fall upon the Federals at Seven Pines. Johnston issued verbal, not
written, orders. The ground and roads were muddy. When the advance
began on the morning of May 31, there was immediate confusion and delay.
About 30,000 Confederates never got into action. To make matters worse,
Federals were crossing the Chickahominy despite the flood, reinforcing their
comrades south of the river.[31]

Late that morning Hampton's brigade helped secure the Confederate
left near the river as battle was joined down at Fair Oaks. By late afternoon
he, too, was ordered to the attack. His brigade advanced on the left, parallel

to the Nine Mile Road, through woods and across a shallow swamp choked with rotting logs. A five-gun Federal battery began lobbing shells and spherical case shot into the advancing Southerners. At a range of 500 yards the Yankee artillery opened up with canister. Confederates returned fire, but the range was too far to be effective.[32] Hampton rode out in front of his North Carolina veterans. "Do not fire a shot until you can feel the enemy on your bayonets. Forward!" A soldier of the Legion saw two young friends fall, one shot through the forehead, another hit in the temple. The Yankees had been reinforced from across the Chickahominy by troops of Maj. Gen. Edwin V. Sumner's corps, who feared that Hampton's men were intent on turning their right. "We made three charges under terrible fire, through the woods," reported a South Carolinian. Confederates got to within fifteen or twenty yards of the enemy line, but each time were forced to fall back. At one point Preston Hampton grabbed the fallen flag of the Legion and cheered on the men.[33]

Colonel Hampton was leading when a minie ball hit the sole of his boot and tore into his foot. The bullet was immediately removed by Surgeon E. S. Gaillard. Despite the pain, Hampton remained on the field, under fire, and in command.[34]

Around twilight Johnston himself was shot in the right shoulder and then struck in the chest by a shell fragment. Falling from his horse, he was carried to safety. Maj. Gen. Gustavus Woodson Smith took temporary command. Repulsed—but unpursued—Confederates fell back to positions they held prior to the battle. Southerners assumed that Seven Pines was a victory, although losses of 6,134 exceeded by more than a thousand those of the enemy. More ominously, Confederates still had their backs to the wall. At two o'clock on the afternoon of June 1, President Davis appointed Robert E. Lee to command the army.[35]

Hampton's foot was badly swollen, and for two days he was in great pain, unable even to sit up. "The ball is mashed up," he wrote to his sister, "and *the bones feel pretty much in the same condition.*" Still, "God has indeed been merciful to spare not only my life, but the lives of my dear boys." As for the Legion, "it fought as only the best troops can fight. . . . They have left a name which will live in History."[36]

In his report of the battle, Smith ignored Hampton's refusal of promotion. "General Hampton, on this as on many previous occasions, was remarkable for coolness, promptness, and decided practical ability as a leader of men in difficult and dangerous circumstances." His praise was extraordinary. "In those high characteristics of a general he has few equals and perhaps no superior."[37]

Lee ordered Hampton's and two other brigades into a reserve under Maj. Gen. Ambrose Powell Hill. Hampton's command had suffered 329 battle casualties. Many men had also fallen ill, reducing the combat effectiveness of these organizations. In his order, dated June 11, Lee also referred to Hampton as "General."[38]

By the second week in June, Hampton had decided to take the promotion offered him by Davis, even as he yielded to the inevitable breakup of his beloved Legion. He had apparently arrived at an understanding with the president that the Legion—or at least part of the Legion—would continue to be brigaded with Hampton's command. According to 2nd Lt. James Washington Moore the new general said he "would not be parted from us" because "he had made that an article of agreement on accepting his commission." "The President wrote a handsome letter after the battle," said Col. James Conner, "and there has been a general smoking of the calumet of peace, and the Colonel has accepted."[39]

Brigadier General Hampton headed home to recuperate from his wounds. A hero's welcome awaited him. "What heroism!" said one Columbian of the wounded Hampton's refusal to leave the field. "No, what luck," replied another. "He is the luckiest man alive. He'll never be killed. He was shot in the temple. That did not kill him! His soldiers believe in his luck."[40] He certainly relished these precious days with wife Mary, the children, and the rest of his family.

Less agreeable were his social obligations. An elaborate reception for Hampton was held at the home of Governor Pickens. The governor's beautiful young wife, Lucy Holcombe, met the limping general at the door, took away his crutch, making him lean upon her shoulder for support. "Her blue eyes were aflame," recounted a guest, "and in response poor Wade smiled and smiled, until his face hardened into a fixed grin of embarrassment and annoyance. He is a simple-mannered man, you know, and does not want to be made much of by women."[41]

Prior to secession Pickens had represented the United States at the Romanov court in Saint Petersburg. Lucy was overheard telling Mary Hampton that she thought Wade "the handsomest man in the world, except the czar, emperor of Russia."

"Do you?" said Mary. "I don't."

"Oh, don't be modest," protested Lucy. "I own that I think Governor Pickens very handsome."

"Do you?" blurted Mary. "I don't."

An amused Mary Chesnut called Mrs. Hampton "a martyr to truth."[42]

Wade Hampton was himself something of a wit. On a hot June morning toward the end of his furlough, he and James Chesnut Jr. attended worship services together. Sitting in front of them was a young girl wearing gold earrings shaped like tiny ladders. There in his pew Hampton improvised and jotted down a doggerel composition.

> Lydia swears her prudish ear
> No word of love shall ever reach—

Hampton initially declined promotion to brigadier general in the Confederate Army, the rank he wears in this image, in an effort to preserve his beloved Hampton Legion. In the wake of the battle of Seven Pines, after being promised that at least part of the Legion would remain under his command, a wounded Hampton acquiesced. *Collection of the New York Historical Society.*

Then—tell, I pray, why doth she wear
What does another lesson teach?
A sign that's plain to every eye
She's not as deaf as any adder,
And he who hopes to climb so high,
Has but to use a golden ladder—[43]

Every armchair strategist in Columbia had a plan for winning the war, but Hampton's views were heard with respect. "If we mean to play at war as we play a game of chess—West Point tactics prevailing—we are sure to lose the game." Hampton had come to realize how superior were the numbers and resources of the North. "They have every advantage. They can lose pawns ad infinitum—to the end of time—and never feel it." Faced with long odds the South's only hope was to gamble on her soldier's "hot-headed dash, reckless gallantry, spirit of adventure—readiness to lead forlorn hopes."

Mary Chesnut thought she was making but a "pleasant remark" when she said to him, "Oh, general! The next battle will give you a chance to be major general."

"I was very foolish to give up my Legion," he replied with genuine sadness.[44]

JOHN ESTEN COOKE was ordnance officer on the staff of cavalryman James Ewell Brown Stuart. A gifted writer, Cooke had the opportunity to observe and size up many high-ranking Confederates, and Wade Hampton came under his scrutiny. Unlike his exuberant friend Stuart, "Hampton smiled oftener than he laughed, never sang at all that I ever heard, and had the composed demeanor of a man of middle age." The South Carolinian's "plain gray coat, worn, dingy, and faded" contrasted with his chief's flamboyant uniform.

Cooke described in some detail the Hampton he remembered.

What the eye saw in those days [July 1862] was a personage of tall stature and "distinguished" appearance. The face was browned by sun and wind, and half covered by dark side-whiskers joined in a long moustache of the same hue; the chin bold, prominent, and bare. The eyes were brown, inclining to black, and very mild and friendly; the voice low, sonorous, and with a certain accent of dignity and composure. . . .

After being in his presence for ten minutes, you saw that he was a man for hard work, and not for display. . . . The General was as courteous to the humblest private soldier as to the Commander-in-Chief. . . . He did not act at all, but lived his character. . . .

An officer long associated with him said to me one day: "I do not believe there ever was a General more beloved by his whole command; and he more than returns it. General Hampton has *a real tenderness,* I do believe, for every soldier who has ever served under him.". . . Many a brave fellow's family was kept from want by him; and a hundred instances of his liberality are doubtless recorded in the grateful memories of the women and children whom he fought for, and fed too, in those dark days. This munificence was nowhere else recorded. The left hand knew not what the right hand did. . . .

His staff were devoted to him. . . . General Hampton liked to laugh and talk with them around the camp fire . . . and to play chess, draughts [checkers], or other games, in the intervals of fighting or work. One of his passions was hunting. This amusement he pursued upon every occasion. . . .

It was impossible to imagine anything coarse or profane in the action or utterance of the man. An oath never soiled his lips. "*Do* bring up that artillery!" or some equivalent exclamation, was his nearest approach to irritation even. . . . On the field Hampton was noted for his coolness. This never left him. It might almost be called repose, so perfect was it. He was never an excitable man; and as doubt and danger pressed heavier, his equanimity seemed to increase. You could see that this was truly a stubborn spirit. I do not think that anybody who knew him could even imagine Wade Hampton "flurried." His nerve was made of invincible stuff.[45]

6

"THE PEOPLE HAVE SURRENDERED CHAMBERSBURG"

Hampton Joins the Cavalry

The streets of the Confederate capital were crowded with wounded soldiers as General Hampton stepped from the car at the Richmond station on Thursday, June 26, 1862. He could hear the distant rumble of artillery. McClellan's army—100,000 strong—was nearly in the suburbs.

It had been less than four weeks since Lee took charge of 72,000 Confederates. He quickly ordered his men to stack arms and pick up spades, strengthening the city's defenses with earthworks. Detective Allan Pinkerton, McClellan's "spymaster," feared that Lee commanded at least 200,000, intelligence that made Little Mac more cautious than ever. In mid-June Lee ordered cavalryman J. E. B. Stuart to make a daring reconnaissance. Riding completely around McClellan, Stuart not only embarrassed the Yankees, but he brought back information that convinced Lee the Union right was vulnerable. Lee recalled General "Stonewall" Jackson from the Shenandoah Valley, where his 18,000 veterans had just won a series of stunning victories. As Confederate preparations for an offensive were going forward, the Federals attempted their own reconnaissance-in-force on June 25 at Oak Grove, gaining 600 yards by giving up 626 casualties.[1] The Seven Days Campaign had begun.

Undeterred by the enemy's aggressive stance, the next day Lee ordered the divisions of major generals Ambrose Powell Hill, Daniel Harvey Hill, and

James Longstreet to attack across the Chickahominy River. They were thrown back with heavy losses near a settlement called Mechanicsville, but McClellan's confidence melted when he learned that Jackson had not been engaged and still threatened his right. The Federals withdrew to a strong position at Gaines' Mill where Confederates renewed their offensive on June 27. All day the Southerners were repulsed, suffering nearly 8,000 casualties.[2] Finally, near dusk, the Union line began to give way. Lee could claim his first victory.

Hampton, still a general without a command, raced to join Longstreet's division as they were about to cross the Chickahominy late on the afternoon of June 26. As the infantry advanced Confederate batteries fell silent, fearful of hitting their own men. Hampton thought he could help. Longstreet reported,

> Brigadier-General Hampton volunteered to give directions and positions to our heavy batteries opposite Mechanicsville, now become useless, and to follow the movements of our army down the river. The battery followed our movements and played upon the enemy's lines with good effect.[3]

One of Jackson's most promising officers, Col. Samuel Vance Fulkerson, was killed at Gaines' Mill while commanding the Third Brigade. On Saturday, June 28, Hampton was placed in temporary command of the brigade. Made up of the Tenth, Twenty-third, and Thirty-seventh Virginia infantry regiments, and Wooding's battery from Danville, Virginia, the Third Brigade was ordered to W. H. C. Whiting's division and placed in reserve. There, they were reinforced by Capt. Hugh R. Garden's company of South Carolina light artillery.[4]

Confederate major general John Bankhead Magruder fought rearguard actions on June 29 at Allen's Farm and Savage's Station as the Federals, encumbered by long wagon trains, slowly withdrew toward the protection of their gunboats on the James River. Jackson seemed uncharacteristically lethargic as unhurried repairs were made to Grapevine Bridge over the Chickahominy. McClellan's army seemed vulnerable as it stretched southward from White Oak Swamp almost to the James River. Lee planned to strike eastward with most of his forces on Monday, June 30. Moving south, Jackson's assignment was to find the Federal right flank, get behind it if possible, and roll it up. Arriving at White Oak Swamp at about ten o'clock that morning, Jackson found that the retreating Federals had burned the bridge over the creek and that their artillery, hidden by trees, commanded the crossing. He directed Hampton to repair the bridge, but enemy fire soon persuaded him to countermand the order. Confederate guns returned fire, although Maj. Edward Porter Alexander thought the duel "a useless burning of both daylight and ammunition," as no advantage was gained and time was wasted.[5]

Hampton put his brigade in position and ordered the men to protect themselves by lying down. He then decided to reconnoiter. Accompanied by his son Lt. Wade Hampton, Maj. Theodore G. Barker, and other staff officers, Hampton rode into the swamp and later reported

> to my surprise [I] found no difficulty in crossing it. This I did and I came out on the opposite side, just in rear of the right flank of the enemy. Carefully reconnoitering them I recrossed and reported the results of my observation to General Whiting and afterwards to General Jackson.

Hampton emphasized to Jackson how easy it would be to surprise and flank the enemy at this newly discovered crossing. He asked permission to make the attack with his own brigade. Stonewall seemed not to understand the import of Hampton's discovery. Jackson, in Hampton's words,

> enquired if I could make a bridge across the stream, to which I replied that I could make one for infantry, but not for artillery, as in attempting the latter my presence would be detected, owing to the fact that we should have to cut down trees in order to clear a road for wheels. General Jackson directed me to make the bridge, and taking a detail of 50 men I put it up in a very short time. It may be well to state too that the stream here was so narrow and shallow that it offered in reality no obstruction to the passage of troops.

The superfluous bridge completed, Hampton again rode across the creek and found the enemy, "in the same position and totally unsuspicious of our presence, though I approached their line to within 100 or 150 yards." He went to Jackson a second time and found the general sitting on a pine log, cap over his eyes, apparently napping. Awakened, Stonewall acknowledged Hampton's presence. Hampton repeated his report. Jackson made no reply, but closed his eyes again. "He sat in silence for some time, then rose and walked off in silence." The situation was awkward. Hampton returned to his brigade to await attack orders that never came.[6]

The next day, July 1, Lee made one more assault on Federals strongly entrenched on Malvern Hill. Confederates were bloodily repulsed, mainly by artillery fire, but McClellan continued his withdrawal. Finally on the move again, Jackson ran into the retreating enemy about two and a half miles south of White Oak Swamp. Hampton's brigade was held in reserve on the left, his men exposed to artillery fire, although casualties were light. The campaign was grinding to a halt. In one week Southerners had suffered over 20,000 casualties.[7] There had been confusion, misunderstanding, and missed opportunity. Still, Lee had saved the capital and seized the initiative.

What was the cause of Jackson's failure at White Oak Swamp? The answer seems to have been simple exhaustion. At supper on the evening of June 30, he had fallen asleep at the table with a biscuit in his teeth. In a letter to his wife, he complained of suffering from "fever and debility." "Nothing," concludes a Jackson biographer, "but a sense of duty on June 30 kept him in command." Pondering the wasted opportunities, "it is enough to make one cry to go over the story of how they were all lost," said artillery officer Porter Alexander. "And to think too that our *Stonewall Jackson* lost them." Hampton did not understand Jackson's decision not to attack, "nor do I venture to criticise the great and good soldier who made it. I only state facts, facts which in justice to General Lee should be known."[8]

In the aftermath of the Seven Days Campaign, Lee reorganized the Army of Northern Virginia. There would be two corps of infantry under Jackson and Longstreet and a division of cavalry commanded by J. E. B. Stuart, recently promoted to major general. This division would be made up of two brigades, and Stuart chose West Point–educated Fitzhugh Lee of the First Virginia Cavalry Regiment to command one of them. Lee was but twenty-seven and Robert E. Lee's nephew. For command of the other brigade, the commanding general wanted Wade Hampton. Hampton agreed, but let Lee understand that he did not consider the assignment permanent. He may have had his mind on future service in Mississippi or on the South Carolina coast. Orders were issued on July 28.[9]

In a letter to sister Mary Fisher nine days earlier, Hampton made no mention of the impending transfer to cavalry service.

> "There is no news here. You ask why "my brigade" [Jackson's Third] is not mentioned in the papers! One reason is that *we did nothing.* Or at any rate we had none of the desperate fighting to do, though we were constantly exposed. . . . I trust that we shall not have any more hard fighting to do, for the battles here were enough to shock any one. But I wish we had killed 25,000 Yankees as I could stand *that shock* very well.

He wrote again on July 26, informing her that "I have nothing to do as yet though I expect orders today." He shared her sadness at the death of a mutual friend. "Many very many of our best citizens have been cut off & I fear many more are to follow. We can only hope & pray & *fight.* All looks brighter for us just now & I hope the worst is past."[10]

On the very day that Hampton was assigned to the cavalry, Robert E. Lee intervened to correct Stuart's organization of his new division. Stuart had designated Fitzhugh Lee's command as the First Brigade, Hampton's as the Second. Lee quickly set him straight. "The brigade commanded by General Hampton will . . . be First Brigade, as he is the senior brigadier."[11] It was an inauspicious beginning for Hampton and Stuart.

Stuart was twenty-nine years old, a United States Military Academy graduate, bold, ostentatious, always in pursuit of glory and praise. Above all, he was a Virginian. "He had strong feelings for place," wrote a biographer, "and identified 'home' with southwestern Virginia. Everywhere else he went was exile. He left Virginia to perform deeds and win honors that would impress people whose opinion of him really mattered—his friends and family in Virginia."[12]

If the war was to Hampton an evil that must be borne, to Stuart it was "a splendid and exciting game," according to John Esten Cooke, his admiring friend. "I have never seen a man who looked his character more perfectly than Stuart," continued Cooke. "You saw . . . at a single glance, that Stuart was a cavalryman—in his dress, voice, walk, manner, everything." Stuart's spirit was irrepressible.

> In the midst of a rain-storm, when everybody was riding along . . . cowering beneath the flood pouring down, he would trot on, head up, and singing gaily. . . . He never moved on the field without his splendid red battle-flag; and more than once this prominent object, flaunting in the wind, drew the fire of the enemy's artillery. . . . Lent was not his favourite season. Life in his eyes was best when it was all flowers, bright colours, and carnival.[13]

Johann August Heinrich Heros von Borcke, Prussian Army officer and a volunteer on Stuart's staff, was in a position to observe both Stuart and Hampton. "Of a calm, dignified nature and friendly but very reserved mien," wrote the German, Hampton "formed a strong contrast to Stuart, whose unfettered, extremely fresh and somewhat loud manner he did not find very attractive." Both were natural leaders and courageous fighters. Hampton was "calm and prudent," "cool in the face of danger," and "an excellent organizer." "He took inexhaustible interest in the care of his people, both during and after a fight, and for that they were completely devoted to him." Von Borcke and his friend Hampton disagreed "only in our judgment of Stuart, whom he, in my belief, did not value highly enough for a long time."[14] There was no open breach. Hampton remained cordial, but cool, toward his superior. Stuart admired Hampton's abilities, even if he could not quite forgive the forty-four-year-old for not having been born in Virginia.

All across the South men like Hampton and Stuart had grown up in the saddle, a way of life that gave the Confederate cavalry a tremendous initial advantage. The Union army actually postponed expansion of its prewar cavalry force because to put a properly mounted, equipped, and trained regiment in the field cost over half a million dollars. Southern cavalrymen rode off to war on their own horses, any deficiencies they might have in arms and equipment more than made up for by their reckless dash and enthusiasm. Confederate War Department regulations stipulated that they wear a gray coat or shell jacket—trimmed in yellow—light-blue trousers, and a yellow kepi. In a blockaded South with few factories, regulation uniforms soon became a rare sight indeed. As prewar militia garb wore out, captured blue would combine with gray and all shades of butternut. Southern individualism was expressed in flamboyant headgear. Nor was there much uniformity in arms and equipment. Civilian saddles might be replaced with those taken from the enemy. Rope was sometimes used instead of leather, and sacks of all descriptions served in the place of saddle bags. A Southern cavalryman in the eastern theater was typically armed with a saber, one or two revolvers, and a carbine. If a trooper lost his horse, he was required to find a replacement—or transfer to the infantry. Shortages of all kinds were regularly made good at the expense of the Yankees.

A Confederate cavalry regiment was, at least in theory, composed of ten companies (sometimes called squadrons), each with from sixty to eighty enlisted men and three officers. Strength declined as the war progressed. Squadrons were commanded by a captain, regiments by a colonel. A brigade might be made up of from four to six regiments or battalions (organizations somewhat smaller than regiments). Southerners thought themselves unsurpassed horsemen and invincible fighters, but there was still much for a new cavalry officer to learn. On the eve of war the U.S. Army commissioned Brig. Gen. Phillip St. George Cooke to write *Cavalry Tactics,* and soon novices North and South were poring over its contents. There was instruction on such things as the training of horses for battle, saber exercise, pistol practice, saddling, and skirmishing. Cooke chose for his cavalry doctrine what he considered "the best points in the systems of France, Russia, Prussia, Austria, and England."[15] Ironically, Union general Cooke was the father-in-law of J. E. B. Stuart.

Hampton's First Brigade was initially made up of the Cobb's Legion cavalry battalion (from Georgia), commanded by Col. Pierce M. B. Young; the Second South Carolina Cavalry Regiment (which now included the cavalry of the Hampton Legion), commanded by Col. Matthew C. Butler; the cavalry of Mississippi's Jeff Davis Legion, commanded by Col. William T. Martin; the First North Carolina Cavalry Regiment, commanded by Col. Laurence S. Baker; the Tenth Virginia Cavalry Regiment, commanded by Col. J. Lucius Davis; and Hart's Battery (formerly of the Hampton Legion), commanded by Capt. James F. Hart.[16]

"My men seem very anxious to carry out all orders & are very much pleased to be in my Brigade," Hampton boasted to his sister. "Even some of the privates of [Fitzhugh] Lee's own Regt. have complained to my men of not being put in this Brigade."

Hampton reported on a conversation he overheard. "There is Wade Hampton: he is a chip off the old block," said the first soldier.

"Yes," replied the second, "he is a true son of his father."

It was, said Hampton, "as high praise as So. Ca. soldiers could give *to me*."[17]

Hampton's first assignment was to patrol the breadth of the peninsula, monitoring the Union army, as Lee shifted the bulk of his forces to northern Virginia. McClellan had fortified Harrison's Landing on the James River and made it his new base. Neither side dared risk an all-out attack. There were occasional skirmishes, but in August Federals began evacuating. On the morning of August 17 Hampton made a reconnaissance with troops from the First North Carolina. They found deserted Federal camps and abandoned Yankee supplies. Late in the day they ran into Union pickets. Across fields of corn and wheat they spied enemy cavalry drawn up in formation. The Carolinians prepared to attack. "General Hampton's clear, calm voice, rang out," remembered a veteran, " 'Charge them.' Sabers leaped from their scabbards, and the whole regiment by squadrons went dashing through the standing corn." The enemy horsemen turned and fled. That night and the next Hampton's Confederates captured a few stragglers as they cautiously approached the last line of Federal fortifications. Guarding the parapet, at regular intervals, were blue–clad scarecrows fashioned of rags and straw.[18] The Yankees were gone.

On August 29 and 30, on the old field of Manassas, Lee met a new Union army now under Maj. Gen. John Pope. Two days earlier Stonewall Jackson had turned Pope's right after a forced march and destroyed his supply base. The Third Brigade, now under the command of Brig. Gen William Booth Taliaferro, covered itself with glory in the ensuing combat at Groveton. At the second battle of Manassas Longstreet's corps joined Jackson's in beating back repeated Union attacks along an unfinished railroad embankment between Sudley Springs and the Warrenton Turnpike, inflicting terrible casualties. At the end of the second day, Pope's defeated army was in full retreat.

Hampton's brigade was still patrolling the peninsula when battle began on the banks of Bull Run, but was quickly ordered to this new front. Hampton and Stuart joined in pursuit of fleeing Federals on September 2. Hart's Battery found a high hill from which to fire upon the foe. "Mending their pace at every step, they plunged on to get beyond the reach of our murderous missiles that were crashing through their ranks," said one pursuer. "Heavy columns of black smoke were to be seen rising from their rear—evident signs of a commissary sacrifice." Prisoners were corralled. At nine o'clock that night the reinforced Yankees made a stand that brought an end to the chase. Hampton's losses were described as "miraculously slight."[19]

Back in South Carolina Sally Baxter Hampton, Frank's wife, had been fighting a desperate battle of her own with tuberculosis. Wade Hampton was kept apprised of Sally's decline. "I wish poor Frank could be here, as I want him made Lt. Col. Poor fellow. I feel deeply grieved about him & I hope God will have mercy on him." To be nearer his ailing wife, Capt. Frank Hampton was serving with the Third Battalion of South Carolina cavalry on James Island, south of Charleston. Wade Hampton wrote again to Mary Fisher in mid-August. "Always give the latest news from Sally, for I am very anxious about her. Her fate was indeed a sad one & I pity her greatly." He hoped that her New York family might somehow be able to visit, and he recommended the cooler air of a mountain retreat. Even as he penned the words, Sally was growing weaker. She died at Millwood on September 10, leaving four children, the oldest but six years old.[20] Grieving, Frank would soon join his brother in Virginia.

Lee would not wait for yet another federal march on Richmond. Confederate victory north of the Potomac River might bring foreign recognition of Southern independence and hasten the end of the war. On September 4 the Army of Northern Virginia began fording the river, crossing unopposed into the United States. One of Hampton's men said they "felt like strangers in a strange land." Troops cheered as bands played "My Maryland." Southerners cherished the hope that the liberation of that state might add a fourteenth star to the Confederate flag. General Lee's proclamation to the people of Maryland read,

> Our army has come among you, and is prepared to assist you with the power
> of its arms in regaining the rights of which you have been despoiled. . . . It
> is for you to decide your destiny, freely and without restraint. This army will
> respect your choice, whatever it may be.[21]

Confederate forces concentrated around Frederick City as Lee developed a bold strategic plan. He would send Stonewall Jackson's corps to Harpers Ferry, Virginia, to capture the Federal garrison there and open lines of supply

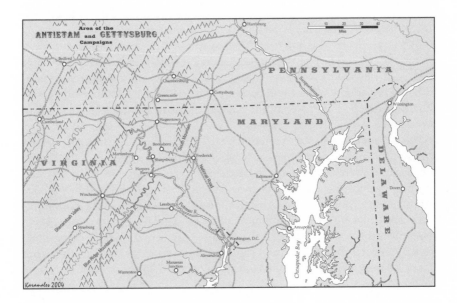

southward. Jackson would then rejoin Lee, and the entire army would march through Maryland into Pennsylvania. It would be the job of Stuart's cavalry to screen Lee's army, provide intelligence, and impede the enemy's movements. Demonstrations were made against federally-occupied Alexandria, Virginia, and Georgetown, in Washington, D.C., before the cavalry rode to Leesburg, Virginia, crossing into Maryland on the night of September 5. The small bands of Yankee cavalry they encountered were easily dispersed.[22] On September 7 the Union Army of the Potomac—under the command of George McClellan—left Washington, marching northwestward through Maryland in pursuit of Lee.

Sentiment for secession was strongest in Baltimore and on the Eastern Shore, still under the heel of Union occupation. Although there were those who came out to cheer the arrival of Hampton's horsemen, in western Maryland most remained loyal to the Union. Just as Hampton's command neared the outskirts of Urbana, a prosperous farmer met an advance party of the Confederate Quartermaster Department. They wished to buy feed for the horses. "The war must go on, the Government must be kept up, and the horses must be fed," enthused the old unionist, not recognizing with which army he was contracting. Ordering two of his slaves to load wagons with barrels of corn, he asked where it might be delivered, "as I am a man that goes in for accommodating the Government."

"I see the command moving up now," replied the officer, "and will gallop down and ascertain where General Hampton will locate the camp."

Alarmed, the farmer shouted for him to stop. "What? Who? What General Hampton?"

"General Wade Hampton, of South Carolina," replied the amused officer. "It's his cavalry you see yonder; it's him you agreed to feed."[23]

The cavalry held a line from Urbana to the Potomac, monitoring all of the roads coming out of Washington. Hampton held the left, Fitzhugh Lee the right. There were "various little skirmishes" with the enemy, said Hampton, his brigade "driving them back on every occasion." As the Confederate infantry marched northwestward to Hagerstown, the cavalry fell back to Frederick City.[24]

At Frederick City on September 12, Hampton, with three guns and a detachment of 150 men, prepared to fight a rearguard action with the Yankee cavalry in the streets of the town. Enemy cannoneers, supported by infantry, were firing into the city. It was about noon. Both unionist and secessionist banners were hanging from balconies. Through raised windows Hampton's men could hear women singing "Dixie" and "The Bonnie Blue Flag." Hampton and his men charged the cavalry, "scattering them in every direction," silenced the cannon, and captured the colonel of the Twenty-eighth Ohio Infantry Regiment. As Hampton galloped down the street in pursuit of fleeing Yankees, a shot rang out. A would-be assassin had fired at the general from a window as he rode past, but the bullet missed. The Confederates continued to withdraw in safety, taking up positions on high ground to the west.[25]

The next day two Union soldiers found three cigars wrapped in a paper lying on the ground outside of town. Apparently dropped by a careless staff officer, the paper was a copy of Lee's orders. McClellan now knew his enemy's strategic plan—and that Lee's already outnumbered forces had been divided. A civilian overheard McClellan boasting of his find. The Confederate sympathizer brought the alarming news to Stuart, who then informed Lee.[26] Invasion of the North was out of the question. Lee was now on the defensive.

Looking toward Frederick City from the gap where the road passes over Catoctin Mountain, Hampton and his men could see McClellan's approaching infantry and artillery. When they were within one and a half miles, Hampton ordered his cannon to open fire with solid shot. An artillery duel ensued that kept the Yankees at a distance. Probing Union cavalry were driven off by artillery fire and the carbines of Hampton's troopers, fighting dismounted. By midafternoon of September 13, Hampton's Confederates began to abandon the gap, withdrawing to Burkittsville, near the southernmost pass in South Mountain. Col. Laurence S. Baker's First North Carolina Cavalry fought a gallant holding action. Hart's Battery poured a punishing fire upon the pursuers.

"Take care of my overcoat, Preston," ordered Hampton as he drew his saber to lead Cobb's Legion in a charge. Preston, the general's aide-de-camp, promptly tossed the coat into a fence corner and followed his father into battle.

"I came to Maryland to fight Yankees," he declared, "not to carry father's overcoat."

Only with difficulty was Hampton able to call off Colonel Young's Georgians as they continued to slash their way through Yankee cavalry.[27]

With Jackson at Harpers Ferry and two of Longstreet's divisions near Hagerstown, Lee had only one infantry division and Stuart's cavalry to hold the passes of South Mountain. Daniel Harvey Hill's infantry blocked the National Road at Turner's Gap and also held nearby Fox's Gap. Some five miles to the south at Crampton's Gap the federal attack stalled, again broke through, then was finally halted. The gallant stand at South Mountain bought time for Confederates to regroup at Sharpsburg, Maryland.

Hampton's cavalry had been posted near the Potomac where they saw little action as they supported Gen. Lafayette McLaws' division as it marched on Harpers Ferry. Hampton and his men arrived at Harpers Ferry the day after the Yankees pulled down their garrison flag, surrendering to Jackson's encircling forces. Confederates captured 11,000 prisoners, 13,000 small arms, 73 cannons, 200 wagons, great quantities of ammunition, and supplies of all kinds. The cavalrymen rested briefly, as one said, "foraging our famished

horses on the vast quartermaster garners."[28] Encouraged by Jackson's success, Lee decided to fight at Sharpsburg, east of Antietam Creek. Jackson
joined him after a forced march, leaving one division in possession of Harpers
Ferry. Hampton recrossed the Potomac on the morning of September 17 and
reported to Stuart. The cavalry was ordered to secure the Confederate left. It
was a mission they performed without being drawn into the developing
infantry struggle.[29] Although he outnumbered Lee almost 2–1, McClellan's
attacks were uncoordinated, and his delays allowed Lee to shift troops to
meet each threat. At the end of the bloodiest single day of the war, more
than 26,000 Americans had been killed, wounded, or were missing. His first
invasion of the United States thwarted, on the night of September 18–19, Lee
withdrew into Virginia.

The Confederate cavalry, posted far to the left, was unable to recross the
Potomac near Shepherdstown with the rest of the army. To create a diversion,
Hampton's brigade crossed into Virginia on the evening of September 18,
recrossing the Potomac the next day to join Stuart at Williamsport, Maryland,
on the afternoon of September 19. The following day Stuart ordered Hampton to ride around Hagerstown, then ford the river again some ten miles
upstream. Patrols had captured prisoners from several federal divisions, con-
vincing Hampton that he faced much of the enemy army. It would be suicidal, he said, to make such an attempt. Stuart insisted, sending von Borcke
to Hampton with the orders. "This intrepid General instantly gave the command to move forward," recounted the Prussian, "to what he so justly considered certain destruction, saying to me, 'Good-bye, my dear friend; I don't
think you will ever see me or a man of my brave brigade again.'" A terrific
Union cannonade soon persuaded Stuart that he had made a mistake, and he
sent von Borcke to countermand the order. Unable to break through enemy
lines—and unwilling to sacrifice his men uselessly—Hampton had already
ordered a retreat. By eleven o'clock that night the Confederate horsemen
were able to make a successful, if hazardous, fording of the Potomac—falling
back to Martinsburg, Virginia. The crossing was made in darkness "in water
over girth-deep and filled with rock, brush and every possible obstruction,"
remembered one officer. "This was even worse than fighting." Skirmishing
and probing continued for the next few days, before the cavalry settled into
the routine of picket duty.[30]

Neither Hampton nor Stuart made direct reference to the sharp differences in their written reports. Stuart commended many of his subordinates,
but had not a word of praise for Hampton. Hampton's pride seemed hurt. A
few days later—in an unrelated matter—he made a lengthy defense of his
brigade's conduct during a minor Martinsburg skirmish. He did not wish,
said Hampton, "to detract from any commendation you [Gen. Robert E.
Lee] have bestowed on [Fitzhugh] Lee's Brigade; my only object is to vindicate my own."[31] Hampton's superiors surely thought him overly sensitive.

The weather in mountainous northern Virginia was growing cooler, forage for the horses was getting scarce, and the men complained of mail from home not reaching them. Hampton wrote to his sister on October 5, again expressing gratitude for God's protection of him and his family. "I pray that we may still be spared, but if this is not to be, I pray that I may be able to discharge my duty faithfully, so as to merit the 'well-done' not only from my country, but from my God." His brother, so recently a widower, was now at his side. "Frank has taken his position as Lt. Col. Poor fellow. I feel very sorry for him. He seems calm & I have no doubt but that his duties here, will serve to distract his mind from his sorrow." And still the carnage continued. "My heart has grown sick of the war, & I long for peace. If it does not come this winter, there is no saying when we may look for it. As long as the madness of the Yankees continues, so long will this fearful war."[32]

Hampton found time to thank the ladies of Fredericksburg, Virginia, for a guidon they made and sent to his brigade, responding, "It shall be cherished most sacredly; it shall be borne proudly; it shall be defended whilst there is an arm to strike in its defence or a heart to remember the noble women who gave it to us."[33]

That flag had arrived just in time to accompany Hampton on a raid. From each cavalry regiment the best men and mounts were chosen, about 1,800 total. Maj. John Pelham's four-gun battery would go along. Stuart charged his little command with strict obedience to orders even as he kept their mission secret. At two o'clock on the afternoon of October 9, they left Martinsburg, headed north. One remembered that "Hampton rode along at his usual easy trotting style, as though he was just going out to look over his broad cotton fields."[34] But this was to be much more than another scouting of the enemy's Potomac River defenses. The troopers did not yet know it, but their destination was Pennsylvania.

They rode to within a mile of the river and halted for the night. Hampton led a party to the ford, discovering that federal pickets were posted only on the Maryland side. A predawn attack by Hampton's advance guard scattered the Yankees and quickly the entire Confederate force crossed into Maryland. A federal signal station was captured. On the main highway Confederate cavalrymen surprised a column of marching infantry, taking ten stragglers and a stand of colors.[35]

The raiders rode "through a rocky, bleak, and almost barren region, with here and there a lonely cabin to relieve the wild scenery," remembered a veteran. The day was cloudy and dark, with a cold wind scattering and swirling the falling leaves. The mountains gave way to hills, until at last only flat and fertile land stretched before them. Quietly, confidently, on a seldom-traveled road, the raiders entered the Keystone State.

Quickly orders were issued. Each command detailed one-third of its men to capture horses and other property. Receipts would be given to all private citizens, who could then seek reimbursement from their own government for their losses. In accordance with orders from General Lee, local politicians and officeholders were to be arrested that they might be exchanged for imprisoned Confederate civilians. There would be no theft or destruction of private property and no violence against civilians. Stuart went so far as to issue instructions that ladies encountered traveling on the road be allowed to pass freely.[36]

"The unsuspecting inhabitants met and hailed us as Union troops," remembered a raider, "and no assertion to the contrary was likely to disabuse their minds of the fact that we were rebels." Standing by his commodious brick barn, one Dutch farmer was dismayed to see troopers emptying his stables. The Pennsylvania Home Guard had recently impressed those very animals, sending them back, said their owner, "all sore and skint up." He declared that he would rather "old Shackson" take the guardsmen than that the guardsmen again take his horses. Mistaking Hampton's men for the Keystone Militia, he cursed them in his thickest brogue. Finally they made him understand that this time Jeff Davis wanted his horses. "Sheff Tavis! Sheff Tavis! Mine Gott . . . he vill never send tem pack!"[37]

At Mercersburg an advance guard from Matthew C. Butler's command fitted themselves with the finest boots one haberdasher had in stock. The smiling shopkeeper realized the identity of his free-spending customers only when they tendered Confederate receipts. A band of militiamen later fired an ineffective volley at the raiders from the cover of a building, then promptly surrendered. After a short rest the Confederate column continued up the road, entering St. Thomas.[38] It was late afternoon and a cold rain was falling. Hundreds of captured horses made the raiding party seem larger than it was. Frantic reports estimated Stuart's force to be from 2,500 to 6,000 strong. One panic-stricken civilian guessed their number at 16,000! Still, federal military authorities were blind to what was happening. That "Rebels" might take Chambersburg "was too absurd to be considered," declared the Union commander at Hagerstown.[39]

After sundown on October 10 raiders reached the outskirts of Chambersburg. The streets were dark. Since federal troops might be there, "I deemed it prudent," said Hampton, "to demand the surrender of the town before taking my men into it." Two guns were unlimbered. Troopers prepared to attack, as men from Butler's regiment, led by Lt. Thomas Lee, rode toward town. A delegation of three prominent Chambersburg citizens came out to meet the invaders. Alex K. McClure, one of the party, described what happened.

> After traveling a mile westward we were brought to a halt by a squad of mounted men, and were informed that General Hampton was one of the party to whom we should address ourselves. . . . Upon being informed that

we were a committee of citizens, and that there was no organized force in the town, and no military commander at the post, he stated, in a respectful and soldier-like manner, that he commanded the advance of the Confederate troops, that he knew resistance would be vain, and he wished the citizens to be fully advised of his purpose so as to avoid needless loss of life and wanton destruction of property. . . . He assured us that he would scrupulously protect the citizens, would allow no soldiers to enter public or private houses, unless under command of an officer upon legitimate business; that he would take such private property as he needed for his government or troops . . . and would give receipt for the same. . . . All property belonging to or used by the United States he stated he would use or destroy at his pleasure."

Quickly they accepted his terms, and hundreds of Confederate cavalrymen galloped into town. One raider remembered how "the whole population seemed confounded at our presence. Houses, public and private, were immediately closed." Municipal authorities were no where to be found. The local banker, upon hearing rumors of the impending raid, had been prudent enough to send his deposits away for safekeeping. Most of the troopers bivouacked outside of town as General Stuart appointed Wade Hampton "military governor" of Chambersburg.[40]

Late that night in Washington, U.S. Secretary of War Edwin Stanton was handed a telegram from Pennsylvania's Republican governor Andrew G. Curtin. It contained but five words. "The people have surrendered Chambersburg."[41]

McClure got home in time to see the Southerners take his horses. Confederates scouted up the road toward Shippensburg, returning with more mounts, camping on the road in front of his home. Troopers came to the door, politely asking for coals to start their cooking fires and for permission to pump water. He distrusted "this uniform courtesy," but was relieved to discover that—except for a fence they used for kindling and some corn eaten by horses—his property remained unmolested. "They did not make a single rude or profane remark even to the [black] servants." At about one o'clock in the morning, a group of officers came to his door asking for coffee, offering to pay in Confederate dollars. "They were wet and shivering, and seeing a bright, open woodfire in the library, they asked permission to enter and warm themselves until their coffee should be ready." Around the fire they opened up "a general conversation on politics, the war, the different battles, the merits of generals of both armies." The one topic they avoided, for reasons of security, was the raid itself. "Most of them were men of more than ordinary intelligence and culture, and their demeanor was in all respects eminently courteous. I took a cup of coffee with them, and have seldom seen anything more keenly relished."

McClure, although not in uniform, was a federal officer. His name was on a list of those that Stuart wanted to capture. Hampton had assured him, McClure told Capt. Hugh Logan, that all officers would be paroled. "Well," replied Logan, "Hampton is a gentleman, and if you can get to him he will parole you, but Jeb wants you damn bad."

At four o'clock on the morning of October 11, the Confederates at McClure's door mounted up and rode into Chambersburg. After daybreak McClure followed them.

> General Stuart sat on his horse in the centre of the town, surrounded by his staff, and his command was coming in from the country in large squads, leading their old horses and riding the new ones they had found. . . . His demeanor to our people was that of a humane soldier.

McClure heard of several cases of attempted theft, but in each instance the perpetrators "were arrested by General Stuart's provost-guard."[42]

That provost-guard—the Confederate "police force"—was under the command of Capt. James P. Macfie of the Second South Carolina Cavalry. At least one incident escaped their vigilance. That morning a large U.S. flag was seen flying from the third story of a Chambersburg residence. For some the sight was too much to endure. Two North Carolina troopers forced their way past the building's owner and "another grim, determined-looking personage," climbed the stairs, and ripped down the flag. The two civilians chose not to become martyrs. One Confederate said

> At every corner could be seen groups of old and young, conversing in an undertone, evincing symptoms of the deepest mortification. The sight of the new *blue* clothing that dotted every company in the command, and the bright United States weapons dangling at our sides, was indeed a sore tax upon their pride. But notwithstanding this, not the least insult was offered us.[43]

At the Chambersburg hospital 280 Union soldiers, all patients, were paroled. Telegraph lines came down in every direction. Railroad tracks were obstructed. Warehouses filled with 5,000 rifles, pistols, sabers, ammunition, and army clothing—all that could not be carried away—were torched. "The extensive machine-shops and depot buildings of the railroad and several trains of loaded cars were entirely destroyed," reported Stuart. "The flames wrapped the building," remembered a raider, "and for an hour the explosions were terrific, shaking the earth." A detachment was dispatched towards Harrisburg to burn a railroad trestle, but returned frustrated. The structure was made of Pennsylvania iron![44]

Hampton and his command formed the rear guard as the raiders abandoned Chambersburg on Saturday, October 11. They headed straight towards Gettysburg to confuse pursuers, then turned south and recrossed the Mason-

Dixon Line into Maryland. They were cheered by the inhabitants of Emmitsburg. Admiring young girls snatched Confederate buttons for souvenirs. As the raiders forded the rain-swollen Potomac on Sunday morning, Hampton's troops, augmented by one cannon, fought a sharp skirmish that kept the enemy at bay. Soon all had crossed safely into Virginia, arriving back at Martinsburg on October 12.

Only two Confederates were missing, presumably captured. A few were wounded, although none had been killed. About 1,200 Pennsylvania horses were added to the Rebel cavalry. Stuart reported,

> A number of public functionaries and prominent citizens were taken captives and brought over as hostages for our unoffending citizens. The results of this expedition, in a moral and political point of view, can hardly be estimated, and the consternation among property holders in Pennsylvania beggars description.

Stuart thanked his entire command, which included Hampton of course, "for their coolness in danger, and cheerful obedience to orders."[45] Still, tension remained. Hampton was restless. On October 23 he wrote to President Davis asking for reassignment to Mississippi. Nothing was said of Stuart in the letter, only that Hampton feared that advancing Union troops would target his property in the Magnolia State. In response, Davis said that he would assign Hampton to Mississippi when affairs permitted, but that Lee could best determine when he might be spared. "Suggest application to him," Davis concluded. Col. William T. Martin of the Jeff Davis Legion was soon promoted to brigadier general and sent to Mississippi. "He is a first rate man, and I shall miss him greatly," wrote Hampton.[46] His own transfer he did not pursue.

At the end of October the Union army began crossing the Potomac in force, requiring that Confederate cavalry fall back from their advanced positions. Converging at Barbee's Cross-Roads, Stuart beat off one federal cavalry attack. A series of skirmishes followed. "In one of these," reported Stuart, "near Gaine's Cross-Roads, a portion of Hampton's command behaved with great gallantry, and routed the enemy." He thanked Hampton and other subordinates "for the zeal and ability displayed."[47]

On November 10 the cavalry was reorganized. William Henry Fitzhugh "Rooney" Lee, Robert E. Lee's son, would command a third cavalry brigade. Hampton lost for a time the Jeff Davis Legion, but was promised the First South Carolina Cavalry Regiment and the Phillips Legion cavalry battalion from Georgia.[48] On November 22 Hampton wrote to his sister from Brandy Station on the Orange and Alexandria Railroad, six miles from Culpeper. "The country is exhausted and I do not see how we are to live," he complained. "But Genl. Stuart never thinks of that; at least as far as my Brigade is concerned. He has always given us the hardest work to perform and the worst places to camp at."[49]

It was not only Hampton's men who were suffering. All of the cavalry brigades were short on resources and diminished in strength—but still required to keep on fighting. On November 27 Hampton and 158 picked men forded the Rappahannock. At four o'clock the next morning they made a surprise attack on encamped federal cavalry. Captured were 92 prisoners, 100 horses, weapons, supplies, and 2 guidons. Four severely wounded Yankee soldiers were left behind. "General Hampton and his gallant command deserve the highest praise for this handsome affair," wrote Stuart, "and are warmly commended to the notice of the commanding general." General Lee forwarded the captured guidons to the War Department, informing Secretary James A. Seddon that Hampton's "energy and courage" were "deserving of high commendations." The secretary later informed Lee that the trophies had been put on display in the War Office in Richmond. "You will convey to General Hampton," Seddon wrote Lee, "in such mode as you may deem appropriate, assurance of due appreciation by the Department of this dashing exploit."[50]

With snow covering the ground on December 10, Hampton and 520 of his men set out on a raid toward Dumfries, north of Fredericksburg. He cut telegraph lines, took fifty prisoners, and captured twenty-four wagons—again without a loss. "Candies, syrups, pickled oysters, lobsters, smoked beef tongues, Westphalia hams, coffee, sugar, lemons, oranges, plums, nuts, and a fine little bit of everything" were among the liberated delicacies. A cask containing bottles of fine champagne labeled "A Christmas Present to Gen. A. E. Burnside" found its way to Hampton's tent. Lee was delighted when he heard of the raid's success. "Brigadier-General Hampton," wrote Stuart, "with a command thinly clad and scantily fed, displayed, amid the rigors of winter . . . an activity, gallantry, and cheerful endurance worthy of the highest praise and the nation's gratitude."[51]

Maj. Gen. Ambrose Everett Burnside lost more than a cask of Christmas champagne in December of 1862. Only weeks before Lincoln had given him the Army of the Potomac. In command of 130,000 men, he determined to overwhelm Lee's 75,000 troops entrenched on hills overlooking Fredericksburg. He ordered a frontal assault against Southern troops dug in on Marye's Heights, but wave after blue wave went forward only to be cut down. Two days later Burnside withdrew, having thrown away 12,653 men. Lee lost 5,309. One of the dead Confederates was Brig. Gen. Maxcy Gregg of South Carolina, Hampton's friend from college days. Lee would offer command of Gregg's brigade to Hampton, but Hampton declined to rejoin the Infantry.[52]

Yet another raid by 465 of Hampton's troopers began on December 17 towards Occoquan. They took 150 prisoners, 20 wagons, food, weapons, 300 pairs of boots, and 1 stand of colors. Forty-one Yankee pickets strung out along eight miles of road were bagged one at a time before any could give the alarm. Hampton suffered no losses and brought back information on enemy troops dispositions. Federals reeled in confusion, estimating the raiders' strength at 1,000. "General Hampton has again made a brilliant dash," wrote Stuart. "Please express to General Hampton," replied Lee, "my high sense of his service, my just appreciation of the conduct of the officers and men of his command, and my congratulations on his complete success without the loss of a man." The secretary of war jotted an endorsement on the bottom of Hampton's report. "A very gallant affair and modestly reported. To be remembered in estimating merit for promotion."[53]

A major raid began, with Stuart in overall command of 1,800 horsemen, the day after Christmas. They rode toward Dumfries, but Hampton and his men were soon dispatched in the direction of Occoquan. As Hampton passed the Tenth Virginia—once part of his command—and "as no noise was permitted the men could not cheer, but every one, waved his hat wildly as I passed down their lines. This reception gratified me very much, especially as it came from a Va. Regt."[54]

During the raid Stuart inflicted considerable punishment upon the enemy, taking 300 prisoners. One federal officer stated that since he was sure he faced no fewer than 8,000 Rebels, "led by three well-known generals Stuart, Fitzhugh Lee, and Hampton, I am astonished that we did not suffer more." At Burke Station on the Orange and Alexandria Railroad—a mere fifteen miles from the District of Columbia—Stuart captured the telegraph and its operator. Before wrecking the apparatus and blocking the tracks, Stuart sent one final message. It was directed to U.S. Army quartermaster general Montgomery C. Meigs and complained, in Stuart's words, of "the bad quality of the mules lately furnished, which interfered seriously with our moving the captured wagons."[55]

Less flamboyantly, Hampton captured eight wagons and twenty-three prisoners. At one point he led a charge into Yankee cavalry. He told his sister,

They fired on me all around but the two first blows I struck brought down a man each & the others scattered. The first poor devil had his skull frightfully fractured . . . while the other was badly cut. Another was about to shoot me, but I scared him out of it by demanding his surrender. I was not touched, & I am again called on to thank God for his mercy in sparing me. I have been in *forty-three* fights, & yet the hand of God has saved me in all of them. The prayers of those who love me, must have been my shield. I hope the same hand will guide & guard me still. I am sick of the horror of war.[56]

By New Year's Day Hampton and Stuart had returned to camp. Lee issued a general order extolling the cavalry's gallant service. Hampton confided to his sister that he thought the latest raid a failure, inasmuch as but little was accomplished & many horses ruined. My men think Stuart came up here because my expeditions had been successful & he was jealous of my Brigade. On the scout he gave my men the hardest work to do, & cut them off from their chance of distinction.

In another letter he was more cheerful and optimistic.

My men are pretty well worn out, by their recent raids. This sort of work is very hard, but we have been very well paid by our captures. We have stirred up the Yankees greatly of late and they swear that my raids shall be stopped. But I shall teach them, that it is hard to catch me, on the ground I know so well. Gen. Lee has complimented me very highly on my late successes and my Brigade is very proud of their recent work. We have all sorts of nice things, Christmas presents sent by the Yankees to their friends in the Army. I have been drinking Burnside's champagne and find it very good. . . . I wish you had some of our lemons and other nice things.[57]

Hampton's men kept to their policy of ceaseless activity, even as they went into winter quarters. All manner of shelters were constructed by the ingenious cavalrymen at their camp near Stevensburg. "Rain, rain, sleet, sleet, snow, snow, alternately," was the weather one remembered. "Variegated modes of architecture could be seen, to suit the energy and convenience of the builder." There were wigwams, lean-tos, and cabins—all too often decorated with icicles. Long-range enemy shelling might send them scurrying, until Hart's Battery responded and scouting parties took more Yankee prisoners. Hampton wrote,

The spirit of my men is very fine, & they are constantly doing some gallant thing. The other day, three of them charged seven Yankees & killed three and captured three, after a hard fight. They understand that I expect them to fight always, & they are all very proud of their Brigade.

Two weeks later he mentioned that "one man took *five* of them, all armed and brought them into camp. Yesterday we killed four and wounded a good many."[58]

Hampton continued to complain about Stuart. He wrote to Mary Fisher in mid-January,

As long as the enemy are in my front, my Brigade will not be moved, even if all my horses starve to death. The other two Brigades are having a good time, whilst we are left out here to scuffle for ourselves. But we have the satisfaction of knowing that we have done more this winter than all the Va. cavalry put together.

He was proud of the prowess of his men and not unmindful of his own reputation. Even as he prayed for peace, Hampton the warrior wanted recognition—especially if it could be had at Stuart's expense. "When we came through Warrenton the other day, there was a large crowd of ladies, to whom Stuart was talking. They proposed & gave 'three cheers for Genl. Hampton,' which S. did not seem to like." Hampton wrote directly to Lee in January, bypassing Stuart, complaining about the lack of forage for his horses. "Some time ago," he later complained privately, "I wrote to Gen. Stuart, to say that I anticipated the very *movements, they [the enemy] have since made*, and Genl. Lee accordingly made the proper dispositions to meet them."

"God grant us peace!" was Hampton's plea in January 1863.[59] That he might have peace among his subordinates was surely the prayer of Robert E. Lee.

7

"HAVE ALL THE
SABRES SHARPENED"

Brandy Station and Gettysburg

O n February 6 enemy cavalry attempted to burn the railroad bridge
over the North Fork of the Rappahannock River, but were forced
to retreat by Hampton's men, fighting dismounted. "I regret,"
Hampton reported to Stuart, "that the condition of my horses did not allow
me to follow them."

"All my time & correspondence of late have been taken up in quarreling
with Stuart," wrote Hampton to his sister, "who keeps me here doing all the
hard work while his Virginia Brigades are quietly doing nothing." Other
letters Hampton directed to seats of political power. He complained to Confederate States Senator Louis Wigfall of unfair army regulations that compen-
sated a trooper if his horse was killed, but not if lost in any other way. Such
a man "should at least be allowed to retain any captured horse as his private
one."[1] The senator would lend a sympathetic ear to Hampton's views on
many topics.

Wigfall was two years older than the general. Born in Edgefield District,
South Carolina, he had graduated from South Carolina College a year after
Hampton. A decade later Wigfall migrated to Texas where he advanced in
politics and came to espouse the secessionist cause. In a letter to the senator
on February 16, Hampton expressed his bitterness and frustration. "My brigade is at last ordered to rest after it is so broken down that it can do nothing
more to keep the Va. Brigades off duty. As nothing is going on, I shall ask

for a furlough. If I get one, I will try to see you as I pass through Richmond."
Hampton predicted that the enemy might open a major offensive on the
coast of North or South Carolina. Should that happen, he asked Wigfall's
help in being transferred there. Hampton suggested that a new division made
up of troopers from the Carolinas and the Gulf States—under his own leadership—could perform valuable service. This hypothetical new command
Hampton referred to as the "Southern Cavalry." He felt too that because of
his seniority, "I have some claim to promotion." Hampton was heartily tired
of serving under Stuart.

> The Va. Cavalry being, according to the Va. papers, the best in the service,
> should be kept by itself, & Stuart could thus have his Division composed
> altogether of troops from his own State (which would be a great matter for
> him, *if he ever runs for Gov. of Va.*).[2]

That Hampton continued to serve in Virginia may have been due in no
small measure to the quiet influence of Robert E. Lee. Hampton was, in
Lee's view, "an officer of standing and gallantry." That his brigade might
regain its strength, it was finally pulled out of the front lines and ordered to
southern Virginia in the late winter of 1863. There they went "wandering
over several of the lower counties of Virginia," as one soldier described their
"recruiting mission."[3] Hampton himself managed to secure that long-
delayed furlough and arrived in South Carolina during late February.

"General Wade Hampton is on a visit home at present," noted the *Daily
Southern Guardian* of Columbia on February 27. "We welcome him amongst
us." It had been nearly a year since he had been home, and he enjoyed these
few weeks with family and friends. Still, there was no escaping the war. Beauregard, defender of Charleston, was marshaling his forces for an expected
enemy attack. The Union navy was active, and federal infantry on Folly Island
threatening the city numbered 12,000, far more than Beauregard had to
oppose them.[4] "Brigadier General Wade Hampton, of Stuart's Cavalry Division, is now on furlough, and on a visit to his family," announced the editor
of Charleston's *Daily Courier* in mid-March. "In expectation of an attack on
this city, he proposes to improve his furlough, and has offered his services to
General Beauregard." Six days later the same newspaper reported General
and Mrs. Hampton's arrival at the Mills House Hotel. Hampton met with
Beauregard and offered what was probably unsolicited advice on Fort Sumter, suggesting "the propriety & the means of rendering it impregnable."[5]

Back in Columbia on April 6, Hampton telegraphed the secretary of war
asking for permission to aid in Charleston's defense. At the same time he let
Beauregard know, "About 150 of my men were sent home to procure horses
and they report here today. . . . All now have horses but they would go as
sharpshooters if that is more desirable." It took two days for permission to

arrive from Richmond. "Lead your furloughed men and any others eager for the fray to Charleston," wired Secretary Seddon, "and God speed you." The Yankees began their attack on the afternoon of April 7. A fleet of heavily armed ironclad vessels opened fire on Forts Sumter and Moultrie. Within hours it was over. Confederate gunners scored 520 hits on the "impregnable" warships, sinking one and sending the rest out to sea. There would be no land invasion for Southern infantry or cavalry to repel. Hampton had rushed his little squadron to Charleston only to arrive late and unneeded.[6] He soon headed back to the front in Virginia.

Hampton and other Southern military leaders were largely unaware of changes and improvements that had been taking place in the cavalry of the United States. No longer were Northern horse soldiers victims of budget constraints. New regiments were forming. As horses were lost the War Department had the resources to replace them, and Union cavalrymen never lacked for weaponry. Traditional prewar dress uniforms and lances were by now little more than a memory. Arms and equipment had been pared down to less than sixty pounds per trooper. Federal cavalry officers began to embrace more flexible tactics, and troopers were learning to fight both dismounted and on horseback. Well-equipped, better trained, and greatly increased in numbers, the United States cavalry lacked only confidence. For two years Confederate horsemen had reigned supreme. Now the South was finding it increasingly difficult to replace horses, men, and the supplies that kept its formidable force in the field.[7]

The first test of the new Union cavalry began April 29. Maj. Gen. Joseph Hooker, latest commander of the Army of the Potomac, ordered cavalry chief Maj. Gen. George Stoneman to lead his 10,000 horse soldiers on a raid. Hooker had succeeded in marching 75,000 infantrymen around Lee's left flank, ten miles behind the Southern lines. At Fredericksburg another 40,000 Federals remained to confront Lee's 60,000 Confederates. Stoneman's troopers were to insure Union victory by cutting Lee's lines of supply and communication.

Hampton and his brigade were near Lynchburg, Virginia, when news of the Stoneman raid was received. On orders from the secretary of war, he hurried his men toward Charlottesville. Stoneman's force was huge and well supplied, but on this occasion poorly led. Officers continually worried that Rebel cavalry were about to appear. Four days after the raid began, before Hampton's reinforcements could get at them, the raiders were in retreat. But there was even bigger news to report. "A decisive victory," Secretary Seddon wired Hampton on May 3.[8] He would learn the amazing details later. Taking a tremendous risk, Lee left but 10,000 to hold the line at Fredericksburg, marching 50,000 towards Hooker's main force near a crossroads called Chancellorsville. When Stuart discovered that Hooker's right was in the air, Lee again split his army, sending 26,000 under Jackson to hit the enemy flank. On

May 2 Jackson attacked. The surprise was complete. Union troops panicked, running away into the enveloping darkness. Hooker's retreating army suffered 17,287 casualties. As he was outnumbered 2–1, Lee's triumph was perhaps the greatest victory in American military history. Tragically, one of his 12,764 casualties was Stonewall Jackson. Victim of a night-time friendly-fire incident, Jackson died on May 10.

With Hooker defeated, Lee planned once again to go on the offensive. In preparation for another invasion of the United States, he decided that his cavalry must be augmented. From the Shenandoah Valley rode the brigade of Brig. Gen. William E. Jones, a command made up entirely of Virginia regiments. Also from the valley came a smaller mounted force under Brig. Gen. John D. Imboden that would operate independently on the army's western flank. Leading the way in the invasion would be a cavalry brigade of western Virginias under Brig. Gen. Albert G. Jenkins. Brought up from North Carolina were two fresh regiments commanded by Brig. Gen. Beverly H. Robertson. The horse artillery battalion, under Maj. Robert F. Beckham, boasted twenty guns. But Stuart put his greatest confidence in those battle-tested veterans—the brigades of Hampton, Fitz Lee, and Rooney Lee. With an effective mounted force of some 2,200 offices and men, Hampton's brigade was now the largest.[9]

Although reinforcements were coming in, many of the cavalry commands remained understrength. In the midst of reorganization there was talk of transforming Stuart's division into a corps. Hampton complained of Stuart's trying "to have himself made Lt. Genl." Still, if a division were to be formed of troopers from states other than Virginia, "I intend to ask for it," said Hampton. "This will bring up the question of my promotion [to major general]." On May 30 Robert E. Lee put an end to Stuart's immediate hopes of an expanded command. He decided that it would be pointless to create new brigades and divisions from existing manpower. "It would give me great pleasure," wrote Lee to Stuart, "to see brigadiers and colonels promoted who have served the country long and well, but nothing is accomplished by their promotion unless they can get enlarged commands with it."[10]

Hampton's brigade camped near Orange Court House on May 13, but the general expected "that we will soon be on the old line of the Rappahannock, catching pickets." Citizens, he boasted to his sister, vowed that had Hampton been there "the Yankees never would have got across the river." He gloried too in the loyalty and spirit of his troopers. "My first order to the men is to have all the sabres sharpened, so we are preparing for work." By May 19 they were around Culpeper Court House. "All the cavalry are near here," he wrote Mary Fisher, "so that we are strong enough for Mr. Stoneman should he advance again." Six days later he assured her that Hooker's men "are not much in the notion of crossing the river again. Our cavalry are collecting here, & we shall soon have a large body ready for work. The Yankees have a large body of cavalry opposite to us, but they do not come across the river."[11]

Stuart, now in command of nearly 10,000 troopers, thought it time to stage a grand review. On a huge field near Brandy Station, at eight o'clock on the morning of June 5, heralded by buglers, Stuart and his staff made their entrance. They rode past a mounted line that stretched for two and a half miles. Taking his place on a knoll, Stuart watched as the cavalry passed in review. Young girls scattered flowers in their path, and local citizens cheered, as three bands played. The horsemen then doubled back. With drawn sabers and rebel yells, they charged past the reviewing stand as the artillery fired blank charges. "At the sight of this impressive show," said von Borcke, "the spectators were seized by a veritable storm of enthusiasm." Many in the appreciative audience were young ladies who would attend that evening's ball. Disappointed that Robert E. Lee had been unable to attend his review, Stuart staged an encore performance for him on June 8. Fitz Lee also invited Maj. Gen. John Bell Hood "and any of your people." Hood came and brought along his entire division. "It was a grand picture," remembered Col. Matthew C. Butler. "We broke into column of companies from the right, Hampton's Brigade occupying the right of the line, and passed in review at a walk in front of General Lee."

Butler believed Stuart's reinforced division to be "the largest body of horsemen ever assembled at one place on the continent."[12] Yet at that moment, across the Rappahannock, a similar force of blue-clad horsemen was concentrating. Fearful that Stuart was about to set out on another of his raids, Hooker decided to strike first. Maj. Gen. Alfred Pleasonton, now commanding the cavalry corps of the Army of the Potomac, headed south with an 11,000-man force. Pleasonton was a little man, fond of fine uniforms, struggling to impress, and scrambling to get ahead in rank. His First Division was commanded by Brig. Gen. John Buford, described by a colleague as "straight-forward, honest, conscientious, full of good common sense, and always to be relied on in an emergency." Col. Alfred N. Duffie led the Second Division; Brig. Gen. David M. Gregg the Third. Col. Hugh Judson Kilpatrick, commanding one of Gregg's brigades, drove his men so hard that troopers called him "Kilcavalry."[13] Stoneman's raid a month earlier had failed. Now the Union horsemen would have another chance to prove their mettle.

Stuart made his headquarters on Fleetwood Heights, a ridge just above the Brandy Station depot, four miles from the Rappahannock River. Confederate brigades camped on both sides of a nearby railroad track. Attacking at four-thirty on the morning of June 9, Federals achieved complete surprise at the river. Pickets were overwhelmed. Hart's Battery was nearly captured by Buford's men pouring across Beverly Ford. Hearing the distant gunfire, Hampton ordered his men to Brandy Station as he rushed to Stuart's headquarters. Stuart quickly ordered Robertson's brigade to ride south to Kelly's Ford. The Second South Carolina remained to hold the depot. Hampton and Stuart, with the rest of Hampton's brigade, rode toward the sound of battle at Beverly Ford.

Arriving at the front, Hampton deployed 200 dismounted sharpshooters on the right of the artillery. Pushing the enemy back, they were met with

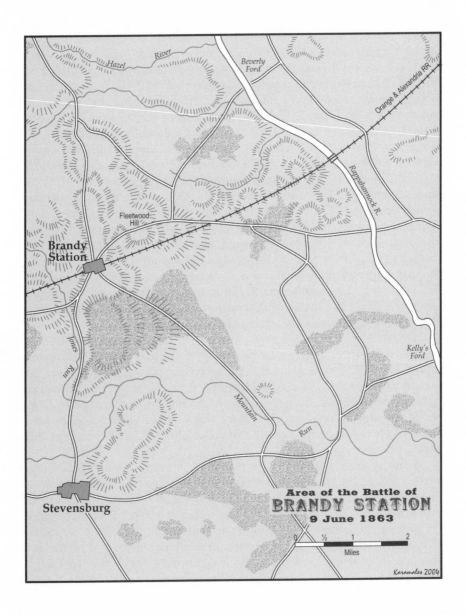

Area of the Battle of
BRANDY STATION
9 June 1863

infantry fire and a cavalry charge. The Jeff Davis Legion checked the drive. "The sharpshooters again advanced," reported Hampton, "regaining their lost ground, and were pressing forward, when, to my surprise, I discovered the enemy in my rear, attacking the hill upon which the headquarters of General Stuart were located." Gregg's cavalry had bypassed Robertson at Kelly's Ford and rushed to surround Stuart. The unionists were being held at bay by a single Confederate artillery piece on Fleetwood Heights.[14]

Fortunately for the Confederates, Buford decided at this moment to halt while he brought up supporting infantry and artillery. The lull allowed Stuart to pull Virginia regiments from the line facing Beverly Ford and race with them back toward Brandy Station. Other units just arriving would take their place. Hampton too began turning his men around when he received urgent messages from Stuart. His Virginians were taking a beating at Brandy Station and needed help. Immediately, Hampton ordered a charge on Kilpatrick's center by Cobb's Legion and the First South Carolina. At the same time he directed the First North Carolina and the Jeff Davis Legion to turn the enemy right. "The leading regiments (Cobb's Legion and First South Carolina) charged gallantly up the steep hill upon which the enemy were strongly posted," reported Hampton, "and swept them off in a perfect rout without a pause or check." The First North Carolina and Jeff Davis Legion—led by Hampton himself—met the retreating blue column "and disbursed it in every direction." Prisoners were taken, abandoned enemy guns were seized, and the flag of the Tenth New York was captured—along with that regiment's commanding officer. By now it was midafternoon. Kilpatrick ordered the Second New York to counterattack, but it, too, was thrown back by Hampton's men. The First Maine then went forward, pushing the Confederates. Hampton rallied his men and again swept the heights.[15]

Two of Hampton's regiments, the First South Carolina and Cobb's Legion, were ordered by Stuart to protect the artillery. "I found myself deprived of two of my regiments," Hampton complained in his report, "at the very moment they could have reaped the fruits of the victory they had so brilliantly won." Earlier the Second South Carolina "was ordered off by General Stuart without notifying me." Even when reinforcements later became available, Hampton complained that Stuart simply had him hold the hill, thus ending offensive operations.[16]

South of Brandy Station about five miles, at the village of Stevensburg, another federal column that had crossed at Kelly's Ford ran into elements of the Second South Carolina. There, Lt. Col. Frank Hampton led just fourteen men in a charge that initially scattered the surprised advance guard. The colonel then stationed some of his troopers in an abandoned seminary. A handful of reinforcements joined them. He was in fact holding the end of Butler's thin line and was under orders from his commander "to charge anything" that attacked. Colonel Hampton took his responsibility very seriously. Seeing a large force of Yankee troopers advancing toward his position, he ordered his thirty-six men to meet them head-on. Amid flashing sabers, the little band was quickly overwhelmed. Frank Hampton was slashed in the head and shot in the stomach. The Yankees pressed on, pushing back the main body of the Second South Carolina and the just-arrived Fourth Virginia. The Virginians rallied briefly, then dashed away in panic. An enemy artillery shell exploded in front of Colonel Butler, tearing off his right leg. Victorious at Stevensburg, another backdoor opened for the Yankee invaders. Yet, they failed to press their advantage. By late afternoon all federal cavalry were withdrawing across the river.

Frank Hampton was carried to the home of John S. Barbour, just outside Stevensburg, where he died late that day. The body would lie in state in the Confederate capitol before being transported back to Columbia for burial. Mary Chesnut chose to view the remains just before the casket was closed. "How I wished I had not looked!" she wrote later. "I remember him so well in all the pride of his magnificent manhood. He died of a saber cut across the face and head and was utterly disfigured." The editor of the *Daily South Carolinian* announced Colonel Hampton's death. "The community mourns the sacrifice of a gallant and valued citizen to the wretched representatives of Lincolnism and tyranny."[17]

Wade Hampton blamed the Fourth Virginia and their commander, Col. Williams C. Wickham, for the tragedy. Butler insisted that he had asked Wickham to support Colonel Hampton, but the Virginian had failed. The Fourth Virginia had broken and run to be sure, but so had many troopers of the Second South Carolina. To his credit, Wickham tried valiantly to rally his men, remaining on the field almost alone. Wade Hampton's grief over his brother's death, combined with his distrust of Virginians, clouded his judgment. For his part, Stuart reported that all the brigade commanders, Hampton included, "were prompt in the execution of orders, and conformed readily to the emergencies arising." He regretted that the Fourth Virginia "broke in utter confusion without firing a gun, in spite of every effort of the colonel to rally the men to the charge."[18]

The battle of Brandy Station remains the largest cavalry engagement ever fought in the New World. Pleasonton brought some 11,000 men across the Rappahannock. Stuart had just over 9,500. Federals suffered 866 casualties, Confederates 500. Rooney Lee was wounded and later captured. His brigade would be assigned to Col. John Chambliss Jr.[19] Yet, Pleasonton failed to delay the Confederate invasion, and Stuart held the field of battle, giving him the age-old right to claim victory. Robert E. Lee expressed satisfaction at his cavalry's conduct. Still, Brandy Station was a turning point. Federal cavalry had surprised the Southerners, pushed them back, fought with a new confidence, and proven that they could hold their own. On Fleetwood Heights and at Stevensburg, the Northern cavalry came of age.

Lee's offensive went forward on schedule. By June 15 he had cleared the Shenandoah Valley of the enemy, and the Army of Northern Virginia began crossing the Potomac. Hooker sent Pleasonton's cavalry on a reconnaissance that found no Confederate infantry east of the Blue Ridge Mountains. Pleasonton skirmished with Southern cavalry at Aldie, Virginia, on June 17. The next day at Middleburg, with Stuart in command, Yankees were routed. Lee would advance northward on the western side of the mountains as Hooker attempted to keep his army between invading Confederates and the cities of Washington and Baltimore.[20]

Another cavalry engagement occurred at Upperville on June 21. After the Confederate advance guard was repulsed, Hampton arrived. His troopers retreated, rallied, and retired to new positions as they battled an enemy armed with repeating Spencer carbines. A staff officer from the Second South Carolina remembered Hampton "as calm and composed as if no battle was in progress." Then, as the general issued orders, there was a tremendous explosion. A limber chest belonging to Hart's Battery had blown up, dismounting one of those imported Blakely guns. The officer described how "an immense cloud of smoke arose obscuring all for the instant, and the next moment the four horses came galloping out, hurrying to escape the scene of death behind them. Hampton quietly remarked: 'Well, I am afraid Hart has lost a gun this time.'" Confederates had been pushed back, but fortunately their enemies did not pursue. Maj. Henry B. McClellan, Stuart's assistant adjutant general, applauded Hampton and his men for their stout resistance at Upperville. In five days Southerners had suffered about 500 casualties, inflicting 860—virtually the same as the losses for both sides at Brandy Station.[21]

Stuart wanted to add to his string of exploits by riding around Hooker's army, scooping up supplies, and causing as much damage as possible. Lee consented, but only if Stuart was certain that Hooker was moving northward and not a threat to Richmond. Stuart was to terminate the expedition should the enemy block his path, and he must not stray too far. Once on the soil of Pennsylvania, Lee would need every man. Confederate partisan leader John Singleton Mosby informed Stuart that the Union army was now stretched out for twenty-five miles and virtually stationary. It would be as easy to ride *through* the enemy as to go *around* them. Hampton and Fitz Lee liked the plan. Stuart detached the brigades of Robertson and Jones—about 3,000 troopers—to guard the rear and flanks of Lee's army. Longstreet would later complain that Stuart was simply ridding himself of two brigades that he did not like, that he should have left behind someone reliable—like Hampton.

Hampton's brigade, on the recommendation of a civilian guide, crossed the Potomac at Rowser's Ford. The river was up two feet and a mile wide, but the crossing was made without incident. Stuart followed with the remainder of the cavalry. Near Rockville on June 28 Southern troopers captured 125 U.S. Army wagons loaded with supplies. Stuart would find himself slowed by those wagons, delayed by spending the next day destroying railroad tracks, and later held up by the unexpectedly fierce resistance of a small band of federal cavalry at Westminster. He knew he was getting behind schedule and falling out of touch with Lee. Stuart did not realize, however, the near panic he was causing in the city of Washington. Thousands of Confederate cavalrymen less than eight miles northwest of the District of Columbia could see the Capitol dome. In the streets of the city, barricades were being thrown up. Clerks were scrambling to pack government records for evacuation. Telegraph lines to the west were down. Had he turned to attack, it is just possible that Stuart could have raised the Confederate flag—at least temporarily—over Lincoln's White House.[22]

The Confederate cavalry crossed the Pennsylvania state line on the last day of June. At Hanover there was a sharp fight with federal horsemen. Hampton's men were in charge of that slow-moving wagon train, the artillery, and about 400 prisoners. By two o'clock that afternoon Hampton brought up sharpshooters and opened with the artillery, clearing the town. Riding all night, out of food, desperate to find Lee's army, Stuart passed through Dover and Dillsburg, reaching Carlisle on the afternoon of July 1. Scattering a force of militia in that town, Stuart learned that Lee was engaged in battle at Gettysburg, some thirty miles to the south. Orders were issued to Hampton's brigade to move immediately. The other brigades would quickly follow.[23]

Hampton and his men arrived at Hunterstown, about five miles northeast of Gettysburg, on July 2. First ordered by Stuart to take position on the Confederate left, Hampton learned that a large force of enemy cavalry was attempting to get behind that flank. Stuart ordered him to put a stop to the threat.

Hampton reported,

> Pursuant to these orders, I moved back, and met the enemy between Hunterstown and Gettysburg. After skirmishing for a short time, he attempted a charge, which was met in front by the Cobb Legion, while I threw in the Phillips Legion and the Second South Carolina as supporting forces on each flank of the enemy. The charge was most gallantly made, and the enemy were driven back in confusion to the support of his sharpshooters and artillery, both of which opened on me heavily.

Near dark two guns of the Louisiana Guard Artillery came to Hampton's aid. "Night coming on, I held the ground until morning, when I found that the enemy had retreated from Hunterstown."

At dawn on July 3 Hampton's brigade, with that borrowed artillery, advanced through Hunterstown. Moving south, they crossed the tracks of the Gettysburg and Hanover Railroad and soon ran into the enemy. Hampton held the center of the Confederate line. Rooney Lee's old command was on his right, Fitz Lee's brigade on his left. Sharpshooters were thrown out, and the three brigades stood ready to do battle.[24]

For two hours that fateful afternoon they all heard the thunder of artillery as Porter Alexander's guns, some four miles to the west, prepared the way for the charge of Maj. Gen. George Pickett's division. Stuart attempted to move his troopers, shielded by woods, into a position where they might hit the enemy's rear. Wishing to show his commanders the situation, Stuart sent for Hampton and Fitz Lee. "Thinking that it would not be proper for both of us to leave the ground at the same time," said Hampton, "I told General Lee that I would go to General Stuart first, and, on my return, he could go." Unable to locate Stuart, Hampton galloped back to find that his brigade had been ordered by Lee to charge. "This order I countermanded," said Hampton, "as I did not think it a judicious one, and the brigade resumed its former position."[25]

A general cavalry engagement finally broke out about midafternoon, Hampton's troopers tangling with the Seventh and Fifth Michigan regiments belonging to Brig. Gen. George Armstrong Custer. The First North Carolina and the Jeff Davis Legion were ordered forward in support of Chambliss' brigade, but, Hampton said,

> in their eagerness they followed him too far. Seeing the state of affairs at this juncture, I rode rapidly to the front, to take charge of those two regiments, and, while doing this, to my surprise I saw the rest of my brigade (excepting the Cobb Legion) and Fitz. Lee's brigade charging."[26]

There could be no turning back now. "Hampton, cool, with his noble eye flashing fire," in the words of a veteran, "rings out: '*Charge them, my brave boys, charge them.*'"

Capt. Walter S. Newhall, a federal staff officer, rallied one group of twenty-one Yankee troopers, and led them directly toward the flag of Hampton's brigade. As Newhall neared the flag, the man grasping it lowered the staff and ran it full-force into the captain's face, tearing off his jaw.

"Hand to hand," in the words of one Confederate, "they bear up against the opposing odds. The tall form of Hampton is conspicuous in the fight, he too plies his sabre with the men, at the same time encouraging the men to stand firm." Two saber-wielding troopers of the Jeff Davis Legion, privates Moore and Dunlap, saved their general's life by downing Yankee attackers. "Now still gleaming sabres from several arms are playing over his head, already spirting from gore, his unerring pistol sends another reeling from his saddle; frantic with rage they press him back against the fence." Wade Hampton is fighting for his life. On the other side of that fence, he might be safe. Sgt. Nat Price of the First North Carolina and Private Jackson of Cobb's

Legion "recklessly dash into the unequal contest; a sure shot from the pistol
of the former blows the nearest one through just as he is repeating a blow
upon the general's bleeding head." Price and Jackson position themselves
between Hampton and the enemy troopers. "General, general," Price
shouts, "they are too many for us; for God's sake leap your horse over the
fence; I'll die before they shall have you." As he leaped the fence on his horse
Butler, a bullet hits Hampton's hip.[27]

According to another account Hampton was handicapped by a revolver
that misfired, even as his vision was obstructed by his own blood. After the
enemy trooper inflicted a second saber wound on Hampton, the general
brought down his own huge blade, cleaving the Yankee's head from crown
to jaw.[28]

"The charge did not last ten minutes," wrote one of Hampton's men
the next day, "but it was desperate and bloody. . . . The [Cobb] Legion did
its duty as usual . . . and we drove the enemy back in splendid style. . . .
General Hampton was seriously wounded, two sabre cuts on the head and
shot in the thigh."[29]

Both sides began to fall back. As Hampton was being carried from the
field, he placed the senior officer, Colonel Baker, in command of his brigade.
He was first taken to a nearby house where Dr. Benjamin W. Taylor administered aid. "The struggle was bitter and determined, but brief," said John
Esten Cooke. "Ten minutes before I had conversed with the noble South
Carolinian, and he was full of life, strength, and animation. Now he was
slowly being borne to the rear in his ambulance, bleeding from his dangerous
wounds." Hampton himself assumed that he was dying.[30]

On July 4 Robert E. Lee made a brief preliminary report to President
Davis. Longstreet's infantry had charged Cemetery Ridge, but the enemy's
"numbers were so great and his position so commanding, that our troops
were compelled to relinquish their advantage and retire." Diplomatic words
to describe defeat. Lee concluded with a message about his losses and said,
"General Wade Hampton was severely wounded in a different action in
which the cavalry was engaged yesterday."[31] Lee began his retreat on July 4,
and ten days later was safely back across the Potomac. The injured Hampton
traveled nearly 200 miles in an ambulance over the rutted roads of the Shenandoah Valley, through Staunton, to the Confederate General Hospital at
Charlottesville, Virginia.

Hampton wrote to Senator Wigfall on July 16,

> I have been handled pretty badly, having received two sabre cuts on the
> head—one of which cut through to the tables of my skull—and a shrapnel
> shot in my body, which is there yet. But I am doing well & in a few days I
> hope to be able to go home.[32]

Hampton was surprised to be alive. He joked with sister Mary Fisher and promised an early departure for Columbia.

> If I stay here much longer, my wounds will get well and then there will be no excuse for me to go home. My head is well, *externally*, but seems tender inside; perhaps it is only *weak*. The penitentiary style in which my hair is cut, half the head being shaven, is striking, if not beautiful. It suits all kinds of weather, as one side of my head, is sure to be just right, either for cool, or for hot weather. But the flies play the mischief, as they wander over the bald side. When I get home, I will shave my whole head, to be uniform at least. Don't you feel mortified that any Yankee should be able, on *horse back*, to split my head open? It shows how old I am growing, and how worthless.[33]

Finally back in Columbia, he found that his injuries healed slowly. "Hampton I fear will not soon be with us," wrote Stuart. "His wound must have been very severe."[34] Hampton's furlough was to expire on August 24, but an examination that month by a Columbia physician "gives me no hope of being fit for duty at that time."[35] Dr. J. Chisolm found that the general's wounds "will incapacitate him for military duty . . . for at least thirty [more] days and it may be for a much longer period."[36] In an August 22 letter to Senator Wigfall, Hampton confessed to not having yet been able even to leave the house, but "I hope to be fit for duty in two weeks."[37]

From his sickbed Hampton issued opinions on the progress of the war. Gettysburg, he declared to Wigfall, was a

> terrible & *useless* battle. The Yankees will be defeated, if we can get at them on fair ground. We could better have stormed the Heights of Stafford than there at Gettysburg. I am thoroughly disgusted & nothing but a sense of duty would take me back to my unpleasant position.[38]

He predicted the imminent fall of Fort Sumter and Yankee shelling of the city of Charleston.[39] "My latest news from Hood is favorable," Hampton wrote to Wigfall on October 2, "& I have written to beg him to come to my home, as soon as he can move." Hood's left arm had been rendered useless by shell fragments at Gettysburg, and he had lost his right leg at Chickamauga. Confederate Gen. Braxton Bragg had failed to take advantage of his victory at Chickamauga on September 20.

> God grant that he [Hood] may get well, for our success would be dearly bought by his loss. Affairs went well in the west, up to a certain point, but the usual *finale* of our western battles seems about to follow the last. I greatly fear the result, for if Bragg waits much longer, his opportunity will be lost. Is there no way to get [Joseph E.] Johnston into the field? If we could only concentrate a force in Tenn now, we could win the greatest success of the War. I hope for the best, but we are too slow.[40]

Despite his gloom and discontent, Hampton looked forward to becoming a major general. On August 1 Lee reversed his previous opinion, perhaps because he now felt that promotions were more than ever needed to reward merit and maintain morale in the cavalry. He had argued in May against transforming Stuart's division into a corps as there were not enough men to justify the move. Now, he proposed to the president that two divisions be created, one to be led by Hampton, the other by Fitzhugh Lee. Corps commander would be Stuart. Lee recommended that the new divisional commanders be promoted to major general.

> General Hampton, I think, deserves it both from his services and his gallantry; of General Fitz. Lee I do not wish to speak so positively, but I do not know any other officer in the cavalry who has done better service. I should admire both more if they were rigid in their discipline, but I know how difficult it is to establish rigid discipline in our armies, and therefore make allowances.[41]

Davis planned at this time to promote four men to the rank of major general: Hampton and Fitzhugh Lee (their promotions to date from September 1), Cadmus Wilcox (to date from August 12), and Stephen Dill Lee (to date from August 3).[42]

Hampton on August 22 assured Wigfall that he would remain in the army, as "this is no time . . . to embarrass the authorities or to consult ones own wishes, & in the next place my attachment to my Brigade makes me very loath to leave it." However, if he were offered promotion with a date-of-rank inferior to that of Stephen Lee, he would refuse. Lee, although a professional soldier, had entered the Hampton Legion as a mere battery commander. Hampton declared to Wigfall that though

> I am willing for the sake of our cause & for my Brigade to suffer the mortification of being passed over, I will not forfeit my own self respect by *accepting* a position lower than I think myself fairly entitled to. . . . I have dismissed the subject from my thoughts & I am now only looking forward to a resumption of my hard duties in the field."[43]

President Davis recognized Wade Hampton's value as a leader and appreciated his contributions to the Confederate war effort. Perhaps at Wigfall's prompting, Davis saw to it that the list was reshuffled.

> Genl. Hampton wishes to have his appointment take the same date as that of Genl. Stephen D. Lee. The Secretary of War learning the feeling of Genl. Hampton on this subject is desirous of carrying out the views of Genl. Hampton. To give Genl. Hampton however the date of 3d August would make him senior to Genl Wilcox who ranked Hampton as Brigadier. It is

Maj. Gen. Wade Hampton in late 1864. Hampton appears more youthful in this photo than his equestrian statue, depicting him during the same period, would indicate. *William A. Turner.*

proposed to give all the date of 3d August so that they will take their positions as Major Generals according to their rank as Brigadier Genl.

The appointments were made by the president on September 3—to rank from August 3—and routinely confirmed by the Senate on January 25, 1864.[44] Stuart would not be promoted to lieutenant general. "A very curious arrangement has been made," commented Hampton, "by which *three* Maj. Genls. are placed in charge of *two* divisions. I wish my command was detached."[45]

Passed over for promotion, Stuart made no complaint.[46]

8

"I Would Not Care if You Went Back to South Carolina"

Reinforcing the Division

In their victory at Gettysburg, the Union army sustained 23,049 casualties. Southern losses were 20,451. Wade Hampton was one of eight Confederate generals wounded; three more had been captured, and six were killed. His own brigade lost 316 men.[1] Both Union and Confederate armies, devastated by the carnage, remained relatively inactive.

Casualties—and promotions—made reorganization necessary. Hampton's brigade would be given to newly promoted Brig. Gen. Matthew C. Butler. During the late summer Butler had traveled through South Carolina searching for recruits as he recovered from his terrible Brandy Station wound. "He has served as a cavalry officer under my command for two years," read Hampton's recommendation of Butler's promotion, "& I have not seen a better officer in this service." In addition to Butler's brigade, Hampton's new division would initially be assigned the brigades of Laurence Simmons Baker and William Edmondson "Grumble" Jones. The division in October reported a strength of 8,789 men, although fewer than 4,000 of that number were "present for duty."[2]

In September Robert E. Lee had detached Longstreet's corps to reinforce Gen. Braxton Bragg's Army of Tennessee, the move contributing to the Confederate victory at Chickamauga. For his part, Lee managed to push

George Meade's lines back forty miles. Personally commanding Hampton's division, Stuart coordinated an attack on Hugh Judson Kilpatrick's troopers on October 19 near Buckland Mills. "They at first resisted my attack stubbornly," reported Stuart, "but once broken the rout was complete." The Yankees ran away "at full speed" and "in great confusion." Prisoners, wagons, horses, and equipment were taken. Hampton regretted not being there himself, but was gratified that "my men were."[3] Although a relatively minor affair, the "Buckland Races" encouraged Stuart and his men, reminding them of the war's earlier triumphs.

Hampton returned to the army hospital in Charlottesville in mid-September, there to be examined by the surgeon in charge. He was found still "unfit for duty because of two wounds . . . one saber cut penetrating the skull . . . the other a gunshot wound . . . in which the ball has not been extracted." Resumption of duty before fifty days would be an "imminent risk and danger to his health and probably to his life." Back in Columbia by October 2, Hampton expressed a desire at least to return to Richmond, if not to active duty, in a week.[4] He was far too optimistic. Not until November 3 was he able to report for duty at the adjutant and inspector general's office in the Confederate capital. It had been a four-month convalescence. Soon after his return Hampton confessed to being still "very tired" and to suffering from pain in his wounded hip. He also telegraphed for a replacement saber blade "as mine is broken."[5]

He would not need it. There was little combat near Hampton's Verdiersville headquarters as fall turned to winter. The "irksome," yet necessary, details of commanding a division took up much of his energy. "Sometimes I have to sign one hundred papers and that is the most tiresome kind of writing," Hampton told Mary Fisher. "After getting through with this, I like to ride out to take exercise or to go shooting." The partridges he bagged supplemented a diet of bacon, bread, and water. His troopers picketed the Rapidan and Rappahannock rivers as far as Fredericksburg on the right of the infantry. Soon Hampton moved his headquarters to Guiney's Station south of that city. By December his command would be made up of Butler's and Gordon's brigades, Brig. Gen. James Byron Gordon having taken charge of those North Carolinians formerly led by Baker. Jones' Virginia troopers were now commanded by Brig. Gen. Thomas Lafayette Rosser. "General Hampton cannot now be spared," President Davis informed Gen. Joseph E. Johnston, who was planning to reorganize the Army of Tennessee and wanted the South Carolinian.[6]

Wade Hampton IV had been serving on the staff of General Johnston since November 1861. General Hampton's son Preston was his father's aide-de-camp and remained at his post during his father's convalescence. Preston was seriously wounded, probably in the Buckland engagement, and admitted to the Charlottesville hospital on October 23. Four weeks later he was released and furloughed for thirty days, too weak to return to duty due to "the effect of a Gunshot wound of the Right Forearm severing the Radial artery and causing profuse loss of blood."[7] At about this time General Hampton learned that his younger children were ill, adding to his worries. He wrote to Mary Fisher,

> News of sickness at home gives me more pain than anything else. When all are well, I can bear cheerfully all the hardships of camp life, but when I hear that some of those I love, are sick, I grow restless & discontented. Would to God peace would come & that we might all once again be at home in happiness.

In a New Year's Day letter to his sister, Hampton alluded to their brother Frank's death.

> But we have had many mercies given to us and I hope that God will still save and bless us. I trust that we may all be spared to meet again soon in peace and happiness, when we can all gather around our quiet hearth without a dread of war. The war still drags on, but I hope this will be the last year of it. I know true and warm prayers go up constantly for my preservation, and I trust that our Father in Heaven will still keep me as he has done.[8]

On November 26 enemy cavalry crossed the Rapidan, and Stuart immediately made plans and issued orders to meet them. When Hampton did not arrive as quickly as he wished, Stuart personally took command of Rosser's brigade. On November 29 at Parker's Store, the enemy were surprised and scattered, their camp destroyed, and prisoners taken. It was clear that corps commander Stuart would never be content to issue orders and wait for his subordinates to act. Hampton complained that all he could do was race to catch up in "the absence of all orders, and without any intimation of the direction or destination of Rosser's brigade, which had been taken by General Stuart."[9]

A situation developed in early February that would prove embarrassing to Hampton. Initiated by the men of Hart's Battery, among others, a movement arose in the Confederate armies to declare that every man would "continue in arms until independence is achieved." All would reenlist for the duration of the war, if they had not already done so. Lee issued a general order encouraging his men to "imitate this noble example and evince to the world that you never can be conquered." Stuart was sure that "the patriotic spirit of the cavalry is not inferior to that of any portion of our army." He expressed the hope that Hampton's division, "representing in States almost the entire confederation, will unite their voices to those of their comrades in arms in this swelling chorus, and go in for the war." Hampton's command responded, except for the Second South Carolina. "I wrote to that Regt.

appealing to it to join the others," said Hampton, "but some of the companies still refused to go in, & now they are conscribed." He did not blame the men.

> This conduct on the part of this Regt. was due to some of the officers who have behaved disgracefully in this matter. I feel mortified about the affair & I shall make those who brought it about, feel still more so, before I am done with them. The old Legion Arty was the *first* company in the confederacy to volunteer again & the Legion has gone in. It is a great pity that a fine Regt like the 2nd should be degraded by having demagogues as its officers.[10]

At month's end Kilpatrick directed a Union cavalry raid against Richmond. While he rode south with 3,500 men, 500 Yankee troopers moved against the capital from the west. Hampton with a small command of but 306 men and two guns attacked a portion of the main body of the enemy as they rested at eleven o'clock on the night of March 1. Many of the Southerners went into action dismounted. Despite darkness and a snowstorm, Hampton reported that "the advance of my men was never checked and they were soon in possession of the entire camp." The enemy ran in confusion, leaving "their provisions, many arms & horses, together *with prisoners from five Regiments* in our hands."

Kilpatrick escaped to Yorktown, evacuating his men by ship, transforming them, in Hampton's words, "into Horse Marines."[11] The smaller enemy force penetrated to the intermediate line of Richmond's defenses before being overwhelmed by Fitzhugh Lee. The commander of this Northern raiding party was Col. Ulric Dahlgren. Killed in the action, he was found to have documents in his possession detailing a plan to assassinate the Confederate president, execute his cabinet, and burn Richmond. Dahlgren's superiors were quick to deny any responsibility for the plot. Hampton wrote,

> I wish Kilpatrick could be taken, & if he authorized the orders under which Dalgreen [sic] was acting I shall give orders that my men shall never take any of his officers alive. There never was a more atrocious plan concocted, & I trust that all concerned will meet their reward.

As for Dahlgren, "he met a fate, far too good for him." For Southerners the affair reinforced a conviction that they struggled against murderers and arsonists. To cries for reprisal, Robert E. Lee urged restraint. "I think it better to do right, even if we suffer in so doing, than to incur the reproach of our consciences and posterity."[12]

Hampton remained dissatisfied and at odds with Stuart. In December Hampton speculated that his division might winter in North Carolina, regaining its strength. Should that happen he hoped to go, at least temporarily, to Mississippi. A few weeks later he confided to Mary Fisher that Stuart had not replied to this proposal, "and I suppose that he intends to keep us here. If he does, my command will be unfit for duty next spring, and in this event, I shall ask to be transferred to some other army, or I will resign." In mid-January he complained again to his sister. "If we are to remain here all winter, I think I shall ask for leave to go to Miss. for a little while." On January 19 Hampton received word, through Stuart, that Robert E. Lee was unwilling for him to transfer temporarily. Lee "would, nevertheless, approve your transfer if it is in accordance with your own desire to command under General Johnston, provided a suitable officer is sent to take your place."[13] Hampton said no more about it.

The relentless Virginia winter was wearing down the Southern cavalry. Horses were perishing. One veteran remembered,

> The privations were among the most severe during the active period of the campaign, but even when that was ended the lack of forage was keenly felt. A more distressing sight than to witness the daily deterioration of the horses under this treatment can hardly be imagined. . . . Where a camp had been located for a few days one would notice the trees to which the horses had been fastened stripped of bark from the ground to as high up as the animals could reach, and where the place was occupied for a week or two many of the smaller trees would be eaten entirely away. Empty bags, scraps of paper, and similar things would often be voraciously devoured.

In February two-thirds of the men in Butler's brigade were without horses. The Second North Carolina could mount but sixty-five men. The situation became so grave that on February 12 Hampton declined to aid Maj. Gen. Arnold Elzey's latest call for help in defending against probing Union cavalry. "I should have moved down at the first notice of the approach of the enemy," Hampton explained to Robert E. Lee, "but for the fact that false alarms constantly came from the Peninsula and my command is in such condition that a hard march would break it down entirely."

Lee could only agree.[14] He was reluctant, however, to approve his subordinate's suggestion to remedy the situation. Hampton wanted to send Butler's brigade back to South Carolina to recruit and regain its strength, exchanging it for four or five cavalry regiments then serving in Beauregard's Department of South Carolina, Georgia, and Florida. Stuart wanted at least two regiments from Beauregard, without giving up Butler's men. Lee thought it best to know first what regiments he could gain before agreeing to any exchange. Hampton waited impatiently as his proposal made its way through channels to the War Department. Outflanking the chain of command, Hampton wrote directly to presidential aide James Chesnut asking his help in having Butler's brigade transferred, for the time being, to Richmond.[15]

It was obvious to John Esten Cooke that Hampton, by his character and heroism, had won Lee's confidence and respect. Hampton, in turn, revered the army commander. "These men seemed to understand each other," concluded Cooke.[16] That understanding may have solidified during a crisis in their relationship, a confrontation that occurred in mid-March 1864.

Lee stationed Butler's worn-down brigade on the lower Rappahannock River, instead of near Richmond as Hampton preferred. Writing to Lee's assistant adjutant general on March 14, Hampton declared that he could not be responsible "for the condition or safety of the brigade if it is placed there." Also, Hampton refused to consent to Stuart's intention to divide the brigade between Butler and Young, unless it was first reinforced. "I have received no orders from competent authority to break up one of my brigades," insisted Hampton. "I respectfully request the commanding general not to authorize any change in my command without at least consulting my wishes on the subject."[17] Lee had long been patient with citizen-soldier Wade Hampton. His forebearance was at an end.

Diarist Mary Chesnut recorded what she learned. On March 15 she had just returned from a drive accompanied by Varina Davis, the president's wife. "When I got home General Hampton came with his troubles." There had been a clash with Stuart.

> General H. complained of this to General Lee—who told him curtly, "I would not care if you went back to South Carolina with your whole division."
>
> Wade said his manner made this speech *immensely* mortifying.
>
> While General Hampton was talking to me, the president sent for him. It seems General Lee has no patience with any personal complaints or grievances. He is all for the cause and cannot bear officers to come to him with any such matters as Wade Hampton came.[18]

Davis summoned Hampton in order to resolve the cavalry crisis.[19] Hampton had for some time hoped to travel home on leave. Now, he would be going back to South Carolina to oversee a plan to bolster his division. Hampton's proposal to exchange worn-out regiments for fresh replacements had essentially been approved. Though his ill-feeling toward Stuart remained, Lee's frown and Davis' favor had subdued the proud Hampton.

The depleted First and Second South Carolina regiments were ordered to Beauregard's coastal command. Those with horses would ride to South Carolina. Those without mounts would travel by rail with the baggage. Beauregard must give up the Fourth, Fifth, and Sixth South Carolina Cavalry, then on picket duty and widely scattered. These three regiments would become Butler's new brigade. Assigned to the Army of Northern Virginia, too, were the Seventh Georgia Regiment and three other companies from that state. The Holcombe Legion would combine with five cavalry companies also from the Palmetto State to form the Seventh South Carolina Cavalry. This new regiment was ordered to Richmond. The Hampton Legion infantry was relieved of duty in Tennessee and sent home to procure horses. Reassembling in Greenville, South Carolina, they would then be assigned to duty on the peninsula in Virginia as mounted infantry. Hampton was himself "charged with the prompt movement of the cavalry" that would become Butler's brigade.[20]

Within a week Hampton was in Columbia. Immediately, he encountered difficulties. "I find most of the cavalry so badly equipped here that there will be some delay in moving them," Hampton reported to the adjutant general. Even more seriously, in a face-to-face meeting with Hampton around April 1, Beauregard balked at giving up the Fourth South Carolina. Withdrawal of that regiment would, he claimed, leave the Charleston and Savannah Railroad open to attack. Rather than relieve them from duty, Beauregard threw the responsibility—and its consequences—on Hampton. If they were under Hampton's orders, Hampton would have to order them away himself. As this "made me in fact answerable for the picket lines of General Beauregard," Hampton declined. On April 1, Hampton wrote a brief letter to Brig. Gen. Thomas Jordan, Beauregard's adjutant. He once again requested, this time in writing, that Beauregard obey the orders of the War Department. Backed by a timely telegram from Richmond, Beauregard relented.

In his communication with Confederate adjutant general Samuel Cooper, Hampton had fretted that his "leave" would soon expire. Cooper was surprised. "His leave has already expired by his assignment to this important duty," wrote Cooper, "from which he cannot be separated until that duty is performed."[21] There was much to do. The Fourth South Carolina arrived in Columbia on April 15 where, along with elements of the Fifth and Sixth South Carolina, they were reviewed by Hampton. Among the reinforcements were the Charleston Light Dragoons. "The Dragoons were easily to be distinguished from the other companies," remembered a veteran, "by their superior uniforms, equipments, and horses. When the General galloped down the lines, looking every inch a chieftan, the air rang with the shouts of the soldiers."[22] Hampton found time to write to the adjutant general, recommending Col. Martin Witherspoon Gary for promotion. "He has commanded the Regt. [the Hampton Legion infantry] in many of its hardest battles with skill and gallantry." To a friend he reported, "My whole time has been given up to those Regiments which are *en route* to Va., & in fact, so far from being 'on leave' I have had a most vexatious tour of duty."[23]

In Columbia Hampton met a cavalry scout named Wallace Miller riding a fine thoroughbred mare. The general suggested that Miller leave the animal at home "to raise colts," as the war "would last at least ten years longer." The Yankees have good horses, said Hampton, and "you scouts know how to get them." To Mrs. Mary Singleton he gave a sober assessment. "If we are successful *now,* in Va. I hope & think that we shall have seen our 'darkest day.' I look to success *there,* with such confidence, that I sometimes shudder when I reflect what failure would bring."[24]

There was at least one high point during his visit home. On Friday, April 22, a "Grand Demonstration" of support was held for Hampton and his men. Despite shortages, Columbians managed to honor them with an impressive celebration and send-off. The *Daily South Carolinian* reported the event in a unique two-page supplement. On the broad grounds behind the brick walls of the state asylum, three tables were set up, each over 200 feet long. Flowers were everywhere. Confederate flags flew from windows, poles, and trees. The old flag of the Hampton Legion, "torn and battle stained," was displayed above a bandstand "almost buried in evergreens and flowers." Over the speaker's table was hung the Legion's Matanzas banner. At one end of the long dining tables was erected an arch of green, decorated with captured Yankee flags. Through that arch the soldiers marched to the banquet. Signs were displayed. One read "Welcome home, our brave defenders—our Hampton forever!" Other posters proclaimed famous Hampton battles such as Brandy Station. "[W]e immediately stationed ourselves at this point," jested the reporter, "but didn't see any brandy." Another motto displayed by the ladies promised, "None but the brave deserve the *fare!*" Delicacies included "pies and patties, pigs and poultry, chocolate, coffee, cakes and custards, salads, syllabubs and sausages, blanc mange, bread and butter, pies, pickles and preserves."

At one o'clock in the afternoon, the speech making began. Dr. Benjamin Morgan Palmer, Presbyterian minister, made a patriotic address. At its conclusion he turned to General Hampton and declared, "to you is allotted a noble destiny. It is given to you, with your brave command, to carve your name with the point of your sword upon the history of your country." He then strode over to the general and pinned on his chest "an exquisite Palmetto badge, interwoven with a miniature Confederate flag."

"There was scarcely a dry eye in the vast assembly, and the brave soldier himself could not restrain the tears." Soldiers and civilians chanted, "Hampton, Hampton."[25]

The general boarded the train for Richmond on the night of April 27. His mounted troopers took to the highways, although their baggage and rifles went by rail. The Charleston Light Dragoons had their own going-away party, "with none of the fair sex present," according to a soldier, "but with oceans of old Madeira to sustain one's spirits in their absence. Recollections of matters and things towards the close are a little vague, consisting chiefly of lights and decanters dancing the can-can." The Fourth South Carolina would go by way of Camden, South Carolina, to have their horses shod there. "The 'Drags' on leaving Columbia were loaded with flowers, as well as with less sentimental gift, and were continually waving farewells as they rode along the streets."

Each of the regiments traveled to Virginia by a different route, making it easier to supply the men and find forage for their mounts. They progressed about twenty-five miles per day. One Dragoon explained,

> The quartermaster and commissary of course preceded the column for the purpose of making the necessary arrangements for rations and camping, and when the regiments reached their destination at night, it was occasionally found that the country people had got up a gratuitous 'spread' for the boys, as best they could, and gave them kindly honest welcome.

Curious civilians visited their camp, where troopers slept on the ground with only "a blanket stretched along a stick" for shelter. "On one occasion an old lady, who was being shown through the camp, at length exclaimed, 'But where do you undress?' It had to be delicately explained, that a cavalryman was supposed to be *robe de nuit* when he had unbuckled his spurs."[26]

In Richmond on May 1 Hampton ran into Mary Chesnut. "He told me again the story of his row with General Lee."[27] The chastisement still stung.

Hampton arrived at Milford the next day and reported to Stuart by telegraph. Three days earlier Gordon's brigade had been transferred to a new division being formed for Rooney Lee. Hampton's assistant adjutant general wrote to the reassigned Gordon, expressing "the surprise with which he [Hampton] has received the orders and the pain it causes him to execute them." Hampton's other regiments were widely scattered. The reinforcements from South Carolina were still on the road. "The effective force here numbers 673 enlisted men," Hampton reported from his Milford headquarters on May 2. With all the troopers he could muster, Hampton joined Stuart at Shady Grove on May 7 to fend off federal cavalry demonstrations. "From the start Lee's cavalry was aggressive," remembered a federal officer, "and by its ceaseless activity in that densely wooded region reminded one of a swarm of bees suddenly disturbed by strange footsteps."[28]

It was soon determined that Union major general Philip H. Sheridan was moving on Richmond with 12,000 blue-clad cavalrymen. Hampton would remain to cover the infantry. Stuart took Gordon's brigade, joined forces with Fitz Lee, and reached Yellow Tavern on Telegraph Road, just six miles from the Confederate capital. He had but 4,500 men. In desperate fighting on May 11, charge was met by countercharge, but the Confederates held the line.

Late that afternoon a dismounted Yankee cavalryman spotted Stuart on horseback, turned, aimed his pistol, and fired, bringing down the Virginian. Evacuated to Richmond in great pain, throughout the next day Stuart steadily grew weaker.

The president was among his visitors. "General, how do you feel?" Davis asked, taking Stuart's hand.

"Easy, but willing to die, if God and my country think I have fulfilled my destiny and done my duty," replied the thirty-one-year old.

Within hours he was dead.[29]

"My Heart Is Sorely Bruised"

Stuart's Successor

W hile Hampton hurried to rejoin his men, Robert E. Lee again faced a host of blue-clad invaders. Their new commander, fresh from triumphs in the West, was Ulysses S. Grant. He vowed to crush the "rebellion" in only months. His 120,000-man Army of the Potomac was twice the size of Lee's, and recruits were pouring in.

On May 5 Grant advanced two columns into the wilderness—seventy square miles of dense woods west of Fredericksburg. Lee withstood his attacks, inflicting 18,000 casualties, while sustaining 10,800 of his own. Rather than back away to rest and regroup, Grant pressed on, moving south in an attempt to get between Confederate defenders and Richmond. Lee was ready for him. Near Spotsylvania Court House on May 10, Grant threw three corps at the Southern entrenchments. There was desperate combat at a Confederate salient called the Bloody Angle. Losses on both sides were horrendous. "I propose to fight it out on this line," said Grant, "if it takes all summer." Lincoln had finally found a commander willing to pay the price in blood—to spend the lives of his own men—to achieve success. Lee withdrew to new positions. Federals attacked him on May 16 and were again repulsed. Grant moved once more to the southeast and was checked by Lee near Hanover Junction, close to the North Anna River. "Lee's army is really whipped," concluded Grant as he ordered his infantry to assault Southerners near a crossroads east of Richmond curiously called Cold Harbor. In only minutes thousands of Grant's exhausted attackers went down in a hail of lead. When Grant ordered that the battle be renewed, all along the line Union troops refused to budge. Commanded to charge, demoralized soldiers instead hugged the ground. Rebuked, they fired volleys into the air. "For the present," conceded Grant, "all further offensive operations will be suspended." In seven weeks he had lost more than 65,000 men, but was no nearer Richmond than McClellan had been two years earlier.[1]

As the infantry slugged it out, Confederate cavalry engaged in reconnaissance. With Stuart dead, all three cavalry division commanders would for now report directly to Lee. For missions involving more than one division, Hampton, as the senior officer, would command. In mid-May Rosser's brigade of Hampton's division rode on the Confederate left, pushing back probing Union cavalry and gathering information on enemy strength. Hampton was ordered to support an infantry demonstration on May 19. In this action the footsoldiers were nearly overwhelmed, until a battery of artillery that accompanied Hampton checked the enemy advance.[2]

On May 27 Lee ordered the cavalry to investigate Grant's movements south of the Pamunkey River. For this mission most of the troopers would come from Rosser's and Butler's brigades of Hampton's division. Butler himself was absent, and only the Fifth South Carolina and part of the Fourth were with the brigade. Of these men, few had ever seen combat. Early that morning troopers mounted up and set out. Old veterans were quick to make fun of the green horsemen from South Carolina. "I say, Parson, let me have your long-shooter and I'll bite off the end," was one jest. Lt. Col. William Stokes of the Fourth attempted to clear wagons off the road by shouting that his men had come "to follow Hampton." One survivor of earlier battles replied, "They'll soon have enough of following Hampton!"[3]

On the next morning they ran into the Second Federal Cavalry Division near Haw's Shop. Hampton had his men fight dismounted in the wooded, uneven terrain. Rosser was on the left, Brig. Gen. William Carter Wickham of Fitz Lee's division in the center, Butler's two regiments on the right. Rooney Lee's division was ordered to follow a road to the left in hopes of turning the Yankee flank, but that proved impossible. An enemy attack on Hampton was repulsed. Reinforced by Custer's brigade of the First Division, the unionists returned to the fray. Fighting went on for seven hours, neither side gaining an advantage, but the hottest part of the field being the Confederate right. Custer was sure, from the volume of fire he was receiving, that he faced great numbers of mounted infantry.[4]

Having determined that federal foot soldiers had indeed crossed the Pamunkey, Hampton's mission was complete. He tried to break off the engagement. Word to withdraw did not reach the Fourth South Carolina on the extreme right, a succession of couriers having been killed in the attempt to bring it. Finally, Hampton himself went and brought them out. They had suffered terrible casualties, but impressed the veterans with their performance and earned the commendation of their general. One of the last men to return was Sgt. Ben Huger. Shot in the upper arm, he had been forced to drop his carbine. Huger feared that he might face amputation. As he stumbled to the rear, he gripped a pistol in his good hand, refusing to give it up, although headed for a field hospital. "I want that to shoot a surgeon," he explained.[5]

On June 1 Hampton led Rosser's brigade in ambushing an enemy cavalry advance. "Rosser fell upon their rear," reported Lee to the War Department, "charged down the road toward Ashland, bearing everything before him." Hampton was glad to pass along Lee's commendation, adding thanks of his own for Rosser's "skill and gallantry."[6]

Although Hampton was not yet formally in overall command, he had already begun changing the tactics of the Army of Northern Virginia's cavalry. By the opening of the 1864 campaign, enemy horse soldiers were numerous, well mounted, excellently trained, and armed with repeating rifles. Hampton knew that for outnumbered and outgunned Confederates to charge such a force on horseback would seldom be feasible. His alternative was to begin fighting dismounted. "He could dash his forces, mounted, to favorable points with great celerity," wrote a veteran, "dismount and rush in, and if advisable, draw them out as quickly and hurl them fiercely on some other weaker position." This often required detailing up to one-quarter of his men as "horse-holders" during action. Still, Hampton successfully transformed his troopers into "good, hard-fighting infantry . . . and at the same time preserved intact all their good qualities as cavalry." Muzzle-loading rifles were undeniably a disadvantage in rapidity of fire, but they tended to be more accurate, had a greater range, and inflicted more damage. And there was a Hampton habit his men came to appreciate. One remembered,

> while General Stuart would attempt his work with whatever force he had at hand, and often seemed to try to accomplish a given result with the smallest number of men, Gen. Hampton always endeavored to carry every available man to his point of operation, and the larger his force the better he liked it.

Hampton's "style of generalship," he concluded, won the "unwavering confidence" of those serving under him. If "under Stuart stampedes were frequent, with Hampton they were unknown."[7]

Those new tactics and their originator were about to be tested again. On June 7 Sheridan led 6,000 blue-clad horsemen across the Pamunkey at New Castle Ferry. The next day Hampton was sent in pursuit with 5,000 men of his and Fitz Lee's division. Rooney Lee's division remained with the infantry. Secrecy was so complete that some of the men speculated that they were perhaps going to raid far-off Washington.[8] On the night of June 10, Hampton's men galloped up to the tracks of the Virginia Central Railroad in the vicinity of Trevilian Station. Fitz Lee reached Louisa Court House, also on the railroad, but some five miles to the southeast. The plan was to converge the next day on Clayton's Store, five miles to the north. At dawn on June 11 Generals Rosser and Butler rode together to Hampton's headquarters at Netherland's house, half a mile from Trevilian Station. Receiving his orders to cover the left, Rosser returned to his brigade. Generals Hampton and Butler rode forward to reconnoiter, but were soon met by Confederate pickets driven in by the enemy. Hampton ordered Butler to attack with his brigade, and immediately word was received that Fitz Lee too was going into action. Butler's men, fighting dismounted, pushed the enemy back. When resistance stiffened Hampton ordered Young's brigade into action. Butler confessed that he "paid little attention" to his right flank "as I supposed it was protected by Lee's division."[9]

Custer's brigade ran into Lee's men, withdrew, and then slipped down a road between Lee's left and Hampton's right. Soon Custer was in Hampton's rear, capturing wagons, ambulances, and horses. When he heard what was happening, Hampton withdrew Butler and Young. "Dismount and protect that battery," he commanded. He ordered Rosser to hit Custer's marauders and push them against Lee. The courier dispatched by Hampton galloped up to Rosser and delivered the message. "Give the general my compliments," replied Rosser, "and tell him we are giving 'em hell." Returning to Hampton, the courier saluted and repeated the reply. "General Rosser is a magnificent fighter," said Hampton, "and has done much to turn the tide in our favor today." The wagons and mounts were retaken. Lee even captured Custer's headquarters wagon. Custer escaped, but his command was "severely punished," in Hampton's words.[10]

The next day Sheridan rode to Hampton's left and attacked, dismounted, but was repeatedly repulsed. "It was a spirited infantry attack," said Rosser, "and a stubborn infantry resistance." Lee managed to strike the enemy's right flank, and Sheridan withdrew after dark. "Sheridan was not only whipped by Hampton at Trevilian, but routed and panic-stricken," concluded Rosser.

Hampton would come to fault Fitz Lee for failing to stop Custer in the first place. "Lee returned to Louisa C. H. just after Rosser's charge," wrote Hampton years later, "& he did not join me until 2 P.M.—the next day!!" Fitz Lee's men did good work the second day, said Hampton, but "I really did not know at first how greatly he had failed on the first day & my regard for Genl. R. E. Lee, induced me to omit all mention of misconduct on the part of Fitz."

Hampton's total losses were around 1,100 men; Sheridan's were about the same. Federals damaged the railroad in several places, but not seriously. Southerners could claim yet another cavalry victory.[11] "The weather was hot," remembered a Union officer, "and the roads were heavy with dust, causing the weaker horses to drop out; in all cases where this occurred the disabled animals were shot by the rear-guard." As many as 2,000 federal horses were destroyed to avoid their capture by Southern pursuers. Confederates needed those mounts. In Butler's brigade alone 1,600 men were without horses, those troopers assigned to a dismounted organization derisively referred to as the "Stud Horse Battalion," or simply the "mob."[12]

Skirmishing continued as the Union and Confederate cavalries moved along parallel lines down the Pamunkey toward White House Landing. There the Federals rested and resupplied under the protective guns of the U.S. Navy. Hampton had begged for infantry help—troops he must have known were not available—exhibiting an aggressive spirit. The Union cavalrymen then rode overland, crossed the Chickahominy, and by June 24 were ready to give battle at Nance's Shop and Samaria Church, some sixteen miles southeast of Richmond. The brigades of Martin Witherspoon Gary and John Chambliss hit the enemy flank while Fitz Lee advanced against the main line. Soon the bluecoats gave way, leaving their dead and wounded on the field. Hampton then ordered the Phillips and Jeff Davis legions to charge on horseback. "This they did most gallantly," reported Hampton, "driving the enemy for 3 miles in confusion." The Federals lost 357 men, the Confederates perhaps half that number. Three days later Hampton attacked the enemy at Sappony Church south of Petersburg, pushing them to Ream's Station. There, the infantry of Southern brigadier general William Mahone cut them to pieces. Many prisoners were taken.

"When the general commanding takes into consideration the disparity in numbers of the troops engaged," Hampton wrote to Lee, "the many disadvantages under which my men labored, their hard marches, their want of supplies, their numerous privations, and the cheerfulness with which these were borne, he will, I trust, be satisfied with the results accomplished."[13]

Hampton found himself still troubled by Lee's words spoken months earlier, and he continued to unburden himself to friends. "Let them alone," James Chesnut advised wife Mary on July 26. "It will all come right. There is really nothing the matter." Unknown to Hampton, Lee had written President Davis on July 2 requesting that Hampton be given formal command of the cavalry corps.

> You know the high opinion I entertain of Gen Hampton and my appreciation of his character and services. In his late expedition he has displayed both energy and good conduct, and although I have feared that he might not have that activity and endurance so necessary in a cavalry commander, and so imminently possessed by Gen Stuart . . . I request authority to place him in the command.[14]

"I am rejoiced at your success," Robert E. Lee wrote to Hampton after the action at Samaria Church. Over the next few weeks, there were conferences with the commanding general as Hampton's men harassed Union gunboats on the James River. "We have been wonderfully quiet of late," he wrote to his sister on July 22. "We have killed three deer, so we are living finely." Most importantly, the "Yankee cavalry has not stirred out, since it was whipped."[15]

Hampton acquired a small, ivory-handled Colt revolver from a captured Yankee lieutenant and decided to try it out. The target was a tree, no larger than a man's arm, some twenty yards away. He opened fire and every bullet hit the tree. Staff officer Nathan Davis complimented the general on his marksmanship, but said he personally preferred the heavier Colt Navy pistol. Hampton replied that he expected to use his new weapon only in close quarters, adding that he never sighted a handgun, only looked at his target and opened fire. Captain Davis agreed, saying that was his method too, and it had proven to be quite effective.[16]

Lt. Wade Hampton IV arrived in Virginia on October 4 to join his father's staff. Twenty-three-year-old Wade had served as aide to Gen. Joseph E. Johnston until Johnston was replaced as commander of the Army of Tennessee in July. Two and a half years younger than brother Wade, Thomas Preston Hampton had been on his father's staff since 1862.[17]

On August 11 Lee made known a decision, approved by the president, that by now seemed a foregone conclusion. Maj. Gen. Wade Hampton would command the cavalry corps of the Army of Northern Virginia. The position was his by both seniority and performance. Hampton's subordinates recognized his strengths. "He never lost his head and rarely lost his temper," said Butler. And "he never seemed to realize what fatigue was." A lifetime spent out of doors gave Hampton a "topographical instinct," insisted Butler, and he knew the value of secrecy and speed. A young soldier remembered that Hampton was "as dauntless as Stuart, and, if anything, a more distinguished-looking man." Although it was obvious that he was a "born aristocrat," still "his manners and bearing with the troops were so thoroughly democratic, and his fearlessness in action so conspicuous, that no man ever excited more enthusiasm." Another acknowledged how Hampton "seemed to be acquainted with every private, remembering faces and names in a wonderful manner." He even knew their horses, noticing "when a man was riding an animal other than his own."[18]

On that same August day, Lee ordered his new cavalry chief to Culpeper that he might threaten the federal flank. No sooner had Hampton started than he received new orders. "Halt your command and return toward Richmond." The city was in danger. On the morning of August 16, Hampton arrived at White Tavern on the Charles City Road, no more than seven miles from the Richmond suburb of Rocketts. Hampton's old division, now commanded by Butler, came to the aid of Gary's brigade and Rooney Lee's division. Fighting raged for two days before federal infantry were pushed back.

Many prisoners were taken by Confederates. Brigadier General Chambliss died rallying his men.[19]

Robert E. Lee quickly directed the cavalry to assist Lt. Gen. Ambrose Powell Hill in making an assault on the federal lines at Ream's Station, seven miles south of Petersburg, on the Weldon and Petersburg Railroad. Hampton had reported the vulnerability of Federals at that point, disorganized as they were in tearing up tracks. Hill would signal the attack by two quick artillery shots on the morning of August 25. On cue, Hampton's cavalry crossed Malone's Bridge and fell upon the federal left flank. Targetted too by well-directed Confederate artillery fire, the Yankees were driven back toward the station. The fighting was hard, the ground obstructed by cut timbers, but after twelve hours enemy defenses were overrun. Hampton took 781 prisoners and reported burying 143 enemy dead. His own losses were far smaller. Chambliss' old brigade took three stands of colors. Although the attack had failed to regain the railroad, the enemy had taken a beating. Lee urged Hampton to rest his men, but prepare "to intercept and punish" any new enemy incursions. "The conduct of the cavalry is worthy of all praise," concluded the army commander.[20]

"That old fellow Hampton is a rusher," an infantryman was heard to say. "He helped us mightily." Praise came too from corps commander Hill. The commanding general told Hampton that "the cavalry *always* fight well now." Hampton was pleased to discover that Lee "is very civil to me." A month earlier Lt. Gen. Jubal Anderson Early had raided Maryland, even threatening Washington. Hampton wished that he could have been part of that adventure. After all, "I am in command of *all* the cavalry which belong to this army." His clothes were wearing out, he told Mary Fisher. Everyone knew the Yankees were well supplied. "Perhaps I may have the chance to run up to Md. Or Penn yet." That was not part of Lee's plans, but he "must not calculate on my storming any more breastworks, for it is not the work for cavalry."[21]

Lee had other intentions. On September 3 he pointed out to Hampton the vulnerability of the enemy's rear areas, as reported by scouts. "I wish you would have the matter closely inquired into," wrote Lee. "A sudden blow in that quarter might be detrimental to him." Two days later Hampton received a lengthy, richly detailed report from his own scout, Sgt. George Shadburne. Shadburne had been as far as Coggins Point on the south side of the James River. He advised Hampton on federal troop dispositions, work being done, what streams were impassable, even which Yankee colonel was under arrest for drunkedness. Of greatest interest, there was a herd of cattle at Coggins Point, "attended by 120 men and 30 citizens, without arms."[22] Confederate troops were hungry Although it was far behind enemy lines, Hampton wanted that herd.

He shared his ambitious plan with an apprehensive Robert E. Lee. Lee conceded that Hampton might penetrate the Union lines, but feared for his safe return, "embarrassed with cattle or wagons." He promised to order a diversionary attack on the appointed day, but urged caution.[23]

"The affair was guarded with perfect secrecy, until Hampton *struck,*" remembered a North Carolina veteran. "I affirm as a fact . . . that *no one* but Hampton, R. E. Lee and Hampton's scouts, unless it was Hampton's own generals, *knew* anything about Hampton's purpose."[24]

Hampton and 3,000 raiders bivouacked on Rowanty Creek, south of Petersburg. On the morning of September 14, they headed east across Jerusalem Plank Road and the ruins of the Norfolk and Petersburg Railroad. Confederate engineers replaced a burned bridge over Blackwater Creek. Then, by separate routes, Rooney Lee's division and Rosser's brigade were directed to converge on Sycamore Church, site of the strongest federal force and only two miles from the herd. There was a sharp fight there and many Yankee prisoners were taken. Brig. Gen. James Dearing's brigade covered the movement of the other Southern columns. To maintain secrecy, civilians encountered were quietly sent to the rear. Achieving complete surprise on the morning of September 16, Rosser fell upon the federal camp. The First District of Columbia Cavalry fought "stubbornly," said Hampton. "But the determination and gallantry of Rosser's men proved too much," resulting in a rout. Half-dressed prisoners were corralled. Lee on the left and Dearing on the right quickly secured their objectives. Rosser sent forward a special detachment assigned to round up the cattle, then stampede toward the James River. By eight o'clock that morning the "beeves" and all three columns were headed to distant Confederate lines. The raiders recrossed the bridge, then destroyed it. One remembered how they "called to the Yankees to come over and get their bulls, and they bellowed at them in derision." Federal pursuers were repulsed near Ebenezer Church. Hampton had lost sixty-one men while riding one hundred miles in seventy-two hours. He returned with 304 prisoners, 11 U.S. Army wagons, 3 captured guidons, and much property. Yankee camps had been burned, and enemy soldiers killed and wounded.

Most importantly, Hampton delivered 2,486 head of cattle—nearly two million pounds of beef—to a hungry army.[25]

"The cattle stretched along the road for seven miles," said one Confederate scout. "I never saw such a sight in my life." One officer thought them "the finest I ever saw. The largest will weigh 1500 pounds, the smallest not less than 400 lbs. All are western cattle and recently arrived to Grant's army." Lee's men would be eating "Hampton steaks" for weeks. The Southern press was ecstatic. "To make his way unobserved to such a point, and bring off so large a number of these slow-moving creatures," wrote the editor of the Richmond *Whig,* "was an achievement that entitles Gen. H. and his gallant followers to the grateful thanks of the country." The Richmond *Examiner* called Hampton's raid "one of the boldest and most brilliant things of the war." Robert E. Lee joined in the praise, noting their "courage and energy."[26]

"If the enemy make so rich a haul as to get our cattle herd he will be likely to strike far to the south, or even to the southeast to get around with it," Grant telegraphed George Meade. Ignoring Grant's poor directions, Meade complained, "Hampton's force is so superior to ours and he had so much time" that pursuit was futile. The Washington *Herald* was astonished that "the rebels have succeeded in this bold maneuver, and have actually taken from beneath our very noses sufficient beef to supply their army for weeks."[27]

On September 27 Rosser's hard-fighting brigade was sent to the Shenandoah Valley. The rest of Hampton's cavalry remained on the line south of the James. Two days later Butler's division was attacked and driven from its entrenchments on the Vaughan Road. With the help of Brig. Gen. Rufus Barringer's brigade of Rooney Lee's division, the line was restored. The next morning Dearing's brigade was driven out of its position. Rooney Lee personally led two of his regiments in retaking the line, bagging 900 prisoners and capturing no fewer than ten enemy flags. "The whole affair was one of the handsomest I have ever seen," said Hampton. In fighting the next day Brig. Gen. John Dunovant was killed while leading the brigade of South Carolinians that once belonged to Butler. Dr. J. B. Fontaine, cavalry corps medical director, was mortally wounded by an exploding shell as he rushed to Dunovant's aid.[28]

Hampton continued to think of ways he might improve the effectiveness of the cavalry corps. So many of his men remained without horses that he proposed that they be "organized into regiments to form a brigade to act as infantry with the cavalry." He preferred this expedient to losing troopers permanently to the infantry. Yet, even men with mounts were too often forced to take on the responsibilities of infantrymen, holding static positions, as the siege tightened around Richmond and Petersburg. Robert E. Lee regretted the necessity. "But the difficulty is to get the men," he explained to Hampton. The role of the mounted arm must for now conform to circumstances "as it is absolutely necessary for us to fill up our infantry regiments." By late October the total strength of the Army of Northern Virginia's cavalry had fallen to fewer than 5,000 men.[29]

Hampton wrote to Mary Fisher in early October,

> We gain successes, but after every fight there comes in to me an ominous paper, marked *"Casualties"* and in this I often find long lists of "killed" and "wounded." Sad, sad words which carry anguish to so many hearts. And we have scarcely time to bury the dead ere we press on in the same deadly strife. I pray for peace. I would not give *peace* for all the military glory won by Boneparte.[30]

Hampton's cavalry held their share of the trenches in siege lines around Burgess's Mill, some eight miles to the southwest of Petersburg. Throughout the month they had helped the infantry of Maj. Gen. Henry Heth's division in constructing earthworks.[31] A massive attack came on the morning of October 27. Grant sent six federal infantry divisions and one division of cavalry, supported by artillery, against the Southerners. His objective was to break through the Confederate lines, advance northwestward, and cut the South Side Railroad. If successful, Lee might be forced to abandon Petersburg and the Confederate capital.

Butler faced the enemy as they advanced to Boydton Plank Road. Hampton directed men on the Quaker Road as he positioned Rooney Lee's division on the right that it might attack the enemy's rear. Dearing was ordered by Hampton to put his mounted men on the Plank Road. As Heth did not have time to replace Dearing's troopers with infantry, the withdrawal left a gap in the lines. An officer sent to alert Hampton of the danger was captured, and Hampton soon discovered the enemy in his rear. Ordering his men to new positions, Hampton formed a line across White Oak Road with the left on Burgess's Mill Pond, and there repulsed one attack. Infantry reinforcements arrived. It was determined that the enemy must not be allowed to remain so dangerously near to the railroad. A plan was quickly put together to dislodge and force them back. About four o'clock in the afternoon, the counterattack began. As soon as he heard the rattle of musketry, Hampton ordered his men forward, dismounted.[32] General, field grade, and staff officers led on horseback. Maj. Theodore G. Barker, Capt. Nat Butler, and Lt. Preston Hampton rode with the advancing men, waving their hats and cheering them on.

"Hurrah, Nat!" Preston shouted. Just then Preston was hit and fell to the ground, shot in the groin. Another officer, bullets ripping his own clothes, saw him fall and rushed over. General Hampton, son Wade, and others galloped up, jumped from their horses, and went to his aid.

"My son, my son," murmured the general as he lifted Preston's head and kissed him, whispering words to his boy that the others were unable to hear. Preston seemed conscious, but could not reply.

General Butler rode up to the group and asked who had been hit. There was agony on Hampton's face and tears in his eyes as he looked up. "Poor Preston has been mortally wounded."

Butler called for a nearby wagon to be brought over. Bullets whined through the air. The crowd that had gathered around Preston was drawing fire. Four more were hit, including Lt. Wade Hampton, shot in the back. Quickly, young Wade was put on a horse and led to safety. General Hampton rode beside the wagon that carried Preston to the rear. Dr. Benjamin W. "Watt" Taylor supported Preston's head on his shoulder.

"Too late, doctor," said the father.

"I learned right there my first great lesson of life from General Hampton," remembered one witness, "which is self control."

Charging Southerners swept the enemy from the field. Hampton rode to Hart's Battery. Captain Hart had been severely injured. Hampton took over, personally directing artillery fire until dark. That evening Hampton relinquished command to Rooney Lee that he might spend the night by the side of his dead boy. An officer remembered that "his voice was broken and his brave old heart was wrenched with grief . . . so that he could scarcely suppress his tears."[33]

Wade Hampton would recover, although he was badly hurt, probably more seriously than first thought. Dr. Taylor had begun to dress his wound when Capt. James Lowndes entered the hut that served as a field hospital. Lowndes was by now a seasoned veteran, but seeing his friend covered in blood, he lost consciousness and dropped to the ground, adding to the hard-pressed doctor's list of patients.[34]

The casket containing Preston's body, draped with the old Legion flag, was sent by rail to Columbia for burial next to his mother in the graveyard at Trinity Episcopal Church. Sarah Buchanan "Buck" Preston, a twenty-two-year-old Hampton cousin, ran out of the funeral service. "I can't bear to think of Preston," she cried. "Can't bear to hear any more moaning, and weeping and wailing—if I do, I shall die." Condolences arrived from everywhere. Hampton's wife Mary came to Virginia for an extended visit. "God only knows how much I need comfort, for my heart is sorely bruised," Hampton wrote to his sister on November 14. "It cries out for my beautiful boy, all the time, & I cannot become resigned to his loss. It is very, very hard to lose him, but I pray that God has taken him to His eternal rest."[35]

"I was dreadfully shocked at Preston Hampton's fate—his untimely fate," wrote Varina Davis to Mary Chesnut. "I know nothing in history more touching than Wade Hampton's situation at the supremest moment of his misery." It was said that Hampton would not permit young Wade to return to his staff after his recovery, anxiety for his safety being simply more than he would be able to bear.[36]

Mary Hampton set up housekeeping with her husband at "a nice little old-fashioned cottage." Young Wade and daughter Sally visited for a time. There was little enemy activity in November, only the routine of command. Hampton tried to provide Maj. Gen. Lunsford Lomax with the supplies he needed in the Shenandoah. He directed Lt. Col. John S. Mosby to procure cavalry weapons then in the hands of civilians for the use of inadequately armed recruits. On the political front Hampton asked Benjamin Perry to support Brig. Gen. John S. Preston for election to the office of South Carolina governor. Andrew G. Magrath would emerge the winner of that contest. At a military review near Petersburg on November 8, Hampton met twenty-four-year-old Katherine Hammond Gregg and introduced her to his officers,

Lt. Preston Hampton, one of the general's sons. *Edward L. Wells, Hampton and His Cavalry in '64 (Richmond, Va.: B. F. Johnson Pub. Co., 1899).*

welcoming a cousin he may not have seen since her childhood. Whatever his feelings toward her father Hampton harbored no ill will against this daughter of James Henry Hammond. Ironically, former governor Hammond would die at his Redcliffe home just five days later.[37]

There were cavalry clashes on December 8 and 9 from Stony Creek Depot down to Belfield, forty miles south of Petersburg. Once again the enemy was driven back and the railroad saved. "As soon as their retrograde movement became evident," said a North Carolina trooper, "Hampton mounted his men, who up to that time were dismounted and in the trenches, and went in pursuit." Only when Confederate cavalry ran into a wall of enemy infantry did they pull back. Hampton reported his losses as "slight, while those of the enemy were considerable," including 300 prisoners. He regretted that the slow-moving infantry allowed so many to escape. Confederate lines were stretched nearly to the breaking point. On one occasion the Yankees got within three miles of where Mary was staying. "Gen. Lee was kind enough to send for her," Hampton told his sister, "& he kept her advised of my movements all the time I was absent. He has been remarkably polite to Mary."[38]

Southern manpower shortages had become so critical by 1864 that Confederate authorities entered their prisoner-of-war camps searching for recruits. Considered prime prospects for switching sides were the foreign-born and disenchanted Midwesterners. Although many questioned the true feelings and doubted the reliability of those who chose to become "Galvanized Rebels," two experimental battalions were recruited for Confederate service. In October of 1864 the First Foreign Battalion, commanded by Lt. Col. Julius G. Tucker, went into training in Columbia, South Carolina. They quickly gained a shady reputation. One citizen thought them "the lowest and most debased looking set of men I ever saw," frankly concluding that "I would rather have them in the Federal army than in our own."[39] In late November, while Mary Hampton was in Virginia, her home near Columbia was burglarized. "General Hampton's house has been robbed," Mary Chesnut recorded, "all of his wife's jewelry taken, everything valuable stolen." To make matters worse, the intruders left behind "derisive notes" reading "Hang Hampton," "Rebel," and "Cattle Stealer." All eyes turned to the First Foreign Battalion. After more nighttime thefts, and even assaults, there was talk of forming a "vigilance committee" in Columbia. A petition circulated demanding the immediate removal of the experimental organization. After the battalion departed in January, at least some of Mary Hampton's stolen jewelry and silver was found in the abandoned tent of a "foreigner."[40]

Both Foreign Battalions were intended for that thin Confederate line facing William Tecumseh Sherman. After a long campaign Sherman had captured Atlanta on September 2. Ten weeks later he burned much of the city, then set out on a march through Georgia, laying waste to everything in a swath sixty miles wide. He reached the outskirts of Savannah on December 10, occupying that city after a siege of but eleven days. Confederate forces under Lt. Gen. William J. Hardee escaped into South Carolina. There they waited—demoralized and hopelessly outnumbered.

Rumors that Hampton might return to South Carolina with a cavalry force provoked a flurry of letters between Grant and Meade in late November. "I am looking with the most profound interest to our state and Geo.," Hampton wrote to South Carolina governor Milledge L. Bonham on December 4. "Surely if active and proper measures are taken, Sherman can be destroyed. He should not be allowed to cross the Savannah [River]." Roads might easily be obstructed to delay him, advised Hampton, somehow under the impression that time was on the Southern side. "I wish that I could be there, for I should like to strike a blow on the soil of my own state."[41]

Through January Sherman remained in Savannah as South Carolinians fretted over where he might turn next. "You all seem to be in a great excitement in Columbia," Hampton wrote to his sister on January 10. He tried to calm her fears. If Confederate troops were sent from Virginia, something he probably expected, "Columbia will be as safe as any other place." Sometime in mid-January Hampton conferred with his commander. "I am going out to see if I can do anything for my state," he wrote to Mary Fisher after the meeting, "as Genl. Lee thinks that I can do good there." He and Mary planned to depart by rail about January 20 or 21 on the thirty-six-hour trip. Before they left Hampton wrote a letter to four-year-old Daisy, then staying with her aunts at Millwood. "As I cannot see you to give you a kiss on your birthday, I write a letter to tell you how much I love you and how I hope that you will be a good girl." He promised to purchase a doll for her in Richmond. "When she gets home, you must name her *Virginia,* because she was born here."

"It will give me great happiness to see you all once more, and to have the rest of home even for a few days," Hampton told his sister on the eve of their return to South Carolina. "Do have the house fixed for us."[42]

10

"THE GRAND SMASH HAS COME"

Defeat in the Carolinas

"We are passing through a fiery ordeal," Hampton wrote to Senator Wigfall on January 20, "but if we 'quit ourselves like men' we must be successful. I do not allow myself to contemplate any other than a successful issue to our struggle." So many had died, including a brother and a son. Such sacrifice could not have been in vain. Hampton continued,

> I have given far more than all my property to this cause, and I am ready to give *all*. I am going to fight for my State and I am willing to fight anywhere. The record of the cavalry which has fought under my command is an honorable one, and I take great pride in it. They have been successful in *every* fight—not a few—have captured large supplies of arms and taken not less than 10,000 prisoners. So I leave the record good.

As to the future, "I shall fight as long as I can wield my sabre."[1]

Robert E. Lee was willing to send Butler's division to South Carolina with Hampton on the condition they return in time for the spring campaign. Preparations went forward in secrecy. Troopers would be transported to Columbia by rail, leaving their horses behind. Hampton assured Lee that he could find mounts for the men once they were in South Carolina. "General Butler, with his division, is on his way to the aid of our State," proclaimed the new governor, Andrew G. Magrath. "Hampton is with him. He needs horses and I told him he shall have them." Col. Christopher Hampton, the general's brother, was responsible for "receiving with thanks, all that will be sent; of taking all that are withheld." Payment was to be made. "No one shall suffer from his devotion to the State," concluded the governor. What had been Butler's brigade, now commanded by Col. B. H. Rutledge, counted but 940 men. Young's brigade had fallen to 586. Despite the insignificant numbers he could add to South Carolina's defense, Lee had hopes that his cavalry chief might help in reversing Confederate fortunes there. "I think Hampton will be of service in mounting his men and arousing the spirit & strength of the State & otherwise do good," he told President Davis. Hampton reported to Lt. Gen. William J. Hardee on February 7.[2]

One week earlier Sherman had launched his invasion of South Carolina. Most thought Charleston would be his objective, but it soon became clear that Columbia was the target. He commanded an army of over 60,000 well-fed, well-supplied veterans. Confederates opposing him, scattered and demoralized, numbered fewer than 20,000. Southerners made a gallant stand on the Salkehatchie River on February 2–3, but outnumbered 10–1, they were flanked and forced to withdraw. The battle of Rivers Bridge was to be the only major resistance Sherman would face in South Carolina. The way seemed clear for a campaign of unparalleled destruction.[3]

One Yankee soldier crossing into the Palmetto State had turned to the troops behind him and shouted, "Boys, this is old South Carolina, let's give her hell." That determination was shared by the entire chain of command. The state was a "viper nest of rebellion" according to U.S. Army Chief of Staff Henry Halleck, "and ought to be punished and that sternly and severely." Sherman agreed. "The whole army is crazy to be turned loose in Carolina," he confided to Halleck. "I judge that a months sojourn in South Carolina would make her less bellicose." On the eve of his assault, he wrote to Grant. "The truth is the whole army is burning with an insatiable desire to wreak vengeance on South Carolina. I almost tremble at her fate but feel that she deserves all that seems in store for her." To Maj. Gen. Henry Slocum, one of his corps commanders, Sherman made his intentions very clear.

> Don't forget that when you have crossed the Savannah River you will be in South Carolina. You need not be so careful there about private property as we have been. The more of it you destroy the better it will be. The people of South Carolina should be made to feel the war, for they brought it on and are responsible more than anybody else for our presence here. Now is the time to punish them.

That theme echoed down the ranks. One soldier wrote that "we have laid a heavy hand on Georgia, but that is light compared to what South Carolina will catch." "We are on her borders," wrote another, "ready to carry fire and sword into every part of that state." "Nearly every man in Sherman's army say they are for destroying everything in South Carolina," explained one Northern private.[4] Issuing orders was unnecessary. The men knew what to do.

Kilpatrick commanded Sherman's cavalry. When asked how he might let his commander know where he was on the march, Sherman joked, "Oh, just burn a bridge or something and make a smoke, as the Indians do on the plains." Kilpatrick understood. "In after years," he wrote, "when travelers passing through South Carolina shall see chimney-stacks without houses, and the country desolate, and shall ask, 'Who did this?' some Yankee will answer, 'Kilpatrick's cavalry.'"[5]

Homes, barns, churches, villages, and towns were all put to the torch. Sometimes Sherman, almost whimsically, pleaded his innocence. He conceded that his men may have burned Blackville after he left, but "it was not destroyed when I was there," adding that "it was a dirty little hole anyway." He claimed that his troops did not set Orangeburg on fire as they departed, repeating a tale that "some Jew" did it.[6]

As Sherman was entering Orangeburg District, the men of Butler's division jumped from the train in Columbia. Citizens were relieved to see them, few though they were. Confederate flags flew from balconies and windows as the troopers made their way down Richardson Street, the main business district. A veteran remembered that "from the old State House the colors waved to the breeze as if signaling to every son of South Carolina to rally to the defense of the old town and its old men, women and children." The division crossed the bridge over the Congaree River and made its camp west of town.[7]

A party of three scouts set out to locate Sherman's army. Returning from the mission, scout J. D. Hogan was captured and brought before Union division commander Alpheus S. Williams. "Where is Hampton and Butler?" demanded Williams.

"I cannot answer that question, General, but you will find them in the proper place at the right time."

Hogan was then brought to Sherman's nearby headquarters where he encountered a deserter anxious to tell all he knew of Columbia's defenses. "I rebuked him and denounced him as a cowardly traitor," said the scout, who then quickly got into an argument with his captors. Sherman demanded that Hogan tell him the number of Southern troops in Columbia.

"You will find an army there that will defend the city and defeat your army," he replied.

Sherman was not misled by the bravado of one rebel scout and told him the war would soon be over. "A man of your determination should be engaged in a better cause."

"The cause is good enough for me," shot back Hogan, "and if it goes down I will go down with it."[8]

Southern defenses were crumbling. On February 14 Confederates began evacuating Charleston for fear of being cut off by Sherman's advance into the center of the state. There would be a general withdrawal toward North Carolina. Hampton had argued earlier for the abandonment of Charleston and for putting that city's defenders into action against Sherman. Confederates would still have been outnumbered at least 2–1, but might have done Sherman enough damage to force his retreat. "I pressed the same views on Governor Magrath," said Hampton, "telling him that, important as Charleston was to us, Branchville, the junction of the railroads from Columbia, Augusta, and Charleston, was far more important." Now it was too late. Sherman was already approaching the outskirts of Columbia. The remnants of Maj. Gen. Carter Stevenson's infantry division and of Maj. Gen. Joseph Wheeler's and Butler's cavalry—a total of about 5,000 men of all arms—were strung out from three miles above Columbia to twenty-one miles south of the city. Confederate troopers from east and west met for the first time. "Very few of Wheeler's cavalry had sabres," remembered one of Hampton's men. "I had one to ask me one day what kind of thing that was strapped to my saddle. I told him he would not be with Hampton long before he would see them used and would probably wish their men had not discarded them."[9]

A skirmish was fought along Congaree Creek, a tributary on the west bank of the Congaree River, before Confederates withdrew. During the night a battery of Southern guns opened fire from across the river on Federals camped west of the Congaree. "This provoked me very much at the time, for it was wanton mischief," complained Sherman, having apparently concluded that resistance was a crime. "I have always contended that I would have been justified in retaliating for this unnecessary act of war."[10]

Rivers were Columbia's only natural defensive barriers, so Confederates burned the bridges spanning the Congaree, Broad, and Saluda. On the morning of February 16, federal batteries on the west bank of the Congaree began firing on downtown Columbia. "You could see the cannons every time they would fire," said a Columbia teenager, "and hear the shells whistle through the air. Some of them would explode in the air and others would not." Sherman ordered Captain De Gres, battery commander, to shift his aim. "I instructed him not to fire any more into the town, but consented to his bursting a few shells near the depot, to scare away the negroes who were appropriating the bags of corn and meal which we wanted, also to fire three shots at the unoccupied State House." The State House was struck six times by the efficient captain. It is not known how many hungry civilians were hit, but an old lady and a child were killed. A total of 325 rounds of shot and shell were thrown into the capital.[11]

Columbia mayor Thomas Jefferson Goodwyn said that "this shelling continued nearly all day." The city was still under the control of the Confederate army, but Sherman opened fire "without any notice, or demand of surrender." General Beauregard informed the mayor that Confederate forces would evacuate before sunrise on February 17. That morning Goodwyn went to Town Hall and prepared to raise a white flag, "but Gen. Hampton requested that it should not be done until he gave the order," said the mayor. "About 8 o'clock that morning he rode up to the Hall and said the flag could be raised."[12]

Some Confederate troopers wanted to stay and fight, preferring one last suicidal charge to abandoning Columbia. Hampton would not allow it. With Young's brigade he left Columbia on the Winnsboro Road. Other troopers retreated up the Camden Road. Mayor Goodwyn, accompanied by four aldermen, rode by carriage to meet the advance guard of the conquering army. He presented a letter surrendering the city, asking for "a sufficient guard in advance of the army to maintain order." Sherman himself entered Columbia about two-thirty in the afternoon. He met the mayor that evening "and promised me most faithfully that our City should be protected."[13]

"Stores were broken open within the first hour after their arrival," said one Columbia resident. Yankee soldiers accosted citizens, taking their hats, coats, shoes, watches, purses—all "in the twinkling of any eye."[14] Troops broke ranks to break open liquor stores.[15] Cotton bales stacked in the streets were ignited by Union soldiers, but extinguished by fire fighters before the flames could spread. "A thousand Federal troops looked on," remembered a citizen. "Then, led by a drunken soldier, they bayoneted the hose."[16] By midafternoon columns of smoke could be seen east of the city as outlying homes were burned. The Hampton family properties of Millwood, Woodlands, and Diamond Hill were soon engulfed in flames.[17]

The night before the evacuation, Beauregard had met with Hampton to decide, among other things, what to do with the blockaded cotton stacked in the streets. Since Sherman would be unable to remove the cotton, burning it would serve no purpose and only endanger the city, thought Beauregard. Hampton issued orders that no cotton be burned, and none was on fire when Confederate troops left.[18]

As darkness fell on the evening of February 17, fires broke out all over the city. Troops were seen "carrying from house to house balls of rags or cotton saturated with [burning] spirits of turpentine," said one witness. "I spent almost the entire night in the streets and witnessed many houses fired by the soldiers," remembered another.[19] The Rev. Peter J. Shand of Trinity Episcopal Church was forced by approaching flames to flee his home. He and a servant tried to carry to safety a trunk containing the communion plate of the church. They were stopped by soldiers who stole it—and Shand's watch—at gunpoint. Seventy-two-year-old Agnes Law watched in horror as what she thought were "well-behaved and sober" guards "took lighted candles from the mantelpiece" in her home and set her curtains on fire. "I have been for over fifty years a member of the Presbyterian Church. I cannot live long. I shall meet General Sherman and his soldiers at the bar of God, and I give this testimony against them in full view of that dread tribunal."[20]

When the sun rose the next morning, Columbians could scarcely believe their eyes. Much of their city, including the State House, Town Hall, and the entire business district, lay in blackened ruins. Homeless refugees crowded city parks and gardens. When Mayor Goodwyn and a delegation went to Sherman asking for food and protection, he gave them a lecture on their folly in having started the war. "It is true our men have burnt Columbia," a witness reported Sherman as saying, "but it was your fault." Columbians, he told them, had provided liquor to his soldiers.[21]

Sherman in his official report wrote that "without hesitation I charge General Wade Hampton with having burned his own city of Columbia . . . filling it with lint, cotton, and tinder."

"The cotton, instead of burning the houses, was burned by them," countered Edwin J. Scott. "If a transaction that occurred in the presence of forty or fifty thousand people can be successfully falsified, then all human testimony is worthless."[22]

Sherman, in his *Memoirs,* explained why he had pointed the finger at Hampton. "In my official report of this conflagration, I distinctly charged it to General Wade Hampton, and confess I did so pointedly, to shake the faith of his people in him, for he was in my opinion boastful, and professed to be the special champion of South Carolina." For two more days Sherman's army remained in the Columbia area tearing up railroad tracks, destroying foundaries and factories. "Having utterly ruined Columbia," Sherman concluded, "the right wing began its march northward."[23]

Both the officers and the men of the Union army were adamant that South Carolina "thoroughly deserved extirpation," said Sherman. "I know that the general judgment of the country is that no matter how it began," he wrote to his brother of Columbia's destruction, "it was all right." Another officer called it "just retribution."[24]

After the war Hampton confronted one of Sherman's corps commanders, Oliver O. Howard. "General Howard," demanded Hampton, "who burned Columbia?" The Medal of Honor winner laughed. "Why, General, of course we did." But not, he was careful to add, under orders.[25]

Even without orders, "the country was converted into one vast bonfire" wrote a Union war correspondent. "Vandalism of this kind, though not encouraged, was seldom punished." A soldier summarized the South Carolina campaign: "We have had a glorious time in this state. Universal license to burn and plunder was the order of the day."[26]

It was probably on the eve of Columbia's evacuation that Wade Hampton received news of his promotion to lieutenant general. Nominated by President Davis on February 14, he would take rank from that day. A letter from Secretary of War John C. Breckinridge accompanied the nomination, recommending Hampton's promotion that he might "command the Cavalry Corps, Army of Northern Virginia." Senate confirmation came the next day. "As you were not advised of the nomination," Davis wrote on February 16, "you may not have anticipated such action, but will understand it as an expression of my appreciation of your past services and confidence in your ability and future usefulness. You have my best wishes for you personally, and highest hopes for you officially." Hampton's promotion left no ambiguity as to who held the highest rank among Confederate cavalry in the Carolinas, though Joseph Wheeler had to admit that the new lieutenant general "exercised his authority with all possible deference."[27]

Despite Davis's hopes for the future and Breckinridge's expectation that Hampton would return to command Lee's cavalry, Mary Chesnut saw only gloom. "Hampton [is] Lieut. Genl. Much good it may do him. The grand smash has come."[28]

On February 23 Gen. Joseph E. Johnston was placed in command of those scattered, depleted, and dispirited Confederate commands converging on North Carolina. Johnston's failure to stop Sherman's advance upon Atlanta the previous summer had prompted Davis to remove him, placing the audacious John Bell Hood in charge. Hood's aggressive stance could not save that city, and his ill-advised invasion of Tennessee in the fall of 1864 all but destroyed the army. Hood had nearly become a member of Hampton's extended family. Until she finally broke off the relationship, Hampton cousin Sarah Buchanan "Buck" Preston had been the object of Hood's affections. "Buck, the sweetest woman I ever knew," wrote Mary Chesnut, "had a knack of being 'fallen in love with' at sight and of never being 'fallen out of love' with." Wade Hampton admired Hood's bravery and considered him a friend. Still, Hampton was a firm Johnston supporter. "Says *Joe* is equal to even Gen. Lee—if not superior," wrote Mary Chesnut.[29]

"Delay the enemy" and "concentrate" were Hampton's words of advice. "If all the infantry can be put together we can punish Sherman greatly," he said. Johnston well understood that unless Sherman was stopped, it was only a matter of time before he marched his army to Virginia and fell on Lee's flank. Hampton felt that the last, best hope for Confederate success would be for Johnston's army to travel by rail to Virginia and join with Lee to hit Grant's left.[30] That kind of swift, undetected movement was by now beyond Southern logistical capabilities.

As he moved through the South Carolina upcountry, Sherman was informed that two parties of foragers near Feasterville in Fairfield District had been captured and killed. They were found with a sign proclaiming "Death to all foragers." Sherman penned a letter to Hampton on February 24, asserting his right to collect provisions "directly of the people." He had "no doubt this is the occasion of much misbehavior on the part of our men," but threatened to begin killing Southerner prisoners if it happened again. Sherman prepared to execute eighteen Confederates held at the Lancaster Courthouse. Hampton fired back a reply. He denied issuing any orders to kill foragers after capture, but emphasized that every man had a right to defend his home and family, "and from my heart I wish that every old man and boy in my country who can fire a gun would shoot down, as he would a wild beast, the men who are desolating their land, burning their homes, and insulting their women." His anger rising, Hampton excoriated Sherman for turning his artillery on Columbia, for robbing its citizens, for burning it after it had been surrendered. "Your line of march can be traced by the lurid light of burning houses," concluded Hampton. He implied too that Sherman's men were guilty of rape. For every prisoner killed by Sherman, Hampton promised to execute two Yankees, "giving in all cases preference to any officers who may be in my hands."

The only time he ever saw Hampton "lose his temper, or make use of bad language," remembered a veteran, was when five of Sherman's foragers, men captured in the act of pillaging a farm house, were taken to the general. "As the Yankees were brought out to the road where he was sitting on his horse, he commanded[,] 'What in the h-l did you bring them to me for?'" The soldier understood Hampton to mean that these criminals should not have been captured alive; because they had been brought in, he was now forced to treat them as prisoners of war. "Sherman had no just cause for making any complaint whatever to Gen. Hampton at this time or on any like occasion," the soldier concluded. "I approve your order to that vandal Sherman," agreed Beauregard.[31]

On March 8 Hampton brought together the troopers under his command and made plans for an attack. A captured Union officer had divulged Northern cavalry dispositions around a little settlement just over the North Carolina State line called Monroe's Cross Roads. On the cold, rainy dawn of March 10, Hampton surprised Kilpatrick's camp. There were no pickets, or even a camp guard, so careless had Kilpatrick become. "Hampton set on his horse only a few paces in front of my company," remembered one. "Drawing his sabre from his scabbard he gave the command in ringing tones, 'Attention, draw sabres, charge!' . . . Gen. Hampton was about the first man to enter the camp, and fought as though a private." The Yankees were driven into a swamp, their commander fleeing in his nightshirt. A few hours later the reinforced unionists counterattacked and retook their wagons and guns. Confederates were able to capture some 475 of the enemy, as well as to liberate over 100 of their own men in federal hands. "The cavalry have had some very severe fighting this campaign," admitted one of Kilpatrick's men.[32]

On the morning of March 11, while the Confederate army was crossing the Cape Fear River, Hampton rode into Fayetteville, North Carolina. He was on his way to a hotel hoping to find some breakfast when a column of Yankee cavalry surprised him and the few men with him. Federals were threatening to cut off the Confederate rear guard.

"General, there are not over ten or fifteen Yankees here," said Hugh Scott. "Give me four or five men, and I will whip them out of town."

"That boy so inspired me," Hampton recalled later, "that I said, 'You scouts follow me.'"

"Charge them," commanded Hampton.

The Yankees were soon on the run, "up one street and down another," in Scott's words. The attack was so bold that the Federals thought themselves outnumbered. "After we had killed or captured most of this squad we were after, I looked and saw some behind us." He yelled a warning to Hampton.

"Men, sit still and pick them off one by one as they are coming down," instructed the general. They did, and soon it was over. The only Southern casualty was a dead horse. That day in the streets of Fayetteville thirteen Yankees were killed and twelve captured by a Confederate lieutenant general, two staff officers, and five privates. "I saw General Hampton cut down two with his sabre that morning," remembered an admiring Scott.

One of those captured Federals was dressed in Confederate gray, a ruse punishable by death. The young man, presumably a spy, was questioned briefly by Hampton. "I said that I had no time to attend to him," remembered the general, "but that when we crossed the River I would hang him." Placed in the custody of a regiment of junior reserves, the man in gray soon escaped.[33]

Johnston could only guess Sherman's immediate intentions. He placed his infantry in the vicinity of Smithfield, between Raleigh and Goldsboro. Wheeler's cavalry guarded the road to Raleigh while Butler covered the route to Goldsboro. On March 15 Wheeler was pushed back. Hampton informed the commanding general that Sherman's objective was Goldsboro, and Johnston determined to stop him near a village called Bentonville. He hoped to defeat one wing of the Federal army at a time. Hampton had Butler's troopers dig entrenchments south of town in order to buy time for Hardee's men to arrive. Johnston had come to rely on Hampton's good judgement, and left the planning of the battle largely up to his cavalry commander. Skirmishing began on the morning of March 18, but by afternoon Hampton's outnumbered force fell back. Hampton remembered,

> It was vitally important that this position should be held by us during the night, so I dismounted all of my men, placing them along the edge of the woods, and at great risk of losing my guns I put my artillery some distance to the right of the road, where, though exposed, it had a commanding position.

"Old Hampton is playing a bluff game," laughed a private, "and if he don't mind Sherman will call him."

The bluff worked for a time. After "a rather feeble demonstration," the enemy withdrew for the night. The next day the battle was renewed, and Confederates were pushed back. Johnston counterattacked, but made little progress. Each side held its ground, as Sherman brought up more troops. Led by Hampton's cavalry and a few hundred Georgians, Johnston parried a flanking maneuver to his left on March 21. Still, the plan had failed. Johnston was now outnumbered more than 3–1. Two days later Maj. Gen. John M. Schofield would link up with Sherman, bringing the federal army's strength to 90,000. "Sherman's course cannot be hindered by the small force I have," Johnston telegraphed to Lee. "I can do no more than annoy him."[34]

Hampton told his sister on March 22,

> I have not been able to write to you for a long time, for I have been on the 'go' all the time, & we have had hard work with some hard fighting. We have injured Sherman a good deal so that he cannot boast of getting through free. I have captured almost 2000 of his rascals & killed many others. It has been a great distress to me hearing that Millwood was burned. It distressed me more than the loss of my own house. We must not worry at these things if God will only spare us all and give us peace.[35]

It may have been at Wigfall's instigation that the Confederate Senate on March 9 passed a resolution of thanks to Hampton. The House of Representatives approved the joint resolution the same day, without referral to committee. It was signed by the president four days later.[36]

On the last day of March, Hampton wrote again to Mary Fisher. He had just turned forty-seven.

> You must not worry & fret about me, for it grieves me greatly to think of you doing so. Your faith should be strong enough to make you *know* that God orders all things for the best. I am in his keeping & you should be quite content to trust me there. I hope & believe that He will keep me for those who are so dear to me & whose prayers go up so constantly for me. But I am sure that whatever happens, is wisely ordered. Let this hope sustain you: place your confidence in God, & having asked Him to answer your prayers, leave the issue to Him.[37]

On April 5 the men of Johnston's army heard that their government had fled Richmond three days earlier. On April 1, Grant overwhelmed Confederate defenders at Five Forks, Virginia, forcing Lee to abandon the Petersburg and Richmond lines. Lee wanted to transport his army by rail to Danville, there to unite with Johnston, but Grant moved too quickly. The railroad was cut. Lee lost a quarter of his starving, exhausted men in battle at Saylor's Creek. Retreating westward, he was trapped at Appomattox. There was no way out. On the afternoon of April 9, 1965, he met with Grant in the home of Wilmer McLean and there surrendered the Army of Northern Virginia.

That same day Hampton reported to Johnston that Sherman was preparing to move on Raleigh. At one o'clock on the morning of April 10, a telegram from President Davis in Danville reached Johnston at his camp near Battle's Bridge on the Neuse River. It conveyed the staggering news of Lee's surrender. Three days later Davis met with Generals Johnston and Beauregard and cabinet members in Greensboro. His military leaders told him bluntly that their position was hopeless, that the cause was lost. Davis could not agree, but permitted Johnston to open negotiations for a general cessation of hostilities. With a cavalry escort the president left Greensboro on the morning of April 15, headed to Charlotte. Under orders from Johnston, Hampton the next day sent a message to Kilpatrick arranging for a meeting between their two commanders. At that conference, in the home of farmer James Bennett, Sherman informed Johnston of the Lincoln assassination. They agreed, in general, to the necessity of ending the war. At a second meeting a memorandum was submitted by Sherman. His terms were fair—as were Grant's to Lee—but went further than the first surrender to guarantee the political rights of Southerners and recognize their state governments once they took an oath of loyalty to the United States. Under the proposal all remaining Confederate forces would lay down their arms, not just Johnston's army.[38]

Riding to a parley at the Bennett house, Kilpatrick came up to Hampton and apparently initiated something of a dare. Witnesses saw Kilpatrick's horse attempt to jump a rail fence, only to come down "belly to rail" and struggle over. Hampton, astride his favorite mount Butler, easily cleared the fence. Wade Hampton was in no mood to surrender. A soldier noticed tears in his eyes. He could barely remain civil in the presence of his enemies as they met under a flag of truce. A Northern reporter wrote that Sherman "looked at ease," puffing on a cigar while Johnston was "care-worn," yet dignified. Hampton and Kilpatrick stole the show. The newsman reported,

> Wade Hampton looked savage enough to eat little Kil, with a grain of salt; while the latter returned his looks most defiantly.
>
> It was evident that they would break out. At length Hampton taunted Kil about his recent surprise of his camp.
>
> Kil replied that he had to leave faster than he came, without being able to carry off a color.
>
> Words grew hot—both parties expressing a desire that the issue of the war would be left between their cavalry. The affair was becoming too personal; so Sherman and Johnston had to interfere.
>
> After this the conference went on pleasantly enough.[39]

On April 19 Hampton sat down and wrote a letter to President Davis. "Having seen the terms upon which it is proposed to negotiate, I trust that

I may be pardoned for writing to you in relation to them." The military situation was "very gloomy," Hampton conceded, but "by no means desperate." He had a plan. Men who had left the Army of Northern Virginia before Lee's surrender might yet return to the ranks. If Confederates still under arms on both sides of the Mississippi River could unite, they would form a powerful force. Hampton proposed mounting as large a body of men as possible and taking them across the Mississippi. "When we cross that river we can get large accessions to the cavalry, and we can hold Texas. As soon as forces can be organized and equipped, send this heavy cavalry force into the country of the enemy, and they will soon show that we are not conquered." Davis should go with him. A Confederate army in the field would keep alive the hope of foreign intervention. Surrender was unthinkable. "No suffering which can be inflicted by the passage over our country of the Yankee armies can equal what would fall on us if we return to the Union.

"My own mind is made up as to my course," concluded Hampton. "I shall fight as long as my Government remains in existence; when that ceases to live I shall seek some other country, for I shall never take the 'oath of allegiance.'" His officers shared his feelings. "If you will allow me to do so, I can bring to your support many strong arms and brave hearts—men who will fight to Texas, and who, if forced from that State, will seek refuge in Mexico rather than in the Union.

"All officers and men of the Cavalry Corps of the Army of Northern Virginia, who have escaped capture, and are not now upon parole, are earnestly called upon to join me at once, mounted or dismounted, and strike another blow for the defence of their country." Somehow Hampton had managed to have these handbills printed for distribution on April 20. "Our cause is not desperate, if our men will rally around and cling to the old battle flags which so often have led them to victory."[40]

Andrew Johnson, the new U.S. president, rejected Sherman's plan for a cessation of hostilities. His response was probably what Davis had expected. Johnston would have to surrender his army without a comprehensive political settlement; he must lay down his arms on the same terms accepted by Lee.

On April 22 Hampton wrote again to his president. He repeated arguments against "peace founded on a restoration of the Union." With men "ready to follow me anywhere," his objective was to carry on the struggle from Texas. "If I can serve you or my country by any further fighting you have only to tell me so."

"Wish to see you as soon as convenient," replied Davis from Charlotte, "will then confer."[41]

Hampton met Davis in Charlotte. General Wheeler was there too. The president agreed to Hampton's plan, giving him

a letter authorizing me to join him with all the men who were willing to accompany us. . . . Having the authority of the President to carry out the plans which had been agreed on, I returned to Hillsborough, arriving there at 11 o'clock P.M. on the 26th April, and I found that the army had surrendered.

Hampton immediately wrote to Johnston, pointing out that he had been absent during the final round of surrender talks. Hampton also said that he had been ordered by Breckinridge on April 25 to meet an enemy threat across the state line in South Carolina, "and I was carrying out this order when I was notified of your surrender." Because of this, Hampton did not consider himself part of the agreement. He would, however, abide by the decision of the secretary of war on the matter.[42] Hampton was groping for some way to extricate himself from the surrender, without letting Johnston know the true reason.

Many of Hampton's troopers, and one battery of artillery, had already galloped off to join Davis and continue the fight for independence. Wheeler was putting together a similar force of about 600, "men who would be willing to stand by Jefferson Davis to the death." Johnston was furious. "You must obey my orders, unless you have contrary orders from higher authority," he wired. Wheeler apparently never received the message and continued on his way. Johnston ordered Hampton to return with his men. At nine-forty-five on the evening of April 27, Hampton replied. He finally explained his agreement with the president, but led Johnston to believe that his mission was to allow Davis merely "to leave the country," not continue the war. Since he and his command were included in the surrender, "I shall not ask a man to go with me," wrote Hampton. He had given President Davis his own word, however. "If I do not accompany him I shall never cease to reproach myself, and if I go with him I may go under the ban of outlawry. I choose the latter, because I believe it to be my duty to do so." He would not order his surrendered command to follow him. "Should any join me, they will be stragglers like myself and, like myself, willing to sacrifice everything for the cause and for our Government."

Hampton left at midnight, after dispatching a courier to overtake his men. He was having second thoughts about suggesting that any follow his lead in violating the surrender. At sunrise he caught up with them on the road to Greensboro. With tears streaming down his face, Hampton removed his hat and broke the news that they had been included in Johnston's capitulation. "There is a day coming when we will all meet and fight again," he concluded. "It was a sad occasion for all of us," remembered a trooper, "but we felt a thrill of pride in our fearless general." Hampton let them believe that he was himself "acting under the orders of President Davis, and was therefore free to join him." The general's staff and an escort—about thirty men—would go on. "After a most painful interview, which brought tears, not only from the eyes of many of these true soldiers, whom it had been my pride to command, and with my little escort we pushed on towards Charlotte, where I hoped to meet President Davis."

The chief executive was gone, headed for Yorkville, South Carolina. Hampton left his escort in Charlotte with instructions to follow in the morning. He then mounted a fresh horse and rode through the night, swimming the Catawba River and reaching Yorkville in the early morning hours of May 2. Davis had gone on to Abbeville, but Hampton found wife Mary waiting for him in Yorkville, relieved that he was safe. Wheeler was there, too, and met him in the morning, "shocked at the broken appearance of my fellow officer. He was harassed in mind, and worn in body." Mary Hampton, Wheeler remembered, "insisted that in his condition, worn as he was by arduous service, he ought not to attempt to overtake Mr. Davis. I fully concurred in this."

He "finally yielded," said Wheeler. Hampton was emotionally drained and physically exhausted. Still, he handed Wheeler a letter addressed to Davis. "My own movements will depend on your orders & wishes," Hampton wrote. "It will give me great pleasure to assist you if I can do so & you may rest assured that I shall stick to our flag as long as any one can be found to uphold it." Later in the day Hampton's staff arrived from Charlotte. Two couriers were dispatched by Hampton bearing the same message for Davis.[43]

The president would finally be captured by federal cavalry on May 10 near Irwinville, Georgia. Wheeler himself was also made a prisoner.

The war was over, but Hampton found himself unable to accept defeat. Nor did he consider himself part of the surrender. "Nothing can be done at present," he wrote to a fellow officer on May 10, "either here, or elsewhere, so I advise quiet for a time. If opportunity offers, later, we can avail ourselves of it. If I determine on any course you shall hear from me."[44]

11

"I Am Not Reconstructed Yet"

Surrender Brings No Peace

April's flowering dogwood boughs shimmered in the Carolina forest, promising an end to the threat of frost. By early May roses bloomed again, then lemon-scented magnolias. So welcome, so familiar. Yet the season was unique in the memory of Southerners who experienced it— this final, fifth Confederate spring. Four years earlier Wade Hampton had raced across the state organizing his Legion. Twelve months later he had commanded an infantry brigade on the Virginia peninsula. In the spring of 1863 Confederate cavalry had prepared for their great invasion of the North. A year later the general had come home to South Carolina for reinforcements—he and his troopers feted by the citizens of Columbia. Hampton had never allowed himself to confront the possibility of defeat. There seemed always a way to overcome the odds, grasp a victory, buy more time. Lee permitted his cavalry commander to come south on the condition that he return in time for the 1865 spring campaign. Now the end had come. All the major Southern armies were disbanded, the Confederate government was swept away, President Davis was in custody, and much of South Carolina was in ruins. From the Palmetto State alone, 71,000 men had marched off to war. One in five never returned.[1]

Mary Hampton, the children, and Wade's sisters probably remained in Yorkville during May as the general returned to Columbia. Still unsurrendered, many looked to Hampton for leadership. The word went around that survivors from the cavalry would report for duty on May 20. "A little farce," scoffed Mary Chesnut, "to let themselves down easily. They know it is all over." Hampton was in Camden on May 10, and there met Mrs. Chesnut. "I quietly take up Gnl. Hampton's tone—& 'wish they were *all* dead—all Yankees.'"[2]

On the evening of May 3, South Carolina governor Andrew Magrath returned to Columbia from Greenville, ordering state officials to resume their duties. The old State House in ashes, the new structure but a shell, South Carolina had no capitol. Maj. Gen. Mansfield Lovell, the last Confederate commander in South Carolina, advised the governor that he was powerless to provide protection. William Gilmore Simms wondered if indeed South Carolina was still a state or had fallen to territorial status. The editor of the Columbia *Daily Phoenix* contended that the people accepted defeat, and there was, therefore, no need for federal troops to garrison Columbia. "We have neither arms nor munitions of war. No banner of the Confederacy now flouts the sky. No commander calls upon troops either to flight or fight." No matter. A detachment of Union soldiers arrived in Columbia on May 25 and promptly arrested the governor. A large crowd stood by helplessly. "There is now no other authority here," concluded the *Phoenix*, "than a military authority."[3]

On May 21 Mary Chesnut heard that Wade Hampton had agreed to be paroled. He may have met the Union contingent in Columbia and there signed the agreement not to bear arms against the United States until formally exchanged. "General Hampton is home again," a friend informed Mrs. Chesnut. "He looks crushed. How can he be otherwise? His beautiful home is in ruins, and ever present with him must be the memory of the death . . . of his glorious boy, Preston!"[4]

A Yankee traveling to Columbia wrote that "in no other city that I have visited has hostility seemed to me so bitter." Devastation was everywhere. "No South-Carolinian with whom I have spoken hesitates an instant in declaring that it was the most beautiful city on the continent," said another visitor, and "they charge its destruction directly to General Sherman." Columbia "is now a wilderness of ruins," he continued. "Its heart is but a mass of blackened chimneys and crumbling walls. Two thirds of the buildings in the place were burned, including, without exception, everything in the business portion." Many residences escaped the flames, as did the campus of South Carolina College. The rest of Columbia was a "town of chimneys—nothing else standing," wrote a shocked James Conner. "Such a sight I have never seen." One Northerner reported that "on the Congaree, just out of Columbia, there remained, for six weeks, a pile of sixty-five dead horses and mules, shot by Sherman's men. It was impossible to bury them, all the shovels, spades, and other farming implements of the kind having been carried off or destroyed."[5]

The Hampton family returned during the summer to take up residence in a rented house in an unburned Columbia neighborhood. Christopher Hampton started building a home for his sisters about one mile from the ruins of Millwood. Kit Hampton was a forty-five-year-old widower with one daughter. He took care of his sisters during the war, serving also as an aide to the governor. Wade Hampton began construction of a modest home he would call "the cottage" on his own property. A friend would christen it "Southern Cross" because of its eventual configuration. Mary Hampton called it "Sand Hills." Both new homes would take months to complete. For part of the summer, the family retreated to the cool and quiet of Cashiers, North Carolina.[6]

On June 24 Hampton's twenty-year-old daughter, Sally, wed twenty-two-year-old John Cheves Haskell. A grandson of Langdon Cheves, young Haskell had risen to the rank of lieutenant colonel in the artillery. He lost his right arm in Confederate service. The wedding was held at Trinity Episcopal Church with the Reverand Shand presiding, the church on the very edge of the ruins of downtown Columbia. The couple would make their new home in Mississippi.[7]

Some defeated Confederates began to consider a permanent escape from despair and federal despotism. Defiant to the end, men like Maj. Gen. John Bankhead Magruder and naval specialist Matthew Fontaine Maury fled to Mexico. Others chose to make a new home in Brazil. A flurry of postwar books and articles recommended immigration by ex-Confederates. Columbia surgeon J. M. Gaston, encouraged by Brazilian authorities, would make an extended tour of that country. "We find people in Brazil capable of appreciating the Southern character," concluded Dr. Gaston, "and ready to extend a cordial greeting to all who come." He, his wife, and their six children became Brazilians. Perhaps as many as 20,000 from across the South made the same decision. The city of Americana was one of their principal settlements. "Certain Amazon Indian tribes decorate their pottery with the Confederate flag," wrote a descendant of Southern immigrants, "the result of having encountered the colonists who chose to settle in that vast jungle." Called *Confederados,* those immigrants would steadfastly cling to their Southern roots, "Lee" and "Hampton" being the most popular names given their Brazilian-born children.[8]

Whether Wade Hampton seriously considered emigration for himself or was simply asked by others for guidance, he did make inquiries. A correspondent in New York contacted the Brazilian consul general, who reported to Hampton. It was found that no land grants were available, but public land would be sold on credit to Southern immigrants, and their agricultural implements would be admitted free of duty. Slavery still existed in Brazil, but "slaves are very dear and holders will not sell," cautioned the diplomat.[9]

From the pages of the *Daily Phoenix* on July 27, 1865, Wade Hampton responded to those who had asked for his opinion. "The desire to leave a country which has been reduced to such a deplorable condition as ours, and whose future has so little of hope, is doubtless as widespread as it is natural." Still, he firmly rejected immigration as an option for himself and hoped others would follow his lead. "The very fact that our State is passing through so terrible an ordeal as the present, should cause her sons to cling the more closely to her." Rebuilding their homes and cities, educating their youth, restoring law, and maintaining order must be their immediate goals. From the depths of defeat only weeks earlier, Hampton's views had evolved rapidly. He was adapting to the new situation. Hope was returning. "To accomplish these objects," he continued, "I recommend that all who can do so should take the oath of allegiance to the United States Government." It was a matter of expediency, a recognition of the new order of things. "War, after four years of heroic but unsuccessful struggle, has failed to secure for us the rights for which we engaged in it. To save *any* of our rights—to rescue anything more from the general ruin—will require all the statesmanship and all the patriotism of our citizens." For ex-Confederates to refuse to take the oath would leave the state to those few who "forsook" South Carolina in "her hour of need." Patriots must now devote themselves "to the rescue of whatever liberty may be saved from the general wreck." Should they fail, "we can then seek a home in another country." Because of the obligations he felt to his state and to his family, he could not "leave the country *at present*," but would continue to gather information on establishing a Brazilian colony, should it come to that. "I invoke my fellow citizens—especially those who have shared with me the perils and the glories of the last four years—to stand by our State manfully and truly."

Within a week Hampton took his own advice by signing an application for amnesty. "I have only to add," he wrote to President Johnson, "that I make this application from a sense of duty & that it is my purpose, if it is acceded to, to devote myself honestly and zealously to the restoration of law & order in my state & to the interests of my country." South Carolina's provisional governor, appointed by the president on June 30, was Benjamin F. Perry. Perry endorsed Hampton's application, informing Johnson that the former general was advising friends to "become loyal citizens and remain in their country. I know likewise that he has determined to pursue that course himself and his example will have good influence in determining the course of others." The governor added, in conclusion, that "General Hampton was no agitator of the Rebellion."[10]

Perry was a man South Carolinians trusted. Although opposed to secession in 1860, he remained loyal to his state and became a firm supporter of the Confederate cause. In the summer of 1865, he was perhaps the most prominent man in South Carolina with "unionist" credentials. "It was with the greatest satisfaction that I saw your appointment as Governor," Hampton wrote to Perry in late July, "& I hail it as the only gleam of sunshine which has fallen on the state since this black cloud has spread over our horizon." Perry was charged with convening a convention to draft a new state constitution and take the steps mandated by Washington to return South Carolina to the Union. Hampton, in his July 27 letter in the *Phoenix*, referred to his old friend Perry as "an honest man and a true patriot." Hampton urged that voters select for the constitutional convention men "who laid *their all* upon the altar of their country."[11]

Over the objection of congressional Republicans, Johnson set out to bring the defeated South back into the Union with the least possible delay. His plan required that former Confederate states repudiate secession, ban slavery, and refuse to pay debts incurred during the war. Upon taking an oath to "faithfully support, protect, and defend the Constitution of the United States and the Union of the States thereunder," amnesty would be granted to ex-Confederates. Fourteen classes of individuals were not eligible. Hampton was disqualified on two counts—he had been a Confederate general officer and he was a "Rebel" with more than $20,000 in taxable property. Still, those excluded by the provisions of the general amnesty could make "special application."[12]

South Carolinians had operated for seventy-four years under the constitution adopted in 1790. Reflecting the views of the founding generation, it was a conservative document requiring that office holders be property owners, and apportioning seats in the legislature was based on both white population and on the amount of taxes paid. Authority was concentrated in the general assembly. The governor was elected by those lawmakers and had few powers. Because of the importance of their calling, clergymen were not eligible to serve in any political office.[13] The constitution of 1790 was carefully designed to protect property rights, establishing a strictly republican form of government. Its framers understood that the unrestrained will of the majority—democracy—could be as tyrannical as rule by a despot. These ancient values were in decline in postwar America, and few expected that anything like the old state constitution would be allowed to survive in South Carolina.

Wade Hampton was willing to acknowledge Confederate defeat, but he would dispute the victorious North every step of the way as they attempted to impose their values on his people. He insisted that Southern states must have the same status, and the same authority over their own affairs, as Northern states. He expressed these views privately in an August 20 letter to James G. Gibbes, the mayor of Columbia. As a tactical matter Hampton questioned the wisdom of even convening a constitutional convention. "Is it desirable that the people of the state should take *any* action looking to a restoration of civil government at present? I think not." He reasoned that South Carolina must either be a state, a territory, or a conquered province. If a state, "she has the right to administer her government under such a constitution and by such laws as she chooses." If she is a territory or a conquered province, it is the duty of the United States to provide "a proper government." The best policy "is to remain passive until such government is given to her, or is forced upon her."

He believed that in the current state of affairs, delegates elected to a constituent assembly would not truly reflect the will of South Carolina. The only kind of constitution acceptable to Washington that they could produce would be one "representing *not* the views and interests of the people of S.C., but those of Mass." He was unwilling to adopt a fundamental law that would "ignore all the teachings of the past . . . subvert the whole order of society . . . commit political suicide." Rather than attempt to write such a document, rather than come begging for readmittance to the Union, Hampton recommended doing nothing for the time being. Washington "will, doubtless in good time provide a government for you." Let the cartridge box and bayonet of the U.S. Army rule South Carolina. "It is better to be governed by these than to give your State a constitution which misrepresents . . . humiliates . . . debases . . . degrades."[14]

That said, Hampton retreated to his Cashiers mountain home for the remainder of the summer. On September 11 he heard that he had been elected as a delegate from Richland District to the convention that would convene in Columbia in only two days. He had led the voting in a field of nine. As he advocated publicly in July, all four delegates elected from Richland were Confederate veterans. Hampton quickly wrote a letter to the presiding officer, promising "that I shall do myself the honor to take my seat as soon as I can reach Columbia." He never made it. It took his letter two weeks to travel the 150 miles to South Carolina's capital.[15]

The convention met at Columbia's Baptist Church, site of the first meeting of the 1860 secession convention, one of only a few such buildings still standing. The *Daily Phoenix* covered the opening session, reporting that Wade Hampton had been nominated for president of the body. "Gen. Hampton was not present, and we are doubtful, if, considering the embarrassments in the way of communication, he has been yet apprised of his election as a member. His more immediate friends declined the nomination for him." Even with his name withdrawn and himself absent, five delegates voted for him.[16]

A Northern newspaperman noticed that some delegates were clad in homespun clothing. "Many coats show Confederate buttons," he wrote, "from the necessity of poverty rather than the choice of disloyalty, I judge." That reporter, Sidney Andrews of the Boston *Daily Advertiser,* gave his impression of the delegates. "They are subdued Rebels, some of them are even conquered Rebels; but few are anything more."[17] Under the president's plan of reconstruction, former Confederate states were required to declare their acts of secession "null and void." Without debate—and in silence—the

South Carolina convention voted to *repeal* the Ordinance of Secession.[18] There was much wrangling over the wording of the clause in the new constitution that would ban slavery, but it passed overwhelmingly. The constitution that emerged provided for a popularly elected governor and lieutenant governor, and their terms were extended from two to four years. Property qualifications for office holding were dropped. Presidential electors would be chosen by the people, one reform that Hampton had advocated a decade earlier. Delegate James Lawrence Orr, once Speaker of the U.S. House of Representatives and a former Confederate senator, urged his associates to support Johnson. The president's terms were liberal, compared to the vindictive policies demanded by radicals in Congress.

> He is the dike between us and the waves of Northern fanaticism. Let us be wise men. Let us strengthen his hands by graceful and ready acquiescence in the results of the war. So shall we strengthen ourselves, and soon bring again to our loved State the blessings of peace and civil rule.[19]

A few delegates expressed privately their view that educated blacks might at some point be permitted to vote. Most, including Perry and Orr, were opposed. A convention of blacks meeting in Charleston that same month petitioned for "perfect equality before the law," but not for universal suffrage. Their tone was moderate and their goals conservative. "We know the deplorable ignorance of the majority of our people . . . and we ask not at this time that the ignorant shall be admitted to the exercise of a privilege which they might use to the injury of the State." These blacks rejoiced in their release from slavery, but expressed "sorrow that freedom to us and our own race is accompanied by the ruin of thousands of those for whom, notwithstanding the bitterness of the past, and of the present, we cherish feelings of respect and affection."[20]

During the war many Southern blacks stood by their country—the Confederate States. One South Carolina veteran was "impressed at the physical courage" displayed by blacks who accompanied their masters to the front, and by "their apparent loyalty to the cause." These men could have had their freedom "by simply stepping across the line into Yankee soldierdom. Yet we never knew of such an instance." After the war Kit Goodwyn, Wade Hampton's wartime servant, could be found on Saturdays at Trinity churchyard "dusting and cleaning the tombs of former army friends, playmates, and young masters." The Boston newspaperman who covered the 1865 convention wrote,

> [That] there are many kind-hearted planters—men who made slavery in very truth a sort of patriarchal institution, and who are now endeavoring in all sincerity and earnestness to make the negro's situation not only tolerable,

but comfortable—is as true as it is that there are many negroes who cling to the old places and the old customs, and are doing their work just as faithfully and unselfishly as ever. These men, on either side, are, I am convinced, the exceptions.[21]

With the coming of emancipation, thousands of former slaves moved around, seeming to enjoy the very novelty of being able to. Towns and cities began to grow as they came in from the country and congregated there. The black death rate increased alarmingly. Many, particularly older blacks, assumed that their former masters would continue to take care of them—with no work required on their part. Others refused to labor, expecting to be given land of their own. With a shortage of laborers, crops failed or were never planted. Theft increased and was often excused, even by black preachers.[22] "On two points they [the freedmen] have very lax notions," complained a white observer, "the sacred obligations of the marriage relation and the sanctity of an oath." Whites told of problems created by blacks in uniform. These troops regularly harassed whites, verbally abusing and pushing them off sidewalks. To avoid trouble many whites simply remained at home. Black soldiers were criticized too for encouraging fellow freedmen to avoid work. "The presence of black troops . . . demoralizes labor, both by their advice and by furnishing in their camps a resort," said General Grant after a tour of the South. The freedman, concluded Grant, "seems to be imbued with the idea that the property of his late master should, by right, belong to him, or at least should have no protection from the colored soldier."[23]

Deeply resented by Southern whites was the Freedmen's Bureau, an agency most thought meddlesome and corrupt. Established in March 1865 and funded by the War Department, the bureau distributed food, clothing, and fuel to the needy, and provided some medical care. Bureau agents were charged with overseeing "all subjects" that might concern newly freed slaves. Often agents confessed to being overwhelmed with the trivial disputes and complaints brought to them. The bureau became responsible for negotiating and enforcing labor contracts between planters and black workers. A fee was paid by the planter for each contract signed, charges that increased dramatically during 1865. Brig. Gen. Robert Scott threatened to seize the land and crops of planters he suspected of unjustly dismissing workers. In June 1866 Scott reported "theft, drunkeness, and vagrancy" among freedmen under his charge. His response was to issue orders that any black breaking a labor contract would be arrested and put to work on the public roads. The following month freedmen in Charleston were informed by federal authorities that idleness would not be tolerated. Those forced to work would see their children given "to such persons as will take care of them and learn them the habits of industry." An "island prison" was to be set up, where the recalcitrant would be forced to labor from "sunrise to sunset." These threatening orders were read in black churches and published in the newspapers.[24]

Dishonesty was rife within the bureau. It was revealed, for example, that Brig. Gen. Ralph Ely—in charge of a five-county district headquartered in Columbia—had neglected his duties. He simply did not have time, as he was renting five plantations, making agreements with his black sharecroppers, and issuing them government rations. Maj. Gen. Oliver Howard, head of the bureau, would be investigated on a number of charges having to do with mismanagement of government funds. The most shameful episode involved the Freedmen's Savings and Trust Company, a nongovernmental institution operated by Freedmen's Bureau officials. Thousands of poor blacks who struggled to accumulate some savings lost their deposits. Frederick Douglass became president, but resigned in disgust at the company's dishonesty and waste.[25]

Hampton was back in Columbia by early October 1865. A notice soon appeared in the *Phoenix* inviting men to meet, "in accordance with the call of Gov. Perry," to reorganize the militia. The advertisement was signed by Hampton, Mayor James G. Gibbes, and five others. On the morning of October 11, they met in a room over the store belonging to Gibbes. Hampton spoke, reported the *Phoenix,* "urging the policy of organization of military companies, to repress disorder and insure tranquility." There were to be four companies formed in Richland—two of infantry in the city and two cavalry companies for rural neighborhoods. Hampton encouraged those interested to enroll at one of two designated Columbia places of business. "Upwards of one hundred volunteers have already come forward," he reported.[26]

Another institution close to Hampton's heart was his alma mater. With students flocking to the army, South Carolina College shut its doors in 1862. The buildings were used as a hospital during the war and came close to destruction by Sherman's incendiaries. Faithful Union guards, and the tall brick wall surrounding the school, kept arsonists at bay. Homeless families later replaced hospital patients in the dormitory rooms. The state House of Representatives and Senate met for a time on campus. Governor Perry made reopening the school by the first of the new year one of his goals. Hampton continued a family tradition with his election to the board of trustees. He began attending meetings in November. The board wanted the college to reemerge as the University of South Carolina.[27]

Hampton had feared that in reestablishing state government in 1865, South Carolinians would feel pressured to cast aside their own unique character and ancient traditions. These thoughts were expressed privately, but explain his reluctance to become involved in the 1865 convention. The constitution they wrote was probably better than what he expected. His reentry into public life as organizer of the local militia and as university trustee evidence a certain optimism. The people continued to look to him for leadership.

In September convention delegates had urged Orr to run for governor under the new constitution. "He is pre-eminently the leader of the progressives," said the Boston reporter covering the meeting. "That he will be elected I do not doubt. A few men are advising that Wade Hampton be also brought into the field. He has many warm personal friends, and is popular with the masses, but I think the people will not elect him, even if he is a candidate." For South Carolina to choose a man of Hampton's conservative reputation and Confederate record might well encourage a backlash in the North. Hampton refused to be a candidate. He had a family to support and must somehow make his plantations productive again. He understood, too, the repercussions his election would have. On October 13 he ran a notice in the *Daily Phoenix*.

> Several nominations of Gen. Wade Hampton, for the office of Governor, having been made in the Charleston and other papers of the State, we are authorized to state that, for various reasons, he cannot consent to be a candidate for the office. Highly appreciating the confidence of his fellow citizens throughout the State, it is proper to make this announcement, to prevent embarrassment to his friends and those who are disposed to vote for him for Governor.[28]

Many still considered him the best man for the office, and it began to appear possible that even without running, he would garner more votes than the uninspiring Orr. Governor Perry thought it wise to inform the president so as to soften the shock of a Hampton victory. Hampton was an "admirable" man, insisted Perry, "honorable, frank and open-hearted," and a supporter of Johnson's plan of reconstruction. Few voters turned out for South Carolina's first popular election of a chief executive. Orr was announced the winner by fewer than 700 votes. Many contended that Hampton actually won, but enough ballots were discarded to insure victory for the candidate acceptable to the North. "It is the general impression that General Wade Hampton was elected by a considerable majority. I have heard that fact asserted positively," said Brig. Gen. Rufus Saxton, a Freedmen's Bureau official. Martin W. Gary confided later that Orr himself told him that Hampton won. "The rebels almost forced Wade Hampton into the gubernatorial chair," claimed the New York *Tribune,* "merely because such action would be a defiance to the President."[29]

Two weeks after the election, Hampton explained in the pages of the *Phoenix* his reasons for bowing out. He felt a "profound sense of honor" in the vote given him, but had declined to run because the convention had endorsed Orr, and he had no desire to contest their decision. He recognized, too, that his election might undermine the president's efforts to resist the radicals. Hampton's own long-neglected plantations demanded his time. He had by now abandoned any notion of South Carolinians remaining passive, however.

Every association of the past, every duty of the present, every hope of the future, bid us still to stand "shoulder to shoulder." The work before us demands all the patriotism, all the courage, all the endurance of our whole people. Let no party strife, no minor issues, no petty politics, divert us from the great and pressing work of the hour. That of reanimating, as far as possible, our prostrate and bleeding State.

He saw hope amid the ruins of the Confederacy.

That barque, which was launched a few years ago, amid such joyous acclamations, which was freighted with such precious hopes, and which was wafted on by such earnest prayers, has suffered shipwreck. It behooves us, as wise men, to build of its broken timbers, as best we may, a raft, whenever we may hope to reach a haven of rest and safety.

"Above all, let us stand by our State," Hampton said in conclusion. "Here we have worshipped the God of our father's; here amid charred and blackened ruins, are the spots we once fondly called our homes; and here we buried the ashes of our kindred. All these sacred ties bind us." The votes he had received Hampton understood as an expression of confidence.

This I shall cherish as one of the proudest recollections of my life, for it assures me of your belief that I have tried to do my duty. It only remains for me, in bidding you farewell, to say that whenever the State needs my services she has only to command and I shall obey.[30]

On November 22 Hampton spoke to blacks and whites gathered at Richland Fork. He had advice for both races. Their world had changed, but life had to go on. "Our fields must be tilled. Unless this is done speedily, famine will destroy what little has escaped fire and the sword." White landowners could secure a reliable labor force "by dealing with the negro fairly, frankly and equitably. Let him see that we not only recognize his newly acquired rights, but that we will protect him in the enjoyment of those rights." Hampton spoke plainly to blacks in the audience.

You are free—free to seek your own happiness—free to do the best you can for yourselves—free to work, and *free to starve if you do not work*. Freedom has its duties as well as its pleasures. And the first duty of every free man is to support himself and his family.

Most of his former hands were staying with him to work for wages, and Hampton urged "all of you, who have good masters, to stay where you are. Be orderly, quiet, attentive and industrious, and you will do well. The law will protect your rights, and you will then find your best friends in us."

On the way to his Mississippi plantations, Hampton stopped in Montgomery, Alabama, on December 11. The legislature was in session, and Hampton was invited to address the lawmakers. In the building that had served as the Confederacy's first capitol, Hampton made a few remarks on Alabama's gallant record in the war. He was given an enthusiastic welcome, an ovation that some in the North viewed with jaundiced eye.[31]

Wade Hampton wrote to Mary Fisher from Mississippi in January 1866. He complained of mail delivery less reliable than it had been even during the war. He planned to have wife Mary make the journey from Columbia accompanied by Wade Jr. and suggested that Mary Fisher come too. "The negroes all seem delighted to see me," he reported. "There are a good many here, who have relations in S.C., and they are very anxious that they should come out." Hampton promised to pay the way for all who wished to make the move. He needed one hundred additional farm hands, and son Wade wanted fifty more. Hampton reported success in hiring his former slaves. "Did you tell Tom Taylor to engage for me all the negroes who wanted to come out? . . . Mine are doing well & I hope to make something this year, if the Yankees do not interfere with me."[32]

The editor of the *Phoenix* mentioned Hampton's success in contracting black laborers.

> We see it stated that every able-bodied negro, who was once Wade Hampton's slave, is now hired by him; men at $10 per month and women at $8, without board. He expects to raise 300 bales of cotton this season—and means to give free negro labor a fair trial.

For most planters the labor problem would be solved only with the adoption of sharecropping. Under that arrangement tenant families would work a parcel of land with seed, equipment, animals, and shelter supplied by the owner—and receive a share of the crop at harvest. This freed the land owner from many responsibilities and, most importantly, gave the tenant a powerful motive for working.[33]

Most planters quickly found the old "gang system" a failure. The freedmen too often neglected their contracts and disliked working under white supervision. "The planters generally entertain but little faith in their ability to make a crop next year under the present system of labor," wrote one South Carolinian in the fall of 1865. "But something must be done to enforce and secure regular, systematic, and reliable labor, or this country will become a wilderness." South Carolina and other Southern states would soon pass laws that came to be known as the "Black Codes." Freedmen were forbidden to leave their employers without good cause. Other provisions limited their right to testify in court or assemble in public. Although the laws guaranteed blacks some rights, the provisions looked like a rewrite of antebellum slave

Hampton thought this photograph of himself in New Orleans during the winter of 1865–1866 "frightful." His family considered it a good likeness. *Manly Wade Wellman, Giant in Gray (New York: Charles Scribner's Sons, 1949)*.

codes. Penalties for violating labor contracts seemed less draconian than some punishments threatened by those in charge of the Freedmen's Bureau; still, the Black Codes caused a furor in the North and gave ammunition to radicals in Congress. At Governor Orr's insistence, almost all such provisions of the South Carolina code were repealed in 1866, but the damage had been done.[34]

White South Carolinians feared losing control of their state government to the black majority should congressional radicals triumph. The U.S. Supreme Court had, less than a decade earlier, ruled that blacks could not become citizens. They were, wrote Chief Justice Roger Taney, "regarded as beings of an inferior order; and altogether unfit to associate with the white race, either in social or political relations; and so far inferior that they had no rights which the white man was bound to respect." When South Carolina's provisional governor Benjamin Perry reminded Congressional radicals that "this is a white man's government, and intended for white men only," he was expressing a truism of American life up to that point. "The African has been, in all ages, a savage or a slave," said Perry. "God created him inferior to the white man in form, color, and intellect, and no legislation or culture can make him his equal." According to Boston newspaperman Sidney Andrews, to think that Southerners might "voluntarily grant the ballot to the negro during this generation seems to me to qualify yourself for the insane asylum."[35]

Andrews, an abolitionist and critic of the white South, found himself expressing views uncharacteristic of a Massachusetts Republican.

> The negro is no model of virtue or manliness. He loves idleness, he has little conception of right or wrong, and he is improvident to the last degree of childishness. He is a creature—as some of our own people will do well to keep carefully in mind—he is a creature just forcibly released from slavery. The havoc of war has filled his heart with confused longings, and his ears with confused sounds of rights and privileges: it must be the nation's duty, for it cannot be left wholly to his late master, to help him to a clear understanding of those rights and privileges, and also to lay upon him a knowledge of his responsibilities.[36]

When the war ended there were but five states—all in New England and all having minuscule black populations—that permitted equal voting rights. Minnesota, Wisconsin, Connecticut, Ohio, and Kansas each rejected black suffrage when that issue was raised after the war. An 1865 referendum in the District of Columbia found 35 voters willing to allow freedmen the right to vote, and 6,951 opposed. "You complain of the disfranchisement of the negro in the southern States," said President Johnson to a Cleveland audience, "while you would not give them the right of suffrage in Ohio today." Johnson recommended that Southern blacks be allowed to vote only when they could read and write and owned property. He thought it ironic that "intelligent, worthy, patriotic foreigners" seeking to become citizens had to spend time becoming familiar with American laws and institutions, then prove their fitness, while radicals demanded that all the rights of citizenship be bestowed immediately on former slaves.[37]

One Freedmen's Bureau official declared that blacks "must be allowed their civil rights: to sue and be sued and to testify in courts, but nineteen in twenty are no more fit for the political responsibilities and duties of a citizen than my horse." Regimental chaplain of the 128th U.S. Colored Troops, stationed in Beaufort, South Carolina, stated that "the more intelligent" of his men believed there should be a literacy qualification for voting, as "you ought never to undertake a job unless you know *how* to do it." The editor of the *Phoenix* thought it strange that many Northerners considered blacks incompetent to make their own labor contracts, yet insisted that they were qualified to become voters. Black voting rights had nothing to do with "justice and humanity," confessed Maryland Republican Henry Winter Davis. Black votes were needed to overcome "the power of those who rebelled. . . . It is a question of power, not of right."[38]

Robert E. Lee saw what was happening and lent his voice to those opposed to unrestricted black suffrage. The general said,

> But this opposition springs from no feeling of enmity, but from a deep-seated conviction that, at present, the negroes have neither the intelligence nor the other qualifications which are necessary to make them safe depositories of political power. They would inevitably become the victims of demagogues, who, for selfish purposes, would mislead them to the serious injury of the public.[39]

If Republicans were to open up the vote to Southern freedmen, they would add to their majorities in both houses of Congress. If not, Southern delegations returning to Washington would be largely Democratic and opposed to Republican tariffs and railroad subsidies. Lawmakers, not the president, must superintend Reconstruction, declared Congress's joint committee on the subject. Having been vanquished, "rebels were at the mercy of the conquerors;" Southern states "disorganized communities, without civil government, and without constitutions." Senator Charles Sumner held that in seceding, Southern states had "committed suicide," reverting to territorial status, and were thus under the control of Congress. Sumner even proposed that the federal government seize—without compensation to property owners—400 million acres in the South. Each adult freedman would be given forty acres; the remainder would be auctioned to retire the Northern war debt.[40] It never came to pass. But neither did the U.S. government make an effort to encourage the independence of ex-slaves by purchasing land for them to farm. Critics noted that over a ten-year period, from 1862 to 1872, the government loaned tens of millions of tax dollars and awarded one-hundred million acres of western lands to railroad corporations. Republican congressmen seemed far more interested in securing black votes than they did in helping freedmen get on their feet. To give the vote without giving land, said the black intellectual W. E. B. DuBois, was to end "a civil war by beginning a race feud."[41]

Georgia humorist Bill Arp summed up the feelings of Southern whites in early 1866. "If they [the radicals] be for peace, it must be the peace that passeth all understandin, for we can't fathom it in these regions."[42]

During March 1866 Wade Hampton continued to be preoccupied with his Wild Woods, Mississippi, property and his family. Receiving word that Mary had taken ill as she traveled from South Carolina, Hampton went to Montgomery. By mid-month the family was finally reunited in New Orleans. "Mary stood the journey well and has improved much," he reported to Mary Fisher. "McDuffie is quite well and he takes possession of everybody and every place. I scarcely ever see him here, as he is on the rampage all the time." Hampton continued to enjoy outdoor sports. "In my last three hunts we have killed 5 bears, one panther, and one wild turkey," he reported to his sister. "McDuffie goes out hunting with me sometimes." They were delighted to meet Varina Davis and other Confederate friends in New Orleans. Late that summer, when the imprisoned Jefferson Davis was finally permitted visitors at his cell in Fort Monroe, Virginia, Hampton was among those who rushed to see the former president. Varina Davis remembered that friends "came to dinner in the casemate, and chairs being scarce, they sat on candle-boxes, and talked of their and our past, and toasted in silence the glorious dead and less happy living heroes."[43]

On May 25 Hampton wrote to John Parsons Carroll, chairman of a Columbia committee gathering facts on the burning of the city. "The charge of that scoundrel Sherman, that I burned the city . . . makes me very solicitous that the truth should be clearly set forth. My reputation is the only thing, that I have left, and I am jealous of its preservation." Hampton recommended the names of a number of people who might testify. "The *very first order* I gave, was that the cotton which had been placed in the streets by order of Genl. Beauregard, *should not be burned*."[44] The committee would have no difficulty in finding witnesses to the fact that the arsonists wore uniforms of blue.

"I may have to go home by Washington, or perhaps N.Y. to attend to some business," Hampton confided to Mary Fisher a few weeks before his departure. "If I do I suppose the Yankees will abuse me considerably." His reason for traveling to New York was probably to confer with John Mullaly. Editor of the *Metropolitan Record and New York Vindicator,* the Irish Catholic Mullaly had long been sympathetic to the South. The *Record* described

itself as "a Democratic paper" and "a truthful and unswerving exponent of
State Rights." During the war Mullaly had been jailed for opposing the draft
and his paper forced to close down.[45] Now, in the summer of 1866, Hampton
prepared to publish in Mullaly's *Record* an open letter to President Andrew
Johnson.

That letter appeared in the issue of August 25—to coincide with a presidential visit to New York City—and it was also published as a broadside. In
it Hampton began by thanking the president. "But for you the South would
have found in peace far greater horrors than she encountered during war."
The fact that representatives from the South were still kept out of Congress
was not the president's fault, said Hampton, but due to "that malignant spirit
of fanaticism, which demands as the price of reunion, the complete degradation and the absolute ruin of the South." Still, Johnson had not done all that
Hampton thought he could.

Hampton insisted that Southerners had "accepted terms" in laying
down their arms. Defeated Confederates recognized the permanency of the
Union. Southerners had abandoned slavery, adopted new state constitutions,
even repudiated the Confederate debt. Yet, still they were excluded from the
halls of Congress. Throughout the war the North professed to be fighting for
a restoration of the Union, but now Southerners found themselves victims of
"the bitterest and most vindictive hatred." Governors had been imprisoned
and state governments overthrown. "Then came the appointment of Provisional Governors, an anomaly, heretofore unknown." Conventions, once
"the great high courts of a free people," came together only to ratify federal
decrees. "Each convention was followed by its own bastard offspring, the
Legislature." Hampton said that he meant no criticism of the patriotic individuals who served, but in these bodies, "all subjects were strictly tabooed
save such as were dictated from Washington."

He went on to complain of depradations committed by "brutal negro
troops under their no less brutal and more degraded Yankee officers." Southern soldiers returning home after the war had been harassed, assaulted, some
even killed by these "black devils who were charged with the preservation of
peace and maintenance of order." Black troops were guilty of "the whole
calendar of crime, ranging from petty larceny to murder." Hampton
denounced too "that Hydra-headed Monster, the Freedmen's Bureau," for
"swindling the negro, plundering the white man and defrauding the government."

Congress, in which the South was not represented, submitted to the
states for ratification a constitutional amendment that affected only those
excluded states. The Thirteenth Amendment abolishing slavery had to be
ratified by states not in the Union as a condition for their return.

> The Amendment has been adopted, but the gates of the Union are still
> closed in our faces. We are *States* whenever our votes are needed to ratify a

Constitutional Amendment, but in all other respects we are only *Conquered Provinces!* We enjoy to the utmost the privileges of *taxation,* but we are denied the right of representation!

Four million slaves had been freed, "but to secure their freedom, eight millions of whites are made slaves!"

The continued imprisonment of Jefferson Davis served to anger and alienate the South. The ex-president had been confined now for well over a year, even shackled for a time, and was still denied a trial. "We do not ask *mercy* for him, at your hands," wrote Hampton, "we only demand *justice.*"

Slavery was gone, and Southerners would not have it return if they could, said Hampton. "The negro, whilst he was a slave, was happy, useful, honest and industrious. But his unfortunate association with the Yankee, has corrupted him . . . and we turn him over willingly to those who imported him from Africa, sold him to us, and then stole him to make him free."

In conclusion, Hampton expressed the feelings of a defeated, but still proud, former Confederate.

The South unequivocally "accepts the situation" in which she is placed. Everything that she has done, has been done in perfect good faith, and in the true and highest sense of the word, she is *loyal.* By this I mean, *that she intends to abide by the laws of the land honestly; to fulfill all her obligations faithfully and to keep her word sacredly.* And I assert that the North has no right to demand more of her. You have no right to ask, or to expect that she will at once profess unbounded love to that Union, from which for four years she tried to escape, at the cost of her best blood and all her treasure. Nor can you believe her to be so unutterably hypocritical, so base as to declare that the "Flag of the Union" has already usurped in her heart the place which has so long been sacred to the "Southern Cross." The men at the South who make such professions are renegades, or traitors and they will surely betray you if you trust them. But the brave men who fought to the last in a cause which they believed *and still believe* to have been a just one, who clung to their colors as long as they waved and who when their cause was lost, acknowledged their defeat and accepted the terms offered to them—as they were true to their convictions in the one case, they will prove to their obligations in the other. Many sacrifices have been demanded of the South, as the price of a restoration of the Union. These she has made; but she will abase herself for no earthly consideration. She will not return to the Union an unequal partner. She will accept no left-handed alliance. She regards herself as fully the peer in honor, in reputation, in character, and in glory of any other portion of the Republic, and she will never consent to tarnish her name, by inscribing on her scutcheon with her own hand, that she has been guilty.[46]

Hampton returned to Columbia in the summer of 1866. Rebuilding was progressing slowly. "Main Street—the one great thoroughfare and business mart—is deserted," reported a visitor in June. "Its sidewalks are obstructed by huge mounds of bricks and mortar." Surviving stores and businesses were concentrated on Gervais and Assembly streets. Mail delivery continued to be slow or nonexistent. Yet, people seemed optimistic. "I never knew so much real social enjoyment," remembered Professor Joseph LeConte. "As everybody was poor the gatherings were almost wholly without expense, and therefore frequent." But not all meetings were permitted by federal authorities. "Associations or assemblages, composed of persons who served in the rebel forces," read General Order Number 7, "having for their object . . . the commemoration of any of the acts of the insurgents . . . will not be permitted."[47]

That Confederate veterans might be remembered for their "bravery and devotion," Robert E. Lee began gathering information for a history of his army. Lee sent a circular letter to former commanders asking for their assistance.[48] Hampton was delighted to help. During those months in Mississippi, he had corresponded with other officers, and on July 21 he wrote to Lee, asking what form his report should take.

> I have nothing to do this Summer, and it would give me great pleasure to contribute all in my power to the success of your undertaking. And it will be a pleasure, though a melancholy one, to pay the last tribute in my power to those brave men who stuck to their colors to the last. You must bear in mind, though, my dear General, that I *am not reconstructed yet,* and in what I shall write every word will be dictated by Southern feelings and come from a Southern heart.

Hampton expressed his admiration and concern for Lee, the general's family, and for the state of Virginia. "Could I leave my own poor, desolate, stricken State, I should assuredly make my home in Va., but I can not forsake a people who have given me so many proofs of their love as these have done." He informed his old chief that he had turned down one recent job offer. Rumanian independence was threatened by the Ottoman Empire, and a call went out for help.

> Genl. Beauregard, who has been offered two positions in the European War, one a command of 100,000 men, has written to offer me the command of all his cavalry, with the rank of Maj. Genl. if he concludes to accept. But whilst appreciating his confidence, I have declined; I shall never draw my sword again, except for *my own country.*[49]

Lee replied, gallantly offering the opinion that had Hampton and his cavalry been with the Army of Northern Virginia in 1865 "the result of Five Forks would have been different."[50] When Hampton delivered his prelimi-

nary report to Lee, he began with a tribute to the veterans, noting that gratitude from their countrymen and the satisfaction of having done their duty

> are the only rewards they can ever receive. The country for which they
> fought is obliterated from the map of the world—the Nationality they
> sought to establish is extinct, & the government which should have
> rewarded them is—like their hopes—dead. It is therefore eminently due to
> them, that their heroic deeds, their sufferings, & their sacrifices, should be
> recorded, so that in after years, their children may not be ashamed to claim
> their descent from men who are now denounced as rebels. Let "the truth,
> the whole truth & nothing but the truth" be placed upon record & we may
> then confidently commit our cause to the impartial judgment of posterity.[51]

South Carolina "unionism," according to the editor of the *Phoenix,*
should be understood simply as patriotism—a devotion to the Constitution—certainly not adherence to New England radicalism. "Gen. Hampton
is the South Carolina type of that kind of Unionism," he concluded, "brave
in war, noble in defeat, and accepting with that self respect and dignity which
true manhood furnishes to its possessor." A national union convention was
to meet that summer in Philadelphia. Delegates would come from North and
South to rally in opposition to the radicals. If they failed, said Governor Orr,
President Johnson might be impeached and driven from office. The *Phoenix*
recommended that men like Orr, Perry, Pickens, and Hampton represent
South Carolina. At the state convention that preceded the national gathering,
Orr was elected president and Hampton one of four vice presidents. Hamp-
ton chose not to serve as a delegate to the Philadelphia meeting, however.[52]
That convention would prove a disappointment, failing to mount a strong
challenge to the Republicans as the fall election approached.

President Johnson's "firm purpose and his indomitable will" had done
much to strengthen the conservative cause, said Hampton. The president
may not have accomplished as much for the South as he and others had
hoped, "but we cannot forget that he has been the only bulwark to stand
between our unhappy country and certain, irretrievable ruin." Hampton
made his comments in Walhalla, South Carolina, in late September, speaking
to the Soldiers' Association. It was an opportunity to share with a predominantly white, upcountry audience his views on slavery, race relations, and the
struggle he saw coming.

Although forced to give up slavery, Hampton again said that Southerners
would not now return blacks to bondage even if they had that power.

> He came to us a heathen, we made him a Christian. Idle, vicious, savage in
> his own country; in ours he became industrious, gentle, civilized. . . . A great
> responsibility is lifted from our shoulders by his emancipation. . . . As a slave
> he was faithful to us; as a freedman, let us treat him as a friend. Deal with

him frankly, kindly, and, my word for it, he will reciprocate your kindness.
. . . If you wish to see him contented, industrious, useful, aid him in his
effort to elevate himself in the scale of civilization, and thus fit him, not only
to enjoy the blessings of freedom, but to appreciate its duties.

A former Confederate lieutenant general speaking to an assembly of
Southern veterans might well be construed as a violation of General Order
Number 7. Hampton advised his hearers to obey the laws of the land, but
not give up "the inalienable right of freedom of speech and of opinion." He
thanked them for "the spontaneous and unsolicited compliment you paid me
a year ago at the ballot-box." The South must not forget "the political faith
taught by her great Apostles of Liberty. I repudiate as heretical and damnable
that morality which inculcates a 'higher law' than the Bible teaches." Hampton's words echoed the sentiments he had expressed years earlier in his speech
against reopening the slave trade. "Pursue this course steadily; bear with
patience and dignity those evils which are pressing heavily upon you. Commit
yourselves to the guidance of God, and, whatever may be your fate, you will
be able to face the future without self-reproach."[53]

In the fall elections Republicans captured 143 seats in the U.S. House of
Representatives, Democrats but 49; in the new Senate 11 Democrats faced 42
Republicans.[54] There would be no stopping the radical agenda when the Fortieth Congress convened in 1867. Southerners seemed to be on the verge of
losing the vestige of self-rule they retained.

As Hampton worried about the future of the country, tragedy struck his
family. On December 12 Mary Fisher Hampton died. According to family
tradition she came down with fever while nursing the aged Mauma Nelly, a
longtime family servant. Mary Fisher's funeral was held at Trinity Episcopal
Church at four o'clock on the afternoon of Thursday, December 13. She was
almost thirty-four. Like her sisters, she never married.[55] She hero-worshipped
her brother Wade, and he grieved deeply over her death.

Only days after his sister's funeral, Hampton contacted a Methodist minister in Columbia and gave him a sum of money intended for a needy
acquaintance.[56] Now thirty-eight, poet Henry Timrod was suffering from
tuberculosis. Discharged from Confederate service as medically unfit, he had
done his best to support his wife and infant son by writing for the *Daily South
Carolinian*. The burning of Columbia destroyed his home and all he owned,
leaving him destitute. His son Willie died in 1865. Timrod had been deeply
stirred by the Southern struggle for independence. He expressed his love for
South Carolina and the Confederacy in such poems as "Ethnogenesis,"
"Carolina," "The Cotton Boll," "Charleston," and "Ode," which he wrote
just after the war to consecrate Confederate graves at Charleston's Magnolia
Cemetery. The poet would die within a year.

"The struggle has unquestionably entailed upon us and our posterity a long train of evils," wrote one South Carolinian. "We are now only entering the threshold of a penal experience which will be protracted into coming years." The First Reconstruction Act passed Congress on March 2, 1867, and became law over the president's veto. Claiming that "no legal State governments or adequate protection for life or property now exists in the rebel States," the former Confederacy was divided into five military districts. Constitutions, although less than two years old, would have to be thrown out and new ones written. Each state was required to ratify what would become the Fourteenth Amendment to the U.S. Constitution. That proposed amendment, designed to solidify federal supremacy over the states, had previously been rejected by southern legislatures. Not surprisingly, the cornerstone of congressional Reconstruction as unrestricted black suffrage, the votes of freedmen guaranteeing Republican domination. On these terms the South could return to Congress.[57]

Hampton would meet the challenge head-on. Although blacks outnumbered whites in South Carolina 2–1, he thought radicals should not assume that the black vote—and political supremacy—belonged to them. Hampton believed freedmen might be reasoned with and persuaded to vote with white South Carolinians for conservative candidates.

Hampton's chance to make that appeal came on March 18. In response to a notice in the press, "the colored citizens of the District assembled in large numbers at the African M. E. Church," reported the *Phoenix*. They marched through the streets of Columbia "headed by a band of music, to the vacant square on Plain Street." There they would be addressed by black entrepreneur Beverly Nash and by Reverend D. Pickett, a local black minister. Also invited to say a few words were five whites, including Wade Hampton.

"No personal motives can possibly sway me for I am no longer a citizen of the United States or of the Confederate States" Hampton told the assembled multitude. "The bill which gives the right of suffrage to you, disfranchises me." Some in the audience that day were undoubtedly former Hampton slaves.

> From many of you I have met not only kindness, but affection. I cannot forget how faithfully some of your people clung to me through all the perils and privations of the war. I cannot forget that it was one of you [Kit Goodwyn], who was always the first at my side when I was wounded, and the last to leave me. Such affection is not often met with, nor is it easily forgotten, and while I have a crust of bread it shall be shared with this well-tried, this true, this trusty friend.

Hampton told of an incident before the war when he and his family were in Philadelphia. At the train station he purchased tickets, including two for the black servants traveling with them. The ticket agent informed Hampton that his servants would not be allowed in the same car, as Pennsylvanians "did not like to ride with negroes." Hampton protested. He had been required to pay full price for their tickets "and one of them is the nurse of my children." The agent still refused. The slave master from South Carolina was out of patience with Philadelphia prejudice. "I told him that I had paid their fare," recounted Hampton, "that I thought them good enough to ride with me, and therefore quite good enough to ride with his fellow-citizens, and that they should get into my car. So I brought them in and kept them there."

Hampton said that he had been the first Southern white to address a colored audience, "nearly two years ago, in the lower part of this district." He insisted that his advice given at Richland Fork was unchanged, and he repeated the plea for racial peace that he had delivered at Walhalla.

> Why should we not be friends? Are you not Southern men, as we are? Is this not your home as well as ours? Does not that glorious Southern sun above us shine alike for both of us? Did not this soil give birth to all of us? And will we not all alike, when our troubles and trials are over, sleep in that same soil.

Looking to the future, the *Phoenix* reported,

> Hampton spoke of the vast importance of the present movement—not only to the colored, but to the white man. He advised the freedmen to give their friends at the South a fair trial, and if they were found wanting, it was time enough to go abroad for sympathy. It was to their interest to build up the South; for as the country prospered, so would they prosper. The present state of affairs was not brought about by the action of the Southern people— white or black; therefore neither was responsible for it.

Nash and Pickett agreed that black voters should "look to merit alone" in choosing among candidates. Nash favored universal suffrage while Pickett wanted restrictions based on education and property ownership. That evening there was a torchlight parade, the newspaper reporting that all day the "strictest order prevailed."[58]

Reaction to the rally came quickly from across America. The New York *Times* was astonished that a former Confederate general, and others, "all imminent and leading men of the State," would gather "to applaud and encourage" negro voters. The *Times* noted,

> Two colored men of note also made addresses, and the whole spirit of the meeting is represented to have been of the most cordial good feeling . . . That, in the heart of South Carolina—a State in which the blacks are largely in the majority—one of the foremost of the Confederate Generals, and him-

self once the largest slaveholder in the country, should meet his former chattels in this frank and manly style, and so unreservedly accept the situation, is a fact to out-weigh volumes of hostile invective and misrepresentation.

His appeals "are producing a marked impression."[59] The Richmond *Times* also applauded Hampton. "Comprehending at a glance his duty to the whites of South Carolina, he has sought to rescue the freedmen of that state from the greedy clutches of that base class of white men who are intent upon degrading and disfranchising their own race." Hampton "has recognized the vital importance of the negro being advised, taught and guided by those who are still his only sincere and true friends."[60]

The *Tribune* of New York dismissed the meeting as a "farce," denouncing Beverly Nash and his followers as "black copperheads."[61] Black radicals in South Carolina were incensed with Nash. The Northern-born Rev. Benjamin F. Randolph, speaking in Charleston, called him "a traitor to his God—a cowardly dupe to the enemies of the Union. He would have all his friends, no doubt stand upon Wade Hampton's platform and submit to Wade Hampton."[62] Nash had said that ex-Confederates should be allowed to vote, declaring "I am a Union man, but a *South Carolinian*." For expressing this conciliatory theme, one letter writer called Nash a "dead dog," one "unfit to be with the lowest of the earth" and "a betrayer of his race." The radical *Advocate* of Charleston bluntly rejected Hampton's appeals.

> Wade Hampton is one of those deep-dyed rebels who staked his all and lost it in an attempt to fasten the chains of slavery upon the neck of the colored man. . . . We want it distinctly understood that we desire that the greatest friendship may exist . . . but we want it as distinctly understood that the freedman is no mercenary tool to be used by sweet words against his own interests.[63]

Withered by the criticism, Nash would make but a feeble attempt to defend himself before abandoning moderation and joining the radical camp.[64]

Hampton remained hopeful. He was encouraged by former Confederate Alfred M. Waddell, a prominent North Carolinian with views similar to his own. In a letter to James Conner Hampton urged him to

> shrink from no duty, no sacrifices. All who can do so should vote, and every good man who can go to the Convention, even if sent by negroes and with negroes, should go. We can control and direct the negro if we act discretely, and in my judgment the highest duty of every Southern man is to secure the good will and confidence of the negro. Our future depends on this. The meeting here the other day was one of the most extraordinary I ever saw, and if it is followed up, great good will come from it.

Hampton believed that the vast majority of freedmen were not qualified, not responsible enough, to make political decisions. They might be led, however, by conservative whites who could govern wisely in the best interests of all. He saw no deception in his paternalistic approach. "Say to the negroes, we are your friends," and even if the Supreme Court should throw out the Reconstruction Act, "we are willing to let the educated and tax paying among you vote." Hampton was at this point concerned solely with control of state government. "I am willing to send negroes to Congress. They will be better than any one who can take the oath and I should rather trust them than renegades or Yankees." Hampton claimed to have no political ambitions for himself. "Disfranchised, an unpardonable and unrepentant rebel, I live solely to try to help my State, and failing that, to suffer with her."[65]

In a letter to New Yorker Mullaly at the end of the month, Hampton said that the South was

> struggling for bare life. If we cannot direct the wave it will overwhelm us. Now how shall we do this? Simply by making the Negro a Southern man, and if you will, a Democrat, anything but a Radical. Beyond these motives for my action I have another. We are appealing to the enlightened sense and justice of mankind. We come forward and say, we accept the decision rendered against us, we acknowledge the freedom of the negro and we are willing to have one law for him and for us.

Southerners must not merely wait and hope for rescue by a favorable Supreme Court decision, Hampton told Mullaly two weeks later. "In short our condition is simply this: the negroes will certainly vote; *how* they vote depends greatly on us. . . . God send us deliverance."[66]

Struggle on the battlefield may have ceased two years earlier, but the enemy was determined to carry on a political war. At the end of March, Hampton expressed his feelings to sister-in-law Elizabeth Preston Carrington.

> The war was full of sorrows & griefs to me, but *peace* has been worse; so much that I often wish I had fallen when our flag was waving in triumph. But as it has pleased God to keep me here, I accept my position & I shall try to fulfill my duties.[67]

12

"WE SHALL NOT GIVE
UP OUR COUNTRY"

Battle against the Radicals

"G eneral Hampton and his friends," said Benjamin Perry, "had just as well try to control a herd of wild buffaloes . . . as the Negro vote." Radical appeals, promises, and prejudices were to prove irresistible to the newly enfranchised. The state's black electorate became the foundation of the Republican Party and began to provide a few of its leaders. From the North came those called carpetbaggers. Black and white, some were idealists determined to build a new order from the ruins of slavery. Most simply saw politics as a way to make their fortunes and were taking advantage of opportunities for advancement. Particularly despised by native whites were scalawags—Southerners who broke ranks to join the Republicans.[1] It was a pattern repeated across the defeated Confederate states.

This coalition of blacks, opportunists, and turncoats owed its existence to the Republican leadership in Washington. The new congressional agenda went far beyond Lincoln's original aim of "preserving the Union." Sen. Charles Sumner of Massachusetts nursed a long-standing hatred of the South. Benjamin F. Wade of Ohio, president pro tempore of the Senate, was a bitter enemy of President Johnson and his conciliatory policies. Radicals in the House were led by Thaddeus Stevens of Pennsylvania, an advocate of Southern land confiscation and stern punishment for ex-Confederates. Republican partisans were determined to block the South's return to Congress until they could be sure that those delegations would be free of Democrats. Many radical Republicans had even more ambitious goals. They wanted a complete break with the past and an overthrow of the Constitution. "They aimed, ultimately," wrote one historian, "at establishing a centralized parliamentary government for the Union."[2]

White South Carolinians shook their heads in astonishment and disgust when they beheld their new leaders. From Ohio, for example, came Benjamin Franklin Randolph. A black Methodist preacher and former chaplain of the Twenty-sixth U.S. Colored Troops, Randolph remained in South Carolina to edit the Charleston *Advocate*. He would go on to represent Orangeburg in the state Senate, where he championed state schools and laws prohibiting racial discrimination. Alonzo Jacob Ransier, a Charleston free black, worked as a shipping clerk before the war. In 1868 he took his seat in the South Carolina House of Representatives, one of a handful of black legislators able to read and write. Benjamin F. Whittemore of Massachusetts, an Amherst graduate and Freedmen's Bureau official, would sit in the state Senate before moving on to the U.S. House of Representatives. Expelled from Congress for selling military academy appointments, he was promptly reelected. Another white, Franklin Moses, lawyer and planter, had a long and honorable political career in antebellum South Carolina. Joining the Republicans in 1868, he became Supreme Court chief justice. His son, Franklin Moses Jr. would follow his father into the camp of the philistines, reaping even richer rewards.[3] Hundreds rose from obscurity to prominence—to lead or be led—as radicals strove to keep "the bottom rail on the top."

A most useful tool was the Union League. Beginning as a patriotic club in the wartime North, the league was initially introduced to the coast of South Carolina, promoted by Freedmen's Bureau agents and black soldiers. Meetings were held in black churches, schools, homes, or even in woods and fields. Ritual was central. A Bible, a copy of the Declaration of Independence, perhaps an anvil symbolizing labor—all were placed on a table. With armed guards standing by, prospective members solemnly pledged to vote Republican. Radical newspapers were read aloud for the illiterate majority, candidates were endorsed, and militia duty was encouraged. South Carolina's Union League president was Francis L. Cardozo, a free-born mulatto. The league was almost entirely black, and virtually every black voter was a member.[4]

Hampton's hope of recruiting significant numbers of black voters to the Democratic Party was by the summer of 1867 clearly a failure. Whites were in a quandary. Congress mandated a new state constitution, but required that the convention that would write it be called by a vote of the people. Blacks were registering in anticipation and easily outnumbered whites. A group of sixty prominent whites wrote an open letter to Hampton asking for his advice.[5] He replied in a letter published in newspapers across South Carolina. "Our State conventions were mistakes; so were the changes in our constitutions; greater than all others was the legislation ratifying the amendment of the United States Constitution known as Article 13." He was not advocating a return to slavery, but pointing out that slavish obedience to federal dictates had gained nothing for the South. He now repeated publicly the advice he had offered privately to Columbia mayor James G. Gibbes a year earlier. In Hampton's opinion military rule was preferable to the "illegal, unconstitutional, and ruinous" plan of Congressional Reconstruction. Eligible whites should register and vote against the proposed convention. Hampton reiterated his appeal for racial peace.

> Let our people remember that the negroes have, as a general rule, behaved admirably, and that they are in no manner responsible for the present condition of affairs. Should they, in the future, be misled by wicked or designing men, let us consider how ignorant they necessarily are, and let us, only the more, try to convince them that we are their best friends.

Hampton repeated his willingness "to see impartial suffrage established at the South." He denied that Congress had a right to confer citizenship on blacks, but thought the Southern states should take that step themselves. He recommended that voting requirements be the same for white and black, with "a slight educational and property qualification for all classes."[6]

When the books were closed on September 30, blacks had registered 78,982; whites, 46,346. In only ten of the state's thirty-one counties—mostly in the upcountry—did whites have a majority. The plebiscite on holding a convention was set for November 19 and 20. The law stipulated that the decision would not stand unless a majority of registered voters took part. Whites decided that their best course was simply to stay home. If enough blacks neglected to vote the convention would never meet. The tactic failed. Although only 2,211 whites turned out, the 68,876 blacks who came to the polls and voted yes more than constituted a majority of the electorate. The total white vote in favor of the convention—probably a fair estimate of the number of white Republicans then in the state—was 130.[7]

"Intelligence, virtue, and patriotism are to give place, in all elections, to ignorance, stupidity, and vice," complained the Democratic Executive Committee, of which Hampton was a member. The constitutional convention convened on January 14, 1868, at the Charleston Club House. President Albert G. Mackey proclaimed it "the only legitimate convention" in South Carolina's history, its delegates chosen "by all the people," except, of course, "traitors." There were seventy-six blacks and forty-six whites. The majority of the blacks, but fewer than half of the whites, were native South Carolinians. Most black delegates chosen to write a new constitution were illiterate.[8] The *Mercury* sarcastically reported on the body's daily deliberations under the heading, "The Great Ring-Streaked and Striped Negro Convention."

The paper's reporter was assaulted on the floor of the convention and then expelled. Among extraneous resolutions adopted by delegates, one recommended that laws eventually be passed banning terms like "negro," "nigger," or "Yankee." The constitution they wrote was modeled on Ohio's. The exercise went on for fifty-three days and cost taxpayers $110,000.[9]

Whites stood by in sullen contempt as they watched political leadership pass to former slaves and outside adventurers. "It is as certain as anything in politics can be," warned the radical *Nation*, "that before long the whites will reassume their old ascendancy. The worst enemies of the blacks are those who deceive themselves on this point."

The state Central Executive Committee of the Democratic Party, chaired by Wade Hampton, issued its own "address to the colored people of South Carolina." Its words echoed the warnings of *The Nation*.

> Your present power must surely and soon pass from you. Nothing that it builds will stand and nothing will remain of it but the prejudices it may create. It is therefore a most dangerous tool that you are handling. Your leaders, both white and black, are using your votes for nothing but their individual gain.

Although whites were now nearly powerless, Democrats continued,

> We shall not give up our country, and time will soon restore our control of it. But we earnestly caution you and beg you in the meanwhile to beware of the use you make of your temporary power. Remember that your race has nothing to gain and everything to lose if you invoke that prejudice of race which since the world began has ever driven the weaker tribe to the wall. Forsake, then, the wicked and stupid men who would involve you in this folly, and make to yourselves friends and not enemies of the white citizens of South Carolina.[10]

If Hampton did not write the address, he certainly shared the sentiments it expressed. The following month he spoke at the Democratic Club of Richland. He meant his words to convey caution, not a threat. "Let the coloured man be told God's truth, that if he expects to escape the fate of the Indian, he should go in with the Democratic or Conservative party."[11]

The black majority remained unmoved. In April they elected Robert K. Scott, Ohio native and Union army veteran, as South Carolina's governor. The new general assembly was mostly black and overwhelmingly Republican. Few of the legislators owned any taxable property. Illiterate lawmakers relied on a cadre of party leaders to tell them how to vote. Paid per diem, all favored the longest possible legislative sessions. Republicans elected to the U.S. Congress were nonentities, officeholders treated as "poor relations" by their northern brethren.[12]

In March House members in Washington had voted to impeach President Johnson for violating the Tenure of Office Act in his firing of Secretary of War Edwin Stanton. The president was also charged with attempting to "bring into disgrace, ridicule, hatred, contempt and reproach the Congress of the United States." On May 16 the Senate returned a guilty verdict of 35–19, one vote short of the number needed to remove Johnson from office.[13] Radicals were disappointed, but had demonstrated their power. President Johnson would finish Lincoln's term with little further influence on the course of events. Southerners came to despair of the Supreme Court's delivering them from congressional Reconstruction. They would turn again to the political arena, staking their hopes on a triumph by the Democratic Party in the presidential election of 1868.

For the first time since 1860, when the Democratic national convention had been held in Charleston, the state's Democrats chose representatives to their party's nominating convention. "To my surprise," wrote Hampton to Perry, "my name was presented as one of the delegates. Though I did not desire this, as the nomination showed a spirit of conciliation I thought it best not to decline."[14] The national convention met at noon on July 4 in New York's Tammany Hall. Southern delegates kept a relatively low profile, not wishing to embarrass the party and hamper its chances for electoral success in the North. Hampton served on the platform committee. On Tuesday, July 7, the platform was adopted by acclamation.[15] Calling for a restoration of constitutional government and amnesty for ex-Confederates, radicals were denounced for their "unparalleled oppression and tyranny," reducing peaceful states "to military despotism and negro supremacy." The very existence of the states was in danger and "we regard the reconstruction acts so called, of Congress, as such an usurpation, and unconstitutional, revolutionary, and void." The platform included praise for Union veterans, thanks to President Johnson, and sympathy for the rights and interests of workingmen.[16]

Voting for the presidential nomination took three days and twenty-three ballots. Horatio Seymour, fifty-eight-year-old former New York governor, reluctantly became the party's compromise standard bearer. Choosing the vice presidential candidate proved to be much easier. Francis P. Blair Jr., formerly a corps commander under Sherman, was opposed to congressional Reconstruction. Hampton spoke enthusiastically in favor of Blair. *Harper's* reported that Hampton "said that he had met General Blair on more than one field. It was due to the Federal soldier that they [Union veterans] should have second place on the ticket, and he, for his State, most cordially seconded the nomination." Backed by border and Southern state delegations, New York came out for Blair, other candidates withdrew, and the general was nominated on the first ballot.[17]

Democrats adjourned, excited and hopeful about their prospects for victory in November. Just after the convention Hampton was called upon to make a few remarks to the crowd gathered in front of the Democratic Association at Union Square. Standing on the balcony, he had just begun to speak—thanking New Yorkers for their kindness and cordiality—when paper lanterns behind him caught fire. They were quickly extinguished, and the general began again, joking, "I do not like to have a fire in my rear." He explained that Southerners had been careful to take "no prominent part" in party proceedings for fear of harming the Democratic cause. He said that he had voted to nominate President Johnson, but now enthusiastically supported Seymour. He went on to tell sympathetic New Yorkers of South Carolina's Reconstruction woes. "Hisses and cries of shame" greeted his account of how nontaxpaying blacks dominated the general assembly and spent the people's money.[18]

Other New Yorkers were less congenial. *Harper's Weekly* claimed that "Wade Hampton, the rebel, and Vanlandingham [Clement Vallandingham], the copperhead, combined and ruled the convention." Hampton advocated that Seymour be forced into office "at the point of the bayonet," according to *Harper's*. Soon *The Nation* and the *Times* repeated the "bayonet" rhetoric.[19] Hampton spoke again in Baltimore on July 16. "I am going home now with a great load lifted off my heart," he said, moved by the friendship and encouragement he had encountered. "When I return to South Carolina I shall tell my beloved people they will again hear the bugle of the old Maryland line, and see her sons fighting shoulder to shoulder under the constitution for liberty." The New York *Herald* pretended to detect rebellion in his imagery, declaring that Hampton "still rang a strain to the same old secesh tune." The *Mercury* dismissed the *Herald's* bombast, reminding all that Hampton "is a thoroughly conservative man; he always has been, both by nature, and habit of thought."[20]

Hampton arrived in Charleston on July 24 where he was met at the railroad terminal and escorted by a delegation of citizens to James Conner's home. At eight-thirty that evening a Democratic rally began in front of the Charleston Hotel on Meeting Street. Crowds stretched for two blocks, from Hasell to Hayne streets. Hampton spoke, although laryngitis made him hoarse, appealing to South Carolinians to follow Seymour, Blair, and their other Democratic friends in the North. The line in the platform declaring that the party regarded the Reconstruction Acts of Congress "unconstitutional, revolutionary, and void" was "my plank in the platform," said Hampton. Daniel S. Henderson, a College of Charleston student in the crowd that night, understood Hampton to mean that he had "induced the Convention" to insert those words. Hampton had to cut short his comments, handicapped as he was by a failing voice. One reporter noticed "400 colored conservatives, who behaved with the greatest propriety throughout the meeting, and, at the close, marched off in a column of fours, cheering for Hampton."[21]

Four days later Hampton campaigned in Columbia. Again "colored Democrats" were present. There was a fireworks display. Thirty-seven young ladies dressed in white represented the states in the Union. Hampton was, of course, the main attraction, repeating his Charleston speech in favor of Seymour. "The hold he has on all who come within the reach of his influence is perfectly wonderful," reported the press, "the enthusiasm is ever the same, and scarcely knows any bounds." Near the end of his remarks, Hampton expressed outrage that carpetbaggers and scalawags had taken the seats of "Hayne, Calhoun, McDuffie and Preston" in South Carolina. "He said he would have much preferred to see colored men in those positions, as they could have filled them without any degradation to themselves."[22]

Once again, Northern Republicans pounced on Hampton's words alleging that the "extreme position" in the Democratic platform denouncing the Reconstruction Acts had been the work of none other than Wade Hampton. Hampton replied that it was "my plank" in the sense that it was "the plank to which I, as well as any other Southern man, clung for safety." By harping on Hampton's supposed "dictation" of the platform, Republicans hoped to put Northern Democrats on the defensive. The battleground in the presidential contest was the Midwest—states that the Democrats knew they must carry to win in November.[23] Hampton was learning that political warfare at this level could be as relentless as combat on the battlefield. He presented a series of resolutions to the Democratic state convention in Columbia on August 7. Despite the evils of Reconstruction, "we rely with confidence upon the constitutional agencies and peaceful instrumentalities alone to bring us the relief we seek and the reform we need." Hampton hoped to reassure Northern voters that he had been misquoted and misrepresented. Resolutions thanking President Johnson and praising "generous spirits" in the North were passed by the state party at Hampton's insistence.[24]

Other Democratic campaign rallies went on around the state. A "mass meeting and barbeque" in Sumter on October 8 was attended by thousands of black and white voters. Speeches were made by Hampton and several others, including one black Democrat. The band of a traveling circus that happened to be in town "contributed much to the entertainment of the crowd," said an observer.[25]

In an attempt at sectional reconciliation—and to demonstrate moderation—Hampton's committee sent a letter to John Quincy Adams II of Massachusetts, inviting him to speak in South Carolina. "Would it not be as if the past were speaking to the present? Would it not seem as if the grave had given up her dead, and they were holding counsel of the future?" The letter was signed by Hampton and four others. Son of Charles Francis Adams, grandson and great-grandson of the two Presidents Adams—John Quincy Adams II had, since the war, broken tradition to support the Democratic cause. In his reply to Hampton's committee, Adams agreed to come, but minimized his own importance. He promised to speak "frankly rather than agreeably" and to avoid election-year partisanship.[26]

Adams spoke in Columbia on October 12. He made it clear that he had supported Lincoln, hated slavery, and opposed secession. He pointed out the irony of radicals now taking the Confederate position in their insistence that Southern states had in fact legally seceded from the Union. Congress, by that reasoning, now considered Southerners "alien enemies; your country conquered territory; yourselves prisoners of war, and your rights of every kind forfeited." "Possess your souls in patience," Adams advised. "Call to your aid that grandest of human qualities, self-control, and all will yet be well." The press reported that his remarks were "well received" and that he was applauded frequently.

Wade Hampton, "being loudly called for," responded to Adams. The general conceded that slavery and the right of secession were gone "forever" and took the occasion to again answer his Northern critics. "I have been the victim of great, willful, and malicious misrepresentation," he said regarding the reporting of his role in framing the party platform. "I did *not* dictate it. I *did* say that it was my plank in the platform, and it is the plank of every Southern gentleman." Hampton, reported the *Phoenix,* "wrought his hearers up to the highest pitch of enthusiasm." South Carolina Democrats, he told Adams, are willing to support not universal suffrage, but "the same suffrage that he [the black man] was given in Massachusetts." Speaking later in Charleston, Adams said of Hampton, "if he is a rebel, he is just such a rebel as I am and no more."[27]

On October 15 the news that had flashed down the telegraph wires was published in papers across South Carolina. In state elections held two days earlier in Ohio, Pennsylvania, and Indiana, Republicans swept the field. These were states that Seymour needed to win in November. South Carolina Democrats were glum. Their fellow partisans in the North were in despair—so desperate, in fact, that there was even talk of changing candidates at this eleventh hour.[28]

Days later news came that might further harm the Democratic cause in South Carolina. Benjamin Franklin Randolph, a black state senator and chairman of the Republican Executive Committee, was gunned down at Hodges Depot near Cokesbury. He had been on an election tour in Abbeville County. Democratic newspapers described him as "obnoxious" and "a persistent advocate of the social equality idea." Three men fired at Randolph on the crowded railroad platform, then calmly rode away, leaving the senator shot in the head. Eleven days earlier Republican lawmaker James Martin of Abbeville had been murdered on a highway outside of that town.[29] But it was the assassination of Randolph that seemed to galvanize the state and conjure up the specter of a race war.

On October 23 the state Democratic Executive Committee issued a proclamation, written by Hampton, denouncing the killings and calling for "peace and the preservation of order." They blamed "a few lawless and reckless men" for bringing "discredit on the character of our people. . . . No cause can prosper which calls murder to its assistance, or which looks to assassination for success." The statement went on to quote the late George McDuffie, Hampton's father-in-law, in warning against lawless violence.

> We ask those who are opposed to us, politically, to unite with us to check and discountenance all incendiary language, whether uttered in public or private, and to join us in the efforts we are making for the preservation of peace, the supremacy of law, and the maintenance of order.[30]

Soon after the Randolph killing, Governor Scott asked Hampton to meet with him. At a second conference on Thursday, October 27, Hampton came to Scott's Columbia home, this time accompanied by L. D. Childs and James G. Gibbes. The purpose of their gathering was to put a stop to the violence and promote a climate of peace in the state. Hampton, perhaps sensing weakness in the governor that he might exploit, made four suggestions:

1. Since the election of Grant was certain, how South Carolina voted would not affect the outcome. But if the state were to go for Seymour, argued Hampton, it would do much to calm Democrats. Scott should "use his influence" to see to it that Seymour carried South Carolina. It was assumed by all present that the Republican governor had the power to insure that result.
2. Scott should "endeavor to induce" some blacks to resign from the legislature that they might be replaced by white Republicans. Having fewer blacks in the general assembly, Hampton reasoned, would help calm racial feelings that had been running high since the constitutional convention in January.
3. The governor should appoint at least a few Democrats to office.
4. Scott should issue his own proclamation calling for peace, and he should commend the Democrats for their address on the subject.

Scott, according to Hampton and his friends, agreed to all four points.[31]

On October 30 a proclamation signed by Scott was published in newspapers across the state, along with a "manifesto" from the Republican Party. The governor congratulated the citizens of South Carolina "upon the beneficial results that have ensued from the admirable and well-timed address of General Hampton and the executive committee of the Democratic Party. In honest and impressive terms they have called on the people to support the laws, to preserve the peace, and to denounce those crimes." His Excellency went on to express "unfeigned pleasure" at the Democrats' "patriotic counsels," urging his own party to follow "the pacific policy so admirably inculcated by the Democratic leaders." The Republican manifesto denounced the murders, as well as attempts made on the lives of Democrats and arson attacks against the homes of whites. Republicans were urged "to abstain from all acts of retaliation and violence." Echoing the governor, it said, "We hail with satisfaction the address of the democratic State central committee as the harbinger of better and more quiet times."[32]

On election day Grant won by a landslide, capturing 214 electoral votes to Seymour's 80.[33] South Carolina was in Grant's column. Scott had reneged on his promise or had been unable to deliver. The complexion of the general assembly remained unchanged, and no Democrats were to serve by gubernatorial appointment. "As Governor Scott has broken faith with me," Hampton said two years later, "I no longer regard the communication he made as confidential." Scott denied making any agreement, but the two witnesses backed Hampton's story.[34] Hampton would reveal that the Republican governor had even allowed his own proclamation to be written for him by the Democratic Executive Committee.[35]

Hampton remained optimistic about his personal financial future, although a heavy load of debt continued to grow. In the spring of 1867, he again asked a creditor for "a small advance," explaining that "I have brought out to my place upwards of 40 hands, nearly all young men, & this increase of force will enable me to plant about 250 to 300 acres more of cotton." Yet, there never seemed to be enough income from planting to repay the loans.

The year 1867 proved to be one of personal tragedy too. Mary gave birth to a girl the parents named Catherine Fisher, but the infant soon died.[36] She "only lived long enough to make us love her," Hampton confided to Robert E. Lee in July. "Mrs. Hampton has not left her room, since her sickness, & I have written only by her bedside." Mary Hampton had given birth to four children in nine years. She would never get completely well, suffering from chronic symptoms caused by an enlarged, swollen uterus. Dr. Daniel H. Trezevant continued to care for her, although she saw at least one other physician when away from Columbia. That doctor, Josiah Clark Nott, "was kind enough to come from New York [to Baltimore] to see her," Hampton wrote to Trezevant, "& you will be gratified to learn that his opinion coincides with yours . . . that hysteria is the disease under which she suffers."[37]

By the end of 1868, Wade Hampton's financial situation had become untenable. At the beginning of the war, he had owned, by his own estimate, some 12,000 acres and 900 slaves. Invading Federals had destroyed his Columbia home and emancipation had swept away his work force. Labor problems, high taxes, and the vagaries of weather had plagued him and all others who farmed during the postwar years. He had a family to support and a wife who required special care. The political struggle consumed Hampton's time and energy. Faced with these demands and liabilities, perhaps even an entrepreneur of extraordinary shrewdness—a businessman such as the first

Wade Hampton—would have failed. Wade Hampton III, like his father, possessed no such gifts.

To Armistead Burt, Hampton was able to unburden himself. An Abbeville lawyer and former congressman, the sixty-five-year-old Burt was the kind of man others felt comfortable confiding in. He was a long-time Hampton family friend.

> At the close of the war it was my hope that my property here [in Mississippi] could be put in such condition as would render it saleable for something approximating its real value, in which event I could have met my liabilities, which were very heavy. But the unsettled aspect of affairs, has made land here valueless, for the present, & some of my creditors have brought suit against me. I have nothing but my land & I have been keeping it solely for the benefit of my creditors. If they press me I can only surrender all I have, in which case those who hold mortgages on the land will be the only ones who will receive any thing. It has been very repugnant to me to take benefit of the Bankrupt Act, & I should not do so voluntarily, but there seems no choice left to me. I am more than willing to give up everything, but it is worse than death to feel that my debts cannot be paid. . . . I will give up all I possess with far greater pleasure than I ever experienced in the acquisition.

Even as Hampton shared his financial woes, Mary Hampton was penning her own letter to Burt. She asked for a loan of "one hundred dollars till Mr. Hampton comes home. He has been away two months longer than I thought he would & I do not know exactly when to expect him."

On Christmas Eve, 1868, in the District Court of the United States, Southern District of Mississippi, Wade Hampton filed a petition for bankruptcy. He listed creditors holding mortgages on his properties in the amount of $645,103. Unsecured claims by banks and individuals came to an additional $367,225, bringing his total debt to an astronomical $1,012,328. Hampton's interest in his South Carolina, Mississippi, and North Carolina lands totaled $235,500 and he listed but $7,905 in personal property. Of that amount $2,875 was in stock he held in the Commercial Bank of Columbia. He felt that his library was worth $1,000. Other items listed were a rifle, a carbine, his gold watch, farm tools, animals, and silverware. Some fifteen months later Judge R. A. Hill granted the bankruptcy, freeing Hampton "from all debts and claims . . . which existed on the 29th day of December 1868."

Hampton's modest home on land outside of Columbia was sold to Hampton himself for $100. That the property remained "subject to encumbrances for more than market value" may have discouraged other potential purchasers. Perhaps for the same reason he was also able to retain possession of Wild Woods. At 835 acres it had been the smallest of his Mississippi holdings—but Hampton's favorite.[38] In any case the family would not have to

move, although Hampton still had substantial obligations. He rented his
Mississippi lands to sharecroppers. He wrote to James Conner in the spring
of 1869,

> You will be glad to hear I have been able to put matters in such shape as to
> give me reasonable ground to hope that I may in time pay off my debts.
> The hope of my life is to do this, and I shall devote all my energies to its
> accomplishment.[39]

On November 17 Hampton was in Macon to deliver an address at the
Georgia State Fair. He spoke on education. He advised white Georgians to
encourage the freedman. "Try to elevate him in the scale of true manhood,
of civilization and Christianity, so that he may be better fitted for the grave
duties and high responsibilities forced upon him by his new position."

Leaving Macon, Hampton took his family to Memphis. Hampton served
on the board of directors of the Southern Life Insurance Company. In Memphis he met with Jefferson Davis, who had just been elected by the board of
the Carolina Life Insurance Company to its presidency.[40] Davis put Hampton
in charge of the Baltimore branch office. Other company executives included
John S. Preston in Virginia, Dabney Maury in Tennessee, Braxton Bragg in
New Orleans, W. T. Walthall in Alabama, and Jeremy F. Gilmer in Georgia.[41]
The company seemed to be in difficulties almost immediately. The entire life
insurance industry in the United States suffered in the decades after the war,
due in no small part to the unanticipated long-term effects of wounds and
disease on surviving veterans. Davis attributed his own company's problems
to the higher-than-expected mortality rate of policy holders. From 1868 to
1870 twenty-three American life insurance companies went out of business.
During the next seven years, eighty-one more would go under.[42]

Carolina Life was part of that unfortunate trend. Hampton did his best,
recommending men like former Confederate major general Robert F. Hoke
as state agent for North Carolina. "The Co. relies confidently on your personal exertions," Hampton wrote to Hoke in May 1872, promising a guarantee of $100, per month plus commissions and modest expenses. "As this
Dept. has been left in my sole charge," Hampton said later, "I am very solicitous to make our success complete." In October he again exhorted Hoke,
"Help us along as far as you can, & we shall want your name as an influence
in N.C."[43]

His board sent Davis to New York in the summer of 1873 in search of a
loan for $150,000 to keep the company afloat. By then the country was in a
recession, and he was unable to borrow the money. At one point Hampton
offered his own meager resources to buy a little time for the company. They
had already closed the Baltimore office. In July Davis would travel to Baltimore hoping to make a deal with the Piedmont and Arlington Company to

purchase Carolina Life. These negotiations fell through. The next month Davis was in Richmond conferring with Hampton when a telegram arrived announcing that the company had been sold to Southern Life. The action had been taken without Davis's knowledge and, he thought, "at a ridiculous compensation." It is not known when Hampton left the Southern board of directors, but he called the sale a "trick." Davis believed it "a blunder," and resigned in protest.[44]

In late summer 1873 Hampton wrote to Davis for advice. The Southern Life home office was failing to pay agents and ignoring Hampton's letters. "They have treated you worse than anybody except myself," replied Davis, "and the only obligation I feel is to the innocent creditors whom I regard as lambs turned over to the care of wolves." Three years later Southern Life would itself go into bankruptcy.[45]

Hampton remained close to Robert E. Lee, continuing to write to his old commander, gathering information for Lee's proposed history. Hampton attended the Washington College commencement in 1868 and spoke before the college's literary societies. Hampton was one of a small circle with whom Lee seemed able to talk freely and frankly about the war.[46] Lee's sudden death in Lexington two years later affected Hampton deeply. A memorial service was held in Columbia on the morning of October 13, 1870, only a day after South Carolina learned of his passing. Columns in the *Daily Phoenix* were bordered in black. Even the radical press seemed subdued and respectful. Hampton spoke first at the memorial. "The foremost man of all the world is no more," he told fellow mourners. "I dare not venture to speak of him as I feel."[47]

A year later, on the first anniversary of Lee's death, Hampton spoke in Baltimore at the invitation of the Maryland Society of Confederate Soldiers and Sailors. His "Address on the Life and Character of General Robert E. Lee" was lengthy, covering the Virginian's noble ancestry and illustrious military career. "It would ill become any Confederate soldier, who is not a renegade to the faith for which he fought, to refuse to deck the honored grave of Lee," said Hampton. He implied that the South's sufferings after the war may have hastened Lee's death. Hampton remembered the days of secession as a time when with "heartfelt reluctance the South, driven to desperation, severed the bonds, no longer fraternal" with the North. Hampton felt his tribute to Lee inadequate, but it was published by popular demand.[48]

Hampton was active in organizing Confederate veterans back home in South Carolina. He headed the Richland Survivors' Association, and as president of the Survivors' Association of South Carolina, he asked that veterans' names be recorded and rosters be preserved "as it is a matter of great historical importance."[49]

At the unveiling of a monument honoring the men of Charleston's Washington Light Infantry, Hampton, their old legion commander, was asked to speak. On the afternoon of June 16, 1870, 6,000 gathered under rainy skies at Magnolia Cemetery. Confederates, insisted Hampton, "fought to vindicate the great truths enunciated in '76, and to defend those inalienable rights established by our fathers, and bequeathed to us by our noblest heritage." Those rights had been valiantly defended, but now seemed lost in the federal triumph. "We see virtue trampled into dust by vice. We see liberty prostrate at the feet of tyranny. We see religion superseded by fanaticism. We see intelligence, virtue, patriotism thrust aside, while ignorance, vice and selfishness usurp the high places of the earth." Christians must not despair, however. Believers are not promised that "virtue shall here triumph, while vice is punished." Hampton accepted Confederate defeat, but warned against the common assumption that might makes right.

> The sword has never, nor will it ever, decide a principle or establish a truth. It can, as it has often done, overthrow a just cause, and make might take the place of right; but it can never reverse the immutable laws of God, and make what is evil appear right in His sight. A noble cause, upheld heroically by honor, courage and patriotism, may die along with its supporters. A great truth never dies.

He concluded,

> It is right and proper that you should preserve the memory of our dead heroes. Would that we could erect to them a monument whose foundation should be as eternal as the great truths for which they died; lofty as their fame; pure as our love; lasting as our gratitude; rising proudly from the earth that holds their clay, and pointing with its spotless shaft to that Heaven where we devoutly trust that they are now at rest.[50]

There would be no rest for those survivors, like Hampton, who struggled to redeem South Carolina from her enemies. In two years of radical rule, the state debt had risen 343 percent, to $18,575,033. Legislators could not balance their budget, although taxes were up. Despite a vaunted commitment to education, little money was actually reaching schools or teachers. The Land Commission, mandated to buy property for the landless, was lining the pockets of its officials. A barroom in the State House served free refreshments at the taxpayers' expense to thirsty politicians. Votes in the legislature were openly bought and sold. Lawmakers appropriated a large sum to furnish the capitol lavishly, but the items purchased found their way into the rooms of representatives and senators. They even voted to fund a state census in 1869, one year before the U.S. Census would be taken. The more detailed federal census was performed on schedule, yet cost far less than the state's superfluous head count. Redistricting seemed almost pointless. In 1868 congressional districts had been jerrymandered to nullify the upcountry's concentration of white voters.[51]

Hampton continued in 1868 to serve as trustee of the University of South Carolina. In May he reported that his "Committee on papers" had examined reports submitted and determined that the school was in a "satisfactory condition." Radicals elected their own board the following year. They integrated the institution, prompting white South Carolinians to flee. Soon but eight undergraduates remained.[52]

Corruption in state government had become so brazen and widespread that a few concerned Republicans broke ranks. A convention in Columbia on June 15, 1870, established the Union Reform Party. R. B. Carpenter, circuit court judge, was nominated for governor. Carpenter was a native of Kentucky, had long been a Republican, and owed his court appointment to that party. Now, he made common cause with the Democrats. Gen. Matthew C. Butler was nominated for lieutenant governor, and there would be a full slate of candidates for seats in the general assembly. Reformers directed an appeal to blacks, nominating black candidates in many races.[53]

Governor Scott wanted a second term. The Republican candidate for lieutenant governor was Alonzo J. Ransier, a Charleston-born black. Scott refused Carpenter's challenge to debate. The incumbent governor's campaign strategy was to organize and arm thousands of black militiamen. Not only did his appointment of militia officers open up a new field for patronage, but these forces could be deployed to suppress Reform Party meetings. At a Chester rally they kept Carpenter from speaking. Most important was the influence the militia had on blacks who might be tempted to listen to the reformers. Carpenter complained that those wanting to vote for him were threatened.[54] Reformers faced other handicaps. "As a rule," said Carpenter, "the commissioners fixed the voting-places to accommodate the colored people, and to be as far off and inconvenient for the white people as they could. In certain counties the white people would have to travel forty miles to the nearest precinct to vote."[55]

The official count gave Scott 85,071 votes, Carpenter, 51,537. The margin in the Butler-Ransier contest was similar. Blacks had again voted Republican overwhelmingly. The new House of Representatives would have 104 Republicans and only 20 Democrats. Republicans would dominate the state Senate 26 to 5. Carpenter charged fraud. He had expected to carry Laurens County, for example, but was shocked at the announced outcome. "It was a round thousand against everybody on our ticket, and a thousand in favor of everybody on the other ticket. I do not think they ever counted the ballots."[56]

The Nation, a New York journal of news and opinion, dismissed South Carolina's 1870 general assembly as "one of the most corrupt assemblages of men that ever legislated for a State, and one of the most contemptible in point of ability." In the spring of 1871, in response to a call by the Charleston

Chamber of Commerce, a taxpayers' convention met in Columbia. Although Hampton was not directly involved, most of the officers and organizers were Democrats. A few Republicans came, concerned about continued corruption. The legislature's printing bill, for example, was an inflated $45,000 in 1869. The following year it soared to $173,000, and to $450,000 the next. Little of the money was actually spent publishing the journals of the House and Senate. Most found its way into the pockets of "public servants." One original idea to come from the taxpayers' convention was that of cumulative voting—the concept of giving voters as many votes as there were seats to fill in the legislature. A minority party might by this device concentrate on a few candidates and, thereby, increase their representation in the general assembly. The Republican Party would, of course, retain a majority of seats. But a bolstered Democratic presence might, it was hoped, "shame them into decency, or frighten them from crime."[57]

"What are we to do?" Hampton asked Armistead Burt from his Mississippi home. "The objects of our reform friends were praiseworthy, but their whole plan of battle was wrong." Hampton believed that Southerners must look to the electoral success of the national Democratic party for their deliverance. In the meantime "if we can secure a majority, or even a strong minority in our Legislature, we will be on the road to permanent relief." The first step must be to reform the election laws "to insure a fair expression of popular opinion."[58]

Suggestions and protests caused little concern to those in power. Corruption continued unabated. The following year there were a few feeble calls in the legislature to impeach Governor Scott and state treasurer Niles G. Parker for unlawfully issuing bonds and falsifying reports. The governor quickly bought the silence of his legislative critics with money embezzled from the state's military budget.[59]

It was said that fellow Republicans asked carpetbagger John Patterson if he did not think it expedient at least to feign reform. "Honest John," as he was called, only scoffed. "Why gentlemen, there are five years of good stealing in South Carolina yet."[60]

The wave of violence that rolled over the state two years earlier now returned. Faced with militia outrages, and expecting no justice from the authorities, Ku Klux Klan members took the law into their own hands. Newspaper publicity had prompted a rapid spread of the secret order since its postwar founding in Tennessee. Beginning as a whimsical social club, members found that their outlandish regalia frightened freedmen. There had been Ku Klux violence in South Carolina in 1868, but then their vigilantism was largely limited to warnings and beatings. Even now Ku Klux activity remained confined to the upcountry. But it had become much more serious. In January 1871 black militiamen murdered a white teamster when he refused to surrender a cargo of whiskey. Arrested, the militiamen were jailed in the town of

Union. Fearing that they would escape punishment, Klansmen took two from jail and killed them. Six weeks later, before the remaining suspects could be transported to safety in Columbia, more than 500 mounted Klansmen rode into Union and executed them all. "We want and will have Justice," read their message, "and this cannot be till a bleeding fight for freedom is fought. Until then the Moloch of Iniquity will have his victims, even if the Michael of Justice must have his martyrs."[61]

Congress responded to Ku Klux activity in the South by creating a joint select committee to investigate. Subcommittees traveled to each of "the late insurrectionary states" to take testimony. One such group would stop in Columbia before moving on to the upcountry towns of Spartanburg, Union, and Yorkville. Chairman of this three-man subcommittee was Senator John Scott, a forty-seven-year-old Pennsylvania Republican. Lawyer Job Evans Stevenson, also a Republican, represented Cincinnati in Congress. Although of military age, Stevenson had avoided Union army service by election to the state Senate. The only Democrat on the subcommittee was Congressman Philadelph Van Trumph of Lancaster, Ohio. In the course of his long political career, the sixty-year-old Van Trumph had been a Whig, a member of the American Party, then a supporter of the Constitutional Unionists in 1860. He was now serving his third term in the House.[62] It is likely that he arranged for Hampton to testify in order to place on record the case against South Carolina's Reconstruction government.

Hampton's testimony began on July 21, 1871. Van Trumph was permitted by Senator Scott to begin the examination of Hampton. The Democrat first asked questions designed to bolster Hampton's credibility in the eyes of Northerners by establishing him as a moderate on the issues of secession and the coming of war. Hampton, although careful to avoid perjury, went along.[63] Van Trumph soon led his witness to the reason for his testimony. Hampton presented facts showing that most members of the radical establishment paid few taxes. Property-owning white people, the taxpayers of the state, had become virtually powerless. The result was "taxation without representation and representation without taxation." Bribery, too, had become routine in the State House. South Carolina, said Hampton, was ruled by "not only freedmen without property, but vagrant whites without character."[64]

Representative Stevenson countered by arguing a variety of points with Hampton, but the general held his ground. One "very grave mistake that you gentlemen in the North make," instructed Hampton, is "in taking it for granted that every white man in the South was a rebel and every negro loyal [to the Union]." He recounted how in 1865 Gen. Johnson Hagood had appealed to the patriotism of his slaves, "and every man who was capable of bearing arms on that plantation enlisted to go and serve in the Confederate army." Hampton pointed out too that before the war free blacks in South

Carolina held a considerable amount of property, and some were even slave owners themselves.[65]

Under questioning by Chairman Scott, Hampton revealed that he had written a letter to Grant soon after the president's election, "expressing my fears that there would be a collision of the races in the State. Those fears are not yet removed; and that has been the main reason why I have deprecated rousing any antagonism between the two races." In Hampton's opinion, if the black majority "were to chose good men and have the government administered economically," white people of the state would wait patiently for the return of their rights. They would not submit, however, to living indefinitely "under a rule where persons so entirely ignorant, so venal, so corrupt, have the management of their State government." Hampton went on to lecture his interrogators.

> You gentleman do not know the negro at all, and there is the great difficulty. You all think the negroes are actuated by the same feelings as the white man, but that is a mistake. I do not pretend to say why it is, but they are not. They have been dependent for a long time; they have no provision; they have no forethought at all; they are content to live from hand to mouth; they do not pretend to lay up anything; they are very credulous; they have an exaggerated opinion of their own power. . . . I am not speaking of the more intelligent ones, but of the great mass of laborers.[66]

Stevenson, showing his irritation, asked if "the fancy of the negro as to his ability to put down everybody" was "any more unreasonable than the fancy prevailing at the South, before the war, that a southern man cold whip ten Yankees?"

"No sir," Hampton replied, "I do not think that fancy prevailed before the war. I did not put the numbers as large as that."

Nevertheless, was there not a "considerable disproportion?" snapped Stevenson.

"I think the result of the war proved that we were not so very wrong," said the general, "so far as the fighting was concerned."

The congressman had no further questions.[67]

13

"STRAIGHT EVERY TIME"

Hampton Is Nominated for Governor

On October 12, 1871, President Grant, in response to the congressional investigation, issued a proclamation suspending habeus corpus in nine upcountry South Carolina counties. Many suspected of Ku Klux Klan activity fled the state and 533 were arrested. Democrat Van Trumph issued a sharply worded minority report. Lawlessness in South Carolina was, in his view, "the clearest natural offspring of as corrupt and oppressive a system of local state government as ever disgraced humanity, and utterly unparalleled in the history of civilization."[1]

The South Carolina Republican Party in August 1872 nominated Franklin Moses Jr. for governor and R. H. Gleaves, a black man, for lieutenant governor. Concerned about blatant corruption in state government, a number of Republicans left the party to nominate the relatively unknown Reuben Tomlinson. Democrats offered no candidate for governor. Many conservatives thought Tomlinson the lesser of two evils, while others simply boycotted the election. The *Edgefield Advertiser* dismissed the contest as "a struggle between thieves and plunderers." The alternatives were a "black dog and a monkey," said the *Chester Reporter*. By now election laws had been amended to provide a degree of honesty, there being little further need to defraud hopelessly outnumbered Democrats. Moses beat Tomlinson by an almost 2–1 margin,[2] and the corruption continued. In two years the governor pardoned 457 convicted criminals. Pennsylvania native John Patterson bribed his way to a U.S. Senate seat, spending some $40,000 for the votes of South Carolina legislators. Those lawmakers also supplemented their incomes by ordering

"Gov. Franklin Moses Jr. views the Promised Land from Mount Ruin" in this period
political cartoon. Rampant corruption in Moses's administration undercut the
credibility of the federal government's Reconstruction efforts. *Harper's Weekly.*

"supplies" that went beyond pens, paper, and postage stamps. Literally any-thing they wanted—from food to furniture—was charged to the taxpayers. These expenses went from $822,608 in the 1870–1871 legislative session to $1,533,574 the next. For two sessions it never dropped below $900,000 annu-ally. The liquor bill for one session was $125,000, according to the clerk of the House. "South Carolina has no right to be a state," sneered carpetbagger C. P. Leslie, "unless it can take care of its statesmen." All newspapers in South Carolina were paid to publish government notices and acts of the legis-lature. Republican papers, despite small circulations, were grossly overpaid for these services, and lawmakers received subscriptions to radical journals at state expense. Nearly all of the owners and editors of these subsidized Repub-lican newspapers were officeholders. "History fails to cite an instance which can be compared with such a carnival of fraud and extravagance," concluded later investigators.[3] A Northern visitor wrote in his journal after talking with Hampton in February 1872,

> I asked him could he forecast the future of the negro rule. He said he could not. He complained of the oppressive taxation, which he said they would not complain of if the proceeds were devoted to any useful purpose. But they were not. They were stolen by the adventurers who led the negroes.

Hampton went on to explain that blacks would no longer work for wages, but wanted a half share of the crop. He blamed this system for a substantial decline in production due to "idleness & mismanagement" on the part of blacks.

Hampton made his comments during an agricultural convention,[4] prob-ably sponsored by the Grange. The Order of Patrons of Husbandry was founded soon after the war by those in the North and South concerned about economic and other issues affecting farmers. The Grange also became an important center of social activity for farm families. Hampton decided to join. By 1875 there were 341 active Granges in South Carolina, with a membership of 10,922. David Wyatt Aiken of South Carolina was on the organization's National Executive Committee.[5]

The Amnesty Act that became law in 1872 finally removed the Fourteenth Amendment's restriction on ex-Confederates voting and holding office. Still, Wade Hampton stood aloof from politics. Disillusioned with radicalism and scandals that were surfacing in the Grant administration, reform-minded Republicans nominated newspaperman Horace Greely as the presidential candidate of the Liberal Republican Party. Hampton privately agreed with Mullaly that Democrats should not split the anti-Grant vote by putting for-ward a third choice. Greely—a man who had made a reputation attacking all things Southern—was hardly Hampton's ideal. He hoped that Greely would at least prove himself acceptable to Southern conservatives by avoiding "civil rights" rhetoric. "I have made no public declaration of my preferences," Hampton told Mullaly, "because experience has taught me that my Rad friends are prone to misinterpret all I say, and hence my support of Greely, would do him more harm than good." Greely, although he became the nominee of both the Democrats and liberal Republicans, was overwhelmed by Grant on election day. Except for Texas, every Southern state still under radical domination ended up in the President's column.[6]

Hampton continued to be anxious about wife Mary. In November 1872 he described her as "very weak and nervous." She had been diagnosed as suffering from hysteria, the term used in the nineteenth century for a poorly understood disease affecting women. One authority described patients "unable to attend to the duties of life and sources alike of discomfort to themselves and anxiety to other." Emotional, restless, victims might swing from laughter to tears in moments. Appetite declined, every activity became wearisome, until the patient became an invalid. Once they were bedridden, other physical symptoms and disabilities inevitably followed. It was thought that victims were born with a disposition for the disease, that it usually made its appearance before age thirty, and that it was activated by an emotional shock.[7] The first evidence we have of Mary Hampton's affliction is postwar, but it may well have begun earlier.

Trips between Columbia and Baltimore were becoming extremely difficult for Mary as she was usually confined to her room. Hampton's brother-in-law Thomas L. Preston was employed by Carolina Life in Richmond. He and wife Anna lived in a large home near Charlottesville. In the spring of 1873, Hampton asked the childless couple if their home might become a refuge for Mary. "The noise and confinement of a [Baltimore] boarding house are hurtful to Mary and I want to get her to the country," he wrote to Thomas. "If she consents to this move, could you and Anna let us board with you for some time?" Hampton insisted on paying expenses, and urged him to respond "frankly." Anna Preston was most agreeable. "My only fear in going to your house," Hampton replied, "is that you will worry and fatigue yourself." They would arrive with a party of six that included twelve-year-old daughter Daisy and the servants. "Two rooms will be sufficient," Hampton was sure, "if you can pack me away anywhere, when I am there."

Again and again in letters, Hampton repeated his desire "to have Mary in the country." In June she arrived at the Preston's home, but her decline continued, and her husband found himself unable to leave her for long. Letters were written from her bedside. "Mrs Hampton is still an invalid," he said in November, "& this confines me greatly." The life insurance business surely suffered by his absence. On February 18, 1874, Hampton confessed to Mullaly that "I have seen nothing and known but little of public affairs for the past two years and a half for during that time my wife has been such an invalid, that my whole time has been devoted to her."[8] Just ten days after he wrote this letter, Mary died. The news reached Columbia on March 2. "The sympathy of our whole community are [sic] extended to General Hampton and family in this severe affliction," said the *Daily Phoenix*. Her funeral was held at noon on Wednesday, March 4, at Trinity Episcopal Church, and she was buried in the Hampton family plot. "I have seen enough of the fortitude of your nature," wrote Matthew C. Butler, "to know that you will bear this trying calamity with that resignation which comes from entire faith in the wisdom of God's dispensations."[9]

Hampton remained in Columbia for a time after the funeral, "living in the utmost quiet." When spring turned to summer, the family retreated once again to the North Carolina mountains.[10] Politics seemed even further from his mind.

Back in February, as Mary was dying, a second taxpayers' convention met in Columbia. Most delegates were, of course, Democrats, although five black and a few white Republicans attended. Resolutions were passed complaining "of the wrongs which we suffer, by reason of the frauds and extravagance of our State Government." Taxpayers appealed to Congress to intervene and put a stop to the abuses. Martin W. Gary stated that the battle was not partisan, but racial. Whites should encourage European immigration to South Carolina in order to overcome the black majority. All attempts at compromise had been futile, insisted Gary. He criticized Hampton for declining to run for governor against Orr back in 1865. Neither did he approve of Hampton's advocacy of even limited black suffrage.[11] A committee from the convention was dispatched to present the delegates' case to the president. Grant was in no mood to hear them. Congress also declined to become involved in the conservative's dispute with South Carolina's rulers.

"The South Carolina government is the worst in the world," said the New York *Journal of Commerce* in commenting on the taxpayers' gathering. Not only were land owners and businessmen bearing the burden of bad government, but the "humblest blacks and whites suffer from the wolves of Columbia, and should be glad to join forces with the taxpayer to exterminate them politically." Congress was responsible for the situation, and the New York editor agreed that Congress should help end it. But "the job of purgation would be clearer and more satisfactory and stay longer done, if it could be wrought out by the tempestuous and irresistible uprising of South Carolina themselves."[12]

South Carolina Democrats, or conservatives, as they had begun calling themselves, again chose not to enter a candidate in the 1874 race for governor. In July the state Republican Executive Committee admitted that their party had not kept campaign promises, that "sound policy has been discarded and reckless extravagance manifested." The national party "admonishes us to at once retrace our steps and vindicate . . . the integrity of Republicanism."

When the Republican convention met in September, delegates chose Daniel H. Chamberlain to be their standardbearer; he defeated Judge John T. Green by a vote of 72–40.[13] Chamberlain, a Massachusetts native, was formerly attorney general of South Carolina, but had been out of office for two years. His attendance at the first taxpayers' convention gave him at least the veneer of reform. A talented speaker and writer, the Yale graduate was remembered by one as "a brilliant man, cold and impassive, with chiseled features and a smile which always seemed to be of special sweetness." Critics remembered that Attorney General Chamberlain had overlooked corruption all around him and that he was closely associated with the worst men in office. Lieutenant Governor Gleaves was renominated, despite his own sordid reputation. Gleaves overcame a challenge in the convention by another black man, Martin R. Delany. Honest, educated, and well-respected even by his political enemies, Delany was especially critical of white carpetbaggers who used black votes simply to advance and enrich themselves.[14]

Independent Republicans soon held their own convention and nominated Green and Delany. The Independents stated frankly that they were "not hostile to the domination of the Republican party in South Carolina," merely that they wanted to clean up corruption. Green and Delany asked for the votes of white Democrats, and James Chesnut's "citizens in favor of honest and good government" quickly endorsed the ticket. Chamberlain won by 11,585 votes, a closer margin than might have been expected. Judge Green died suddenly in January. Had he and Delany been elected, Delany would have become South Carolina's first black chief executive—the candidate of conservative whites.[15]

Chamberlain got off to a good start as governor. A number of individuals were indicted for corruption, some made it to trial, and at least a few were convicted. The governor was cautious in the exercise of his pardoning power. Taxes became more uniform and slightly lower, and expenditures were reduced. "News of an honest and economical administration of the State Government of South Carolina is good news indeed," wrote the Philadelphia *Ledger*. "South Carolina sadly needs it." Still, there were questions about Chamberlain's sincerity. He had submitted false figures on the state debt to the first taxpayers' convention. As a member of Governor Scott's Financial Board, some thought he profited from the sale of stock owned by the state in the Greenville and Columbia Railroad. In his private law practice, it was charged that he had been overpaid for work he did on behalf of the Republican Printing Company. Chamberlain's concern for reform had at least as much to do with the survival of his party as it did with the good of his adopted state.[16]

Hampton remained out of politics, but he continued to encourage the writing of history by Southerners. "We wish to put on record in an enduring form," he told James Conner, "the truths regarding our struggle for freedom, and thus preserve our glorious position and our heroic deeds." Hampton became embroiled briefly in Joseph Johnston's long-running feud with Jefferson Davis. Johnston wrote to Hampton, asking if it was true that Lee had advised Davis to remove Johnston from command. Hampton replied in the negative, a response interpreted by Davis as an "endorsement of complaints against" him. Hampton had to patch things up with Davis, assuring that "upon no occasion, nor in any manner have I made or endured complaints against yourself." Hampton truly admired Davis, even as he attempted to remain on good terms with the former president's detractors. Hampton had his own continuing war of words with Sherman over Columbia's destruction. "I want to nail Sherman's lies to the counter forever," said Hampton.[17] It was one battle he would win.

Although Hampton accepted Confederate defeat, he was not about to concede that the cause of the South had been wrong. Speaking to the Southern Historical Society in 1873, he expressed the hope that one day people might come to understand that the struggle between North and South went back to the very founding of America. Confederates had nothing to be ashamed of. Southern children must be taught "that their fathers were neither traitors nor rebels; that we believed as firmly as in the eternal word of God, that we were in the right." *The Southern Magazine* of Baltimore applauded Hampton's attitude. "National restoration is no more possible, with self-abasement, that resurrection when there is no soul."[18]

John S. Preston created a furor in July 1875 when he spoke to the graduating class at the University of Virginia. Now sixty-six, Preston had been a signer of South Carolina's Ordinance of Secession and a Confederate brigadier. He called the war "a mortal struggle for truth and liberty," but many thought he went too far in disparaging the North. "Will not the God of truth forbid that your liberties shall be judged forever by other men's consciences?" he asked. Some called his words "extreme," but Hampton thought the "indiscretion was in the time and place of delivering the speech and not in the speech itself."[19]

That month Hampton delayed his departure for Cashiers in order to attend a Columbia reunion of the Hampton Legion. A reporter from the Republican *Daily Union Herald* was there, ready to pounce upon any evidence of an un-Reconstructed attitude. Hundreds were present, the veterans wearing blue ribbons emblazoned with "Hampton Legion" in letters of gold. The general presided, but made no address. The reporter was surprised by the moderate tone of the speeches he heard. The band played "Dixie," of course, but he conceded that the song "is now a national air." All considered, he noted an "absence of the Confederate ghost," the term the *Union Herald* had coined for Preston's evocation of the Lost Cause.[20]

At the beginning of 1876, most white South Carolinians probably felt that recapturing the reins of state government was a cause no less lost. There seemed to be simply no way for Democrats to overcome the black majority vote. Conservative "fusionists" argued that they might maximize their influence by joining forces with the better type of Republicans, men such as Chamberlain. The governor's reputation with conservatives was then at a high point. Just before Christmas the legislature had elected W. J. Whipper and Franklin J. Moses Jr. to vacant court judgeships. The election of two of the state's most notorious "corruptionists" was meant by legislative radicals to be a slap in the face to the governor. One black lawmaker jumped up on his desk shouting, "Chamberlain can't veto this!" Instead, the governor refused the new judges' commissions on a technicality, and his action was backed up by the state supreme court. Whipper threatened to seize his Charleston courthouse by force, and Democrats rallied to the governor. In Sumter, where Moses would preside, whites threatened armed resistance. "The election of these two men to judicial office sends a thrill of horror throughout the State," Chamberlain told President Grant. The governor welcomed the backing of white conservatives,[21] and fusionists were optimistic.

Democratic support for Chamberlain was especially strong in Charleston. "All that stands between us and the degradation of the bench," said James Conner at a Hibernian Hall rally, "is the wise and bold action of the Governor." Other fusionists included Generals Joseph Brevard Kershaw and Johnson Hagood. Even former governor Perry thought Chamberlain "honest, wise and patriotic." The Charleston *News and Courier,* the largest newspaper in the state, became an enthusiastic defender of Chamberlain and an eloquent exponent of fusion. "To him," read an editorial, "thanks eternal for interposing the shield of executive authority between the chieftans of the robber band in Columbia and the people of the low country of South Carolina." It was in this atmosphere that the state Central Executive Committee of the Democratic Party met on January 6, 1876, in Columbia. Hampton was still a member, although not present. Matthew C. Butler was chairman. Over Martin W. Gary's objections, the committee applauded Chamberlain for "reform and retrenchment" and for his stand on the judicial election. All agreed, however, that the Democratic Party should be "revived." Whether in concert with Republican reformers or on their own, in the coming election "we must win. Defeat cannot be borne." The party would be reorganized, and preparations would go forward for a state convention. Only then would they decide what course to take.[22]

Chamberlain would be opposed in the Republican convention in September by his party's worst "corruptionists"—men like U.S. Senator John Patterson and R. B. Elliott, speaker of the South Carolina House. Chamberlain was able to secure renomination through his oratorical abilities, and perhaps by a realization among delegates that the incumbent governor was, after all, their strongest candidate.[23]

At the beginning of 1876, of the former Confederate states, only South Carolina, Louisiana, and Florida remained under Republican control. One by one, conservative southern whites had "redeemed" their state governments. Even Mississippi, with a black majority as large as South Carolina's, had thrown out the radicals. Many Democrats were asking why the same result could not be achieved in the Palmetto State. Martin Delany, candidate for lieutenant governor two years earlier, had warned fellow blacks "that there are no white people, North or South, who will submit that the black rule over the white in America."[24] White Democrats had made a similar prophecy on the eve of congressional Reconstruction. Advocates of South Carolina's redemption were now ready to make their case.

Democrats of all persuasions met in a state convention in Columbia on May 4. "The man who dares, wins; not he who holds back," declared Gary.[25] He was formulating a plan in his own county of Edgefield, based on tactics recently proven successful in Mississippi. Gary insisted that Democrats nominate only those candidates who were willing to give "their time, their money, their brains, their energies and if necessary lay down their lives" to achieve victory. Black voters would be welcomed, but must understand that "their natural position is that of subordination to the white man." Every Democrat should make it his business to control one black Republican voter "by intimidation, purchase, keeping him away [from the polling place]." Campaigning should be carried out as if it were a military operation. Armed Democrats would appear at Republican meetings, get on the platform, and denounce opponents as "liars, thieves and rascals" who were "only trying to mislead the ignorant Negroes." There should be no attempt to reason with blacks, as "they can only be influenced by their fears, superstitions and cupidity." Democratic rallies were to "make an imposing spectacle," demonstrating the inevitability of victory. On election day every Democrat must vote and an honest count be ensured. If fraud or violence occurred, radical leaders had to understand that they would be held personally responsible. No individual radical should be threatened; "the necessities of the times require that he should die." Armed men would go to Columbia, if necessary, to see to it that victorious Democrats were allowed to take office. The Edgefield Democratic Executive Committee objected to Gary's advocacy of violence, and those points were dropped. The remainder of the plan was endorsed and distributed statewide.[26]

Matthew C. Butler agreed with Gary. "The only possible way to redeem the state," he told the Democratic convention, "is to nominate a true, liberal, moderate native [for governor], with a like ticket, and carry the war into Africa. Go into the swamps and bogs of the low country and carry your Democracy with you." It would take more than words to undo the Reconstruction Acts of Congress. "They may have been unconstitutional and revolutionary," said Gary, referring to the ill-fated platform of 1868, "but they were not null and void."[27] Gary and his followers called themselves "straight-outs"—conservatives who refused to compromise, Democrats who would win or lose as Democrats, in one straight-out bid for victory.

Straightouts made their point in the convention, but the majority remained cautious and unconvinced. After much debate, early on the morning of Saturday, May 6, delegates could only agree on a resolution permitting the Executive Committee to call a second convention at a later date. Democrats were for now too divided to choose a platform or nominate candidates. Straightouts were bitterly disappointed. Fusionists, led by the *News and Courier*, expressed relief that delegates were "cool and determined," rather than "rash and impulsive." "Paradoxically enough," concluded the Charleston editor, "to do nothing was the wisest thing that the Convention could do."[28]

Wade Hampton remained at Wild Woods, Mississippi, during May, seemingly disinterested and little aware of the debate back home. Other than to join his family at Cashiers, "I have made no plans for the summer." On Friday, June 16, he was in Columbia, accompanied by daughter Sally Haskell and her young children. The entire family would soon gather at their mountain retreat, but Hampton himself must follow later. He had promised to attend ceremonies in Charleston commemorating the one-hundredth anniversary of Col. William Moultrie's victory over the British at the beginning of the Revolutionary War.[29]

A century earlier patriots under the command of Moultrie had hastily erected a fort of palmetto logs on Sullivan's Island, protecting Charleston Harbor. On June 28, 1776, a British fleet of nine warships dueled with those defenders before being driven away. South Carolinians liked to believe that news of the event prompted a wavering continental congress to declare American independence. The palmetto tree on South Carolina's flag commemorated the victory, and June 28 was known thereafter as "Carolina Day."

For the centennial a grand patriotic celebration was planned, a nonpartisan event that all might be proud to take part in. On June 27 the Boston Light Infantry and the New York Old Guard arrived by ship. As their vessel tied up at the dock, a band on board struck up "Dixie." The next morning they joined a long parade of military units from Georgia and South Carolina that even included a contingent of Mexican War veterans. All were under the honorary command of Wade Hampton. The general wore the uniform of the Palmetto Guards. "It is putting it mildly to say it was hot," reported the *News and Courier*. "The traditional 4th of July weather was frosty in comparison." After the parade there was speech making across the harbor at Fort Moultrie, a rowing regatta, sailboat races, and cannon salutes. Banners of every description and nationality flew throughout the old city, including one Confederate battle flag at the Queen Street armory of the Charleston Light Dragoons.[30] Hibernian Hall on Meeting Street was centennial headquarters, and there, on the evening of Carolina Day, a banquet was held.

Maj. G. Lamb Buist, commanding officer of the Palmetto Guard Rifle Club, presided. On his right sat Wade Hampton, to his left, Daniel Chamberlain. Some would later claim that the arrangement was intentional and politically motivated, although few probably thought so at the time. The occasion was a love feast. The governor made handsome, patriotic remarks that were loudly applauded. Toasts were made to South Carolina, Massachusetts, and other states. After each toast followed an eloquent response. Then C. Rutledge Holmes proposed a toast to Wade Hampton. The *News and Courier* reported,

> Gen. Hampton rose to acknowledge it, and, as soon as the cheering could be hushed, said in a voice and with a manner which betrayed considerable emotion: "Gentlemen, I acknowledge this greeting of me by my fellow citizens as adding another to the many obligations under which the people of South Carolina have placed me, and if devotion and loyalty to her can give me any claim on the good will of my friends of South Carolina, then I may not be altogether unworthy of the affection they bestow upon me."

Hampton remembered that Moultrie and his men did battle "under a flag whereon was inscribed the word 'Liberty,' and we shall prove false to the blood that flows in our veins if we fail to maintain the principles for which they fought." Speaking to the Northerners present, Hampton reminded them that for "nearly a century" South Carolinians firmly held that they had a right to peacefully withdraw from a union they had freely joined. He made it emphatically clear that he accepted "the decision of the war as final." But the North must credit the South's motives and not ask former Confederates to give up "our honor" or "self respect." "When this is done, we can agree to disagree on the questions that led to war."[31]

Next day, on the train from Charleston back to Columbia, Hampton found himself in the company of former generals Gary, Kershaw, and Hagood, all traveling home from the Moultrie centennial. Gary had for weeks been encouraging Butler to run for governor as he garnered allies for his straightout strategy. Talking privately now with Hampton, Gary found that Hampton, too, was sympathetic to the idea that Democrats contest the election as Democrats. Gary had a flash of inspiration. Would Hampton be willing to run for governor himself? Butler had, of course, not been consulted. Hampton replied that he did not want to run, but would if chosen by the Democratic convention. That was enough for Gary. He took Hampton over to where Generals Kershaw and Hagood, both prominent fusionists, were sitting and announced that Hampton had consented to run, if nominated, as a straightout. "Well, if the general is nominated, I will fall into line and support him," replied a smiling Kershaw. "I always obey orders from headquarters." The quartet parted at Branchville; Gary and Hagood going to Augusta as Hampton and Kershaw continued on to Columbia, where Hampton would spend but one night before traveling to Cashiers. Once alone, Hagood confided to Gary that his question to Hampton and Hampton's reply had destroyed all of his fusionist plans.[32]

Less than a week later, public opinion statewide was polarized by a race riot in the all-black village of Hamburg. The place already had a dark reputation. Two years earlier a crew of railroad repairmen had been arrested and confined "by a posse of negroes, headed by a few Hamburg constables," motivated by nothing but a desire "to show their power." On July 4, 1876, black militiamen harassed two white travelers on the main street of Hamburg. Four days later, a confrontation, at which Matthew C. Butler was present, led to the shooting death of a white man and the retaliatory killing of seven blacks. Chamberlain immediately sided with the blacks, denounced Butler, and asked President Grant for troops. Black carpetbagger Richard H. "Daddy" Cain threatened statewide vengeance. "Remember that there are 80,000 black men in this State who can bear Winchester rifles and know how to use them," said Cain, "and that there are 200,000 [black] women who can light a torch and use the knife."[33] The prospect of fusion between Democrats and Republicans suddenly began to fade.

During a lull in the violence at Hamburg, a truce had been proposed. "I'll be god damned if I am not tired of these conferences," said Butler.[34] By midsummer 1876 his fellow South Carolinians were no less weary of talk and ready for action.

On July 9 a letter from Butler appeared in the Columbia *Register*. He and Gary had chosen this forum for a withdrawal of Butler's candidacy. Butler recommended that Democrats nominate Wade Hampton, "one of our most prominent, patriotic and popular countrymen." Although Butler said that he had not spoken with Hampton, "he can more completely than any other man reconcile whatever discordant elements there may be in the Democratic party."[35]

There was to be a campaign appearance by Chamberlain in Edgefield on August 12, and Gary invited Hampton to come. Not yet the Democratic nominee, Hampton declined. "Butler has got me into a scrape," he wrote Gary, referring to the public letter of endorsement. Hampton still seemed reluctant to enter the political fray, but understood what was at stake and the absolute necessity that Democrats be united.

> I am satisfied that the convention will be Straight out & we must be gentle with our Charleston friends, appealing to them to go in with us. The News & Courier must either be made to sustain our policy or to quit the party which it is defeating and disgracing.[36]

Two weeks later Hampton wrote a letter to the *Register*, replying in public to Butler's endorsement. He claimed that "my first impulse was to decline the nomination at once and unconditionally." He suggested that his friends find some other candidate. He would run, however, "if this call shall be made with unanimity, and that those making it will be fully prepared, like myself, to make every sacrifice and to devote every energy and every effort to the redemption of our 'Prostrate State.' "[37]

The Edgefield campaign event that Hampton declined to attend proved to be a dress rehearsal for what was to come. Governor Chamberlain was informed by local Democrats that they would attend his outdoor meeting and expected to "divide the time." As promised, Gary, Butler, and 800 mounted men arrived. Gary declared that they would "share the meeting or there would be no meeting." The governor began to speak, promising reform, but was heckled. Part of the stand crashed to the ground. Frustrated, Chamberlain attempted to leave, but Gary told him to sit down or he would make him sit down. Butler then rose. He said that Congressman Robert Smalls and Chamberlain had both accused him of being a Ku Klux Klan leader, and if they were now unable to prove it, "they stood confessed liars." Gary came forward. He called Chamberlain "a cheat, a fraud and a snare"; one who was involved in corruption; a man who appointed thieves to office. All his talk of "reform" was a lie.

"For God's sake, Gary, hold up on him!" whispered Butler. But Gary went on, concluding that "our exemplary Governor had better begin to pack his carpet-bag for he will soon have to quit eating South Carolina rice and return to Massachusetts where he can enjoy codfish." Just then the speakers' stand completely collapsed, sending everyone sprawling except Butler, "perched upon the only point left standing." Democrats cheered, as if it were an omen. What had been billed as a Republican rally broke up in chaos, the angry governor escaping to his waiting railroad car, where he continued to be harassed.[38]

It may have been the same day that Chamberlain was retreating from Edgefield that Hampton received a message at Cashiers, delivered by a black man riding a mule. The next morning the two departed together.[39] Hampton had been invited to join in a deer hunt in the mountains of Oconee County between Cashiers and Walhalla. When the party returned to camp, "lace coffee" was served, an upcountry concoction of strong coffee, sugar, and corn whiskey, served hot. Hampton had never heard of it, but declared the beverage "Gilt-edged." Once in Walhalla he met with local leaders at his room in Biemann's Hotel. When asked how Democrats hoped to win the unequal contest with their Republican foes, Hampton said, "You must just out-vote them."[40]

The convention of the Democratic party came to order in Columbia on August 15 in the house chamber of the capitol. An immediate test of strength for fusionists came on the vote for chairman. W. W. Harllee of Marion, an ally of Gary, defeated fusionist Charles H. Simonton by a vote of 73–66. The

next morning the convention went into secret session to consider the para-
mount question of whether to nominate a straightout Democratic ticket or
to attempt fusion with Republican reformers. After five and a half hours of
behind-closed-door debate, the result was announced. Democrats had
decided, by a vote of 82–65, to nominate a full slate of candidates.[41]

Those who favored Hampton found they must surmount yet another
hurdle. John F. Coyle had been dispatched to Columbia by the National
Democratic Committee to inform delegates that Northern party leaders,
including presidential nominee Samuel J. Tilden, were opposed to Hampton's candidacy. A campaign led by the former Confederate general might
embarrass Democrats in the North. This news had a chilling effect, playing
on the minds of even Hampton's supporters.[42]

The Aiken and Edgefield delegates sat in the front of the hall, on the
right. Just as the galleries were again opened to press and public following
the vote in favor of nominating a full ticket, Gary turned to Butler. "Now is
the time for you to nominate Hampton," he said. Butler replied that Gary
should do it, but nearby delegates lifted Butler to a chair, and he then made
the nomination.[43]

"It was nearly five o'clock," remembered one participant. "Hampton,
who had stood apart, and up to this time had not opened his mouth . . .
arose in the back of the hall. Tall, rather slim (then), neatly dressed, quiet and
cool, and unassuming, he strode to the front; held up his hand," and began
to speak.

Referring to Trinity Episcopal across the street, Hampton said,

> I have claimed nothing from South Carolina but a grave in yonder church
> yard. But I have always said that if I could ever serve her by word or deed
> her men had only to call me and I would devote all my life to her service.

He acknowledged that Tilden and the national party thought his unrepentant Confederate past a liability. "That is the record of 60,000 South
Carolina soldiers; and if I am to forfeit that, and say that I am ashamed to
have been one of them, all the offices in the world might perish before I
would accept them."

Vowing to support whoever was chosen, Hampton then left the hall.
Someone nominated John Bratton of York County, one of those who had
argued for heeding the admonitions of the national party. Bratton quickly
rose to decline in favor of Hampton. Former governor John L. Manning was
nominated, and he too declined in favor of Hampton. Wade Hampton was
then nominated by acclamation.[44]

The nominee was escorted back into the hall amid prolonged applause.
"You are struggling for the highest stake for which a people ever contended,"
said Hampton in accepting, "for you are striving to bring back to your pros-

trate State the inestimable blessings which can only follow orderly and regulated liberty under free and good government." He appealed to "every man in South Carolina who honestly desires reform," to rally to a cause "where our citizens of all parties and all races can stand assured of equal rights and full protection." He closed with a promise. "For myself, should I be elevated to the high position for which you have nominated me, my sole effort shall be to restore our State government to decency, to honesty, to economy, and to integrity. I shall be the Governor of the whole people, knowing no party."[45]

"If there had been a ballot many would have voted against H.," said one Democrat, "but it would have only done harm to oppose him ineffectually." All knew that unity was now essential. The slate of Democratic nominees for statewide offices was well balanced geographically and factionally. James Conner was nominated for attorney general and Johnson Hagood for comptroller general—both were former fusionists. William Dunlap Simpson of Laurens, once a colonel under Stonewall Jackson, was the Democratic candidate for lieutenant governor.[46]

If unanimity among some of the politicians was affected, outside in the summer air it was very different. One witness remembered,

> There was wild rejoicing in Columbia that night. Thousands, cheering, yelling in a pandemonium of joy, and in the glaring flames of a torchlight procession, moved down Main Street to the State House, where, from a stand erected in front of the building, speakers pledged themselves and their hearers to the support of the Democratic ticket.

The enthusiasm was genuine, but the demonstration itself had been planned for over a week, originally as a "Tilden for president" rally.[47] A huge number had gathered at the fairgrounds on Elmwood at six o'clock that evening. Led by perhaps 1,000 horsemen, the crowds poured through Columbia's main business district. One poster read, "No milk, no sugar, no lemon; straight every time." Another bore a likeness of Chamberlain running "straight-out" of the state. There was little anger; the mood of the multitude was joyous, yet determined. Not since the war had there been such a scene in South Carolina's capital. "The nomination of Gen. Wade Hampton for Governor," remembered a supporter, "sent a thrill like electricity through the State, and revived hopes, long drooping and well nigh dead."[48]

"It is impossible to regard the course of the Democrats in South Carolina as anything but reactionary," wrote the New York *Evening Post*. "The name of Wade Hampton, not only in South Carolina, but throughout the country, stands for the old order." That editor was relieved to report it "not likely that Hampton will be elected." Hampton, said *The Nation*, "is neither a statesman nor a politician, nor a man of conciliatory disposition," but merely

Wade Hampton, candidate for governor. *Harper's Weekly*.

a relic of the Old South. William Lloyd Garrison was livid at the news from Columbia. Democrats had shown "their unchanged spirit by the nomination of the leading slaveholder and rebel in the State, General Wade Hampton, as their standardbearer and candidate for Governor of South Carolina!"[49]

"In their commander-in-chief, General Hampton, we are assured of a foeman worthy of our steel," conceded the Republican editor of Columbia's *Union Herald*. Still, Hampton was "the nominee of Edgefield." The "ruffian policy" now adopted by Democrats would surely "plunge the state into a vortex of hate, terror and anarchy."[50]

More thoughtful was the editorial in Columbia's Democratic *Daily Register* the day after Hampton's triumph.

> From our knowledge of the man, we are aware of the extreme reluctance with which he has been compelled to yield to the force of an irresistible public opinion. With the blunt simplicity of a soldier . . . he rose in the convention and stated the objections against himself as a candidate. It is a strange thing in this day to listen to such an argument. It was so strange, indeed, and so new, that the convention broke down under it completely.

Hampton's nomination may have been a misstep by a "too bold" Democratic party, wrote the editor. "Nevertheless, this we will say, that what win popular victories and rule the world are ideas that are throbbed from the heart and burned into the brain of a people or an age."[51]

14

"TO STORM HELL
FOR HAMPTON"

The Red Shirt Campaign

T he prospect of a Hampton victory, wrote one Democrat, was like "the sudden flash of a new day of sunshine and brightness and hope for safety and freedom of life for family and home, of race purity and pride secure and the loved state cleansed of filth and shame and the meanest and foulest and most stinging oppression."[1]

When the convention adjourned candidate Hampton boarded a train for Walhalla. From there he would ride to Cashiers for a few days of rest and planning. At every station along the way, he was met by artillery salutes and "deafening cheers." At Walhalla a band began to play as the crowd chanted his name. He spoke briefly, thanking them and reminding them of his visit a decade earlier at the beginning of congressional Reconstruction. Three times, he said, conservatives had united with Republican "reformers," only to be disappointed. Hampton urged his audience to attend Republican meetings and "hurl back their false accusations, and teach the colored people that the misrepresentations of bad and designing men were leading them to ruin, and that the Democratic party would guarantee equal rights and equal justice to all classes of our citizens."[2]

Closing ranks after the nomination, the formerly fusionist *News and Courier* endorsed the Democratic candidate with a headline reading "Hampton and Victory!" It was, said one, "an audacious, masterly somersault at which everybody laughed, but which everybody approved." That same observer

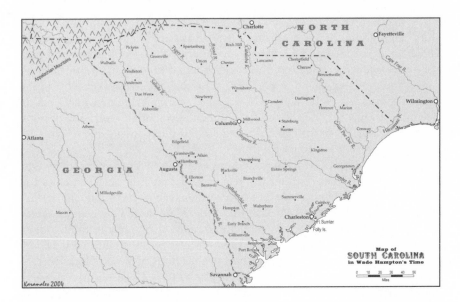

Map of
SOUTH CAROLINA
in Wade Hampton's Time

watched as Charleston celebrated the Hampton nomination with a torchlight parade on August 25. The Republican city government provided police protection "to guard six thousand men who in temper and preparation were as well able to take care of themselves as any people in the world that night."[3]

Earlier the same day in Edgefield, two companies of the U.S. Army's Eighteenth Infantry Regiment arrived from Atlanta. Troops, thought Governor Chamberlain, would surely subdue those Edgefield hotheads. Again, he would be outfoxed. Local Democrats proclaimed that the Federals had come to protect *them*. Soldiers "were surrounded by a shouting, cheering, hurrahing swarm of white men and women," said a reporter. Edgefield Republicans

> found themselves unnoticed and elbowed aside. . . . The men in the ranks, the non-coms and subordinate officers were astonished at first. Looking to encounter a sullen, resentful rebel population, they met the most cordial and enthusiastic welcome they ever had known. They quickly understood, however, and marched to camp through the supposed conquered and hostile crowds grinning broadly.

According to one Northerner, "Sending in troops does no good. They like troops. The more troops they get the better they are pleased."[4]

It may have been at the Charleston torchlight parade that great numbers of Democratic men were first seen wearing red shirts. Oliver P. Morton of Indiana, in a Senate speech castigating the supposed cruelty of the white South, once held aloft a shirt he said had been soaked with the blood of a black victim. Democrats made fun of his theatrics, and "waving the bloody shirt" entered the American political lexicon as slang for such demagoguery. In early August George D. Tillman and Andrew P. Butler had decided that the Sweet Water Sabre Club of Edgefield should don red shirts to mock Morton. At first some objected to a "Tory" color, but the fashion quickly caught on and spread across the state. Women set to work making new garments or dyeing old ones for their men. Ladies themselves often wore red ribbons around their waists or in their hair. Red-shirted riders soon came to symbolize the Hampton campaign of 1876.[5]

In the absence of competent and consistent law enforcement, the white people of South Carolina had for years relied primarily on themselves for protection. Rifle clubs appeared as early as 1869. Members often held no formal rank, nor did they usually wear uniforms. Many were Confederate veterans. Mounted troops, often in rural areas, called their organizations "saber clubs." Unrecognized by the state, often denounced, the clubs were nevertheless respected. In October 1874 two rival factions of armed blacks threatened to riot in Columbia. With nowhere else to turn, Governor Moses asked the Richland Rifle Club for help. The mere assembling of the club proved sufficient to quell the riot. By 1876 Chamberlain guessed that there were 240 rifle clubs in South Carolina with a total membership of 20,000. Other estimates put the number much higher. That year the clubs were organized statewide under James Conner. Theodore Barker commanded the lower division, Samuel B. Pickens the upper.[6] It would at times be difficult to differentiate between rifle club members and Red-Shirt Riders.

The Democratic campaign itself was run almost as a military operation. Alexander C. Haskell, chairman of the State Executive Committee headquartered in Columbia, was in overall charge. Despite the failure and frustration of nearly a decade, Hampton remained convinced that he could reach blacks with his message and persuade them to vote Democratic. This became the keynote of his campaign. Democrats planned to have at least one major meeting in each courthouse town. Hampton would begin his tour, assisted by other speakers, in the predominantly white upcountry. The campaign would build momentum there, then move toward the coastal counties with their black majorities. Few resources would be spent on the presidential contest. Home rule was the only issue that concerned South Carolina Democrats.[7]

The other side of the Edgefield Plan involved constrained intimidation. Republicans would be challenged at their own meetings by Democrats demanding to be heard. This insistence on "dividing the time" was intended to embarrass Republicans and undermine their black support. It worked nearly every time. The incumbent governor, although he was not yet officially the Republican nominee, secretly planned a campaign appearance in Abbeville for August 22. Word was passed by Republicans to friendly blacks, but kept from Democrats. Vigilant railroad men and telegraph operators—loyal

Democrats all—informed J. S. Cothran, leader of the party in Abbeville, that Chamberlain and his entourage were on the way. At the hour appointed for the Republican meeting, the speakers' stand and the assembled black crowd were surrounded by hundreds of armed men on horseback. Democrats demanded to speak first, shouting down Republicans. Before the day was over, fights broke out, and hundreds of shots were fired, but only a few were injured.[8] Another Republican rally had dissolved in chaos.

When Chamberlain appeared in Cheraw three weeks later, he was met by 1,000 mounted Red Shirts, who acted like they were at a "Sunday School picnic." This change in attitude may well have been made at Hampton's instigation. Not wishing to make Chamberlain a martyr in the Northern press or invite federal intervention, Democrats were prepared "to behave like sweet little girls," said a reporter, or "to storm hell for Hampton" should that be required.

Governor Chamberlain "was not effective on the stump—was too precise and restrained." The forty-one-year-old New Englander, bald and pale, had the look of a scholar. The debacles at Edgefield and Abbeville seemed to discourage the governor and derail his campaign even before it could get underway. Railroad men continued to act as spies. When trains carrying Republicans stopped at stations, young boys would shout through the windows or harass campaigners by running through the cars. Although invited to Democratic meetings, Chamberlain declined to attend. At times he failed to show up at his own scheduled rallies. Republican campaign events, with or without Chamberlain, were small and lacked enthusiasm. Intimidated Republicans canceled some of their meetings. Lizzie K. Geiger, a young Lexington County girl, reported not hearing more of a Republican rally that was to have been held at the courthouse in early September. "I believe it has died away. Tomorrow the company [of mounted Democrats] will go down to Sandy Run to attend a Radical meeting."[9]

South Carolina whites believed that they had endured tyranny for a decade, that the government was plundering and oppressing them, that civilization itself was in peril. Radicals had introduced electoral fraud, their regime was propped up by federal bayonets, and corruptionists would do anything to retain power. Revolutionary methods were in order if a revolution was to be effected. Democrats would oppose force with force, backing away only when that might provoke a federal military response. War was merely politics by "other means," according to military theoretician Carl von Clausewitz. In 1876 South Carolina the reverse was equally true.

Hampton began his campaign on Saturday, September 2, in Anderson. Even before daylight cannons were booming, and people were shouting. Every store was closed. A procession began forming at the fairgrounds at nine-thirty that morning, then moved down Main Street to the campus of the Carolina Collegiate Institute. Led by at least 1,500 mounted Red Shirts,

Republican governor Daniel H. Chamberlain. Wade Hampton's challenge of
Chamberlain in the 1876 South Carolina governor's race, coupled with the deadlocked
Hayes-Tilden presidential election, resulted in two of the most controversial political
contests in U.S. history. *Walter Allen, Governor Chamberlain's Administration in
South Carolina (New York: G. P. Putnam's Sons, 1888).*

the parade was more than a mile long. Bands from Pendleton and Anderson played, and the rebel yell was heard again. The crowd was estimated at 6,000, including hundreds of curious blacks. At eleven o'clock Hampton rose to speak, but had to wait for some time before the cheering died down. His theme was "Reconciliation, Retrenchment and Reform." Much of his thirty-five minute address was directed to the blacks in the crowd. "He said that General R. E. Lee told him before the war was over, that no matter which side was successful, the negro would be free," wrote a reporter. Other Democratic speakers followed. Blacks could trust Wade Hampton, said William D. Simpson, for "sooner would the stars fall from the skies than General Hampton would break his word." William Wallace added that "Hampton was now on board the ship of State, and could stop her leaks and steer her safely on her voyage towards the next centennial." Beginning in Anderson and at every meeting that followed, said a witness, "there was [an] artistically arranged balance of hard sense and facts, popular oratory, fire, ginger, humor and soothing syrup precisely right to put [the] crowds in tune."[10]

H. V. Redfield, radical correspondent of the *Cincinnatti Commercial,* was surprised at the impact Hampton made. The candidate's words were "straightforward," not "emotional or dramatic." Still, Redfield witnessed strong, rough-hewn men from the mountains "weeping and squirming and clenching their fists silently while Hampton talked."[11] Clearly, this was no ordinary political contest.

Hampton spoke again before enthusiastic crowds in Walhalla and Pickens before arriving at the Greenville railroad station on the evening of September 5. There he was met by mounted Red Shirts bearing torches and serenaded by the Greenville Cornet Band. The next morning a procession that included between 1,500 and 2,000 on horseback formed at the fairgrounds and marched down Buncombe to Main, and then to Furman University. All businesses were closed. On the university grounds a crowd of 5,000 or 6,000 cheered their hero. A transparency was displayed showing Hampton as an eagle digging his talons into Chamberlain. Another depicted Sioux chief Sitting Bull in the act of scalping one of Custer's men. "Send troops South," read the caption. "They are not needed in the West." A second meeting was held that night. "Cannon roared," remembered a witness, "rockets whizzed and blazed and burst and sparkled overhead, drums beat and horns blared, men and women screamed together and lights and waving flags were everywhere." The Columbia *Register* summed it up. "The Mountain City is ablaze with enthusiasm in the Democratic cause."[12]

As Hampton campaigned in Greenville there was an outbreak of violence on King Street in Charleston. Two black Democrats had been attacked by a mob. Whites came to their aid, but the rioters held the streets for an hour, firing guns and breaking windows. One white man was killed, and seven were injured. Three black policemen were wounded. Two black gangs, the "Hunkidories" and the "Live Oaks" were thought to be the instigators of the trouble. The next day white rifle club members were detailed by their superiors to protect the homes of black Democrats as the violence subsided. Chamberlain ordered that there be no "gathering, assembling or parading" in the city by armed men, an order ignored by the clubs.[13]

Hampton interrupted his speaking tour for a strategy meeting in Abbeville on September 16. James A. Hoyt, secretary of the state party Executive Committee, brought news from what he called "a reliable source" indicating that Democratic presidential candidate Samuel J. Tilden and his advisors were dissatisfied with Hampton and "vehemently opposed" to his "shotgun policy." South Carolina Democrats were an embarrassment to the national ticket.

> This intimation was made almost simultaneously with a direct proposition from Judges [Thomas J.] Mackey and [Thompson H.] Cooke . . . to the effect that a withdrawal of the [Tilden] Presidential electors from the field would undoubtedly secure the support of a sufficient number of influential Republicans to elect the state ticket.

Mackey and Cooke had appeared at the office of the state Democratic Committee on the day of Chamberlain's nomination, announced their support of Hampton, and suggested then that dropping Tilden would bolster Hampton's prospects. Everyone at the Abbeville conference expressed their views as Hampton listened, saying little. Hoyt added that it was characteristic of Hampton "in counsel to weigh carefully the points involved, and not to express himself vehemently." All present, Hampton included, were opposed to withdrawing the Tilden electors, unless Tilden himself instructed them to. Although the state Executive Committee had received only "imperturbable silence" from the national party, it was decided to communicate with Manton Marble, chairman of the national Democratic Executive Committee and a "mutual friend" of Tilden and Hampton.[14]

Hampton wrote to Marble on September 19,

> Our executive committee seems to apprehend that our friends in the North are embarrassed by our alliance with them. If these apprehensions are well founded, how can we best relieve our friends at the North of their embarrassment? Before our convention met I wrote fully to Mr. Tilden, telling him what would probably be its action, and asking his advice so that we could promote the interests of the Democratic party. He did not reply to my letter, and I was forced by irresistible public opinion to accept the nomination for Governor. I have made the canvass thoroughly conservative, and it has been a perfect success so far. With aid from abroad the State can be carried for Tilden. There is no doubt of its being carried for our State ticket, for our opponents would gladly agree to let us elect our men if we withdrew

from the Presidential contest. Of course we are most anxious to aid in the general election, but you can understand our solicitude to find out how we can best do this. If our alliance is a load, we will unload. If our friends desire us to carry on the contest as begun, we shall do so. If you will give me your views on these points I shall be indebted to you.[15]

Marble replied two weeks later in a cryptic, one-sentence telegram to state party chairman Haskell. "It is agreed here that your friend's persistence and his present efforts and plans are wise and advantageous."[16] It was the nearest to an endorsement the national party would give to Hampton. Tilden surely understood that he needed South Carolina Democrats far more than they needed him.

Months later a charge would be made anonymously, quite possibly at Gary's instigation, that Hampton masterminded a plot to abandon Tilden. This charge was vehemently denied by those present at the conference. Hampton had been nominated to redeem the state from radical rule. It might be assumed that the election of a Democratic president would in time accomplish the same goal, but Tilden and the national party had offered South Carolina only discouragement. Cutting ties to Tilden might have been an understandable reaction; still, Hampton remained, in every public utterance, a Tilden supporter. Of the Abbeville meeting Hoyt declared that "Hampton was not responsible for its origin, but he was the exponent of its conclusions."[17]

Judges Cooke and Mackey were the first of many Republicans to come over to the Democratic side. "Crossing Jordan," it came to be called. C. P. Townsend, judge of the Third District, endorsed Hampton on September 19. Martin R. Delany, black independent Republican, had run unsuccessfully for lieutenant governor two years earlier. Now he came out for Hampton. Whites had taken him at his word in 1874, Delany said, and now he would take Hampton at his word. Even Robert Scott, first of the radical governors, refused to support Chamberlain, "indicating a general preference for Hampton."[18]

There was another outbreak of violence in mid-September, this time at Ellenton. Two blacks burglarized a home, brutally beating the white woman they found there with her little boy. Armed blacks resisted the arrest of the suspects, leading whites to take the law into their own hands. Battle would rage for two days and spread over two counties. Black militiamen even tore up tracks, wrecking a train. Two whites and fifteen blacks died before U.S. troops restored order. The Ellenton violence, tragic as it was, could have been much worse. James Conner received a tip that 2,000 Enfield rifles with ammunition were being shipped secretly from Washington to blacks in the riot zone. Again, the informal "spy network" of railroad men and telegraph operators made and reported the discovery. The weapons arrived at an Ashley

River depot in Charleston. Under cover of darkness two watchmen were bound and gagged by rifle club members, who appropriated the weapons for their own armory. It was never discovered who made the shipment. Those responsible could not, of course, complain of the theft.[19]

As Democrats had hoped, the Hampton campaign through the upper part of the state was an unbroken series of triumphs. With momentum building, the candidate campaigned for the first time below Columbia in the town of Darlington on September 23. "With restless sweep," wrote the *News and Courier*, "the wave of Democratic enthusiasm has burst upon Darlington, and today this quiet and pretty village was the scene of a demonstration without parallel in its history." Hampton had arrived in neighboring Florence at midnight, where he was greeted by a brass band and a delegation of citizens. They boarded a special train at nine o'clock on Saturday morning for the ten mile journey to Darlington. A procession that included at least 1,000 Red-Shirt Riders made its way to the grove at St. John's Academy. Expelled congressman Benjamin F. Whittemore watched from an open window. For his benefit demonstrators displayed a transparency that portrayed a hog gobbling ill-gotten gains from selling military academy appointments. A large pavilion served as a speakers' stand. Hampton and 5 others spoke to a crowd of 4,000 that included perhaps 500 blacks. Republicans had been invited to participate, but declined. During the afternoon word came that a riot had broken out in town and 200 mounted men were sent to investigate. They soon returned; the riot having been a brawl between two drunks. Speech making went on until four o'clock in the afternoon and the rally was counted as another great Democratic success. "I care not whether they call me a Republican or a Conservative or a Democrat," Hampton told the Darlingtonians, "I stand on a broader platform than that now—a platform so strong and true, and broad that every South Carolinian can stand with me."[20]

Hampton thought he ought to be the choice of black voters, that all blacks would "cross Jordan" one day. "They will say that they have always been Democrats, but were afraid to say so." Several former Hampton slaves vocally supported his campaign. Francis Davie wrote,

> Seeing you are nominated for governor by the white people, and hearing you have promised the black man all the rights he now has, and knowing you were always a good and kind man to me when your slave. . . . I write to say that I will vote for you and get all the black men I can to do the same. I have bought a piece of land in York County and am trying to make a support for my family, which I can do if we had good laws and low taxes."

Former Hampton bondsman Jonas Weeks was assaulted on one occasion during the campaign simply for being a Democrat. "I told them if I died," Weeks recounted later, "I would die for General Hampton."[21]

Across the state Hampton was making slow, but encouraging, progress in winning black support. Abbeville blacksmith Aaron Mitchell switched to the Democratic Party and spoke before local groups of black voters. Edward Henderson, a forty-eight-year-old carpenter, had been a Democrat since blacks first received the vote. He organized a Democratic club for black voters with 180 members. Thomas Burgess of Hodges rejected carpetbaggers as "rogues" who "fooled us by their false promises." Neighbor Asbury Green agreed. "I can't support my family. I want a change in the government."[22]

Some blacks donned red shirts and rode alongside their white comrades. Thomas Young organized a mounted unit in Abbeville County that was half black. Young, himself white, had known Hampton years earlier in North Carolina and thought him a "straightforward and honest man, and a man who would do justice to the colored man as well as the white man." There were black Red Shirts also in Sumter, Due West, Florence, Fairforest, and Walhalla. Black musical bands contributed to the Hampton campaign in Newberry, Abbeville, Columbia, and elsewhere. At a Kingstree rally blacks carried a banner that pictured a black man kicking a carpetbag-toting white. "Things are too hot for carpetbaggers," read the caption. "Let us go, boys!"[23]

At every Hampton meeting an appeal was made to black voters. Hampton told of an occasion before the war when he had intervened to save a black man accused of murder from a Mississippi lynch mob. He had such confidence in his black neighbors in that state, many his former slaves, that he did not even have a lock on his house. The only protection he said that he needed was those very neighbors. "I am just as safe there as when I was surrounded by my old cavalry company in Virginia." Edwin W. Moise, one of the most effective Democratic campaigners, answered a Republican slander that Hampton had branded his slaves. Moise would tell of good times and friendly relations between the benevolent master and his well-cared-for people. "The only brand Wade Hampton's slaves ever wore," he concluded, "was the name of their master stamped on their loving hearts."[24]

Blacks who openly sided with Hampton often found themselves persecuted. Some were expelled from their churches, shunned by family, or abandoned by wives. The Republican press denounced black Democrats as "jail birds" or "lackeys." Physical threats were common. In Marion County two black Democrats were fired on. Their assailants, also black, were quickly released. Hampton supporter Tom Elsey was badly injured by buckshot in a night ambush. His attackers were never arrested. Another black Democrat, William Black of Yorkville, left his horse at a local stable while he traveled to a political meeting. He returned to find the animal strangled with a rope. White friends collected money to buy a replacement. In upper Orangeburg County a black Democrat was beaten severely, and his home was burned.[25]

Whites did everything possible to win converts. By the one-man-apiece plan individual whites tried to keep black Democrats in the fold. A preference policy was also instituted by Whites, giving their business to black Democrats and often refusing to trade with or hire Republicans. Richard Roman, black Abbeville County farmer, adopted the same policy, employing only black Democrats himself. Cincinnatti reporter H. V. Redfield estimated that 7,000 South Carolina blacks had committed themselves to Wade Hampton. "If the whites can hold all these black men who have enrolled in democratic clubs," he wrote, "they will certainly carry the state." Judging by the degree of hate engendered against them during the campaign, many black Democrats would have faced death or exile in the event of yet another Republican triumph.[26] The most courageous men in South Carolina in 1876 were those blacks who declared for Hampton.

Horry, the northernmost county on South Carolina's coast, had managed to avoid the worst depredations of Reconstruction. Unique among the coastal counties, Horry was predominantly white. Even before the August convention, Thomas W. Beaty, editor of the *Horry News,* made his opinion clear. "Were we a delegate to the Convention we should vote for Gen. Hampton from first to last, unless he knocked us down with a stick." During the last week in September, Hampton made his way to Chesterfield, Cheraw, Bennettsville, and Marion. Finally, on Sunday, October 1, he arrived in Conwayboro, Horry County seat, "then the most sequestered and obscure of all the courthouse towns of the state, quiet, staunch, steady," remembered a reporter.

Not wishing to disturb the Sabbath, Hampton asked that there be no reception or public display. But at dawn on Monday, the stillness was shattered by the salute of a brass six-pounder cannon. The candidate received callers from breakfast until ten o'clock. A huge "Hampton and Tilden" flag was run up a sixty-foot flag pole at the courthouse, and a procession began to form. Soon, 1,000 participants, 300 of them on horseback, marched through the streets of the little town, arriving at a grove of oak trees near the Methodist church. The Central Band of Georgetown provided music. Rev. George T. Harmon delivered the invocation before a crowd that had grown to 3,000, perhaps 500 of them black. The correspondent for the *News and Courier* noted the friendship and good will he observed among blacks and whites. Hampton spoke for a full hour, the longest address he made during the campaign. One reporter declared the event "Horry's greatest meeting, greatest occasion, and greatest day of a century."

That evening, as Hampton ate supper, he was handed a note. Conwayboro blacks politely asked to see him at their church. According to a witness,

> He went immediately, faced a large congregation and spent nearly two hours answering frankly, kindly and sensibly, timely questions, and talking informally on state and national topics and the relations of the races. This incident pleased him vastly. Unhappily, it was one of the kind in the whole campaign.[27]

A Republican meeting at the Horry courthouse the following month drew fewer than 200, many of them Democrats come to "divide the time." The *Horry News* reported that local blacks were planning a boat trip down the Waccamaw River to Georgetown in late October to see Hampton one more time. "All who heard Gen. Hampton speak here," wrote editor Beaty, "want to hear him again, and those who did not hear him are now anxious to hear the words, as they say, from the 'Governor' himself."[28]

From Conwayboro Hampton and entourage traveled to Kingstree and then to Sumter. The meeting at Sumter included an unforgettable tableau. Smiling young girls dressed in brightly colored dresses representing the other states of the Union stood on a stage. Another girl sat on that platform. Dressed in mourning, eyes downcast, wrapped in chains, she represented the Palmetto State. Just as Hampton stepped upon the stage, a transformation occurred. As if by magic, the chains noisily dropped off, the black robes fell away, "and a radiant young woman in pure white stood tall and stately, head up-lifted and eyes shining like stars with excitement and pleasure, a golden coronet on her hair—'South Carolina.' Big men were not ashamed to let tears come," said one witness. "Gen. Hampton was completely overcome with the scene," remembered another.[29]

Just after the meeting in Sumter, Hampton was dining at a private home when a messenger delivered a telegram. He read it, folded the paper, and continued the conversation almost without interruption. Only later did his hosts appreciate Hampton's "Roman self-control." The telegram informed Hampton that Chamberlain had issued a proclamation aimed at the rifle clubs. They must disband, their members "disperse and retire to their homes." President Grant would aid the governor by ordering all U.S. troops in the Military District of the Atlantic to South Carolina. General Thomas Howard Ruger, commanding federal forces in the state, had recently informed General in Chief of the Army Sherman that his nineteen companies were all that were needed. "No special disorder has occurred since [the] Ellenton riot last month," said Ruger. "If I need more troops I will ask for them." It seemed obvious that Chamberlain's proclamation and Grant's order were political measures, designed to intimidate Democrats and bolster their own party. Soon 5,000 federal soldiers were garrisoning the state.[30]

The rifle club ban was denounced by Democrats. They wanted it understood that their party did not control the rifle clubs, even as it appealed to those clubs to obey the law. The ban's "sole object is to irritate and provoke collisions. . . . We counsel our people to preserve the peace, observe the laws and calmly await the day of their deliverance from this wanton despotism." Rifle clubs had been formed for protection, they added, and had been sometimes equipped and sanctioned by the state when needed. They would have been unnecessary but for "the reckless distribution of arms and ammunition among the colored people." The Democratic address was accompanied by statements from members of the state supreme court, circuit court judges, and the sheriffs of Aiken and Barnwell counties, all in agreement that peace prevailed. "We cannot 'disperse,' because we are not banded together—we cannot 'retire to our homes,' because we are already there," Democrats said in conclusion.

"Disbanded, but solid for Hampton," read the banner the Richland Rifle Club stretched across the street in front of its Columbia armory. In reality, the clubs cheerfully ignored the governor's orders. The Columbia Flying Artillery transformed itself into "The Hampton and Tilden Musical Club, with four twelve-pounder flutes." A sabre club voted unanimously to dissolve, then reemerged as "The Allendale Mounted Base Ball Club." Other units chose to rechristen themselves "brass bands," "church sewing circles," even "Mother's Little Helpers."[31]

Soon after the order to disband, Hampton spoke in Edgefield. That evening one group of Red Shirts was ambushed while traveling home. A young man named John Gilmore was killed, shot through the head. A furious Gary ordered men to the scene. There was talk of reprisals, of a bloodletting directed at a nearby black settlement called "Promised Land." Wade Hampton galloped up, "his overcoat billowing from his shoulders," and at his insistence peace prevailed. "Hampton's war record had caused him to be regarded as the personification of the chivalry of the State," remembered a contemporary, "and when he counseled *yielding,* even General Gary had to subside." Homes and other property belonging to prominent Democrats were burned in nearby Abbeville County, but there was no retaliation.[32] Hampton was able to keep the explosive situation under control.

Hampton tried to separate the rifle clubs from the Democratic campaign in the minds of Northerners. "During my canvass of the State I have not seen a single gun or sabre in the possession of these clubs," he wrote to the New York *Tribune,* "and they have not carried such at any meeting at which I have been present." Some critics would conclude that Hampton was insulated from the "revolutionary campaign." Hampton pointed out that the rifle clubs "were formed long before the present canvass began. . . . Nearly all of them have at some time been sanctioned by the acts or words of Gov. Chamberlain. They were in no sense political organizations or used for political purposes." To be sure, Red-Shirt Riders were not necessarily rifle or saber club members, nor did Hampton choose to explain just how commonplace carrying a concealed pistol was in South Carolina. If he found it inexpedient to discuss Edgefield Plan harassment publicly, he did in fact modify Democratic strategy in response to Chamberlain's proclamation and the increased presence of U.S. troops. There would be no more demands for a "division of time" and disruption of Republican meetings. With the election now only weeks away, Democrats were willing to be patient and follow orders to keep the peace. If Hampton lost, however, there was talk of open rebellion—of forcing Washington to replace Chamberlain with a military government.[33]

Chamberlain was to have appeared with Hampton in joint debate at Yorkville on Friday, October 13, but the governor backed out. Having spoken in Camden and Lancaster, Hampton passed through Rock Hill, arriving at Yorkville at one o'clock in the afternoon. "Chamberlain never saw a Hampton meeting," said one who covered the campaign. "If he had gone to Yorkville the heart would have been taken out of him." No fewer than 6,000, many of them blacks, met in a grove just outside of town. A youthful choir sang "The Song of the Hampton Boys" written for the occasion. Hampton was showered with roses thrown by the women as he stood to speak. He urged everyone to welcome federal troops when they came, claiming that the more soldiers Grant sent, the better he liked it. He challenged the many blacks in the audience to advance to a new level of freedom. "You have, ever since emancipation, been slaves to your political masters. As members of the Loyal [Union] League you have been fettered slaves to party." He promised to provide a better system of education in South Carolina. "In coming to us, you are only coming to your own people. You do not desert your true friends, but you are coming to them." Hampton spoke again that night. There were fireworks and huge "Tilden balloons," the band played "Dixie," and crowds chanted Hampton's name.[34]

Hampton was in Chester the next day and in Winnsboro on October 16. That same day in the isolated Charleston County village of Cainhoy, a rare joint debate was scheduled between speakers of both parties. Blacks outnumbered whites 10–1 in rural Cainhoy. White Democrats brought to the meeting black Hampton supporter Martin Delany in hopes that he might be able to win converts. They had no way of knowing that they were walking into an ambush. Almost as soon as the meeting began black Republicans grabbed hidden rifles and opened fire. Four whites and Delany were able to retreat to a brick house and from there scramble to safety. Six whites were killed, and sixteen more were wounded. One old man was captured and beaten to death. Bodies were later found mutilated. When word finally reached the city of Charleston that night, the Palmetto Guard and other rifle clubs chartered boats and hurried to rescue survivors. Not until the danger was past did Chamberlain request federal soldiers be sent to Cainhoy. Clearly, U.S. troops were in South Carolina on a political mission that did not include protecting Democrats. Whites congratulated themselves for disobeying the governor's week-old order to disband their clubs.[35]

On the day of the Cainhoy massacre, a personal tragedy struck the Hampton family. Wade Hampton's eight-year-old granddaughter Sophia, second child of Sally and John Haskell, died in Abbeville. Only the day before Sally had given birth to a son. When Hampton received the telegram informing him of Sophia's death, he rushed to Abbeville. The meeting scheduled

for Lexington on October 17 would have to take place without him. For John
and Sally Haskell, 1876 would be a year of terrible heartbreak. Their fourteen-
month-old baby daughter had died in June. On October 31, near the end
of the campaign, they would also lose three-year-old son Wade Hampton
Haskell.[36]

At the suggestion of Orangeburg County Democratic Party chairman
James F. Izlar, the Hampton campaign declared Thursday, October 26, a day
of fasting and prayer for the deliverance of South Carolina. Response was
quick. Charleston stock brokers and real estate agents announced that they
would do no business that day. Although prayers were to be offered for no
party or candidate, a few clergymen felt that they must refrain, scrupulous to
keep the church above politics or even patriotism. Most, however, gladly
joined in supplications for "justice, peace and prosperity, mercy and truth,
with fellowship and good feeling to all men."[37]

In a little more than nine weeks, tens of thousands of South Carolinians
had been able to see and hear and learn something of Wade Hampton. "General Hampton was not brilliant nor spectacular," wrote a reporter who heard
him almost daily.

> He wrote and spoke strong, clear English, but did not attempt the lofty
> flights of oratory or literature. His speeches . . . were just plain, straight talks.
> When he addressed the negroes, as he invariably did . . . he talked as if he
> had been on the steps of his plantation house reasoning with the people of
> his place . . . He used no passion or fire. When he introduced a bit of humor
> it was natural, incidental, on the suggestion of the moment, such as every-
> body could catch. He never became excited or shouted or gesticulated.

The strongest language he used was an occasional "infernal" when
somebody or something required "special emphasis."

Hampton was an "inveterate tease," although he "never rubbed a really
bad sore spot," said the same reporter. If a fellow campaigner could not keep
up in a procession, for example, or if a speaker stumbled in his delivery, he
would be sure to be the target of Hampton's teasing. During one October
procession, said Conner, the general "was in capital spirits, enjoying the
whole thing and keeping up a running fire of comment on every thing." As
they rode along Hampton recounted that at a recent rally "a very pretty
woman wishing to tell him the time, pulled her watch from her breast and
said, 'Oh, my watch has stopped!' 'That is very natural,' replied the general,
'for I am sure had I been in the watch's place, I would have stopped too.' "[38]

Hampton always had time for fellow Confederates who crowded up to
shake his hand. "He liked to discuss with other veterans incidents and events
of the Civil War," wrote the reporter, "but never so much as hinted at a
boast of his own distinguished part in it." If he was proud of anything, it was
of his horsemanship and of his abilities as a fisherman and hunter.

The newspaperman remembered,

He was a big, powerful, athletic man, with rather small dark blue eyes, the face of a good humored, self confident, fearless fighter, carrying just enough extra flesh to become his fifty-eight years. Probably he weighed 240 pounds. When in the saddle he looked as if he and the horse were one.

In the midst of the campaign our train stalled somewhere between Columbia and Graniteville, and all of us got out and walked about, amusing ourselves firing at targets with revolvers. By the way, Hampton never carried a weapon—possibly the one man in South Carolina who didn't—and on this occasion he borrowed. A farmer living nearby recognized the General and after looking him over, spoke—

"Say Gin'ral, they tell me you're a kind of a dog man. I wisht you'd come over here an look at somethin' I've got.'"

The General joined him and they tramped together to where there was a litter of new hound puppies and through the next hour were in deep, confidential debate on the breeds and builds of hounds . . .

That was characteristic of Hampton. He never posed, never tried to look or do like somebody else—always and everywhere just plain Wade Hampton, simple, unaffected gentleman, dauntless warrior of South Carolina, loving and reverencing his God, his cause and his commonwealth to the last recess of his clean soul.[39]

The Democratic campaign had to meet the challenge posed too by the ever present "flower problem." As they traveled Hampton and his party were given literally thousands of bouquets and wreathes and arrangements. Each gift had been carefully gathered and was lovingly given, often accompanied by notes telling of family members who had served with the general and promising prayers. Obviously, Hampton could not transport a train load of flowers around the state, nor could they be carelessly discarded. As a result, his staff was constantly conducting "flower funerals," discreetly and respectfully hiding arrangements at the side of railroad tracks and roads as they traveled.[40]

Certainly the most difficult stop of the Democratic campaign was in Beaufort on October 26. The meeting had been scheduled originally for Gillisonville, but Beaufort was substituted, and Early Branch was added to the itinerary. Hampton was now in that region of South Carolina where blacks made up 90 to 95 percent of the population. At Early Branch Hampton was met at the station by a Red Shirt escort that included a contingent of blacks. Among these black Red Shirts may have been the "mounted black cadre," a group that traveled to join Hampton at some of his campaign stops around the state. Several in the cadre were black Confederate veterans. The Garden Corner Campaign Club, a black choral group, sang songs "each having as its theme the good time coming when the thieves and disturbers would be sent away, honest folk would conduct the government and the races would be at peace." So many black supporters appeared at Hampton meetings that some

Northern Republicans would claim that they must be servants of the speakers or paid to be there. It was even charged that whites put on burnt cork and donned wigs to impersonate black Democrats.

Peace may have been on Hampton's mind when he declined a mounted escort, choosing to enter Beaufort with only his contingent of Democratic speakers and the newspapermen. He knew there could be trouble. Republican Edmund W. M. Mackey had spoken there a week earlier. Mackey attacked Hampton without mercy, making sure that his audience knew about his bankruptcy, even mentioning the first Wade Hampton's Yazoo land dealings. The Hampton party arrived at ten o'clock on the night of October 25, met by a handful of white residents. The ladies had decorated a speaker's stand near the Beaufort Club House, but during the night vandals made short work of their efforts. There would be no procession. A few ladies watched from the veranda of the club house as Hampton spoke to a group of about 500, two-thirds of them black. The blacks listened in silence even as the Beaufort police tried to create a disturbance by pushing them away from the stand. Hampton called Chamberlain a coward for refusing to debate. Lt. Gov. R. H. Gleaves was in the neighborhood, and Hampton in vain challenged him to come and defend his party's record.

The next speaker was LeRoy F. Youmans, but the audience soon began shouting and calling names. Unable to be heard, Youmans quit and sat down. Thompson H. Cooke then began to speak, and the mood of the crowd became threatening. Judge Cooke lost his temper—and his voice—and gave up. "Then came another marvel," wrote a reporter.

> Hampton advanced again, and again there was silence. He spoke quietly and without show of resentment, like a man rebuking a crowd of disorderly children. He said those before him might be interested to know that a large party of naval officers from the fleet at Port Royal was in the club house and had seen all that had happened and would be able to tell their friends at the North what the conduct of the negroes and Republicans and the officials had been.

The reporter from the *News and Courier* noted eight or ten naval officers had indeed observed the performance. Hampton closed the meeting by telling the unruly crowd "that Beaufort had done more today to elect him than any other county in the State, and bade them farewell." Before leaving town Hampton made the effort to wire General Ruger, asking that troops be sent to protect black Democrats. One of the departing group said he was glad no longer to be "made to feel hatred every minute and at every step." Still, Democrats could hardly complain about the Beaufort rebuff, their own partisans having already made a shambles of the Republican campaign. At the village of Green Pond, a newsman reported "a swirl of light and cheering and welcome, red-shirted horsemen of both colors waving their hats joyously." After another warm welcome and an enthusiastic rally at Walterboro, they were on their way to Charleston.[41]

"Hampton is by all means the strongest man in the State," James Conner wrote to his wife on the eve of the Charleston visit. "His influence over the people is wonderful—and he has shown so much judgment in this canvas, that he has added much to his previous strength." Conner was on the committee planning Hampton's reception in Charleston, but privately expressed doubts over the prospects for Democratic victory. U.S. troops in the upcountry and in the midlands would cost Hampton votes by showing blacks "that there was a power stronger than ours," wrote Conner. "Our chance to carry the negro was not by argument or reason, but by letting him see that we were the stronger—and to impress him with a sense of our power and determination." He now thought the election too close to call.

Hampton spent the night before the Charleston meeting in Summerville. The annual yellow fever outbreak in Charleston had nearly run its course, but staying in the healthful village seemed to his hosts a wise precaution. His party reached the Charleston railroad station at eight-forty on the morning of October 30 and proceeded to the Charleston Hotel. Among the crowd were hundreds of blacks who came to shake Hampton's hand.

The fall weather was perfect. Decorations surpassed even those of the Moultrie Centennial; the old city was covered with flags and flowers. The *News and Courier* estimated that half of Charleston's population of 55,000 was in the streets. The procession that formed on the Citadel green "was the largest demonstration which has ever occurred in the City by the Sea," reported the newspaper. Ten thousand marched to where a stage had been constructed on South Battery. "The appearance of Gen. Hampton aroused a perfect hurricane of cheers," as the candidate rode in a carriage drawn by four matched horses. There were Red Shirts, black and white, from the Cooper River rice fields. Another contingent, again of both races, wore red shirts and black sombreros. The German Hussars paraded in defiance of the governor's ban. The Washington Light Infantry proclaimed that it was "Disbanded but solid for Hampton!" Employees of businesses that had closed for the day paraded in groups. The Workingmen's Democratic Association decorated the engine of Hook and Ladder Company Number 1, which carried thirteen little girls dressed to represent the original states. Each marcher from one political club carried a stalk of sugar cane topped with a little U.S. flag as a way of poking fun at the notorious radical "Daddy" Cain. "Irishmen welcome Hampton" proclaimed a gigantic banner at the Fourth Ward club. "We'll Wade In" and "Ballots not Bayonets" read other signs. The piazza of the Mills House Hotel was elaborately decorated with evergreen wreathes, but the predominant color seen everywhere this day was "Hampton red."

Hampton badges, sold by vendors in the streets for five cents each, "were as plentiful as blackberries in June."

The only building in the city *not* flying a flag was the U.S. Custom House, Republican employees there pointedly furling their banner for the day. Along the parade route black women hurled obscenities and brickbats at black Democrats. At King and Calhoun streets, "Hunkidori rowdies" tried briefly to create trouble. "No serious harm was done," wrote a reporter, "and the [black] Democrats bore with equanimity the cheers of the Republican slaves."

The covered stage was thirty feet long, decorated with 6 vases of roses and a large oil portrait of Hampton. The general was presented with another of those ubiquitous bouquets as all waited for parade participants to gather at South Battery. Hampton expressed joy at being again in the city of his birth. He was encouraged by Charleston's outpouring of support, made optimistic by the number of black Democrats in the parade, and expressed confidence in victory. Hampton again chided Chamberlain for not appearing with him. If he did, said Hampton, "the colored people would come out and hear the truth and be converted." South Carolina's palmetto banner stood for the people and their cause.

> I have taken that flag and I have borne it from where our mountains kiss the sky to where old Ocean beats the shore. I have pleaded only for peace and for South Carolina. . . . Trust in the justice of your cause; lay that cause before the throne of Heaven . . . [and] work earnestly and unceasingly.

That evening after supper a scheduled meeting was held especially for black voters at the Academy of Music. Richard Holloway, a prominent black Democrat, presided over what was described as a "packed house" of 1,000. Hampton and others spoke. Only a month earlier black Democrats in Charleston had been hounded by their enemies, unable to meet in safety.[42]

Hampton made a trip by boat to a meeting in Georgetown, returning to Summerville for a brief appearance on November 2. A stand amid the pine trees was the center of "two hours of cheers, music, marching, flowers, flags and a general swirl of enthusiasm." An unusually large number of black Red Shirts lifted Democratic spirits. The next day a rally was scheduled for Orangeburg, but Hampton left immediately for Columbia. It may have been his only opportunity to spend a few hours with his family, grieving over the loss of yet another grandchild.

Hampton was back in Orangeburg on the morning of Friday, November 3. "As he left the train he barely was able to force his way through the joyous, cheering crowd," wrote a witness. "Orangeburg was determined to see Hampton on horseback . . . and a big grey horse was brought forward" that he might review his mounted men. A parade was held through town, a procession two miles long that included perhaps 500 blacks. The route "literally was an unbroken succession of garlands, flowers, wreathes, banners and inspiring mottoes and inscriptions, with three arches spanning the street to vary the monotony of beauty."

Columbia's *Register* reported a crowd of 3,000, although other estimates were much higher. There were a series of elaborate tableaux along the parade route. In one yard young women stood like statues on an elevated platform, each representing an American state. They surrounded "South Carolina," cowering in rags. When Hampton came by, a participant waved the wand of "Prosperity." Instantly South Carolina arose smiling, discarded her mourning, as "Peace" and "Plenty" came to her side.

During Hampton's Orangeburg speech, he was interrupted by a black man asking unfriendly questions. One credited the Republican with having "nerve and intelligence," reporting that he "was answered courteously and patiently and remained in the crowd undisturbed."[43]

Teenager Lizzie Geiger followed events from her rural Lexington County home. Her father, uncle, and brothers were active in the Red Shirt campaign. On October 30 she wrote,

> the mind of every person seems to be taken up with Hampton. I don't think there ever was so much excitement through the country about an election as at this time. . . . I presume there will be a great enthusiasm on next Saturday in Columbia. That day will end Hampton's campaign.[44]

Preparations had gone on for many days. Although theirs was a far smaller city than Charleston, Columbians were determined to put on a demonstration to rival the coastal metropolis. Hampton Day began with a cannon booming one hundred times. Some noticed that the salute seemed a little too quick and precise. It was found that local "disbanded" club members were being assisted by artillerymen of the U.S. Army garrison. Parade participants gathered on Sumter Street near Trinity Episcopal Church. The procession marched down Gervais Street, turning onto Richardson in front of the State House. At the head of Richardson Street, two huge pillars had been erected, representing the gates of the city. The parade was led by one hundred mounted Red Shirts—fifty white and fifty black. An arch spanning the street at the Wheeler House Hotel had at its peak a replica of a ship under sail with Hampton as helmsman. Someone put up a palmetto tree with a stuffed rattlesnake coiled around it. A raccoon skin nailed to a post was labeled "Chamberlain's Hide." Many out-of-state reporters there to cover the election were amazed at the Columbia display.

Finally reaching the fairgrounds on Elmwood Avenue, Hampton stood before a crowd that refused to stop cheering. "Several times as he opened his mouth to start his speech the cheering burst forth anew," remembered a witness. "It looked as if the people, men and women, did not care to hear him or anybody—just wanted to try to make him understand how much they loved and believed in him and his leadership and his triumph."

"When I stand once more in this county of Richland," Hampton finally began, "where live the playmates of my youth, the associates of my manhood, my friends, my lifelong friends, may understand what a crowd of memories throng my heart." Hampton had traversed his state by rail and by rutted roads, speaking in every county from the mountains to the sea islands. He had stood before farmers in the red hills of the upcountry, bankers and businessmen in Charleston, sullen former slaves in Beaufort. Always his appeal was directed first to the black voter. "I have not said one word," Hampton told the Columbia crowd, "that could hurt the feelings of a colored man or woman." With the day of triumph approaching, "we will owe this victory in great part to the colored man."

"Now, my friends, my work is done. I have gone throughout the whole state in obedience to your command. . . . God save the State and bless the people of Richland." The crowd burst into cheers, the band began to play, and the cannon boomed another salute. That night there would be one last torchlight parade, one final barrage of fireworks.[45] Hampton could not know what election day would bring. His work was only beginning.

15

"I AM GOING THERE TO DEMAND OUR RIGHTS"

Both Sides Claim Victory

Tuesday, November 7, was election day across the thirty-eight united states. Voters would choose between presidential candidates Samuel J. Tilden, the Democrat nominee, and his Republican opponent, Rutherford B. Hayes. All 293 congressional seats were at stake, as were a myriad of state and local offices. Nowhere in America, however, would there be an election like the one in South Carolina. Troops were stationed in all of the state's courthouse towns, and at many other polling places as well. Democrats had been up all night, and at dawn their clubs served breakfast to black supporters and made sure that they voted. In the upcountry and the midlands, gunshots shattered the predawn darkness as Red Shirts rode through the countryside, their fearsome noisemaking bolstering the faithful and, perhaps, prompting a few fainthearted Republicans to stay home. The riders set up camps near polling places and were permitted to demonstrate as long as they threatened no violence. Democrats tried to vote first, crowding the polls as they opened, forcing Republicans to wait.

Each polling place had three managers: two Republicans and one Democrat.[1] There had never been a formal system of voter registration in South Carolina. Edgefield Democrats were determined to overcome the system of intimidation long perfected by local Republicans. The practice had been for large numbers of blacks to pack the polling places, making it impossible for whites to cast ballots. Late in the day the Republicans would disperse in time to vote at least once in their own precincts. This year it would be different. At least fifteen Democratic voters arrived early at the courthouse and at all other Edgefield polling places to insure that whites were not excluded and to challenge black Republicans who tried to vote in precincts other than their own. Election managers ordered the Democratic activists out, but they refused to leave unless voters were permitted to enter in groups of no more than twelve. At one point a ballot box was taken by officials to another polling place, a schoolhouse at the edge of town where blacks had packed the building. Mounted Red Shirts never let the box out of their sight and insisted that only small groups of voters be allowed inside. Blacks, numbering more than 1,000, became unruly, and the U.S. marshal stationed at the polling place sent for federal troops. Soon voting proceeded in an orderly manner.[2]

Republicans would later complain that Democrats had committed fraud in Edgefield and elsewhere by permitting white men under twenty-one to vote, by repeat voting, and even by allowing Georgians to cast votes in South Carolina. Democrats, of course, denied the charges. Some would later concede that illegal votes had been cast, but justified the fraud as a necessary act of revolution. The ever-conservative *News and Courier* would remind readers that "a revolution without irregularities is as rare as fire without heat." Still, for Democrats to have gotten away with widespread fraud in the presence of U.S. marshals, federal troops, and Republican election managers seems dubious. Democrats charged their opponents with intimidating black Hampton supporters in Darlington, Orangeburg, and Charleston counties. Blacks wanting to vote Democratic were threatened and beaten in Beaufort. Thomas J. Robertson, South Carolina's Republican senator in Washington, said that he suspected Chamberlain's vote total in Charleston alone was padded by 3,000. In the overwhelmingly black counties, it had long been the practice, one Democrat observed, for black Republicans to "vote as often as they liked and at as many precincts as they could reach." Democrats charged that one precinct in Barnwell County closed early, then reported a 2,000 vote majority for Chamberlain. They had but 400 voters. It was said that black women and boys cast ballots for Chamberlain, while off duty soldiers voted for Hampton.[3]

As soon as each precinct closed, the votes were counted publicly by the three managers and the results sent to the Board of County Managers. Each county's statement, along with precinct returns and supporting documents, was sent to the state Board of Canvassers. The state board transmitted the results of the legislative and other races to the secretary of state. The results of the contests for governor and lieutenant governor were sealed, to be opened by the house and senate in joint session. The vote count itself was not secret, of course, being reported by the press.[4]

Yet, those returns came in very slowly. On November 9 the *Register* reported Hampton leading by nearly 3,000 votes. The Democratic vote in the coastal counties was disappointing, but on November 10 Hampton still held a statewide lead of almost 2,000 out of a total of 182,707 votes cast. Crowds waited at newspaper offices for the latest dispatches. Lizzie Geiger reported that her brothers remained in Columbia until very late. Finally, Democrats declared victory.

> Bro. said when the flag was put through the window of the Democratic Hall with Hampton's portrait on it, and the words "Our Governor" written above, the crowd at the door appeared almost wild, they were so excited, the [federal] troops shouted for Hampton and appeared to be as proud of Hampton's Election as our own people.

A witness remembered people going "stark, staring crazy with joy . . . everybody quit work and proceeded to celebrate. It was a wild time. So far as I can recollect, nobody north of Orangeburg went to bed in a week." Another confessed to being "so full of, not politics, but, an intense desire for freedom from Radical rule, that, poor as we are, we can think of but little else."[5]

In Columbia on the evening of November 10, Hampton made a formal statement. He thanked and congratulated the people for "the grand victory they have won." He urged them to maintain the peace.

> Let us show that we seek only the restoration of good government, the return of prosperity and the establishment of harmony to the whole people of our State . . . In the hour of victory we should be magnanimous, and we should strive to forget the animosities of the contest by recalling the grand results of our success.

Hampton was then carried down Richardson Street on the shoulders of black supporters. "We have won a great victory," he wrote to Armistead Burt, "but we shall have to face heavy responsibilities and arduous duties."[6]

Even as crowds waited on the streets of Charleston for election results, fights broke out, shots were fired, and soon another riot engulfed the city. A committee of citizens, on the advice of Hampton and with the consent of the Republican mayor, asked for federal troops to take charge, assisted by the rifle clubs. The soldiers soon cleared the streets, while 500 rifle club members served as a reserve. When word reached Washington that Col. Henry J. Hunt had accepted help from the clubs, he was transferred.[7]

Democrats had also elected the lieutenant governor and other state officers by narrow margins. South Carolina Democrats, for the first time since 1860, even elected a pair of U.S. congressmen. The new state house of representatives would be made up of sixty-four Democrats and sixty Republicans. In the state senate Democrats added twelve seats for a total of fifteen.

Although outnumbered by three in the senate, Democrats commanded a majority of one in joint session. The general assembly was scheduled to convene on November 28.

All seven of South Carolina's Republican presidential electors, each elector running independently, were victorious by margins of but a few hundred votes.[8]

The state Board of Canvassers consisted of five members, all Republicans, and they had no intention of accepting Chamberlain's defeat. Under the state constitution their responsibility was simply to authorize the secretary of state to issue certificates of election to those house and senate candidates who had received the highest number of votes. If there were challenges the constitution stipulated that "each house shall judge of the election returns and qualifications of its own members." The constitution also empowered the general assembly to determine the winner of a contested gubernatorial race. Democrats expected trouble from the board. At the request of Alexander C. Haskell, the state supreme court issued a writ of mandamus requiring the board to issue certificates to those house and senate candidates who had received the most votes. The board learned that the writ was coming, so before it arrived they threw out the returns from Laurens and Edgefield counties, then quickly adjourned. The court issued warrants for the arrest of board members on contempt charges. They were all apprehended and jailed by the Richland County sheriff, but soon released by a sympathetic federal judge.[9]

The action of the board "can have no force whatever," said Hampton, urging calm. "Your cause . . . the cause of constitutional government in this country, has been carried to the highest Court of the State, and we are willing to abide by its decision." The supreme court of South Carolina promptly issued certificates of election to every winning candidate, including those from Laurens and Edgefield. Democrats elected to the state house of representatives caucused in Columbia on November 25 at Carolina Hall and again two days later at the State House. They were trying to decide what action to take should the two disputed delegations be denied their seats. They expected a battle, but no one realized just how far the Republicans would go to hold on to power.

Chamberlain wanted U.S. troops, and his president did not hesitate to provide them. On November 26 Grant ordered Secretary of War James D. Cameron "to sustain Governor Chamberlain in his authority" against "resistance too formidable to be overcome by State authorities." Cameron telegraphed Brig. Gen. Thomas H. Ruger, instructing him to "advise with the Governor, and dispose of your troops in such manner as may be deemed best." Chamberlain deemed it best to garrison the State House. A company of soldiers arrived late on the night of November 27 and took up their positions in South Carolina's capitol.[10]

For over a decade radicals had taxed and borrowed and spent millions, but they had little to show for it. They had inherited a State House under construction, put a roof on it, and moved in. It had no stone steps, no portico, no dome. "The building looked like a huge, ugly, decaying barn," someone said. Outside lay blocks of granite and unfinished stone, just as workmen had left them in 1861. The grounds were crisscrossed with muddy paths through the weeds.[11] Still, the building was a symbol. Now, it might become the scene of battle.

On the morning of Tuesday, November 28—the day set for the convening of the general assembly—word spread through Columbia and was telegraphed across the state. Troops were in the State House! Some Democratic house members, expecting something like this, had gone to the house chamber the night before, intending to stay and let themselves be surrounded. At the last minute "our advisors induced us to leave," said young Aiken representative Claude E. Sawyer. Democratic house members gathered just before noon at Carolina Hall, their meeting place in downtown Columbia, then marched together to the State House. Although all but the Edgefield and Laurens delegations had certificates from the secretary of state, it was agreed that everyone would present their certificates from the supreme court. Arriving at the door on the west side, they were stopped by an army officer with orders to admit only those with certificates from the secretary of state, but after some wrangling he let them all into the building. They were asked to surrender any pistols they might be carrying, although no Republican was similarly instructed. When Democrats reached the entrance to the house chamber, they were halted by a doorkeeper backed by twelve soldiers. The Edgefield and Laurens men were not to be allowed in, so a formal protest was read, and the Democrats left the building. William H. Wallace of Union County stayed behind to keep an eye on the Republicans, but once he had been admitted to the floor of the house, they refused to let him leave. Republicans were struggling to come up with a quorum, and only when Wallace threatened them with indictment for false imprisonment did they relent.[12]

On the muddy grounds outside the state house, a crowd had formed of over 5,000 "sunburned and hard faced men and they were not shouting nor saying such," said a witness. "They were tightening their belts and straightening up and flexing their shoulders, as men do when preparing for a desperate rush." Chamberlain told Ruger to find Hampton and have him do something. The multitude outside looked like a Confederate infantry division about to charge. Hampton was at that moment inside the building. "I was passing through the corridor," he said later, "when the officer in charge of the troops asked me to help him in quieting a crowd which had assembled in front of the Capitol threatening an attack."

Hampton walked just outside the door of the State House, found something to stand on, and began to speak.

It is of the greatest importance . . . that peace should be preserved. . . . One act of violence may precipitate bloodshed and desolation. . . . I beg all of my friends to disperse, to leave the grounds of the State House, and I advise all the colored men to do the same. Keep perfectly quiet, leave the streets, and do nothing to provoke a riot. We trust to the law and the Constitution, and we have perfect faith in the justness of our cause.

To Hampton's great relief the disappointed crowd gave a cheer and within three minutes was gone. "Nothing which had yet happened to us was so appalling as that mob," said the general, "which was friendly to me."

Baltimore attorney and former Confederate brigadier Bradley T. Johnson was there and feared another Fort Sumter. If Hampton had but raised his hand, "Ruger's garrison would have been swept off the face of the earth." Johnson credited Hampton's "moral force" for controlling the situation. A reporter from the New York *Herald* estimated the crowd at 8,000, understood them to be armed, and was certain they could have quickly overwhelmed the 300 troops. "It is fortunate that they have a leader so strong, so sagacious, so self-possessed and so thoroughly trusted as Wade Hampton. He perfectly understands the situation, and as we may judge by his conduct yesterday, he will make no mistake." The New Haven, Connecticut, *Register* agreed. "He has shown himself a leader worthy to be followed—one of whom South Carolina and the whole South may be justly proud."[13]

Hampton asked that Congress remove Grant's troops from the State House. Chamberlain countered, pleading that his government be protected from "domestic violence now threatened by Wade Hampton and others." South Carolina Republicans were losing credibility with their Northern supporters. *The Nation* concluded that "there is not in this case the slightest foundation for the pretense that there is any domestic violence in the State. The people of South Carolina are displaying great moderation and self-control." The editor was appalled at the scene in Columbia. "Has the spectacle ever been witnessed out of the United States of an armed corporal of the guard passing on the validity of election certificates at the door of a legislature?"[14]

When Democratic house members reached the security of Carolina Hall, they organized themselves as the state's lawful house of representatives, electing William H. Wallace as speaker. Their sixty-four members constituted a majority and, therefore, a quorum. Republicans argued that *they* held a quorum of those *elected*, as they considered Edgefield and Laurens unrepresented. Edmund William McGregor Mackey, one of only three whites in the Republican house, was chosen as their speaker. The Mackey house then voted to unseat also those Democrats elected from Abbeville, Aiken, and Barnwell—replacing them with their defeated Republican opponents. Now, Republicans would claim that they had a majority of the whole House. Only hours later, however, Republicans W. H. Reedish of Orangeburg and J. W. Westberry of Sumter abandoned Mackey and took seats in the Wallace house. Within two days three more Republicans left what was being called the "Bayonet house." Wallace could now claim a majority of the whole house, even without counting the delegations from Edgefield and Laurens.[15]

On November 30 Democrats made another attempt to take possession of the house chamber in the State House. Members departed Carolina Hall in groups of two and three, some walking down Sumter Street, others down Richardson. They expected the soldiers at the capitol entrance to reject those without certificates from the secretary of state, but surprisingly, all were admitted. Troops insisted that no weapons be carried inside. Claude Sawyer came to the door with a revolver in each pocket of his overcoat and carrying a walking cane. When asked by an officer if he was armed, Sawyer held up the cane and said, "I am if you call *that* armed." The officer smiled and said, "Pass on." When they reached the entrance to the house chamber, there were no troops, only two doorkeepers blocking the way. James L. Orr, giant of a man, son of the former governor, pushed the door open and all rushed in.

One witness recounted,

> The members of the Mackey House were on the side of the hall to the left as one enters. They stared open mouthed and wide eyed at the sudden invasion, while the Democrats trooped to the right side and selected desks and seats. General Wallace marched straight to the speaker's desk and took the chair there, his Sergeant-at-arms and Clerk with him. General Hampton arrived at the door and asked for admission, but the doorkeepers had recovered their wits, or received new orders, and refused him. Two or three white men stepped forward to remove the doorkeepers, but Hampton asked that they desist and walked away.[16]

Within minutes Mackey "hurried in, breathing hard," charged up to Wallace and politely demanded that he vacate the speaker's chair. Wallace refused. Each ordered his sergeant-at-arms to remove the other. "Hands crept towards hip pockets and holsters," remembered a reporter. Democratic assistant sergeants-at-arms lined one wall, ready for action. "Nothing happened. [Each] two Sergeants-at-arms . . . saluted his own Speaker, reported that he was unable to obey the order and stepped back." A chair was brought for Mackey. Both speakers had their clerks begin reading the journals for the previous day's session, two legislative bodies pretending to do business in the same chamber at the same time, each claiming to be the house of representatives of South Carolina.

Alex Haskell was chairman of the Democratic Executive Committee, but he held no government office. Mackey saw him on the stand and demanded to know why he was there.

"Mackey, you know I never go armed, but I'm armed now, and for the purpose of killing you if trouble starts in this House; and I tell you, as man to man, if trouble does start, you'll be the very first to die."[17]

Two speakers, two clerks, and two sets of legislators sat side by side. Speech making went on simultaneously. Throughout the afternoon there was a cacophony of name calling, laughter, denunciation, and song. Neither side would retreat. The Wallace house journal summarized the impasse.

> The said Mackey, protected by a negro constabulary or police, appointees of D. H. Chamberlain, Governor *so-called*, supported by United States soldiers under orders of General Ruger, continued to annoy and disturb the House, from day to day, in divers ways, although frequently called to order by the Speaker.

Tension began to subside as the day wore on. Hampton directed a telegram to President Grant complaining that Ruger was planning to expel the members from Edgefield and Laurens forcibly. Hampton made it clear that Democrats had no intention of overturning the state's electoral vote for Republican Rutherford B. Hayes. "We seek only a constitutional legislature peacefully assembled for the good of the state."[18]

Democratic members with certificates from the secretary of state were permitted to leave the building and return. They brought back food, blankets, and pillows, providing for their Edgefield and Laurens neighbors. More guns and ammunition were also smuggled in. One newspaperman remembered,

> As night came on, Republicans went out and bought a dozen candles, which were stuck about on desks on their side, giving a sickly light. The credit of the state with the gas company had been exhausted months before. The Democrats sent an order for the gas to be turned on and soon had the hall brightly lighted.

That night Ruger received orders not to intervene, so the Edgefield and Laurens delegations remained at their desks undisturbed. The next day Mackey repeatedly instructed his sergeants-at-arms to remove the Wallace house Democrats. Each time the Democrats would endure the formality of being asked to leave. Each time their response was silence. Had there been a serious attempt at forcible expulsion, bloodshed would have surely followed. The dual occupation continued on Friday and Saturday.[19] On Sunday afternoon, December 3, Haskell and Wallace received an anonymous letter from someone identifying himself as a Republican. The writer warned that Chamberlain had arranged for between fifty and sixty armed men, some of them members of the Charleston Hunkidori gang, to be sworn in as state constables and secretly brought inside the capitol. At a given signal they would attempt either to eject or, preemptively, to gun down the entire Wallace house. Their bloody work completed, Republicans would meet in joint session to declare Chamberlain governor.

Reporters verified that more than 100 of the "constables" were indeed hidden inside the State House. Newsmen sitting at their desk in front of the speaker's platform began eyeing escape routes should shooting begin. Hampton notified Ruger of the plot and then fired off a 650-word telegram to U.S. Secretary of State Hamilton Fish explaining the situation and including the text of the anonymous note. "We deprecate resort to violence & desire to abide decision of lawful authorities. Chamberlain will precipitate conflict here unless restrained by orders from Washington—in the interest of peace, in the name of the Constitution I invoke such orders."[20]

Democratic house members expected someone "to discharge a pistol on the floor then say we started it," remembered Claude Sawyer. "We were greatly outnumbered. We each selected a man to kill. We were to back up against the East side wall and take deliberate aim, keep cool and get his man." When the correspondent from the London *Times* told a colleague that he had no weapon, "he stared at me much as in England a man might have stared if I had said I did not own a tooth-brush." At eleven o'clock on this fourth night of the dual occupation, the speech making died down. Men tried to sleep in their chairs or on the floor, the silence "broken by murmured conversations here and there and constant coughing. Nearly everybody had a cold," remembered a reporter. No one knew what daylight might bring, or if they would even survive the cold December night.[21]

That Sunday evening telegraphic messages had been sent out, many in a prearranged code, spreading the alarm across the state. Men who had campaigned hard for Hampton were not about to sit by while Republicans staged a bloody coup. "I happened to see the message that went to Greenville," said a newspaperman. "It read: 'Ship first train 200 game chickens state fair, with sufficient gaffs.' When the chickens arrived most of them wore red shirts and the gaffs were not lacking."

At dawn those inside the house chamber could hear the whistle of a freight train arriving at the Gervais Street depot of the Greenville and Columbia Railroad. On board were Red Shirts from Newberry. The Prosperity Rifle Club rode through the night. Rifle and saber clubs from Richland, Lexington, and Fairfield counties were converging on the State House. Some wore red shirts, some civilian dress, but all came well armed. Regular and special trains arrived all day. The same reporter wrote,

> By noon there were twenty-five hundred to three thousand and before night between four and five thousand, enough to annihilate all the Hunkidories Mackey could bring, and the troops also, if necessary. . . . In the hall the Democrats were smiling and jubilant, Republicans bewildered, depressed, demoralized. The sudden show of strength too overwhelming to be resisted

made it evident that an attempt to expel the Democratic members by force would result in the death of every prominent Republican in the city, if not in the state.[22]

Several members of the Wallace house wanted to hold their position, come what may. The majority took the advice of wiser heads and voted to seize this opportunity to withdraw. At noon Monday, exactly four days after they had forced entrance, Democrats marched out with heads held high. That evening about 5,000 cheering men assembled on Richardson Street in front of Hampton's second-story office. He came down to the street and stood on a box to speak to them.

> "We'll leave everything we've got with you and tear down the State House with our hands, if you'll just give us the word, General!" one cried out. Others shouted agreement.
> "When the time comes to take the State House I'll lead you there," replied Hampton, to more cheers.
> "I am glad to see you all here," he smiled, "come to see the State Fair. There is very good stock out there and I hope you will go to see it, and be very particular to behave in an orderly and quiet manner. I want you all to remember that I have been elected Governor of South Carolina, and by the God above I intend to be Governor. Go home and rely on that. I'll send for you whenever I need you."

For the second time in a week, Hampton had calmed and dispersed such a crowd, promising them that his way—patient maneuvering—was best. The wisdom of that strategy was confirmed by a message Bradley Johnson wired from Washington. "Grant and [Secretary of War James D.] Cameron angry because Wallace left house without fight. . . . Grant wants outbreak. Advise avoid collision . . . for any reason."[23]

Hampton received a letter from one W. H. Jones, a Confederate veteran living in Conwayboro, that expressed the feelings of many supporters. Jones had campaigned for Hampton, even neglecting his business, "only to see the Rads act so much fool. I wanted them put out of the way at once." His first impulse had been "to come up there & with Gen Gary *kill* out all the Rads in and around the city and install you in the grandest style." There were thousands of impatient men like Jones willing to go to war again, restrained now only by their leader's orders. The *Times* of London correspondent gave Hampton sole credit for keeping the peace.

> General Hampton had but to utter one word, and the State House would have been stormed long ago, or rather he had only to maintain silence, and this silence would have been construed into a permission to do what some of the rank and file have been longing for and arguing should be done. But

he has an extraordinary control over the whole of his Party, the wildest spirits among them obeying his slightest word.[24]

During the week several more Republicans joined the Wallace house. At noon on December 6, Samps Bridges, Republican of Newberry County, took the oath amid a storm of applause. With his defection the Wallace house now had sixty-three members—*not counting all five of the excluded counties*—an unassailable majority. The South Carolina Supreme Court declared the Wallace house the state's lawful house of representatives, but a delegation to Ruger was rebuffed. The general said that his troops must continue to obey the instructions of the Republican doorkeepers.[25]

The state senate remained in undisputed Republican control, but was "divided against itself," observed the London reporter. That body had refused to seat three Democratic senators-elect, including Gary of Edgefield. Democrats there were left with twelve members. Republicans held eighteen seats.[26] On December 5 the senate and the Mackey house met in joint session. Having thrown out the returns from Edgefield and Laurens, they declared Chamberlain the victor by 3,145 votes, Lieutenant Governor Gleaves by 4,089. The work was done by candlelight. After the Democrats had left, the utility had again cut off the gas.[27]

Two days later Chamberlain rode to the State House in his guarded carriage. With the curtains drawn, the vehicle was said to resemble "half a hearse." The ceremony itself was closed to the general public, the oath of office administered by a probate judge. "The inauguration was in the hall of the House and was like something being done in the shadow of death," wrote a Democratic newspaperman, "the hall dark, untidy, dismal, the attendance fifty-one alleged representatives, sixteen senators, eighty-seven negro spectators and six newspaper men." Chamberlain denounced his opponent's campaign as "a deliberate and cruel conspiracy . . . to overcome by brute force the political will of a majority of 30,000 of the lawful voters of this State." Applause was slight.[28]

Hampton made one call for assistance at this point that proved to be counterproductive. Former Confederate John Singleton Mosby practiced law in Virginia and had joined the Republican Party, although he never embraced the radical agenda. Thinking Mosby might be able to influence Grant, Hampton sent the colonel a telegram on December 11. Mosby immediately went to the White House. "I showed him Hampton's telegram," reported Mosby. "Grant assured me that he would only use military force to preserve peace and save the State from anarchy. I wrote Hampton what Grant said." Mosby's interview with the president was disappointing. Even worse, news of the exchange became public, bringing sharp criticism on Hampton from Southern newspapers for his having asked the help of a scalawag. Hampton subsequently distanced himself from Mosby, hurting the colonel's feelings.

Democrats had the legitimate house of representatives, but only a minority vote in the senate. Republicans controlled a lawful senate, but operated a rump house. On joint ballot, with all legislators casting individual votes, Democrats commanded a majority. It was on joint ballot that U.S. senators were chosen. Incumbent U.S. Sen. Thomas J. Robertson was retiring after one term. The Mackey house and the Republican state senators met in joint session and, after several ballots, picked David T. Corbin. The Wallace house and Democratic state senators met and elected Matthew C. Butler. The U.S. Senate itself would spend nearly a year wrangling over which man to seat. In other ways South Carolina Republicans tried to carry on as they had for so many years, but things had changed. State bank accounts were overdrawn. Republican legislators had not been paid. Even the railroads had canceled their free passes. On top of county and special taxes, Chamberlain's general assembly tried to raise the state property tax.[29] Republicans did not seem to realize that their power had all but slipped away, that they were no longer able to collect those taxes. Now, they controlled only their stone fortress in the heart of Columbia.

On December 13 John S. Richardson, unsuccessful Democratic candidate for the U.S. House of Representatives, asked Secretary of State H. E. Hayne for certified copies of election returns for 1874 and 1876. The Republican secretary promptly complied, likely assuming that Richardson wanted the figures to appeal his recent loss. Included in those numbers were the results from Edgefield and Laurens counties. The Republican secretary of state had unwittingly furnished Democrats with officially certified returns showing that Hampton had won the governorship by 1,134 votes! The Wallace house and the Democratic senators met on December 14 and declared that Hampton had been elected governor and Simpson Lieutenant governor. A delegation was sent to officially inform the governor-elect.[30]

Wade Hampton's inauguration was held that day on a stand built in front of Carolina Hall in downtown Columbia. A crowd filled the lot in front of the building and extended down neighboring streets. People watched from windows and roof tops. Flags were everywhere. Wreathes of green had replaced the flowers of the summer–fall campaign. The Columbia Flying Artillery fired their guns, having renamed their battery the "Hampton Saluting Club."[31]

> It is with feelings of the profoundest solicitude that I assume the arduous duties and grave responsibilities of the high position to which the people of South Carolina have called me. It is amid events unprecedented in this Republic that I take the chair as Chief Magistrate of this State.

Hampton credited "the honest people of this State, without regard to party or race" for demanding an end to "years of misrule, corruption and

Celebration in the streets of Columbia upon news of Hampton's inauguration. *Leslie's Weekly.*

anarchy, brought upon us by venal and unprincipled political adventurers." Federal occupation of the capitol was something that "the civilized world has looked on with amazement, disgust and horror." He promised that his administration would support public education. Conservatives recognized "that all citizens of South Carolina, of both races and both parties, should be regarded as equals in the eyes of the law." "We owe much of our late success to those colored voters who were brave enough to rise above the prejudice of race and honest enough to throw off the shackles of party, in their determination to save the State." In fact, Hampton may well have received more than 10,000 black votes. Of those who did not vote for him, he said, "we should not be vindictive but magnanimous." In conclusion, Hampton hoped that God would "shower the richest blessings of peace and happiness on our whole people."[32]

As he finished speaking, Hampton turned to Judge Thomas J. Mackey. "Now, sir, I am ready to take the oath of office to which I have been elected." As the judge walked up to Hampton "a pin might have been heard to fall," wrote a reporter, "so perfect was the silence, so impressed were all present with the solemnity of the occasion."

"As I looked around me," said the correspondent of the Baltimore Gazette, "I saw silent tears creep into the eyes of old gray-headed men, and they brushed them away and bit their lips to restrain their feelings." The inauguration over, Gov. Wade Hampton was placed in a chair and carried through the cheering crowd to his hotel.

The Columbia Register noted,

Many persons must have seen the brilliant meteor which shot across the sky just as the inaugural ceremonies were completed yesterday afternoon. It is the first that we have ever seen in the broad daylight, and we hope that its brightness is typical of the future of our State.

The astronomical report was headlined "Happy Omen."[33]

Governor Hampton set up his office in rooms over a downtown Columbia store. He chose nephew Wade Hampton Manning as his secretary, assisted by a clerk. On December 18 Hampton sent a letter to Chamberlain requesting the seal of the state, public records, and the capitol. Chamberlain, of course, refused. Each signed his letter as South Carolina's governor. Each addressed the other as "Esquire." Hampton also addressed identical letters to Hayes and Tilden, enclosing copies of his inaugural address. The people, said Hampton, "are not wanting either in the spirit or the means to maintain their rights of citizenship," but still have faith enough to leave the issue "to the proper legal tribunals." He wanted it understood that although their patience was being severely tested, Democrats would not themselves resort to "the exhibition of armed force."[34]

Nearly two weeks before on December 6, both Republican and Democratic presidential electors had met in Columbia and voted for their candidates. As close as the presidential vote was in South Carolina, it seemed clear that the Hayes electors had won. It was suggested that, even now, were Hampton to make a statement acknowledging Hayes to be the winner in

South Carolina, troops might be removed in response. Hampton refused. In addition to South Carolina, both Florida and Louisiana had competing sets of electors. And one Hayes elector in Oregon was being challenged. If but a single elector in any one of those four states were counted for Tilden, the Democrat would be elected president. To resolve the impasse Congress created an electoral commission of fifteen members, made up of eight Republicans and seven Democrats. That commission, voting strictly along party lines, decided every disputed contest in favor of the Republican candidate. Rutherford B. Hayes was president-elect of the United States.[35]

The fate of South Carolina now seemed to be in the hands of the new chief executive. Hampton's letter to Hayes was delivered personally by Judge Mackey. "The letter is not of much importance," wrote Hayes in his journal, "except as it indicates General Hampton's views of duty in case of armed resistance by the Democrats." Hayes had been warned about Mackey, but thought him "a fluent and florid talker. His representations are such as lead one to hope for good results by a wise policy in the South."[36]

On December 20 the Wallace house "requested, instructed, and admonished" that property owners pay no taxes to the Chamberlain government. By resolution the Democratic legislators authorized Hampton to ask taxpayers to advance immediately one quarter of what their tax bill had been the preceding year. That amount voluntarily submitted now would be deducted from what came due later. Hampton thought the amount too high and asked for just 10 percent in a January 1 address. The response was gratifying. Mass meetings were held, with taxpayers pledging to support the Hampton government and promising to give nothing to Chamberlain. Dr. James Woodrow of Columbia's Presbyterian Publishing House offered to meet all of the Democratic government's publishing needs on credit.[37] Soon Republican-controlled state agencies were coming to Hampton. Dr. J. F. Ensor, superintendent of the lunatic asylum, was the first. This Republican addressed a letter to "Governor Hampton," asking for help. His institution had received but a fraction of its operating budget during the past two years and would soon have to close its doors. Hampton responded with the needed funds. Ironically, twenty years earlier state senator Wade Hampton had made the asylum his special concern. The penitentiary was next in line for assistance, followed by the Deaf, Dumb and Blind Institute and the orphan asylum. The salaries of judges were to be paid under the terms of the house resolution. "I suppose that I am only authorized to recognize claims accruing since the 14th Dec. last," Hampton wrote Chief Justice Moses, "but I propose to pay for the quarter ending after that date." During an eleven-week period more than $120,000 was paid to the Hampton government in voluntary taxes. Almost $38,000 had been disbursed, and the remainder was on deposit in eight separate banks in Columbia and Charleston.[38]

A U.S. Army engineer sent a letter to Hampton on February 9 requesting

Despite Hampton's inauguration, his opponent, Governor Chamberlain, initially refused to leave office. Supportive citizens voluntarily sent their taxes to Hampton as a show of support and, despite offers of mob assistance in toppling Chamberlain's government, Hampton insisted on a peaceful solution. In this period cartoon, an increasingly powerless Chamberlain attempts to goad Hampton into violence so that he can justifiably call federal troops in to settle the matter. Hampton, with the power of the treasury beneath him, refuses to oblige.

Chamberlain: "Will you come down and fight, so that I can call in the troops to suppress you?"
Hampton: "No!"
Chamberlain: "Well, then, stay where you are."
Leslie's Illustrated Weekly.

title to the land upon which a lighthouse was to be erected. Capt. W. A. Jones addressed the missive simply to the "Governor of South Carolina."[39] Grant was still commander in chief, and the captain did not want to invite trouble by formally addressing Hampton as governor. But he knew where to send his letter.

A test case was arranged to strengthen Hampton's claim on the office. Tilda Stephens, alias Tilda Norris, penitentiary convict number 2114, was pardoned by Hampton. She had served fourteen months of a two-year sentence for manslaughter. By prearrangement the superintendent refused to recognize Hampton's pardon, and the case went to the supreme court. Chief Justice Moses was very ill. The case would have to be decided by his two associates. Justices A. J. Willard and Jonathan J. Wright issued an order freeing Norris. Pressure was put on Wright by Republicans to change his decision. He did—before the order was filed, but after he had signed it. Justice Willard went ahead and processed the order for Norris's release, thus recognizing Hampton as the lawful governor, and the superintendent obeyed. In a case brought over a Chamberlain pardon, Judge R. B. Carpenter of the Fifth Circuit Court ruled that neither Hampton nor his rival had been legally elected. Hampton won yet another pardon case.[40] It became obvious that judicial sparring would bring no resolution.

Messages began to arrive on Hampton's desk from citizens begging for better law enforcement and from rifle clubs tendering their services. As Republican county treasurers, trial justices, and other local officials were removed from office, there were rumblings from the black militia.[41] Fortunately, no immediate crisis arose. Hampton commissioned officers of Charleston's Washington Artillery and the German Fusiliers, the Sumter Guard, and Orangeburg's Edisto Rifles. These and other units had planned to parade, along with U.S. troops, on Washington's birthday. At the last minute President Grant issued an order forbidding the white militias from marching. Once again Hampton called on South Carolinian Democrats to swallow their pride and postpone their celebration, obeying Grant "in deference to the office he holds."[42]

There seemed scant hope that before leaving office Grant would resolve the issue by withdrawing support for the Chamberlain government. Just before adjourning for the year, the Wallace house had gone into secret session, on December 21, to consider a "memorial to President Grant and the Congress of the United States," pressing the cause of South Carolina Democrats. Hampton was willing to travel to Washington, if that might help. "Your presence here would not expedite action might delay it," Matthew C. Butler telegraphed on December 21. Butler seemed optimistic, however. "Cabinet meets tomorrow on S. C. I have it authoritatively that no government in S.C. will be sustained which cannot sustain itself."[43]

Still, the stalemate continued. At a series of conferences held in Washington in February, assurances were given that the incoming Hayes administration would withdraw troops, allowing the remaining Republican regimes in the South to surrender to the inevitable. The agreement was unofficial, but it was understood that in return Democrats were only required to guarantee peace and protection for blacks and to promise not to persecute political enemies. Hayes took office on March 5 and in his inaugural address seemed conciliatory toward the South. He said he wanted sectionalism forgotten. A message from friends of the new administration to Chamberlain asked him to accept troop removal, but the governor balked. T. J. Mackey was in Washington to represent the Hampton government in negotiations with the White House. Democrats now controlled the U.S. House of Representatives. The U.S. Senate remained in Republican hands and was then in special session considering a long list of presidential nominations. Hayes preferred to wait until Senate adjournment, expected in a week, before taking action on the controversial "Southern problem."[44] The very fact that he chose to wait seemed to auger well for South Carolina Democrats.

On March 10 Judge Mackey met with President Hayes and his nominee for secretary of state William M. Evarts. Mackey telegraphed Hampton immediately, informing him that Evarts

> desired to know whether Chamberlain could visit Washington without impairing his position in Columbia. I replied that Chamberlain is simply the ward of the military but that if requested by President you would not attempt to disturb the status quo during his temporary absence. I insisted on an early decision as essential to the maintenance of public order.

Evarts promised that a decision would come soon. "I have no doubt that favorable action will be taken by next Thursday [March 15]," concluded Mackey.[45]

Senator John Patterson suggested to the president that new elections be held in South Carolina, something Mackey refused to consider. Judge Carpenter was also in Washington, "active for Chamberlain," reported Mackey, but "the police arrested him with other gamblers at a gambling den Sunday night." Remaining members of the Chamberlain team claimed that South Carolina would acquiesce "if he [Chamberlain] is recognized" by the president. Mackey told Hampton that he replied to that by saying "to recognize Chamberlain is to impel armed resistance to his authority by relieving you [Hampton] of any obligation to be active in maintaining the peace."[46] Hampton wanted it known that Democrats would take possession of the State House without violence if U.S. troops would simply stand aside. The situation in Washington, said Butler, is "very anxious and uncertain."[47] The Senate had adjourned March 17, but still the White House was silent.

On Wednesday, March 21, Butler again telegraphed Hampton. "Everything looks blue; there seems to be no hope for South Carolina. It looks like another game of 8 to 7," referring to the Electoral Commission's partisan vote putting Hayes in the White House.

"Shall I come to Washington?" wired Hampton. "Do you think I can do anything by coming?"

"No," telegraphed Butler. "Stay where you are. You can do no good here, and you cannot tell what a day may bring forth in South Carolina."[48]

Hayes's cabinet rejected the idea of sending a presidential commission to South Carolina, and on March 23 the president decided to invite both Hampton and Chamberlain to see him in Washington. Hampton had already decided that he would not leave South Carolina unless the president asked him to come.[49] Even so, many friends were against his going. "Don't commit yourself until I can learn what it means," telegraphed Butler. "Wait till I see you [before deciding to come]," Butler wired just before he boarded a train for Columbia.[50]

Identical invitations were sent to Hampton and Chamberlain by W. K. Rogers, Hayes's secretary, on Friday, March 23. "It is the earnest desire of the President to be able to put an end as speedily as possible to all appearances of intervention by the military authority of the United States in political derangements which affect the Government and afflict the people of South Carolina." The wording could not have cheered Chamberlain. Secretary Evarts had already made it clear to Chamberlain that his intransigence was embarrassing the party. Hayes recorded in his journal that it was not a president's duty "to decide contested elections in the States." The federal government must "keep the peace," but otherwise not intervene.[51]

Mackey was encouraged Saturday by a conversation he had with Secretary of War George W. McCrary. The president's purpose in inviting Hampton to the White House was not to investigate election returns, said McCrary, but to ask Hampton about the policies he would pursue as governor. Secretary McCrary even "referred to you as Governor," wired Mackey to Hampton, "and expressed hope that your administration would prove the wisdom of Presdts policy." Mackey expressed even greater optimism in a telegram he sent to Hampton on Sunday, assuring him that all the president required was an assurance that a "vindictive policy will not be pursued towards Republicans" by a Hampton administration. "Come," begged Mackey, "and end our long agony peacefully."[52]

On Monday morning Hampton sent a telegram to President Hayes accepting his invitation. All that was required for the "peaceful and orderly" organization of state government was "the withdrawal of the federal troops from our state house." Hampton assured Hayes that "no discrimination shall be made in the administration of justice and that all citizens of both parties and both races shall be regarded as fully protected."[53] Chamberlain was in

Washington on Tuesday having his interview with the president as Hampton prepared to leave Columbia.

> I go to Washington simply to state before the President the fact that the people of South Carolina have elected me Governor of that State. I go there-fore to say to him that we ask no recognition of any President. We claim the recognition from the votes of the people of the State. I am going there to demand our rights—nothing more—and, so help me God, to take nothing less.

Republican circuit court judge L. C. Northrop said,

> I have never seen such profound excitement and inflexible resolution. It is a kind of frenzy that possessed the people of Paris in 1793. It has been waiting like a chained tiger on the first movement of Hampton's finger or lips. If that movement had been made, the whole Army of the United States would have business on its hands.

Accompanied by Butler, Conner, and a large delegation of business leaders, Hampton's journey to the District of Columbia was a triumph. Stations all along the line of the Wilmington, Columbia, and Augusta Railroad asked for his itinerary that people might come out. Crowds and bands met his train in Wilmington, Goldsboro, Wilson, and Weldon in North Carolina and in Petersburg and Richmond in Virginia.[54]

They arrived in Washington at three o'clock on the morning of March 29. From his room that morning in Willard's Hotel, Hampton wrote the president a letter that would be hand-delivered to the White House. Hampton again stated his intention to respect the rights of all, particularly "the political rights of colored citizens."[55] The president's private secretary came to Hampton's hotel and arranged for the interview. Hampton would be received by Hayes that day, accompanied by South Carolina attorney general Conner and Georgia senator John B. Gordon.

Conner boasted to his wife,

> When we drove to the White House we were received in state, met by the President's son and escorted by the private secretary to the library. The Cabinet was in session. In a few moments the President came out. We were introduced and invited into the Cabinet room and introduced to all the Cabinet. . . . We chatted for a quarter of an hour I suppose, then the President went back with us to the Library and I suppose we talked over the situation and things generally for an hour or an hour and a half. Mrs. Hayes put her head in for a moment and was about to withdraw when the President called her in and presented us all.

Hayes invited them to have lunch, and Hampton escorted the First Lady to the dining room. "Mrs. Hayes sat at the center of the table, on one side, and the President opposite," continued Conner, "the Governor on her right, I on her left." After they dined, President Hayes invited Hampton to go on a drive with him while the others departed on their own. Later, Secretary Evarts also met with Hampton.[56]

It was not disclosed what was said. Hampton found a crowd waiting for him at Willard's Hotel, but he refused to make a speech and discouraged their demonstration of support. "Wade Hampton's presence in Washington," said the New York *Tribune*, "excites more attention than that of any other public man since Pres. Hayes came."[57] Apparently, Hampton had not yet received a schedule, or even definite assurance, of a troop withdrawal. On the evening of March 30, he wrote a note to Hayes. "Several telegraphic communications have come to me today from Columbia demanding immediate answer," said Hampton, "but I can give none until I have a conference with yourself." On March 31, from his hotel room, Hampton wrote a letter to Hayes reiterating "in the fullest & most definite form the assurances given to you verbally." Again, he made it clear that upon removal of troops from the State House, there would be no violence, that the rights of all would be respected. Hampton expressed confidence that "the wise & patriotic policy announced in your inaugural, will, as soon as it takes shape in action produce such fruits—that the whole country will enjoy the blessings of peace, prosperity & harmony."[58]

The next day, Sunday, Hampton was again invited to the White House, and this time all his questions were resolved. "Everything satisfactorily and honorably settled," he wired Lieutenant Governor Simpson. "I expect our people to preserve absolute peace and quiet. My word is pledged for this. I rely on them." News of the impending troop removal spread quickly. Chamberlain was shocked. His partisans in Columbia were disbelieving. "Senator Patterson and other South Carolina Republicans called upon Wade Hampton before he left," reported the New York *Times,* "and admitting they were finally defeated, cordially expressed a purpose to support his Administration."

Said the New York *Tribune,*

> Gov. Wade Hampton returns to Columbia one of the most important men in the U.S. The future of the whole South may be said to depend in great measure upon him. He can confirm the federal administration in its new policy of non-interference, or he can provoke a reaction in public opinion.[59]

Hampton was riding high in Southern sentiment. He began his trip home on April 5, and, again, the journey became a continuous ovation. A special train met him in Charlotte, where he was sent on his way by an enthusiastic crowd and a military escort. One reporter said,

> The locomotive and entire train were covered with wreaths and flowers. The car reserved for the Governor was carpeted especially and upholstered with flowers, growing flowers in every window. Over in South Carolina the country people had built great arches spanning the track over which the train was to run. At Rock Hill, Chester, Winnsboro were arches, profusions of flowers, cheering crowds, bands, rockets.

The flower-laden train rolled to a stop in Columbia at four-thirty on the afternoon of Saturday, April 7. The crowd that met Hampton at the station was "enormous and enormously happy." Rifle clubs stood in formation. The band of the Eighteenth U.S. Infantry Regiment played. The state was wild with joy. Hampton's message was simple. "Forget we are Democrats or Republicans, white or colored, and remember only that we are all South Carolinians."[60]

Chamberlain declared to fellow Republicans, and anyone else who would listen, that he was still the legal governor, but could not hold on to his office without federal support. At noon on April 10 Lieutenant Haynes of Company B, Second Regiment, ordered his twenty men to assemble in the downstairs corridor of the State House. They then marched out by way of the south door into the fresh air of a Carolina spring. The constables were nowhere to be seen. The capitol was almost empty. The next day there was one final exchange of notes, with Hampton demanding the governor's office and Chamberlain agreeing to leave. At noon Wade Hampton Manning, the governor's secretary, walked to the State House, and Chamberlain's secretary handed him the keys. There was no crowd, no demonstration. "Perfect peace prevails," Hampton telegraphed to Senator Gordon at three-thirty that afternoon. "The troops have been withdrawn, and Chamberlain surrenders South Carolina. Thank you."

"A squad of convicts from the Penitentiary was busily engaged today in the very necessary labor of scouring the floors of the rooms which had been thoroughly defiled by Chamberlain's special constables during their occupancy," reported the *News and Courier* on April 13. "This herculean task will have to be performed throughout the entire building."[61]

ON APRIL 9, just before the federal evacuation of the State House, young Charleston reporter Alfred Williams was sent by his editor to interview Hampton. Williams hired a buggy and two horses at a Columbia livery stable and told the driver to take him to Hampton's home on the outskirts of town.

It was getting dark. The horses were hard to handle, but the driver finally got Williams to his destination. The young man remembered,

> When I found the Governor, and had the talk for which I had been sent, he said he would go to town with me, got in the seat . . . took the reins and gave the most perfect demonstration of understanding by horses of the master hand I ever have seen. He drove with his left hand only and apparently gave to the team no attention; and it trotted into town like a well regulated piece of machinery.
>
> I asked him, not for publication, what he had said to Hayes while they were together. His reply is distinct in my mind. He said Hayes asked him what would happen if Chamberlain were recognized as governor.
>
> "I told him," Hampton answered, "that the first thing would be that every Republican tax collector in the state should be hanged within twenty-four hours."
>
> I suspected a furtive grin beneath this bare faced bulldozing of the President of the United States, but it was dark.
>
> Then I asked him if he really meant that if necessary he would fight the United States government. His reply was solemn and deliberate and I believe he meant every word of it.
>
> "The people of South Carolina gave me their banner to carry. I intended to carry it as far as they would follow me."[62]

DANIEL H. CHAMBERLAIN would move to New York City and there practice law. After the passage of a few years, he returned to visit South Carolina and was cordially received. He died in Italy, where he had gone for his health, in 1907. Robert K. Scott, the other carpetbag governor of South Carolina, went home to Ohio where he died in 1900. The state's only scalawag chief executive, Franklin J. Moses Jr., never stayed anywhere for long. He became a drug addict and spent time in jail for theft, vagrancy, and passing bad checks. In 1885 he was sentenced to three years in a Massachusetts penitentiary. He died in Winthrop, Massachusetts in 1906.[63]

In 1901, the twenty-fifth anniversary of those crucial elections, the *Atlantic Monthly* published a series of articles on Reconstruction. Among the contributors were Princeton professor Woodrow Wilson and Atlanta University historian W. E. B. DuBois. William A. Dunning, Thomas Nelson Page, and a number of other prestigious writers added to the symposium.

One who knew his subject firsthand was the author of "Reconstruction in South Carolina." The writer of this article blamed Republican politicians for "putting the white South under the heel of the black South." Lust for power was their motivation. "If this is a hard saying, let any one now ask himself, or ask the public, if it is possibly credible that the reconstruction acts would have been passed if the negro vote had been believed to be Democratic."

"To this feast of reconstruction, this dance of reunion, rushed hundreds, even thousands, of white and colored men from the North, who had almost as little experience of public affairs as the negroes of the South . . . and [were] not morally the equals of the negroes of the South." Some of these carpetbaggers may have been "unselfish doctrinaires, humanitarians, and idealists," but most were simply opportunists. The result was inevitable.

> In the mass of 78,000 colored voters in South Carolina in 1867, what elements or forces could have existed that made for good government? Ought it not to have been as clear then as it is now that good government, or even tolerable administration, could not be had from such an aggregation of ignorance and inexperience and incapacity[?]
>
> The quick, sure result was of course misgovernment. Let a few statistics tell the tale. Before the war, the average expense of the annual session of the legislature in South Carolina did not exceed $20,000. For the six years following reconstruction the average annual expense was over $320,000, the expense of the session of 1871 alone being $671,000. The total legislative expenses for the six years were $2,339,000.

The state's debt soared to $17,500,000; but without "a single public improvement" to show for it.

> No such result could be possible except where public and private virtue was well-nigh extinct. . . . Public offices were objects of vulgar, commonplace bargain and sale. Justice in the lower and higher courts was bought and sold. . . . State militia on a vast scale was organized and equipped in 1870 and 1871 solely from the negroes, arms and legal organization being denied the white Democrats.

The writer remembered one black county school commissioner who was unable to read or even to write his own name. "He was corrupt, too, as he was ignorant." No Northern state would have tolerated such an official. One morning he was found dead, shot by the "famous and infamous Ku Klux Klan." Their "brutal and murderous" actions were without excuse. "Yet it was symptomatic of a dreadful disease—the gangrene of incapacity, dishonesty, and corruption in public office."

"It has been remarked that South Carolina had no great leader or leaders after Mr. Calhoun," he wrote, but that was true only until the emergence of Wade Hampton in 1876.

> Totally unlike Calhoun, Hampton's strength of leadership lay, not in intellectual or oratorical superiority, but in high and forceful character, perfect courage, and real devotion to what he conceived to be the welfare of South Carolina. Not even Calhoun's leadership was at any time more absolute, unquestioned, and enthusiastic than Hampton's was in 1876; and it was

justly so from the Democratic point of view, for he was unselfish, resolute, level-headed, and determined. He was for the hour a true "natural leader"; and he led with consummate mingled prudence and aggressiveness.

It was often charged that whites used "force and violence" to bring an end to Reconstruction in South Carolina. "What is certain is that a people of force, pride and intelligence, driven, as the white people of South Carolina believed they were in 1876, to choose between violence and lawlessness for a time, and misrule for all time, will infallibly choose the former." The corrupt Republican regime, in power for a decade, "fell in a day."

> If there is any interest still attaching to the writer's own view, he is quite ready now to say that he feels sure there was no possibility of securing good government in South Carolina through Republican influences. . . . The vast preponderance of ignorance and incapacity in that party, aside from down-right dishonesty, made it impossible."

The writer of the article was Daniel H. Chamberlain.[64]

16

"HE HAS KEPT
ALL HIS PLEDGES"

Governor Hampton

With Hampton the undisputed governor, South Carolina Democrats moved to secure their claim on state government. A form
letter had already gone out to Democratic legislative delegations
asking for the names of all those holding county office, inquiring about their
loyalty and competence. Hampton wanted those positions held by men "possessing undoubted ability and integrity—prepared to actively support and
emphatically carry out the much-needed reforms to which we are solemnly
pledged." Hundreds of applications from job seekers poured into the governor's office.[1] Not all appointees would be white Democrats. Edward Henderson, for example, was recommended for the position of jury commissioner
of Abbeville County. "Henderson is a colored man," wrote the one who
nominated him. "There can be no objection to him & the appointment is
well deserved & would give entire satisfaction."[2] It was suggested that black
Democrat Harry B. Scott, an incumbent school commissioner, keep his job.[3]
Republican James Van Tassell was recommended for appointment as auditor
of Orangeburg County. Hampton sent out another form letter to those
appointed to local office, instructing them on the procedures to follow in
claiming their positions.[4]

On April 12 Governor Hampton issued a proclamation calling for a special session of the general assembly to convene twelve days later.[5] Democratic
members met beforehand, agreeing to make their decisions in caucus, then

vote in unity. The house of representatives required former members of the illegal Mackey house to purge themselves of contempt merely by asking for pardon. One Republican refused, two resigned, two were expelled, and seats from Charleston County were declared vacant because of election irregularities. The new house would end up securely in Democratic hands. In the state senate Republican resignations left each party with fifteen seats; Lieutenant Governor Simpson controlled tie votes. During the summer and fall ten more Republican senators chose to depart. Attorney General Conner brought suit against six Republican circuit court judges, and the supreme court agreed to their removal. The general assembly would elect four Democrats and two Republicans to replace them, giving the state six Democratic and two Republican judges. The Reconstruction regime had been swiftly swept away, wrote one observer, and "the Hampton Govt. is now in full possession, [and] it was all done quietly."[6]

Governor Hampton addressed the lawmakers in joint session on April 24. Months of governmental confusion made it difficult for him to give exact figures, but he knew that the state had "an empty treasury and a ruined credit." South Carolina should reduce expenses, cut salaries, and eliminate some offices altogether. Taxes must be "as light as possible, for the resources of our people are well nigh exhausted." Hampton suggested that the state asylum be controlled by a board of regents, with each member an unpaid volunteer. For the time being the state could not afford to operate the University of South Carolina, as it was named during the Radical regime. Closing the doors of his alma mater must have been a difficult decision for Hampton. Primary education had to come first. "Free schools for the poorest as well as the richest, black as well as white" must be "within the reach of all classes." The system as administered by Republicans was "a mere mockery, under which the children have been imperfectly taught. The teachers have been swindled out of their pay, and the money of the people has been squandered." Hampton recommended that a commission be formed to investigate the indebtedness of the state and determine which liabilities were just and which fraudulent. "I cherish the additional hope that you will forget the animosities engendered by political strife, rise superior to the petty considerations of partisanship."[7]

Hampton was determined to demonstrate to Hayes the wisdom of the new president's decision in favor of Southern home rule. Hampton appointed Republicans to demonstrate that "our fight here has not been against Northern men but only against a band of plunderers." Such was Hampton's relationship with Hayes that Edmund W. M. Mackey would later complain that no appointment could be had from the Republican administration in Washington without "the endorsement of the Democrats."[8] Hampton asked that those arrested by federal authorities in the 1876 Ellenton Riot and other cases be released. Dr. J. Rufus Bratton was one prominent example. The Yorkville physician was accused of Ku Klux Klan involvement. Protesting his innocence, Bratton fled to London, Ontario, to avoid arrest. He practiced medicine there, but was soon kidnaped by federal agents. Canadians were outraged at this violation of their sovereignty and demanded his return. Bratton was sent back to Canada, remaining there as Hampton negotiated with Hayes. Finally, Hampton could assure Dr. Bratton's family that all was well. The governor had gone to Washington, and reported,

> I am happy in being able to convey to you the assurance of the President that your brother and all others connected with the Ku Klux troubles can return to the state with perfect safety. Mr. Hayes promises that no action shall be taken against any of those parties.

To avoid political repercussions, there would be no public announcement. But, concluded Hampton, the president "has done all that was necessary, and he has placed the people of the state under additional obligations to him." The state chose to prosecute but a few of the Republicans accused of fraud, and federal charges were dropped in nearly all of the Ellenton cases. "I agree with you," the president wrote to Hampton, "that a general amnesty should extend to all political offenses except those which are of the gravest character."[9]

Hampton was to become the most widely traveled of South Carolina's governors. During June and July he was in New York negotiating a loan to pay interest on the state's debt. Hampton kept a low profile in the city, even moving from his hotel to a private residence to avoid publicity. He finally secured the loan. He also found time to pursue amnesty for three South Carolinians, federal prisoners serving sentences in the Albany penitentiary. Hampton wrote to Hayes from New York City requesting clemency.[10]

Later, Hampton would pass on to President Hayes what he knew of a plan by Democrats to reassert their claim of having won the 1876 presidential election. Montgomery Blair, encouraged by the Democratic press, sought a court decision that even now might eject Hayes and install Tilden in the White House. The Democratic U.S. House of Representatives resolved to get involved. Wade Hampton supported the Republican president. He wrote to Hayes,

> You can crush the ambitious politicians who are trying to crush you if you accept the gage of battle they have thrown down. Of course, there are extreme men in the Democratic party, who seek to keep up agitation, but they are powerless. I honestly think that you will secure the almost unanimous support of the South.

Hampton's prediction proved true. The president overcame the challenges with little difficulty, grateful for the support of Hampton and other Southern Democrats.[11]

Hampton's closer relationship with President Hayes was helpful, too, in resolving a situation in the mountains of South Carolina that threatened to become another Whiskey Rebellion. Throughout the mountain South it was difficult, if not impossible, for federal agents to collect the tax on whiskey. Agents often met with violence, and in early July 1878, one revenue officer killed a resident of Pickens County. A state judge insisted on a trial in state court. Hampton urged the president to appoint a new set of Revenue Service officers and declare amnesty for past offenders. The governor appealed to those illegal distillers to "come in and bind themselves to stop their unlawful work." He promised to try to halt the prosecutions of those who did so, and soon twenty-five had come forward. Hayes was determined to enforce the laws, but appreciated Hampton's help in calming the situation and avoiding a collision between state and federal authority. "Governor Hampton is a conservative man," the president wrote in his journal, "and wishes to see the laws enforced without violence."[12]

In 1877 Hampton visited White Sulphur Springs, Greenbriar County, West Virginia. There on August 16 he was welcomed by the governor of that state, reviewed local militia units, and spoke to a sympathetic crowd. He was glad to report that South Carolina was no longer the "Prostrate State," but once again the "Palmetto State." The former Confederate general noticed that the militiamen of the West Virginia Guards wore blue uniforms. "Time was when he had not been so glad to meet the blue," wrote a reporter of Hampton's reaction, "though he always gave them as warm a reception as he could."

The South Carolina governor was in Washington on September 1, staying at the Arlington House Hotel, when he received a telegram from the mayor of Louisville, Kentucky. The president was scheduled to visit the Louisville Industrial Exposition on September 17, and Hampton was invited to come too. "Your presence will be highly appreciated and do much good," urged another message.[13] Hampton added Louisville to his itinerary, but he also had other obligations. After briefly returning to Columbia, on September 12 he arrived in Chicago. A reporter from the Chicago *Times* found him at the Palmer House Hotel late that night and was granted a brief interview. The newsman thought the fifty-nine-year-old governor was "about 45," describing his hair as "tinged with gray." Hampton was on his way to Rockford, Illinois, a town some twenty miles from the Wisconsin state line. The governor revealed that he had received an anonymous letter threatening death should he come to Rockford, but he seemed unconcerned. Hampton praised the Republican president. "He has done all that Tilden could have done; indeed, in my judgment, he has done more than would have been possible for him to do."

Hampton traveled to Rockford at the invitation of that city's Agricultural Association to address a crowd at the Winnebago County Fair. His theme was sectional reconciliation. He praised from firsthand experience the fighting prowess of Illinois volunteers. And he disingenuously distanced himself from South Carolina's original secessionists. "I obeyed the command of my own State as you did yours; and you, men of the North were guided by your own consciences, as we of the South were guided by ours." The crowd in the home state of Lincoln was friendly, at times even enthusiastic.[14]

Hampton headed south to meet President Hayes at the Louisville Exposition. Kentucky had been divided in loyalty on the eve of war and was quickly overrun by Union armies. Still, some 25,000 from the Bluegrass State would become "orphans" by fighting for the Confederacy. "My friends, my Confederate friends," the president asked the multitude in Louisville, "do you intend to obey the whole Constitution and Amendments?" Their cheers signified acceptance. "Received everywhere heartily," Hayes recorded in his journal. "The country is again one and united! I am very happy to be able to feel that the course taken has turned out so well."[15] In these days spent with President Hayes, Hampton would deepen his friendship with the chief executive. And the South Carolinian was himself becoming known by thousands outside the South.

In possession of his office for only five months, Hampton now prepared to address the general assembly for the first time in regular session since the end of Reconstruction. Lawmakers assembled on November 28. "No human wisdom could have brought us safely through the danger that beset us on all sides," said Hampton, "and we should reverently give thanks to Him who alone wrought this great deliverance." That South Carolinians might continue to receive God's blessings, they must prove themselves worthy. "The first step in this direction is for us to observe, in perfect good faith, the pledges made during the canvas which resulted in our success."[16]

Promises had thus far been kept. Governor Hampton appointed competent blacks to county offices. R. H. Gleaves and Martin R. Delany were trial justices. Another black, Charles McDuffie Wilder, was appointed to the board of the state orphan asylum, and that board elected him its chairman. The Charleston Democratic Party nominated three blacks to run in a special election for vacant house seats. South Carolina's first radical governor, Robert K. Scott, confessed that Hampton was "honestly carrying out the promises he made" and had in a few months "already appointed more colored men to office than were appointed during the first two years that I was Governor."[17]

Hampton hoped one day to reopen the University of South Carolina and create a "similar institution for the black," but the present demand for economy made it impossible. A decade of radical control had nearly destroyed confidence in the university among the white people of the state. For the time being the library was put in the custody of Robert W. Barnwell, and faculty residences were rented. All state institutions were encouraged to become more self-supporting.[18] Only by careful control of the purse strings could Democrats support the fledgling system of public education.

Despite the focus on economy, Governor Hampton warned against a repudiation of Reconstruction debt. The Wallace house had promised that there would be no repudiation a year earlier, trying to calm the fears of Northern bond holders. In an interview with the New York *Herald,* Hampton had made the same assurance. "You must remember," he told South Carolinians, "that we have the honor of the State in our hands, and her just debts must be paid. *We mean to put the credit of the State where it was before the war.*" Martin W. Gary led those who insisted that South Carolina repudiate the debt, the senator voting against that portion of the appropriation bill that set aside $270,000 for interest payments. A bond committee would study the matter and eventually recommend that $3,608,717 of the Reconstruction debt be declared "illegal and void." That compromise, although upheld by a series of court decisions, satisfied neither side.[19]

Another issue that stirred contention was the election of a supreme court chief justice to replace Franklin Moses Sr. Moses had died in March 1877. Hampton let it be known that he favored Amiel J. Willard, the court's senior associate justice, who had sided with the Democrats during the months of dual government. Promoting a New York–born Republican to lead South Carolina's high court would conciliate critical Northerners. "There ought to be no hesitation," said Hampton, "in acting with magnanimity and justice toward a gentleman whose acts have been in striking accord with a sense of duty and the promotion of good government." Many Democrats wanted to replace Moses with a man of their own party, and Samuel McGowan emerged as their favorite. Senator Gary worked hard for McGowan, but a Democratic caucus narrowly backed Willard. Gary then attempted to have the general assembly vote against the wishes of the caucus and the governor, but again he failed. "I am surprised at the course Genl Gary is pursuing," wrote a colleague. "Yesterday Gary voted squarely with the Radicals, he was the only Democrat [to do so]. He is injuring himself here very much, with his former friends."[20]

Martin Witherspoon Gary, a Harvard-educated lawyer with an outstanding Confederate war record, first led Company B of the Hampton Legion infantry, on good terms with his commander, eventually rising to the rank of brigadier general. Now forty-six, Gary opposed many major points of the governor's program, from the debt controversy to the prosecution of radicals. Gary rejected Hampton's conciliatory racial policies. He fought to exclude blacks from Edgefield County's Democratic primary, and the Edgefield party came to agree with him. He did not want taxes that were paid by whites going to the support of black schools. Contentious by nature, Gary had been frustrated in his ambitions and embittered. Governor Hampton was revered as South Carolina's redeemer, and Matthew C. Butler had been elected to the U.S. Senate, while Gary, originator of the Straightout Movement, remained a mere state legislator. He had his sights set on Patterson's Senate seat.[21] In the interim he remained a thorn in Hampton's side.

Governor Hampton enjoyed overwhelming support in the general assembly. During his administration a single act was vetoed by the governor, a measure to put prisoners to work on roads. The house had approved the bill by a vote of 73–24. Hampton thought it unconstitutional, and the house reversed itself, sustaining his veto by a vote of 10–102. The legislature carved up sprawling Beaufort County creating, at the request of residents, a new county and naming it for the governor. In 1879 the town of Hampton was incorporated and became the site of the Hampton County courthouse.[22]

As time neared for reelection Hampton vigorously defended his policies. At a reunion of Hart's Battery on July 4, 1878, in Blackville, Conner was the speaker. Hampton was called for "amid a perfect thunder of cheers and a shower of bouquets." Not expecting to speak, "I would say 'ditto' to everything Conner has said," smiled Hampton. He took the opportunity, though, to warn against any change in Democratic policy. He had Gary in mind as he criticized "office seekers" and "extreme men, who will tell you that the glorious platform of 1876 was very well as a promise to be kept only to the ear and broken to the heart." Blacks by the thousands had supported the Democratic party.

> And now would you turn your back upon them, and, after trying for ten years to convince the colored man that his true interests lay with the Democratic party, would you say, "Now we have no use for you. You shall not vote even at the primary elections?" If this be the policy of South Carolina, then I am sadly mistaken in the people of South Carolina and the people are mistaken in me, because *I can carry out no such policy as that. I stand where you put me in 1876*. I have not deviated one *iota*.

Hampton rejected any thought of using illegal methods to retain power. "I tell you, people of Barnwell [County], and people of South Carolina, that if you once countenance fraud, before many years pass over your heads you will not be worth saving, and will not be worthy of the State you live in." He was certain that those now in charge of elections were honorable men who "would rather die before they would perjure themselves by placing men wrongfully in office."[23]

Speaking in Greenville, Gary insisted that South Carolina's divide was racial, not partisan. The Edgefield senator would prefer to exclude blacks from voting and office holding altogether. The governor's protection of political rights for blacks would lead to social equality, warned Gary, and "we will next hear of dining or dancing with the colored brothers and sisters as events the natural result of *Hampton* Democracy." The *News and Courier* was quick to defend Hampton, declaring that Gary's remarks put him outside the Democratic Party. "Hampton Democracy, the only true Democracy in South Carolina, means honest and unreserved concession to the colored people all of their public and private rights." To sit together in the Senate, to march in the same militia parade, to accept black votes, and to educate black children did not, said the *News and Courier,* constitute "miscegenation."[24]

Part of Gary's strategy in his feud with Hampton was to encourage rumors that the governor was unopposed to social equality. The basis for this charge came from an incident in the summer of 1878 when the governor traveled to Orangeburg with Superintendent of Education Hugh S. Thompson. They were invited to dine with the white president of Claflin University. Claflin had been established by Methodists for black students, and by state mandate its board of trustees oversaw federal Morrill Act funds. When Hampton and Thompson arrived at President Edward Cooke's home, they discovered that two blacks had also been invited. "Wade looked at me and I looked at him," remembered Thompson, then they sat down and acted as "perfect gentlemen." They had been, wrote one historian, either "entrapped by an unworthy trick," or were "traitors to the white race," according to who told the story.[25]

Gary's behind-the-scenes maneuvering for a U.S. Senate seat depended, he thought, on confusing and dividing the opposition. He wanted Hampton to be reelected governor, but surrounded by a new set of officeholders because "the way to get up a political furor is to cater to the ambitions of men all over the state." He would engage in no "personal fight against the present State ticket, except under cover of correspondents." To his chagrin, the state Democratic convention in August renominated the entire set of incumbents, and party unity seemed secure. Understanding that Hampton had only to ask for the senatorship to be elected, Gary now promoted a campaign to convince South Carolinians that they could not afford to lose Hampton as their governor.[26] Matthew C. Butler was from Edgefield, and Gary seemed not to consider just how unlikely legislators were to elect two U.S. senators from the same county. Gary greatly overestimated his own popularity with the people and their representatives.

When asked a year earlier about his political enemies, Hampton answered with a twinkle in his eye. "I believe the opposition includes at present only one man, and he is a gentleman of somewhat eccentric political qualities."[27] By the summer of 1878, Hampton's patience with Gary was running out. At a joint speaking engagement with Hampton in Edgefield, Gary and Butler were most cordial. "I intended to take issue with them on the Edgefield resolutions [excluding blacks] when I accepted the invitation to speak," Hampton confided to Conner. Gary's comments in Greenville had to be answered. "I do not intend to enter in a controversy with him, but I shall denounce his allusions to the results of Hampton democracy as a piece of impertinence. I am tired of his pretended support and covert insolence."[28]

Hampton would respond to Gary in a Greenville speech on September 18. The governor again took issue with Gary's advocacy of violence and fraud to hold on to power. "I believe that it was the conservative character of the last campaign, as contradistinguished from what he calls an 'aggressive' one, that enabled us to carry the State. . . . We cannot do evil that good may come of it."

Hampton spoke plainly to blacks in his Greenville audience. "You must stand on your own footing. You cannot be put upon any better one merely because you are a colored man. We propose to protect you and give you all your rights; but while we do this you cannot expect that we should discriminate in your favor." Despite the Edgefield party's resolutions, blacks who became Democrats "will be welcomed."

His final words were directed to all South Carolinians. "Your children for generations to come will be influenced by your action." He was not

> advocating a policy simply for momentary triumph or personal gratification. No, I have been looking far beyond the present day—for it has seemed to me that I have been able sometimes to catch transient glimpses of the future through the veil that hides it from us—and I have thought that in that far future, in the day when you and I and all of us shall have been gathered to our God, I could see a great and happy State and people. Our children's children—wise by the errors we have committed, chastened by sorrows we vicariously have borne for them, instructed by the experiences we have gained—shall build up South Carolina and place her where God intended her to stand—with a united, free and happy people, walking on the great road to National prosperity and peace. I have seen that future, and I have worked for it; I have prayed for it. And, surely, if in the good providence of God it is given to us after death to look back upon the scene of our labors here, even the pleasures of Heaven would be brightened by such a view. I trust in God it may come. It would be the highest reward that could come to me if in the hearts of those descendants of ours yet unborn they could say that I had worked for South Carolina. . . . And I would want no nobler epitaph to be placed on my tombstone than that I had been true to South Carolina, and in war and in peace had done my whole duty to her. God save our State, and God for all time to come bless her people.[29]

"Brother Wade seems to have won golden opinions everywhere," wrote Kate Hampton. "I trust that a Higher Wisdom than his own may direct him."[30]

During the 1876 campaign Hampton promised to improve public education. Superintendent Hugh S. Thompson had taken over a system in its infancy. During his first abbreviated year, a time of disruption due to the dual government, school attendance of both blacks and whites declined. Those figures soon began to grow, as did tax dollars spent on education. Schools were segregated, as they had been even during radical control, but per capita expenditures were almost exactly the same for students of both races. Thompson recommended consolidating schools, increasing teacher pay, allowing students of all ages to attend, and adopting uniform text books. By the end of 1878 South Carolina had more schools and more teachers than the year before. Attendance was the second highest in the ten years of the system's existence.[31] Despite demands for economy, the opposition of Gary, and the hesitancy of some to support public education at all, Democrats had made a respectable start.

Adjutant and Inspector General Edwin W. Moise found the post-Reconstruction militia in a "deplorable" condition. On taking office he discovered that all portable property, even stationery, had been stolen. Despite years of extravagant spending, only 200 weapons could be accounted for. General Moise sent a requisition for rifles and eight batteries of artillery to the War Department. With a state expenditure of $9,537 and federal help, he felt that he could restore South Carolina's three-division militia force. In 1877 the adjutant general commissioned 192 volunteer companies. The next year fifty more were added.[32]

The *News and Courier* asked state judges for their opinion of crime and law enforcement under the Democratic government. All gave high marks to Hampton. Judge B. C. Pressley "found the criminal dockets very much lighter than they had formerly been." Many of the accused were repeat offenders, "pardoned by former Governors of this State." Judges Alfred P. Aldrich, Joshua H. Hudson, Joseph Brevard Kershaw, Thomas J. Mackey, H. B. Wallace, and Thomas Thompson all agreed that crime in their circuits had diminished under Governor Hampton. "My experience in the Courts," reported Aldrich, "satisfies me that not only has there been a diminution of serious offenses against the law, but greater security is felt among all classes of the people, white and black."[33]

"The colored people urge me to be a candidate for the next term," Hampton wrote to Hayes in the spring of 1878, "& assure me that there shall be no opposition if I will run." Hampton told Armistead Burt that "the opposition has been crushed out."[34] The Union Republican Party met in convention on August 7. Sen. John R. Cochran introduced a resolution backing Hampton. This "apostasy" set off a round of denunciation and speech making by unrepentant radicals. Edmund W. M. Mackey of Charleston and Fred Nix Jr. of Barnwell were reported as "the most ravenous." The next day the convention declared it "inexpedient" to nominate any statewide candidates, then adjourned. The *News and Courier* cautioned Democrats against overconfidence. The editor feared that Republicans might "sneak into power again through the portals of the hall of the House of Representatives."[35]

Still, there was no denying that the opposition was in disarray. "Governor Hampton," said Theodore W. Parmele, "is as good a Republican as I want to see." Black Republicans continued to cross over to Hampton's side. "We are largely indebted to the colored voters," said the incumbent governor. Benjamin A. Boseman, black Charlestonian, expressed confidence in Hampton. "We have no complaint whatever to make. He has kept all his pledges." Columbia's black postmaster, Charles McDuffie Wilder, agreed. "I can't help regarding it as Providential that Wade Hampton became Governor of South Carolina. God only knows what would have become of us if things had kept on the way they were going."[36] A meeting of blacks at Great Cypress Township, Barnwell County, endorsed Hampton's reelection, calling him "the truest friend alike to all classes and conditions of our people." Even Robert Smalls of Beaufort, a Republican congressman, spoke of the "just and liberal course of the Governor which had recommended him to the confidence of the people." Former supreme court justice Jonathan J. Wright, one of those said to have dined with Hampton at Claflin, endorsed the governor's reelection, predicting that he would receive 90 percent of the black vote. "I speak advisedly on that point," said Wright. "There is not a decent negro in the State will vote against him."[37]

Speaking to blacks in Sumter, Hampton reminded them of the Republican lie that Democratic victory meant a return to slavery. Not only did blacks retain all their rights, said the governor, but were more prosperous and lived in a climate of increased good will. At a Hampton rally in Greenville, "the building was fairly shaken to its foundations by uproarious applause," reported one newsman. "I have conversed with colored men, and find the Hampton sentiment unanimous here." South Carolina poet Paul Hamilton Hayne told friend John Greenleaf Whittier of Hampton's amazing support among blacks. If men like Wendell Phillips dismissed Hampton, his was but "the abuse of a willfully wrong-*headed* & wrong-*hearted* man!" said Hayne. "If ever a Statesman of enlightened views & far-reaching sagacity, of unimpeachable *honor* existed in this land, that Statesman is Hampton!"[38]

Red-shirted riders appeared again at rallies across the state. At a parade of 1,000 horsemen in Winnsboro, one quarter was black. On October 11 a group of black and white Democrats disrupted a Republican meeting in Blackville.[39] That was a rarity. The election campaign of 1878 was much quieter than that of 1876. It seemed more a triumphant procession than a political campaign. One of the final stops for Hampton was Beaufort on October 29. The *News and Courier* reported,

> In 1876 the Republicans of Beaufort refused to give Governor Hampton a respectful hearing. Today he came as the guest of these same people, and was treated by them with the utmost courtesy and respect. . . . [E]ven in Beaufort, the hotbed of Radical hate and prejudice, the deeds of a just and good man do not go unnoticed and unappreciated by all.

A British member of Parliament, Sir George Campbell, arrived in Columbia on election day, Tuesday, November 5. "There were a good many negroes about, and they did not look terrorised," wrote Sir George, seeming almost disappointed. He was told about Gary's leadership of "an extreme party opposed to Mr. Wade Hampton." Campbell met Hampton at his State House office the next day. "All his conversation gave one the idea of a very moderate man."[40]

That moderate man had just scored an overwhelming victory, garnering 119,550 votes. Although unopposed, he won about 30,000 more black votes than he had in 1876. Only five Republicans survived in the state senate and three in the house. From Charleston, Colleton, Orangeburg, and Sumter counties came six black Democrats to the new general assembly.[41]

There was little postelection celebrating. Soon after meeting with Campbell, Hampton left his office. He had been invited to join in a deer hunt in the Wateree Swamp east of Columbia. He spent Wednesday night at the home of a friend named Speigner. The next morning Hampton set out alone into the moss-hung wilderness, expecting to meet up with other members of the party. He was riding a borrowed animal, described as "a young half-broken mule." Hearing the baying of hounds, Hampton followed, pushing deeper into the woods. Even at sixty Hampton remained an expert rider, described by a friend as "an iron man physically."[42]

At four o'clock on that November afternoon, he had still not caught up with the other hunters. Hampton spotted a deer, raised his rifle, took aim, and fired. Preparing to dismount, he leaned forward as he threw the reins over a tree limb. Without warning the mule bolted. Hampton had but a moment to react. Rather than remain in the saddle to be pummeled by overhanging branches, he jumped, landing full force on his right foot. The pain was intense. He had broken both bones in his lower leg and the tibia, the large bone, was protruding through the flesh. Blood was flowing from the injury caused by this compound fracture. Hampton lay on the forest floor in desperate need of help.

He still had his rifle and a hunting horn and began to use them to signal. A high wind dissipated the sounds. The far-away hunting party finally heard shots, but it was the frequency of the reports that caught the attention of Col. Thomas Taylor. The colonel sent a black servant to investigate. At about sundown, two hours after the accident, Hampton was found lying on his back with his head resting against the base of a tree.[43]

The rescuers immediately sent for a wagon equipped with a spring suspension and laid a mattress in the bed. They had to cut a crude road through the woods, allowing enough clearance for the vehicle. While they waited with the governor, and before darkness descended, someone noticed that Hampton had not merely been signaling with his rifle shots. Even in his pain he had taken careful aim at a target—and hit the mark every time.

The sixteen-mile journey back to Hampton's home took half the night. Bumping along a dirt road, badly injured, must have brought to mind that agonizing retreat from Gettysburg fifteen years earlier. Dr. Benjamin W. Taylor met his old friend at Hampton's home and there dressed the wound. A newspaperman reported,

> It was found that the small bone of the right leg was broken about six inches above the ankle, that the larger bone had been completely severed just above its terminus at the ankle joint, and that the upper end of the lower section had swerved from its place, and penetrating the surrounding flesh protruded into plain view. This protrusion of the bone had caused considerable loss of blood.

Early on the morning of Friday, November 8, Dr. Taylor was joined by physicians Daniel H. Trezevant and A. N. Talley. Hampton was anesthetized with chloroform as the doctors put the ankle back into position, a procedure that required considerable force and was complicated by the fractures. Hampton slept through the day.[44]

The *Daily Register* on Saturday fretted over what effect Hampton's absence would have because the legislature was about to convene. On November 13, six days after the accident, a proclamation was issued in Hampton's name giving notice of the governor's "physical inability . . . to discharge the power and duties of the office." Lieutenant Governor Simpson would assume the duties of governor, acknowledging the transfer of authority in a proclamation of his own. "In making this announcement," said Simpson, "no words can express the sorrow which pervades this entire Commonwealth at the occurrence of this calamity to our beloved Chief Magistrate."[45] Simpson would address the general assembly on November 26 in his new capacity. The press referred to him as "governor." Simpson considered himself South Carolina's "acting governor."[46] Secretary Wade Hampton Manning remained at his post in the governor's office.

Little news escaped Hampton's sickroom. The *Register* tried to assure readers that their governor was doing as well as could be expected.[47] The *News and Courier* said that on November 10 he had been able to sleep without pain medication. On November 15 there was a slight fever, but his physicians "feel no alarm."[48] The *Newberry Herald* reported that on Friday, November 29, there was a turn for the worse. "Dr. Kinlock, of Charleston, and Dr. Campbell, of Augusta, were telegraphed for, and came." Hampton had been seized with chills, then fever, "and seemed depressed in spirits," said Dr. Kinlock. That Sunday evening all of Columbia's churches met together to pray for the governor. His condition seemed to stabilize. Kinlock and Campbell returned home.[49]

One of the general assembly's most important responsibilities this session would be to elect a U.S. senator to replace Republican John Patterson whose term would expire on March 3, 1879. For months there had been an undercurrent of discussion over the wisdom of sending Hampton to Washington. He had expressed no interest in becoming senator, but the job was his were he to ask for it. Months earlier the *Register* marveled over Hampton's popularity. "Not only has he commanded universal confidence in himself as a man, but he has carried his party on to a higher plane than it ever meant to occupy and holds it there." One more term in the governor's office "would carry the good work beyond the possibility of ever being undone." Election to the U.S. Senate, warned the editor, might undo this.[50] A series of eloquent letters, signed "Cato," appeared in the *Register* arguing that Hampton must remain in South Carolina. "We need him *here* to reconcile the races; we need him to protect the weak; we need him to restrain the strong; we need him to carry out his honest promises." The Greenville *Enterprise and Mountaineer* agreed. "The hitherto incongruous elements here have not become altogether as quiet and peaceful as they should be; therefore his magic wand is still needed to guide the State still farther out into the waters of peace."

Were Hampton elected senator he would still be "in a position to counsel us the best," argued another letter writer. "We are for making Hampton Senator, then, in the interests of the State, the South, and the whole country." That theme of Hampton serving "the interests of the whole country" was repeated by the *Anderson Intelligencer* and others.[51] At a militia review in Greenville during the summer, Adjutant General Moise predicted that in the presidential election year of 1880, "the great heart of the North would call out for Wade Hampton because his country needed him." In October the *Anglo-American Times* of London predicted that in two years Democrats would choose Winfield Scott Hancock, Union hero at Gettysburg, as their standardbearer. If so, Wade Hampton would be an ideal running mate. "Governor Hampton's reputation in the North is almost as good as in the South," wrote the *Times*. "The conduct of the government of South Carolina since the collapse of the carpetbag *regime* has stamped General Wade Hampton as the man for the position." The governor "knows how to conciliate" and serve as "a buffer between conflicting factions." Although Hampton "might prefer a seat in the Senate, [he] may have to bow to public opinion and reserve for himself the nomination that looms ahead."[52]

Hampton "wields an immense influence among conservative men of the North, and they will listen to his words," editorialized the Winnsboro *News and Herald*. The *Darlington News* preferred for Hampton to serve another term as governor, not becoming senator "unless he asks for it." The *Newberry Herald* thought Simpson would make a good governor, and Hampton deserved to be senator "above all others."[53]

On the afternoon of December 4, a party of fifteen, led by the president of the state senate and the speaker of the South Carolina house, rode out to

Hampton's home. Arriving at about two o'clock in the afternoon, they were invited in by Wade Hampton IV. They were there to inform him officially of his election to a second term as the state's chief executive, and to administer the oath of office. "The Governor was lying in bed with an expression of pain upon his countenance," reported a newspaperman. Hampton feebly shook hands with his guests as each approached his bed. "Chief Justice Willard, sitting by his bed side, held a small Bible upon which the Governor held his hand while the oath was being read." At the conclusion Hampton raised the Bible "and gently pressed it to his lips." Not wishing to tire the governor, the committee quickly departed, returning to the State House less than an hour after they had left. "We take off our hat before the touching scene," wrote the editor of the *Register,* "as we shout, with all the force and meaning which the devotion of an admiring people can impart to the experience, '*long live the Governor!*'"[54]

The *Register* said two days later,

> We believe, and believe confidently that if the Governor felt he could be of more service to the State by remaining in the gubernatorial chair, he would not hesitate a moment to say so. We take it, then, that with becoming modesty, he concurs . . . that his true measure of future usefulness, whatever that may be, is in the United States Senate. His profound silence . . . can have no other meaning.[55]

> After the oath taking, little was reported by the press for several days. Rumor had it that infection had spread, threatening Hampton's life. "I hear this morning Gen. Hampton is in a critical condition," William L. Buck wrote to his wife on December 9, "many think he will never survive his present misfortune—it will be a great loss to S.C." Despite the prognosis, state senator Buck predicted Hampton's election to the U.S. Senate.[56]

The vote was scheduled for December 10. At noon that day, Samuel McGowan, house member from Abbeville, was recognized. "Mr. Speaker, I have the honor to nominate for the great office of Senator from South Carolina one whose past history marks with certainty his future course; one who is in the truest sense the embodiment of the brave, just, conservative Democracy of the State." Charles H. Simonton of Charleston seconded Hampton's nomination. Another Charlestonian, Charles Richardson Miles, then asked to read a letter that the governor had dictated only the day before as Miles sat by his bedside. Hampton thanked members for their concern and left the vote for senator "entirely to their judgment." Whether he served another term as governor or went on to the Senate, "I will with equal cheerfulness accord with their desire."

Although nothing was said publicly in the general assembly, word spread that Hampton was that day undergoing amputation of his shattered leg. Many members were in tears.

Two Beaufort Republicans voted for Edmund Mackey. The remainder of the house and a unanimous senate stood by Wade Hampton. The overwhelming vote, said the *Register,* "was a fitting and timely recognition of those great qualities of head and heart which have made the name of Hampton synonymous with truth, justice and integrity throughout the country."

Hampton's doctors had watched in alarm as inflamation spread, but kept their fears from both patient and the public. Early on the morning of December 10, Dr. Taylor told Hampton that they must amputate his lower leg. The news was expected, Hampton said, and he "consented without a murmur." Taylor performed the surgery at one o'clock that afternoon, assisted by six other Columbia doctors. They used "Lister's antiseptic process." Blood loss was minimal. It was discovered that even after a month the broken bones in the damaged limb had not begun to heal.[57] Three days later the press reported Hampton able to "retain nourishment." By December 15 he was sleeping well.[58] His condition was "less favorable," thought the *News and Courier* the day following; his prospects for recovery only "fair." The next day the Charleston paper claimed he had eaten solid food for the first time and had "turned the corner."[59] Other sources told the *Newberry Herald* that Hampton was "delirious all day," concluding "there is scarcely any hope of his recovery."[60]

ON WEDNESDAY, January 15, 1879, five weeks after Hampton lost a leg and became senator-elect, the editor of the *Daily Register* went to Hampton's home for an interview, accompanied by a friend of the governor. Only one and a half miles from downtown Columbia, Hampton's home was a "quaint little brick cottage, with three rooms on a row, and a projecting front entrance." It seemed rather modest for the residence of a governor. "If an old-fashioned log hut in brick can be imagined, we have the 'mansion' to a dot." A driveway circled up to the front door, "bordered by a faintly-developed hedge struggling for life in the thin sandy soil. In this 'circle' of fair dimensions a single stunted magnolia was shimmering its dark green leaves in the bright January sunlight." A servant answered the door, then went to tell Governor Hampton that he had guests. The newsman described the middle chamber where they stood as "a plain, very plain, but comfortably furnished room." Bookshelves stood against every wall. There was one painting, perhaps a survivor from an earlier collection, hanging over the mantle.

Ushered into Hampton's room they greeted the governor, still bedridden, and complimented him on how well he looked. After all he had endured, the encouraging words were welcome. Hampton replied that he had been invited to attend a Washington's birthday celebration in Charleston on February 22 and felt he would "benefit from it."

"How is your appetite now, Governor?"

"Not good at all," he replied, pushing himself up in his bed. "It could not be expected otherwise. Here I have been for ten long weeks suffering or wearily waiting for recovery on this bed, and only in the last few days have I had the power to change my position. Hence one of my usually active habits must surely feel sadly the want of exercise. I am suffering consequently from indigestion."

"You take fresh air sometimes?"

"Oh, yes. Every fair day now I am rolled out on the porch and enjoy the fresh air very much."

"Do you suffer much pain from your limb now?"

"Oh, life, yes! Sometimes I suffer very much. I suffer, strange to say, in *my foot*. My toes seem so cold, and my foot at times is so painful. Then again it itches me beyond endurance, and when half awake I find myself stretching my hand to scratch it, but find its presence a mere delusion. Yet I am doing very well and feel myself on the mend."

"This is a bright, beautiful day. Have you taken the benefit of the fresh air this morning?"

"Not yet. But I shan't miss it, I assure you. I shall see the glad sun before the day is over."

The subject turned to politics. The editor first queried Hampton about the November 1878 general election. The governor insisted that there had been no bullying by Democrats, but "gross intimidation" of voters perpetrated by Republicans. Still, Hampton admitted to "irregularities in our Democratic household."

> It seemed impossible to prevent it in view of the terrible moral obliquity visited on our people by the Radical rule under which they lived since the war. This is a far greater curse to us than all the thefts that have been perpetrated on us. . . . No one can regret this more than I do, and no one could have striven harder to impress its wrongfulness and absolute impolicy upon our people than I have.

The interviewer went on to national questions. Hampton said that he favored "Jackson Democracy." Business in America should be allowed to "expand and contract according to its own necessities and the uncontrollable laws of trade." The "moneyed men in their own interest" must not be permitted to control the financial policy of the United States. Hampton had not given up on the national Democratic Party. After a generation out of the White House, Democrats had a good chance to win in 1880. The basis for victory would be a platform that called for, in Hampton's words, *"constitutional rule, self government and no sectionalism."*

As his guests prepared to leave, Hampton was asked one more personal question. Had he been aware of "the devoted love of your own people" during the illness?

"Ah, yes, sir," Hampton replied, his voice growing deeper. "I believe, as confidently as I do that I live, that the prayers of the people saved my life. I will tell you why I feel and believe it so firmly. Whilst I was lying here at the point of death and had become indifferent whether I lived or died, I got a letter from an old Methodist preacher, one of my old friends. He wrote me a word informing me of the deep and devout petitions put up in behalf of my restoration by the Methodist Conference then in session at Newberry."[61]

The letter writer, Rev. Hugh A. C. Walker, had been attending the denominational meeting when a special prayer service for Hampton was held on Thursday, December 12. Clergy, laymen, and visitors bowed in silence "broken only by the voice of the venerable minister who led and the irrepressible sobs and moans and amens."[62]

"My sister," continued Hampton, "who had tremblingly brought the letter to my bedside and read it to me, then urged me to listen to the kind, loving words of the man of God and to rouse my will to live." In the letter Walker told Hampton that prayers on his behalf were going up from every household, night and day, across the state. Hampton promised his sister he would make an effort to live.

"I fell into a deep sleep that night, and the most vivid dream I ever experienced in my life crossed my slumbers. I dreampt I was in a spacious room, and that in it I was moved to all parts of the State, so that I met my assembled friends everywhere. I remember most distinctly of all old Beaufort, where I had last been. It seemed there were immense assemblages, and as I looked down upon them a grave personage approached me and touched me on the shoulder and said to me: 'These people are all praying for you. Live, live, live!'

"I never realized anything like it before. It seemed a vision. I woke the next morning feeling the life blood creeping through my veins, and I told my family the crisis was passed and I would get better."[63]

"Hampton Has
Nothing to Regret"

United States Senator

Hampton's convalescence took longer than anyone expected. On January 15, 1879, he was able to take a buggy ride for the first time since his accident, as son Wade prepared to return home. On January 17 Hampton was paid a visit, probably a surprise, by Gen. Edmund Kirby Smith, once commander of the Confederate army's Trans-Mississippi Department. Friends were anxious to hurry Hampton's recovery. Col. J. B. Palmer arranged a trip by rail to Jacksonville, Florida, in "an easy and elegant car," followed by hunting and fishing along the Indian River. Hampton did not feel strong enough to accept. Nor was he able to attend the celebration of Washington's birthday in Charleston as he had hoped. A reporter from the *Newberry Herald* found Hampton at home in the care of "a silent, sympathizing attendant" named Tom. The huge cat had been a family pet for years, "and in all but disposition looks every inch a dark young tiger," wrote the newsman. Tom, "contrary to all cat precedent," was Hampton's companion indoors and out.[1]

In a proclamation February 26, Hampton resigned as governor, explaining that he had delayed leaving office in order to finish a few items of business, but his health never permitted the work to be done. "I can only promise to devote whatever of life and ability . . . God may grant me" to continued public service. The first session of the Forty-Sixth Congress began on March 18, 1879, without Wade Hampton. He wrote that very day to Matthew C.

288

Butler, now South Carolina's senior senator, one who had lost a leg at Brandy Station. "It would be very painful to me to travel just now as my leg is extremely tender. The end of the bone is dead, & will have to come off before the leg will heal." Hampton complained of pain and difficulty sleeping, but if needed in Washington, "I will go at a moments notice, & I beg you to telegraph me."[2]

Hampton departed in April, greeted my crowds and militia salutes as he journeyed northward. In the chamber of the upper house on April 16, Butler interrupted a speech by Massachusetts senator Henry L. Dawes, announcing that Hampton was present and prepared to claim his seat. Hampton and Butler advanced to the desk of Vice President William A. Wheeler, where Hampton took the oath of office. "South Carolina won't have as many legs in the next Senate," wrote the *Newberry Herald*, "but she will have as much brains as any."[3]

Hampton was soon appointed to vacancies on three Senate committees: Military Affairs, Mines and Mining, and Transportation Routes to the Seaboard. The freshman senator made his first remarks on June 5, advocating repeal of a Reconstruction-era law designed to keep ex-Confederates from serving on federal juries. Although "reluctant to obtrude my views on the Senate," and laboring under a "physical disability," Hampton felt he must respond to those who continued to berate former Confederates. He noted that there were twenty-two veterans of the Southern army then sitting in the U.S. Senate. "Nearly every man in the South who could bear arms was in her armies and she can scarcely be reproached with justice for trusting and honoring in peace the men who risked their fortunes and their lives for her in war." He refused to apologize for the past. "In the heat of conflict we struck hard blows, and doubtless we spoke hard words. But does remembering or repeating them now bring us any nearer to the peace and harmony for which the whole country so ardently longs?" He wished that there were more Union veterans in Congress. "We learned in a common school how to respect our enemies."

He was interrupted by applause from spectators. The presiding officer warned that the galleries would be cleared should it happen again. Hampton insisted that "constitutional liberty as established by our fathers" be the goal of all, North and South. The war's "painful memories" should remain "buried in our hearts, nor rising to the lips in bitter words." He was again applauded by the public in the galleries.[4]

With Reconstruction over there arose a widespread debate about the future of black participation in American political life. Some Northerners, concluding that black suffrage had proven a failure, felt it best to disfranchise the race formally, a move that would require a reduction in Southern congressional representation as stipulated by the Fourteenth Amendment. Many Southern whites might be relieved to have the threat of black political

U.S. Sen. Wade Hampton. *Edward L. Wells, Hampton and His Cavalry in '64 (Richmond, Va.: B. F. Johnson Pub. Co., 1899).*

supremacy permanently removed, but balked at giving up members of Congress. The *North American Review* published a symposium on the subject in March 1879, and invited Wade Hampton to participate. The *Review* asked if blacks should have the vote taken from them, and if blacks should have been allowed to vote in the first place. Disfranchising had "been rendered impossible by the action of national and state governments," said Hampton. The question was, therefore, no more than speculative.

> Whatever may have been the policy of conferring the right of voting upon the negro, ignorant and incompetent as he was to comprehend the high responsibilities thrust upon him, and whatever may have been the reasons which dictated this dangerous experiment, the deed has been done and it is irrevocable.

As blacks became better educated and acquired property, they might well become conservative supporters of "good government and home rule," said Hampton. "The result has been shown in the last two general elections in this State, where thousands of negroes voted with their white friends." Blacks could not be denied the right to vote solely because of their race. As citizens, it followed that they would become voters. But Hampton still insisted that universal suffrage, voting rights without an educational or property qualification, gave the vote to those "yet utterly unprepared to exercise it."[5]

The Senate adjourned on July 1, 1879, and Hampton vacationed in West Virginia. The water there "has benefited me very much," he wrote to a friend, and he hoped the warm springs "will do my leg good." Son Wade, now thirty-eight and recently wed, brought his bride to meet her father-in-law for the first time. Her name was Kate Phelan; she was the twenty-three-year-old daughter of a Mississippi lawyer. "She is a charming girl," concluded Senator Hampton, "and I am very much pleased with her." In December of that year, Congress was in its second session when Wade Hampton IV died of malaria at Wild Woods, Mississippi. He would be buried in the family plot at Trinity churchyard in Columbia. "Life seems closed for me," wrote the grieving father, having lost five of his nine children. "I have nothing but duty to live for. God's will be done."[6]

Duty meant politics. After the Hayes-Tilden debacle, Democrats were more determined than ever to capture the White House for their party in 1880. In a June 1879 interview, Hampton made no mention of those earlier rumors that he might find himself on the ticket. He had a sober understanding of Northern prejudices. Although the South was solidly Democratic, "we do not intend to ask a place, upon the Presidential ticket for a Southern man," said Hampton. "We want the party in the North to place two good men on the ticket, and we will support it for the national success of the Democratic party." Nevertheless, the first choice of Hampton and many Southerners was Senator Thomas F. Bayard. From the border state of Delaware, this fifty-one-year-old member of a prominent Wilmington family seemed congenial to Southern conservatives.[7] Bayard, who had served in the Senate since 1869, was one of the most senior Democratic members when Hampton took office.

The 1880 Democratic National Convention met in the Cincinnati Music Hall. "Now and then a faint cheer from the audience welcomed some favorite member," wrote a Charleston reporter, "but when Wade Hampton, preceded by Senator Butler, came across the floor on his crutches the applause was vociferous, and cries of 'Hampton, Hampton,' echoed through the air." Bayard's backers were confident that their man could secure the nomination if supporters stood by him for as long as it took for the multitude of marginal candidates to drop by the wayside. On June 23 nominations were made. Unexpected enthusiasm developed when Pennsylvania suggested Winfield Scott Hancock. The attorney general of Delaware had already nominated their favorite son Bayard when South Carolina's turn came. Hampton said that the state had no other name to put forward. Cheering delegates shouted for him to come to the platform, and there Hampton made a short speech. He thought it a "happy omen" that both South Carolina and Massachusetts supported Bayard. "The South asks for no place, no power, no patronage, no office," insisted Hampton. He had confidence in Hancock, but preferred Bayard only "because we believe him to be the strongest candidate." On the first ballot Hancock led with 171 votes, Bayard captured 163.5. Seventeen other nominees shared the remainder. It appeared that many ballots might be required before any candidate garnered the necessary two-thirds majority.

The next morning balloting resumed. Tilden had received only thirty-eight votes, but withdrew amid much fanfare. Even as the second ballot was being taken, Wisconsin asked to change its vote to Hancock. New Jersey did the same. The stampede was on as state after state jumped on board the Hancock bandwagon. It was proposed that the nomination be made unanimous, and speakers came forward to second that motion.

"In response to loud calls," reported a Charleston correspondent, "Wade Hampton advanced to the platform and said, in behalf of the solid South, which was once arrayed against the gallant soldier, he pledged to him its solid vote." The Republican press feigned shock at Hampton's reference to a "solid South" backing the Democratic candidate.[8]

The News and Courier blamed Bayard's defeat on a lack of "fire and force" in his campaign. "It was strictly deliberate and unsentimental." And sectionalism played a part in that too many party strategists "felt that Delaware would be regarded as a strictly Southern State, and he as a Southern man."

Hampton in a letter to Bayard wrote that "all the opposing elements were concentrated that night [June 23] against you, & the influence of Tilden's friends was brought to bear solely to defeat you." Southern delegates had unwisely scattered their votes "until it could be ascertained what your Northern strength was." That tactic had been "a great mistake. It led to the accidental position Hancock obtained & then the galleries nominated him." Some good had come of Bayard's failed candidacy, thought Hampton. "Your strength defeated Tilden & his friends, & for this, at least, I am delighted."[9]

Weeks later Hampton spoke at Staunton, Virginia, campaigning for Hancock and his vice presidential running mate, William H. English of Indiana. Hampton began by mentioning his own grandfather, Virginia-born Anthony Hampton, and telling the audience that during the Confederate struggle "almost every male descendant of his who could then buckle on a sword came hither to fight and die for Virginia and Virginians." Hampton invoked the memory of Jefferson and Madison, of Lee and Jackson, in appealing to Virginians to vote for Hancock. "Consider what Lee and Jackson would do were they alive," said Hampton. "These are the same principles for which they fought for four years." The irony of a former Confederate corps commander urging Southerners to put a former Union corps commander in the White House could not have been lost on is hearers. "When Hancock was nominated," Hampton continued, "Bayard wrote to me that he was perfectly satisfied—that Hancock . . . was one against whom the bloody shirt could not be waved." With a Democratic victory "the Republican party will go to pieces like a rope of sand. Their mission is ended, if they ever had a mission. . . . The Republican party is the party of hate, the party of rank and rabid sectionalism."

As if to prove Hampton correct, there soon appeared a Republican pamphlet entitled "Rebel Echoes." With his appeal for a solid Democratic vote in the South, and in his mention of Virginia's Confederate heroes, Republicans charged that Hampton showed himself to be an unrepentant secessionist.[10] Presidential politics had not changed. And despite Democrats' best efforts, Republican James A. Garfield narrowly won the contest.

From almost his first appearance in the U.S. Senate, Hampton was assailed by Northern Republicans. In a public speech Hampton had observed that Hungarians, although subjugated by the Austrians, rose to influence within that empire. He remembered too that even Napoleon's conquests had proven temporary. Maine senator James G. Blaine claimed that Hampton's words could only mean that defeated rebels were educating "the rising generation of the South for another conflict." Massachusetts-born John Ingalls, senator from Kansas, complained again that Chamberlain had been cheated of his victory. Minnesota senator William Windom brought up once more that shopworn charge of Hampton's having "dictated" the anti-Reconstruction plank in the 1868 Democratic platform.[11]

Years earlier George Edmunds of Vermont had accused both Hampton and Butler of being "connected with" the Ku Klux Klan in South Carolina.

Hampton wrote at that time, demanding proof. His letter was ignored. Now Hampton, standing on the floor of the Senate, wanted it understood "that if there was one man in America who had no knowledge of, no connection with, no sympathy with anything like the Ku-Klux organization, it was myself." His words brought an immediate apology from the Vermont senator. The charge against Hampton, confessed Edmunds, "was entirely unfounded, coming from somebody who either had it second-hand from somebody who invented it or suspected it, or manufactured it out of the whole cloth."[12]

In 1882 the Committee on Military Affairs, of which Hampton was a member, reported to the Senate a bill to repeal an old law banning former Confederates from U.S. Army service. Edmunds thought the ban should remain as an "everlasting monument" to the victory of the "right side." Texas senator Samuel Maxey demurred. "The war has been over for seventeen years, and a man who served in the confederate army is . . . declared by this statute to have committed the unpardonable sin." George G. Vest of Missouri, former Confederate congressman, reminded the Vermont senator that Southern states were supposed to have been received back into the Union as equals. Vest asserted that Edmunds could not claim that "he believes my professions of loyalty to this country when he heaps upon my brow the ban of proscription and of hate." Not even victors should "agree with the opinion of Napoleon that Providence always fights on the side of the heaviest battalions," said Hampton. "Now, sir, no great question of right ever was settled in the world, and none ever will be settled as long as the world lasts, by the sword."[13]

Senators Hampton and Butler were usually found on the same side of most issues, but disagreed over an 1884 proposal that the federal government provide aid to education. Butler opposed the measure, as did many Southerners, as unconstitutional. Hampton respected that objection, although he disagreed. South Carolinians had found themselves deeply in debt at the end of Reconstruction, Hampton reminded his colleagues, but still managed to devote 71 percent of their entire state budget to education. "These public schools, maintained at so heavy a cost, are open to all, and no distinction is made on account of race or color." Although the majority of students was black, whites contributed 95 percent of all tax revenue. This was spent without discrimination, said Hampton, "and I would not have it otherwise." But in fairness, he concluded, South Carolina taxpayers "are authorized to ask aid of the General Government in behalf of these people who were made citizens and adopted as wards by it." Hampton was applauded by the *Daily Register,* that editor agreeing that if only whites were to be educated, no help would be needed.[14]

Higher education in South Carolina had again become the concern of state government. South Carolina College, no longer a university, opened its doors in 1880 for the first time since the end of Reconstruction, but soon became the target of criticism. Free tuition at the state institution seemed unfair to the backers of denominational schools. In order to bolster support for South Carolina College, trustees in the spring of 1885 created a board of visitors. Among those chosen to serve on that board were Wade Hampton, Ellison Capers, J. L. Murray, and Joseph Earle. Hampton became chairman, and was soon involved in reporting on conditions at the college.[15]

Hampton frankly disliked much of the routine work required of a U.S. senator. During his first recess he went deer hunting with son McDuffie. "There is much more fun in doing that," he wrote to Butler, "than in listening to dry speeches!" To Stephen D. Lee he expressed a desire to give up public life altogether. "It is even worse than fighting," he said. When John S. Preston died in May 1881, Hampton excused himself from a special session of the Senate to attend the funeral. Kate Hampton reported that Wade "will not return to Washington, unless it is absolutely necessary to do so."[16]

During his years in Washington, Hampton would see no fewer than five men occupy the White House. President Hayes had been succeeded in 1881 by James A. Garfield. Although Garfield had a long record of Reconstruction radicalism, Hampton thought that a conciliatory South might "modify his feelings." Hampton once invited him to visit Spartanburg, South Carolina. Garfield politely declined.[17] Just weeks later the president was mortally wounded by an assassin, a mentally disturbed office seeker, in the nation's capital. Vice President Chester A. Arthur served out the remainder of Garfield's term. Senator Hampton's daughter Daisy, as yet unmarried, kept her father's home and accompanied him to Washington social events. In January 1885 they dined at the Arthur White House. At this banquet Att. Gen. Benjamin H. Brewster sat to Daisy's right, Adm. David Dixon Porter on her left.[18] These were unforgettable times for the senator's daughter.

Arthur would leave office only weeks after this social gathering. The Republican Party passed him over as their 1884 standardbearer, choosing instead James G. Blaine of Maine. New York governor Grover Cleveland quickly emerged as front-runner for the Democratic nomination. Many South Carolinians thought him an attractive candidate, although Hampton continued to prefer Bayard of Delaware. On the eve of the convention, it was revealed that Bayard had made a speech in Dover in June of 1861 that now became a political liability. "Why may not two American confederacies exist side by side without conflict," wondered young Bayard. "With such a sickening alternative of civil war, why should not the experiment at least be made?" Hampton defended his friend. "We [Southerners] should be the last people in the world to attempt to strike him down because of his fidelity to us in our days of trouble and to the Constitution. If he is unacceptable to the North we can't help it."[19] It was no use. Bayard's cause was lost. On the first ballot Cleveland led Bayard 388–173, but 159 short of the required two-thirds majority. Then supporters of minor candidates began to switch to Cleveland, and the New York governor was nominated on the second ballot. He went on to claim the presidency by carrying his own state by a razor-thin margin. The victory, the first by a Democrat in twenty-five years, was cause for special celebration in the South.[20] Hampton was delighted of course, despite his long-time support for Bayard.

Hampton wrote to the president-elect a month before he took office, encouraging Cleveland to consider the appointment of Southerners to his cabinet. He made no specific recommendations, but assured Cleveland that "such action on your part will go far to unite the whole country." Hampton surely was satisfied with the independent-minded chief executive's choices. Bayard became Cleveland's secretary of state. The Interior Department was put under Mississippi's Lucius Quintus Cincinnatus Lamar, and Augustus H. Garland of Arkansas became attorney general. Both Lamar and Garland were former Confederate leaders.[21]

In the Senate Hampton introduced little legislation of his own, but on December 18, 1885, he proposed that no senator or representative be allowed to recommend or solicit the appointment of any individual to federal office. Only months earlier he had inadvertently offended a friend by recommending someone else for a postmastership. There were still problems with civil service, despite the passage of the Pendleton Act in 1883. Hampton sought the advice of Garland in framing his own civil service bill. "I long since determined that I should not enter the scramble," wrote Hampton, "for I do not regard it as a duty of a Senator to become an attorney for office-seekers." Despite his best efforts, Hampton's bill died in committee.[22]

Hampton supported treaties with western tribes that he thought might avert further conflict and "do justice to the Indian." And he backed a bill to reimburse Freedmen's Bank depositors, victims of one of Reconstruction's first swindles. The South Carolina senator agreed that the U.S. government had no legal liability, but because the cheated depositors were innocent, credulous former slaves, some of them his, he supported the measure. "I want to see those people paid who were . . . so faithful during the whole war to our women and children, and who have been deceived; and if it is a gratuity from the United States Government, I for one shall vote for it with infinite pleasure."[23]

The year 1886 would bring more personal sadness to Wade Hampton. On April 4 he wrote to Grover Cleveland from Columbia explaining that "I have been detained here by the desperate & I fear hopeless illness of my eldest daughter." Three days later forty-one-year-old Sally died. She left widower John Cheves Haskell and four children. Hampton had just been appointed to West Point's board of visitors, representing the Senate at the annual examination of cadets, but had to be excused. On June 8 his brother Christopher died in Mississippi at age sixty-four. The next day Butler asked for and received a Senate leave of absence for Hampton due to the "terrible family affliction." During Congress's summer recess Hampton was resting at Natural Bridge, Virginia, when he heard of a death in the family of old friend Dr. Benjamin W. Taylor. Hampton long ago learned "that no human consolation can be given." Still, he expressed "how deeply I feel for your wife and yourself . . . & I hope that the Father of us all may comfort and console you. He alone can do it & friends can only offer condolence & sympathy."[24]

One long-term Hampton labor of love was completed in 1886. Two years earlier the cornerstone had been laid for an Episcopal church at Cashiers, North Carolina. Several families contributed, and the chancel furniture, pulpit, and stained-glass windows were gifts of the Hamptons. It was no doubt gratifying to see the work finished. On August 31, 1886, a destructive earthquake shook Charleston, killing ninety-two . Hampton urged in vain that the president journey to the city and that he do so without being asked. "Coming of your own accord, to visit your fellow citizens who have suffered so greatly, would gratify them more than if you came on a formal invitation." Hampton himself traveled in November of that year to Mississippi for the wedding of twenty-seven-year-old McDuffie, first-born of Wade and Mary Hampton, to twenty-two-year-old Heloise Urquhart.[25]

Hampton found time while in office to stay in touch with Confederate friends both in and out of Congress. He developed a close relationship with Joseph E. Brown, Georgia's wartime governor and John B. Gordon's successor in the Senate. Virginia governor Fitzhugh Lee accompanied Hampton on deer-hunting excursions.[26] Animosity between the two generals had faded over the decades. Senator Hampton even backed the appointment of his old nemesis Judson Kilpatrick as U.S. ambassador to Chile. Hampton saw less of Jefferson Davis, but they continued to correspond to the end of the former Confederate president's life.[27] Confederate cavalry veteran Heros von Borcke visited America in 1884. The German confessed that he was

> quite surprised to find my old friend and comrade waiting for me on the platform when my train arrived in Washington. He was wearing a very well made cork leg and could move about so easily and naturally that one could hardly tell that it was not his own. He was able to ride with it and could even continue to follow his passion for hunting and fishing.

Von Borcke and Hampton visited a home for Union veterans near Washington. There the old soldiers "greeted with exquisite politeness the general who had formerly been their enemy."

Senator Hampton once gave Washingtonians something to talk about. Lucy Durr of Alabama was amused to see the senator in a theater box night after night, enjoying the performance of a beautiful French actress. "She spoke English with a charming French accent," remembered Lucy, "which added to her whirlwind of charm." Although the old man's infatuation was "entirely proper," the mademoiselle "swept Senator Hampton off of his remaining foot." For a time Hampton was the talk of the town, even replacing "Yankees and white supremacy" as the favorite topics of Southern conversation. Lucy could only conclude that "the human heart is uncertain in its emotions, and not to be trusted, be one's hair gold or gray."[28]

A close Hampton friend in the Senate was Missouri Democrat George Vest. One morning Hampton told Vest of an incident that had occurred during the war. Hampton and an orderly came upon a Yankee soldier bathing in a creek, his blue uniform on the bank. Informed that he was a prisoner, the naked man began to plead for mercy. He claimed that he was a mere clerk in the commissary department, not a combat soldier, and only the night before had been granted a furlough to visit his sweetheart. Trying to keep a straight face, Hampton told the man he could go. With many thanks, the Yankee began to don his clothes. Hampton ordered him to stop, explaining that the Confederacy needed those garments. The man started for the Union lines naked, but Hampton had had his joke and called him back, telling him to dress. "He was profuse in his thanks," the smiling Hampton told Vest, "and said he would name his first boy after me. Last evening, when I started up on the elevator at my hotel, a well dressed young fellow spoke to me and inquired if I was not Senator Wade Hampton." Hampton said that he was. The young man asked if the senator remembered the soldier he had captured naked and then released. Surprised, Hampton replied that he did.

"Well, that prisoner was my father," said the man, "and my first name is Wade Hampton. Good evening, sir."

The stranger stepped from the elevator and disappeared, leaving Hampton speechless.[29]

With the passions of war now a generation in the past, Cleveland in 1887 approved the Army adjutant general's request that captured Confederate flags be returned to the governors of the Southern states. It seemed an appropriate and timely gesture of reconciliation. There were more than 500 such banners "decaying rapidly" in the basement of a War Department building. But organized Union veterans and Republican politicians protested so loudly that the president was forced to send the flags back into storage.[30] Even more politically dangerous than irate veterans, Cleveland faced opposition from Tammany Hall in the 1888 election. Machine politics denied him the electoral vote of New York state. Despite garnering fewer popular votes than Cleveland, Republican Benjamin Harrison won the presidency, taking office in March 1889.

As the decade began, so it ended—with a debate in America over race. Senator Butler had introduced a bill to provide federal funds to promote black emigration from the southern states. He said that his object was to help only those blacks who might choose to relocate and had nothing to do with "deportation." Still, he thought it would be "advantageous to both races" if the number of blacks would be reduced in the South by their settlement elsewhere. Senator Zebulon Vance, former North Carolina governor, spoke in opposition to the bill. He agreed that blacks were "incapable of attaining to and keeping up with the civilization of the race to which we belong." The black presence had created so many problems, said Vance, that "I should be happy to know that there was not one of them in the United States." Butler's bill, however, was impractical. "It would result in no relief, few negroes would go from the country under its provisions and those would probably be the best." Nevertheless, Vance hoped blacks would choose to migrate to the North and West. "If the negro is a good thing we are willing to divide him up," he said, to the laughter of other senators. "There is plenty of him to go around."

A month earlier Hampton had told the *News and Courier* that it would be in "the best interests of both races that they be permanently separated, leaving each to work out its own destiny. Of course I do not contemplate the removal of the negroes against their wills, nor would I be willing to see them leave the country empty-handed." The *Washington Star* quoted Hampton as saying that a black exodus would "involve inconvenience, but no injury" to the South. "It would deprive us of much of our labor, and make it a little harder for the present generation, but it would be the salvation of the future."

His views had been misconstrued, Hampton now told fellow senators, as a call for the "forcible expulsion" of blacks.

> Never for one moment has such a solution of this question occurred to me as desirable or practicable. I recognize as fully as anyone the political rights of our colored fellow-citizens, and amongst those rights is that supreme one, allowing every citizen of the Union to choose his home. The forcible expulsion of the negroes would not only be unlawful, but impolitic, unjust, and cruel.

Wade Hampton wanted to make it clear, however, as it was clearly understood by nearly all in 1890, that America belonged to the white race. If there were no blacks in the United States, he asked rhetorically, would anyone advocate that they now be brought in? "Every race, save the Caucasian, is and ought to be regarded as alien in the United States." That included Indians, "the former owners of this broad land of ours," as well as the newly arrived Chinese. "The declared and wise policy of the country is that of exclusion of all alien races." He approved Harrison's restrictive immigration policy. Hampton agreed with the president when he said, "We are clearly under a duty to defend our civilization by excluding alien races whose ultimate assimilation with our people is neither possible nor desirable."

Hampton came to believe that the presence of blacks in America had been "the sole disturbing cause" leading to the Civil War. There exists, he said,

> a deep-seated, ineradicable race antagonism, and it is idle for us to shut our eyes to this fact and endeavor to conceal it. This feeling exists among the blacks in even a greater degree than it does among the whites. . . . Philanthropists may deplore it and fanatics deny it, but it has existed from time immemorial.[31]

Hampton continued this theme in an article he wrote for a magazine of opinion. Allowing "so large a mass of ignorant voters" to control government was "a great crime against humanity, civilization, and Christianity." He went on to catalog public crimes resulting from Reconstruction in his own state. Hampton quoted Abraham Lincoln's words from a debate with Stephen Douglas in 1858. Lincoln had then denied that blacks had a right to vote, serve as jurors, hold office, or mix with whites. While the two races lived together, said Lincoln, "there must be a position of superior and inferior; and I, as much as any other man, am in favor of having the superior position assigned to the white race." Hampton, no less than Lincoln, thought of himself as "a sincere friend of the colored race." Though Lincoln's views might have changed, had he lived, Hampton had even gone beyond Lincoln, advocating that political rights not be withheld from blacks. But, like Lincoln, Hampton was unwilling to see whites dominated by blacks.[32]

Hampton wrote more on "The Race Problem" in an article by that name in *The Arena* four months later. He began by asserting what was generally accepted as fact in his age—that "the masterful, the conquering, and the unconquerable Caucasians" could never be governed by an inferior black race. "If any proof is necessary to show that the negro is incapable of self-government, one need only turn to the history of Liberia, San Domingo, and Hayti, to have all his doubts dispelled." He criticized Republicans for bringing upon America the "calamity" of unrestricted voting rights.

> In their senseless advocacy of universal suffrage, they have not only thrown wide open the doors leading to American citizenship, admitting thus the Anarchist, the Communist, the Nihilist, and all the other scum of European nations, but they have injected into our body politic millions of ignorant, uneducated blacks, who have no more comprehension of our system of government than their African forefathers had.

But he again rejected the idea of revoking black citizenship. And although it might solve America's dilemma if blacks were to leave the country, it would alleviate the South's difficulties if blacks would simply "scatter over the land. If they will do this, going to the fertile fields of the great West, or to New England, the home of his special friends, he will lift a great burden from the South, where his presence is a menace to our institutions." Other states would then "have the benefit of their presence, or learn by actual experience how baleful an influence they exercise." "This continent belongs to those who conquered the wilderness," wrote Hampton in conclusion, "who have taught to the world how a people can govern themselves, and who want no foreign element, white or black to control their destiny, or to debase their civilization."[33]

Federally aided deportation never came to pass, of course, but over the years Southern blacks did begin an exodus to the cities of the North and West, searching for better jobs. In the census of 1930, four decades after Hampton's comments, South Carolina for the first time since 1820 reported a white-majority population.

Hampton had been elected to a second Senate term in 1884 with only token Republican opposition, but new political winds were blowing in South Carolina. Criticism of Hampton continued to surface occasionally, sometimes by ex-radicals, more often by Martin Gary partisans. Gary, Hampton nemesis, died in 1881.[34] Soon a new leader arose, also from Edgefield, to challenge the conservative status quo in the Palmetto State.

Benjamin Ryan Tillman was a successful farmer from a family long prominent in that section. Illness in 1864 had cost him an eye, and nearly his life, making army service impossible. He played an active part in the 1876 campaign as a Gary lieutenant. Now Tillman began to voice many of the frustrations felt by white farmers in the state. In a speech to the Agricultural and Mechanical Society at Bennettsville in 1885 Tillman attacked conservative politicians. He denounced that "seedbed of aristocracy," South Carolina College. He agitated for the establishment of a new school where the sons of farmers might learn the latest techniques of agricultural science. And while Tillman shared prevailing racialist views, he despised conservative paternalism. Hampton recognized the myriad problems of a racially diverse society, but Christian convictions kept him from embracing solutions that involved coercion or violence. He vowed to secure black voting rights, maintain protection under the law, and provide opportunities for all to go to school. Hampton did not make and keep these promises because he believed in racial equality. His commitments were grounded in fair play, and he followed through because he had pledged his word. For Tillman the ends justified the means. To maintain white supremacy he favored stripping blacks of their voting rights—by repealing the Fifteenth Amendment if possible, by violence if necessary. He openly advocated lynching blacks accused of rape. To Tillman, money spent on black schools was wasted because "in educating a negro you spoil a good field hand." "I drew a sword and threw the scabbard away," said Tillman, "and I have never looked for it since. I have attacked friend or foe, whoever got in the way."

In June of 1890 a manifesto, written by Tillman but signed by G. Wash Shell of Laurens, was addressed to the "Democracy of South Carolina." From the days when King Charles II granted land to the Lords Proprietors, argued Tillman, the state had been ruled by aristocrats. Whenever a "champion of the people" had arisen, he had been bought with an office or simply destroyed. Now, there was a movement within the Democratic Party dedicated to securing "the needs and rights of the masses." He denounced "the continuance of men in office as political pensioners, after their ability or willingness to serve the people is gone." Such "pandering to sentiment" was "a crime." Democrats must remove from office those "wedded to ante-bellum ideas, but possessing little of ante-bellum patriotism and honor." The "common people" had redeemed the state in 1876, according to Tillman, only to see it run by a few for their own interests.

Two months later the Farmers' Association met and "suggested" a slate of candidates for statewide office. That list was led by Tillman for governor. Tillman toured the state whipping up support in preparation for the September convention of the state Democratic Party.[35]

Hampton and Tillman appeared on the same platform in debate at the Columbia fairgrounds on June 24. In arranging the confrontation conservatives hoped at last to put Tillman in his place before an unfriendly crowd. The senator arrived after a trip of four days by rail from Canada, where he had probably been salmon fishing in Quebec. The crowd this day was not large—just over 1,000—but spectators were ready to see their hometown hero Hampton deal with the upstart Tillman. Hampton rose to speak first and was greeted by "hoarse yells" and a band playing "Dixie." "For several minutes," said one reporter, "the applause was so loud he could not utter a word." Hampton asked that all speakers be given a respectful hearing and warned against division in Democratic ranks. There was, he cautioned them, an election bill then pending in Congress "framed by our bitter enemies, which will leave the federal elections practically in the hands of United States supervisors."

Tillman had proposed primary elections statewide as a more Democratic way of choosing party candidates. Hampton said that he had no objection to replacing nominating conventions with direct primaries. But he emphatically denied that South Carolina was ruled by an aristocracy.

> I do not know what aristocracy is. God knows I do not know. I do not recognize anybody in South Carolina as common people. . . . If there is any man here who followed me during the war, I appeal to him to bear me witness that I have treated every man in the ragged jacket as well as I did the man who wore the stars upon his coat.

His words were met with confirming cheers.

The general assembly to be elected in November would decide if Hampton should serve a third term in the Senate, but he claimed to have "no personal interest" in the election. "My career must soon close," said the seventy-two-year-old. "In the natural course of events I cannot hope to be here much longer." He expressed the wish that South Carolinians would become "a happy, prosperous and united people."

Then, it was Ben Tillman's turn. Hampton's conservatives he taunted as "innocent lambs, that they never saw such a thing as an aristocrat!" He lectured them on "a little South Carolina history," pointing out the undemocratic elements in the antebellum constitution. The crowd tried to shout him down, but Hampton came forward, asking that Tillman be heard. Soon a downpour of rain threatened to break up the meeting. Tillman continued to rail against conventions that left the common people "tied and handcuffed." He successfully parried the question of how he missed Confederate service. The ill-mannered, but fearless, farmer had faced his enemies on their own turf and held his own. "The grand mogul here," said Tillman of Hampton, "who ruled supremely and grandly cannot terrify me." A few days later Hampton was himself shouted down by Tillmanites at a rally in Aiken.[36]

Tillman took control of the Democratic convention and secured his party's nomination for governor. Some appalled conservatives broke ranks to nominate former party stalwart Alex C. Haskell as an independent to oppose Tillman in the general election. Yet, Hampton formally endorsed Tillman rather than back his old friend Haskell. "No one who knows Col. Haskell can doubt his sincerity," Hampton wrote to John L. M. Irby, Tillman lieutenant. But Hampton would not ask Democrats to vote for someone other than the nominee of the party. "I am impelled to support the . . . ticket because it was nominated by the Democratic convention, and because the other ticket lacks that endorsement." He had attended the meeting at the Columbia fairgrounds to promote unity, Hampton insisted. Furthermore, South Carolinians must "avoid all semblance of violence in the conduct of the election" so as to give no ammunition to proponents of "the odious Federal election bill now pending before Congress."

Tillman won the governorship with 59,159 votes to Haskell's 14,828. And the new general assembly would be dominated by Tillman's followers.[37]

Hampton was feeling his years and his infirmities. He was slowing down. If his Senate career had been unexceptional, most would agree that he had adequately represented the state. But his enemies did not bring up the issues of age or performance in office. Tillman later claimed to have been miffed by Hampton for his not riding in the same carriage with him at the Aiken rally. Hampton said that the treatment he received there, "when the Tillman roughs howled me down," led him to retire from the fray. The fact of the matter was that Tillman would brook no opposition, least of all from the state's archconservative. Although Hampton endorsed Tillman, he had not a single good word to say for him. One "prominent Tillmanite" interviewed by the press predicted Hampton's defeat for reelection. "The course of Senator Hampton in the recent bitter Haskell campaign in Carolina gave offense to the whole Tillman following." "If our Senator is not elected," said the new governor, "he can attribute his defeat to his own acts." Years later Tillman denied that he dictated the outcome of Hampton's reelection, "though I confess that I exerted what influence I had against him in that fight."

Hampton had not campaigned for election to the Senate in 1878, and he would not ask to be reelected now. Senator Butler was in the State House in late November lobbying for the junior senator. "I think he is entitled to reelection," pleaded Butler, a sentiment that Hampton certainly agreed with. In the meantime, legislators who favored electing Irby in his place circulated a paper "suggesting" his election, listing his qualifications and "fitness for the position."[38] Tillmanites found themselves split between Irby and Milton L. Donaldson. On the first ballot in the general assembly the top three candidates were Irby with fifty-five votes, Donaldson with forty-eight, and Hampton with forty-five. The next day in a second ballot Irby made gains. On Thursday, December 11, four more ballots were taken. Donaldson supporters continued to go over to Irby. The final tally was Irby 105, Donaldson 10, Hampton 42. "The Tillmanites are in a state of quiet exultation," wrote the *Washington Post*. Tillman said that to have reelected Hampton "would have been to stultify the reform movement and confess that its attack on the oligarchy was wrong."[39]

Conservatives were horrified. "Blot out Wade Hampton from the history of South Carolina for the past thirty years," wrote one, "and you blot out South Carolina." Pierce M. B. Young compared the vote to "but one other glaring event of history during the last hundred years that would rival it, and that was the shooting of Marshall Ney by the French people." The *News and Courier* thought "it was too much to expect the present General Assembly to rise above itself to a just appreciation of the gravity of the situation." The Charleston editor blamed Tillmanite Farmers' Alliance politicians for Hampton's ouster, not the people of South Carolina. Hampton's hold on the affection of the people was still strong,

> and when the sound of the fantastic parade has died away in the distance and the people begin to ask themselves and the men whom they trusted to represent them why Wade Hampton was driven out of public life, there will be a casting up of accounts between the people and the powers that be.

"Hampton has nothing to regret," said the editor in conclusion, "nothing of which to be ashamed; he did not ask for votes, he will not beg for charity."[40]

"The Alliance having 'shelved' me, I must resume the life of a planter though [it is] late in the day to do so," Hampton wrote to Butler shortly after his defeat. Despite a professed disinterest in remaining in public life, Hampton could not help but feel hurt, even bitter, at the rebuff.

> Base methods were used to defeat me: the ordinary methods of Tillman and his followers—misrepresentations, detraction & lying, but I prefer defeat at their hands, rather than to have been successful by sacrificing my independence and self-respect. I am hurt that the old soldiers turned against me, for I did not expect that at their hands.

Nearly all of his Senate colleagues, even Republicans, "have expressed sincere regret at my defeat," Hampton told Theodore G. Barker. "I am content, and if the people will rebuke the representatives, who misrepresented their constituents, I shall be satisfied."[41]

Hampton would remain South Carolina's junior senator for almost three more months. There was still the matter of the "force bill," the measure pending in the Senate that would reintroduce federal management of elections. On the evening of January 16, 1891, Hampton made his last Senate speech.

That the bill's supporters would "camp outside the Constitution" Hampton took for granted. Based on his own experience, Hampton was sure too that federal interference would rekindle bitterness and lead to violence, "for a law as immutable as that which guides the planets in their orbits decrees that when people of different races are brought into contact or collision the weaker race is invariably the sufferer." As senator, Hampton had responded favorably to the petitions of black constituents, at times recommending even the appointment of Republicans. He rejoiced that some blacks had made progress, and "I shall always be glad to lend them a helping hand when this can properly be done." But, as Hampton saw it, these blacks were the exceptions that proved the rule.

> [The] vast majority are still in dense ignorance, an ignorance so profound as to render them not only unfit to govern great and free States, but unfit to meet the responsibilities or discharge the duties of citizenship. I do not say this by way of reproach, for no blame attaches to them on this account, nor do I think to us.

Blacks in South Carolina were still allowed to vote, said the senator, and some held office in the state, but most were simply no longer interested in politics. According to Hampton, "many of them have lost their certificates of registration, and without one of these no citizen can vote, as I discovered in my own case at the last election. I suppose my friends on the other side would say that my vote was suppressed."

His concluding words brought applause from both the galleries and fellow senators.

Mr. President, my public career will in all human probability soon close for-ever. During its long continuance I have never sought office. I have accepted it only when my people called on me to serve them, and I shall retire to private life without one regret, save that caused by the severance of the many ties of friendship formed here. No political ambition can animate me in the future, as none has done in the past. The sole ambition that has ever stirred my heart has been to serve faithfully the people who in that past honored me by their confidence and support, and, while doing this, to promote the welfare of our common country.

During the time I have had the honor to represent my State in this body not one word of recrimination, nor one calculated to keep alive sectional animosity, has escaped my lips. The thunders of war had scarcely ceased to reverberate when I, in opposition to the feelings and apprehensions of many of my fellow-citizens, urged them, not only to deal justly with the negroes, but to accord to them all the rights which would necessarily follow their enfranchisement. From that day to the present I have steadily and constantly advocated the same policy, not because it was politic, but because it was right.[42]

The *News and Courier* applauded the speech, again expressing regret that Hampton was about to leave office. Not only would South Carolina lose "an able and worthy representative," but "the country will miss the counsel of one of the wisest and most conservative statesmen of his generation."[43]

On May 13 ex-senator Hampton was invited to speak at ceremonies in Columbia celebrating that city's centennial as South Carolina's capital. Also on the platform was Gov. Benjamin R. Tillman. When Hampton rose to speak, he was greeted "with deafening cheers" by this local crowd. Toward the end of his address, he took the opportunity to bid farewell to South Caro-lina politics.

In every position to which the partiality of my fellow-citizens has called me, I have tried, honestly and sincerely, to discharge the duties imposed upon me to the best of my ability. How my duty to the State has been performed is not for me, but for my fellow-citizens, to judge. From their verdict I shall never appeal. My political career is ended, my public work is finished.

Throughout the remarks, reported the press, Tillman sat six feet behind Hampton, "perfectly quiet for the whole time, except for an occasional smile."[44] Gary had his revenge.

"MEMORIES OF THE PAST"

Railroad Commissioner, Southern Symbol

Only days after Hampton left the Senate, he was interviewed in Petersburg, Virginia, by a reporter from the New York *Sun*. Unusual for the time, that journalist was a black man. T. Thomas Fortune's questions centered on sectionalism. Twenty-six years after Appomattox, Hampton well understood how sensitive the issue remained in American politics. The Democratic Party during the 1888 election had erred, thought Hampton, in sending Southern speakers to the North. "The voters resent it. If Northern speakers should be sent into the South we should resent it."

"What about the speakership of the next house?" asked Fortune.

"I think it will be a mistake to elect a Southern man as speaker," Hampton replied. "I think some good Northern or Western man should be selected."

John Carlisle of Kentucky had been House Speaker during the Fiftieth Congress, and Southern Democrats now dominated committee chairmanships. Hampton feared that this hurt the party nationally.

"What is your opinion," asked the reporter, "of the future of the races in the South?"

"Most hopeful," said Hampton. Friction would decrease as all "understood the mutuality of their interests." He predicted that in South Carolina "the best elements among the colored people would cooperate with the best elements among the white people" to defeat Tillmanism.

"That being the case," said the newsman, "would you not feel it a public duty to accept the gubernatorial nomination if offered to you?"

Hampton had perhaps said too much. The seventy-three-year-old did not feel strong enough physically or politically to lead another crusade, this time against Tillman Democrats.

"I must straighten out my personal affairs," concluded Hampton.

Fortune did not press him further, as "he really looked as if he wished not to be called upon to make other sacrifices prejudicial to his personal interests. As the cars sped away Southward I could not but think pleasantly of the fine old type of Southern gentlemen."

Within weeks of returning home, Hampton received word that Gen. Joseph E. Johnston, last of the Confederacy's army commanders, was dead. Cleveland had appointed Johnston railroad commissioner in 1885. The funeral was in Washington on March 24, 1891, and Hampton was there. "To an honored grave the thoughts of Joe Johnston's old soldiers will follow his body," wrote editor Narciso G. Gonzales of the Columbia *State*, "and then will resolutely and hopefully turn to the duties of the present and the making of the future."[1]

Gonzales had founded the *State* soon after Tillman's election in order to speak out against the governor and his "farmers' movement." Conservatives focused on defeating Tillman's bid for reelection in 1892. In a March 3 letter to the *State*, also published in other papers around South Carolina, Hampton added his voice to calls for a statewide primary election. He wanted conservatives to unite and recapture the Democratic Party. Former Haskell supporters must join with "farmers who have learned by bitter experience how grievously they have been deceived by false promises." Hampton was especially intent that those who bolted two years earlier return to give battle within the party. "Rally to Hampton!" was the title of the *State* editorial endorsing those sentiments. "We want that corps to aid in the fight," wrote Gonzales, "and when it is urged by an old commander like Wade Hampton to double-quick to the front, we believe it will do so." Conservatives met in a "peace and unity" convention on March 24, endorsing former governor John C. Sheppard to replace Tillman, but vowing to support the nominee of the party. Hampton was chairman of the platform committee. That document called for a "safe and conservative government." Tillman was accused of destroying the credit of the state. He had created a "servile Legislature and an intimidated judiciary." The governor himself was becoming "the master and king of the people instead of their servant." After a hard fought campaign, Tillman beat Sheppard by a landslide in the series of local primaries held on August 27 to choose convention delegates.[2]

Although Hampton saw his candidate go down to defeat, Democrats on the national stage were resurgent. Grover Cleveland had been renominated by his party's convention on the first ballot, going on to defeat the incumbent

Benjamin Harrison. Cleveland was the first American president to be elected to two nonconsecutive terms. Irby had voted against him in the convention. Neither did Tillman have any liking for Cleveland, claiming his nomination was "dictated by Wall Street."[3] Most South Carolinians rejoiced in the New Yorker's comeback—no one more than Wade Hampton.

Hampton was in a jovial mood at the Sumter, South Carolina, "Cleveland celebration" held soon after the victory. Governor Tillman and Senator Irby had been invited, but were "unable to be present." Despite a steady rain Hampton spoke to a crowd of 5,000. "I could not resist the invitation of a town which merits what Burns said: 'No town surpasses for honest men and bonnie lasses.' I regret that so many of the latter were driven away by the inclement weather, unless they have chosen to stay here and be 'reining bells.'"

Cleveland's win, said Hampton, meant that America would enjoy "peace, prosperity and happiness. The workingman will not have his hard-earned gains taken away to enrich the plutocrats of the North." And Southerners could rest easy knowing that the Republican "force bill" was at last dead. The rain grew heavier, but the crowd shouted for more. "I want to tell you that this night has waked in my heart the memories of '76." Hampton concluded with words of blessing on his state.[4]

The following month Hampton received a letter from his friend Senator Vest. Vest said that he had spoken to President-elect Cleveland at Lakewood, New Jersey, and recommended Hampton's appointment as commissioner of railroads. Hampton would serve with "honesty and ability," Vest assured Cleveland, and he deserved the position that he might "pass his declining years in comfort." Cleveland replied "that nothing would give him greater pleasure." He would announce the appointment soon after naming his cabinet. The railroad commissioner's annual salary of $4,500 was quite comfortable, and Hampton needed the income. He probably provided at least partial support for his sisters, as well as taking care of himself and daughter Daisy. The position had been vacant since the death of General Johnston. Hampton replied to Vest on December 20, thanking him, and accepting "for my means are very slender." "It would please me, too, to let the demagogues who struck me in the back see that the head of the Democratic party thinks me worthy of recognition." He would never serve in state office again, Hampton told Vest, "for my reward for my sacrifices has been sufficient to teach me that gratitude is short-lived."[5]

"During a period of temporary aberration of mind," wrote the Houston Post, "South Carolina turned her back on Wade Hampton, the hero, scholar, patriot and statesman. Now every Democrat in America would rejoice to see Mr. Cleveland give him an appointment." In early March it became known that the wish was to become reality. The State reported Cleveland as saying "Wade Hampton could have any office he wished," and when he spoke of the general, "his eyes filled with tears." Every U.S. senator (except Irby, who was not asked) signed a letter requesting the nomination, but Hampton would not let the document be sent to the president, keeping it himself, "among his cherished possessions." The appointment, one of many, went to the Senate on March 21. Hampton's former colleagues confirmed the nomination unanimously, without reference to committee.[6]

He began his duties immediately. One of Hampton's first chores was to hire a private secretary. "I feel that I have been very much honored by this appointment," wrote Charles E. Thomas to his mother. Thomas had been working for John C. Haskell, who recommended the young man.

> The duties of the Railroad Commissioner are to supervise all railroads in which the Government is interested, which are almost altogether west of the Missouri. . . . He goes over this territory about twice a year and makes a statement of the condition of these roads to the Secretary of the Interior. . . . Of course on these trips I will accompany him, and it will cost me nothing. He wrote that he expected to go to California between now and July. . . . I certainly am fortunate in getting this excellent opportunity.[7]

The continent had been conquered on May 10, 1869, when tracks of the Union Pacific and Central Pacific met at Promontory Point, Utah, at last linking the nation by rail. Other lines followed. Construction of railroads to the Pacific coast was financed by federal loans and generous land grants, but over the years terms for repayment had not been met. The Thurman Act of 1878 tried to correct the situation. Under its provisions the Government would retain the amount it owed the railroads for carrying mail and other cargo and apply it to the debt. No less than 25 percent of annual company net earnings was also to be used to reduce the balance. Yet, even this failed to solve the problem. Railroad executives were creative in their definition of what constituted "net earnings" and kept their lawyers busy filing litigation. By 1893 the Pacific railroads still owed over $115,000,000. A proposal in Congress suggested refinancing the debt at low interest rates for a period of 100 years. "The roads," sneered one Western editor, "prefer that Uncle Sam run around barefooted on the tie path while the Goulds and Huntingtons [railroad barons Jay Gould and Collis P. Huntington] ride on vestibuled private cars." Some advocated that the U.S. government should pay off other outstanding mortgages, foreclose, then own the railroads outright.

Congress would have to decide. It was the responsibility of the railroad commissioner to examine the financial records of railroads indebted to the government, inspect company assets, and submit an annual report to the secretary of the interior. Hampton's first report was due on November 1, which was just seven months away. After organizing his small staff, Hampton prepared to make an inspection tour to the West Coast. This trip would involve pleasure as well as business. Ironically, most of the expense would be borne by the railroad companies themselves. Although these trips were required by law, very little money was budgeted to pay for them.[8]

Late on the night of Tuesday, May 16, Hampton and a party of guests left their rooms at the Metropolitan Hotel and headed for the Washington station of the Baltimore and Ohio Railroad.[9] Waiting for them was a private car provided for their use by the Union Pacific. Accompanying Hampton were secretary Thomas, W. M. Thompson (a former commission employee on his way to San Francisco), and Dr. Benjamin W. Taylor. Ladies in the group included Hampton's thirty-two-year-old daughter Daisy and his twenty-seven-year-old granddaughter Ann Hampton Haskell. Both were unmarried. They brought along friends Lucy T. Herndon and Virginia T. Long of Fredricksburg and Charlottesville, Virginia, respectively. The eight passengers were looked after by Levi Kean, "combination porter and cook." The car was coupled to the scheduled B&O train bound for Chicago, and soon they were on their way.

For almost two days they passed through the states of West Virginia, Ohio, and Indiana, arriving in Chicago on the morning of Thursday, May 18. The car would serve as their hotel while they toured Chicago and the just-opened World's Columbian Exhibition. "My impression of the Fair," wrote Thomas, "was that it was a wonderful thing, and the buildings were simply grand, but the exhibits were not half completed and that served to disappoint us a great deal." At noon on Saturday they were off again, this time attached to a train of the Chicago and Northwestern Railroad.

They crossed the Mississippi River at Clinton, Iowa, and the Missouri at Council Bluffs. Thomas described Omaha, Nebraska, as "quite a western looking town, with wide streets, electric cars, and some very fine buildings." There they transferred to a special train, made up of engine, baggage car, their private car, and a superintendent's car, provided by the Union Pacific. They would travel now only by daylight, so as to inspect the railroad and enjoy as much western scenery as they could. Impressed with Denver, Colorado, "we unanimously voted it the nicest city we had seen since we left Washington." Former Colorado senator Horace Tabor gave Hampton and his party two boxes at a Denver theater for a performance of a comedy called "The Prodigal Father."

The *Rocky Mountain News* recounted the welcome Hampton had received earlier in Sterling, Colorado. A veteran, one of Hampton's men, determined to give the general a true military reception. Jim May put on his "old butternut uniform and lovingly girded it around as much of his person as it would encompass," then marched down Main Street to the depot "amid the acclamation of the populous." When Hampton arrived May saluted, gave three cheers, then boarded the train for an emotional reunion with his old commander. The reporter wrote,

Maybe it was a foolish sort of an affair, but the big crowd at Sterling was very quiet while it was going on and when old Jim May, with a suspicious lump in his throat, marched back up the street to his work he got a cheer that could be heard out on the prairie.[10]

Side trips were arranged, allowing the Hampton party to visit the mining towns of Forks Creek, Idaho Springs, Black Hawk, Silver Plume, and Golden. They were amazed at the engineering skill required to lay track through the towering peaks. On an excursion to Manitou Springs, the ground was covered with a blanket of snow, although it was now late spring. On May 25 their private cars were coupled to a regular train of the Union Pacific, and by early afternoon they arrived in Cheyenne, Wyoming.

Commissioner Hampton was tired of talking to newsmen, so the four ladies answered a reporter's questions. The men looked over the Cheyenne railroad shops where an electric crane "lifts an 85 ton engine with the greatest ease and moves it anywhere about the shed."

"You will find that father does not talk much," Daisy explained to the man from the *Daily Sun.*

"Then," said the reporter, "the four young ladies began to talk, all at once, of course, and they fired impertinent questions. For instance, they wanted to know if the women in Wyoming were not all positive and self-conscious beyond endurance?" Unique in America, while still a territory Wyoming had given women the right to vote.

"The women's rights women I know are unbearable," said Lucy.

Just then Hampton appeared. "Do you know," smiled the commissioner, "these young ladies worry the life out of me? I can have no peace of mind. If we stop but five minutes at a station everyone of these bound out of the car and on to the platform and I am afraid the train will pull out and leave them behind."

Hampton, concluded the newsman, "is a hale and hearty man." As for the ladies, "Their dispositions are as sunny as the land from which they come."[11]

The next morning those ladies were mortified to discover that every word they expressed was now in black and white for all to read. "We had the laugh on them," said Thomas, "and held that interview over them the whole balance of the trip, so that they became frightened even at the mention of the word 'Reporter,' and fled whenever one appeared."

Soon they were again on their way, accompanied for a time by John E. Osborne, the thirty-four-year-old governor of Wyoming, who was traveling to his home in Rawlins. Passing through Ogden, Hampton and his companions arrived in Salt Lake City, Utah, where they were given a tour in carriages provided by the railroad. They saw the Mormon Temple and the Tabernacle. "Some of these Mormon houses have a front door for each wife," observed

Thomas, "where the wives all live in the same house." Hampton, Thomas, and a railroad superintendent set out on a fishing expedition in Idaho, leaving the others in Salt Lake City. The scenery in Idaho was magnificent, but fishing in Billinger Creek and Malad River proved unproductive. "General Hampton is a large, fine-looking man, of some seventy-five years of age, but is still hale and vigorous," wrote the *Deseret Evening News.* "He represents in all departments of life the genuine quality of chivalry so much spoken of but so seldom encountered."[12]

Transferring to a Central Pacific train, the Hampton party continued into Nevada, described by Thomas as "the dryest and most desolate looking [place] imaginable." They soon tired of the scenery and passed the time playing cards. Thomas had nothing but praise for the food and accommodations provided by the railroad. They traveled through Elko, Carlin, Battle Mountain, and Reno. At Carson City Hampton received a delegation of prominent citizens. Early on the morning of June 1, he and two railroad officials went on a fishing trip while the others toured Lake Tahoe. Thomas thought Tahoe the highlight of the trip, and the women declared it "just lovely." Hampton happily came in with a large string of fish from Donner Lake.

Soon their train was climbing over the Sierras, at one point traversing a snow shed thirty-two miles long. These engineering wonders kept the tracks clear of snow, which even in June was still over ten feet deep. They stopped in Colfax, California, and there found a store that sold tropical fruit. "This is what California is famed for the world over," wrote Thomas, "in two hours you can go from Vermont to a Florida climate." The warmth and vegetation in Sacramento reminded him of Charleston. By sundown they were in San Francisco, arriving by ferry from Oakland, and found they again needed their overcoats. "Eastern people can hardly understand these sudden changes in climate when they first visit California," Thomas concluded.

Staying at the "very large and magnificent" Palace Hotel, Hampton and his entourage slept late, then set out on an afternoon tour of the city and its surroundings. They especially enjoyed Golden Gate Park and the view from the Cliff House Hotel. A reporter from the *Examiner* caught up with Hampton.

> Yes, this is my first visit to San Francisco. More than that, it is my first trip west of the Mississippi. I am just beginning to realize the magnitude of the country, and the more I travel the more I see, and the more I wish I was young again.[13]

That evening Hampton stayed behind to rest while the young people went to China Town. The next day he was still not feeling well and let the others ride cable cars up and down California Street and enjoy a comedy at Stockwell's Theater.

On Tuesday, June 6, the general was well enough to host a hotel reception for the many Confederate veterans then living in the Bay Area who wanted to greet him. Former Hampton scout George D. Shadburne, now a San Francisco attorney, met him there, "and it was with pleasure we reviewed the past," said Shadburne. He had seen Hampton in Washington five years earlier and now noticed "the marks of time with him."[14]

The next day Hampton and his party boarded a train headed south. They passed through San Mateo. At Menlo Park they stopped and were taken in carriages to the home of Leland Stanford. Stanford was then sixty-nine years old. He had served as Republican governor during the Civil War, made a fortune in railroads, and since 1885 represented California in the U.S. Senate. Hampton was driven over the grounds of the Stanford estate, shown a farm and stables that kept 600 horses, and given a tour of Stanford University. Returning to the Stanford home, wrote Thomas,

> We were entertained by a most elegant luncheon. The table was beautifully decorated with flowers and fruits, all grown on the Senator's place there, as were also his wines. . . . The house is the most magnificently furnished I ever saw, the ceilings being frescoed in imitation of Persian rugs in a most perfect manner. Senator Stanford is estimated to be worth forty millions.

Back aboard the train that afternoon, they traveled to Del Monte, near Monterey, there to spend the night. The following day they went sightseeing through Monterey and Pacific Grove and along the scenic coast in horse-drawn conveyances. Later, they traveled north to Santa Cruz, touring the town and riding on the beach. They boarded a private railroad car in San Jose and reached Tracy by dark. There Dr. Taylor left to return to Columbia, much to everyone's regret. The train carrying Hampton and the remainder of his party rumbled on through the night. At morning light, they found themselves in the Mojave Desert, "a sandy plain covered with the Yucca tree," according to Thomas. After a brief stay in Los Angeles, they started south again, passing through orange groves, enjoying the view of the Pacific where the tracks ran along the coast. In the San Diego vicinity, they saw Coronado and the ruins of Mission San Juan Capistrano. The next day they returned by the previous route until reaching Orange. From there they traveled to Riverside, through groves of orange, lemon, and olive trees, and spent the night.

In the morning they rode through Colton, past Mission San Gabriel, to Los Angeles. Side trips were made to San Pedro and Santa Monica. They walked on the Santa Monica pier and spent the night in their railroad car on a siding near the beach. "The whole party went out in the evening," remembered Thomas, "and watched the breakers coming in, and all night we could hear them roar."

Soon they traveled north again, back up the Central Valley through Stockton to Sacramento. Interviewed by the Sacramento *Daily Record-Union*, Hampton was described as "wonderfully well preserved, genial and handsome," and "an expert fisherman." "They say he can throw a fly sixty feet and hit the size of a four-bit piece every time."[15] They stopped at Vina Vineyard, owned by Stanford, were given a tour by the superintendent, and sent on their way with a complimentary selection of wine. Hampton tried fishing along the way in the Sacramento and later in the Klamath and Rogue rivers, but had little success. Near Oregon City he fished for salmon from a boat. "The General hooked a 12 pound salmon and played it for half an hour," said Thomas, "and just as they were pulling it in the boat they let it get away, much to the disappointment of all of us."

The next few days were spent in the Portland area. They marveled at views of Mt. Saint Helens, Mt. Adams, Mt. Hood, and even the distant Mt. Tacoma. The weather for sightseeing was perfect, "such a day as is seen in Portland but a few times a year," learned Thomas. On Thursday, June 22, Hampton and his secretary spent the morning answering letters while the others toured the city. It was probably then that they read in the paper that Leland Stanford had died the day before in Palo Alto. Later, they crossed the Columbia River on a ferry and in the middle of the night arrived in Tacoma, Washington.

On Saturday, June 24, Hampton's car was coupled to the Cannon Ball Express, and soon they were climbing the Cascades, headed east. The next day they sped past Spokane, through Idaho, and into Montana. On the morning of June 26, they were preparing to tour Yellowstone. For two days these Southerners stared open-mouthed at a succession of hot springs, bizarre mineral formations, "paint pots," and geysers. On their final day at Yellowstone, Hampton and Thomas went on one more fishing expedition,

> leaving the ladies to look around. We rode two miles up the river and hitched our horses and started in. We fished until nearly 8 o'clock, and between us caught a dozen fine two pound trout . . . [T]he General was much elated and only stopped when we could not see any longer.

Having traversed the Badlands of North Dakota, crossed the Missouri River, and gone through Bismarck, Hampton found himself in Minneapolis on July 1. He remained behind while the younger travelers toured that city and St. Paul. "Returning to the car in time for dinner," said Thomas, "we found the General very lonely and very impatient for us to return." The next day Thomas and Hampton spent the morning again writing letters before the train set out. They passed Oshkosh and Fond du Lac, Wisconsin. On the morning of July 3, they were again in Chicago.

After breakfast all headed for the grounds of the World's Fair, but Hampton chose to go by himself, rather than slow down the young people. He was tired. As he walked around the exposition, his thoughts may have wandered back to another July 3, exactly thirty years before, when he thought his life was ending on a field in Pennsylvania. "While he seemed cheerful and com- paratively happy," Shadburne remembered from their June meeting, "I could plainly see the marks of sadness, and I regret that, as he said to me in one of his letters, there is little left to him but the memories of the past."[16]

On July 7 they were on their way again, crossing the states of Indiana, Ohio, and West Virginia, reaching the District of Columbia on the afternoon of July 8. "We were all very sorry that the trip had come to an end," said Thomas, "and the parting was a sad one." In eight weeks Hampton had traveled 10,200 miles by rail and hundreds of additional miles on side trips through eighteen states and one territory. "He is looking much better and is ten pounds heavier than when he left Washington," reported the *State*.[17]

Hampton found the Union and the Central Pacific properties "to be in excellent physical condition." Included in his report was a meticulously detailed inspection by the commissioner's engineer, a 20,000-word analysis that came to the same general conclusion. Unfortunately, the position of engineer had been cut by Congress, and his responsibilities would in future devolve upon the commissioner.

In the West Hampton had tried to avoid comment on policy matters. "Understand," he told a San Francisco reporter, "I am not out here to hear arguments, to receive railroad delegations or to make recommendations to Congress. I am here . . . to learn all I can about these roads and report what I learn to Washington." Now that time had come.

In this first report to the interior secretary, Hampton blamed the failure of the Thurman Act on shortcomings in the law itself. There were now five transcontinental railroads. "The completion and opening of these roads to traffic revolutionized the conditions which prevailed" a generation earlier. Foreclosure was a poor solution to the problem. Hampton recommended that the president be allowed to appoint a commission "with full power to settle the indebtedness." If Congress would not agree to that, he suggested that they place *all* of the Pacific railroads under the Thurman Act, and make them pay 50 percent of net earnings, instead of 25 percent as then required. "The companies named are abundantly able to do this," Hampton wrote to Interior Secretary Hoke Smith.[18]

Hampton could only reiterate those recommendations in 1894. An eco- nomic depression that had begun the year before now gripped the country and much of the world. The railroad industry had additional problems. Floods, forest fires, and crop failures in the West combined to reduce their earnings. The strike of the Pullman car workers in Illinois, led by Eugene V. Debs, resulted in rioting and the destruction of property. U.S. troops were called in to restore order and to break the strike. Hampton hoped that Congress would create a board of railway arbitration with binding authority, "this doing away with the barbarous and brutal methods which were recently resorted to."[19]

Economic conditions improved somewhat the following year, and Hampton reported that American railroads had placed orders for 25,000 new freight cars. During June and July he made his annual inspection of the "roadbed, tracks, bridges, shops, and rolling stock" of the Pacific railroad companies and found no problems. Yet Congress still would not agree on a repayment plan. Hampton repeated his recommendations. His two book-keepers were busily engaged in examining railroad company records.[20] Hampton begged that "a man of practical experience in railroad engineering and operation" be assigned to his office. "A sufficiently accurate, intelligent, and careful inspection . . . cannot be made by a layman."[21]

In the summer of 1896, Commissioner Hampton was in Denver when a former Union army scout paid him a visit. The veteran's name was David Day, and he was then living in Colorado. Day had been in the fight at Fayett-ville—the 1865 skirmish where Hampton's little band killed and captured so many of the enemy. In the course of their reminiscing, Hampton mentioned the gray-clad federal spy whom Confederates had captured, but who had escaped before Hampton could hang him. Day said that he was that man! "I told him that I am glad I did not hang him," Hampton related later to a friend. Day emphatically agreed.[22]

Hampton remained concerned about the political situation in South Car-olina and anxious to do what he could to oppose Tillman. Hampton wished the state party were more in line with the conservative national Democratic party. He was particularly disgusted with Tillman's dispensary.[23] Effective July 1, 1893, state government became the sole legal proprietor of liquor in South Carolina. All saloons and public bars were closed. Spirits were now sold in bottles bearing the emblem of the palmetto. It was Tillman's way of controlling the consumption of intoxicants—and of making a tidy profit. In a February 1894 letter to political ally Narciso Gonzales, Hampton could not resist telling of an experience he had while traveling to Washington with Till-man crony John Gary Evans. Evans "traveled on a pass & was drunk all the way from Charlotte here."[24] Within months this nephew of Martin W. Gary would succeed Tillman as governor.

Even from his post as railroad commissioner, Hampton continued to have influence with those making federal appointments. On December 4, 1893, he asked President Cleveland to name Charles H. Simonton to a federal judgeship. "I think Simonton's record on the bench justifies his promotion . . . & his appointment would be a rebuke to the Tillman Legislature which has just turned out all the best judges in the State." Only days earlier, in a speech before the general assembly, Tillman had referred to Simonton as a "puissant Judge, whose satrapy is South Carolina." To Hampton, such "shameful language" was without excuse. Cleveland immediately appointed Simonton a federal circuit court judge.[25]

Hampton often received letters recommending—or warning against—federal job applicants.[26] Once, in October 1897, he had the assistant secretary of the Navy wait a full hour in President William McKinley's office on behalf of a job applicant. That assistant secretary's name was Theodore Roosevelt.[27] On an earlier occasion Hampton told White House secretary Henry T. Thurber of an encounter he had with Ruth Cleveland. The president's daughter was not yet three years old. "I had the pleasure of meeting Ruth yesterday as I was coming out, who after greeting me very pleasantly and cordially, pointed to the elevator and said, 'Now go.' She must have thought I was an office seeker!"[28]

Secretary Thomas wrote his mother,

> The General and I have become very "chummy," and I often leave the office and stay in his [hotel] room with him half the day. He is never happy unless he is engaged in one of three or four occupations: fishing or fixing fishing tackle, cutting and scraping a long handled gourd, making fans out of turkey feathers, or trimming walking canes from the natural stick cut in the woods. He is certainly a lovely old man, and I am very much attached to him.[29]

William McKinley had defeated Democrat William Jennings Bryan for president in the election of 1896, but the Republican chief executive allowed Hampton to remain at his post. It was rumored that McKinley wanted Hampton to stay indefinitely, despite pressure to replace him with a Republican. But Hampton submitted his final report on November 1, 1897, and resigned a week later. He was succeeded by another ex-Confederate, one with Republican credentials, James Longstreet. Only after Hampton left office did Congress finally settle with the Pacific railroads. A series of reorganizations eventually allowed the government to collect the principal, if not all of the interest, due on its claims.[30]

Hampton was soon home and reported to be in "fine spirits." His resignation had come as no surprise to President McKinley, said Hampton, and he denied rumors that he planned to write a history of the cavalry of the Army of Northern Virginia, although he had been approached to do so many times. "He seems to be enjoying excellent health despite his increasing years," reported the *State*.[31]

During his nearly two decades in Washington, Hampton had been one Southerner with a national outlook, proud of America and wanting his own state to share in the country's prosperity and greatness. He knew that Confederates had fought for principles—constitutional government, states' rights—handed down from the founders of the Republic. He asked of former foes only that they give him the measure of respect he accorded them, by acknowledging that each had struggled for his own vision of American liberty.

Hampton told Confederate veterans in Savannah,

> If we were wrong in our contest, then the Declaration of Independence of 1776 was a grave mistake, and the revolution to which it led was a crime. . . . If Washington was a patriot, Lee cannot have been a rebel; if the enunciation of the grand truths in the Declaration of Independence made Jefferson immortal, the observance of them could not have made Davis a traitor.

He was not bitter. "We acknowledge that the stern, irrevocable verdict of war has been rendered against us. . . . [W]e claim to be honest and loyal citizens." Still, Confederate Southerners remained, in a sense, citizens of two countries.

> I am aware that in certain quarters it is the fashion to tell our people that these are all dead issues, and that they should be forgotten as we press on in that new and glorious era which is dawning on the reconstructed South . . . that we must forget and forgive! . . . What are we to forget? Must we forget that we are the sons of men who gave their blood to establish the liberty of America. . . . Can the father forget his son, struck down by his side, in the prime of manly strength and youthful beauty? . . . Time may teach us to forgive, but it can never make us forget.

Hampton claimed that Southerners had the right

> to justify our cause, to vindicate our motives, and to honor our dead. . . . If our faith in the justice of our cause was so strong that we risked life and all that made life desirable on the dread issue of war, surely we should strive to justify ourselves in the eyes of the world.

He plead for Southern women to

> teach their children that their fathers fought for the right; that they were inspired by as just a cause as ever fired the hearts or nerved the arms of patriots, and that though that cause has gone down in disaster, in ruin, in blood, not one stain of dishonor rests upon it.[32]

The general continued this theme in a speech before the Sons of Confederate Veterans in Charleston. "It will be the task of your organization and kindred ones . . . to preserve the honor and to preserve from detraction the memory of those who sacrificed everything." He warned them against a

> false doctrine . . . which tells you that because of the failure of our cause there was no truth or justice in it. Any human undertaking, however just it

The ruins of Millwood, burned by Sherman's advancing troops, in a photograph taken before 1899. The man by the column may be Wade Hampton. *Edward L. Wells, Hampton and His Cavalry in '64 (Richmond, Va.: B. F. Johnson Pub. Co., 1899).*

may be, may fail, but the everlasting principle of right and justice can never be blotted out. A great truth, like the God-head whence it emanates, is eternal, and it will live "till the last syllable of recorded time."

He went on to remind his audience of one great triumph of justice.

I have a right to feel some pride in the result of that memorable political contest of '76—in my judgment the most memorable ever waged on this continent, for home rule, for personal liberty and States' rights, for it was my good fortune to bear the standard placed by our people in my hands to victory, and whatever Fate may have in store for me, nothing can ever deprive me of the honest pride I feel that I contributed, in part, to the glorious victory won then by the people of my State.[33]

In retirement Hampton continued to attend Confederate meetings and memorial observances. In May 1899 he was looking forward to the national reunion of Confederate veterans in Charleston. The city had even constructed a new auditorium for the event. Stephen D. Lee, Joseph Wheeler, Clement Evans, and Ellison Capers were a few of the thousands expected to attend.[34] Just a week before the gathering, Hampton, now eighty-one, would endure yet another affliction.

At three o'clock on the morning of May 2, Hampton awoke to see what he thought was light from the morning sun under the door of his room. Quickly, he realized he was seeing the glow of flames! He put on his trousers, slippers, and his artificial leg. Daisy, staying with her father, was alerted and escaped. Black neighbors came running and were able to pull out a few pieces of furniture and other items. Hampton saved swords belonging to his grandfather, father, and himself. All his papers, books, and most of his possessions were lost.

Southern Cross was gone. In its original form the house had served as the gardener's cottage for Diamond Hill, far enough away from the main house to have been overlooked by Sherman's incendiaries. It had been comprised of one brick selection of four rooms and an addition of wood. Hampton had no insurance. Once again, he was homeless.

A reporter from the *State* found him the next morning in a surviving two-room utility shed, "chatting pleasantly," wearing the trousers and slippers he had donned when he fled the flames. Two Columbia policemen guarded the ruins of his home. The old man had reentered the inferno in a futile attempt to save a puppy, and as a result his mustache, eyebrows, and hair were burned. "The general told the story modestly," wrote the newsman, "merely relating it as an incident."

"Well, I have had many hard knocks in my life," said Hampton, "and I do not know any one better able to stand it than I am."

Friends were of course concerned about him, and some questioned if he would attend the Charleston reunion, now only days away. "I have saved some clothes, my gun, and fishing tackle," he replied to one. "We are in an outhouse, quite comfortable. If I had only saved my tent, I would be all right." He went to Charleston as planned and was given "one of the grandest ovations of his life."[35]

Almost immediately after the fire, admirers from across the state began collecting money to purchase a comfortable home for the old man. The *State* said that Hampton's losses were especially serious "because while he is rich in honor and affections of a grateful people, he is poor in purse." The first contributions were raised in Darlington. Newspapers in Sumter, Chester, Timmonsville, Union, Kingstree, Augusta, Spartanburg, and elsewhere publicized the effort.

Quickly, Hampton responded with a public letter thanking all for their sympathy, but declining the help. "I cannot accept from my friends a testimonial of regard such as they propose, but the affection shown by them in wishing to reimburse me for my loss can never be forgotten, for it is prized by me higher than any gift from them could ever be." The *State* published his letter with "much regret." Describing Hampton as "a very poor man," even "destitute," editor Gonzales likened the building project "to the gift of a son to his father." There must be some way to overcome his refusal of help "and we commend this problem to the ingenuity of the general's friends in the hope that a solution may be found."[36]

Hampton may not have been literally penniless, but what little cash he had would certainly not permit him to live independently, even in his customarily modest style. A committee was formed and circular letters mailed. "He served his State in war and in peace during the best years of his life," read one, "spending generously and lavishly his mental and physical resources for her welfare, and giving away his money with a free hand and a warm heart to the needy and unfortunate." To help him now "is their right and their duty" as South Carolinians. Recipients of the letter were cautioned to avoid publicity, but quietly to raise a "creditable" sum. "We can then show General Hampton that it is his duty to accept what the conscience and love of the people prompt them to offer." The goal was to have all funds raised by June 15, just six weeks after the fire.

Faced with such an outpouring, Hampton relented.[37] A lot was purchased in Columbia at the corner of Barnwell and Senate Streets, and a home was built. He would be only a few blocks from his church and near to neighbors and friends.

The sight of the old man sitting on the porch of his new home became a familiar sight to Columbians. Hampton continued to express himself on the issues of the day. The fight for independence from British rule by the South African Republic and the Orange Free State attracted his sympathy. America's brief and nearly bloodless acquisition of the Spanish empire seemed to him hardly even a war. He was proud of Maj. Gen. Joseph Wheeler's part in the conflict "because you ended your career as a Confederate soldier as a member of my command."

Once a cavalry veteran asked Hampton how many Yankees he had personally dispatched in hand-to-hand combat during the war. The old man remembered eleven, "two with my sword and nine with my pistol."

"How about the two at Trevilian Station?" he replied, trying to jog the general's memory.

"Oh, well, I did not count them, they were running."[38]

Hampton was briefly involved in one more political brouhaha. As President McKinley began his second term, Republican strategists dreamed of building a "respectable," white Republican Party in the South. According to press reports, McKinley would "get rid of the negro altogether." Southern businessmen would then perhaps be attracted to the GOP. Point man for this pioneering effort was South Carolina's U.S. Senator John McLaurin. In a speech to the Manufacturer's Club in Charlotte, he declared himself still a Democrat, but he emphasized the development of Southern industry and commerce. William Jennings Bryan feared that McLaurin foreshadowed the "commercialism which has debauched municipal and state government in the north [and] will soon be apparent in the south." Tillman thought

McLaurin was either beginning his "passage into the Republican camp" or wished the Democratic Party to "become an echo."

McLaurin's apparent first goal was to recruit respectable Southern Democrats to the Republican Party by offering lucrative federal appointments. It was reported that he sent an emissary to Hampton in the spring of 1901, offering him the postmastership of Columbia. Presumably, he expected Hampton to switch his party allegiance. When questioned by a reporter, Hampton was reluctant to comment. Told that the information had come from one "in close touch" with McLaurin, Hampton responded in "his usual firm way."

"I would not accept anything in the world from that source."

McLaurin in 1890 had seconded Irby's nomination for U.S. senator in the contest to unseat Hampton.

Hampton paused, said the reporter, "and after a moment continued with significant emphasis:

" 'The people of South Carolina ought to know by this time that I cannot be bought.' "

"The best way for the Democracy of South Carolina to rebuke McLaurin," wrote one irate editor, "is to retire him from the United States Senate and send the peerless Hampton back."[39]

Hampton rode on horseback from his home to ceremonies at Elmwood Cemetery on Confederate Memorial Day, 1900. He had not been well for several months, but still made the effort.[40] After Memorial Day activities the following year, a crowd, many of them veterans, marched from the State House to Hampton's residence. The column stretched four blocks. They gathered in front of his home, shouting for their hero. Rebel yells split the air. James Hart, once a major commanding the Legion artillery, presented the men. "I have . . . heard that Rebel yell often before," smiled the old warrior, "and when I heard it from my own men, from the men I had the honor to command, I knew that we were safe." From his porch he spoke again of their common heritage.

> I want you to try to teach to your children and to your children's children that ours was not a lost cause. I want you to tell them that we were fighting for the right. . . . The greatest honor that I felt during the war was once when I came upon a poor private who was dying. I stopped beside him and he said: "I am happy to die fighting and I am proud to die fighting under you." . . . I pray God to bless you.[41]

Hampton's last public appearance was at a Charleston gathering of the alumni of South Carolina College in December 1901. He was the oldest graduate, the one surviving member of the class of 1836. While there he caught a cold that lingered. Far more serious, Dr. Taylor knew that his friend was suffering from valvular heart disease.[42]

Soon after the first of the year, Hampton felt he should put his affairs in order, making final changes to his will. Most of the estate he would leave to Daisy, the daughter who had devoted herself to caring for him for so many years.[43] March 28, 1902, was Hampton's eighty-fourth birthday. On April 1 he enjoyed a carriage drive down Main Street, but when he returned home, his strength left him.

His mind remained clear. Bishop Ellison Capers came. "From my heart," said Hampton, "I forgive all my enemies, if there are any men in South Carolina who are my enemies."

The *State* took note of his decline. "During the past few days Gen. Hampton's condition has been causing his friends much uneasiness," the paper reported on April 10. "Dr. Taylor late last night said that the general's condition was 'very low,' and that the worst might happen at any time."

The next day the general slept with the help of pain medication. The only nourishment he was able to take was a little milk. The family gathered around his bedside. Sisters Kate and Caroline, daughter Daisy, sons McDuffie and Alfred were among those there. Hampton knew the end was near. He spoke of his funeral, asking for simplicity, and that his favorite hymn, "Lead, Kindly Light," be sung at the service.

"All my people, black and white—God bless them all," was his benediction, his prayer for South Carolina.

A little later, half-conscious, he began to whisper something. They listened intently. "All is black—My children on the field—Heroes forever! forever!"

One gently asked if he meant sons Preston and Wade.

He nodded yes. The searing memory of that dark day at Burgess's Mill haunted him still.

Wade Hampton's pulse gradually grew weaker. The end came peacefully. So quiet was his last breath that Dr. Taylor had to tell the family that the old warrior was gone. It was eight-fifty on the morning of Friday, April 11, 1902.[44]

> And with the morn those angel faces smile
> Which I have loved long since, and lost awhile.

Notes

CHAPTER I

1. *State,* 11, 12, 13, and 14 April 1902; *Times and Democrat,* 16 April 1902; *News and Courier,* 12, 13, and 14 April 1902; V. L. Pendleton, "Last Words of Confederate Heroes" (Raleigh, N.C.: The Mutual Publishing Co., 1913), 7; Louis Albert Banks, *Immortal Hymns and Their Story* (Cleveland, Ohio: The Burrows Brothers Co., 1897), 31–32. The funeral is given detailed coverage in the Columbia and Charleston dailies on April 14. The editorial is from the *News and Courier,* 12 April 1902, 1.

2. Virginia G. Meynard, *The Venturers: The Hampton, Harrison, and Earle Families of Virginia, South Carolina, and Texas* (Easley, S.C.: Southern Historical Press, 1981), 1; Stebbing Shaw, *The History and Antiquities of Staffordshire*, vol. 2, part 1, (London: J. Nichols and Son, 1798–1801), 51. A broad picture of Wolverhampton and surroundings is found in D. M. Palliser, *The Staffordshire Landscape* (London: Hodder and Stoughton, 1976).

3. Meynard, *Venturers*, 2–3; Charles S. McCleskey, *The Hampton Connection: Descendants of John Hampton the Tailor* (Baton Rouge, La.: privately printed, 1975), 11; Katie Weatherford Anderson, *Standing in the Doorway of a Day Long Ago* (n.p.: privately printed, 1963), 90; Luther Wightman Hampton Jr., *Genealogy of Hampton, Boulware, Setzler, Goodwin and Related Families* (n.p.: privately printed, 1983), 1; Carey P. McCord, *The Pratt Family* (n.p.: privately printed, n.d.), 39. Of genealogical studies dealing with the Hampton family easily the best is Meynard's *Venturers*.

4. Meynard, *Venturers*, 6–27, passim.

5. Ann Fripp Hampton, "The Hampton Family of South Carolina," *The Carolina Herald*, vol. 3, no. 3 [1975], 19; Meynard, *Venturers*, 50. According to Ann Fripp Hampton ("Hampton Family," 19), "this was not the first time the names Wade and Hampton had been united, for John's [John Hampton Jr.'s] aunt had also married a Wade, and among her descendants was Hampton Wade who lived in Lunenburg County, Virginia, shortly before the Revolution."

6. Meynard, *Venturers*, 58–70, passim; Ronald Edward Bridwell, "The South's Wealthiest Planter: Wade Hampton I of South Carolina, 1754–1835" (Ph.D. dissertation, University of South Carolina, 1980), 18–19, 32, 34; Chapman J. Milling, *Red Carolinians* (Chapel Hill, N. C.: University of North Carolina Press, 1940), 313–314.

7. Joseph Johnson, *Traditions and Reminiscences Chiefly of the American Revolution in the South* (Charleston, S.C.: Walker and James, 1851), 442–443; Meynard, *Venturers*, 72–73; Milling, *Red Carolinians*, 314–315; George M. Folk, *Folk Family Tree* (n.p.: privately printed, n.d.), 215–217; Samuel Edward Mays, *Genealogy of the Mays Family and Related Families to 1929 Inclusive* (Plant City, Fl.: privately printed, 1929), 145; Ella Mulkey Range, *The Life of Reverend Philip Mulkey, His Ancestors and Descendants, 1650–1950* (n.p.: privately printed, n.d.), 11; Bridwell, "Wade Hampton I," 61, 70. The story of the Hampton massacre is part of the folklore of South Carolina and has been told in many variations. The short recounting here contains the details that seem best supported and most plausible.

8. Bridwell, "Wade Hampton I," 64–67, 72.

9. Bridwell, "Wade Hampton I," 1–2.

10. Bridwell, "Wade Hampton I," 11, 13; "Wade Hampton," *Biographical Directory of the American Congress, 1774–1927* (Washington, D.C.: Government Printing Office, 1928), 1055; Edward Hooker, *Diary of Edward Hooker 1805–1808*. In *Report of the Historical Manuscripts Commission of the American Historical Association for 1896* (Washington, D.C.: Government Printing Office, 1897), 845–846.

11. Bridwell, "Wade Hampton I," 86–88, 93, 105; Joan Schreiner Reynolds Faunt, et al., comp., *Biographical Directory of the South Carolina House of Representatives*, vol. 3 (Columbia: University of South Carolina Press, 1981), 310.

12. Bridwell, "Wade Hampton I," 117, 127, 128–129.

13. Bridwell, "Wade Hampton I," 138–141; Robert D. Bass, *Gamecock: The Life and Campaigns of General Thomas Sumter* (New York: Holt, Rinehart and Winston, 1961), 136, 145.

14. Bridwell, "Wade Hampton I," 148–149, 152, 160–162; Bass, *Gamecock*, 197.

15. Henry Lumpkin, *From Savannah to Yorktown: The American Revolution in the South*

(Columbia: University of South Carolina Press, 1981), 218; Bass, *Gamecock*, 210; Bridwell, "Wade Hampton I," 180–181.

16. Lumpkin, *Savannah to Yorktown*, 221; Bridwell, "Wade Hampton I," 194, 196, 203; Bass, *Gamecock*, 217.

17. Meynard, *Venturers*, 75, 100, 101; Bridwell, "Wade Hampton I," 380–381.

18. Meynard, *Venturers*, 108–109; Bridwell, "Wade Hampton I, " 381–382, 383; Harry Hampton, *Woods and Waters and Some Asides* (Columbia: State Printing Company, 1979), 388–391.

19. Bridwell, "Wade Hampton I," 319–320; 323–324, 379–386, 405–408; Meynard, *Venturers*, 104. "Charles Town" officially became "Charleston" in 1783.

20. Meynard, *Venturers*, 111, 113, 142.

21. Joseph S. Ames, "The Cantey Family," *The South Carolina Historical and Genealogical Magazine*, vol. xi, no. 3: 253; Meynard, *Venturers*, 117, 143; Bridwell, "Wade Hampton I," 557.

22. Bridwell, "Wade Hampton I," 387–388, 391, 419–422, 770–772.

23. "Wade Hampton," *Biographical Directory of Congress*, 1055; Bridwell, "Wade Hampton I," 230–235, 253–255; Meynard, *Venturers*, 75.

24. Bridwell, "Wade Hampton I," 271–272, 499; Hooker, *Diary*, 848, 850; Meynard, *Venturers*, 75.

25. Bridwell, "Wade Hampton I," 505, 511–512, 516, 518, 536–537.

26. Bridwell, "Wade Hampton I," 630, 632; Meynard, *Venturers*, 127.

27. Pierre Berton, *Flames across the Border: The Canadian-American Tragedy, 1813–1814* (Boston: Little, Brown and Co., 1981), 214–215; Bridwell, "Wade Hampton I," 673–674, 676.

28. Berton, *Flames*, 216–218.

29. Bridwell, "Wade Hampton I," 694–695, 697–699; Berton, *Flames*, 221–228.

30. Bridwell, "Wade Hampton I," 503, 657, 706–709.

31. Bridwell, "Wade Hampton I," 664, 744–748; Meynard, *Venturers*, 146–148; Benjamin F. Perry, *Reminiscences of Public Men with Speeches and Addresses* (Greenville, S.C.: Shannon & Co., 1889), 108–109; Edward L. Wells, *Hampton and His Cavalry in '64* (Richmond: B. F. Johnson Publishing Co., 1899), 20–21; Wade Hampton to Edward L. Wells, 17 June 1895 and 20 June 1899 (Edward L. Wells Correspondence, Charleston Library Society).

32. Bridwell, "Wade Hampton I," 557–560; Anonymous manuscript, n.d. (HFP).

33. Meynard, *Venturers*, 148–150; Charles E. Cauthen, ed., *Family Letters of the Three Wade Hamptons, 1782–1901* (Columbia: University of South Carolina Press, 1953), 9; Thomas M. Stubbs, "Garner's Ferry Road," *Names in South Carolina* vol. I, no. 2 (Winter 1954): 10. One story making the rounds had the parson who performed the ceremony receiving $500 delivered to him the following morning in a silver cup. See Bridwell, "Wade Hampton I," 754n.

34. *Times*, 13 March 1818; *City Gazette and Commercial Daily Advertiser*, 8 and 9 April 1818; Philip Freneau, "On the Emigration to America and Peopling the Western Country," *The Treasury of American Poetry* (Garden City, N.Y.: International Collectors Library, 1978), 25; Meynard, *Venturers*, 194. The Fitzsimons' home, now 54 Hasell Street, may be the oldest existing residence in the city. See Samuel Gaillard Stoney, *This Is Charleston: A Survey of the Architectural Heritage of a Unique American City* (Charleston, S.C.: Carolina Art Association, 1970), 57 and Junior League of Charleston, comp., *Historic Charleston Guidebook* (Charleston, S.C.: Nelson's Southern Printing, 1971), 85.

Chapter 2

1. Manly Wade Wellman, *Giant in Gray: A Biography of Wade Hampton of South Carolina* (New York: Charles Scribner's Sons, 1949), 17–18. This story of a family tradition was related to Wellman by Mrs. Susan Howze Hampton (1874–1959). A shorter version is in Harry Hampton, *Woods and Waters and Some Asides* (Columbia: State Printing Co., 1979), 376.

2. Anonymous manuscript, n.d. (HFP); Virginia G. Meynard, *The Venturers: The Hampton, Harrison, and Earle Families of Virginia, South Carolina, and Texas* (Easley, S.C.: Southern Historical Press, 1981), 193.

3. Meynard, *Venturers*, 195; Edward L. Wells, *Hampton and Reconstruction* (Columbia: The State Co., 1907), 14.

4. John Hammond Moore, *Columbia and Richland County: A South Carolina Community, 1740–1990* (Columbia: University of South Carolina Press, 1993), 112, 170–171; Lawrence Fay Brewster, *Summer Migrations and Resorts of South Carolina Low-Country Planters* (Durham, N.C.: Duke University Press, 1947), 75; Jane Kealhofer Simons, *A Guide to Columbia, South Carolina's Capital City* (Columbia: Columbia Chamber of Commerce, 1945), 72; Catalog, 1830 (Richland School manuscript, SCL).

5. Helen Kohn Hennig, ed., *Columbia, Capitol City of South Carolina, 1786–1936* (Columbia: The Columbia Sesqui-Centennial Commission, 1936), 92–93, 94, 135, 137, 142, 228–229, 267.

6. Maximilian LaBorde, *History of the South Carolina College* (Charleston, S.C.: Walker, Evans & Cogswell, 1874), 172, 187; Daniel Walker Hollis, *South Carolina College*, vol. 1, *The University of South Carolina* (Columbia: University of South Carolina Press, 1951), 94, 109–116, 119; Minutes, 27 November 1833 (Minutes of the Board of Trustees of the South Carolina College, SCL).

7. Edwin L. Green, *A History of the University of South Carolina* (Columbia: The State Co., 1916), 45; LaBorde, *College*, 242–243, 246; Hollis, *College*, 127–128.

8. LaBorde, *College*, 211–212, 214, 263.

9. LaBorde, *College*, 221, 270, 271, 273, 274.

10. LaBorde, *College*, 224–227.

11. Hollis, *College*, 180; LaBorde, *College*, 418–419.

12. Frank Freidel, *Francis Lieber: Nineteenth Century Liberal* (Baton Rouge: Louisiana State University Press, 1947), 129, 132; Hollis, *College*, 182–183, 187, 188; Francis Lieber, *The Life and Letters of Francis Lieber*, ed. Thomas Sergeant Perry (Boston: James R. Osgood and Co., 1882), 285.

13. Hollis, *College*, 183; LaBorde, *College*, 430–431.

14. Wade Hampton III to Peter Della Torre, 4 January 1835 (HFP); Records of members, 1835 (Clariosophic Society records, University of South Carolina Archives); Andrew Charles Moore, comp., *Roll of Students of South Carolina College, 1805–1905* (Columbia: The State Co., 1905), 15; "A Carolina Cavalier," *Program of Alumni Meeting* (n.p.: 1900).

15. LaBorde, *College*, 207.

16. Wade Hampton III to Peter Della Torre, 4 January 1835 (HFP); Treasurer's reports, 1835–1836 and receipt books, 1835–1836 (Clariosophic Society records, University of South Carolina Archives); LaBorde, *College*, 512–513.

17. *Catalogue of the Trustees, Faculty and Students of the South Carolina College* (Columbia: 1836); *Laws of the South Carolina College* (Columbia: A. S. Johnston, Printer, 1848), 57; "Order of Exercises at Commencement," filed in the faculty minutes, 1836 (Minutes of the faculty of South Carolina College, SCL). The Thomas Cooper Library at the Univer-

sity of South Carolina has on its shelves Henry Stebbing's three-volume *Lives of the Italian Poets*. Published in London in 1832, each volume bears the gold imprint "South Carolina College"; this may be one of the works consulted by Hampton.

18. *Telescope*, 14 January 1837.

19. Edward L. Wells, *Hampton and His Cavalry in '64* (Richmond: B. F. Johnson Publishing Co., 1899), 19–20; Robert W. Gibbes, *A Memoir of James De Veaux* (Columbia: J. C. Morgan's Letter Press Print, 1846), 13–14, 23.

20. Edwin J. Scott, *Random Recollections of a Long Life, 1806–1876* (Columbia: Charles A. Calvo Jr., Printer, 1884), 61; Benjamin Franklin Perry, *Reminiscences of Public Men with Speeches and Addresses* (Greenville, S.C.: Shannon & Co., 1889), 111, 112; Anonymous manuscript, n.d. (HFP).

21. Wade Hampton II to Wade Hampton I, many dates (HFP); Ronald Edward Bridwell, "The South's Wealthiest Planter: Wade Hampton I of South Carolina, 1754–1835" (Ph.D. dissertation, University of South Carolina, 1980), 749, 768; Scott, *Recollections*, 61; Wells, *Cavalry*, 16–17.

22. Bill of Josiah C. Nott, 21 December 1834 (HFP); Bridwell, "Wade Hampton I," 780–781. A story circulated years later that Wade Hampton II inherited the entire estate, a falsehood that has "given offense to some of the younger [family] members." See Kate Hampton to Means Davis, 8 July 1902 (HFP).

23. Bridwell, "Wade Hampton I," 748n; Ernest M. Lander Jr., "Dr. Thomas Cooper's Views in Retirement," *South Carolina Historical Magazine* vol. LIV (1953): 183; John B. Irving, *The South Carolina Jockey Club* (Charleston: Russell & Jones, 1857), 177, 178, 181.

24. Ann Fitzsimons Hampton to Margaret Preston, 9 June 1830 (HFP); Brewster, *Migrations*, 95; Perceval Reniers, *The Springs of Virginia: Life, Love, and Death at the Waters, 1775–1900* (Chapel Hill: University of North Carolina Press, 1941), 120.

25. Meynard, *Venturers*, 172; Perry, *Reminiscences*, 110; Anonymous manuscript, n.d. (HFP).

26. N. Louise Bailey, et al., *Biographical Directory of the South Carolina Senate, 1776–1985* (Columbia: University of South Carolina Press, 1986), vol. 1, 654 and vol. 3, 1852, 1854; Committee book entries (South Carolina Senate Committee Book, 1803–1830, SCDAH).

27. Walter Brian Cisco, *Taking a Stand: Portraits from the Southern Secession Movement* (Shippensburg: Pa.: White Mane Books, 1998), 2–3, 27; *Report of the Special Committee of the Senate of South Carolina on the Resolution Submitted by Mr. Ramsey on the Subject of State Rights* (Washington, D.C.: Duff Green, 1828), 17.

28. Henry Steele Commager, ed., *Documents of American History* (New York: Appleton-Century-Crofts, 1968), 250–251.

29. Margaret L. Coit, *John C. Calhoun: American Portrait* (Boston: Houghton Mifflin Co., 1950), 186; *Senate Journal*, 17 December 1828 (Journal of the Senate of South Carolina, 1828, SCDAH).

30. Cisco, *Stand*, 32.

31. Wade Hampton I to Goodhue & Co., 6 February 1831 (HFP); Cisco, *Stand*, 36–37.

32. Meynard, *Venturers*, 156.

33. Hampton, *Woods and Waters*, 380; Edward L. Wells, *Hampton and Reconstruction* (Columbia: The State Co., 1907), 15–18. Harry Hampton (*Woods and Waters*, p. 380) repeats an uncorroborated family story that Wade Hampton III was color blind.

34. Meynard, *Venturers*, 197; Charles E. Cauthen, ed., *Family Letters of the Three Wade Hamptons, 1782–1901* (Columbia: University of South Carolina Press, 1953), 28; James De Veaux to Wade Hampton III, 1 November 1838 (James De Veaux Papers, SCL).

35. Meynard, *Venturers*, 981, 982.

36. Meynard, *Venturers*, 978–980; *State*, 1 September 1935; Wells, *Reconstruction*, 15, 25; Jonathan Daniels, *Tar Heels: A Portrait of North Carolina* (New York: Dodd, Mead & Company, 1941), 238.

37. Paul Schullery, *The Bear Hunter's Century*, (New York: Dodd, Mead & Company, 1988), 70, 77, 83; Alfred B. Williams, *Hampton and His Red Shirts: South Carolina's Deliverance in 1876* (Charleston, S.C.: Walker, Evans & Cogswell, 1935), 90. Written when he was twenty-two years old, Hampton's letters are filled with discussion of hunting dogs. Wade Hampton III to Alexander Williams, 29 July 1840 and 24 August 1840 (Alexander Williams Papers, Duke).

38. Meynard, *Venturers*, 197; Margaret Hampton to Lavelette Floyd, 18 June 1844 (George Frederick Holmes Papers, Duke).

39. Julian A. Selby, *Memorabilia and Anecdotal Reminiscences of Columbia, S.C. and Incidents Connected Therewith* (Columbia: R. L. Bryan Co., 1905), 125–126; Hennig, *Columbia*, 382. "Columbia's first extensive fire," according to Hennig, occurred in 1842. Selby's detailed account is of an 1841 fire. He was but nine years old at the time, but claims to have "a wonderful memory."

40. *Trinity Church, Columbia, S.C.: One Hundred and Twenty-Fifth Anniversary, 1937* (Columbia: The State Co., 1937), 17; Peter J. Shand, *Address at the Laying of the Corner Stone of the New Episcopal Church, Columbia, S.C.* (Columbia: I. C. Morgan, 1845), 7, 8; Cauthen, *Letters*, 32; Meynard, *Venturers*, 169.

41. Carol Bleser, ed., *Secret and Sacred: The Diaries of James Henry Hammond, a Southern Slaveholder* (New York: Oxford University Press, 1988), 188; Carol Bleser, *The Hammonds of Redcliffe* (New York: Oxford University Press, 1981), 3–5; "James Henry Hammond" *Biographical Directory of the American Congress, 1774–1927* (Washington: Government Printing Office, 1928), 1054.

42. Bleser, *Secret and Sacred*, page 16–18. A study of 440 South Carolina slaveholders found but 12 for which there is "traditional or legal evidence of habitual cohabitation with mulatto mistresses, and it is significant that in no instance was it condoned by their neighbors." Only two in the study "enjoyed reputations as reprobates in their own time." Chalmers Gaston Davidson, *The Last Foray: The South Carolina Planters of 1860: A Sociological Study* (Columbia: University of South Carolina Press, 1971), 5.

43. Cauthen, *Letters*, 27, 30.

44. Meynard, *Venturers*, 172; Drew Gilpin Faust, *James Henry Hammond and the Old South: A Design for Mastery* (Baton Rouge: Louisiana State University Press, 1982), 243.

45. Bleser, *Secret and Sacred*, 169, 171, 176, 180.

46. Faust, *Hammond*, 243, 244; Bleser, *Secret and Sacred*, 171.

47. Bleser, *Secret and Sacred*, 120, 126, 134.

48. Bleser, *Secret and Sacred*, 172, 173, 175, 269.

49. Bleser, *Secret and Sacred*, 132, 171, 185, 234; Mary C. Simms, et al., comp. and ed., *1845–1849*, vol. II, *The Letters of William Gilmore Simms* (Columbia: University of South Carolina Press, 1953), *1845–1849*, 175, 218–219, 235–236.

50. Benjamin F. Perry, *Reminiscences of Public Men*, vol. II, *The Writings of Benjamin F. Perry* (Spartanburg, S. C.: The Reprint Co., 1980), 227; Francis W. Pickens to Lucy Holcombe, 6 December 1857 (Francis W. Pickens Papers, SCL).

51. Meynard, *Venturers*, 193. In his journal Hammond quotes an unnamed bachelor as saying that "after all the fuss made no man who values his standing could marry one of the Hampton girls." Bleser, *Secret and Sacred*, 181.

52. *The Book of Common Prayer and Administration of the Sacraments and Other Rites and Ceremonies of the Church* (New York: A. Hanford, 1838), 107.

Chapter 3

1. Virginia G. Meynard, *The Venturers: The Hampton, Harrison, and Earle Families of Virginia, South Carolina, and Texas* (Easley, S.C.: Southern Historical Press, 1981), 198–199, 516, 522, 566; Charles E. Cauthen, ed., *Family Letters of the Three Wade Hamptons, 1782–1901* (Columbia: University of South Carolina Press, 1953), 33. The tortured history of Houmas ownership is told in appendix II of Meynard's book.

2. Wade Hampton III to G. G. Skipwith, 27 June 1846 (James McDowell Papers, Duke); Wade Hampton III to Margaret Hampton, 27 July 1846 (HFP). Hampton called the museum "Madam Jureaud's."

3. Wade Hampton III to Margaret Hampton, 30 July, 1 August, and 13 August 1846 (Wade Hampton Papers, SHC); Cauthen, *Letters,* 34–36. Hampton planned to visit Paris, but there is no evidence that he did.

4. Harry Hampton, *Woods and Waters and Some Asides* (Columbia: State Printing Co., 1979), 377.

5. Meynard, *Venturers,* 527, 562; James 4:14.

6. Meynard, *Venturers,* 200, 562; Wade Hampton II to Mary Fisher Hampton, 24 December 1853 (HFP).

7. Philip M. Hamer, *The Secession Movement in South Carolina, 1847–1852* (New York: Da Capo Press, 1971), 3–4, 14, 16–17, 22; Margaret L. Coit, *John C. Calhoun: American Portrait* (Boston: Houghton Mifflin, 1950), 481; *Mercury,* 14 May, 15 May, and 16 May 1849.

8. Hamer, *Secession,* 69; Wade Hampton III to James Chesnut, 27 September 1850 (James Chesnut Papers, South Carolina Historical Society); *Proceedings of the Meeting of Delegates from the Southern Rights Association of South Carolina* (Columbia: Johnson & Cavis, 1851), 14; *Journal of the State Convention of South Carolina; Together with the Resolutions and Ordinance* (Columbia: Johnson & Cavis, 1852), 18–19.

9. U.S. Congress, *Testimony Taken by the Joint Select Committee,* vol. 2 (Washington, D.C.: Government Printing Office, 1872), 1218; Wade Hampton III to Mary Fisher Hampton, 8 March 1858, 24 April 1857, and 2 September 1855 (HFP); Wade Hampton III to Mary Fisher Hampton, 6 May 1857 (John C. Haskell Papers, SHC).

10. Ann Fripp Hampton, ed., *A Divided Heart: Letters of Sally Baxter Hampton, 1853–1862* (Spartanburg, S.C.: The Reprint Co., 1980), xi–xiv; Gordon N. Ray, ed., *The Letters and Private Papers of William Makepeace Thackery,* vol. 3 (Cambridge, Mass.: Harvard University Press, 1946), 556–557.

11. Hampton, *Divided Heart,* 29–30.

12. Hampton, *Divided Heart,* 22–23.

13. Edmund L. Drago, *Hurrah For Hampton!: Black Red Shirts during Reconstruction* (Fayetteville: University of Arkansas Press, 1998), 61; Coit, *Calhoun,* 447.

14. Julia Ward Howe, *Reminiscences, 1819–1899* (New York: Negro Universities Press, 1969), 234–235.

15. Wade Hampton III to James Henley Thornwell, 13 January 1853 (HFP); Maximilian LaBorde, *History of the South Carolina College* (Charleston, S.C.: Walker, Evans & Cogswell, Printers, 1874), 570.

16. Anonymous manuscript, n.d. (HFP); Hampton, *Woods and Waters,* 386–387.

17. Cauthen, *Letters,* 55, 58–59, 61; Wade Hampton to Mary Fisher Hampton, 27 February 1858 (HFP).

18. Ralph Henry Fletcher, "George McDuffie: Orator and Politician" (Master's thesis, University of South Carolina, 1986), 260, 266, 277; Wade Hampton III to Mary Singleton

McDuffie, 1 March 1856 (Wade Hampton Papers, Duke); Clyde N. Wilson, *Carolina Cavalier: The Life and Mind of James Johnston Pettigrew* (Athens: The University of Georgia Press, 1990), 75–76; Hampton, *Divided Heart,* 40.

19. Poem "To Miss Mary McDuffie" by Wade Hampton III, 14 February 1857 (HFP).

20. Cauthen, *Letters,* 50, 63–65, 67; Meynard, *Venturers,* 194, 579, 983; Wade Hampton to James Johnston Pettigrew, 28 May 1858 (Pettigrew Family Papers, North Carolina State Archives); Benjamin F. Perry, *Biographical Sketches of Eminent American Statesmen* (Philadelphia: The Ferree Press, 1887), 565–566; Wade Hampton to Maria Clopton, 19 September 1860 (Clopton Family Papers, Duke).

21. Wade Hampton to Mary Fisher Hampton, 30 September 1859 (HFP). Hampton had been on his way to an unnamed convention and was anxious that the reason for his absence be known, asking his sister to have a brief explanation put in the Columbia newspaper.

22. Wade Hampton [III] Papers (CSR); Meynard, *Venturers,* 200; Joan Schreiner Reynolds Faunt, et al., comps., *Biographical Directory of the South Carolina House of Representatives,* vol. 1 (Columbia: University of South Carolina Press, 1974), 366–369.

23. J. H. Easterly, ed., 1790 Constitution, Article I, Section 10 *Basic Documents of South Carolina History* (Columbia: Historical Commission of South Carolina, 1952); Faunt, *House Directory,* page 366; *Journal of the House of Representatives of South Carolina Being the Annual Session of 1855,* December 14.

24. N. Louise Bailey, et al., *Biographical Directory of the South Carolina Senate, 1776–1985* (Columbia: University of South Carolina Press, 1986), 666; *House Journal 1854,* 216–217; *House Journal 1855,* 162–164; *Journal of the Senate of South Carolina Being the Annual Session of 1859,* 57.

25. Wilton Hellams, "A History of South Carolina State Hospital (1821–1900)" (Ph.D. dissertation, University of South Carolina, 1985), 7, 12, 22–25, 31, 40, 61; *House Journal 1853,* 129, 179–180; *House Journal 1855,* 268–270; *Senate Journal 1859,* 55.

26. *House Journal 1856,* 35–36.

27. *House Journal 1856,* 51–55; 163–165.

28. Benjamin M. Palmer, *The Life and Letters of James Henley Thornwell* (Richmond: Whittet and Shepperson, 1875), 422–423.

29. Wade Hampton to James Johnston Pettigrew, 28 May 1858 (Pettigrew Family Papers, North Carolina State Archives); Bailey, *Senate Directory,* 1884; Francis Lieber, *The Life and Letters of Francis Lieber* (Boston: James R. Osgood and Co., 1882), 303–304.

30. Senate Speech of Wade Hampton, 10 December 1859 (HFP). The notion that Hampton had doubts about slavery was promoted by a grandson, but evidence is lacking. See U.S. Congress, *Acceptance and Unveiling of the Statue of Wade Hampton* (Washington, D.C.: Government Printing Office, 1929), 26.

31. Palmer, *Thornwell,* 594–595.

32. Senate Speech of Wade Hampton, 10 December 1859 (HFP).

33. *Senate Journal 1859,* 98, 136.

34. The facts do not sustain the oft-repeated characterization of Hampton as a conditional unionist in 1860. Edward Wells's claim that Hampton did not believe the election of Lincoln sufficient grounds for secession, is contradicted by Hampton's own words. See Edward L. Wells, *Hampton and Reconstruction* (Columbia: The State Co., 1907), 33. Matthew C. Butler also assumed that Hampton "was opposed to secession in 1860–61," concluding that he must have been a cooperationist because he possessed a "conservative, sedate temperament." South Carolinians of all temperaments chose to abandon the Union in 1860, and of course cooperationists were themselves in the secessionist camp. See Edwin Anderson Alderman and Joel Chander Harris, eds., vol. 5, *Library of Southern Literature*

(New Orleans, La.: The Martin & Hoyt Co., 1907), 2062. Benjamin F. Perry's remembrance of Hampton as "a Union man till his beloved native State seceded" is an accurate description of himself, not his friend. See Perry, *Biographical Sketches*, 566. Like the overwhelming majority of South Carolinians, Hampton found secession the appropriate response to Lincoln's election in 1860.

35. Walter Brian Cisco, *Taking a Stand: Portraits from the Southern Secession Movement* (Shippensburg, Pa.: White Mane Books, 1998), 80–81.

36. Steven A. Channing, *Crisis of Fear: Secession in South Carolina* (New York: Simon and Schuster, 1970), 246; Charles Edward Cauthen, *South Carolina Goes to War, 1860–1865* (Chapel Hill: University of North Carolina Press, 1950), 53.

37. Wade Hampton to Mary Fisher Hampton, 22 October and 4 November 1860 (HFP); *Daily Courier*, 26 November 1860. Although absent, on November 7 Hampton was appointed a member of the Senate Standing Committee on Federal Relations. *Mercury*, 8 November 1860.

38. Channing, *Crisis*, 245; Cauthen, *War*, 57; *Senate Journal 1860*, 15.

39. Lillian A. Kibler, "Unionist Sentiment in South Carolina in 1860," *Journal of Southern History* vol. IV, no. 3 (August 1938): 356–357; Walter Brian Cisco, *States Rights Gist: A South Carolina General of the Civil War* (Shippensburg, Pa.: White Mane Publishing Co., 1991), 44–46.

40. Channing, *Crisis*, 271; Cauthen, *War*, 46–47, 57; *Southern Enterprise*, 1 November 1860; Constitution of the Minute Men for the Defense of Southern Rights, Columbia, 7 October 1860 (Minute Men of Richland District Manuscript, SCL); *Constitution of the Minutemen for the Defence of Southern Rights* (Camden, S.C.: *Camden Weekly Journal* Press, 1860).

41. *Senate Journal 1860*, 22; Cauthen, *War*, 59–61.

42. Wade Hampton [III] Papers, (CSR): Bailey, *Senate Directory*, 1886; *Senate Journal 1860*, 3.

43. Reprinted in the *Daily Courier*, 26 November 1860; U.S. Congress, *Testimony*, vol. 2, 1218. Hampton retained the honorary title of "colonel" bestowed on him by the governor in 1837.

44. *Daily Courier*, 26 November 1860; Cauthen, *War*, 66; John Amasa May and Joan Reynolds Faunt, *South Carolina Secedes* (Columbia: University of South Carolina Press, 1960), 177.

45. *Senate Journal 1860*, 81; *Daily Southern Guardian*, 28 November 1860.

46. *Senate Journal 1860*, 114, 120. It has been suggested that secessionists somehow invented the smallpox scare to move the convention to a location more sympathetic to their cause. Evidence shows that the epidemic was real. Some seventy cases were reported, students and legislators evacuated, nearby residents refused to enter Columbia even to mail a letter, and the unprotected received vaccinations. As a more populous city, Charleston might host larger demonstrations, but in December 1860 Columbia was no less secessionist. Moving the convention and the legislature injured Columbia's civic pride. It in no way affected South Carolina's decision to secede. See Hampton, *Divided Heart*, 77, 79, 84; Cauthen, *War*, 69; *Daily Courier*, 22 December 1860.

47. Hampton, ed., *Divided Heart*, 74–76.

48. Hampton, ed., *Divided Heart*, 76.

49. Palmer, *Thornwell*, 592.

50. Mrs. Roger A. Pryor, *Reminiscences of Peace and War* (New York: The Macmillan Co., 1904), 111. Mrs. Pryor, writing more than forty years after the event, mistakenly identifies the party crasher as S.C. congressman Laurence Keitt. Keitt was that day in Charleston

signing the ordinance. See Elmer Don Herd Jr., "Chapters from the Life of a Southern Chevalier: Laurence Massillon Keitt's Congressional Years, 1853–1860" (Master's thesis, University of South Carolina, 1958), 182–183. Buchanan knew of course that South Carolina had called a convention, but was "very anxious for the Act of secession not to take effect" until he left office. See L. Washington to James Chesnut, 10 December 1860 (James Chesnut Papers, South Carolina Historical Society).

CHAPTER 4

1. E. Milby Burton, *The Siege of Charleston 1861–1865* (Columbia: University of South Carolina Press, 1970), 2, 9–16, 18–19.

2. Ann Fripp Hampton, ed., *A Divided Heart: Letters of Sally Baxter Hampton, 1853–1862* (Spartanburg, S.C.: The Reprint Co., 1980), 97; *Journal of the Senate of South Carolina Being the Annual Session of 1861*, 191.

3. *Mercury,* 30 April 1861; Alexander K. McClure, *Recollections of Half a Century* (Salem, Mass.: The Salem Press, 1902), 408; *Daily Courier,* 29 December 1860; Edwin Anderson Alderman and Joel Chandler Harris, eds., *Library of Southern Literature* vol. 5 (New Orleans: The Martin & Hoyt Company, 1907) 2061; Virginia G. Meynard, *The Venturers: The Hampton, Harrison, and Earle Families of Virginia, South Carolina, and Texas* (Easley, S.C.: Southern Historical Press, 1981), 196; U.S. Congress, *Testimony Taken by the Joint Select Committee,* vol. 2 (Washington, D.C.: Government Printing Office, 1872) 1218.

4. Walter Brian Cisco, *States Rights Gist: A South Carolina General of the Civil War* (Shippensburg, Pa.: White Mane Publishing Co., 1991), 31–33, 50–51.

5. Walter Brian Cisco, *Taking a Stand: Portraits from the Southern Secession Movement* (Shippensburg, Pa.: White Mane Books, 1998), 84, 105, 107–112.

6. C. Vann Woodward, ed., *Mary Chesnut's Civil War* (New Haven, Conn.: Yale University Press, 1981), 51.

7. Wade Hampton to Mary Fisher Hampton, 27 March and 9 April 1861 (HFP).

8. P. G. T. Beauregard to Jefferson Davis, 21 April 1861 (P. G. T. Beauregard Papers, LC). Hampton's appointment was finally confirmed by the Provisional Congress of the Confederate States on 15 February 1862, to take rank from 12 July 1861. See *Journal of the Congress of the Confederate States of America, 1861–1865,* vol. 1 (Washington, D.C.: Government Printing Office, 1904) 437, 839.

9. Wade Hampton to Mary Fisher Hampton, 24 April 1861 (HFP); Mark Mayo Boatner, III, *Encyclopedia of the American Revolution* (New York: David McKay Co., Inc., 1975), 615; Woodward, *Civil War,* p. 55.

10. Note from Mary Fisher Hampton to Mary McDuffie Hampton on the envelope of Wade Hampton's letter to Mary Fisher Hampton, 24 April 1861 (HFP); Charles E. Cauthen, ed., *Family Letters of the Three Wade Hamptons, 1782–1901* (Columbia: University of South Carolina Press, 1953), 73.

11. *Daily Courier,* 3 May 1861. Also in U.S. War Department, comp., *War of the Rebellion: A Compilation of the Official Records of the Union and Confederate Armies,* ser. 4, vol. 1 (Washington, D.C.: Government Printing Office, 1880–1901), 303–305.

12. Cauthen, *Letters,* 73; *Daily Courier,* 3 May 1861.

13. *Official Records,* ser. 4, vol. 1, 296; *Daily Courier,* 29 May 1861.

14. William C. Davis, ed., *The Confederate General* vol. 2 (n.p.: National Historical Society, 1991) 17; Frank Freidel, *Francis Lieber: Nineteenth Century Liberal* (Baton Rouge, La.: LSU Press, 1947), 306.

15. Clement A. Evans, ed., *South Carolina*, vol. 5, *Confederate Military History* (Atlanta: Confederate Publishing, 1899), 395; Patricia L. Faust, ed., *Historical Times Illustrated Encyclopedia of the Civil War* (New York: Harper Perennial, 1991), 301.

16. N. Louise Bailey, et al., *Biographical Directory of the South Carolina Senate, 1776–1985* (Columbia: University of South Carolina Press, 1986), 1045.

17. *Daily Courier*, 28 June 1861; Janet B. Hewett, ed., *South Carolina Confederate Soldiers 1861–1865*, vol. 2 (Wilmington, N.C.: Broadfoot Publishing Co., 1998), 537; Henry J. Smith Papers (CSR-SC).

18. Benjamin F. Perry, *Biographical Sketches of Eminent American Statesmen* (Philadelphia: The Ferree Press, 1887), 567; John Coxe, "Wade Hampton," *Confederate Veteran* vol. XXX, no. 12 (December 1922): 460; *Southern Enterprise*, 8 November and 20 December 1860.

19. *Daily Courier*, 28 June 1861; John Coxe, "The Battle of First Manassas," *Confederate Veteran* vol. XIII, no. 1 (January 1915): 24; William L. M. Austin Papers (CSR-SC).

20. U. R. Brooks, *Butler and His Cavalry in the War of Secession, 1861–1865* (Columbia: The State Co., 1909), 62; Davis, ed., *General*, vol. 1, 151.

21. Coxe, "Hampton," 460; Wade Hampton to Benjamin F. Perry, 20 Mary 1861 (Benjamin F. Perry Papers, Alabama Department of Archives and History).

22. Thomas E. Screven Papers, (CSR-SC); Hewett, *Soldiers*, vol. 2, 80; Cisco, *Gist*, 20–21.

23. Hewett, *Soldiers*, vol. 2, 81. Some unsuccessful applicants for membership in the Legion included the Charleston Riflemen, the Campbell Rifles of Yorkville, and the Cowpens Cavalry of Spartanburg. See Ron Field, *The Hampton Legion, Part 1: Regimental History* (Gloucestershire, England: Design Folio, 1994), 55n.

24. U. R. Brooks, *Stories of the Confederacy* (Columbia: The State Co., 1912), 246–247; *Daily Courier*, 7 June 1861; Bailey, *Senate Directory*, 683–684; Herman Hattaway, *General Stephen D. Lee*, (Jackson: University Press of Mississippi, 1976), 28.

25. *Daily Courier*, 13 and 15 June 1861.

26. *Daily Courier*, 29 May 1861, 20 and 27 June 1861; Coxe, "Hampton," 461; Brooks, *Stories*, 248; Field, *Hampton Legion*, 52.

27. Wade Hampton to William Porcher Miles, 14 December 1861 (William Porcher Miles Papers, SHC); Bailey, *Senate Directory*, 825; *Daily Courier*, 13 June 1861; Hewett, *Soldiers*, 533; Brooks, *Cavalry*, 556.

28. Mary Conner Moffett, ed., *Letters of General James Conner, C.S.A.* (Columbia: R. L. Bryan Co., 1950), 26–29.

29. Coxe, "Hampton," 460; Coxe, "Manassas," 24; Field, *Hampton Legion*, 37–39.

30. Moffett, *Conner*, 34.

31. Wade Hampton to P. G. T. Beauregard, 10 June 1861 (Wade Hampton Papers, Duke); Moffett, *Conner*, 31–33.

32. *Daily Courier*, 28 June 1861; Moffett, *Conner*, 31, 33.

33. Coxe, "Manassas," 24; Moffett, *Conner*, 31–33; *Daily Courier*, 4 and 6 July 1861.

34. Coxe, "Manassas," 24; Woodward, *Civil War*, 91; Brooks, *Stories*, 248; Cauthen, *Letters*, 74; C. Vann Woodward and Elizabeth Muhlenfeld, eds., *The Private Mary Chesnut: The Unpublished Civil War Diaries* (New York: Oxford University Press, 1984), 90.

35. Douglas Southall Freeman, *Lee's Lieutenants: A Study in Command*, vol. 1 (New York: Charles Scribner's Sons, 1942), 94; Coxe, "Hampton," 460; Woodward, *Civil War*, 102. Hampton dismissed rumors that any in the Legion were guilty of "mutinous conduct." See Wade Hampton note, n.d. (HFP).

36. Coxe, "Manassas," 24; Cauthen, *Letters*, 74; Richard Habersham to Bernard and

Emma Habersham, 19 July 1861 (Habersham Family Papers, LC); Isabella Middleton Leland, ed., "Middleton Correspondence, 1861–1865," *The South Carolina Historical Magazine* vol. 64 (1963): 99–100; Moffett, *Conner,* 35; *Richmond Enquirer,* 19 July 1861.

37. The myriad details of First Manassas are masterfully brought together by William C. Davis, *Battle at Bull Run: A History of the First Major Campaign of the Civil War* (Mechanicsburg, Pa.: Stackpole Books, 1977).

38. Coxe, "Manassas," 24; Richard Habersham to Bernard and Emma Habersham, 19 July 1861 (Habersham Family Papers, LC).

39. Richard Habersham to Emma Habersham, 26 July 1861 (Habersham Family Papers, LC); Coxe, "Manassas," 24; Samuel Elias Mays, "Sketches from the Journal of a Confederate Soldier," *Tyler's Quarterly Historical and Genealogical Magazine* vol. V (1924): 45, 47; Moffett, *Conner,* 37.

40. Coxe, "Manassas," 24–25; *Daily Courier,* 7 and 8 August 1861.

41. *Official Records,* ser. 1, vol. 2, 566; *Daily Courier,* 8 August 1861; Coxe, "Manassas," 25; Richard Habersham to Emma Habersham, 26 July 1861 (Habersham Family Papers, LC).

42. *Official Records,* ser. 1, vol. 2, 559, 566; Kate Virginia Cox Logan, *My Confederate Girlhood* (Richmond: Garrett & Massie, Inc., 1932), 173.

43. *Official Records,* ser. 1, vol. 2, 567; Logan, *Girlhood,* 121.

44. James Lowndes to "Cousin Mattie," 26 July 1861 (James Lowndes Papers, SCL): William Parker Snow, *Southern Generals, Their Lives and Campaigns* (New York: Charles B. Richardson, 1866), 494–495; *Richmond Enquirer,* 26 July 1861.

45. *Official Records,* ser. 1, vol. 2, 567; *Daily Courier,* 7 August 1861; JoAnna M. McDonald, *"We Shall Meet Again:" The First Battle of Manassas (Bull Run) July 18–21, 1861* (Shippensburg, Pa.: White Mane Books, 1999), 206n.

46. *Official Records,* ser. 1, vol. 2, 406, 567; *Daily Courier,* 7 August 1861; Cox, "Manassas," 26; John Bratton to his wife, 23 July 1861 (John Bratton Papers, SHC); Cauthen, *Letters,* 75.

47. Logan, *Girlhood,* 128–129; *Official Records,* ser. 1, vol. 2, 474, 491–492, 500.

48. *Official Records,* ser. 1, vol. 2, 567. "The Cavalry and the Arty of the command," wrote Hampton, "did not reach Manassas in time to share in the great honor won by their comrades & they as well as myself regretted their absence." Wade Hampton note, n.d. (HFP).

49. Woodward and Muhtenfeld, *Private,* 100, 115; Woodward, *Civil War,* 147; Shelby Foote, *The Civil War: A Narrative,* vol. 1 (New York: Vintage Books, 1986), 84; Wade Hampton to Mrs. [Mary] Singleton, 5 September 1861 (HFP).

50. Woodward, *Civil War,* 106.

51. Cauthen, *Letters,* 74–75; John Bratton to his wife, 25 July 1861 (John Bratton Papers, SHC); Mary Hampton to "Aunt Martha," 2 September 1861 (Mary S. McDuffie Papers, Duke); Brooks, *Stories,* 248. Doctors may have later suggested to Hampton that the missile exited the wound. Only many years after the war did physicians confirm that the object was indeed still there and might be surgically removed. "But I told them," said Hampton, "that as I had carried that ball since July 21, 1861, with very little inconvenience, I would continue to carry it to the end." See Coxe, "Hampton," 462.

52. Wade Hampton to Mrs. [Mary] Singleton, 5 September 1861 (HFP).

CHAPTER 5

1. Quoted in the *Daily Southern Guardian,* 30 July 1861; William K. Bachman to James Lowndes, 16 February 1864 (CSR-SC).

2. John Coxe, "Wade Hampton," *Confederate Veteran* vol. xxx, no. 12 (December 1922) 461; U. R. Brooks, *Stories of the Confederacy* (Columbia: The State Co., 1912), 278–279; William J. Rivers, *Rivers' Account of the Raising of Troops in South Carolina for State and Confederate Service, 1861–1865* (Columbia: The Bryan Printing Co., 1899), 17.

3. Samuel Elias Mays, "Sketches from the Journal of a Confederate Soldier," *Tyler's Quarterly Historical and Genealogical Magazine* vol. V, (1924) 45–53; Ron Field, *The Hampton Legion, Part 1: Regimental History* (Gloucestershire, England: Design Folio, 1994), 39–48.

4. Coxe, "Hampton," 460–461.

5. Coxe, "Hampton," 461; Charles E. Cauthen, ed., *Family Letters of the Three Wade Hamptons, 1782–1901* (Columbia: University of South Carolina Press, 1953), 76; Field, *Hampton Legion,* 10. In the spring of 1862 Hampton responded to his sister's complaint that he had neglected to write as often as she thought he should. "Now for the record. Since I went to Richmond [about two months earlier] I have written 18 letters to Mary and 5 to you." He explained how busy he was, promised to write more often, and assured her of his love. Hampton's letters to wife Mary may have been lost when Sherman's troops burned his home in 1865. Millwood and Woodlands were also burned. An accidental fire destroyed Hampton's residence in 1899. It is fortunate that any letters survived.

6. James Lowndes to "Cousin Mattie," 13 September 1861 (James Lowndes Papers, SCL); Muster roll, James Lowndes Papers (CSR-SC).

7. Coxe, "Hampton," 461; U.S. War Department, comp., *War of the Rebellion: A Compilation of the Official Records of the Union and Confederate Armies,* ser. 1, vol. 5 (Washington, D.C.: Government Printing Office, 1880–1901), 779; *Daily Courier,* 2 October 1862; U.S. War Department, comp., *War of the Rebellion: A Compilation of the Official Records of the Union and Confederate Navies,* ser. 1, vol. 4 (Washington, D.C.: Government Printing Office, 1894–1931), 689; Cauthen, *Letters,* 77.

8. Coxe, "Hampton," 461; *Official Records,* ser. 1, vol. 5, 913, 961; Wade Hampton to P. G. T. Beauregard, 17 November 1861 (Galesburg, Ill.: Sang-Lee Civil War Collection, Knox College).

9. *Official Records,* ser. 1, vol. 5, 1002; Cauthen, *Letters,* 80; Wade Hampton to Mary Fisher Hampton, 15 January 1862 (HFP).

10. Wade Hampton to William Porcher Miles, 10 December 1861 (William Porcher Miles Papers, SHC); Wade Hampton to Mary Fisher Hampton, 17 December 1861 (HFP); Cauthen, *Letters,* 78.

11. *Daily Courier,* 30 November 1861 and 11 March 1862.

12. *Official Records,* ser. 1, vol. 5, 986–987.

13. Cauthen, *Letters,* 78–81; Wade Hampton to Mary Hampton, telegram dated 13 January 1862 (HFP).

14. *Official Records,* ser. 1, vol. 5, 1030; *Official Records,* ser. 1, vol. 2, 483; Cauthen, *Letters,* 85.

15. *Official Records,* ser. 4, vol. 1, 902, 907.

16. Wade Hampton to Mary Fisher Hampton, 25 March 1862 (HFP); *Daily Southern Guardian,* 16 May 1862.

17. Douglas Southall Freeman, *Lee's Lieutenants: A Study in Command,* vol. 1 (New York: Charles Scribner's Sons, 1942), 171–173.

18. Freeman, *Lee's Lieutenants,* 171–173; Kevin Conley Ruffner, "Before the Seven Days: The Reorganization of the Confederate Army in the Spring of 1862," in *The Peninsula Campaign of 1862: Yorktown to the Seven Days,* ed. William J. Miller, vol. 1 (Campbell, Calif.: Savas Woodbury Publishers, 1995), 69; Wade Hampton to Mary Fisher Hampton, 25 March 1862 (HFP).

19. Freeman, *Lee's Lieutenants*, vol. 1, 134–135, 136n.

20. *Official Records*, ser. 1, vol. 5, 533–534, 535, 1082.

21. *Official Records*, ser. 1, vol. 5, 530.

22. Freeman, *Lee's Lieutenants*, vol. 1, 140–141, 155, 174, 188; *Official Records*, ser. 1, vol. 5, 1106.

23. *Official Records*, ser. 1, vol. 2, pt. 1, 602; *Daily Southern Guardian*, 29 May 1862.

24. Freeman, *Lee's Lieutenants*, vol. 1, 193–194; *Official Records*, ser. 1, vol. 2, pt. 1, 628–633; *Official Records*, ser. 1, vol. 2, pt. 3, 500.

25. *Official Records*, ser. 1, vol. 5, 1058; Wade Hampton to Mary Fisher Hampton, 25 March 1862 (HFP).

26. Wade Hampton to Mary Fisher Hampton, 21 May 1862 (HFP). He did not at this time consider political office to be his "business." In August 1861 Hampton had been mentioned as a possible Confederate States Senate candidate, although there is no evidence of his interest in the position. On 8 October 1861 he resigned his seat in the state senate. See C. Vann Woodward and Elizabeth Muhlenfeld, eds., *The Private Mary Chesnut: The Unpublished Civil War Diaries* (New York: Oxford Universities Press, 1984), 121–122; N. Louise Bailey, et al., *Biographical Directory of the South Carolina Senate, 1776–1985* (Columbia: University of South Carolina Press, 1986), 666. What is supposed to be the text of Hampton's senate resignation letter is printed in Edwin Anderson Alderman and Joel Chandler Harris, eds., *Library of Southern Literature*, vol. 5 (New Orleans, La.: The Martin & Hoyt Co., 1907) 2062. The actual one-sentence letter appears in the *Senate Journal* for 8 October 1861.

27. Marcus J. Wright, *General Officer's of the Confederate Army* (New York: The Neale Publishing Co., 1911), 82; *Journal of the Congress of the Confederate States of America, 1861–1865*, vol. 2 (Washington, D.C.: Government Printing Office, 1904), 298–299, 392; *Official Records*, ser. 1, vol. 2, pt. 3, 543. Congress was in adjournment when Hampton was promoted. His and many other nominations were confirmed by the Senate on 30 September 1862,.

28. *Daily Courier*, 12 June 1862.

29. Freeman, *Lee's Lieutenants*, vol. 1, 211; Wade Hampton to Mary Fisher Hampton, 21 May 1862 (HFP).

30. Wade Hampton to Mary Fisher Hampton, 26 May 1862 (HFP).

31. Freeman, *Lee's Lieutenants*, vol. 1, 225–231; Stephen W. Sears, *To the Gates of Richmond: The Peninsula Campaign* (New York: Ticknor & Fields, 1992), 138.

32. Robert Underwood Johnson and Clarence Buel, eds., *Battles and Leaders of the Civil War*, vol. 2 (New York: The Century Co., 1884–1887), 242, 245–246; Sears, *Gates*, 137; Gustavus W. Smith, *The Battle of Seven Pines* (New York: C. G. Crawford, 1891), 87.

33. Walter Clark, ed., *Histories of the Several Regiments and Battalions from North Carolina in the Great War 1861–'65*, vol. 1 (Raleigh, N.C.: E. M. Uzzell, 1901), 772; Smith, *Seven Pines*, 88; Alexander S. Webb III, *The Peninsula: McClellan's Campaign of 1862* (New York: Charles Scribner's Sons, 1881), 111–113; *Daily Courier*, 10 June 1862; Cuathen, *Letters*, 86.

34. C. Vann Woodward, ed., *Mary Chesnut's Civil War* (New Haven, Conn.: Yale University Press, 1981), 373; Clement A. Evans, ed., South Carolina, vol. 5, *Confederate Military History* (Atlanta: Confederate Publishing, 1899), 56.

35. Gilbert E. Govan and James W. Livingwood, *General Joseph E. Johnston, C.S.A.: A Different Valor* (New York: Bobbs-Merrill Co., Inc., 1956), 156, 157; Freeman, *Lee's Lieutenants*, vol. 1, 263.

36. Cauthen, *Letters*, 85–86; Wade Hampton to Mary Fisher Hampton, 8 June 1862 (HFP).

37. *Official Records,* ser. 1, vol. 2, pt. 1, 991.

38. *Official Records,* ser. 1, vol. 2, pt. 3, 589; Smith, *Seven Pines,* 101.

39. Journal of James Washington Moore, 13 June 1862 (Journal of James Washington Moore, SCL); Mary Conner Moffett, ed., *Letters of General James Conner, C.S.A.* (Columbia: R. L. Bryan Co., 1950), 99.

40. Woodward, *Civil War,* 376.

41. Woodward, *Civil War,* 395.

42. Woodward, *Civil War,* 342.

43. Woodward, *Civil War,* 396–397.

44. Woodward, *Civil War,* 391–392, 393.

45. John Esten Cooke, *Wearing of the Gray* (Bloomington: Indiana University Press, 1959), 51–55. In 1865 Hampton was described as having blue eyes, a dark complexion, dark hair, with a height of 5′ 11.5″. See John Hope Franklin, *Reconstruction: After the Civil War* (Chicago: University of Chicago Press, 1961), 23 opposite.

CHAPTER 6

1. Stephen W. Sears, *To the Gates of Richmond: The Peninsula Campaign* (New York: Ticknor & Fields, 1992), 189–190.

2. Sears, *Gates,* 210, 249.

3. U.S. War Department, comp., *War of the Rebellion: A Compilation of the Official Records of the Union and Confederate Armies,* ser. 1, vol. 11, pt. 2 (Washington, D.C.: Government Printing Office, 1880–1901), 756.

4. Official Records, ser. 1, vol. 11, pt. 2 484, 592–593; *Official Records,* ser. 1, vol. 51, pt. 2, 585. The Third Brigade had previously been commanded by Brig. Gen. William Booth Taliaferro (pronounced Tarl-iver). Hampton said that he was given two of Jackson's brigades, but the other "had to be sent back to guard prisoners." Charles Marshall, *An Aide-de Camp of Lee* (Boston: Little, Brown and Co., 1927), 110.

5. Gary W. Gallagher, ed., *Fighting for the Confederacy: The Personal Recollections of General Edward Porter Alexander* (Chapel Hill: University of North Carolina Press, 1989), 105, 108; Marshall, *Aide-de-Camp,* 111; Edward Porter Alexander, *Military Memoirs of a Confederate* (Bloomington: Indiana University Press, 1962), 148.

6. Alexander, *Memoirs,* 150–151; Gallagher, *Fighting for the Confederacy,* 108–109; Marshall, *Aide-de-Camp,* 111–112.

7. *Official Records,* ser. 1, vol. 11, pt. 2, 593; Sears, *Gates,* 343.

8. James I. Robertson, *Stonewall Jackson: The Man, the Soldier, the Legend* (New York: Macmillan Publishing USA, 1997), 495, 498; Gallagher, *Fighting for the Confederacy,* 109; Marshall, *Aide-de-Camp,* 112.

9. Douglas Southall Freeman, *Lee's Lieutenants: A Study in Command,* vol. 1 (New York: Charles Scribner's Sons, 1942), 643; *Official Records,* ser. 1, vol. 21, 1067; *Official Records,* ser. 1, vol. 11, pt. 3, 657.

10. Charles E. Cauthen, ed., *Family Letters of the Three Wade Hamptons, 1782–1901* (Columbia: University of South Carolina Press, 1953), 87; Wade Hampton to Mary Fisher Hampton, 26 July 1862 (HFP).

11. *Official Records,* ser. 1, vol. 12, pt. 3, 920.

12. Emory Thomas, *Bold Dragoon: The Life of J. E. B. Stuart* (New York: Harper & Row, 1986), 62.

13. John Esten Cooke, *Wearing of the Gray* (Bloomington: Indiana University Press, 1959), 7, 12–13.

14. Heros von Borcke and Justus Scheibert, *The Great Cavalry Battle of Brandy Station, 9 June 1863* (Winston Salem, N.C.: Palaemon Press Ltd., 1976), 119–120.

15. Stephen Z. Starr, vol. 1: *From Fort Sumter to Gettysburg, 1861–1863, The Union Cavalry in the Civil War,* 3 vols. (Baton Rouge: Louisiana State University Press, 1979, 65, 66, 218, 219, 228, 232; Michael Blake, *American Civil War Cavalry* (London: Almark Publishing Co., 1973), 4, 5, 7, 18, 40, 51; Phillip St. George Cooke, *Cavalry Tactics or, Regulations for the Instruction, Formations, and Movements of the Cavalry of the Army and Volunteers of the United States* (Philadelphia: J. B. Lippincott & Co., 1862), 1. "*Every man* in the Laurel Brigade," Brig. Gen. Thomas Rosser would later state, "was equipped with saddle, bridle, halter, saddle pockets, carbine, sabre and pistol captured from the Yankees." See Thomas Rosser to Edward L. Wells, 25 May 1898 (Edward L. Wells Correspondence, Charleston Library Society).

16. Walter Clark, ed., *Histories of the Several Regiments and Battalions from North Carolina in the Great War 1861–'65* (Raleigh, N.C.: E. M. Uzzell, 1901), 421; U. R. Brooks, *Stories of the Confederacy* (Columbia: The State Co., 1912), 67.

17. Wade Hampton to Mary Fisher Hampton, 11 August 1862 (HFP).

18. *Official Records,* ser. 1, vol. 11, pt. 2, 957–958; Brooks, *Stories,* 70–72.

19. *Official Records,* ser. 1, vol. 12, pt. 3, 942; *Official Records,* ser. 1, vol. 51, pt., 2, 609; Brooks, *Stories,* 76–77.

20. Wade Hampton to Mary Fisher Hampton, 11 August 1862 (HFP); Virginia G. Meynard, *The Venturers: The Hampton, Harrison, and Earle Families of Virginia, South Carolina and Texas* (Easley, S.C.: Southern Historical Press, 1981), 532–533; *Official Records,* ser. 1, vol. 14, 575. Frank Hampton's name appears on a November 1862 petition requesting that his Second South Carolina Regiment be sent to South Carolina. See Frank Hampton Papers (CSR-SC).

21. Hudson Strode, *Jefferson Davis: Confederate President* (New York: Harcourt, Brace & World, Inc., 1959), 301; James Simons Journal, 6 September 1862 (James Simons Papers, South Carolina Historical Society).

22. *Official Records,* ser. 1, vol. 19, pt. 1, 814, 822; Brooks, *Stories,* 77.

23. Brooks, *Stories,* 79–80.

24. *Official Records,* ser. 1, vol. 19, pt. 1, 815, 822.

25. *Official Records,* ser. 1, vol. 19, pt. 1, 822–823; *Stories,* 81–83; U. R. Brooks, *Butler and His Cavalry in the War of Secession, 1861–1865* (Camden, S.C.: Gray Fox Books, n.d.), 64–65.

26. Freeman, *Lee's Lieutenants,* vol. 2, 173.

27. *Official Records,* ser. 1, vol. 19, pt. 1, 816–817, 823–824; Brooks, *Stories,* 83–84; *Southern Historical Society Papers,* vol. xxv (1897): 148. Preston's words are put in the first person, rather than in the odd third person quotation given in the source.

28. *Official Records,* ser. 1, vol. 19, pt. 1, pp. 818–819, 824; Freeman, *Lee's Lieutenants,* vol. 2, 199; Brooks, *Stories,* 90.

29. *Official Records,* ser. 1, vol. 19, pt. 1, 819–820.

30. *Official Records,* ser. 1, vol. 19, pt. 1, 820–821, 824; Heros von Borcke, *Memoirs of the Confederate War for Independence,* vol. 1 (New York: Peter Smith, 1938), 251–256; Clark, *N.C. Regiments,* 421.

31. *Official Records,* ser. 1, vol. 19, pt. 1, 821; *Official Records,* ser. 1, vol. 19, pt. 2, 12–14.

32. Brooks, *Stories,* 96–97; Wade Hampton to Mary Fisher Hampton, 5 October 1862 (HFP).

33. "Correspondence between Colonel S. Bassett French and General Wade Hampton," *Southern Historical Society Papers* vol. II (1876): 31–32.

34. H. B. McClellan, *The Life and Campaigns of Major-General J. E. B. Stuart* (Boston: Houghton, Mifflin and Co., 1885), 136–137; *Official Records*, ser. 1, vol. 19, pt. 2, 52, 57; Brooks, *Stories*, 97.

35. *Official Records*, ser. 1, vol. 19, pt. 2, 52, 57; Brooks, *Stories*, 98; Edward L. Wells, *Hampton and His Cavalry in '64* (Richmond: B. F. Johnson Publishing Co., 1899), 64.

36. Wells, *Hampton*, 99–100; *Official Records*, ser. 1, vol 19, pt. 2, 55, 56; McClellan, *Life and Campaigns*, 140.

37. Brooks, *Stories*, 100–101.

38. McClellan, *Life and Campaigns*, 140; *Official Records*, ser. 1, vol. 19, pt. 2, 57. Hampton reported the Home Guard skirmish as occurring at St. Thomas. A veteran writing two years later (reprinted in Brooks, *Stories*, 101) remembered shots being fired in Mercersburg.

39. *Official Records*, ser. 1, vol. 19, pt. 2, 59, 60, 61, 62, 64; *Times and Democrat*, 14 May 1902.

40. *Official Records*, ser. 1, vol. 19, pt. 2, 52, 57; Brooks, *Stories*, 102; Brooks, *Butler and His Cavalry*, 81; Wells, *Hampton and His Cavalry*, 57–58; McClellan, *Life and Campaigns*, 142–143. Demanding the surrender of Chambersburg prior to its occupation and sending in a flag of truce were actions that both Hampton and Stuart in their individual reports claimed as their own.

41. *Official Records*, ser. 1, vol. 19, pt. 2, 65.

42. McClellan, *Life and Campaigns*, 144–146; Alex K. McClure to Edward L. Wells, 16 May 1907 (Edward L. Wells Correspondence, Charleston Library Society); Freeman, *Lee's Lieutenants*, vol. 2, 287, 290.

43. *Official Records*, ser. 1, vol. 19, pt. 2, 57; Brooks, *Stories* 102–103.

44. *Official Records*, ser. 1, vol. 19, pt. 2, 51, 52, 53, 54, 58–59; Brooks, *Stories*, 106; Clark, *N.C. Regiments*, 421.

45. *Official Records*, ser. 1, vol. 19, pt. 2, 53–54, 58; Brooks, *Stories*, 107.

46. Lynda Lasswell Crist, ed., *The Papers of Jefferson David*, vol. 8, (Baton Rouge: Louisiana State University Press, 1995), 463; Cuathen, *Letters*, 87–88.

47. *Official Records*, ser. 1, vol. 19, pt. 2, 143–145.

48. *Official Records*, ser. 1, vol. 19, pt. 2, 712–713; *Official Records*, ser. 1, vol. 51, pt. 2, 648.

49. Cauthen, *Letters*, 87.

50. *Official Records*, ser. 1, vol 21, 15–16, 1051.

51. *Official Records*, ser. 1, vol 21, 689–691; Brooks, *Stories*, 120–121.

52. *Official Records*, ser. 1, vol. 21, 1067.

53. *Official Records*, ser. 1, vol 21, 694–697; Freeman, *Lee's Lieutenants*, vol. 2, 399.

54. *Official Records*, ser. 1, vol. 21, 731–732, 735–736; Wade Hampton to Mary Fisher Hampton, 2 January 1863 (HFP).

55. *Official Records*, ser. 1, vol. 21, 713, 734. The veteran (D. B. Rea) who wrote "Sketches of Hampton's Cavalry" (Brooks, *Stories*, 125) had the telegram directed to Lincoln himself and included the text.

56. *Official Records*, ser. 1, vol. 21, 736; Wade Hampton to Mary Fisher Hampton, 2 January 1863 (HFP).

57. *Official Records*, ser. 1, vol. 21, 1114–1115; Wade Hampton to Mary Fisher Hampton, 2 January 1863 (HFP); Cauthen, *Letters*, 89–90.

58. Brooks, *Stories*, 127–128; Wade Hampton to Mary Fisher Hampton, 12 January 1863 (HFP); Cauthen, *Letters*, 92

59. Wade Hampton to Mary Fisher Hampton, 12 January 1863 (HFP); Cauthen, *Letters*, 92.

CHAPTER 7

1. U.S. War department, comp., *War of the Rebellion: A Compilation of the Official Records of the Union and Confederate Armies*, ser. 1, vol. 25, pt. 1 (Washington, D.C.: Government Printing Office, 1880–1901), 9; Wade Hampton to Mary Fisher Hampton, 27 January 1863 (HFP); Wade Hampton to Louis T. Wigfall, 19 January 1863 (HFP).

2. Wade Hampton to Louis T. Wigfall, 16 February 1863 (HFP).

3. *Official Records*, ser. 1, vol. 25, pt. 2, 654; U. R. Brooks, *Stories of the Confederacy* (Columbia: The State Co., 1912), 129.

4. *Daily Southern Guardian*, 27 February 1863; E. Milby Burton, *The Siege of Charleston, 1861–1865* (Columbia: University of South Carolina Press, 1970), 141. Wade and Mary Hampton's son Alfred was born in 1863. Virginia G. Meynard, *The Venturers: The Hampton, Harrison, and Earle Families of Virginia, South Carolina and Texas* (Easley, S.C.: Southern Historical Press, 1981), 588.

5. *Daily Courier*, 14 and 20 March 1863; Wade Hampton to Louis T. Wigfall, 22 August 1863 (Louis T. Wigfall Papers, The Center for American History).

6. Wade Hampton to P. G. T. Beauregard, 6 April 1863 (Wade Hampton [III] Papers, CSR); *Official Records*, ser. 1, vol. 14, 890; Burton, *Siege*, 140; *Daily Courier*, 10 April 1863.

7. Edward G. Longacre, *The Cavalry at Gettysburg* (Cranbury, N.J.: Associated University Presses, 1986), 58–60.

8. *Official Records*, ser. 1, vol. 25, pt. 1, 1047; *Official Records*, ser. 1, vol. 25, pt. 2, 771–772.

9. Longacre, *Cavalry*, 17–18; *Official Records*, ser. 1, vol. 25, pt. 2, 825.

10. *Official Records*, serv. 1, vol. 25, pt. 2, 836; Charles E. Cauthen, ed., *Family Letters of the Three Wade Hamptons, 1782–1901* (Columbia: University of South Carolina Press, 1953), 93.

11. Wade Hampton to Mary Fisher Hampton, 13 May 1863 and 25 May 1863 (HFP).

12. Longacre, *Cavalry*, 40–41; Douglas Southall Freeman, *Lee's Lieutenants: A Study in Command*, vol. 3 (New York: Charles Scribner's Sons, 1944), 1–3; U. R. Brooks, *Butler and His Cavalry in the War of Secession, 1861–1865* (Columbia: The State Co., 1909), 151; Heros von Borcke and Justus Scheibert, *The Great Cavalry Battle of Brandy Station, 9 June 1863* (Winston-Salem, N.C.: Paleamon Press, 1976), 82.

13. Longacre, *Cavalry*, 48–50, 53, 62–63.

14. Longacre, *Cavalry*, 62–73; *Official Records*, ser. 1, vol. 27, pt. 2, 721.

15. Longacre, *Cavalry*, 74–80; *Official Records*, ser. 1, vol. 27, pt. 2, 722.

16. *Official Records*, ser. 1, vol. 27, pt. 2, 682, 722.

17. Longacre, *Cavalry*, 81–83; Brooks, *Butler and His Cavalry*, 152–153, 165–168; *Official Records*, ser. 1, vol. 27, pt. 2, 729; C. Vann Woodward, ed., *Mary Chesnut's Civil War* (New Haven, Conn.: Yale University Press, 1981), 452; *Daily South Carolinian*, 11 June 1863.

18. Brooks, *Butler and His Cavalry*, 169; *Official Records*, ser. 1, vol. 27, pt. 2, 683; Longacre, *Cavalry*, 83.

19. Longacre, *Calvary*, 87, 93; H. B. McClellan, *The Life and Campaigns of Major-General J. E. B. Stuart* (Boston: Houghton, Mifflin and Company, 1885), 293.

20. Longacre, *Cavalry*, 109, 112.

21. Longacre, *Cavalry*, 126–128, 132; McClellan, *Life and Campaigns*, 311–312; Brooks, *Butler and His Cavalry*, 177, 184.

22. Longacre, *Cavalry*, 150–151, 154, 155–156; *Official Records*, ser. 1, vol. 27, pt. 2, 693–694.

23. Longacre, *Cavalry*, 175; *Official Records*, ser. 1, vol. 27, pt. 2, 695–697.

24. *Official Records,* ser. 1, vol. 27, pt. 2, 497, 724. According to one postwar account, Hampton was receiving a report from courier David Flenniken when the trooper shouted, "Look to your right!" Seeing a Yankee aiming his rifle, Hampton rode him down and sabered him. Upon meeting Flenniken in 1876 Hampton said, "Well! Here's the boy who saved my life at Gettysburg!" There seems to be no way to place this episode in the chronology. See Alfred B. Williams, *Hampton and His Red Shirts: South Carolina's Deliverance in 1876* (Charleston, S.C: Walker, Evans & Cogswell, 1935), 288.

25. *Official Records,* ser. 1, vol. 27, pt. 2, 697, 724.

26. Longacre, *Cavalry,* 237; *Official Records,* ser. 1, vol. 27, pt. 2, 698, 725.

27. Brooks, *Stories,* 176–177; Longacre, *Cavalry,* 239; Edward L. Wells, *Hampton and His Cavalry in '64* (Richmond: B. F. Johnson Publishing Company, 1899), 19. In letters to his sister Hampton refers to the wound being in his "hip." See Cauthen, *Letters,* 96, 98. The author of "Sketches of Hampton's Cavalry" (in Brooks' *Stories of the Confederacy*) was a veteran and wrote his narrative within a year of the events described. In contrast is the problematic account of T. J. Mackey ("Hampton's Duel," *Southern Historical Society Papers* vol. xx, 122–126). This tale, oft repeated since, has Hampton giving a federal private abundant opportunity to shoot him, claims the general was also wounded on July 2, and includes a conversation with Frank Hampton ten years after the Colonel's death.

28. Wells, *Hampton,* 75.

29. William G. Deloney to Rosa Deloney, 4 July 1863 (William Gaston Deloney Papers, Hargrett Library).

30. *Official Records,* ser. 1, vol. 27, pt. 2, 725; Theodore G. Barker to Wade Hampton, 8 July 1896 (HFP); *Daily Courier,* 10 October 1866.

31. *Official Records,* ser. 1, vol. 27, pt. 2, 298.

32. Wade Hampton to Louis T. Wigfall, 15 July 1863 (Louis T. Wigfall Papers, The Center for American History). It is unlikely that Hampton was hit by a fragment from an exploding shell, as implied by his use of the word "shrapnel." General Hampton, courageously dueling hand to hand with men half his age, still preferred to think he was hit with a piece of random metal than admit to having been shot in the backside.

33. Wade Hampton to Mary Fisher Hampton, 16 July 1863 (HFP).

34. Mrs. D. Giraud Wright, *A Southern Girl in '61: The War-Time Memories of a Confederate Soldier's Daughter* (New York: Doubleday, Page & Co., 1905), 148.

35. Wade Hampton to Robert Hall Chilton, 8 August 1863 (Wade Hampton [III] Papers, CSR).

36. Statement of Dr. J. Chisolm, _____ August 1863 (Wade Hampton [III] Papers, CSR).

37. Wade Hampton to Louis T. Wigfall, 22 August 1863 (Louis T. Wigfall Papers, Center for American History).

38. Wade Hampton to Louis T. Wigfall, 15 July 1863 (Louis T. Wigfall Papers, Center for American History). Stafford Heights was high ground held by the federal army opposite Fredericksburg.

39. Wade Hampton to Louis T. Wigfall, 22 August 1863 (Louis T. Wigfall Papers, Center for American History).

40. Wade Hampton to Louis T. Wigfall, 2 October 1863 (Louis T. Wigfall Papers, Center for American History).

41. *Official Records,* ser. 1, vol. 27, pt. 3, 1069.

42. Memo of J[efferson] D[avis], n.d. (Wade Hampton [III] Papers, CSR).

43. Wade Hampton to Louis T. Wigfall, 22 August 1863 (Louis T. Wigfall Papers, Center for American History). The dispute involved no personal ill will between Hampton and

Stephen D. Lee. Lee thought Hampton's "noble traits surpassed any one I ever knew, unless it be Robert E. Lee." Stephen D. Lee to Matthew C. Butler, 11 April 1907 (Stephen D. Lee Papers, Duke).

44. Memo of J[efferson] D[avis], n.d. (Wade Hampton [III] Papers, CSR); Marcus J. Wright, *General Officers of the Confederate Army* (New York: The Neale Publishing Co., 1911), 35, 156; *Journal of the Congress of the Confederate States of America, 1861–1865,* vol. 3 (Washington, D.C.: Government Printing Office, 1904), 530, 618.

45. Wade Hampton to Louis T. Wigfall, 2 October 1863 (Louis T. Wigfall Papers, Center for American History).

46. John W. Thomason Jr., *Jeb Stuart* (New York: Charles Scribner's Sons, 1930), 459.

Chapter 8

1. Douglas Southall Freemen, *Lee's Lieutenants: A Study in Command,* vol. 3 (New York: Charles Scribner's Sons, 1944), 190; U.S. War Department, comp., *War of the Rebellion: A Compilation of the Official Records of the Union and Confederate Armies,* ser. 1, vol. 27, pt. 2 (Washington, D.C.: Government Printing Office, 1880–1901), 334.

2. Freeman, *Lee's Lieutenants,* vol. 3, 210, 215; *Official Records,* ser. 1, vol. 29, pt. 1, 401; *Daily Southern Guardian,* 8 September 1863; Wade Hampton to _____, n.d. (M. C. Butler Papers, CSR).

3. *Official Records,* ser. 1, vol. 29, pt. 1, 438–439; Wade Hampton to Edward L. Wells, 25 January 1900 (Edward L. Wells Correspondence, Charleston Library Society).

4. Certificate of the Surgeon-in-Charge, 20 September 1863 (Wade Hampton [III] Papers, CSR); Wade Hampton to Louis T. Wigfall, 2 October 1863 (Louis T. Wigfall Papers, Center for American History).

5. *Official Records,* ser. 1, vol. 29, pt. 2, 817; Wade Hampton to Mary Fisher Hampton, 12 November 1863 (HFP); Charles E. Cauthen, ed., *Family Letters to the Three Wade Hamptons, 1782–1901* (Columbia: University of South Carolina Press, 1953), 96.

6. Cauthen, *Letters,* 96; Wade Hampton to Mary Fisher Hampton, 12 November 1863 (HFP); Wade Hampton to [Robert E. Lee], n.d. (HFP); *Official Records,* ser. 1, vol. 29, pt. 2, 902; Dunbar Rowland, ed., *Jefferson Davis, Constitutionalist: His Letters, Papers and Speeches,* vol. 6 (Jackson: Mississippi Department of Archives and History, 1923), 93.

7. Personnel Data (Wade Hampton [IV] Papers, CSR); Medical Information (Preston Hampton Papers, CSR).

8. Wade Hampton to Mary Fisher Hampton, 15 December 1863 (HFP); Cauthen, *Letters,* 99.

9. *Official Records,* ser. 1, vol. 29, pt. 1, 899–902.

10. *Official Records,* ser. 1, vol. 33, 1144–1145, 1170; Wade Hampton to Mary Fisher Hampton, 21 February 1864 (HFP).

11. *Official Records,* ser. 1, vol. 33, 201–202; Freeman, *Lee's Lieutenants,* vol. 3, 334; Edward L. Wells, *Hampton and Reconstruction* (Columbia: The State Co., 1907), 43; Wade Hampton to [Robert E. Lee], n.d. (HFP). Late in life Hampton remembered having but 250 men—100 dismounted and 150 mounted. See Wade Hampton to Edward L. Wells, 10 May 1898 (Edward L. Wells Correspondence, Charleston Library Society).

12. Wade Hampton to Mary Fisher Hampton, 9 March 1864 (HFP); Wade Hampton to [Robert E. Lee], n.d. (HFP); Louella H. Bales, *Confederate Cavalry: Last Days of Chivalry* (Jacksonville, Fla.: privately printed, 1989), 217.

13. *Official Records,* ser. 1, vol. 29, pt. 2, 863; Cauthen, *Letters,* 100, 101; *Official Records,* ser. 1, vol. 33, 1100.

14. Edward L. Wells, *Hampton and His Cavalry in '64* (Richmond: B. F. Johnson Publishing Co., 1899), 100–101; *Official Records*, ser. 1, vol. 33, 1153, 1162–1163, 1186.

15. *Official Records*, ser. 1, vol. 33, 1153–1154; Manly Wade Wellman, *Giant in Gray: A Biography of Wade Hampton of South Carolina* (New York: Charles Scribner's Sons, 1949), 136.

16. John Esten Cooke, *Wearing of the Gray* (Bloomington: Indiana University Press, 1959), 57.

17. *Official Record*, ser. 1, vol. 33, 1229–1230.

18. C. Vann Woodward, ed., *Mary Chesnut's Civil War* (New Haven, Conn.: Yale University Press, 1981), 587–588.

19. Wade Hampton to [Robert E. Lee], n.d. (HFP).

20. *Official Records*, ser. 1, vol. 33, 1231–1232.

21. Wade Hampton to J. A. Seddon, 24 March 1864 (HFP); *Official Records*, ser. 1, vol. 33, 1243, 1258–1260.

22. Janet B. Hewett, ed., *Supplement to the Official Records of the Union and Confederate Armies*, vol. 6 (Wilmington, N.C.: Broadfoot Publishing Co., 1998), 446; Edward L. Wells, *A Sketch of the Charleston Light Dragoons* (Charleston, S.C.: Lucas, Richardson & Co., 1888), 32.

23. Wade Hampton to Samuel Cooper, 29 March 1864 (M. W. Gary Papers, CSR); Wade Hampton to Mary Singleton, 24 April 1864 (HFP).

24. U. R. Brooks, *Butler and His Cavalry in the War of Secession, 1861–1865* (Columbia: The State Co., 1909), 67; Wade Hampton to Mary Singleton, 24 April 1864 (HFP).

25. *Daily South Carolinian*, supplement, 23 April 1864. The reporter covering the event was probably associate editor Henry Timrod. See Jay B. Hubbell, *The Last Years of Henry Timrod 1864–1867* (Durham, N.C.: Duke University Press, 1941), 18, 40.

26. Hewett, ed., *O.R. Supplement*, vol. 6, 446–447; Wells, *Dragoons*, 32–33.

27. Woodward, *Civil War*, 602.

28. *Official Records*, ser. 1, vol. 36, pt. 2, 941; Walter Clark, *Histories of the Several Regiments and Battalions from North Carolina in the Great War 1861–1865*, vol. 3 (Raleigh: E. M. Uzzell, 1901), 592–593; Wells, *Hampton Cavalry*, 136; Robert Underwood Johnson and Clarence Buel, eds., *Battles and Leaders of the Civil War*, vol. 4 (New York: The Century Co., 1884–1887), 189.

29. Freeman, *Lee's Lieutenants*, vol. 3, 420–424; H. B. McClellan, *The Life and Campaigns of J. E. B. Stuart* (Boston: Houghton, Mifflin and Co., 1885), 413–417.

CHAPTER 9

1. James M. McPherson, *Battle Cry of Freedom: The Civil War Era* (New York: Oxford University Press, 1988), 725–742.

2. Douglas Southall Freeman, *Lee's Lieutenants: A Study in Command*, vol. 3 (New York: Charles Scribner's Sons, 1944), 436; Edward L. Wells, *Hampton and His Cavalry in '64* (Richmond: B. F. Johnson Publishing Co., 1899), 152.

3. U.S. War Department, comp., *War of the Rebellion: A Compilation of the Official Records of the Union and Confederate Armies*, ser. 1, vol. 36, pt. 2 (Washington, D.C.: Government Printing Office, 1880–1901), 1001; Edward L. Wells, *A Sketch of the Charleston Light Dragoons* (Charleston, S.C.: Lucas, Richardson & Co., 1888), 38.

4. Wells, *Hampton Cavalry*, 157–158; Freeman, *Lee's Lieutenants*, vol. 3, 499.

5. Janet B. Hewett, ed., *Supplement to the Official Records of the Union and Confeder-*

ate Armies, vol. 6 (Wilmington, N.C.: Broadfoot Publishing Co., 1998) 449; Wells, *Dragoons,* 45.

6. *Official Records,* ser. 1, vol. 36, pt. 3, 867.

7. Wells, *Hampton Cavalry,* 150; Edward L. Wells, *Hampton and Reconstruction* (Columbia: The State Co., 1907), 49; Frank M. Myers, *The Comanches: A History of White's Battalion, Virginia Cavalry, Laurel Brig., Hampton Div., A.N.V.* (Baltimore: Kelly, Piet & Co., 1871), 291.

8. Freeman, *Lee's Lieutenants,* vol. 3, 516–518; *Official Records,* ser. 1, vol. 36, pt. 1, 1095.

9. Robert Underwood Johnson and Clarence Buel, eds., *Battles and Leaders of the Civil War,* vol. 4 (New York: The Century Co., 1884–1887), 237; Freeman, *Lee's Lieutenants,* vol. 3, 519–520.

10. *Official Records,* ser. 1, vol. 36, pt. 1, 1095; Olin Fulmer Hutchinson Jr., ed., *"My Dear Mother & Sisters:" Civil War Letters of Capt. A. B. Mulligan, Co. B, 5th South Carolina Cavalry—Butler's Division—Hampton's Corps 1861–1865* (Spartanburg, S.C.: The Reprint Co., 1992), 183; Walbrook Davis Swank, ed., *Battle of Trevilian Station: The Civil War's Greatest and Bloodiest All Cavalry Battle* (Shippensburg, Pa.: Burd Street Press, 1994), 65.

11. Freeman, *Lee's Lieutenants,* vol. 3, 521–522, 522n; Wade Hampton to Edward L. Wells, 18 January and 22 February 1900 (Edward L. Wells Correspondence, Charleston Library Society); U. R. Brooks, *Butler and His Cavalry in the War of Secession 1861–1865* (Columbia: The State Co., 1909), 256.

12. Johnson and Buel, *Battles and Leaders,* vol. 4, 237; U. R. Brooks, *Stories of the Confederacy,* (Columbia: The State Co., 1907), 392; Brooks, *Butler Cavalry,* 301, 380.

13. *Official Records,* ser. 1, vol. 36, pt. 1, 1096–1098; U.S. Navy Department, comp., *Official Records of the Union and Confederate Navies in the Rebellion,* ser. 1, vol. 10 (Washington, D.C.: Government Printing Office, 1894–1927), 165, 166; Wade Hampton to Braxton Bragg, 20 June [1864] (Wade Hampton Papers, Duke); Freeman, *Lee's Lieutenants,* vol. 3, 551n. "Samaria" is also called "Saint Mary's" Church.

14. C. Vann Woodward, ed., *Mary Chesnut's Civil War* (New Haven, Conn.: Yale University Press, 1981), 625; Douglas Southall Freeman, *Lee's Dispatches* (New York: Knickerbocker Press, 1915), 268–269.

15. *Official Records,* ser. 1, vol. 36, pt. 3, 903; *O.R. Navy,* ser. 1, vol. 10, 283, 298; Wade Hampton to Mary Fisher Hampton, 22 July and 7 August 1864 (HFP).

16. Brooks, *Butler Cavalry,* 435–436.

17. Charles E. Cauthen, ed., *Family Letters of the Three Wade Hamptons 1782–1901* (Columbia: University of South Carolina Press, 1953), 108; John Cheves Haskell, *The Haskell Memoirs* (New York: G. P. Putnam's Sons, 1960), 131n; Personnel Data (Thomas Preston Hampton Papers, CSR).

18. *Official Records,* ser. 1, vol. 42, pt. 2, 1171; Matthew C. Butler's tribute to Wade Hampton, August 1902 (Butler Family Scrapbook, SCL); John S. Wise, *The End of an Era* (Boston: Houghton, Mifflin and Co., 1899), 333; Wells, *Hampton Cavalry,* 249.

19. *Official Records,* ser. 1, vol. 43, pt. 1, 996, 999; Wells, *Hampton Cavalry,* 271–274.

20. *Official Records,* ser. 1, vol. 42, pt. 1, 942–944; Brooks, *Butler Cavalry,* 303–304; *Official Records,* ser. 1, vol. 42, pt. 2, 1204–1205.

21. Cauthen, *Letters,* 107–108.

22. *Official Records,* ser. 1, vol. 42, pt. 2, 1233–1236.

23. *Official Records,* ser. 1, vol. 42, pt. 2, 1242.

24. Walter Clark, ed., *Histories of the Several Regiments and Battalions from North Carolina in the Great War 1861–1865,* vol. 3 (Raleigh, N.C.: Uzzell, 1901), 625.

25. *Official Records,* ser. 1, vol. 42, pt. 1, 944–946; Brooks, *Butler Cavalry,* 317, 320; Thomas L. Rosser, *Riding with Rosser* (Shippensburg, Pa.: Burd Street Press, 1997), 41–42.

26. Rosser, *Riding,* 111; Day Book of Hugo G. Sheridan, 20 September 1864 (Orangeburg County Historical Society); *Daily South Carolinian,* 22 September 1864; *Official Records,* ser. 1, vol. 42, pt. 1, 952.

27. *Official Records,* ser. 1, vol. 42, pt. 2, 852–853; *Richmond Examiner,* 23 September 1864.

28. Wells, *Hampton Cavalry,* 312; *Official Records,* ser. 1, vol. 42, pt. 1, 947–948; Cauthen, *Letters,* 108–109.

29. *Official Records,* ser. 1, vol. 42, pt. 3, 1161–1162, 1176, 1198–1199.

30. Cauthen, *Letters,* 109.

31. *Official Records,* ser. 1, vol. 42, pt. 3, 1161–1162.

32. *Official Records,* ser. 1, vol. 42, pt. 1, 949–950; Wells, *Hampton Cavalry,* 330.

33. Brooks, *Butler Cavalry,* 352, 359; Haskell, *Memoirs,* 164n; Wells, *Hampton Cavalry,* 345–346; Reminiscences, n.d. (Fred C. Foard Papers, North Carolina State Archives).

34. Brooks, *Butler Cavalry,* 359–360.

35. Woodward, *Civil War,* 665, 674; Wade Hampton to Mary Fisher Hampton, 14 November 1864 (HFP).

36. Woodward, *Civil War,* 665–666. Many years after the war, Hampton wrote a brief sketch of the cavalry for a Charleston newspaper. He noted that "comrades of the infantry had their jest that no dead man with spurs on was ever seen! But that this harmless jest was without foundation is proved by the graves of many of the noblest men of the South who fell in the cavalry & by many a mourning heart through the breadth of the Southern land." Wade Hampton to the editor of the *News and Courier,* n.d. (HFP).

37. Wade Hampton to Mary Fisher Hampton, 14 November 1864 (HFP); *Official Records,* ser. 1, vol. 43, pt. 2, 923, 926; Wade Hampton to Benjamin F. Perry, 29 November 1864 (Benjamin F. Perry Papers, Alabama Department of Archives and History); Carol Bleser, *The Hammonds of Redcliffe* (New York: Oxford University Press, 1981), 128.

38. *Official Records,* ser. 1, vol. 42, pt. 1, 950–952; Reminiscences, n.d. (Fred C. Foard Papers, North Carolina State Archives); Wade Hampton to Mary Fisher Hampton, 14 December 1864 (HFP).

39. Walter Brian Cisco, "Galvanized Rebels," *Civil War* vol. viii, no. 5 (October 1990): 48–52.

40. Woodward, ed., *Civil War,* pp. 678, 702; *Daily South Carolinian,* 29 December 1864.

41. *Official Records,* ser. 1, vol. 42, pt. 3, 748–749; Cauthen, *Letters,* 112.

42. Wade Hampton to Mary Fisher Hampton, 10 January 1865 (HFP); Cauthen, *Letters,* 112–113.

CHAPTER 10

1. Mrs. D. Giraud Wright, *A Southern Girl in '61: The War-Time Memories of a Confederate Senator's Daughter* (New York: Doubleday, Page & Co., 1905), 222–223.

2. Douglas Southall Freeman, ed., *Lee's Dispatches* (New York: Knickerbocker Press, 1915), 314–318; *Daily South Carolinian,* 24 January 1865; Edward L. Wells, *Hampton and His Cavalry in '64* (Richmond: B. F. Johnson Company, 1899), 389; U.S. War Department, comp., *War of the Rebellion: A Compilation of the Official Records of the Union and Confederate Armies,* ser. 1, vol. 47, pt. 2 (Washington, D.C.: Government Printing Office, 1880–1901), 1112.

3. J. Tracy Power and Daniel J. Bell, *Rivers Bridge State Park: Visitors Guide* (n.p.: South Carolina Department of Parks, Recreation and Tourism, 1992), 1, 10.

4. John F. Marszalek, *Sherman: A Soldier's Passion for Order* (New York: The Free Press, 1993), 320–321; Michael Fellman, *Citizen Sherman: A Life of William Tecumseh Sherman* (New York: Random House, 1995), 222–223.

5. G. Wayne King, "The Civil War Career of Hugh Judson Kilpatrick" (Ph.D. dissertation, University of South Carolina, 1969), 234.

6. Fellman, *Sherman*, 231.

7. U. R. Brooks, *Butler and His Cavalry in the War of Secession 1861–1865* (Columbia: The State Co., 1907), 403.

8. Brooks, *Butler Calvary*, 403–406.

9. Robert Underwood Johnson and Clarence Buel, eds., *Battles and Leaders of the Civil War,* vol. 4 (New York: The Century Co., 1884–1887), 700–701; C. M. Calhoun, *Liberty Dethroned: A Concise History of Some of the Most Startling Events before, during, and since the Civil War* (n.p.: privately published, n.d.), 172.

10. William Tecumseh Sherman, *Memoirs of General W. T. Sherman* (New York: The Library of America, 1990), 759.

11. J. F. Williams, *Old and New Columbia* (Columbia: Epworth Orphanage Press, 1929), 120–121; Sherman, *Memoirs,* 759; Christie Zimmerman Fant, *The State House of South Carolina: An Illustrated Historic Guide* (Columbia: The R. L. Bryan Co., 1970), 22; Calhoun, *Liberty Dethroned,* 173.

12. Thomas Jefferson Goodwyn to Colin Campbell Murchison, 8 June 1866 (Thomas Jefferson Goodwyn Papers, SCL).

13. Brooks, *Butler Cavalry,* 459, 466–477; Thomas Jefferson Goodwyn to Colin Campbell Murchison, 8 June 1866 (Thomas Jeffrson Goodwyn Papers, SCL).

14. William Gilmore Simms, *Sack and Destruction of the City of Columbia, S.C.* (Columbia: Power Press of Daily Phoenix, 1865), 37.

15. Edwin J. Scott, *Random Recollections of a Long Life, 1806 to 1876* (Columbia: Charles A. Calvo Jr., Printer, 1884), 176.

16. Statements of Peter J. Shand, 8 January 1866 and 5 June 1866 (Peter J. Shand Papers, SCL); Williams, *Old and New,* 122; James G. Gibbes, *Who Burnt Columbia?* (Newberry, S.C.: Elbert H. Aull Co., 1902), 7.

17. Gibbes, *Columbia,* 7; Scott, *Random,* 179; Simms, *Sack,* 41; Earl Schenck Miers, ed., *When the World Ended: The Diary of Emma Le Conte* (New York: Oxford University Press, 1957), 44.

18. Rawlins Lowndes to Wade Hampton, 15 August 1866 (Daniel Heyward Trezevant Papers, SCL); Gibbes, *Burnt,* 118–119; James Wood Davidson, "Who Burned Columbia?—A Review of General Sherman's Version of the Affair," *Southern Historical Society Papers* vol. vii (1879): 190; A. R. Chisolm, "Beauregard's and Hampton's Orders on Evacuating Columbia," *Southern Historical Society Papers* vol. vii (1879): 249–250; Calhoun, *Liberty Dethroned,* 174.

19. Scott, *Random,* 186; Gibbes, *Burnt,* 9; Simms, *Sack,* 41.

20. Nell S. Graydon, *Tales of Columbia* (Columbia: R. L. Bryan Company, 1964), 134; Agnes Law, "The Burning of Columbia—Affidavit of Mrs. Agnes Law," *Southern Historical Society Papers* vol. xii (1884): 233–234.

21. Scott, *Random,* 183–184.

22. *Official Records,* ser. 1, vol. 47, pt. 1, 21–22; J. F. Carrol, "The Burning of Columbia, South Carolina—Report of the Committee of Citizens Appointed to Collect Testimony," *Southern Historical Society Papers* vol. viii (1880): 212–214.

23. Sherman, *Memoirs*, 767–768.

24. Earl Schenck Miers, *The General Who Marched to Hell: William Tecumseh Sherman and His March to Fame and Infamy* (New York: Alfred A. Knopf, 1951), 348; Rachel Sherman Thorndike, ed., *The Sherman Letters: Correspondence between General and Senator Sherman from 1837 to 1891* (New York: Charles Scribner's Sons, 1894), 266; Richard Harwell and Philip N. Racine, eds., *The Fiery Trail: A Union Officer's Account of Sherman's Last Campaign* (Knoxville: University of Tennessee Press, 1986), 131–132.

25. Scott, *Random*, 186; Julian A. Selby, *Memorabilia and Anecdotal Reminiscences of Columbia, S.C. and Incidents Connected Therewith* (Columbia: R. L. Bryan Co., 1905), 122.

26. David P. Conyngham, *Sherman's March through the South with Sketches and Incidents of the Campaign* (New York: Sheldon and Company, 1865), 311; Graydon, *Tales*, 136. Savannah's survival proved that Sherman "could control his men when it suited his purpose to do so," wrote one historian. "The real difference between Savannah and Columbia was that Sherman needed the Georgia port as a base. Columbia was merely a stopover in a general swath of destruction. Sherman had no more use for Columbia than he had for Atlanta, a city he had burned in 1864 to cover his rear. . . . Sherman may have issued no order [to burn Columbia] but his failure to control his men constituted probable tacit consent." See Allan D. Charles, "The Burning of Columbia," *Southern Partisan* vol. 1, nos. 3–4 (Spring–Summer 1981): 9. *"There is no doubt whatsoever,"* wrote another scholar, *that Union soldiers were to blame for what happened, some with intent, others by default in their drunken stupor"* [Emphasis in the original]. See John Hammond Moore, *Columbia and Richland County: A South Carolina Community, 1740–1990* (Columbia: University of South Carolina Press, 1993), 203, 208. British claims of $1,206,821 against the U.S. government were disallowed because Columbia's destruction "was not to be ascribed to either the intention or default of either the federal or confederate officers." U.S. Department of State, *Papers Relating to the Treaty of Washington*, vol. 6 (Washington, D.C.: Government Printing Office, 1874), 50. Sherman is not without his apologists. See Marion Brunson Lucas, *Sherman and the Burning of Columbia* (College Station: Texas A&M University Press, 1976).

27. Jefferson Davis to Samuel Cooper, 14 February 1865 (Wade Hampton [III] Papers, CSR); Marcus J. Wright, *General Officers of the Confederate Army* (New York: The Neale Publishing Co., 1911), 18; *Journal of the Congress of the Confederate States of America, 1861–1865*, vol. 4 (Washington, D.C.: Government Printing Office, 1904), 563–564; *Official Records*, ser. 1, vol. 47, pt. 2, 1207; Mark L. Bradley, *Last Stand in the Carolinas: The Battle of Bentonville* (Campbell, Cal.: Savas Pub. Co., 1995), 85.

28. C. Vann Woodward and Elisabeth Muhlenfeld, eds., *The Private Mary Chesnut: The Unpublished Civil War Diaries* (New York: Oxford University Press, 1984), 234.

29. C. Vann Woodward, ed., *Mary Chesnut's Civil War* (New Haven, Conn.: Yale University Press, 1981), 430–431; Woodward and Muhlenfeld, *Private*, 225.

30. *Official Records*, ser. 1, vol. 47, pt. 2, 1211, 1218, 1317; Johnson, *Battles and Leaders*, vol. 4, 701.

31. *Official Records*, ser. 1, vol. 47, pt. 2, 546, 596–597, 1300; Richard H. McMaster, *The Feasterville Incident: Hampton and Sherman* (Washington, D.C.: n.p. 1955), 3, 12; Calhoun, *Liberty Dethroned*, 177–178.

32. Edward L. Wells, *Hampton and Reconstruction* (Columbia: The State Co., 1907), 62–65; Calhoun, *Liberty Dethroned*, 179–181; Joseph E. Johnston, *Narrative of Military Operations* (Bloomington: Indiana University Press, 1959), 380–381; Robert Winn to his sister, 25 March 1865 (Robert Winn Papers, Filson Historical Society).

33. Brooks, *Butler Cavalry*, 112–113; Edward L. Wells, *A Sketch of the Charleston Light*

Dragoons (Charleston, S.C.: Lucas, Richardson & Co., 1888), 91–92; Wells, *Hampton Cavalry*, 30–36; Charles E. Cauthen, ed., *Family Letters of the Three Wade Hamptons, 1782–1901* (Columbia: University of South Carolina Press, 1953), 161–162; Wade Hampton to Edward L. Wells, 20 December 1897 (Edward L. Wells Correspondence, Charleston Library Society). There is some minor disagreement about the numbers engaged and the federal casualties.

34. Johnston, *Narrative*, 382–394; Bradley, *Last Stand*, 303; Johnson, *Battles and Leaders*, vol. 4, 701–705; Gilbert E. Govan and James W. Livingwood, *General Joseph E. Johnston, CSA: A Different Valor* (New York: Bobbs-Merrill Co., 1956), 358.

35. Wade Hampton to Mary Fisher Hampton, 22 March 1865 (HFP).

36. *Journal of Confederate Congress*, vol. 4, 676, 721.

37. Wade Hampton to Mary Fisher Hampton, 30 March 1865 (HFP).

38. Johnston, *Narrative*, 395–397; *Official Records*, ser. 1, vol. 47, pt. 3, 234; Govan and Livingwood, *Johnston*, 363–366.

39. Brooks, *Butler Cavalry*, 288–289; Conyngham, *March*, 365.

40. *Official Records*, ser. 1, vol. 47, pt. 3, 813–814; Head Quarters Cavalry handbill, 20 April 1865 (Heartt-Wilson Papers, SHC).

41. Fellman, *Sherman*, 245–246; *Official Records*, ser. 1, vol. 47, pt. 3, 829–830. Davis's telegram begins, "Letter not received." This is almost certainly an error, perhaps on the part of the telegrapher. Hampton believed "not" was used instead of "just." See Wade Hampton, "An Effort to Rescue Jefferson Davis: Statement of General Wade Hampton," *Southern Historical Society Papers* vol. xxvii (1899): 134.

42. Joseph Wheeler, "An Effort to Rescue Jefferson Davis," *The Century Magazine* vol. LVI, no. 1 (May 1898): 86; *Official Records*, ser. 1, vol. 47, pt. 3, 841, 845, 846.

43. Hampton, "Effort," 134–135; *State*, 11 May 1908; *Official Records*, ser. 1, vol. 47, pt. 3, 846; Wheeler, "Rescue," 86–87; Hudson Strode, ed., *Jefferson Davis: Private Letters, 1823–1889* (New York: Harcourt Brace & World, 1966), 160.

44. Cauthen, *Letters*, 114.

CHAPTER II

1. Archie P. McDonald, ed., *A Nation of Sovereign States: Secession and War in the Confederacy* (Murfreesboro, Tenn.: Southern Heritage Press, 1994), 8.

2. Virginia G. Meynard, *The Venturers: The Hampton, Harrison, and Earle Families of Virginia, South Carolina, and Texas* (Easley, S.C.: Southern Historical Press, 1981), 245; C. Vann Woodward, ed., *Mary Chesnut's Civil War* (New Haven, Conn.: Yale University Press, 1981), 806; C. Vann Woodward and Elisabeth Muhlenfeld, eds., *The Private Mary Chesnut: The Unpublished Civil War Diaries* (New York: Oxford University Press, 1984), 243.

3. Joel R. Williamson, "The Disruption of State Government in South Carolina during the Magrath Administration" (Master's thesis, University of South Carolina, 1951), 83–85, 87, 88; *Daily Phoenix*, 18 May 1865.

4. Woodward and Muhlenfeld, *Private*, 250; Mary Boykin Chesnut, *A Diary from Dixie* (Gloucester, Mass.: Peter Smith, 1961), 404.

5. John Richard Dennett, *The South as It Is: 1865–1866* (New York: The Viking Press, 1965), 230; Sidney Andrews, *The South since the War* (Boston: Houghton Mifflin Company, 1971), 33; Mary Conner Moffett, ed., *Letters of General James Conner, C.S.A.* (Columbia: R. L. Bryan Co., 1950), 167; J. T. Trowbridge, *The South: A Tour of its Battle Fields and Ruined Cities* (Hartford, Conn.: L. Stebbins, 1866), 564.

6. Wade Hampton to Benjamin F. Perry, 27 July 1865 (Benjamin F. Perry Papers, Alabama Department of Archives and History); Meynard, *Venturers*, 245, 246, 530–531, 983; Mary Hampton to Armistead Burt, 20 October 1870 (Mary S. McDuffie Papers, Duke).

7. Meynard, *Venturers*, 246, 564–565; *Daily Phoenix*, 27 June 1865.

8. J. McF. Gaston, *Hunting a Home in Brazil* (Philadelphia: King & Baird, 1867), 290, 374; Cyrus B. Dawsey and James M. Dawsey, *The Confederados: Old South Immigrants in Brazil* (Tuscaloosa: University of Alabama Press, 1995), 18, 160, 247–252; Eugene C. Harter, *The Lost Colony of the Confederacy* (Jackson: University Press of Mississippi, 1986), 12, 71.

9. ——— to Wade Hampton, 20 July 1865 (HFP).

10. *Daily Phoenix*, 27 July 1865; Wade Hampton to Andrew Johnson, 3 August 1865 and Benjamin F. Perry to Andrew Johnson, 9 August 1865 (Wade Hampton [III] File, Applications from Former Confederates for Presidential Pardons, 1865–1867, U.S. National Archives). This application is reproduced in John Hope Franklin, *Reconstruction: After the Civil War*, (Chicago: University of Chicago Press, 1961), 23 opposite.

11. Wade Hampton to Benjamin F. Perry, 27 July 1865 (Benjamin F. Perry Papers, Alabama Department of Archives and History); Henry Steele Commager, ed., *Documents of American History* (New York: Appelton-Century-Crofts, 1968), 458–459; *Daily Phoenix*, 27 July 1865.

12. Commager, *Documents*, 457–458.

13. J. H. Easterly, ed., "1790 Constitution" *Basic Documents of South Carolina History* (Columbia: Historical Commission of South Carolina, 1952), 2.

14. Wade Hampton to James G. Gibbes, 20 August 1865 (HFP).

15. *Daily Phoenix*, 6, 7, and 27 September 1865.

16. *Daily Phoenix*, 14 September 1865; Andrews, *South*, 42.

17. Andrews, *South*, 40, 48.

18. John Porter Hollis, *The Early Period of Reconstruction in South Carolina* (Baltimore: The Johns Hopkins University Press, 1905), 37–38; Andrews, *South*, 53–54; *Journal of the Convention of the People, Held in Columbia, S.C., September, 1865* (Columbia: J. A. Selby, 1865), 27–29.

19. Andrews, *South*, 57–67, 83–84.

20. Andrews, *South*, 86, 89–90; Thomas Holt, *Black over White: Negro Political Leadership in South Carolina during Reconstruction* (Urbana: University of Illinois Press, 1977), 21–22.

21. U. R. Brooks, *Butler and His Cavalry in the War of Secession, 1861–1865* (Columbia: The State Co., 1909), 185, 370; Andrews, *South*, 96–97.

22. Eric Foner, *Reconstruction: America's Unfinished Revolution, 1863–1877* (New York: Harper & Row, 1988), 80–81, 106–107, 202.

23. John Hammond Moore, ed., *The Juhl Letters to the Charleston Courier: A View of the South, 1865–1871* (Athens: University of Georgia Press, 1974), 47; Walter L. Fleming, ed., *Documentary History of Reconstruction* (Cleveland, Ohio: The Arthur H. Clark Company, 1906), 48–49, 363–364; Commager, *Documents*, 460–461.

24. Foner, *Reconstruction*, 68–70; Martin Abbott, *The Freedmen's Bureau in South Carolina 1865–1872* (Chapel Hill: University of North Carolina Press, 1967), 71, 73, 74; Moore, *Juhl Letters*, 103n.

25. Abbott, *Bureau*, 28–29; Fleming, *Documentary*, 379–381, 386–389.

26. *Daily Phoenix*, 8, 11, and 14 October 1865.

27. Daniel Walker Hollis, *The University of South Carolina*, vol. 2 (Columbia: University of South Carolina Press, 1951), 4–5, 8–9, 19–20; Minutes, 29 November 1865 (Minutes of the Board of Trustees of the South Carolina College, SCL). Although Hampton was

among those formally elected to the Board of Trustees on 18 December 1865, he is listed as a member—and present—beginning in the minutes of 29 November.

28. Andrews, *South,* 96; *Daily Phoenix,* 13 October 1865.

29. Ellis Paxson Oberholtzer, *A History of the United States since the Civil War,* vol. 1 (New York: The Macmillan Co., 1936), 124–125; *Daily Phoenix,* 1 November 1865; U.S. Congress, *Report of the Joint Committee on Reconstruction* (Washington, D.C.: Government Printing Office, 1866), 216–217; *News and Courier,* 15 August 1878; Hollis, *Early Reconstruction,* 43n.

30. *Daily Phoenix,* 15 November 1865. Perhaps because he was concerned that Hampton would indeed be elected governor, President Johnson had his attorney general "forward to this office the pardon of Wade Hampton of South Carolina." See president's secretary to James Speed, 13 November 1865 (Wade Hampton File, Applications from Former Confederates for Presidential Pardons, 1865–1867, U.S. National Archives).

31. Oberholtzer, *History,* vol. 1, 124; *Daily Phoenix,* 27 December 1865 and 21 January 1866.

32. Charles E. Cauthen, ed., *Family Letters of the Three Wade Hamptons, 1782–1901* (Columbia: University of South Carolina Press, 1953), 117–118; Wade Hampton to Mary Fisher Hampton, 31 January 1866 (HFP).

33. *Daily Phoenix,* 10 October 1865; Foner, *Reconstruction,* 173–174.

34. Moore, *Juhl Letters,* 53; Holt, *Black over White,* 24.

35. Alfred Kelly and Winfred A. Harbison, *The American Constitution: Its Origins and Development* (New York: W. W. Norton & Co., 1970), 384–389, 391–393; Andrews, *South,* 86, 396; Holt, *Black over White,* 25.

36. Andrews, *South,* 396.

37. Foner, *Reconstruction,* 222–223, 240, 315; Fleming, *Documentary,* 177, 226; Commager, *Documents,* 467–468.

38. Moore, *Juhl Letters,* 71–72; Holt, *Black over White,* 34; *Daily Phoenix,* 30 August 1865; Foner, *Reconstruction,* 221.

39. Douglas Southall Freeman, *R. E. Lee: A Biography,* vol. 4 (New York: Charles Scribner's Sons, 1935), 376.

40. Samuel Eliot Morison and Henry Steele Commager, *The Growth of the American Republic,* vol. 2 (New York: Oxford University Press, 1955), 33; Commager, *Documents,* 468–469; Foner, *Reconstruction,* 232, 235.

41. Foner, *Reconstruction,* 467; Morison and Commager, *American Republic,* vol. 2, 21; Abbott, *Bureau,* 65.

42. *Daily Phoenix,* 12 January 1866.

43. Cauthen, *Letters,* 118–120; Hudson Strode, *Jefferson Davis: Tragic Hero* (New York: Harcourt, Brace & World, 1964), 295; Varina Howell Davis, *Jefferson Davis, Ex-President of the Confederate States of America,* vol. 2 (New York: Belford Co., Publishers, 1890), 772–773; Wade Hampton to Mary Fisher Hampton, 1 March 1866 (HFP).

44. Cauthen, *Letters,* 120–121.

45. Cauthen, *Letters,* 122, 124n; Undated copy of *Metropolitan Record and New York Vindicator* (HFP); Frank L. Klement, *Lincoln's Critics: The Copperheads of the North* (Shippensburg, Pa.: White Mane Books, 1999), 97, 101.

46. Cauthen, *Letters,* 123–141; *New York Times,* 28 August 1866.

47. Moore, *Juhl Letters,* 100–101; Joseph Le Conte, *The Autobiography of Joseph Le Conte* (New York: D. Appleton and Company, 1903), 236; Fleming, *Documentary,* 211.

48. Freeman, *Lee,* vol. 4, 213.

49. Wade Hampton to Robert E. Lee, 21 July 1866 (HFP); Alfred Roman, *The Military*

Operations of General Beauregard, vol. 1 (New York: Harper & Brothers, 1884), 10. Beauregard overestimated Rumania's troop strength. See Stefan Pascu, ed., *The Independence of Romania* (Bucuresti: Editura Academiei Republicii Socialiste România, 1977), 49.

50. Wade Hampton to the editor of the Charleston *News and Courier,* n.d. (HFP); Robert E. Lee to Wade Hampton, 1 August 1865 (Edward L. Wells Correspondence, Charleston Library Society).

51. Wade Hampton to Robert E. Lee, 11 November 1866 and n.d. (HFP).

52. *Daily Phoenix,* 25 July, 2 and 16 August 1866.

53. *Daily Courier,* 10 October 1866; *Daily Phoenix,* 17 October 1866.

54. David C. Whitney, *The American Presidents* (Garden City, N.Y.: Doubleday & Co., 1978), 487.

55. Meynard, *Venturers,* 251, 530; *Daily Phoenix,* 13 December 1866. A decade earlier Mary Fisher Hampton exhibited symptoms—cough and hemorrhages—that might suggest tuberculosis. See Wade Hampton II to William A. Williams, 18 June 1857 (Alexander Williams Papers, Duke).

56. Jay B. Hubbell, ed., *The Last Years of Henry Timrod 1864–1867* (Durham, N.C.: Duke University Press, 1941), 64–65.

57. Moore, *Juhl Letters,* 44; Fleming, *Documentary,* 401; Foner, *Reconstruction,* 269, 276.

58. *Daily Phoenix,* 19 March 1867; *Daily Courier,* 23 March 1867.

59. Quoted in the *Daily Phoenix,* 22 March 1867; *New York Times,* 28 March 1867.

60. Quoted in the *Daily Phoenix,* 26 March 1867.

61. Quoted in the *Daily Phoenix,* 27 March 1867.

62. *Daily Courier,* 22 March 1867.

63. *Daily Phoenix,* 31 March 1867; *Advocate,* 23 March 1867.

64. *Daily Phoenix,* 21 March 1867; N. Louise Bailey et al., *Biographical Directory of the South Carolina Senate, 1776–1985,* vol. 2 (Columbia: University of South Carolina Press, 1986), 1191–1193.

65. Wade Hampton to Alfred M. Waddell, 3 April 1867 (Alfred Moore Waddell Papers, SHC); Wade Hampton to James Conner, 24 March 1867 (HFP).

66. Cauthen, *Letters,* 141–143; Wade Hampton to John Mullaly, 11 April 1867 (HFP).

67. Wade Hampton to [Elizabeth Preston] Carrington, 28 March 1867 (HFP).

CHAPTER 12

1. Hampton M. Jarrell, *Wade Hampton and the Negro: The Road Not Taken* (Columbia: University of South Carolina Press, 1950), 18; Eric Foner, *Reconstruction: America's Unfinished Revolution, 1863–1877* (New York: Harper & Row, 1988), 295–296; 302–303.

2. David Duncan Wallace, *South Carolina: A Short History, 1520–1948* (Columbia: University of South Carolina Press, 1951), 569–570; Samuel Eliot Morison and Henry Steele Commager, *The Growth of the American Republic,* vol. 2 (New York: Oxford University Press, 1955), 43.

3. Thomas Holt, *Black over White: Negro Political Leadership in South Carolina during Reconstruction* (Urbana: University of Illinois Press, 1977), 132–133; N. Louise Bailey et al., *Biographical Directory of the South Carolina Senate, 1776–1985* (Columbia: University of South Carolina Press, 1986), vol. 2, 1159–1161, 1335–1337, and vol. 3, 1718–1720.

4. Foner, *Reconstruction,* 110, 283–285; Holt, *Black over White,* 31, 113.

5. Martin E. Mantell, *Johnson, Grant, and the Politics of Reconstruction* (New York:

Columbia University Press, 1973), 25; "South Carolina," *The American Annual Cyclopedia and Register of Important Events,* 1867, 696–697; John Porter Hollis, *The Early Period of Reconstruction in South Carolina* (Baltimore: The Johns Hopkins University Press, 1905), 76–77.

6. *Mercury,* 29 August 1867.

7. Hollis, *Early Reconstruction,* 78–82.

8. State [Democratic] Central Executive Committee, *The Respectful Remonstrance on Behalf of the White People of South Carolina* (Columbia: Phoenix Book and Job Power Press, 1868), 6; William Watts Ball, *The State That Forgot: South Carolina's Surrender to Democracy* (Indianapolis: The Bobbs-Merrill Co., 1932), 145; Wallace, *South Carolina,* 573.

9. *Mercury,* 15 January and 30 January 1868; Walter L. Fleming, ed., *Documentary History of Reconstruction* (Cleveland, Ohio: The Arthur H. Clarke Co., 1906), 450; Ball, *State That Forgot,* 146, 149.

10. Jarrell, *Hampton,* 24–25.

11. U.S. Congress, *Testimony Taken by the Joint Select Committee to Inquire into the Condition of Affairs in the Late Insurrectionary States,* vol. 2 (Washington, D.C.: Government Printing Office, 1872), 1232; *Mercury,* 6 May 1868.

12. Foner, *Reconstruction,* 359, 360, 450.

13. Mantell, *Politics of Reconstruction,* 88, 96–97.

14. Wade Hampton to Benjamin F. Perry, 10 June 1868 (HFP).

15. Jarrell, *Hampton,* 166; "The Democratic Convention," *Harper's Magazine* vol. xxxvii, no. ccxx (September 1868): 567–568; U.S. Congress, *Testimony,* vol. 2, 1235.

16. Donald Bruce Johnson and Kirk H. Porter, comp., *National Party Platforms 1840–1972* (Urbana: University of Illinois Press, 1973), 37–39.

17. "Convention," *Harper's,* 569–570; Mantell, *Politics of Reconstruction,* 122, 128.

18. *Daily Phoenix,* 14 July 1868.

19. Jarrell, *Hampton,* 29; Mantell, *Politics of Reconstruction,* 130.

20. *Mercury,* 20 July and 25 July 1868.

21. *Daily Phoenix,* 26 July 1868; P. F. Henderson et al., eds., *Life and Addresses of D. S. Henderson* (Columbia: The R. L. Bryan Co., 1922), 142.

22. *Mercury,* 30 July 1868. Hampton refers to Robert Young Hayne (1791–1839) and William Campbell Preston (1794–1860).

23. U.S. Congress, *Testimony,* vol. 2, 1234–1235; Mantell, *Politics of Reconstruction,* 114. Republican warhorse James G. Blaine was still exercised about the "Hampton plank" nearly two decades later. See James G. Blaine, *Twenty Years of Congress: From Lincoln to Garfield,* vol. 2 (Norwich, Conn: The Henry Bill Publishing Co., 1886), 400–401.

24. *Daily Phoenix,* 8 August 1868.

25. John Hammond Moore, ed., *The Juhl Letters to the Charleston Courier: A View of the South, 1865–1871* (Athens: University of Georgia Press, 1974), 256.

26. *Massachusetts and South Carolina: Correspondence between John Quincy Adams and Wade Hampton and Others of South Carolina* (Boston: J. E. Farwell & Co., n.d.), 1–2, 7; Paul C. Nagel, *Descent from Glory: Four Generations of the John Adams Family* (New York: Oxford University Press, 1983), 241.

27. *Mass. and S.C.,* 8, 23, 25, 28–29; *Daily Phoenix,* 13 October 1868; Claude G. Bowers, *The Tragic Era: The Revolution after Lincoln* (New York: Blue Ribbon Books, 1929), 233.

28. *Mercury,* 15 October 1868; Mantell, *Politics of Reconstruction,* 140–141.

29. *Daily Phoenix,* 18 October 1868; U.S. Congress, *Testimony,* vol. 2, 1256.

30. U.S. Congress, *Testimony,* vol. 2, 1221, 1248–1249.

31. *Daily Phoenix,* 11 October and 19 October 1870. The governor appointed three com-

missioners of election in each county who named managers. Managers had three days to count the ballots. Commissioners then had ten days to "revise and tabulate the returns." Corruption was assumed. See Alfred B. Williams, *Hampton and His Red Shirts: South Carolina's Deliverance in 1876* (Charleston, S.C.: Walker, Evans & Cogswell, 1935), 24–25.

32. U.S. Congress, *Testimony,* vol. 2, 1264–1265.

33. Mantell, *Politics of Reconstruction,* 143.

34. *Daily Phoenix,* 11 October and 19 October 1870.

35. U.S. Congress, *Testimony,* vol. 2, 1233.

36. Wade Hampton to Jonathan S. Gaines, 17 April 1867 (HFP); Virginia G. Meynard, *The Venturers: The Hampton, Harrison, and Earle Families of Virginia, South Carolina, and Texas* (Greenville, S.C.: Southern Historical Press, 1981), 284.

37. Wade Hampton to Robert E. Lee, 16 July 1867 (HFP); Wade Hampton to Daniel H. Trezevant, 2 October 1872 (HFP). In July of 1867 there was talk, too, of forty-three-year-old Catherine Pritchard (Kate) Hampton's engagement to "Mr. Nathan Davis who has been attentive to her for 20 years." The marriage never took place. Davis had been one of General Hampton's staff officers. See Louis P. Towles, ed., *A World Upside Down: The Palmers of South Santee, 1818–1881* (Columbia: University of South Carolina Press, 1996), 553.

38. Wade Hampton to Armistead Burt, 13 March 1868 (Wade Hampton Papers, Duke); Mary Hampton to Armistead Burt, March [1868] (Mary S. McDuffie Papers, Duke); Bankruptcy Records of Wade Hampton (HFP). Typewritten copies were made by the district court in 1938 from originals that had become "almost illegible." Meynard, *Venturers,* 979.

39. Wade Hampton to Armistead Burt, 2 January 1871 (Wade Hampton Papers, Duke); Wade Hampton to Daniel Harvey Hill, 11 October 1869 (Daniel Harvey Hill Papers, SHC); Mary Conner Moffett, ed., *Letters of General James Conner, C.S.A.* (Columbia: R. L. Bryan Co., 1950), 203.

40. *Yorkville Enquirer,* 31 August 1876; Capt. Robert E. Lee, *Recollections and Letters of General Robert E. Lee* (New York: Doubleday, Page & Company, 1904). 376–377; Hudson Strode, *Jefferson Davis: Tragic Hero* (New York: Harcourt, Brace & World, Inc., 1964), 357, 363; Hudson Strode, ed., *Jefferson Davis: Private Letters, 1823–1889* (New York: Harcourt, Brace & World, Inc., 1966), 324; *Daily Phoenix,* 25 July 1871.

41. Wade Hampton to Daniel H. Trezevant, 27 December 1872 (HFP); Strode, *Tragic Hero,* 363; William C. Davis, *Jefferson Davis: The Man and His Hour* (New York: Harper Collins, 1991), 664; Felicity Allen, *Jefferson Davis: Unconquerable Heart* (Columbia: University of Missouri Press, 1999), 507.

42. Strode, *Tragic Hero,* 382–383; Carlyle R. Buley, *The American Life Convention, 1906–1952: A Study in the History of Life Insurance,* vol. 1 (New York: Appleton-Century-Crofts, Inc.,. 1953), 91.

43. Wade Hampton to Robert F. Hoke, 24 May, 2 July, and 1 October 1872 (Robert F. Hoke Papers, North Carolina State Archives).

44. Strode, *Tragic Hero,* 379, 382–383, 385; Wade Hampton to Jefferson Davis, 23 July 1873 (Sang-Lee Civil War Collection, Seymour Library, Knox College); Davis, *Jefferson Davis,* 664; *Daily Phoenix,* 25 February 1874.

45. Jefferson Davis to Wade Hampton, 20 September 1873 (HFP); U.S. District Court of West Tennessee, Notice of meeting and list of creditors of the Southern Life Insurance Company, 14 July 1876 (Bratton Family Papers, SCL).

46. Wade Hampton to Robert E. Lee, 16 July 1867 (HFP); Douglas Southall Freeman, *R. E. Lee: A Biography,* vol. 4 (New York: Charles Scribner's Sons, 1935), 367.

47. *Daily Phoenix,* 13 October and 14 October 1870.

48. Wade Hampton, *Address on the Life and Character of Gen. Robert E. Lee* (Baltimore: John Murray & Co., 1871), 4, 11, 54–55; Wade Hampton to Col. Johnston, 21 November 1871 (Johnston Family Papers, Filson Historical Society).

49. *Daily Phoenix,* 26 October 1871; Form Letter of Wade Hampton, Pres. of Survivor's Association of S.C., 1 July 1870 (HFP).

50. Washington Light Infantry Charitable Association, *Proceedings on the Occasion of Unveiling the Monument Erected in Memory of Their Comrades Who Died in the Service of the State* (Charleston, S.C.: Walker, Evans & Cogswell, 1870) 4, 5, 14–16.

51. Wallace, *South Carolina,* 574, 579; James S. Pike, *The Prostrate State: South Carolina under Negro Government* (New York: D. Appleton and Co., 1874), 197, 199, 205, 207, 208, 211. South Carolina taxpayers finally retired the Reconstruction debt in 1943! See Jarrell, *Hampton,* 38.

52. Minutes, 7 May 1868 (Minutes of the Board of Trustees of the University of South Carolina, SCL); Daniel Walker Hollis, *The University of South Carolina,* SCL); Daniel Walker Hollis, *The University of South Carolina,* vol. 2 (Columbia: University of South Carolina Press, 1951), 70.

53. Wallace, *South Carolina,* 580; Pike, *Prostrate State,* 231.

54. Wallace, *South Carolina,* 580–581; Foner, *Reconstruction,* 439; Pike, *Prostrate State,* 189, 226.

55. Pike, *Prostrate State,* 233.

56. Daily Republican, 9 November and 11 November 1870; Pike, *Prostrate State,* 189–190.

57. Jarrell, *Hampton,* 33; Wallace, *South Carolina,* 583–584; *Proceedings of the Tax-Payers' Convention of South Carolina* (Charleston, S.C.: Edward Perry Printer, 1871), 54, 61.

58. Wade Hampton to Armistead Burt, 2 January 1871 (Wade Hampton Papers, Duke).

59. Wallace, *South Carolina,* 585–586.

60. *News and Courier,* 10 January 1876. The story is told in several variations.

61. Stanley F. Horn, *Invisible Empire: The Story of the Ku Klux Klan, 1866–1871* (Montclair, N.J.: Patterson Smith, 1969), 9, 17, 21, 216, 217, 219; Wallace, *South Carolina,* 581–582.

62. Horn, *Invisible Empire,* 232; *Biographical Directory of the American Congress, 1774–1927* (Washington, D.C.: United States Government Printing Office, 1928), 1502, 1568, 1646.

63. U.S. Congress, *Testimony,* vol. 2, 1218–1219.

64. U.S. Congress, *Testimony,* vol. 2, 1219–1230, 1238–1248.

65. U.S. Congress, *Testimony,* vol. 2, 1230–1232.

66. U.S. Congress, *Testimony,* vol. 2, 1236. There are no letters to or from Hampton in the Library of Congress' Grant papers. See Library of Congress, *Index to the Ulysses S. Grant Papers* (Washington, D.C.: Library of Congress, 1965).

67. U.S. Congress, *Testimony,* vol. 2, 1238.

CHAPTER 13

1. Richard Zuczek, *State of Rebellion: Reconstruction in South Carolina* (Columbia: University of South Carolina Press, 1996), 98, 99; Stanley F. Horn, *Invisible Empire: The Story of the Ku Klux Klan, 1866–1871* (Montclair, N.J.: Patterson Smith, 1969), 234–239.

2. Francis Butler Simkins and Robert Hilliard Woody, *South Carolina during Reconstruction* (Gloucester, Mass.: Peter Smith, 1966), 465–468.

3. Simkins and Woody, *Reconstruction,* 136, 138–139; David Duncan Wallace, *South Carolina: A Short History, 1520–1948* (Columbia: University of South Carolina Press, 1951),

591; Henry T. Thompson, *Ousting the Carpetbagger from South Carolina* (Columbia: R. L. Bryan Co., 1926), 41, 63; Zuczek, *Rebellion*, 136; Robert H. Woody, *Republican Newspapers of South Carolina* (Charlottesville, Va.: The Historical Publishing Co., 1936), 55–57, 59; *Reports and Resolutions of the General Assembly of the State of South Carolina at the Regular Session, 1877–1878* (Columbia: Calvo & Patton, 1878), 631–642, 1019.

4. James S. Pike Notebook, No. 28, entries for 16–23 February 1872 (James S. Pike Notebook, Raymond H. Fogler Library).

5. D. Sven Nordin, *Rich Harvest: A History of the Grange, 1867–1900* (Jackson: University Press of Mississippi, 1974), 4, 30–32; Joel Williamson, *After Slavery: The Negro in South Carolina during Reconstruction, 1861–1877* (New York: W. W. Norton & Co., Inc., 1965), 121n.; O. H. Kelly, *Origin and Progress of the Order of the Patrons of Husbandry in the United States: A History from 1866 to 1873* (Philadelphia: J. A. Wagenseller, 1875), 421.

6. Richard Nelson Current, *Those Terrible Carpetbaggrs* (New York: Oxford University Press, 1988), 192; Wade Hampton to John Mullaly, 19 May 1872 (HFP); William B. Hesseltine, *Ulysses S. Grant: Politician* (New York: Dodd, Mead & Company, 1935), 289.

7. Wade Hampton to Armistead Burt, 14 November 1872 (Wade Hampton Papers, Duke); Ilza Veith, "Four Thousand Years of Hysteria." In *Hysterical Personality,* ed. Mardi J. Horowitz (New York: James Aronson, Inc., 1977), 50–51; Ilza Veith, *Hysteria: The History of the Disease* (Chicago: University of Chicago Press, 1965), 216, 243.

8. Wade Hampton to Mrs. Parker, 1 March 1872 (HFP); Wade Hampton to Stephen D. Lee, 7 November 1873 (Stephen D. Lee Papers, SHC); Charles E. Cauthen, ed., *Family Letters of the Three Wade Hamptons, 1782–1901* (Columbia: University of South Carolina Press, 1953), 145–148.

9. *Daily Phoenix,* 3 March and 4 March 1874; Matthew C. Butler to Wade Hampton, 16 March 1874 (HFP).

10. Cauthen, *Letters,* 149.

11. *Daily Phoenix,* 18 February 1874; William Arthur Sheppard, *Red Shirts Remembered: Southern Brigadiers of the Reconstruction Period* (Atlanta: Ruralist Press, Inc., 1940), 14–17.

12. Wallace, *South Carolina,* 591–592; *Daily Phoenix,* 4 March 1874.

13. Wallace, *South Carolina,* 592; Simkins and Woody, *Reconstruction,* 471–473.

14. Thompson, *Ousting,* 3–4; Wallace, *South Carolina,* 592; Simkins and Woody, *Reconstruction,* 472.

15. Simkins and Woody, *Reconstruction,* 472–473; Wallace, *South Carolina,* 592.

16. Simkins and Woody, *Reconstruction,* 476–477; Walter Allen, *Governor Chamberlain's Administration in South Carolina* (New York: G. P. Putnam's Sons, 1888), 36–37; Wallace, *South Carolina,* 594–595.

17. Mary Conner Moffett, ed., *Letters of General James Conner, C.S.A.* (Columbia: R. L. Bryan Co., 1950), 204; Dunbar Rowland, ed., *Jefferson Davis, Constitutionalist: His Letters, Papers and Speeches* (Jackson: Mississippi Department of Archives and History, 1923), vol. 7, 399–400 and vol. 9, 366; Cauthen, *Letters,* 145.

18. "Transactions of the Southern Historical Society," *The Southern Magazine* (January 1874) 12, 15, 18; "General Wade Hampton's Warrenton Address," *The Southern Magazine* (August 1873): 249.

19. *Daily Phoenix,* 10 July and 11 July 1875; Cauthen, *Letters,* 152.

20. *Daily Union-Herald,* 22 July 1875.

21. Wallace, *South Carolina,* 596; Sheppard, *Red Shirts,* 38, 39; Thompson, *Ousting,* 88–89; Simkins and Woody, *Reconstruction,* 478.

22. Sheppard, *Red Shirts,* 40, 43, 53–54; *The Free Citizen,* 4 December 1875; *News and Courier,* 8 January 1876.

23. Thompson, *Ousting*, 97.

24. Thompson, *Ousting*, 79.

25. *News and Courier*, 5 May and 6 May 1876.

26. Sheppard, *Red Shirts*, 46–51, 54.

27. *News and Courier*, 6 May 1876.

28. *News and Courier*, 8 May 1876; Thompson, *Ousting*, 98.

29. Cauthen, *Letters*, 153; Wade Hampton to Anna Preston, 18 June 1876 (HFP).

30. *News and Courier*, 28 June and 29 June 1876. "I don't take any stock in the Centennial," Hampton confessed privately in January, speaking of the national event. Wade Hampton to Stephen D. Lee, 31 January 1876 (Stephen Dill Lee Papers, SHC).

31. Thompson, *Ousting*, 2, 5; *News and Courier*, 29 June 1876; *Daily Register*, 12 July 1876.

32. *News and Courier*, 15 August 1878; U. R. Brooks, *Stories of the Confederacy* (Columbia: The State Co., 1912), 372–373; Sheppard, *Red Shirts*, 89.

33. *Daily Phoenix*, 14 March 1874; Sheppard, *Red Shirts*, 90–92; *Daily Register*, 20 July 1876; *Daily Union-Herald*, 19 July 1876; Samuel J. Martin, *Southern Hero: Matthew Calbraith Butler* (Mechanicsburg, Pa.: Stackpole Books, 2001), 211.

34. Statement of Joseph Thomas, 27 July 1876 (Martin W. Gary Papers, SCL).

35. *Daily Register*, 9 July 1876.

36. Wade Hampton to Martin W. Gary, 25 July 1876 (HFP).

37. *Daily Register*, 9 August 1876.

38. *Daily Register*, 16 August 1876; Sheppard, *Red Shirts*, 97–109. "I spoke to him in rude and rough language," said Gary, "in order that the rude and rough negro might understand it." *News and Courier*, 15 August 1878.

39. Statements of James Willis Bradley, 18 May 1926 (Statements Concerning the 1876 Election, SCDAH). Bradley thought the messenger came with a telegram summoning Hampton to Columbia.

40. R. T. Jaynes to W. P. Houseal, 17 February 1926 (Statements Concerning the 1876 Election, SCDAH).

41. Sheppard, *Red Shirts*, 116; Thompson, *Ousting*, 102.

42. Sheppard, *Red Shirts*, 110, 112–114.

43. P. F. Henderson et al., *Life and Addresses of D. S. Henderson* (Columbia: The R. L. Bryan Co., 1922), 149.

44. Henderson et al., *Henderson*, 149; *Daily Register*, 17 August 1876.

45. Thompson, *Ousting*, 103–104.

46. Williamson, *After Slavery*, 408; Thompson, *Ousting*, 103.

47. Thompson, *Ousting*, 104; *Daily Register*, 8 August 1876; Alfred B. Williams, *Hampton and His Red Shirts: South Carolina's Deliverance in 1876* (Charleston, S.C.: Walker, Evans & Cogswell, 1935), 85.

48. Lizzie K. Geiger to W. Leaphart, 15 August 1876 (Lizzie K. Geiger Papers, SCL); *Daily Register*, 17 August and 18 August 1876; John A. Leland, *A Voice From South Carolina* (Charleston, S.C.: Walker, Evans & Cogswell, 1879), 160–161.

49. Allen, *Chamberlain*, 337, 405.

50. *Daily Union-Herald*, 17 August and 21 August 1876.

51. *Daily Register*, 18 August 1876.

Chapter 14

1. Alfred B. Williams, *Hampton and His Red Shirts: South Carolina's Deliverance in 1876* (Charleston, S.C.: Walker, Evans & Cogswell, 1935), 162.

2. *Daily Register,* 23 August 1876.

3. Williams, *Red Shirts,* 79, 104–105.

4. Williams, *Red Shirts,* 106–107.

5. Williams, *Red Shirts,* 105, 134; P. F. Henderson et al., *Life and Addresses of D. S. Henderson* (Columbia: The R. L. Bryan Co., 1922); 146; Edward L. Drago, *Hurrah for Hampton! Black Red Shirts in South Carolina during Reconstruction* (Fayetteville: University of Arkansas Press, 1998), 10.

6. Henry T. Thompson, *Ousting the Carpetbaggers from South Carolina* (Columbia: R. L. Bryan Co., 1926), 69–71, 121, 121n.; Williams, *Red Shirts,* 252, 303.

7. Thompson, *Ousting,* 110, 113.

8. Thompson, *Ousting,* 115–116; Williams, *Red Shirts,* 88; Lowry Ware, *Old Abbeville* (Columbia: SCMAR, 1992), 132–135.

9. Williams, *Red Shirts,* 91, 187, 291, 303; Thompson, *Ousting,* 112; U.S. Senate Subcommittee of the Committee on Privileges and Elections, *South Carolina in 1876. Report on the Denial of the Elective Franchise in South Carolina at the State and National Elections of 1876* (Washington, D.C.: Government Printing Office, 1877), 469; Lizzie K. Geiger to W. Leaphart, 7 September 1876 (Lizzie K. Geiger Papers, SCL).

10. *Daily Register,* 5 September 1876; *News and Courier,* 4 September 1876; Williams, *Red Shirts,* 161–165.

11. Williams, *Red Shirts,* 180.

12. *Daily Register,* 7 September and 8 September 1876; Williams, *Red Shirts,* 167.

13. Thompson, *Ousting,* 119; Williams, *Red Shirts,* 119–121, 156–157.

14. Statement of James Allen Hoyt, c. January 1880 (James Allen Hoyt Papers, SCL); D. D. Wallace, "The Question of the Withdrawal of the Democratic Presidential Electors in South Carolina in 1876," *Journal of Southern History* vol. viii, no. 3 (August 1942): 377.

15. William Arthur Sheppard, *Some Reasons Why Red Shirts Remembered* (Greer, S.C.: privately published, 1940), 8n.

16. Wallace, "Electors," 379.

17. *Chronicle and Sentinel,* 10 January 1877; William Arthur Sheppard, *Red Shirts Remembered: Southern Brigadiers of the Reconstruction Period* (Atlanta: Ruralist Press, Inc., 1940), 141; Edward L. Wells, *Hampton and Reconstruction* (Columbia: The State Co., 1907), 179; Statement of James Allen Hoyt, c. January 1880 (James Allen Hoyt Papers, SCL).

18. Williams, *Red Shirts,* 223, 248; *Yorkville Enquirer,* 5 October 1876.

19. Thompson, *Ousting,* 119; Williams, *Red Shirts,* 206–208, 209, 212, 225–226.

20. *News and Courier,* 25 September 1876; Williams, *Red Shirts,* 218–220; *Daily Register,* 24 September 1876.

21. Wade Hampton, *Free Men! Free Ballots! Free Schools!!!*)n.p.: [Democratic Executive Committee, 1876]), 8; Williams, *Red Shirts,* 201; Drago, *Black Red Shirts,* 59.

22. Drago, *Black Red Shirts,* 23, 24, 25.

23. Drago, *Black Red Shirts,* 13, 14, 16, 22, 39; R. T. Jaynes to W. P. Houseal, 19 February 1926 (Statements Concerning the 1876 Election, SCDAH).

24. Hampton, *Free Men!,* 5, 7; Williams, *Red Shirts,* 229.

25. Drago, *Black Red Shirts,* 27, 39–40, 41, 42; Williams, *Red Shirts,* 224, 227, 259, 353; Lizzie K. Geiger to W. Leaphart, 13 November 1876 (Lizzie K. Geiger Papers, SCL).

26. Williams, *Red Shirts,* 237, 348–349; Drago, *Black Red Shirts,* 21, 23.

27. *Horry News,* 5 August 1876; *News and Courier,* 7 October 1876; Williams, *Red Shirts,* 241–243.

28. *Horry News,* 21 October and 28 October 1876.

29. C. M. Calhoun, *Liberty Dethroned: A Concise History of Some of the Most Startling events before, during, and since the Civil War* (n.p.: privately published, n.d.), 341–342; Williams, *Red Shirts*, 244.

30. John A. Leland, *A Voice from South Carolina* (Charleston, S.C.: Walker, Evans & Cogswell, 1879), 165; Thompson, *Ousting*, 124, 125, 127; Williams, *Red Shirts*, 263.

31. Thompson, *Ousting*, 122, 125–126, 126n.; Williams, *Red Shirts*, 246, 358; Drago, *Black Red Shirts*, 37.

32. Williams, *Red Shirts*, 261, 297–299; Leland, *Voice*, 165.

33. *New York Tribune*, 3 November 1876; U.S. Senate Subcommittee, *South Carolina*, 137–138; Williams, *Red Shirts*, 296, 316, 331.

34. *Yorkville Enquirer*, 19 October 1976; Williams, *Red Shirts*, 279–282.

35. Thompson, *Ousting*, 119–120; Williams, *Red Shirts*, 272–274.

36. Virginia G. Meynard, *The Venturers: The Hampton, Harrison, and Earle Families of Virginia, South Carolina, and Texas* (Easley, S.C.: Southern Historical Press, 1981), 568; Williams, *Red Shirts*, 295. the child born on 15 October, John Cheves Haskell Jr., would die in only two years.

37. Williams, *Red Shirts*, 309–311; Thompson, *Ousting*, 127.

38. Williams, *Red Shirts*, 89–90, 217, 235; James Conner to his wife, 10 October 1876 (HFP).

39. Williams, *Red Shirts*, 90, 91, 235.

40. Williams, *Red Shirts*, 178–179.

41. Williams, *Red Shirts*, 321, 324–329; U.S. Senate Subcommittee, *South Carolina*, 139–140; Drago, *Black Red Shirts*, 15; *News and Courier*, 27 October, 1876.

42. Mary Conner Moffett, ed., *Letters of General James Conner, C.S.A.* (Columbia: R. L. Bryan Co., 1950), 220–225; Williams, *Red Shirts*, 339–343; *News and Courier*, 31 October 1876.

43. *News and Courier*, 4 November 1876; Williams, *Red Shirts*, 354–356; *Daily Register*, 6 November 1876.

44. Lizzie K. Geiger to W. Leaphart, 30 October 1876 (Lizzie K. Geiger Papers, SCL).

45. Williams, *Red Shirts*, 357–359; *Daily Register*, 6 November 1876.

CHAPTER 15

1. Alfred B. Williams, *Hampton and His Red Shirts: South Carolina's Deliverance in 1876* (Charleston, S.C.: Walker, Evans & Cogswell, 1935), 364–365; Henry T. Thompson, *Ousting the Carpetbagger from South Carolina* (Columbia: R. L. Bryan Co., 1926), 129.

2. Hampton M. Jarrell, *Wade Hampton and the Negro: The Road Not Taken* (Columbia: University of South Carolina Press, 1950), 168–170.

3. U.S. Senate Subcommittee of the Committee on Privileges and Elections, *South Carolina in 1876. Report on the Denial of the Elective Franchise in South Carolina at the State and National Elections of 1876* (Washington, D.C.: Government Printing Office, 1877), 335–336, 345, 349; Wade Hampton, *Reply of Wade Hampton, Governor of South Carolina, and Others to the Chamberlain Memorial* (Columbia: Presbyterian Publishing House, 1877), 4–6; Thompson, *Ousting*, 133–134; Edward L. Wells, *Hampton and Reconstruction* (Columbia: The State Co., 1907), 184; Williams, *Red Shirts*, 240, 365, 379–380; *News and Courier*, 20 January 1879.

4. Wells, *Reconstruction*, 148–151.

5. *Daily Register*, 9 November and 11 November 1876; Lizzie K. Geiger to W. Leaph-

art, 13 November 1876 (Lizzie K. Geiger Papers, SCL); Williams, *Red Shirts,* 372; Oliver _____ to William H. Witherow, 13 November 1876 (W. H. Witherow Papers, SCL).

6. Thompson, *Ousting,* 132; Williams, *Red Shirts,* 374; Wade Hampton to Armistead Burt, 17 November 1876 (Wade Hampton Papers, Duke).

7. Williams, *Red Shirts,* 368–372; Thompson, *Ousting,* 130–131.

8. Thompson, *Ousting,* 132; Williams, *Red Shirts,* 383.

9. Williams, *Red Shirts,* 387–388; Thompson, *Ousting,* 136–137.

10. Thompson, *Ousting,* 137–139.

11. Claude E. Sawyer to W. P. Houseal, 17 November 1926 (Statements Concerning the 1876 Election, SCDAH); Williams, *Red Shirts,* 375.

12. Williams, *Red Shirts,* 394; Claude E. Sawyer to W. P. Houseal, 17 November 1926 (Statements Concerning the 1876 Election, SCDAH).

13. Williams, *Red Shirts,* 394; Thompson, *Ousting,* 141–142; *Daily Register,* 8 December 1876.

14. Thompson, *Ousting,* 159–160; *The Nation,* 30 November and 7 December 1876.

15. Thompson, *Ousting,* 140, 140n., 143–144; Williams, *Red Shirts,* 395–396.

16. Williams, *Red Shirts,* 399–401; Thompson, *Ousting,* 144–147; Claude E. Sawyer to W. P. Houseal, 17 November 1926 (Statements Concerning the 1876 Election, SCDAH).

17. Williams, *Red Shirts,* 401–402; Claude E. Sawyer to W. P. Houseal, 17 November 1926 (Statements Concerning the 1876 Election, SCDAH).

18. Williams, *Red Shirts,* 404–406; *Journal of the House of Representatives of the State of South Carolina Being the Annual Session of 1876,* 30 November; Wade Hampton to U. S. Grant, 30 November 1876 (WHC).

19. Williams, *Red Shirts,* 406–407.

20. Wade Hampton to Hamilton Fish, 3 December 1876 (WHC); Williams, *Red Shirts,* 408.

21. Claude E. Sawyer to W. P. Houseal, 17 November 1926 (Statements Concerning the 1876 Election, SCDAH); London *Times,* 20 December 1876; Williams, *Red Shirts,* 411.

22. Williams, *Red Shirts,* 409, 415–416.

23. Claude E. Sawyer to W. P. Houseal, 17 November 1926 (Statements Concerning the 1876 Election, SCDAH); Thompson, *Ousting,* 149; Bradly Johnson to J. B. Gordon, 10 December 1876 (Bradly Johnson Papers, Duke). The New York *Times* on 5 December 1876 claimed that only "the presence of the military preserves the peace."

24. W. H. Jones to Wade Hampton, 29 December 1876 (Records of Governor Wade Hampton, SCDAH); London *Times,* 28 December 1876.

25. Williams, *Red Shirts,* 419–420; Thompson, *Ousting,* 149; *House Journal 1876,* 8 December.

26. Thompson, *Ousting,* 143; London *Times,* 1 January 1877.

27. Thompson, *Ousting,* 151; Williams, *Red Shirts,* 420.

28. Williams, *Red Shirts,* 419, 421; Wells, *Reconstruction,* 170; Thompson, *Ousting,* 151.

29. Wade Hampton to John S. Mosby, 11 December 1876 and undated Mosby note (John W. Daniel Papers, Duke); Wells, *Reconstruction,* 171; Williams, *Red Shirts,* 423–425.

30. Williams, *Red Shirts,* 425; *House Journal 1876,* 38.

31. Williams, *Red Shirts,* 426; Thompson, *Ousting,* 152–153.

32. *News and Courier* ("Extra" supplement), 14 December 1876. Hampton claimed that 17,000 blacks voted for him. Adjutant General Moise estimated the number at 16,000; Democratic Party chief Haskell said 15,000. Chamberlain conceded that 3,000 blacks voted for his opponent, a number far greater than Hampton's margin of victory. See DeWitt Grant Jones, "Wade Hampton and the Rhetoric of Race: A Study of the Speaking of Wade

Hampton on the Race Issue in South Carolina, 1865–1878" (Ph.D., dissertation, Louisiana State University, 1988), 167–168; George B. Tindall, *South Carolina Negroes, 1877–1900* (Columbia: University of South Carolina Press, 1952), 30.

33. *Daily Register,* 15 December and 27 December 1876; New York *Times,* 15 December 1876; *New York Tribune,* 15 December 1876.

34. Thompson, *Ousting,* 153–154; Wade Hampton to Rutherford B. Hayes, 23 December 1876 (WHC).

35. Wells, *Reconstruction,* 153–154; Thompson, *Ousting,* 162n.; *News and Courier,* 3 January 1877.

36. Charles Richard Williams, ed., *Diary and Letters of Rutherford Birchard Hayes, Nineteenth President of the United States,* vol. 3 (Columbus: The Ohio State Archaeological and Historical Society, 1924), 396.

37. *House Journal 1876,* 20 December; *News and Courier,* 2 January 1877; Williams, *Red Shirts,* 424.

38. *News and Courier,* 16 December 1876; Wade Hampton to Franklin Moses, 15 January 1877 (Letterbook #1, Records of Governor Wade Hampton, SCDAH); Receipts and Disbursements, 14 December 1876 to 2 March 1877 (Proclamation Book, Records of Governor Wade Hampton, SCDAH).

39. Capt. W. A. Jones to Governor of South Carolina, 9 February 1877 (Records of Governor Wade Hampton, SCDAH).

40. Theodore Parmele to Wade Hampton, 2 March 1877 (Records of Governor Wade Hampton, SCDAH); *Reports and Resolutions of the General Assembly of the State of South Carolina at the Regular Session, 1877–1878* (Columbia: Calvo & Patton, 1878), 576; Thompson, *Ousting,* 158–159; Williams, *Red Shirts,* 436–437; *News and Courier,* 30 January 1877.

41. L. R. Ragsdale to Wade Hampton, 13 January 1877 and J. R. Byrd to Wade Hampton, 20 February 1877 (Records of Governor Wade Hampton, SCDAH); *Daily Register,* 20 December 1876; Benjamin Stuart Williams to Wade Hampton, 3 March 1877 (Benjamin Stuart Williams Papers, SCL).

42. Special Order, 13 April 1877 (Letterbook #2, Records of Governor Wade Hampton, SCDAH); Williams, *Red Shirts,* 438–439; Proclamation of Wade Hampton, 20 February 1877 (Letterbook #1, Records of Governor Wade Hampton, SCDAH).

43. *Daily Register,* 21 December 1876; M. C. Butler to Wade Hampton, 21 December 1876 (Records of Governor Wade Hampton, SCDAH).

44. Paul Leland Haworth, *The Hayes–Tilden Disputed Presidential Election of 1876* (Cleveland, Ohio: The Burrows Brothers Co., 1906), 268–270, 295; Williams, *Red Shirts,* 441; T. J. Mackey to Wade Hampton, 5 March 1877 (Records of Governor Wade Hampton, SCDAH).

45. T. J. Mackey to Wade Hampton, 10 March 1877 (Records of Governor Wade Hampton, SCDAH).

46. T. J. Mackey to Wade Hampton, 13 March, 14 March, and 20 March 1877 (Records of Governor Wade Hampton, SCDAH).

47. Wade Hampton to M. C. Butler, 17 March 1877 (WHC); M. C. Butler to Wade Hampton, 20 March 1877 (Records of Governor Wade Hampton, SCDAH).

48. *Daily Register,* 25 March 1877.

49. T. J. Mackey to Wade Hampton, 22 March 1877 (Records of Governor Wade Hampton, SCDAH); Wade Hampton to T. J. Mackey, 22 March 1877 (WHC).

50. Jonathan Coyle to M. C. Butler, n.d., M. C. Butler to Wade Hampton, 23 March 1877, and M. C. Butler to Wade Hampton, 3:20 P.M., 23 March 1877 (Records of Governor Wade Hampton, SCDAH).

51. Walter Allen, *Governor Chamberlain's Administration in South Carolina* (New York: G. P. Putnam's Sons, 1888), 473; Brainerd Dyer, *The Public Career of William M. Evarts* (Berkeley: University of California Press, 1933), 189; Williams, *Diary,* vol. 3, 429.

52. T. J. Mackey to Wade Hampton, 24 March and 25 March 1877 (Records of Governor Wade Hampton, SCDAH).

53. Wade Hampton to Rutherford B. Hayes, 26 March 1877 (WHC). Hampton's reply was telegraphed at 9:20 A.M. A letter, with the same text, was also mailed.

54. Williams, *Red Shirts,* 443; Thompson, *Ousting,* 164; New York *Times,* 1 April 1877; *Daily Register,* 28 March 1877.

55. Wade Hampton to Rutherford B. Hayes, 29 March 1877 (WHC).

56. Mary Conner Moffett, ed., *Letters of General James Conner, C.S.A.* (Columbia: R. L. Bryan Co., 1950), 233–235 (Conner dated his letter March 28, but he must have meant March 29); Chester L. Barrows, *William M. Evarts: Lawyer, Diplomat, Statesman* (Chapel Hill: University of North Carolina Press, 1941), 315.

57. Undated manuscript quoting the New York *Tribune* (HFP).

58. Jarrell, *Hampton,* 173; Wade Hampton to Rutherford B. Hayes, 31 March 1877 (WHC).

59. Williams, *Red Shirts,* 444; Thompson, *Ousting,* 164; New York *Times,* 5 April 1877; *New York Tribune,* 3 April 1877.

60. Williams, *Red Shirts,* 444–445; Thompson, *Ousting,* 164; Wells, *Reconstruction,* 194.

61. Williams, *Red Shirts,* 446–447; Thompson, *Ousting,* 164–165; *News and Courier,* 11 April and 13 April 1877.

62. Williams, *Red Shirts,* 446–447.

63. Allen, *Chamberlain,* 526; Thompson, *Ousting,* 169–170; *Times and Democrat,* 29 January 1902.

64. Daniel H. Chamberlain, "Reconstruction in South Carolina," *The Atlantic Monthly* vol. LXXXVII (April 1901): 473–481.

CHAPTER 16

1. A. P. Butler to Wade Hampton, 18 December 1876 (Records of Governor Wade Hampton, SCDAH). Surviving letters to Hampton seeking or recommending appointments total 326 in December alone.

2. James Conner to Wade Hampton, 20 December 1876 (Records of Governor Wade Hampton, SCDAH).

3. J. Y. Pope to Wade Hampton, 23 December 1876 (Records of Governor Wade Hampton, SCDAH).

4. James F. Izlar to Wade Hampton, 21 December 1876 and undated form letter from Wade Hampton (Records of Governor Wade Hampton, SCDAH). Hampton even appealed to N.C. governor Zebulon Vance to find a position for a South Carolinian living in Charlotte. See Wade Hampton to Zebulon B. Vance, 10 December 1877 (Zebulon B. Vance Papers, SHC).

5. Proclamation of Wade Hampton, 12 April 1877 (Proclamation Book, Records of Governor Wade Hampton, SCDAH).

6. William J. Cooper Jr., "The Conservative Regime in South Carolina" (Ph.D. dissertation, John Hopkins University Press, 1966), 23–26, 28–29; William L. Buck to Desiah Buck, 1 May 1877 (Simpson Family Papers, SCL).

7. Executive Message No. 1, [24] April 1877 (Records of Governor Wade Hampton, SCDAH).

8. Wade Hampton to William M. Evarts, 13 May 1877 (HFP); Cooper, "Conservative," 33.

9. Cooper, "Conservative," 39–40; Henry T. Thompson, *Ousting the Carpetbagger from South Carolina* (Columbia: R. L. Bryan Co., 1926), 58; Wade Hampton to J. Bratton, 14 June 1878 (Bratton Family Papers, SCL); Rutherford B. Hayes to Wade Hampton, 12 May 1877 (WHC).

10. Wade Hampton to W. D. Simpson, 16 June 1877 (HFP); *Daily Register,* 3 July and 7 July 1877; Wade Hampton to Rutherford B. Hayes, 24 June and 25 September 1877 (WHC).

11. Ari Hoogenboom, *Rutherford B. Hayes: Warrior and President* (Lawrence: University Press of Kansas, 1995), 364–366; Wade Hampton to Rutherford B. Hayes, 9 January 1878 (WHC).

12. Wade Hampton to Rutherford B. Hayes, 15 July and 13 August 1878 (WHC): *News and Courier,* 18 July 1878; Charles Richard Williams, ed., *Diary and Letters of Rutherford Birchard Hayes, Nineteenth President of the United States,* vol. 3 (Columbus: The Ohio State Archaeological and Historical Society, 1924), 492–493.

13. *News and Courier,* 20 August 1877; Charles D. Jacobs to Wade Hampton, 1 September 1877 and Jilson P. Johnson to Wade Hampton, 1 September 1877 (Records of Governor Wade Hampton, SCDAH).

14. *News and Courier,* 17 September 1877.

15. Hoogenboom, *Hayes,* 317; Williams, *Diary,* vol. 3, 443.

16. Message No. 1 from the Governor, 28 November 1877 (Records of Governor Wade Hampton, SCDAH).

17. George Brown Tindall, *South Carolina Negroes 1877–1900* (Columbia: University of South Carolina Press, 1952), 22–23; C. Vann Woodward, *Reunion and Reaction: The Compromise of 1877 and the End of Reconstruction* (Boston: Little, Brown and Co., 1951), 227.

18. Message No. 1 from the Governor, 28 November 1877 (Records of Governor Wade Hampton, SCDAH); Daniel Walker Hollis, *The University of South Carolina,* vol. 2 (Columbia: University of South Carolina Press, 1951), 79, 83.

19. Cooper, "Conservative," 67, 69–70, 73, 74–77.

20. Cooper, "Conservative," 77–82; William L. Buck to Desiah Buck, 5 May 1877 (Simpson Family Papers, SCL).

21. William L. Buck to Desiah Buck, 6 March 1878 (Simpson Family Papers, SCL); Cooper, "Conservative," 83–85.

22. *Journal of the House of Representatives of the State of South Carolina Being the Annual Session of 1877–1878* (Columbia: Calvo & Patton, 1878), 113, 478; The Hampton County Tricentennial Commission, *Both Sides of the Swamp: Hampton County* (Columbia: R. L. Bryan, 1970), 10, 190n.

23. *Daily Register,* 7 July 1878.

24. *News and Courier,* 29 August 1878.

25. Charlestine Romelle Fairley, "A History of Claflin College 1869–1987" (Ph.D. dissertation, University of South Carolina, 1990), vii, 25, 26; David Duncan Wallace, *The History of South Carolina,* vol. 3 (New York: The American Historical Society, Inc., 1934), 329n.

26. Cooper, "Conservative," 86–87, 89, 91.

27. Tindall, *Negroes,* 30.

28. Wade Hampton to James Conner, 5 September 1878 (HFP); Wade Hampton to Milledge Luke Bonham, 28 September 1878 (Milledge Luke Bonham Papers, SCL).

29. *News and Courier,* 20 September 1878.

30. Kate Hampton to [Mrs. James H. Hammond?], 6 June 1878 (HFP).

31. *Reports and Resolutions of the General Assembly of the State of South Carolina at the Regular Session, 1877–1878* (Columbia: Calvo & Patton, 1878), 411–413, 417; *Reports and Resolutions of the General Assembly of the State of South Carolina at the Regular Session of 1878* (Columbia: Calvo & Patton, 1878), 32, 343–345; *Newberry Herald,* 15 January 1879.

32. *Reports and Resolutions 1877–1878,* 733, 735, 740; *Reports and Resolutions 1878,* 448–449, 563.

33. *News and Courier,* 26 August 1878.

34. Wade Hampton to Rutherford B. Hayes, 25 March 1878 (WHC); Wade Hampton to Armistead Burt, 24 March 1878 (Wade Hampton Papers, Duke).

35. *Daily Register,* 8 August and 9 August 1878; *News and Courier,* 9 August 1878.

36. Tindall, *Negroes,* 24–25, 26; *Chronicle and Constitutionalist,* 25 April 1878.

37. *Daily Register,* 7 September 1878; Tindall, *Negroes,* 25.

38. *Daily Register,* 21 September and 24 September 1878; Paul Hamilton Hayne to John Greenleaf Whittier, 17 November 1878 (John Greenleaf Whittier Papers, Duke).

39. Edward L. Drago, *Hurrah for Hampton!: Black Red Shirts in South Carolina during Reconstruction* (Fayetteville: University of Arkansas Press, 1998), 47; Tindall, *Negroes,* 34.

40. *News and Courier,* 31 October 1878; George Campbell, *White and Black: The Outcome of a Visit to the United States* (New York: R. Worthington, 1879), 313, 315, 321.

41. *Reports and Resolutions 1878,* 438; Tindall, *Negroes,* 36.

42. *Anderson Intelligencer,* 14 November 1878; Alfred B. Williams, *Hampton and His Red Shirts: South Carolina's Deliverance in 1876* (Charleston, S.C.: Walker, Evans & Cogswell, 1935), 217.

43. *Anderson Intelligencer,* 14 November 1878; *Daily Register,* 9 November 1878. The Anderson reporter gathered his information from a Hampton relative. The account here combines facts found in both press reports. Edward L. Wells (*Hampton and Reconstruction,* 201) claims that a rotten bridle broke, the mule ran with Hampton astride the animal, causing his leg to hit a tree. Wells published his book twenty-nine years after the accident and five years after Hampton's death.

44. *Anderson Intelligencer,* 14 November 1878.

45. *Daily Register,* 9 November and 14 November 1878.

46. *Daily Register,* 24 November and 27 November 1878.

47. *Daily Register,* 22 November 1878.

48. *News and Courier,* 11 November and 15 November 1878.

49. *Newberry Herald,* 4 December 1878; *News and Courier,* 1 December and 2 December 1878.

50. *Daily Register,* 19 April 1878.

51. *Daily Register,* 24 November and 30 November 1878; *Anderson Intelligencer,* 12 December 1878.

52. *Daily Register,* 20 August 1878; *Anderson Intelligencer,* 28 November 1878.

53. *Daily Register,* 24 November 1878.

54. *Daily Register,* 5 December 1878; *Anderson Intelligencer,* 12 December 1878.

55. *Daily Register,* 7 December 1878.

56. *News and Courier,* 7 December and 9 December 1878; William L. Buck to Desiah Buck, 9 December 1878 (Simpson Family Papers, SCL).

57. *Daily Register,* 11 December 1878; *News and Courier,* 11 December 1878.

58. *News and Courier,* 13 December and 16 December 1878.

59. *News and Courier,* 17 December and 18 December 1878.

60. *Newberry Herald,* 18 December 1878.

61. *Daily Register,* 17 January 1879. The dialog in the *Register* article has been restructured, but the words remain unchanged.

62. *Newberry Herald,* 18 December 1878; *Daily Register,* 2 February 1879.

63. *Daily Register,* 17 January 1879.

CHAPTER 17

1. *News and Courier,* 15, 16, and 17 January 1879; *Daily Register,* 23 February 1879; *Newberry Herald,* 29 January and 5 February 1879.

2. *Daily Register,* 27 February 1879; Wade Hampton to Matthew C. Butler, 18 March 1879 (Matthew C. Butler Papers, SCL).

3. *Daily Register,* 17 April 1879; U.S. Congress, *Congressional Record,* 46th Cong., 1st Sess., 16 April 1879, vol. 9, 483; *Newberry Herald,* 5 February 1879.

4. *Congressional Record,* 46th Cong., 1st Sess., 23 April 1879, vol. 9, 737, and 5 June 1879, vol. 9 1778–1781.

5. Wade Hampton, "Ought the Negro to Be Disfranchised? Ought He to Have Been Enfranchised?" *North American Review* vol CCLXVII (March 1879): 240–243.

6. Wade Hampton to William Pinckney Starke, 26 August 1879 (William Pinckney Starke Papers, SCL); Virginia G. Meynard, *The Venturers: The Hampton, Harrison, and Earle Families of Virginia, South Carolina, and Texas* (Easley, S.C.: Southern Historical Press, 1981), 564; Wade Hampton to Anna Preston, 20 March 1880 (HFP).

7. *Daily Register,* 17 June 1879; Herbert J. Clancy, *The Presidential Election of 1880* (Chicago: Loyola University Press, 1958), 79, 137.

8. *News and Courier,* 23 June and 25 June 1880; *New York Tribune,* 25 June 1880.

9. *News and Courier,* 25 June 1880; Wade Hampton to Thomas F. Bayard, 26 June 1880 (Thomas F. Bayard Papers, LC).

10. *News and Courier,* 2 August 1880; *Chicago Tribune,* 26 August 1880; Clancy, *Election,* 178.

11. *Congressional Record,* 46th Cong., 1st Sess., 19 May 1879, vol. 9, pt. 2, 1458–1459, 20 June 1879, vol. 9, 2207, and 16 May 1879, vol. 9 1358.

12. *Congressional Record,* 6 June 1879, 1811–1812.

13. *Congressional Record,* 47th Cong., 1st Sess., 27 April 1892, vol. 13, pt. 4, 3348–3350 and 2 May 1882, vol. 9 3499.

14. *Congressional Record,* 48th Cong., 1st Sess., 27 March 1884, vol. 15, pt. 3, 2328–2330; *Daily Register,* 30 March 1884.

15. Daniel Walker Hollis, *The University of South Carolina,* vol. 2 (Columbia: University of South Carolina Press, 1951), 131–132; Wade Hampton to Hugh Thompson, 23 June 1885 (HFP).

16. Wade Hampton to Matthew C. Butler, 16 November 1879 (Matthew C. Butler Papers, SCL); Wade Hampton to Stephen D. Lee, 22 February 1882 (Stephen D. Lee Papers, SHC); Charles E. Cauthen, ed., *Family Letters of the Three Wade Hamptons 1782–1901* (Columbia: University of South Carolina Press, 1953), 159.

17. Wade Hampton to Armistead Burt, 28 August 1881 (Wade Hampton Papers, Duke); James A. Garfield to Wade Hampton, 6 May 1881 (James A. Garfield Papers, LC).

18. Wade Hampton to Chester A. Arthur, 16 January 1885, and Seating Arrangement for White House Dinner, 24 January 1885 (Chester A. Arthur Papers, LC).

19. *News and Courier*, 18, 23, and 26 June 1884.

20. *News and Courier*, 11 July and 7 November 1884.

21. Wade Hampton to Grover Cleveland, 5 February 1886 (Grover Cleveland Papers, LC); *Biographical Directory of the American Congress, 1774–1927* (Washington, D.C.: Government Printing Office, 1928), 21, 1001, 1199.

22. *Congressional Record*, 49th Cong., 1st Sess., 18 December 1885, vol. 17, pt. 1, 300; Wade Hampton to Jonathan Leaphart, 4 June 1885 (Janney-Leaphart Family Papers, SCL); Wade Hampton to Augustus H. Garland, 12 June 1885 (Grover Cleveland Papers, LC).

23. Congressional Record, 46th Cong., 2nd Sess., 12 April 1880, vol. 10, pt. 3, 2319 and 49th Cong., 2nd Sess., 26 February 1887, vol. 18, pt. 3, 2326.

24. Wade Hampton to Grover Cleveland, 4 April 1886 (Grover Cleveland Papers, LC); Meynard, *Venturers*, 269; *Congressional Record*, 49th Cong., 1st Sess., 7 April 1886, vol. 17, pt. 3, 3176 and 9 June 1886, vol. 17, pt. 5, 5438; Wade Hampton to Benjamin Walter Taylor, 11 August 1886 (Benjamin Walter Taylor Papers, SCL).

25. Robert R. Brown, *The Mountains in Reply* (n.p.: privately published, n.d.), 2: Wade Hampton to Grover Cleveland, 18 October 1886 (Grover Cleveland Papers, LC); Meynard, *Venturers*, 579.

26. Wade Hampton to Julius L. Brown, 8 December 1889 (Galesburg, Ill.: Sang-Lee Civil War Collection, Knox College); Wade Hampton to Grover Cleveland, 9 August 1887 (Grover Cleveland Papers, LC).

27. Hudson Strode, ed., *Jefferson Davis: Private Letters 1823–1889* (New York: Harcourt, Brace & World, Inc., 1966), 554–555; Dunbar Rowland, ed., *Jefferson Davis, Constitutionalist: His Letters, Papers and Speeches*, vol. 10 (Jackson: Mississippi Department of Archives and History, 1923), 48, 161–162.

28. Heros von Borcke, *Memoirs of the Confederate War for Independence* (New York: Peter Smith, 1938), 122–123; Lucy Durr writings, n.d. (Durr Family Papers, Alabama Department of Archives and History).

29. G. G. Vest, "A Senator of Two Republics," *The Saturday Evening Post* (20 February 1904) 8. There is a slightly different version in Edward L. Wells, *Hampton and Reconstruction* (Columbia: The State Co., 1907), 18–19.

30. Richard Rollins, ed., *The Returned Battle Flags* (Redondo Beach, Calif.: Rank and File Publications, 1995), iii.

31. *Congressional Record*, 51st Cong., 1st Sess., 30 January 1890, vol. 21, pt. 1, 967, 970–972.

32. Wade Hampton, "What Negro Supremacy Means," *The Forum Extra* vol. 1, no. 1 (March 1890): 4, 14.

33. Wade Hampton, "The Race Problem," *The Arena* vol. 2, no. 2 (July 1890): 133, 136, 137.

34. *News and Courier*, 10 December 1884; *Mercury*, 25 January and 29 January 1881; *Daily Register*, 10 April 1881.

35. Francis Butler Simkins, *Pitchfork Ben Tillman: South Carolinian* (Baton Rouge: Louisiana State University Press, 1967), 45, 68, 93, 140–141, 143–146; Howard Dorgan, "'Pitchfork Ben' Tillman and 'The Race Problem from a Southern Point of View.'" In *The Oratory of Southern Demogogues*, eds. Cal. M. Logue and Howard Dorgan (Baton Rouge: Louisiana State University Press, 1981), 56, 63; Stephen Kantrowitz, *Ben Tillman & the Reconstruction of White Supremacy* (Chapel Hill: University of North Carolina Press, 2000), 82–83; *News and Courier*, 23 January 1890.

36. *The World,* 25 June 1890; *Times and Democrat,* 2 July 1890; Francis Butler Simkins, *The Tillman Movement in South Carolina* (Gloucester, Mass.: Peter Smith, 1964), 122. Hampton had been to Canada before. See Wade Hampton to Grover Cleveland, 25 June 1887 (Grover Cleveland Papers, LC.).

37. Simkins, *Ben Tillman,* 163, 164–165, 168n., 201–202; *Times and Democrat,* 29 October 1890; Jerry L. Slaunwhite, "John L. M. Irby: The Creation of a Crisis" (Master's thesis, University of South Carolina, 1973), 59, 79.

38. *News and Courier,* 28 November 1890; *Times and Democrat,* 19 November 1890 and 13 July 1892; Benjamin R. Tillman to J. C. Guinyard, 2 September 1912 (Benjamin R. Tillman Papers, SCL); Simkins, *Movement,* 153.

39. *News and Courier,* 10, 11, and 12 December 1890; *Washington Post,* 12 December 1890.

40. *News and Courier,* 8 and 12 December 1890; Lynwood Mathis Holland, *Pierce M. B. Young, the Warwick of the South* (Athens: University of Georgia Press, 1964), 208.

41. Wade Hampton to Matthew C. Butler, 13 December 1890 (Matthew C. Butler Papers, SCL); Wade Hampton to Theodore G. Barker, 29 January 1891 (HFP).

42. Wade Hampton to Benjamin Harrison, 27 November 1889 and 16 January 1890 (Benjamin Harrison Papers, LC); *Congressional Record,* 51st Cong., 2nd Sess., 16 January 1891, vol. 22, pt. 2, 1418–1422. In losing his registration Hampton was spared the indignity of actually having to vote for Tillman, although Tillman was sure it was deliberate.

43. *News and Courier,* 19 January 1891.

44. *Proceedings of the Centennial Celebration of the First Meeting of the General Assembly of the State of South Carolina Convened in the Town of Columbia in the Year 1791* (Columbia: Centennial Committee, 1893), 28; *State,* 14 May 1891.

CHAPTER 18

1. *State,* 22 and 24 March 1891; Gilbert E. Govan and James Livingwood, *General Joseph E. Johnston, C.S.A.: A Different Valor* (New York: Bobbs-Merrill Co., Inc., 1956), 394.

2. *State,* 7 and 9 March 1892; *Times and Democrat,* 9 and 30 March 1892; Frank E. Jordan Jr., *The Primary State: A History of the Democratic Party in South Carolina 1876–1962* (n.p., n.d.), 13–14.

3. *News and Courier,* 23 and 24 June 1892.

4. *State,* 15 November 1892.

5. G. G. Vest, "A Senator of Two Republics," *The Saturday Evening Post* (20 February 1904) 8; *Report of the Commissioner of Railroads to the Secretary of the Interior. 1893* (Washington, D.C.: Government Printing Office, 1893), 12; *Washington Post,* 21 March 1893.

6. *State,* 8 and 21 March 1893.

7. Charles E. Thomas to Mother, 5 April 1893 (Charles E. Thomas Papers, SCL).

8. *Report of the Commissioner 1893,* 4–7, 217; Nelson Trottman, *History of the Union Pacific: A Financial and Economic Survey* (New York: Augustus M. Kelly, Publishers, 1966), 141–142, 244–246; *Salt Lake City Herald,* 28 May 1893.

9. Unless otherwise noted, quotations and the narrative of the trip are from a record kept by Charles E. Thomas, "A Trip Across the Continent, Made by General Wade Hampton, U.S. Railroad Commissioner, Accompanied by a Party of Friends," 1893 (Charles E. Thomas Papers, SCL).

10. *Rocky Mountain News,* 21 and 24 May 1893.

11. *Wyoming State Tribune,* 25 May 1893; *Cheyenne Daily Leader,* 26 May 1893; *Daily Sun,* 26 May 1893.

12. *Daily Tribune,* 28 May 1893; *Deseret Evening News,* 27 May 1893.

13. *Examiner,* 3 June 1893.

14. U. R. Brooks, *Butler and His Cavalry in the War of Secession, 1861–1865* (Columbia: The State Co., 1909), 261.

15. *Daily Record-Union,* 25 June 1893.

16. Brooks, *Butler and His Cavalry,* 261.

17. *State,* 10 July 1893.

18. *Report of the Commissioner 1893,* 7, 9–12, 103–128; *Examiner,* 3 June 1893; Wade Hampton to Hoke Smith, 19 January 1894 (Grover Cleveland Papers, LC).

19. *Report of the Commissioner of Railroads to the Secretary of the Interior. 1894* (Washington, D.C.: Government Printing Office, 1894), 3–4, 11–12.

20. *Report of the Commissioner of Railroads to the Secretary of the Interior. 1895* (Washington, D.C.: Government Printing Office, 1895), 3, 7, 13–16.

21. *Report of the Commissioner of Railroads to the Secretary of the Interior. 1896* (Washington, D.C.: Government Printing Office, 1896), 11.

22. Wade Hampton to Edward L. Wells, 20 December 1897 (Wells Correspondence, Charleston Library Society).

23. Wade Hampton to Narciso Gonzales, 30 August 1893 (HFP); Andrew Harllee to Wade Hampton, 22 April 1893 (Grover Cleveland Papers, LC); Wade Hampton to Edward Wells, 5 September 1900 (Wells Correspondence, Charleston Library Society).

24. Wade Hampton to Narciso Gonzales, 9 February 1894 (HFP).

25. Wade Hampton to Grover Cleveland, 4 December 1893 (Grover Cleveland Papers, LC); *News and Courier,* 29 November and 12 December 1893.

26. George G. Prince to Wade Hampton, 6 October 1893 and J. P. Poole to Wade Hampton, 19 October 1893 (Grover Cleveland Papers, LC).

27. Private secretary of Theodore Roosevelt to Wade Hampton, 19 and 20 October 1897, and Theodore Roosevelt to Wade Hampton, 26 October 1897 (Theodore Roosevelt Papers, LC).

28. Wade Hampton to Henry T. Thurber, 7 September 1893 (Grover Cleveland Papers, LC).

29. Charles E. Thomas to Mother, 1 November 1895 (Charles E. Thomas Papers, SCL).

30. *State,* 10 November 1897; *Times and Democrat,* 8 May 1901; Trottman, *Union Pacific,* 267–272.

31. *State,* 13 and 15 November 1897.

32. *State,* 27 April 1892.

33. Camp Moultrie, Sons of Confederate Veterans, comp., *Echoes from Hampton Day* (Charleston, S.C.: Walker, Evans & Cogswell), 20–21, 26.

34. *State,* 10 May 1899.

35. *State,* 3 and 10 May 1899; I. D. Martin, "General Wade Hampton at Home," *The New South,* February 1899, 52; Edward L. Wells, *Hampton and Reconstruction* (Columbia: The State Co., 1907), 216.

36. *State,* 5, 15, and 17 May 1899.

37. Circular letters, 22 May 1899 and n.d. (HFP); Wells, *Reconstruction,* 220.

38. Wells, *Reconstruction,* 220; Wade Hampton, "An Effort to Rescue Jefferson Davis: Statement of General Wade Hampton," *Southern Historical Society Papers* vol. xxvii (1899): 132; Brooks, *Butler and His Cavalry,* 494.

39. *Times and Democrat,* 20 and 24 March and 8 May 1901. Hampton's words are

slightly different in G. G. Vest, "A Senator of Two Republics," *The Saturday Evening Post* (20 February 1904): 8. "Please tell them I am not for sale," is the response given in Wells, *Reconstruction*, 223–224.

40. McDuffie Hampton to Annie Laurie Rogers, 4 May 1911 (HFP); Wade Hampton to Edward Wells, 18 January 1900 and Wade Hampton to Rawlins Lowndes, 27 March 1900 (Wells Correspondence, Charleston Library Society).

41. *Times and Democrat,* 15 May 1901.

42. Wells, *Reconstruction,* 224; *News and Courier,* 12 April 1902.

43. Wade Hampton will and codicils (Records of Richland County Probate Court, SCDAH); Wade Hampton Estate Records (Richland County Probate Court).

44. Wells, *Reconstruction,* 225; *State,* 10 April 1902; *News and Courier,* 12 April and 14 April 1902.

Bibliography

MANUSCRIPTS

Arthur, Chester A. Papers. Library of Congress, Washington, D.C.

Austin, William L. M. Papers. Compiled Service Records of Confederate Soldiers Who Served in Organizations from the State of South Carolina. U.S. National Archives, Washington, D.C.

Bachman, William K. Papers. Compiled Service Records of Confederate Soldiers Who Served in Organizations from the State of South Carolina. U.S. National Archives, Washington, D.C.

Bayard, Thomas F. Papers. Library of Congress, Washington, D.C.

Beauregard, P. G. T. Papers. Library of Congress, Washington, D.C.

Board of Trustees of the South Carolina College. Minutes 1833–1836, 1865–1868. South Caroliniana Library, University of South Carolina, Columbia, S.C.

Bonham, Milledge Luke. Papers. South Caroliniana Library, University of South Carolina, Columbia, S.C.

Bratton Family. Papers. South Caroliniana Library, University of South Carolina, Columbia, S.C.

Bratton, John. Papers. Southern Historical Collection, Library of the University of North Carolina, Chapel Hill, N.C.

Butler, Matthew Calbraith. Papers. Compiled Service Records of Confederate General and Staff Officers and Non-regimental Enlisted Men. U.S. National Archives, Washington, D.C.

Butler, Matthew Calbraith. Papers. South Caroliniana Library, University of South Carolina, Columbia, S.C.

Butler Family. Scrapbook 1856–1953. South Caroliniana Library, University of South Carolina, Columbia, S.C.

Chesnut, James. Papers. South Carolina Historical Society, Charleston, S.C.

Clariosophic Literary Society. Records. University Archives, University of South Carolina, Columbia, S.C.

Cleveland, Grover. Papers. Library of Congress, Washington, D.C.

Clopton Family. Papers. Special Collections Library, Duke University, Durham, N.C.

Daniel, John W. Papers. Special Collections Library, Duke University, Durham, N.C.

Durr. Family. Papers. Alabama Department of Archives and History, Montgomery, Ala.

Faculty of South Carolina College. Minutes 1836. South Caroliniana Library, University of South Carolina, Columbia, S.C.

Deloney, William Gaston. Family Papers. Hargrett Library, University of Georgia, Athens, Ga.

De Veaux, James. Papers. South Caroliniana Library, University of South Carolina, Columbia, S.C.

Foard, Fred C. Papers. North Carolina State Archives, Raleigh, N.C.

Garfield, James A. Papers. Library of Congress, Washington, D.C.

Gary, Martin Witherspoon. Papers. Compiled Service Records of Confederate General and Staff Officers and Non-regimental Enlisted Men, U.S. National Archives, Washington, D.C.

Gary, Martin Witherspoon. Papers. South Caroliniana Library, University of South Carolina, Columbia, S.C.

Geiger, Lizzie K. Papers. South Caroliniana Library, University of South Carolina, Columbia, S.C.

Goodwyn, Thomas Jefferson. Papers. South Caroliniana Library, University of South Carolina, Columbia, S.C.

Haberhsam Family, Papers. Library of Congress, Washington, D.C.

Hampton Family. Papers. South Caroliniana Library, University of South Carolina, Columbia, S.C.

Hampton, Frank. Papers. Compiled Service Records of Confederate Soldiers Who Served in Organizations from the State of South Carolina, U.S. National Archives, Washington, D.C.

Hampton, Thomas Preston. Papers. Compiled Service Records of Confederate Soldiers Who Served in Organizations from the State of South Carolina, U.S. National Archives, Washington, D.C.

Hampton, Wade. Correspondence. Rutherford B. Hayes Library, Fremont, Ohio.

Hampton, Wade. Estate Records. Richland County Probate Court, Columbia, S.C.

Hampton, Wade. File. Applications from Former Confederates for Presidential Pardons, 1865–1867. U.S. National Archives, Washington, D.C.

Hampton [III], Wade. Papers. Compiled Service Records of Confederate General and Staff Officers and Non-regimental Enlisted Men, U.S. National Archives, Washington, D.C.

Hampton, Wade. Papers. Southern Historical Collection, Library of the University of North Carolina, Chapel Hill, N.C.

Hampton, Wade. Papers. Special Collections Library, Duke University, Durham, N.C.

Hampton, Wade. Records of the Governor. South Carolina Department of Archives and History, Columbia, S.C.

Hampton, Wade. Will. Records of the Richland County Probate Court, South Carolina Department of Archives and History, Columbia, S.C.

Hampton [IV], Wade. Papers. Compiled Service Records of Confederate Soldiers Who Served in Organizations from the State of South Carolina, U.S. National Archives, Washington, D.C.

Harrison, Benjamin. Papers. Library of Congress, Washington, D.C.

Haskell, John Cheves. Papers. Southern Historical Collection, Library of the University of North Carolina, Chapel Hill, N.C.

Hearett-Wilson. Papers. Southern Historical Collection, Library of the University of North Carolina, Chapel Hill, N.C.

Hill, Daniel Harvey. Papers. Southern Historical Collection, Library of the University of North Carolina, Chapel Hill, N.C.

Hoke, Robert F. Papers. North Carolina State Archives, Raleigh, N.C.

Holmes, George Frederick. Papers. Special Collections Library, Duke University, Durham, N.C.

Hoyt, James Allen. Papers. South Caroliniana Library, University of South Carolina, Columbia, S.C.

Janney-Leaphart Family. Papers. South Caroliniana Library, University of South Carolina, Columbia, S.C.

Johnson, Bradley. Papers. Special Collections Library, Duke University, Durham, N.C.

Johnston Family. Papers. Filson Historical Society, Louisville, Ky.

Lee, Stephen Dill. Papers. Southern Historical Collection, Library of the University of North Carolina, Chapel Hill, N.C.

Lee, Stephen Dill. Papers. Special Collections Library, Duke University, Durham, N.C.

Lowndes, James. Papers. Compiled Service Records of Confederate Soldiers Who Served in Organizations from the State of South Carolina, U.S. National Archives, Washington, D.C.

Lowndes, James. Papers. South Caroliniana Library, University of South Carolina, Columbia, S.C.

McDowell, James. Papers. Special Collections Library, Duke University, Durham, N.C.

McDuffie, Mary S. Papers. Special Collections Library, Duke University, Durham, N.C.

Miles, William Porcher. Papers. Southern Historical Collection, Library of the University of North Carolina, Chapel Hill, N.C.

Minute Men of Richland District. Manuscript. South Caroliniana Library, University of South Carolina, Columbia, S.C.

Moore, James Washington. Journal. South Caroliniana Library, University of South Carolina, Columbia, S.C.

Perry, Benjamin Franklin. Papers. Alabama Department of Archives and History, Montgomery, Ala.

Pettigrew Family. Papers. North Carolina State Archives, Raleigh, N.C.

Pickens, Francis W. Papers. South Caroliniana Library, University of South Carolina, Columbia, S.C.

Pike, James S. Notebook. Raymond H. Fogler Library, University of Maine, Orono, Maine.

Richland School. Manuscript. South Caroliniana Library, University of South Carolina, Columbia, S.C.

Roosevelt, Theodore. Papers. Library of Congress, Washington, D.C.

Sang-Lee Civil War. Collection. Seymour Library, Knox College, Galesburg, Ill.

Screven, Thomas E. Papers. Compiled Service Records of Confederate Soldiers Who Served in Organizations from the State of South Carolina, U.S. National Archives, Washington, D.C.

Senate of South Carolina. Committee Book 1803–1830. South Carolina Department of Archives and History, Columbia, S.C.

Senate of South Carolina. Journal 1828. South Carolina Department of Archives and History, Columbia, S.C.

Shand, Peter J. Papers. South Caroliniana Library, University of South Carolina, Columbia, S.C.

Sheridan, Capt. Hugo G. Day Book. Orangeburg County Historical Society, Orangeburg, S.C.

Simons, James. Papers. South Carolina Historical Society, Charleston, S.C.

Simpson Family. Papers. South Caroliniana Library, University of South Carolina, Columbia, S.C.

Smith, Henry J. Papers. Compiled Service Records of Confederate Soldiers Who Served in Organizations from the State of South Carolina, U.S. National Archives, Washington, D.C.

Spann, James G. Papers. Compiled Service Records of Confederate Soldiers Who Served in Organizations form the State of South Carolina, U.S. National Archives, Washington, D.C.

Starke, William Pinckney. Papers. South Caroliniana Library, University of South Carolina, Columbia, S.C.

Statements Concerning the 1876 Election. South Carolina Department of Archives and History, Columbia, S.C.

Taylor, Benjamin Walter. Papers. South Caroliniana Library, University of South Carolina, Columbia, S.C.

Thomas, Charles E. Papers. South Caroliniana Library, University of South Carolina, Columbia, S.C.

Tillman, Benjamin Ryan. Papers. South Caroliniana Library, University of South Carolina, Columbia, S.C.

Trezevant, Daniel Heyward. Papers. South Caroliniana Library, University of South Carolina, Columbia, S.C.

Vance, Zebulon B. Papers. Southern Historical Collection, Library of the University of North Carolina, Chapel Hill, N.C.

Waddell, Alfred Moore. Papers. Southern Historical Collection, Library of the University of North Carolina, Chapel Hill, N.C.

Washington Family. Papers. South Carolina Historical Society, Charleston, S.C.

Wells, Edward L. Correspondence. Charleston Library Society, Charleston, S.C.

Whittier, John Greenleaf. Papers. Special Collections Library, Duke University, Durham, N.C.

Wigfall, Louis T. Papers. Center for American History, University of Texas, Austin, Texas.

Williams, Alexander. Papers. Special Collections Library, Duke University, Durham, N.C.

Williams, Benjamin Stuart. Papers. South Caroliniana Library, University of South Carolina, Columbia, S.C.

Winn, Robert. Papers. Filson Historical Society, Louisville, Ky.

Witherow, William H. Papers. South Caroliniana Library, University of South Carolina, Columbia, S.C.

Newspapers and Periodicals

Anderson Intelligencer [South Carolina], 1878.

Charleston Advocate, 1867.

Charleston Daily Courier, 1860, 1861, 1862, 1865, 1866, 1867.

Charleston Mercury, 1849, 1860, 1861, 1867, 1868, 1881.

Cheyenne Daily Leader [Wyoming], 1893.

Chicago Tribune, 1880.

Chronicle & Sentinel [Augusta, Ga.], 1877.

City Gazette and Commercial Daily Advertiser [Charleston, S.C.], 1818.

Columbia Daily Register, 1876, 1877, 1878, 1879, 1881, 1884.

Columbia Telescope, 1837.

Constitutionalist [Augusta, Ga.], 1878.

Daily Phoenix [Columbia, S.C.], 1865, 1866, 1867, 1868, 1870, 1871, 1874, 1875.

Daily Record-Union [Sacramento, Calif.], 1893.
Daily Republican [Charleston, S.C.], 1870.
Daily South Carolinian [Columbia, S.C.], 1864, 1865.
Daily Southern Guardian [Columbia, S.C.], 1860, 1861.
Daily Sun [Cheyenne, Wyo.], 1893.
Daily Tribune [Salt Lake City, Utah], 1893.
Daily Union-Herald [Columbia, S.C.], 1875, 1876.
Deseret Evening News [Salt Lake City, Utah], 1893.
Examiner, [San Francisco, Ca.], 1893.
Free Citizen [Orangeburg, S.C.], 1875.
Horry News [Conwayboro, S.C.], 1876.
London Times, 1876, 1877.
The Nation [New York, N.Y.], 1876.
Newberry Herald [South Carolina], 1878, 1879.
News and Courier [Charleston, S.C.], 1876, 1877, 1878, 1879, 1880, 1881, 1890, 1891, 1902.
New York Times, 1866, 1867, 1876, 1877.
New York Tribune, 1876, 1877, 1880.
Richmond Enquirer, 1861, 1864.
Rocky Mountain News [Denver, Colo.], 1893.
Southern Enterprise [Greenville, S.C.], 1860.
State [Columbia, S.C.], 1891, 1892, 1893, 1899, 1902, 1908, 1935.
Times [Charleston, S.C.], 1810, 1818.
Times and Democrat [Orangeburg, S.C.], 1890, 1892, 1894, 1901, 1902.
Washington Post, 1890, 1893.
World [Charleston, S.C.], 1890.
Wyoming State Tribune [Cheyenne, Wyo.], 1893.
Yorkville Enquirer [South Carolina], 1876.

OTHER PRIMARY SOURCES

"A Carolina Cavalier," *Program of Alumni Meeting.* n.p.: 1900.
Alderman, Edwin Anderson, and Joel Chandler Harris, eds. *Library of Southern Literature.* New Orleans, La.: The Martin & Hoyt Co., 1907.
Alexander, E. P. *Military Memoirs of a Confederate.* Bloomington: Indiana University Press, 1962.
Allen, Walter. *Governor Chamberlain's Administration in South Carolina.* New York: G. P. Putnam's Sons, 1888.
Andrews, Sidney. *The South Since the War.* Boston: Houghton Mifflin Co., 1971.
Blaine, James G. *Twenty Years of Congress: From Lincoln to Garfield.* 2 vols. Norwich, Conn.: The Henry Bill Publishing Co., 1886.
Bleser, Carol, ed. *Secret and Sacred: The Diaries of James Henry Hammond, a Southern Slaveholder.* New York: Oxford University Press, 1988.
Book of Common Prayer and Administration of the Sacraments and Other Rites and Cere-monies of the Church. New York: A. Hanford, 1838.
Borcke, Heros von, and Justus Scheibert. *The Great Cavalry Battle of Brandy Station, 9 June 1863.* Winston-Salem, N.C.: Palaemon Press Ltd., 1976.
———. *Memoirs of the Confederate War for Independence.* New York: Peter Smith, 1938.
Brooks, U. R. *Butler and His Cavalry in the War of Secession, 1861–1865.* Columbia: The State Co., 1909.

————. *Stories of the Confederacy*. Columbia: The State Co., 1912.

Calhoun, C. M. *Liberty Dethroned: A Concise History of Some of the Most Startling Events before, during, and since the Civil War*. n.p.: privately published, n.d.

Campbell, George. *White and Black: The Outcome of a Visit to the United States*. New York: R. Worthington, 1879.

Camp Moultrie, Sons of Confederate Veterans, comp. *Echoes from Hampton Day*. Charleston, S.C.: Walker, Evans & Cogswell Co., 1895.

Carrol, J. P. "The Burning of Columbia, South Carolina—Report of the Committee of Citizens Appointed to Collect Testimony," *Southern Historical Society Papers* vol. VIII (1880): 202–214.

Catalog of the Euphradian Society of the South Carolina College. Columbia: J. R. N. Tenhet, 1847.

Catalog of Regular and Honorary Members of the Clariosophic Society of South Carolina College. Columbia: I. C. Morgan, Printer, 1847.

Catalogue of the Trustees, Faculty and Students of the South Carolina College. Columbia: various printers, 1806–1849.

Cauthen, Charles E., ed. *Family Letters of the Three Wade Hamptons, 1782–1901*. Columbia: University of South Carolina Press, 1953.

Chamberlain, Daniel H. "Reconstruction in South Carolina," *The Atlantic Monthly* vol. LXXXVII (April 1901): 473–484.

Chesnut, Mary Boykin. *A Diary from Dixie*. Gloucester, Mass.: Peter Smith, 1961.

Childs, Arney Robinson, ed. *The Private Journal of Henry William Ravenel 1859–1887*. Columbia: University of South Carolina Press, 1947.

Chisolm, A. R. "Beauregard's and Hampton's Orders on Evacuating Columbia," *Southern Historical Society Papers* vol. VII (1879): 249–250.

Clark, Walter, ed. *Histories of the Several Regiments and Battalions from North Carolina in the Great War 1861–'65*. Raleigh, N.C.: E. M. Uzzell, 1901.

Commager, Henry Steele, ed. *Documents of American History*. New York: Appleton-Century-Crofts, 1968.

Constitution of the Minutemen for the Defense of Southern Rights. Camden, S.C.: Camden Weekly Journal Press, 1860.

Conyngham, David P. *Sherman's March through the South with Sketches and Incidents of the Campaign*. New York: Sheldon and Co., 1865.

Cooke, John Esten. *Wearing of the Gray*. Bloomington: Indiana University Press, 1959.

Cooke, Phillip St. George. *Cavalry Tactics or, Regulations for the Instruction, Formations, and Movements of the Cavalry of the Army and Volunteers of the United States*. Philadelphia: J. B. Lippencott & Co., 1862.

"Correspondence between Colonel S. Bassett French and General Wade Hampton," *Southern Historical Society Papers* vol. II (1876): 31–32.

Coxe, John. "The Battle of First Manassas," *Confederate Veteran* vol. XIII, no. 1 (January 1915): 24–26.

————. "Wade Hampton," *Confederate Veteran* vol. XXX, no. 12 (December 1922): 460–462.

Crist, Lynda Lasswell, ed. *The Papers of Jefferson Davis*. Baton Rouge: Louisiana State University Press, 1995.

Davis, Varina Howell. *Jefferson Davis, Ex-President of the Confederate States of America: A Memoir*. 2 vols. New York: Belford Co., Publishers, 1890.

De Forest, John William. *A Union Officer in the Reconstruction*, edited by James H. Croushore and David Morris. New Haven, Conn.: Yale University Press, 1948.

"Democratic Convention," *Harper's Magazine* vol. XXXVII, no. 220 (September 1868): 567–571.

Dennett, John Richard. *The South as It Is: 1865–1866.* New York: The Viking Press, 1965.

Easterly, J. H., ed. *Basic Documents of South Carolina History.* Columbia: Historical Commission of South Carolina, 1952.

Fleming, Walter L., ed. *Documentary History of Reconstruction.* Cleveland, Ohio: The Arthur H. Clark Co., 1906.

Freeman, Douglas Southall, ed. *Lee's Dispatches.* New York: The Knickerbocker Press, 1915.

French, Mrs. A. M. *Slavery in South Carolina and the Ex-Slaves: or, The Port Royal Mission.* New York: Winchell M. French, 1862.

Gallagher, Gary W., ed. *Fighting for the Confederacy: The Personal Recollections of General Edward Porter Alexander.* Chapel Hill: University of North Carolina Press, 1989.

Gaston, J. McF. *Hunting a Home in Brazil.* Philadelphia: King & Baird, 1867.

Gibbes, James G. *Who Burnt Columbia?.* Newberry, S.C.: Elbert H. Aull Co., 1902.

Gibbes, Robert W. *A Memoir of James De Veaux.* Columbia: J. C. Morgan's Letter Press Print, 1846.

Hampton, Ann Fripp, ed. *A Divided Heart: Letters of Sally Baxter Hampton, 1853–1862.* Spartanburg, S.C.: The Reprint Co., 1980.

Hampton, Wade. *Address on the Life and Character of Gen. Robert E. Lee, Delivered on the 12th of October, 1871, before the Society of Confederate Soldiers and Sailors, in Maryland.* Baltimore: John Murphy & Co., 1871.

———. "An Effort to Rescue Jefferson Davis," *Southern Historical Society Papers* vol. XXVII (1899): 132–136

———. *Free Men! Free Ballots! Free Schools!!! The Pledges of Gen. Wade Hampton, Democratic Candidate for Governor to the Colored People of South Carolina.* n.p.: [1876].

———. "General Wade Hampton's Warrenton Address," *The Southern Magazine* (August 1873): 225–249.

———. *Message No. 1 of His Excellency Wade Hampton, Governor of South Carolina, to the General Assembly, Extra Session, Commencing April 24, 1877.* Columbia: Republican Printing Co., 1877.

———. "Ought the Negro to Be Disfranchised? Ought He to Have Been Enfranchised?" *North American Review* vol. CXXVII (March 1879): 239–244.

———. "The Race Problem," *The Arena* vol. II, no. 2 (July 1890): 132–138.

———. *Reply of Wade Hampton, Governor of South Carolina, and Others, to the Chamberlain Memorial.* Columbia: Presbyterian Publishing House, 1877.

———. "What Negro Supremacy Means," *The Forum Extra* vol. I, no. 1 (March 1890): 2–14.

Harwell, Richard, and Philip N. Racine, eds. *The Fiery Trail: A Union Officer's Account of Sherman's Last Campaigns.* Knoxville: University of Tennessee Press, 1986.

Haskell, John Cheves. *The Haskell Memoirs.* New York: G. P. Putnam's Sons, 1960.

Henderson, P. F, D. S. Henderson Jr., and T. R. Henderson, eds. *Life and Addresses of D. S. Henderson.* Columbia, S.C.: The R. L. Bryan Co., 1922.

Hewett, Janet B., ed. *South Carolina Confederate Soldiers, 1861–1865.* Wilmington, N.C.: Broadfoot Publishing Co., 1998.

———. *Supplement to the Official Records of the Union and Confederate Armies.* Wilmington, N.C.: Broadfoot Publishing Co., 1998.

Hooker, Edward. *Diary of Edward Hooker 1805–1808.* In the *Report of the Historical Manuscripts Commission of the American Historical Association for 1896.* Washington, D.C.: Government Printing Office, 1897.

Howe, Julia Ward. *Reminiscences, 1819–1899*. New York: Negro Universities Press, 1969.

Hutchinson Jr., Olin Fulmer, ed. *"My Dear Mother & Sisters": Civil War Letters of Capt. A. B. Mulligan, Co. B, 5th South Carolina Cavalry—Butler's Division—Hampton's Corps 1861–1865*. Spartanburg, S.C.: The Reprint Co., 1992.

Irving, John B. *The South Carolina Jockey Club*. Charleston, S.C.: Russell & Jones, 1857.

Johnson, Donald Bruce, and Kirk H. Porter, comp. *National Party Platforms 1840–1972*. Urbana, Ill.: University of Illinois Press, 1973.

Johnson, Joseph. *Traditions and Reminiscences Chiefly of the American Revolution in the South*. Charleston, S.C.: Walker and James, 1851.

Johnson, Robert Underwood, and Clarence Buel, eds. *Battles and Leaders of the Civil War*. 4 vols. New York: The Century Co., 1884–1887.

Johnston, Joseph E. *Narrative of Military Operations Directed during the Late War Between the States*. Bloomington: Indiana University Press, 1959.

Jones, J. William. *Personal Reminiscences of General Robert E. Lee*. Richmond: United States Historical Society Press, 1989.

Journal of the Congress of the Confederate States of America, 1861–1865. 7 vols. Washington, D.C.: Government Printing Office, 1904.

Journal of the Convention of the People of South Carolina, Held in Columbia, S.C., September, 1865. Columbia: J. A. Selby, 1865.

Journal of the Convention of the People of South Carolina, Held in 1860 –'61. Charleston, S.C.: Evans & Cogswell, 1861.

Journal of the House of Representatives of the State of South Carolina. Columbia, S.C.: various printers, 1852, 1853, 1854, 1855, 1876, 1877–1878.

Journal of the Senate of South Carolina. Columbia: various printers, 1858, 1859, 1860, 1861, 1877–1878.

Journal of the State Convention of South Carolina; Together with the Resolution and Ordinance. Columbia: Johnston & Cavis, 1852.

LaBorde, Maximilian. *History of the South Carolina College*. Charleston, S.C.: Walker, Evans & Cogswell, Printers, 1874.

Law, Agnes. "The Burning of Columbia—Affidavit of Mrs. Agnes Law," *Southern Historical Society Papers* vol. XII (1884): 233.

Laws of the South Carolina College. Columbia: A. S. Johnston, Printer, 1848.

Le Conte, Joseph. *The Autobiography of Joseph Le Conte*. New York: D. Appleton and Co., 1903.

Lee, Capt. Robert E. *Recollections and Letters of General Robert E. Lee*. New York: Doubleday, Page & Co., 1904.

Leland, Isabella Middleton, ed. "Middleton Correspondence, 1861–1865," *The South Carolina Historical Magazine* vol. 64 (1963): 99–100.

Leland, John A. *A Voice from South Carolina*. Charleston, S.C.: Walker, Evans & Cogswell, 1879.

Lieber, Francis. *The Life and Letters of Francis Lieber*, edited by Thomas Sergeant Perry. Boston: James R. Osgood and Co., 1882.

Logan, Kate Virginia Cox. *My Confederate Girlhood*. Richmond: Garrett & Massie, Inc., 1932.

Mackey, T. J. "Hampton's Duel," *Southern Historical Society Papers*, vol. 20 (1894): 122–126.

Marshall, Charles. *An Aide-de-Camp of Lee*. Boston: Little, Brown and Co., 1927.

Martin, I. D. "General Wade Hampton at Home," *The New South* (February 1899): 52.

Massachusetts and South Carolina: Correspondence between John Quincy Adams and Wade Hampton and Others of South Carolina. Boston: J. E. Farwell & Co., n.d.

Mays, Samuel Elias. "Sketches from the Journal of a Confederate Soldier," *Tyler's Quarterly Historical and Genealogical Magazine* vol. V (1924): 45–53.

McClellan, H. B. *The Life and Campaigns of J. E. B. Stuart.* Boston: Houghton, Mifflin and Co., 1885.

McClure, Alexander K. *Recollections of Half a Century.* Salem, Mass.: The Salem Press, 1902.

Miers, Earl Schenck, ed. *When the World Ended: The Diary of Emma Le Conte.* New York: Oxford University Press, 1957.

The Militia and Patrol Laws of South Carolina: To December 1851. Columbia: Johnston & Cavis, 1852.

Moffett, Mary Conner, ed. *Letters of General James Conner, C.S.A.* Columbia: R. L. Bryan Co., 1950.

Moore, Andrew Charles, comp. *Roll of Students of South Carolina College, 1805–1905.* Columbia: The State Co., 1905.

Moore, John Hammond, ed. *The Juhl Letters to the Charleston Courier: A View of the South, 1865–1871.* Athens: University of Georgia Press, 1974.

Myers, Frank M. *The Comanches: A History of White's Battalion, Virginia Cavalry, Laurel Brig., Hampton Div., A.N.V.* Baltimore: Kelly, Piet & Co., 1871.

Oliphant, Mary C. Simms, et al., comps. and eds. *The Letters of William Gilmore Simms.* Vol. 2, *1845–1849.* Columbia: University of South Carolina Press, 1953.

Palmer, Benjamin M. *The Life and Letters of James Henley Thornwell.* Richmond: Whittet and Shepperson, 1875.

Perry, Benjamin F. *Biographical Sketches of Eminent American Statesmen.* Philadelphia: The Ferree Press, 1887.

———. *Reminiscences of Public Men with Speeches and Addresses.* Greenville, S.C.: Shannon & Co., 1889.

———. *The Writings of Benjamin F. Perry.* Spartanburg, S.C.: The Reprint Co., 1980.

Pike, James S. *The Prostrate State: South Carolina under Negro Government.* New York: D. Appleton and Co., 1874.

[Pollard, E. A.]. *The Early Life, Campaigns, and Public Services of Robert E. Lee: With a Record of the Campaigns and Heroic Deeds of His Companions in Arms.* New York: E. B. Treat & Co., Publishers, 1870.

Porter, William T. "Wade Hampton Obituary," *Porter's Spirit of the Times* vol. IV (1858): 139–142.

Proceedings of the Centennial Celebration of the First Meeting of the General Assembly of the State of South Carolina Convened in the Town of Columbia in the Year 1791. Columbia: Centennial Commission, 1893.

Proceedings of the Meeting of Delegates from the Southern Rights Association of South Carolina. Columbia: Johnson & Cavis, 1851.

Proceedings of the Tax-Payers' Convention of South Carolina. Charleston, S.C.: Edward Perry, Printer, 1871.

Pryor, Mrs. Roger A. *Reminiscences of Peace and War.* New York: The Macmillan Co., 1904.

Ray, Gordon N., ed. *The Letters and Private Papers of William Makepeace Thackery.* 4 vols. Cambridge, Mass.: Harvard University Press, 1946.

Report of the Commissioner of Railroads to the Secretary of the Interior. 1893. Washington, D.C.: Government Printing Office, 1893.

Report of the Commissioner of Railroads to the Secretary of the Interior. 1894. Washington, D.C.: Government Printing Office, 1894.

Report of the Commissioner of Railroads to the Secretary of the Interior. 1895. Washington, D.C.: Government Printing Office, 1895.

Report of the Commissioner of Railroads to the Secretary of the Interior for the Fiscal Year Ended June 30, 1896. Washington, D.C.: Government Printing Office, 1896.

Report of the Special Committee of the Senate of South Carolina on the Resolutions Submitted by Mr. Ramsay on the Subject of State Rights. Washington, D.C.: Duff Green, 1828.

Reports and Resolutions of the General Assembly of the State of South Carolina at the Regular Session, 1877–1878. Columbia: Calvo & Patton, 1878.

Reports and Resolutions of the General Assembly of the State of South Carolina at the Regular Session of 1878. Columbia: Calvo & Patton, 1878.

Rivers, William J. *River's Account of the Raising of Troops in South Carolina for State and Confederate Service, 1861–1865.* Columbia: The Bryan Printing Co., 1899.

Roman, Alfred. *The Military Operations of General Beauregard.* New York: Harper & Brothers, 1884.

Rosser, Thomas L. *Riding with Rosser.* Shippensburg, Pa.: Burd Street Press, 1997.

Rowland, Dunbar, ed. *Jefferson Davis, Constitutionalist: His Letters, Papers and Speeches.* Jackson: Mississippi Department of Archives and History, 1923.

Scott, Edwin J. *Random Recollections of a Long Life, 1806 to 1876.* Columbia: Charles A. Calvo Jr., Printer, 1884.

Selby, Julian A. *Memorabilia and Anecdotal Reminiscences of Columbia, S.C. and Incidents Connected Therewith.* Columbia: The R. L. Bryan Co., 1905.

Shand, Peter J. *Address at the Laying of the Corner Stone of the New Episcopal Church, Columbia, S.C., November 26th, 1845.* Columbia: I. C. Morgan, 1845.

Sherman, William Tecumseh. *Memoirs of General W. T. Sherman.* New York: The Library of America, 1990.

Simms, William Gilmore. *Sack and Destruction of the City of Columbia, S.C.* Columbia: Power Press of Daily Phoenix, 1865.

Smith, Gustavus W. *The Battle of Seven Pines.* New York: C. G. Crawford, 1891.

State [Democratic] Central Executive Committee. *The Respectful Remonstrance in Behalf of the White People of South Carolina.* Columbia Phoenix Book and Job Power Press, 1868.

Strode, Hudson, ed. *Jefferson Davis: Private Letters 1823–1889.* New York: Harcourt, Brace & World, 1966.

Sullivan, Nancy, comp. *The Treasury of American Poetry.* Garden City, N.Y.: International Collectors Library, 1978.

Thompson, Henry T. *Ousting the Carpetbagger from South Carolina.* Columbia: R. L. Bryan Co., 1926.

Thorndike, Rachel Sherman, ed. *The Sherman Letters: Correspondence between General and Senator Sherman from 1837 to 1891.* New York: Charles Scribner's Sons, 1894.

Towles, Louis P., ed. *A World Turned Upside Down: The Palmers of South Santee, 1818–1881.* Columbia: University of South Carolina Press, 1996.

"Transactions of the Southern Historical Society," *The Southern Magazine* (January 1874): 12–18.

Trowbridge, J. T. *The South: A Tour of Its Battle Fields and Ruined Cities.* Hartford: Stebbins, 1866.

U.S. Congress. *Acceptance and Unveiling of the Statue of Wade Hampton.* Washington, D.C.: U.S. Government Printing Office, 1929.

————. *Report of the Joint Committee on Reconstruction*. Washington, D.C.: Government Printing Office, 1866.

————. Senate. *Congressional Record,* 46th Cong., 1st session, 1879, vol. 9, pt. 2.

————. Senate. *Congressional Record,* 46th Cong., 2nd session, 1879, vol. 10, pt. 1.

————. Senate. *Congressional Record,* 46th Cong., 3rd session, 1880, vol. 11, pt. l.

————. Senate. *Congressional Record,* 47th Cong., 1st session, 1882, vol. 13, pt. 4.

————. Senate. *Congressional Record,* 48th Cong., 1st session, 1884, vol. 15, pt. 4.

————. Senate. *Congressional Record,* 49th Cong., 1st session, 1885, vol. 17, pt. 1.

————. Senate. *Congressional Record,* 49th Cong., 2nd session, 1886, vol. 18, pt. 1.

————. Senate. *Congressional Record,* 50th Cong., 1st session, 1888, vol. 19, pt. 8.

————. Senate. *Congressional Record,* 51st Cong., 1st session, 1890, vol. 21, pt. 1.

————. Senate. *Congressional Record,* 51st Cong., 2nd session, 1891, vol. 22, pt. 2.

————. *Testimony Taken by the Joint Select Committee to Inquire into the Condition of Affairs in the Late Insurrectionary States.* Vol. 2, *South Carolina.* Washington, D.C.: Government Printing Office, 1872.

U. S. Department of State. *Papers Relating to the Treaty of Washington.* Washington, D.C.: Government Printing Office, 1874.

U.S. Navy Department, comp. *Official Records of the Union and Confederate Navies in the Rebellion.* 31 vols. Washington, D.C.: Government Printing Office, 1894–1927.

U.S. Senate Subcommittees on Privileges and Elections. *South Carolina in 1876. Report on the Denial of the Elective Franchise in South Carolina at the State and National Elections of 1876.* Washington, D.C.: Government Printing Office, 1877.

U.S. War Department, comp. *The War of the Rebellion: A Compilation of the Official Records of the Union and Confederate Armies.* 128 vols. Washington, D.C.: Government Printing Office, 1880–1901.

Vest, G. G. "A Senator of Two Republics," *The Saturday Evening Post,* (February 20, 1904): 8–10.

Washington Light Infantry Charitable Association. *Proceedings on the Occasion of Unveiling the Monument Erected in Memory of Their Comrades Who Died in the Service of the State.* Charleston, S.C.: Walker, Evans & Cogswell, 1870.

Wells, Edward L. *A Sketch of the Charleston Light Dragoons.* Charleston, S.C.: Lucas, Richardson & Co., 1888.

Wells, Edward L. *Hampton and His Cavalry in '64.* Richmond: B. F. Johnson Publishing Co., 1899.

Wheeler, Joseph. "An Effort to Rescue Jefferson Davis," *The Century Magazine* vol. LVI, No. 1 (May 1898): 85–91.

Williams, Alfred B. *Hampton and His Red Shirts: South Carolina's Deliverance in 1876.* Charleston, S.C.: Walker, Evans & Cogswell, 1935.

Williams, Charles Richard, ed. *Diary and Letters of Rutherford Birchard Hayes, Nineteenth President of the United States.* 4 vols. Columbus: The Ohio State Archaeological and Historical Society, 1924.

Wise, John S. *The End of an Era.* Boston: Houghton, Mifflin and Co., 1899.

Woodward, C. Vann, and Elisabeth Muhlenfeld, eds. *The Private Mary Chesnut: The Unpublished Civil War Diaries.* New York: Oxford University Press, 1984.

Woodward, C. Vann, ed. *Mary Chesnut's Civil War.* New Haven, Conn.: Yale University Press, 1981.

Wright, Mrs. D. Giraud. *A Southern Girl in '61: The War-Time Memories of a Confederate Senator's Daughter.* New York: Doubleday, Page & Company, 1905.

UNPUBLISHED STUDIES

Bridwell, Ronald Edward. "The South's Wealthiest Planter: Wade Hampton I of South Carolina, 1754–1835." Ph.D. dissertation, University of South Carolina, 1980.

Cooper Jr., William James. "The Conservative Regime in South Carolina." Ph.D. dissertation, Johns Hopkins University, 1966.

Fairley, Charlestine Romelle. "A History of Claflin College 1869–1987." Ph.D. dissertation, University of South Carolina, 1990.

Fletcher, Ralph Henry. "George McDuffie: Orator and Politician." Master's thesis, University of South Carolina, 1986.

Gettys Jr., James Wylie. "'To Conquer a Peace': South Carolina and the Mexican War." Ph.D. dissertation, University of South Carolina, 1974.

Hellams, Wilton. "A History of South Carolina State Hospital (1821 to 1900)." Ph.D. dissertation, University of South Carolina, 1985.

Herd Jr., Elmer Don. "Chapters from the Life of a Southern Chevalier: Laurence Massillon Keitt's Congressional Years, 1853–1860." Master's thesis, University of South Carolina, 1958.

Jones, De Witt Grant. "Wade Hampton and the Rhetoric of Race: A Study of the Speaking of Wade Hampton on the Race Issue in South Carolina, 1865–1878." Ph.D. dissertation, Louisiana State University, 1988.

King, G. Wayne. "The Civil War Career of Hugh Judson Kilpatrick." Ph.D. dissertation, University of South Carolina, 1969.

Slaunwhite, Jerry L. "John L. M. Irby: The Creation of a Crisis." Master's thesis, University of South Carolina, 1973.

Williamson, Joel. "The Disruption of State Government in South Carolina during the Magrath Administration." Master's thesis, University of South Carolina, 1951.

HAMPTON AND RELATED-FAMILY GENEALOGICAL STUDIES

Ames, Joseph. "The Cantey Family," *South Carolina Historical and Genealogical Magazine* vol. XI, no. 3 (October 1910): 203–258.

Anderson, Katie Weatherford. *Standing in the Doorway of a Day Long Ago.* n.p.: privately published, 1963.

Folk, George M. *Folk Family Tree.* n.p.: privately published, n.d.

Hampton, Ann Fripp. "The Hampton Family of South Carolina," *Carolina Herald* vol. 3, no. 3 ([1975]): 19.

Hampton, Harry. *Woods and Waters and Some Asides.* Columbia: State Printing Co., 1979.

Hampton Jr., Luther Wightman. *Genealogy of Hampton, Boulware, Setzler, Goodwin and Related Families.* n.p.: privately published, 1983.

Mays, Samuel Edward. *Genealogy of the Mays Family and Related Families to 1929 Inclusive.* Plant City, Fla.: privately published, 1929.

McCleskey, Charles S. *The Hampton Connection: Descendants of John Hampton the Tailor.* Baton Rouge, La.: privately published, 1975.

McCord, Carey P. *The Pratt Family.* n.p.: privately published, n.d.

Meynard, Virginia G. *The Venturers: The Hampton, Harrison, and Earle Families of Virginia, South Carolina, and Texas.* Easley, S.C.: Southern Historical Press, 1981.

Range, Ella Mulkey. *The Life of Reverend Philip Mulkey, His Ancestors and Descendants, 1650–1950.* n.p.: privately published, n.d.

SECONDARY SOURCES

Abbott, Martin. *The Freeman's Bureau in South Carolina 1865–1872*. Chapel Hill: University of North Carolina Press, 1967.

‌Allen, Felicity. *Jefferson Davis: Unconquerable Heart*. Columbia: University of Missouri Press, 1999.

Bailey, N. Louise, Mary L. Morgan, and Carolyn R. Taylor. *Biographical Directory of the South Carolina Senate, 1776–1985*. Columbia: University of South Carolina Press, 1986.

Bales, Louella H. *Confederate Cavalry: Last Days of Chivalry*. Jacksonville, Fla.: privately printed, 1989.

Ball, William Watts. *The State That Forgot: South Carolina's Surrender to Democracy*. Indianapolis: The Bobbs-Merrill Company, 1932.

Barrows, Chester L. *William M. Evarts: Lawyer, Diplomat, Statesman*. Chapel Hill: University of North Carolina Press, 1941.

Bass, Robert D. *Gamecock: The Life and Campaigns of General Thomas Sumter*. New York: Holt, Rinehart and Winston, 1961.

Berton, Pierre. *Flames across the Border: The Canadian-American Tragedy, 1813–1814*. Boston: Little, Brown and Company, 1981.

Biographical Directory of the American Congress 1774–1927. Washington, D.C.: Government Printing Office, 1928.

Blake, Michael. *American Civil War Cavalry*. London: Almark Publishing Co., 1973.

Bleser, Carol. *The Hammonds of Redcliffe*. New York: Oxford University Press, 1981.

Boatner III, Mark Mayo. *Encyclopedia of the American Revolution*. New York: David McKay, Co., 1975.

Bowers, Claude G. *The Tragic Era: The Revolution after Lincoln*. New York: Blue Ribbon Books, 1929.

Boykin, Edward. *Beefsteak Raid*. New York: Funk & Wagnalls Company, 1960.

Bradley, Mark L. *Last Stand in the Carolinas: The Battle of Bentonville*. Campbell, Calif.: Savas Pub. Co., 1995.

Brewster, Lawrence Fay. *Summer Migrations and Resorts of South Carolina Low Country Planters*. Durham, N.C. Duke University Press, 1947.

Brown, Robert R. *The Mountains in Reply*. n.p.: privately published, n.d.

Buley, R. Carlyle. *The American Life Convention, 1906–1952: A Study in the History of Life Insurance*. 2 vols. New York: Appleton-Century-Crofts, Inc., 1953.

Burton, E. Milby. *The Siege of Charleston 1861–1865*. Columbia: University of South Carolina Press, 1970.

Cash, W. J. *The Mind of the South*. New York: Alfred A. Knopf, 1941.

Cauthen, Charles Edward. *South Carolina Goes to War, 1860–1865*. Chapel Hill: University of North Carolina Press, 1950.

Channing, Steven A. *Crisis of Fear: Secession in South Carolina*. New York: Simon and Schuster, 1970.

Charles, Allan D. "The Burning of Columbia," *Southern Partisan* vol. 1, nos. 3–4 (Spring-Summer 1981): 8–10.

Cisco, Walter Brian. "Galvanized Rebels," *Civil War* vol. VIII, no. 5 (September-October 1990): 48–54.

———. *States Rights Gist: A South Carolina General of the Civil War*. Shippensburg, Pa.: White Mane Publishing Co., 1991.

———. *Taking a Stand: Portraits from the Southern Secession Movement*. Shippensburg, Pa.: White Mane Books, 1998.

Clancy, Herbert J. *The Presidential Election of 1880*. Chicago: Loyola University Press, 1958.

Coddington, Edwin B. *The Gettysburg Campaign: A Study in Command*. New York: Charles Scribner's Sons, 1968.

Coit, Margaret L. *John C. Calhoun: American Portrait*. Boston: Houghton Mifflin Company, 1950.

Cooper Jr., William J. *The Conservative Regime: South Carolina, 1877–1890*. Baltimore: The Johns Hopkins University Press, 1968.

Current, Richard Nelson. *Those Terrible Carpetbaggers*. New York: Oxford University Press, 1988.

Daniels, Jonathan. *Tar Heels: A Portrait of North Carolina*. New York: Dodd, Mead & Company, 1941.

Davidson, Chalmers Gaston. *The Last Foray, The South Carolina Planters of 1860: A Sociological Study*. Columbia: University of South Carolina, 1971.

Davidson, James Wood. "Who Burned Columbia?—A Review of General Sherman's Version of the Affair," *Southern Historical Society Papers* vol. VII (1879): 185–192.

Davis, Burke. *Jeb Stuart: The Last Cavalier*. New York: Bonanza Books, 1957.

Davis, William C. *Battle at Bull Run: A History of the First Major Campaign of the Civil War*. Mechanicsburg, Pa.: Stackpole Books, 1977.

———, ed. *The Confederate General*. n.p.: National Historical Society, 1991.

———. *Jefferson Davis: The Man and His Hour*. New York: Harper Collins, 1991.

Dawsey, Cyrus B., and James M. Dawsey. *The Confederados: Old South Immigrants in Brazil*. Tuscaloosa: University of Alabama Press, 1995.

Dorgan, Howard. "'Pitchfork Ben' Tillman and 'The Race Problem from a Southern Point of View.'" In *The Oratory of Southern Demagogues*. Edited by Cal M. Logue and Howard Dorgan. Baton Rouge: Louisiana State University Press, 1981.

Drago, Edmund L. *Hurrah for Hampton!: Black Red Shirts in South Carolina during Reconstruction*. Fayetteville: University of Arkansas Press, 1998.

Dyer, Brainerd. *The Public Career of William M. Evarts*. Berkeley: University of California Press, 1933.

Evans, Clement A., ed. *Confederate Military History*. 12 vols. Vol. 5, *South Carolina*. Atlanta, Ga.: Confederate Publishing, 1899.

Fant, Christie Zimmerman. *The State House of South Carolina: An Illustrated Historic Guide*. Columbia: R. L. Bryan Company, 1970.

Faunt, Joan Schreiner Reynolds, Robert E. Rector, and David K. Bowden, coms. *Biographical Directory of the South Carolina House of Representatives*. Columbia: University of South Carolina Press, 1974.

Faust, Drew Gilpin. *James Henry Hammond and the Old South: A Design for Mastery*. Baton Rouge: Louisiana State University Press, 1982.

Faust, Patricia L., ed. *Historical Times Illustrated Encyclopedia of the Civil War*. New York: Harper Perennial, 1991.

Fellman, Michael. *Citizen Sherman: A Life of William Tecumseh Sherman*. New York: Random House, 1995.

Field, Ron. *The Hampton Legion, Part 1: Regimental History*. Gloucestershire, England: Design Folio, 1994.

Foner, Eric. *Reconstruction: America's Unfinished Revolution, 1863–1877*. New York: Harper & Row, Publishers, 1988.

Foote, Shelby. *The Civil War: A Narrative*. 3 vols. New York: Vintage Books, 1986.

Franklin, John Hope. *Reconstruction: After the Civil War*. Chicago: University of Chicago Press, 1961.

Freeman, Douglas Southall. *Lee's Lieutenants: A Study in Command*. New York: Charles Scribner's Sons, 1942.

Freeman, Douglas Southall. *R. E. Lee: A Biography*. 4 vols. New York: Charles Scribner's Sons, 1935.

Freidel, Frank. *Francis Lieber: Nineteenth-Century Liberal*. Baton Rouge: Louisiana State University Press, 1947.

Govan, Gilbert E., and James W. Livingwood. *General Joseph E. Johnston, C.S.A.: A Different Valor*. New York: Bobbs-Merrill Company, Inc., 1956.

Graydon, Nell S. *Tales of Columbia*. Columbia: R. L. Bryan Company, 1964.

Green, Edwin L. *A History of the University of South Carolina*. Columbia: The State Co., 1916.

———. *George McDuffie*. Columbia: The State Co., 1936.

Hamer, Philip M. *The Secession Movement in South Carolina, 1847–1852*. New York: Da Capo Press, 1971.

Hampton County Tricentennial Commission. *Both Sides of the Swamp: Hampton County*. Columbia: R. L. Bryan Co., 1970.

Harley, Lewis R. *Francis Lieber: His Life and Political Philosophy*. New York: AMS Press, 1970.

Harter, Eugene C. *The Lost Colony of the Confederacy*. Jackson: University Press of Mississippi, 1986.

Hattaway, Herman. *General Stephen D. Lee*. Jackson: University Press of Mississippi, 1976.

Haworth, Paul Leland. *The Hayes-Tilden Disputed Presidential Election of 1876*. Cleveland, Ohio: The Burrows Brothers Co., 1906.

Hennig, Helen Kohn, ed. *Columbia, Capitol City of South Carolina, 1786–1936*. Columbia: The Columbia Sesqui-Centennial Commission, 1936.

Hesseltine, William B. *Ulysses S. Grant: Politician*. New York: Dodd, Mead & Company, 1935.

Holland, Lynwood Mathis. *Pierce M. B. Young, the Warwick of the South*. Athens: University of Georgia Press, 1964.

Hollis, Daniel Walker. *The University of South Carolina*. 2 vols. Columbia: University of South Carolina Press, 1951.

Hollis, John Porter. *The Early Period of Reconstruction in South Carolina*. Baltimore: The Johns Hopkins University Press, 1905.

Holt, Thomas. *Black over White: Negro Political Leadership in South Carolina during Reconstruction*. Urbana: University of Illinois Press, 1977.

Hoogenboom, Ari. *Rutherford B. Hayes: Warrior and President*. Lawrence: University Press of Kansas, 1995.

Horn, Stanley F. *Invisible Empire: The Story of the Ku Klux Klan, 1866–1871*. Montclair, N.J.: Patterson Smith, 1969.

Hubbell, Jay B., ed. *The Last Years of Henry Timrod 1864–1867*. Durham, N.C.: Duke University Press, 1941.

Jarrell, Hampton M. *Wade Hampton and the Negro: The Road Not Taken*. Columbia: University of South Carolina Press, 1950.

Jordan Jr., Frank E. *The Primary State: A History of the Democratic Party in South Carolina 1876–1962*. n.p.: privately published, n.d.

Junior League of Charleston, comp. *Historic Charleston Guidebook*. Charleston, S.C.: Nelson's Southern Printing, 1971.

Kantrowitz, Stephen. *Ben Tillman & the Reconstruction of White Supremacy*. Chapel Hill: University of North Carolina Press, 2000.

Kelly, Alfred, and Winfred A. Harbison. *The American Constitution: Its Origins and Development*. New York: W. W. Norton Co., 1970.

Kelly, O. H. *Origin and Progress of the Order of the Patrons of Husbandry in the United States; A History from 1866 to 1873*. Philadelphia: J. A. Wagenseller, Publisher, 1875.

Kennedy, Frances H. *The Civil War Battlefield Guide*. Boston: Houghton Mifflin Company, 1990.

Kibler, Lillian A. "Unionist Sentiment in South Carolina in 1860," *Journal of Southern History* vol. iv, no. 3 (August 1938): 346–366.

King, Alvy L. *Louis T. Wigfall: Southern Fire-eater*. Baton Rouge: Louisiana State University Press, 1970.

Klement, Frank L. *Lincoln's Critics: The Copperheads of the North*. Shippensburg, Pa.: White Mane Books, 1999.

Lander Jr., Ernest M. "Dr. Thomas Cooper's Views in Retirement," *South Carolina Historical Magazine* vol. LIV (1953): 173–184.

————. *Reluctant Imperialists: Calhoun, the South Carolinians, and the Mexican War*. Baton Rouge: Louisiana State University Press, 1980.

Library of Congress. *Index to the Ulysses S. Grant Papers*. Washington, D.C.: Library of Congress, 1965.

Livermore, Thomas L. *Numbers and Losses in the Civil War in America, 1861–65*. Carlisle, Pa.: John Kallmann, Publishers, 1996.

Longacre, Edward G. *The Cavalry at Gettysburg*. Cranbury, N.J.: Associated University Presses, Inc., 1986.

Lucas, Marion Brunson. *Sherman and the Burning of Columbia*. College Station: Texas A&M University Press, 1976.

Lumpkin, Henry. *From Savannah to Yorktown: The American Revolution in the South*. Columbia: University of South Carolina Press, 1981.

Mantell, Martin E. *Johnson, Grant, and the Politics of Reconstruction*. New York: Columbia University Press, 1973.

Marszalek, John F. *Sherman: A Soldier's Passion for Order*. New York: The Free Press, 1993.

Martin, Samuel J. *Southern Hero: Matthew Calbraith Butler*. Mechanicsburg, Pa.: Stackpole Books, 2001.

May, John Amasa, and Joan Reynolds Fant. *South Carolina Secedes*. Columbia: University of South Carolina Press, 1960.

McDonald, Archie P., ed. *A Nation of Sovereign States: Secession and War in the Confederacy*. Murfreesboro, Tenn.: Southern Heritage Press, 1994.

McDonald, JoAnna M. *"We Shall Meet Again:" The First Battle of Manassas (Bull Run) July 18–21, 1861*. Shippensburg, Pa.: White Mane Books, 1999.

McMaster, Richard H. *The Feasterville Incident: Hampton and Sherman*. Washington, D.C.: privately published, 1955.

McPherson, James M. *Battle Cry of Freedom: The Civil War Era*. New York: Oxford University Press, 1988.

Miers, Earl Schenck. *The General Who Marched to Hell: William Tecumseh Sherman and His March to Fame and Infamy*. New York: Alfred A. Knopf, 1951.

Milling, Chapman J. *Red Carolinians*. Chapel Hill: University of North Carolina Press, 1940.

Moore, John Hammond. *Columbia and Richland County: A South Carolina Community, 1740–1990*. Columbia: University of South Carolina Press, 1993.

Morison, Samuel Eliot, and Henry Steele Commager. *The Growth of the American Republic*. 2 vols. New York: Oxford University Press, 1955.

Nagel, Paul C. *Descent from Glory: Four Generations of the John Adams Family*. New York: Oxford University Press, 1983.

Nordin, D. Sven. *Rich Harvest: A History of the Grange, 1867–1900*. Jackson: University Press of Mississippi, 1974.

Oberholtzer, Ellis Paxson. *A History of the United States since the Civil War*. 5 vols. New York: The Macmillan Co., 1936.

Palliser, D. M. *The Staffordshire Landscape*. London: Hodder and Stoughton, 1976.

Pancake, John S. *This Destructive War: The British Campaign in the Carolinas, 1780–1782*. Tuscaloosa: University of Alabama Press, 1985.

Pascu, Stefan, ed. *The Independence of Romania*. Bucuresti: Editura Academiei Republicii Socialiste România, 1977.

Pendleton, V. L. *Last Words of Confederate Heroes*. Raleigh, N.C.: The Mutual Publishing Co., 1913.

Phisterer, Frederick. *Statistical Record of the Armies of the United States*. Carlisle, Pa.: John Kallmann, Publishers, 1996.

Power, J. Tracy, and Daniel J. Bell. *Rivers Bridge State Park: Visitors Guide*. n.p.: South Carolina Department of Parks, Recreation and Tourism, 1992.

Reniers, Perceval. *The Springs of Virginia: Life, Love, and Death at the Waters, 1775–1900*. Chapel Hill: University of North Carolina Press, 1941.

Reynolds, John S. *Reconstruction in South Carolina 1865–1877*. Columbia: The State Co., 1905.

Robertson, James I. *Stonewall Jackson: The Man, the Soldier, the Legend*. New York: Macmillan Publishing USA, 1997.

Rollins, Richard, ed. *The Returned Battle Flags*. Redondo Beach, Calif.: Rank and File Publications, 1995.

Rose, Willie Lee. *Rehearsal for Reconstruction: The Port Royal Experiment*. Indianapolis: The Bobbs-Merrill Company, Inc., 1964.

Ruffner, Kevin Conley. "Before the Seven Days: The Reorganization of the Confederate Army in the Spring of 1862." In *The Peninsula Campaign of 1862: Yorktown to the Seven Days*. Edited by William J. Miller. Campbell, Calif.: Savas Woodbury Publishers, 1995.

Schullery, Paul. *The Bear Hunter's Century*. New York: Dodd, Mead & Co., 1988.

Sears, Stephen W. *To the Gates of Richmond: The Peninsula Campaign*. New York: Ticknor Fields, 1992.

Shaw, Stebbing. *The History and Antiquities of Staffordshire*. 2 vols. London: J. Nichols and Son, 1798–1801.

Sheppard, William Arthur. *Red Shirts Remembered: Southern Brigadiers of the Reconstruction Period*. Atlanta: Ruralist Press, Inc., 1940.

———. *Some Reasons Why Red Shirts Remembered*. Greer, S.C.: privately published, 1940.

Sifakis, Steward. *Compendium of the Confederate Armies: South Carolina and Georgia*. New York: Facts on File, 1995.

Simkins, Francis Butler, and Robert Hilliard Woody. *South Carolina during Reconstruction*. Gloucester, Mass.: Peter Smith, 1966.

Simkins, Francis Butler. *Pitchfork Ben Tillman: South Carolinian*. Baton Rouge: Louisiana State University Press, 1967.

———. *The Tillman Movement*. Gloucester, Mass.: Peter Smith, 1964.

Simons, James Kealhofer. *A Guide to Columbia, South Carolina's Capital City*. Columbia: Columbia Chamber of Commerce, 1945.

Snow, William Parker. *Southern Generals, Their Lives and Campaigns*. New York: Charles B. Richardson, 1866.

Starr, Stephen Z. *The Union Cavalry in the Civil War.* 3 vols. Baton Rouge: Louisiana State University Press, 1979.

Stoney, Samuel Gaillard. *This Is Charleston: A Survey of the Architectural Heritage of a Unique American City.* Charleston, S.C.: Carolina Art Association, 1970.

Strode, Hudson. *Jefferson Davis: Confederate President.* New York: Harcourt, Brace & World, Inc., 1959.

———. *Jefferson Davis: Tragic Hero.* New York: Harcourt, Brace & World, Inc., 1964.

Stubbs, Thomas M. "Garner's Ferry Road," *Names in South Carolina* vol. I, no. 2 (Winter 1954): 10.

Swank, Walbrook Davis. *Battle of Trevilian Station.* Shippensburg, Pa.: Burd Street Press, 1994.

Thomas, Emory. *Bold Dragoon: The Life of J. E. B. Stuart.* New York: Harper & Row, 1986.

Thompson Jr., John W. *Jeb Stuart.* New York: Charles Scribner's Sons, 1930.

Tindall, George Brown. *South Carolina Negroes, 1877–1900.* Columbia: University of South Carolina Press, 1952.

Trinity Church, Columbia, S.C.: One Hundred and Twenty-Fifth Anniversary, 1937. Columbia: The State Co., 1937.

Trottman, Nelson. *History of the Union Pacific: A Financial and Economic Survey.* New York: Augustus M. Kelly, Publishers, 1966.

Veith, Ilza. "Four Thousand Years of Hysteria." In *Hysterical Personality.* Edited by Mardi J. Horowitz. New York: Jason Aronson, Inc., 1977.

———. *Hysteria: The History of a Disease.* Chicago: University of Chicago Press, 1965.

Wallace, David Duncan. *The History of South Carolina.* 4 vols. New York: The American Historical Society, Inc., 1934.

———. "The Question of the Withdrawal of the Democratic Presidential Electors in South Carolina in 1876," *Journal of Southern History* vol. VIII, no. 3 (August 1942).

———. *South Carolina: A Short History, 1520–1948.* Columbia: University of South Carolina Press, 1951.

Ware, Lowry. *Old Abbeville.* Columbia: S.C. Magazine of Ancestral Research, 1992.

Webb III, Alexander S. *The Peninsula: McClellan's Campaign of 1862.* New York: Charles Scribner's Sons, 1881.

Wellman, Manly Wade. *Giant in Gray: A Biography of Wade Hampton of South Carolina.* New York: Charles Scribner's Sons, 1949.

Wells, Edward L. *Hampton and Reconstruction.* Columbia: The State Co., 1907.

Welsh, Jack D. *Medical Histories of Confederate Generals.* Kent, Ohio: The Kent State University Press, 1995.

Whitney, David C. *The American Presidents.* Garden City, N.Y.: Doubleday & Company, 1978.

Williams, J. F. *Old and New Columbia.* Columbia: Epworth Orphanage Press, 1929.

Williamson, Joel. *After Slavery: The Negro in South Carolina during Reconstruction, 1861–1877.* New York: W. W. Norton & Co., Inc., 1965.

Wilson, Clyde N. *Carolina Cavalier: The Life and Mind of James Johnston Pettigrew.* Athens: University of Georgia Press, 1990.

Woodward, C. Vann. *Reunion and Reaction: The Compromise of 1877 and the End of Reconstruction.* Boston: Little, Brown and Co., 1951.

———. *The Strange Career of Jim Crow.* New York: Oxford University Press, 1955.

Woody, Robert H. *Republican Newspapers of South Carolina*. Charlottesville, Va.: The Historical Publishing Co., 1936.

Wright, Marcus J. *General Officers of the Confederate Army*. New York: The Neale Publishing Co., 1911.

Zuczek, Richard. *State of Rebellion: Reconstruction in South Carolina*. Columbia: University of South Carolina Press, 1996.

Index

About the Author

WALTER BRIAN CISCO is the author of *States Rights Gist: A South Carolina General of the Civil War*, an alternate selection of the History Book Club; *Taking a Stand: Portraits From the Southern Secession Movement;* and *Henry Timrod: A Biography.* He lives in Cordova, South Carolina.